Course

Taking Sides: Clashing Views in World History, Vol 1, 5th Ed. by Mitchell/Mitchell

http://create.mheducation.com

ISBN-10: 1121834310 ISBN-13: 9781121834316

Contents

Credits

Unit III 195

Preface

In *Taking Sides: Clashing Views in World History*, we identify the issues that are typically covered in the teaching of world history, using scholarly and readable sources that argue these issues. We have taken care to choose issues that will make this volume multicultural, gender-based, and reflective of current historical scholarship. We frame its issues with introductory and exploratory sections that are user-friendly for both teachers and students. Students who use this volume should come away with a greater understanding and appreciation of the value of studying history as well as enhanced skills in critical thinking.

Plan of the book This book is made up of issues that argue pertinent topics in the study of world history. Each issue begins with *Learning Outcomes* that preview the issue question for the student before moving into an *Introduction* that sets the stage for the debate as it is argued in the YES selections and NO selections that follow. At the end of each selection is a short biography of the contributor(s) that will give you information on the historians and commentators whose views are debated here.

Each issue concludes with *Exploring the Issue*. There are questions for *Critical Thinking and Reflection* that point the way to other considerations related to the issue and a section that asks: *Is There Common Ground?* In reading the issue and forming your own opinions, you should not feel confined to adopt one or the other of the positions presented. There are positions in between the given views or totally outside them, and the *Additional Resources* section that concludes each issue should help you find print, visual, Internet, and other sources to continue your study of the subject.

Using the book Care has been taken to provide issues that are in various ways related. A *Topic Guide* groups the issues for a quick overview. The issues could be used to: (a) compare/contrast those with like/unlike content; (b) show relationships between and among some topics across time, geographic, and cultural boundaries; (c) make connections between past historical events and their contemporary relevance. For example, several issues cover questions concerning some of the oldest civilizations in human history, stretching back to the origins of humankind. Other issues analyze the reasons for the demise of civilizations. Some issues explore the roles played by women at various stages of world history. Some issues evaluate the influence of historical figures. Others explore the historical relationships between followers of different world religions, or examine overseas exploration and expansion. Finally, several issues show the power of ideas in shaping the history of civilizations.

A word to the instructor An *Instructor's Resource Guide with Test Questions* (multiple choice and essay) is available through the publisher for the instructor using *Taking Sides* in the classroom. A general guidebook, *Using Taking Sides in the Classroom*, which discusses methods and techniques for integrating the pro–con approach into any classroom setting, is also available. An online version of *Using Taking Sides in the Classroom* and a corresponding service for *Taking Sides* adopters can be found at www.mhhe.com/createcentral.

Taking Sides: Clashing Views in World History is only one title in the *Taking Sides* series. If you are interested in seeing the table of contents for any of the other titles, please visit the *Taking Sides* website at www.mhhe.com/cls.

Acknowledgments We would like to thank Larry Madaras of Howard Community College—fellow teacher, good friend, coeditor of *Taking Sides: Clashing Views in American History*, and editor of *Taking Sides: Clashing Views in American History since 1945*—for his past and present assistance in making our work possible. Special acknowledgment also goes to David Stebenne of Ohio State University—friend, scholar, teacher, and author of *Arthur Larson: Modern Republican* (Indiana University Press, 2006)—for his suggestions and advice. Thanks also go out to the library staffs of Howard County, Maryland, University of Maryland, College Park, University of Maryland, Baltimore County (UMBC), and Howard Community College, particularly Ela Ciborowska who secured interlibrary loans.

At McGraw-Hill, a debt of gratitude is owed to Managing Editor Larry Loeppke and Senior Developmental Editor Jill Meloy, who guided us through the process of publishing this book, offering advice, support, and encouragement when they were most needed.

A final word We would appreciate any questions or comments that you may have on our work, especially which issues work best in your classroom and which issues you never use. Please contact us at joemitch@bigjar.com. We will use this feedback in shaping future editions.

Helen Buss Mitchell and Joseph R. Mitchell
Howard Community College

Editors

JOSEPH R. MITCHELL is a history instructor at Howard Community College in Columbia, Maryland, and a popular regional speaker. He co-authored a book on the history of the planned city of Columbia, Maryland, *New City on a Hill* (The History Press, 2006). He received an M.A. in history from Loyola College in Maryland and an M.A. in African American History from Morgan State University, also in Maryland. He is the principal co-editor of *The Holocaust: Readings and Interpretations* (McGraw-Hill, 2001) and *Taking Sides: Clashing Issues in Western Civilization* (McGraw-Hill,

2000). He currently serves on the Board of Trustees of the African Art Museum of Maryland.

HELEN BUSS MITCHELL is a professor of philosophy and director of the women's studies program at Howard Community College in Columbia, Maryland. She is the author of *Roots of Wisdom: A Tapestry of Philosophical Traditions*, 6th edition and *Readings from the Roots of Wisdom*, 3rd edition (Wadsworth/Cengage). *Roots of Wisdom* has twice been translated into Spanish and a Chinese translation is underway. She is also creator, writer, and host of a philosophy telecourse, *For the Love of Wisdom*, distributed nationally by Dallas TeleLearning. She has earned numerous degrees, including a PhD in intellectual and women's history from the University of Maryland.

Academic Advisory Board Members

Members of the Academic Advisory Board are instrumental in the final selection of articles for *Taking Sides* ExpressBooks. Their review of the articles for content, level, and appropriateness provides critical direction to the editor(s) and staff. We think that you will find their careful consideration reflected in this ExpressBook.

Topic Guide

Selected, Edited, and with Issue Framing Material by:
Helen Buss Mitchell, *Howard Community College*
and
Joseph R. Mitchell, *Howard Community College*

(Continued)

Correlation Guide

The *Taking Sides* series presents current issues in a debate-style format designed to stimulate student interest and develop critical thinking skills. Each issue is thoughtfully framed with an issue summary, learning outcomes, an issue introduction, and a section on exploring the issue. The pro and con essays—selected for their liveliness and substance—represent the arguments of leading scholars and commentators in their fields.

Taking Sides: Clashing Views in World History, Volume 1: The Ancient World to the Pre-Modern Era, 5/e, is an easy-to-use reader that presents issues on important topics such as the *Scientific Revolution, Martin Luther's reforms* and *Genghis Khan.* For more information on Taking Sides and other *McGraw-Hill Contemporary Learning Series* titles, visit www .mhhe.com/cls.

This convenient guide matches the issues in **Taking Sides: World History, Volume 1, 5/e** with the corresponding chapters in two of our best-selling McGraw-Hill World History textbooks by Bentley/Ziegler and Bentley et al.

TAKING SIDES: World History, Vol. 1, 5/e	Traditions & Encounters: A Global Perspective on the Past, 5/e by Bentley/Ziegler	Traditions & Encounters: A Brief Global History, 3/e by Bentley et al.
Issue: Was an Aryan Invasion Responsible for the Demise of the Indus Valley Civilization?	**Chapter 4:** Early Societies in South Asia	**Chapter 1:** The Foundations of Complex Societies
Issue: Was Sumerian Civilization Exclusively Male Dominated?	**Chapter 2:** Early Societies in Southwest Asia and the Indo-European Migrations	**Chapter 1:** The Foundations of Complex Societies
Issue: Did Egyptian Civilization Originate in Africa?	**Chapter 3:** Early African Societies and the Bantu Migrations	**Chapter 2:** Early African Societies and the Bantu Migrations
Issue: Were the Spartans Fighting for a Compromised View of Freedom at Thermopylae?	**Chapter 10:** Mediterranean Society: The Greek Phase	**Chapter 8:** Mediterranean Society under the Greeks and the Romans
Issue: Should We Deny Alexander III His Title, "The Great"?	**Chapter 7:** The Empires of Persia **Chapter 10:** Mediterranean Society: The Greek Phase	**Chapter 5:** The Empires of Persia **Chapter 8:** Mediterranean Society under the Greeks and Romans
Issue: Did Christianity Liberate Women?	**Chapter 16:** The Two Worlds of Christendom	**Chapter 8:** Mediterranean Society under the Greeks and the Romans **Chapter 9:** Cross-Cultural Exchanges on the Silk Roads
Issue: Were Internal Factors Responsible for the Fall of the Roman Empire?	**Chapter 12:** Cross-Cultural Exchanges on the Silk Roads	**Chapter 9:** Cross-Cultural Exchanges on the Silk Roads
Issue: Did the Byzantine Empire Benefit from the Rule of Justinian and Theodora?	**Chapter 16:** The Two Worlds of Christendom	**Chapter 10:** The Christian Commonwealth of Byzantium
Issue: Did Environmental Factors Cause the Collapse of Maya Civilization?	**Chapter 6:** Early Societies in the Americas and Oceania	**Chapter 4:** Early Societies in the Americas and Oceania **Chapter 17:** Worlds Apart: The Americas and Oceania
Issue: Could the Crusades Be Considered a Christian Holy War?	**Chapter 21:** Reaching Out: Expanding Horizons of Cross-Cultural Interaction	**Chapter 18:** Reaching Out: Cross-Cultural Interactions
Issue: Was Mongol Leader Genghis Khan an Enlightened Ruler?	**Chapter 17:** Nomadic Empires and Eurasian Integration	**Chapter 14:** Nomadic Empires and Eurasian Integration
Issue: Was Zen Buddhism the Primary Influence on the Japanese Samurai?	**Chapter 31:** Societies at Crossroads	**Chapter 12:** The Resurgence of Empire in East Asia
Issue: Did Women and Men Benefit Equally from the Renaissance?	**Chapter 21:** Reaching Out: Expanding Horizons of Cross-Cultural Interaction	**Chapter 18:** Reaching Out: Cross-Cultural Interactions
Issue: Did China's Worldview Cause the Abrupt End of Its Voyages of Exploration?	**Chapter 22:** Transoceanic Encounters and Global Connections	**Chapter 3:** Early Societies in South and East Asia **Chapter 6:** The Unification of China **Chapter 18:** Reaching Out: Cross-Cultural Interactions

(Continued)

TAKING SIDES: World History, Vol. 1, 5/e	Traditions & Encounters: A Global Perspective on the Past, 5/e by Bentley/Ziegler	Traditions & Encounters: A Brief Global History, 3/e by Bentley et al.
Issue: Is Christopher Columbus's Reputation as a Positive Force in World History Still Merited?	**Chapter 21:** Reaching Out: Expanding Horizons of Cross-Cultural Interaction **Chapter 22:** Transoceanic Encounters and Global Connections **Chapter 24:** New Worlds: The Americas and Oceania	**Chapter 18:** Reaching Out: Cross-Cultural Interactions
Issue: Was Gender a Major Issue in Queen Elizabeth I of England's Reign?	**Chapter 23:** The Transformation of Europe	
Issue: Did Martin Luther's Reforms Improve the Lives of European Christians?	**Chapter 23:** The Transformation of Europe	
Issue: Were European Witch Hunts Misogynistic in Nature?	**Chapter 23:** The Transformation of Europe	
Issue: Was the Scientific Revolution Revolutionary?	**Chapter 23:** The Transformation of Europe	
Issue: Did the British Enlightenment Pave the Way for the Modern World?	**Chapter 23:** The Transformation of Europe	

Introduction

What Is History?

History is a dialogue between the past and the present. As we respond to events in our own world, we bring the concerns of the present to our study of the past. What seems important to us, where we turn our attention, how we approach a study of the past—all these are rooted in the present. It has been said that where you stand determines what you see. This is especially the case with history. If we stand within the Western tradition exclusively, we may be tempted to see its story as the only story or the only one worth telling. And whose perspective we take is also critical. From the point of view of the rich and powerful, the events of history take one shape; through the lens of the poor and powerless, the same events can appear quite different. If we take women, or non-Western cultures, or the ordinary person as our starting point, the story of the past may present us with a series of surprises.

Tools of the Historian

Much of the raw material of history consists of written sources. Original sources—from a period contemporary with the events or ideas described—are called *primary sources*. These may include documents of all kinds, including official records as well as personal letters and diaries. The writings of historians reflecting on the past are called *secondary sources*. It is important to keep in mind that primary sources may not automatically be assumed to be free from bias. Each contains historical and personal perspectives. Their principal limitation, however, is that they record what people considered noteworthy about their own age and not necessarily what would most interest us today. As the concerns of the present evolve, the questions we bring to our study of the past will also change. Much of what you read in this book will reflect differences in focus between one historian and another. As Edward Hallett Carr points out, the historian constructs a working model that enables him or her to understand the past. It would be a great mistake to confuse this working model with a photocopy.

Traditional History

Only recently has history considered itself a social science and striven for a kind of scientific accuracy in speaking about the past. For much of human history, until perhaps the late nineteenth century, history was considered a branch of literature rather than a kind of science. It was concerned first of all with narrative, with the telling of a compelling story, and its focus was on the fascinating characters whose lives shaped and defined the past.

Biography, the recounting of the life and times of a powerful man, was regarded as one of the most reliable windows on the past. The so-called great man was credited with shaping and defining his own time. As a result, studying Alexander the Great, Genghis Khan, or Christopher Columbus was assumed to offer one of the most reliable keys to unlocking a specific historical time period.

And, traditional history looked relatively uncritically at the great men from the past. Military heroes, for example, were lauded for their conquests with little or no focus on the carnage that made those conquests possible. Another unspoken assumption was the dominance and superiority of the West as the creator and bearer of human civilization. Divine power was sometimes seen as directing or, at least, approving the actions of powerful nations and men.

The traditional areas of focus for the historian have been political, diplomatic, and constitutional. Political history considers how power has been organized and enforced by the state within human societies. Diplomatic history looks at what has influenced the power struggles between states as they continually struggled for dominance. Constitutional history examines the evolution of national states with special attention to who rules and who or what confers the right to rule.

A related domain of the traditional historian has been that of intellectual history or the history of ideas—in the fields of politics, economics, sociology, theology, and science. Probing the power of world religions, understanding the ideological aspects of conflicts, examining the influence of a worldview on a nation's commercial enterprises—all these are the province of intellectual history. Taking this approach to its widest scope, one might explore the intellectual climate of an entire age, such as the Renaissance, the Reformation, the Scientific Revolution, or the Enlightenment. Which ideas shaped and defined each of these distinct historical periods? And, what marked the change from one to another?

Revisionism

However, history is not a once-and-for-all enterprise. Each generation formulates its own questions and brings new tools to the study of the past resulting in a process called revisionism. Much of what you will read in this book is a product of revisionism as historians reinterpret the past in the light of the present. One generation values revolutions, the next focuses on their terrible costs. One generation assumes that great men shape the events of history, the next looks to the lives of ordinary people to illuminate the past. There is no final answer, but where we stand will determine which interpretation seems more compelling to us. Some issues introduce the tension between traditional and revisionist interpretations of influential figures in world history.

As new tools of analysis become available, our ability to understand the past improves. Bringing events into clearer focus can change the meaning we assign to them. Many of the selections in this book reflect new attitudes and new insights made possible by the tools that historians have borrowed from other social sciences. For instance, finding and deciphering long-hidden manuscripts can shed new light on religious belief systems. And, physical artifacts can help us decode elements of language and culture as we examine explanations for the artifacts and architectural elements they have left behind or even causes for the collapse of their civilizations.

Presentism

While we stand in the present, we must be wary of what historians call presentism, that is, reading the values of the present back into the past. If we live in a culture that values individualism and prizes competition, we may be tempted to see these values as good even in a culture that preferred communalism and cooperation. And, we may miss a key component of an ancient civilization because it does not match what we currently consider worthwhile. In defining the overall context, can the West acknowledge the role of non-Europeans in shaping the modern world? We cannot and should not avoid our own questions and struggles. They will inform our study of the past; and yet, they must not warp our vision. Ideally, historians engage in a continual dialogue in which the concerns but not the values of the present are explored through a study of the past.

At the same time, though, we might bring the moral standards of the present to bear on the past. Cultural relativism, pioneered in the field of anthropology, made us sensitive to the many and varied ways in which civilizations define what is "normal" and what is "moral." So, we remain appropriately reluctant to judge individuals from other times and places by our standards since they were or are, in fact, behaving perfectly normally and morally by the standards of their own time and place. However, from the perspective of the present, we do not hesitate to condemn slaveholding, genocide, or even the zealotry that leads to what the modern world calls "ethnic cleansing."

Changing Historiographical Focuses

All cultures are vulnerable to the narrow mindedness created by ethnocentrism—the belief that my culture is superior to all others. From inside a particular culture, certain practices may seem normative—that is, we may assume that all humans or all rational humans must behave the way we do or hold the attitudes we hold. When we meet a culture that sees the world differently from ourselves, we may be tempted to write them off as inferior or primitive. As an alternative to ethnocentrism, we might want to enter the worldview of another and see what we can learn from expanding our perspective. These issues will offer you many opportunities to try this thought experiment.

Stepping outside the Western tradition has allowed historians to take a more globocentric view of world events. Accusing their predecessors of Eurocentrism, some historians have adopted a multicultural view of world history that explores Africa's influence in ancient Egypt and Mesoamerica. Questions about how civilizations begin and end can be of great relevance to modern peoples. Within the Western tradition, women have challenged the male-dominated perspective that studied war but ignored family. Including additional perspectives complicates our interpretation of past events but permits a fuller picture to emerge. We must be wary of universalism—assuming, for example, that patriarchy has always existed or that being a woman was the same for every woman no matter what her historical circumstances. If patriarchy or the nuclear family has a historical beginning, then there was a time when some other pattern existed. If cultures other than the West have been dominant or influential during the past, what did the world look like under those circumstances?

Social History

Some historians have moved beyond political, diplomatic, military, and constitutional history to explore economics and demographics as well as to study social processes. Moving from a focus on nations and rulers to a close examination of forces and structures that can be studied analytically has opened up the realms of business and the family to the historian. Proponents of the so-called new social history rejected what they called history from the top down. Instead of the great man whose influence shaped his age, they looked to the lives of ordinary people and called what they were doing history from the bottom up. The previous generation of historians, they claimed, had sometimes acted as if only the influential had a role in shaping history. Social history assumes that all people are capable of acting as historical agents rather than being passive victims to whom history happens. With this shift in attitude, the lives of slaves, workers, women of all kinds, and children, too, become worthy subjects of historical investigation.

Because the poor and powerless seldom leave written records, other methods must be used to understand their lives. Applying the methods of social scientists to their own discipline, historians have broadened and deepened their field of study. Archaeological evidence, DNA analysis, the tools of paleoanthropology, computer analysis of demographic data—all these have allowed the voiceless to speak across centuries. Fossil evidence, for instance, and the analysis of mitochondrial DNA—the structures within cells we inherit only from our mothers—may each be employed, sometimes with strikingly different results, to trace the migrations of pre-literate peoples.

What historians call material culture reveals the everyday lives of people by analyzing what they discarded as well as the monuments and other material objects they intended to leave as markers of their civilizations. At certain points in human history, owning a plow made the difference between merely surviving and having some surplus food to barter or sell. What people leave to their heirs can tell us how much or how little they had to brighten their lives while they lived. As we continue to dig, we may find our assumptions confirmed or denied by the fossils of once living organisms. Evidence of sea life on the top of a mountain lets us know that vast geologic changes have taken place. And, in another example, our genetic material has information we are just now learning to decode and interpret that may settle important questions of origin and migration as we learn to read the data locked inside our DNA.

The high speed comparative functions of computers have allowed the historian to analyze vast quantities of data and look at demographic trends. How old are people when they marry for the first time, have a child, or die? Only with the expanded life expectancy made possible by the modern world has it been possible for people to see their children's children—to become grandparents. Looking at the time between marriage and the birth of a first child can help us calculate the percentage of pregnant brides and gain some insight into how acceptable or unacceptable premarital sex may have been in the context of an expected future marriage. If we study weather patterns and learn that certain years were periods of drought or that the glacier receded during a particular time period, we will know a little more about whether the lives of people who lived during these times were relatively easier or more difficult than those of their historical neighbors in earlier or later periods.

Race, Class, and Gender

The experience of being a historical subject is never monolithic. That is, each of us has a gender, a race, a social class, an ethnic identity, a religion (even if it is atheism or agnosticism), an age, and a variety of other markers that color our experiences. At times, the most important factor may be my gender and what happens may be more or less the same for all members of a particular gender. Under other circumstances, however, race may be predominant. Being a member of a racial minority or of a powerful racial majority may lead to very different experiences of the same event. At other times social class may determine how an event is experienced; the rich may have one story to tell, the poor another. And, other factors, such as religion or ethnic identity, even age, can become the most significant piece of a person's identity, especially if prejudice or favoritism is involved. Historians try always to take into account how race, class, and gender (as well as a host of other factors) intersect in the life of a historical subject.

Issues Involved in Historical Interpretation

Often historians will agree on what happened but disagree about why or how something occurred. Sometimes the question is: Were internal or external causes more responsible? Both may have contributed to an event but one or the other may have played the more significant role. Looking at differing evidence may lead historians to varying interpretations. Similarly, historians ponder whether an empire fell because of internal weaknesses or external pressures. A related question is: Was it the circumstances that changed or only the attitudes of those who experienced them? If we find less protest, for instance, can we conclude that things have gotten better or only that people have found a way to accommodate themselves to a situation beyond their control.

Periodization

Even more basically, the student of the past must wonder whether the turning points that shape the chapters in our history books are the same for all historical subjects. The process of marking turning points is known as periodization. It is the more or less artificial creation of periods that chunk history into manageable segments by identifying forks in the road that took people and events in a new direction. Using an expanded perspective, we may learn that the traditional turning points hold for men but not for women or reflect the experiences of one ethnic group but not another. And, if periodization schemes conflict, which one should we use? Several issues examine questions of periodization. If Europe was experiencing a "dark age" while the Islamic world enjoyed a "golden age," which one more accurately describes the time period? And, was there a distinct break at the periods we designate the Renaissance, the Scientific Revolution, and the Enlightenment? If so, did women and men experience these breaks identically?

It is also important to keep in mind that people living at a particular moment in history are not aware of labels that later historians will attach to their experience. People who lived during the Middle Ages were surely not aware of living in the middle of something. Only much after the fact were we able to call a later age the Renaissance. To those who lived during what we call the Middle Ages or the Renaissance, marriage, childbirth, work, weather, sickness, and death were the real concerns, just as they are for us. Our own age will certainly be characterized by future historians in ways that might surprise and shock us. As we study the past, it is helpful to keep in mind that some of our assumptions are rooted in a traditional periodization that is now being challenged.

Continuity or Discontinuity?

A related question concerns the connection or lack of connection between one event or set of events and another. When we look at the historical past, we must ask ourselves whether we are seeing continuity or discontinuity. In other words, is the event we are studying part of a normal process of evolution or does it represent a break from a traditional pattern. Questions of continuity versus discontinuity are the fundamental ones on which the larger issue of periodization rests. Did the Industrial Revolution redefine the lives of workers? Were the periods we refer to as the Renaissance, the Scientific Revolution, or the Enlightenment really more discontinuous with the past than continuous with it? And, if some elements shift while others constitute a seamless web, which is the more significant element for the historian?

Sometimes events may appear continuous from the point of view of one group and discontinuous from the point of view of another. Suppose that factory owners found their world and worldview shifting dramatically, whereas the lives and perspectives of workers went on more or less as they had before. When this is the case, whose experience should we privilege? Is one group's experience more historically significant than another's—and how should we decide? Modern historians are struggling with these questions as the voices of indigenous peoples compete with those praising explorers.

The Power of Ideas

Can ideas change the course of history? People have sometimes been willing to die for what they believe in and revolutions have certainly been fought, at least in part, over ideas. Some historians believe that studying the clash of ideas or the predominance of one idea or set of ideas offers the best key to understanding the past. How significant is a nation's worldview and view of itself? Could this factor be more significant than more practical considerations?

What do you think? Do ideas shape world events? Would devotion to a political or religious cause lead you to challenge the status quo? Or, would economic conditions be more likely to send you to the streets? Historians differ in ranking the importance of various factors in influencing the past. Do people challenge the power structure because they feel politically powerless, or because they are hungry, or because of the power of ideas?

The Timeliness of Historical Issues

When we read the newspaper, log on to online sources, follow blogs or a Twitter feed, or listen to the evening news or comedy shows, there is a confusing array of present day political, economic, religious, and military clashes that can be understood only by looking at their historical contexts. The perennial conflicts in the Middle East, China and India's emerging roles as economic superpowers, the threat posed by religious fundamentalism, the question of whether revolutions are ever worth their costs—these concerns of the global village have roots in the past. Understanding the origins of conflicts gives us the possibility of envisioning their solutions. The issues in this book will help you think through the problems facing our world and give you the tools to make an informed decision about what you think is the best course of action.

In a democracy, an informed citizenry is the bedrock on which a government stands. If we do not understand the past, the present will be a puzzle to us and the future may seem out of our control. Seeing how and why historians disagree can help us determine what the critical issues are and where informed interpreters part company. This offers a foundation for forming our own judgments and acting upon them. Looking critically at clashing views also hones our analytic skills and makes us thoughtful readers of all our textbooks as well as magazines, newspapers, and blogs.

Why Study World History?

You may be wondering why this book deals with world history rather than exclusively with Western civilization. At times the West has felt its power and dominance in the world made only its own story worth studying. History, we are sometimes told, is written by the winners. For the Chinese, the Greeks, the Ottoman Turks, and many other victors of the past, the stories of other civilizations seemed irrelevant, unimportant, not nearly as valuable as their own triumphal saga. The Chinese considered their Middle Kingdom the center of the world; the Greeks labeled all others barbarians; and the Ottoman Turks expected never to lose their position of dominance. From our perspective in the present these stories form a tapestry. No one thread or pattern tells the tale and all seem to be equally necessary for a complete picture of the past to emerge.

Any single story—even that of a military and economic superpower—is insufficient to explain the scope of human history at a given moment in time. Our story is especially interesting to us and you will find many issues specific to Western civilization in this book. However, as we are learning, our story achieves its fullest meaning only when it is told in concert with those of other civilizations that share an increasingly interconnected planet with us. As communications systems shrink the Earth into a global village, we may be ignoring the rest of the world at our own peril. At the very least the study of civilizations other than our own can alert us to events that may have worldwide implications. And, as we are beginning to learn, no story happens in isolation. The history of the West can perhaps be accurately told only within a global context that takes into account the actions and reactions of other civilizations as they share the world stage with the West.

As you read the issues that concern non-Western civilizations, stay alert for what you can learn about your own.

Your textbook may take a global focus or it may be restricted to the study of Western civilization. In either case, the readings in this book will enrich your understanding of how the peoples of the world have understood themselves and their relationships with others. As we become a more clearly multicultural society, we have an additional reason for studying about other civilizations that have blended with our own through immigration. Perhaps the biggest challenge for an increasingly diverse United States of America is to understand its own role in world affairs and its relationship with other countries, which may have different histories, value systems, and goals.

Helen Buss Mitchell and Joseph R. Mitchell
Howard Community College

Unit I

UNIT

The Ancient World

Archaeologists, anthropologists, linguists, and art historians deciphering the meaning of surviving sculptures, and scientists decoding DNA have all shed new light on the world's most ancient cultures. Beginning with the question of the collapse of the Indus River civilization, and the gender fluidity in ancient Sumer, we enter more deeply into the lives of people, through the unearthing of their homes, the translations of their poetry and sacred texts, and the recreation of the texture of their daily lives. Can modern Hinduism trace its origins to Aryans who displaced an indigenous civilization? Did the powerful Goddess worshiped in Sumer make possible greater gender equality for earthly women? Is it possible that in the second millennium B.C.E. *Africans exploring the west coast of their own continent were blown off course and diffused their culture into what would much later be called the New World?*

These new points of view can also open our eyes to new dimensions of the Classical period in Greece and Rome. Knowing that the city-state of Sparta took a suicidal stand in its epochal battle with the Persian Empire at Thermopylae, we might wonder how the slave class of helots experienced this fight to the death. And, in learning about the early life of the man we call Alexander the Great, including his time as the student of the philosopher, Aristotle, we are able to construct a more complex picture of a complex man. Despite his failings as a person and as a leader, are we still willing to call him "Great"?

Through recently uncovered scriptural texts, we enter deeply into the secret world of early Christianity, when it was still persecuted as a cult within the Roman Empire. There is a stark contrast between the fervor and communal nature of the earliest Christians and the more formal, bureaucratic consequences that followed from being declared the official religion of the Roman Empire. Was this a factor in the ultimate collapse of the Roman Empire? Or, were the Huns to blame? Was the empire weakened from within or threatened from without? As the questions become more complicated, history comes alive.

Selected, Edited, and with Issue Framing Material by:
Helen Buss Mitchell, *Howard Community College*
and
Joseph R. Mitchell, *Howard Community College*

ISSUE

Was an Aryan Invasion Responsible for the Demise of the Indus Valley Civilization?

YES: Stanley Wolpert, from *India* (University of California Press, 1991)

NO: Romila Thapar, from *Early India: From the Origins to A.D. 1300* (University of California Press, 2004)

Learning Outcomes

After reading this issue, you should be able to:

- Describe the key features of the Indus Valley cities of Harappa and Mohenjo-daro.
- Describe the key characteristics of nomadic Aryans.
- Understand how archaeological findings, artistic creations, linguistic patterns, and sacred literary texts can provide clues about why the Indus Valley civilization declined.

ISSUE SUMMARY

YES: Historian Stanley Wolpert argues that the Aryan invasion of the Indus Valley did occur and played a role in the demise of the Indus Valley civilization.

NO: Historian Romila Thapar argues that multiple factors were responsible for the demise of the Indus Valley civilization and that the Aryan penetration into India was migratory rather than belligerent, resulting in a fusion of the two cultures.

Which of the world's ancient civilizations was the first? The most advanced? Prior to the 1920s, three civilizations could stake a claim to those titles—Mesopotamian, Egyptian, and Chinese. Circumstances during that decade, however, produced a fourth claimant.

In the 1920s, archaeologists digging in the Indus River Valley (located in present-day Pakistan) discovered the remains of two major cities which they named Harappa and Mohenjo-daro. These sites had the earmarks of urban environments—a well-planned street system, numerous public facilities, and what may have been the world's first indoor plumbing/drainage system. Further archaeological digs in the area produced evidence of other lesser cities and seemed to provide evidence for the existence of a fourth major ancient civilization. Work continues as scholars and scientists attempt to draw a picture of the Indus Valley civilization and determine its proper place in human history.

Information today remains incomplete. Archaeologists agree that this Indus civilization began to develop in the third millennium B.C.E. and reached its apex in the period from 2500 to 1500 B.C.E. There is also consensus that it began to decline soon afterward, disappearing and remaining hidden until it was rediscovered in the last century. What happened during the interim between 1500 B.C.E. and its decline is the subject of this issue.

Who were the original creators of the Indus civilization? Archaeologists can trace their roots to the Neolithic era, when people in the area began to domesticate animals, grow crops, and live in communities. As their settlements grew into a civilization, Indus Valley residents began to trade with their Mesopotamian neighbors to the north, bringing further sophistication to their cities. Eventually the Dravidians, dark-skinned people from what today is south/central India, began to move into the Indus valley. Although there is little evidence available regarding this migration, there is nothing to indicate that it took the form of an invasion; rather it seems to have occurred as a peaceful synthesis of two peoples' cultures.

This situation existed until circa 1500 B.C.E. when the Aryans, a nomadic, warlike people, entered the Indus Valley and perhaps changed the course of Indian history. This Aryan migration was part of a larger movement of Indo-European peoples who eventually settled throughout the European and Asian continents, influencing the development of civilizations wherever they settled.

How the Aryan and the Indus/Dravidian cultures mixed is a subject of scholarly dispute. For most of the twentieth century, based primarily on linguistic and religious sources, it was assumed that the Aryans entered India as conquerors, applied the final blow to a dying civilization, and adopted much of its more advanced civilization. Hinduism, the caste system, and India's sacro/mythological worldview were all products of what Stanley Wolpert has called "India's first cultural synthesis" ("Multiculturalism in History: India, the Multicultural Paradigm," *Orbis* (Fall 1999)).

This theory has, within the last generation, come under scholarly attack. Based on recent archaeological evidence and written sources, a new generation of scholars argues that there is little solid evidence to support the Aryan invasion theory and claims that those who espoused it in the past were misinterpreting the linguistic and religious sources they used as proof. Modern scholars counter that the Aryan migration into the area may have been a peaceful one and assert that the demise of the Indus Valley civilization was caused by a combination of environmental, political, and social circumstances and conditions.

The importance of the question of Aryan influence on Indus Valley civilization extends beyond the boundaries of history. If the "Aryan invasion" theory is true, the major roots of India's civilization, including its language, religion, and social system, developed from a non-Indian source. There are some Hindu nationalists especially who see this not only as a falsification of the historical record but also as an attempt to deny India its true cultural roots (see Issue: Have Afghan Women Been Liberated from Oppression? in Volume 2 of this series).

Historians have a continuing interest in the reasons for the decline and fall of civilizations and they spend much time and effort analyzing and evaluating the reasons for those occurrences. Historically and for professional reasons, they are interested in setting the record straight. Contemporarily, they hope that lessons from the past can be studied and, perhaps, serve as warnings of the potential demise of present civilizations. There are no guarantees that our own civilization can assume indefinite survival. Perhaps it behooves us to study the lessons offered by the past.

There are many civilizations whose demise can be fitted into a decline/fall paradigm. In this book, material is available for a comparative study of the various explanations given for the downfall of the Indus Valley, Roman (Issue: Should We Deny Alexander III His Title, "The Great"?) and Maya (Issue: Were Internal Factors Responsible for the Fall of the Roman Empire?) civilizations. Any of these issues could provide useful information for analysis, as would research into the decline of the Greek, Islamic, Aztec, or Ottoman civilizations. A useful source to consult would be Norman Yoffee and George L. Cowgill, eds., *The Collapse of Ancient States and Civilizations* (University of Arizona Press, 1988), which includes information on many of the civilizations mentioned above, as well as several essays on the general nature and pattern of civilizations and their decline.

In the YES and NO selections, Stanley Wolpert, a long-time student and scholar of Indian history and culture, argues that the Aryan invasion did take place and it resulted in a blending of Aryan and Indo-Dravidian societies from which Indian civilization sprang. Romila Thapar, the author of many books on India's history, states that several factors were responsible for the demise of the Indus Valley civilization, but an Aryan invasion is not one of them. The Aryan presence in southern India, she argues, occurred as the result of a gradual migration that allowed the two cultures to assimilate and over time form the roots of Indian civilization.

A final word of caution: Adolf Hitler and Nazi Germany have made the term "Aryan" fraught with controversy through misuse and falsification. In its Sanskrit origins, the word's meaning is "highborn" or "noble." No more should be derived from the word than its original meaning.

Stanley Wolpert

India

Pre-Aryan Urbanization

More than 4,000 years ago people living along the river Indus and throughout most of what is now Pakistan enjoyed a highly sophisticated, urban, commercial civilization. Thanks to careful excavations at more than fifty sites around the Indus Valley, most important of which were undertaken at the twin "capitals" of Mohenjo-daro and Harappa, we can confidently date this civilization to at least 2300–1700 B.C. The grid patterns of urban planning and the remarkably advanced sewer and septic-tank drainage, as well as hypocaustically regulated baths characteristic of Indus cities attest to the precocity of the builders, rulers, and bureaucrats of Indus Civilization. Its arts were equally advanced, displaying technological as well as creative ingenuity, both of which are embodied in one beautiful bronze "dancing girl" cast by the lost wax process, and in many remarkable seals, whose pictographs remain undeciphered, but whose gods and animals look quite at home in modern India. One seated figure in yogic position appears to be Shiva as "Lord of Beasts," and several humped bulls look alive, or at least as if they were modeled from zebus still walking the streets of any Punjabi town.

Viewed from the air, modern Pakistani homes built close to Harappa, the Northern "capital" of India's first major incarnation, are not only made of bricks burned to much the same hue of salmon, but appear to have been constructed with floorplans similar to those of their most ancient ancestors. Practical-minded Scottish engineers used so many of the bricks they found scattered around ancient Harappa as a bed for their Punjabi railroad in the late nineteenth century that little more than bare floorplans and sewerage drains remain of what must have been solid two-story homes in the ancient city that seems to have supported about 40,000 people. Who exactly those people were, however, remains a mystery—as is the language they wrote and spoke, the precise nature of their polity, and the names of their gods. We assume from various shreds of evidence that they were proto-Dravidians, possibly using a language that was a grandfather of modern Tamil, and that they were ruled by a king, who was worshiped as a god. They also worshiped the male phallus, it appears, symbolizing a fertility god such as Shiva, and the Mother Goddess. They had special reverence of water, which must have played a central role in their ritual. Hindu temples continue to have rectangular tanks, much like the "great bath" found at Mohenjo-daro, and ritual washing is important to Hindus, especially for purification purposes before approaching the icon of any god.

Certain plants, like the pipal tree, were sacred then and have remained so throughout Indian history. The Buddha attained enlightenment while seated in the shade of that great tree at Sarnath. We also find solar symbols, such as the wheel of light rays that in Sanskrit was called *su-asti* ("well-being"), later corrupted and misused by the Nazis as *Swastika,* their symbol of "Aryan purity." We know almost nothing of the social system of Mohenjo-daro, yet the floorplans of houses in some parts of town are much smaller than those found in other quarters, which were themselves small by comparison to the citadel's Great Bath and "temple" structures, reflecting a hierarchy of class or something perhaps like India's more complex "caste" system that emerged later.

The more we study the bronze and stone tools and remains of these remarkable Indus sites, the more it appears that earliest Indic Civilization contained many of the cells of the later Indian socioreligious organism. The seals themselves were obviously used to identify produce, shipped to Mesopotamia along the Makran coast, since several have been found at Sumerian digs and elsewhere. Indus exports probably included cotton cloth, a fragment of which was found at Mohenjo-daro, which still remains India's premier commercial product and export. Indian cotton cloth is now in demand, however, not only throughout Africa and Southeast Asia but also in some of the finest shops of Rome, Paris, London, New York, and Beverly Hills.

Indus Valley planners obviously understood enough secrets of water control to allow their cities to flourish for almost a thousand years, yet not without periodic rebuilding. Mohenjo-daro seems to have been rebuilt no less than ten times and was probably abandoned after the last great flood forced its surviving inhabitants to flee. We obviously don't know what happened in those dark final hours that caught so many Indus residents off guard, their outstretched skeletal remains alone mutely attesting to the panic that must have suddenly seized them. Perhaps earthquake tremors preceded the flood, or possibly triggered it. Tectonic shock might, in fact, have ruptured a major Indus dam, releasing its trapped waters. The coast has fallen since Indus Valley times, immersing the three lowest layers of Mohenjo-daro totally under water, eluding all attempts to shed historic light on their remains. Whatever cataclysmic events caused the fall of Indus urban Civilization, they appear to have come shortly before tribes of wandering pastoral Aryans reached India's western borders, somewhere between 1600 and 1500 b.c. With mighty Indus walls shattered by earth's rumbling surface and most pre-Aryan defenders drowned or forced to abandon her citadels, fleeing south for their lives, the new arrivals found scant resistance as they moved their flocks of goats and kine over the river and through the rubble that had once been a flourishing civilization.

Aryan Conquests and Emerging Synthesis

Devout Hindus believe the Aryans have always lived in India, at least since before the first Ice Age, when they migrated south from the North Pole. Historical scholarship and comparative linguistic studies of the past century and a half give us better reason to hypothesize, however, that Indo-Aryans were the easternmost wing of the once cohesive Indo-European-speaking tribes, whose great dispersion from pastureland somewhere between the Caspian and Black Seas probably occurred around 2000 B.C. That monumental Indo-European dispersion impelled some tribes west to England and Ireland, others to Germany, Greece, and Rome, still others east to Iran, from which Indo-Iranian wing the Indo-Aryan tribes broke away about 1500 B.C., migrating over snow-capped *Hindu Kush* ("Killers of Indians") mountains, down Khyber and Bolan Passes, into the Indus Valley.

All that we know about the early Aryans was preserved through oral tradition by their priestly bards, Brahmans, whose heirs painstakingly memorized thousands of Sanskrit poetic hymns considered sacred, eventually recording their scripture in "Books of Knowledge" called *Vedas,* most important of which is the *Rig*. Vedic prayers were addressed to no less than thirty-three named gods, to whom Kings (*Rajas*) and Warriors (*Kshatriyas*) as well as *Brahmans* and Commoners (*Vaishyas*) appealed for long life, good fortune, heroic sons, and rain. India's early Aryan tribals were hearty, lusty, life-affirming, drinking, gambling, fighting people, who resembled their Homeric cousins much more than they would their Gangetic Valley descendants. Their most important god, Indra, was a young hero, who wielded his *vajra* ("weapon") much the way his Icelandic cousin Thor hurled thunderbolts, using it daily to "pierce" the dark outer "covering" of the cosmic Demon, thereby releasing the sun, waters, and lowing cows.

The Vedas report nothing about the pre-Indian history of the Aryans, nor do they say anything specific concerning the Aryan conquests of Indus Valley Civilization, exept for a few references to "dark" (*dasa*) peoples, who lived in "fortified cities" (*pur*), and had to be "subdued." Indra's daily defeat of demon Vritra may, nonetheless, allegorically reflect the conquest by Aryan forces of light over the demon darkness of pre-Aryan "shells" (fortresses), possibly even King Indra's piercing of pre-Aryan dams, thus releasing their waters. The Vedas, however, were not compiled as histories but as hymnals; hence their disinterest in temporal matters, even such earthshaking events as may have occurred less than a century before those chants were first "heard" by the Rishis. For Rishis and Mahatmas, however, and those Hindus who revere them, this world of rebirth (*samsara*) and pain is, after all, more "illusion" than real. Why bother with names, dates, or even the most dramatic of historic events? The difficulty of firmly establishing dates throughout Indian history is in part attributable to at least such widespread belief in their insignificance by many of India's best and brightest philosophic minds.

What seems clear, however, is that between about 1500 and 1000 B.C., Aryan tribes conquered the remaining pre-Aryan *dasas* throughout the Indus Valley and Punjab, moving as far east as the plains of Delhi. When they first reached India, the Aryans were still pastoral nomads; hence no trace has been found of their villages or huts. By the end of this half millennium, however, no doubt because of much they learned about urban civilization from the *dasas* they enslaved, Aryan cities began to rise on those plains around Delhi, whose first capital was named for Lord Indra (*Indraprastha*).

The Aryans brought the horse as well as cows to India. Aryan Rajas rode to war in horse-drawn chariots, which helped them defeat all who confronted them, as did their well-aimed arrows and hafted axes. Nomadic wandering across the Iranian plateau had toughened them into fierce warriors, and like Indra himself, they must have taken heart from draughts of "divine" Soma, swallowed before doing battle. That nectar of the gods apparently grew wild in the hills of northwestern India, and whether narcotic or psychedelic in nature, the effects of its "juice" [were] such that it "settled in every joint" and was worshiped in Vedic hymns as a deity second only to Indra in power. The most important ritual of Vedic Aryan faith was, in fact, building the annual Soma altar, whose fires were lit just before the monsoon started. Soma libations were deemed essential prerequisites to rain. Cows were used as early Aryan currency, paid to Brahmans who chanted mantras as they poured out Soma juice and clarified butter (*ghi*). Agni, the god of fire, smacked his hot lips and soared toward the sky as he tasted the divine offerings, passing them up to many solar divinities, whose presiding judge-on-high was Varuna.

By about 1000 B.C., iron was discovered in such accessible profusion on the Barabar hills near the Ganga around modern Patna that it could be "peeled" off for use in weapons as well as for axes and ploughs. An era of rapid change was thus launched, as the Aryan expansion eastward accelerated, owing to the conquest of hitherto impenetrable Gangetic Sal forests with iron tools and weapons. As pastoral nomadism was replaced by iron plough agriculture, tribal villages were incorporated into territorial kingdoms. India's two great Epics reflect the courtly life and martial conflicts of this era of rapid change and cultural syncretism evolving from the early integration of Aryan and pre-Aryan cultures.

The longer Epic, *Mahabharata* ("Great Bharata") is the story of a monumental struggle for territorial power around the plains of Delhi among rival Aryan cousins. The five "good" Pandava brothers are pitted in long, often treacherous battle against their 100 "evil" cousins, who initially conspire to oust them from their rightful capital by winning a game with loaded dice. Aryans loved to gamble almost as much as they enjoyed Soma. Even noble Yuddhistira, incarnate "King of Religion or Law" (*Dharma*), eldest of the Pandavas, could never resist a challenge at craps, and kept losing roll after roll, until his kingdom and entire fortune were gone, finally sacrificing even the lovely polyandrous wife of all five brothers, Draupadi. Several times the length of *Iliad* and *Odyssey* combined, *Mahabharata* is uniquely rich in ancient Indian legend, lore, character, and custom. Its heroes are all Kshatriyas, but they wander for years in North India's jungles after losing their court, prior to returning home to fight and win the epic eighteen-day battle that ends the fabulous tale. Shortly before the battle is joined, however, a brief religiophilosophic dialogue was inserted in the earlier epic. Called *Bhagavad Gita* ("Song of the Blessed Lord"), it has since become more important to Hinduism than the rest of the rambling work. Reflecting as it does post-Christian era concepts rather than ideas current in 1000 B.C., the message of the *Gita* will be considered later.

The setting of the shorter Epic, *Ramayana* ("The Story of Rama"), is about 300 miles east of Delhi at Ayodhya, and probably reflects Aryan court life several centuries later than that depicted in the *Mahabharata*. As they advanced to the east and south, Aryans came into contact with and conquered many different peoples, some quite primitive jungle folk. The *Ramayana* may be read as an allegory of what Aryans see as the conquest of "uncivilized demons" who inhabited Southern forests and disturbed the meditations of sadhus seeking enlightenment through yogic concentration. Prince Rama and his perfect wife Sita were also obliged to leave their capital and palace to wander in treacherous jungles for many years, and while so doing beautiful Sita was abducted to the island of Lanka by its demon-king Ravana, darkly as villainous as Rama was virtuous. Subsequent additions to the Epic core turn Prince Rama into an earthly emanation (*avatara*) of solar god Vishnu, sent down to save the world from Ravana's terror and torture. The original story might, however, truly indicate how perilous life in North India was from the tenth to the eighth century B.C., when respectable people could hardly venture beyond their palace walls without risking abduction, robbery, or rape. Earlier episodes of courtly intrigue at Ayodhya among the doting old king's three wives also reflect the sordid politics of harem rule, so common to subsequent eras of Indian history.

Enlisting the aid of jungle birds and beasts, especially monkeys, whose General, Hanuman, is still worshiped as a Hindu deity, Rama finally finds his poor bride and saves her after defeating Ravana in prolonged single combat. The traditionally low and suspect status of Indian women was then made painfully clear, however, since even all-virtuous Rama refused to take his bride back until she first proved her chastity through ordeal by fire. Agni himself emerges golden from the flames as Sita approaches and escorts her to Rama. They fly home together in Rama's "private plane" to inaugurate the era of Ram Rajya. Many years later, nonetheless, courtly tongues started wagging and male chauvinist questions were asked about how it was possible for Sita to live so long in Ravana's palace without once allowing that tall, dark, and handsome demon-king to lay a finger on her beautiful body. King Rama not only listened to such scurrilous gossip, but believed it, once again calling on Sita to "prove" herself. This time, in despair, she cried out to her Mother, Earth's Goddess, for "Sita" means "furrow." At her supplication, the earth opened, and up came Mother Goddess on her throne of gold, taking her lovely daughter up onto her lap, away from such foolishly doubting men.

While Aryan Epics reflect an exalted status of Kshatriyas in this era from about 1000 until 700 B.C., duller "commentaries" on the Vedas were composed by Brahman priests, who exalted themselves and their rituals in prose *Brahmanas*. Every detail of each ritual sacrifice was elaborated in these handbooks of priestly lore, which helped inflate Brahmanic pretentions as well as the cost of ceremonies that soon required as many as sixteen or seventeen Brahmans to carry them out. Rajas and Vaishyas paid the lavish price in cows, Soma, ghi, and other nectar consumed by the flames. Brahmans prospered and emerged by the end of this era as nothing less than "gods on earth," whose sacred feet supposedly never touched common dirt, thanks to Brahmanic powers of levitation. Perhaps because of their status as currency, cows were now also worshiped, as were the mantras chanted by Brahmans; sacred utterances such as "*Om*" came to symbolize the universe, for example. "Sound" itself, *Vach*, was deified, as was demiurge *Brahma*, and a new specially mighty impersonal absolute called *Brahman*.

Rama's defeat of Ravana, however, symbolizing the Aryan conquest of non-Aryan demons in Gangetic forests and farther south, permitted patient sadhus to continue silent yogic meditation in those jungles. Soma sacrifices in the Gangetic valley were more often than not ill-timed to "bring" monsoon rains, and the pretentions as well as inflated costs of Brahmanic ritual started seeming more and more hollow to kings and commoners alike. For where was the Raja who never lost a war, despite all the cows he paid his Brahmans? Or the wealthy merchant who never died? Or the pious prince who never fell ill? Why waste so many valued creatures and resources on "magic" that didn't work? Some Kshatriya princes started asking radically different questions, seeking inner paths to salvation that had nothing to do with ritual sacrifices or the costly and elaborate Brahmanic establishment.

Pre-Aryan wisdom distilled from the "heat" of silent yogic meditation provided Aryan conquerors with new mystic keys to understanding and salvation. After some seven centuries of Aryan and pre-Aryan intercourse, a synthesis of what seems to have been the finest fruit of both systems emerged in scripture called *Vedanta* ("End of the Vedas"), starting by about 800 B.C. The texts of this last stage in Vedic intellectual evolution were compiled in the woods around eastern U.P. and Bihar, mostly by Kshatriyas, and are known as *Upanishads*, meaning "to sit down in front of" in Sanskrit, since that was how these ideas were conveyed, esoterically, by a single guru to his student in forest clearings. Upanishadic dialogues, often brilliant, introduced new concepts that were to become axiomatic to the subsequently emerging Hindu synthesis. The "laws of action" (*karma*) and pessimistic ideas of "reincarnation" (*samsara*) and the material world as "illusion" (*maya*) bubbled up to Vedantic light from pre-Aryan antiquity, or so it would seem, for ideologically Upanishadic thought was as far removed from robust Aryan optimism and nature-worship as Bihar is from the North-West Frontier. The ultimate goal was now "release" (*moksha*) of one's "Soul" (*Atman*) from this veil of material sorrow and pain, and from any imperative of rebirth. Historically, Aryan conquerors by this time appear to have fallen under the spell of deeper pre-Aryan profundity and quiet wisdom. Upanishadic texts, however, continued to pay lip service to Brahmans and their rituals, hence were accepted as Vedic scripture, despite their radical doctrines. Brahmans have long been ingenious assimilators and synthesizers. . . .

STANLEY WOLPERT, professor of history at the University of California in Los Angeles, is a recognized expert in the history of India. Among his many books are biographies of Gandhi and Nehru.

Romila Thapar

NO

Early India: From the Origins to A.D. 1300

The First Urbanization—the Cities of the Indus Civilization

The earliest excavations of the cities of the Indus civilization were at Harappa (Punjab) and Mohenjo-daro (Sind) and these remain the most important urban complexes, larger than the other towns. Many of the latter—large or small—have been excavated, some only partially, such as Kot Diji (Sind), Kalibangan (Rajasthan), Rupar (Punjab), Rakhigarhi, Banawali, Mitathal (Haryana) and the ports of Lothal and Dholavira, and Surkotada (Gujarat). Ganweriwala (Bahawalpur) awaits excavation. The larger cities are approximately a hundred hectares in size and the lesser towns come close to half that size. It has been suggested that if the extensions of the city are included Mohenjo-daro could cover an area of 200 hectares.

The time period of the civilization has in the past been divided into the pre-Harappan (starting in the late fourth millennium and continuing to 2600 B.C.), the Mature Harappan (from *c.* 2600 to 1900 B.C.) and the Late Harappan (to *c.* 1750 B.C.). There is sometimes a preference for the term Early Harappan rather than pre-Harappan, since it suggests continuity into the Mature Harappan. Other labels have also been used in recent studies but there is no final consensus. The cluster of sites in the Bolan area—Mehrgarh, Pirak and Nowshehra—as well as the settlement at Harappa, show an impressive continuity from the pre-urban to the mature urban, and finally the declining phase of the civilization.

The Indus civilization was the most extensive of the ancient riverine civilizations, with sites as far north as Shortughai in the Pamirs, and some activity across the sea southwards in Oman in the Arabian peninsula. It incorporated the north-western mountains and came as far east as the upper *doab,* although the actual area of control is likely to have been more limited. Southwards there was much activity in present-day Gujarat, and some settlements going further into northern Maharashtra. In the first two instances the Harappans, as entrepreneurs in trade, were doubtless searching for valuable raw materials. Lapis lazuli from the Pamirs and the Chagai Hills of eastern Iran was much valued in the trade with Mesopotamia. Copper deposits in Oman were perhaps what attracted the Harappans, given that copper was much in demand further west. Trade with Mesopotamia is evident from the recovery of a few Harappan seals, beads and weights at Mesopotamian sites, and some, which are thought to be Harappan, at sites in the Persian Gulf. The Mesopotamian references to the land of Meluhha and its people might have been intended for the Indus civilization, the products of this land being listed as ivory, carnelian, wood, lapis and gold, all familiar to the Indus cities. Other areas to the east mentioned in Mesopotamian sources were Dilmun and Makan. Coastal shipping from western India along the Gulf to the Tigris-Euphrates delta has been continuously involved in the exchange between India and the Gulf. Contacts with Afghanistan and Iran were maintained through the passes in the north-west mountains, and particularly the Bolan Valley. Other contemporaries were the people of the Sothi-Siswal cultures in Rajasthan and Haryana, as well as the Kayatha culture in central India. The locations of the cities appear to have been chosen with an eye to the availability of resources and the transportation of goods by river or by sea.

Harappan artefacts, or artefacts influenced by Harappan forms, designs and functions, have been found over an extensive area. But this is not an indication that the area had a uniform culture and identical observances. It seems evident from the variations discovered that local cultures functioned and took shape beneath the Harappan system. This interface between the local culture and a wider ranging one is an aspect of the subcontinental cultural life throughout its history.

The cities were maintained from the surplus produced in the countryside, together with other resources gathered or mined in various regions. This process seems to have resulted from co-ordination in obtaining raw materials, working them into commodities and trading them in a systematic manner. Closer to home, copper would be mined in Rajasthan and Baluchistan. Semi-precious stones were available in large quantities from western India, lapis from the Chagai Hills or the Pamirs and were crafted into beads, some perhaps being traded as raw material. Timber such as teak was available in Gujarat, and other wood elsewhere; shell and chank came from the coast and were cut to make ornaments; and there was a range of other items. Harappan pottery is distinctive, with designs in black, of plants, birds and abstract forms, frequently painted on a red surface. Pottery is a clue to locating Harappan sites, but it is likely to have been made, after a fashion, in many local areas.

The cities were centres for the production of crafted items that were traded both overland and across the seas. This was not the work of casual craftsmen and required considerable skill and organization. Bead-making was an extensive industry, using gold, copper, shell, semi-precious stones, steatite, faience and ivory. Bronze and stone tools were largely functional but some were useful for exchange. Workshops for the production of beads and similar objects were located in Harappan cities and the etched carnelian bead was to become a characteristic Harappan object. Such workshops are often identified by the presence of a quantity of unfinished items. Carefully graded weights made of chert occur at Harappan sites, as well as rods for measurement, again suggesting functions linked to exchange and a sophisticated system of weights and measures. Lothal has evidence of a structure that has been described as a dockyard, although this description remains controversial. In its vicinity was a warehouse which was probably a hub of exchange and a place where the finished products of the craft workshops were gathered, stored and transported. Doubtless the profits from trade both within the northern and western areas of the subcontinent, and between the people of this culture and those of the Persian Gulf and Mesopotamia, kept the cities economically viable.

The cities demonstrate a sophisticated sense of civic planning and organization. In most cases the city was divided into the smaller citadel area, frequently to the west, where the essential institutions of civic life were located, possibly together with some places used for public rituals, and the larger residential area to the east. This bifurcation was not continued in the planning of cities of the later historical periods, although the tendency in civic planning to concentrate professions in particular areas remained characteristic. The impression given by the Harappan cities is one of a concern with maintaining urban order and an efficient economic system managing land, labour and water.

Huge man-made brick platforms formed the foundation for the buildings of the citadel, possibly to make them secure against floods and other damage since most of the cities were on the banks of rivers, probably to facilitate the transportation of goods. These structures may also have given direction to the plan of the cities. City-planning roughly followed a grid pattern, with roads oriented approximately to the cardinal directions, which assisted civic facilities, particularly the carefully articulated drainage system where house drains were linked to those of the street. House-plans generally had a courtyard as the focus, with rooms opening on to it. Most houses had individual wells, bathing places and drains. Drains and structures of importance were largely constructed of kiln-fired brick, whereas the houses were of mud-brick. The brickwork shows experience and expertise. Stone was used more extensively in Dholavira. The quarrying, dressing and transporting of stone was more labour-intensive and would have required considerable management. The city-plan of Dholavira differed from that of the other cities. Elaborate arrangements were made, but less for the storage of food and more for the storage of water. Large water reservoirs were built within the fortified part of the city. Architectural requirements for the building of the Harappan cities would have included a knowledge of surveying and geometry. The making of a calendar was necessary for agriculture and this in turn incorporated some knowledge of astronomy.

The citadel area of the city generally had defence walls and bastions, with elaborate entrances that were no doubt appropriately guarded. Sometimes the city was also fortified. Was this demarcation from the surrounding countryside expected in early cities? As a new phenomenon, the city was the focus of wealth that was different in quantity from that of the village, and its management also differed. It required a distinctive way of life unfamiliar to non-urban societies. In comparison with other contemporary cities, the Harappan cities do not display any spectacular wealth in either the houses or the graves. A few impressive gold objects have recently been excavated from a Harappan site, but the totality of jewellery remains small when compared, for instance, to the volume from Mesopotamian cities. The demarcation between town and countryside may also reflect the management of the cities. Did the control over agricultural production, labour and raw materials require that those exercising this authority be protected? Such control would have been more extensive than that based on kinship connections and clan loyalties. This is not to suggest that those inhabiting the cities were aliens, but rather that they gave expression to the kind of authority that had not existed before, and that it was the concept of this authority that may have seemed alien to rural life.

Clearing the surrounding tropical savanna forest around each city may have been necessary in order to extend cultivation sufficiently to support the urban population. This may have resulted in fairly large-scale deforestation. A ploughed field of the period just prior to Harappan urbanization was excavated at the site of Kalibangan, with the field coming up to the edge of the city. Wheat and barley were the staple crops, although rice and millet were also grown where possible. Water conduits, some of which were underground in certain areas, and small-scale inundation canals leading off rivers directed water to where it was needed. These would have required constant maintenance and supervision.

The monumental buildings of the citadel areas have been variously interpreted: granaries, warehouses, collegiate buildings and possibly a ritual centre at Mohenjo-daro, including a tank and its surroundings. The constructing of the platforms and the buildings would have required a large deployment of organized labour with an equally effective system of obtaining and controlling labour. Possibly this was done through regular labour services rather than a tax or tribute. The form that this may have taken remains uncertain, although some attempts have been made to reconstruct the foci of authority. Supervision and control involved many aspects of administration: agriculture to ensure food for the city population; the production of items for trade, such as copper ingots and beads, and seals for stamping goods; labour for the building and maintaining of cities; and above all the organization of the trade itself.

In describing the governing authority it was earlier suggested that it consisted of a single imperial system, with twin capitals at Mohenjo-daro and Harappa, a suggestion that has been superseded by others. The recent idea that the Indus cities were city-states and were the prototypes for the 'autonomous' cities of historical times carries little conviction, given the essential differences in the concept and planning of the early and later cities. It might be more plausible to consider flexible relationships between the cities, given their differentiated size and their authority systems that are apparent, for instance, if the city-plan of Kalibangan is compared with that of Dholavira or Harappa. Governed by chiefs of clans in the early phase, this system would have given way to a more complex one by the Mature period, when representatives of city authorities probably coalesced to ruling jointly in assembly to control a sophisticated system of obtaining labour and co-ordinating urban activities. The structures at Mohenjo-daro point to complex authority systems. Possibly a more centralized administration was adopted and adapted in various regions, interacting with city centres.

The kind of evidence that is associated with the archaic states of west Asia is hardly recognizable in the Harappan state or states. Distinctive buildings cluster in one area in most cities, and there is a striking absence of monumental graves or well-demarcated sacred centres. Even a palace is difficult to discern. The availability of weapons appears to have been limited, with little evidence of disturbed strata to indicate physical destruction arising from warfare. The usual supporting evidence for an organized administration in the form of designations, codes and accounting is unavailable, unless some of the pictograms when deciphered contain information on titles and formal functionaries. The seals may well be tokens of identity of such authorities.

Among the many remains of the Harappan culture, the most puzzling are the seals. They are generally small, flat, square or rectangular, often made of steatite, with a pictorial motif that depicts humans and/or animals or composite figures, and an inscription which remains undeciphered. If the script is pictographic or logographic and not alphabetic, as has been suggested, it could point to the use of more than one language. The possible languages that have been considered include Proto-Dravidian, Indo-Sumerian, Elamo-Dravidian, Indo-Aryan and Austro-Asiatic. Some systematic work in linguistic patterns suggested by the script has attempted to use Proto-Dravidian, but so far without success in decipherment. Attempts to read it as Indo-Aryan are as yet far from systematic. The one certainty is that the signs should be read from right to left. A perforated boss at the back of the seal helps in its handling. Seal impressions on clay indicate that among other uses seals were used to stamp packages. They could therefore have been tokens identifying civic authorities, supervisory managers of long-distance trade, merchants or those bringing raw materials to the cities, or clan affiliations. Signs of identification could relate to professions, religious associations or social organizations. The script also occurs on objects thought to be copper amulets, apart from occasionally being scratched on pots, bangles and suchlike. A short inscription in large-sized letters was unearthed at Dholavira and has been described as a signboard.

Equally puzzling are some of the animals and the scenes depicted on the seals. The most common animal is one that is thought to be a mythical unicorn, although a more mundane identification describes it as a stylized rhinoceros. It is often depicted together with an object that has been variously interpreted, often described as an altar or even a brazier. Among single animals the bull and the elephant were popular. Tigers occur less frequently and more often as part of a scene. The depiction of the horse is absent on the seals. A few bones, said to be of the horse, and small terracotta forms occur in late levels at Pirak (Baluchistan) dating to the early second millennium B.C. The claim that horse bones occur at Surkotada, and at a few other sites at earlier levels, has met with doubt, the bones being identified as those of the ass and the onager. The late arrival of the horse in India is not surprising since the horse is not an animal indigenous to India. Even on the west Asian scene, its presence is not registered until the second millennium B.C. The horse was unimportant, ritually and functionally, to the Indus civilization.

A noticeable difference between the Harappan cities and those of other ancient civilizations is the absence of recognizable religious buildings and of elaborate burials. If there were temples they are difficult to identify, for there is neither the presence of magnificent icons nor specially decorated structures. Temples therefore were not the focus of social bonding. Traditions of ancestral rituals are also not apparent, for people tended to migrate away from the cities when they declined. The cities may not therefore have been the focus of religious worship. Female figurines from the more westerly sites have been viewed as icons for worship with a prevalence of a goddess cult. This possibility is based in part on the continuing worship of various goddesses later in Indian history. Some emphasis on fertility rituals seems evident, but whether these were elaborate ceremonies remains uncertain. Fertility rituals would not be unusual given the prevalence of these in other chalcolithic cultures of the subcontinent. Some small oval structures containing ash have been interpreted as fire altars, but they could equally well be hearths. A shamanistic religion has also been suggested, but the urban character of the civilization is unlikely to have been conducive to shamanism.

A few motifs continue from Harappan times into later history, such as the *pipal*—as a leaf decoration on pottery and as a tree on seals—which was revered by some later religious sects. Much speculation focuses on whether a seated figure on a seal represents a proto-Shiva. The identification of the figure is uncertain and the evidence for the link with Shiva is tenuous. It would perhaps be more apposite to regard these representations as contributing to the evolution of a later religious mythology and iconography, rather than insisting that a later icon be imposed on an earlier period. To explore the meaning of such an icon in its own context would perhaps be more meaningful than to give it an instant label derived from an icon of a much later period. The figure could equally well be identified as depicting a yogic position, as indeed female figures in trees on some seals could be linked to the evolving of the idea of *apsaras,* celestial maidens associated with trees.

Sculptures in stone and bronze have been found, but in sporadic locations not indicating an assembly of images in a temple. Such sculpture shows a refinement of technique and concept that is striking. A small bronze figurine, probably not a ritual object, has the pleasing stance of a young and spirited woman. One among the portrait heads sculpted in stone is evidently of a person of consequence, given the band around his head and the trefoil design on his shawl, together with his curiously semi-closed eyes. Popular interpretation describes him as a priest, but this remains unproven. Terracotta forms range from children's toys to larger representations of animals. There is a noticeable absence of figures reflecting grandiose self-representations, in common with many other civilizations of this period.

Another striking contrast is the simplicity of the burials compared to the tombs of rulers further west. Grave goods are mainly the pottery of daily use with a scatter of other small items. Clearly, they did not expect huge demands on the dead in the after-life, nor were burials occasions for demonstrating status.

Post-Harappan burials of the late second millennium B.C. in what has been called the Cemetery H culture, largely confined to Harappa and the Punjab plains, were accompanied by pottery that was different from the Harappan. The ritual of burial continued even if the culture of these later people was not identical. These burials may point to new arrivals or the emergence of some new traits in the cultures of the region. Such suggestive links through a few items reflect similar hints from earlier times, although the artefacts differed. For instance, connections have been suggested between artefacts found in the Bolan Valley and in the Indo-Iranian borderlands, and still further in Afghanistan and Iran, in the area now being referred to as the Bactria Margiana Archaeological Complex.

The decline of the cities was once ascribed to invading Aryans. However, there is little archaeological evidence for the type of massive invasion that would have led to the collapse of a well-established political and economic system, resulting in a displacement of culture, although the denial of an invasion does not preclude the possibility of migrants bringing the Indo-Aryan language into India. The argument supporting an invasion was based on the subsequent culture of the Vedic corpus, using a language—Indo-Aryan that had affinities with central Asian Indo-European, particularly with Old Iranian. That this language gained currency in northern India was thought to be the result of a conquest of the local population by Indo-Aryan speakers, the evidence being drawn from the hostility of the *arya* towards the *dasa* in the *Rig-Veda.* The reference to Indra attacking the *pur,* enclosed settlements of the *dasas,* was erroneously read as referring to the cities of the Indus civilization. However, there are alternative explanations for the introduction of Indo-Aryan into India and its gradual spread across northern India. These explanations have more to do with the historical context of urban decline, the coexistence of differing cultures or languages, and the filtering of Indo-Aryan speakers into north India through small-scale migrations, than with the overly simplistic theory of an invasion as a historical explanation; or for that matter with the current attempts being made by some enthusiasts to prove the indigenous origin of the Indo-Aryan speakers even though, as we shall see, the evidence points to the contrary.

The skeletons in habitation areas at Mohenjo-daro were earlier interpreted as demonstrating the massacre of citizens, which endorsed the theory of an invasion. But analyses of the skeletons revealed that most of these people had died of diseases such as severe anaemia, indicating a different set of reasons for urban decline. Violent deaths in a limited area do not necessarily mean widespread invasion and could be evidence of local disturbances. Diseases or severe environmental changes as factors in weakening a population have not been sufficiently examined in the context of early Indian history.

Other explanations generally advanced are that the cities declined largely because of environmental changes, such as the long duration of the severe flooding of the Indus in the vicinity of Mohenjo-daro, and climatic change leading to greater desiccation, deforestation and a more generalized deurbanization with the dying out of trade requirements and a consequent political collapse. The extent to which the degradation of the environment caused the decline of the cities remains unclear. Urban decline can only be properly explained by multiple causes, and these were not uniformly applicable to each region. This is also evident from the variant patterns that followed urban decline. Squatters from the countryside occupied some cities in the lower Indus Plain, bringing about a ruralization of the erstwhile urban system. Elsewhere there were migrations away from Harappan centres, as in the migration from the Hakra Plain towards the Ganges-Yamuna *doab,* or from Gujarat to northern Maharashtra. Some settlements in the northwest and Punjab might have been subjected to raids and skirmishes, such as are described in the *Rig-Veda,* or for which there appears to be occasional evidence at some sites, for example Kot Diji.

The decline of the cities did not mean that the Harappan pattern of culture disappeared. Although many urban functions would have ceased, people in rural areas would have continued their activities with marginal changes. The Harappan system was a network linking the urban to the rural and some features could have been maintained in the rural areas, even if these areas suffered administratively and economically from the removal of this protective system. Some archaeological cultures were contiguous in time and space with the Harappan; at other places there were overlaps between the Late Harappan and subsequent cultures. Continuities would therefore not be unexpected, but it is more likely that these were restricted to mythologies, rituals and concepts of tradition, since the material culture does not show continuities.

The second millennium also saw activity along the Indo-Iranian borderlands, including the arrival in north-western India of the horse and the chariot with a spoked wheel, both of which were new to the subcontinent. Occasional comings and goings across these borderlands were gradually to accelerate, a pattern that remained effective until recent times. . . .

The Vedic Corpus

Had these been the only sources available, the reconstruction of the beginnings of Indian history would have been relatively simple. But two other kinds of evidence have contributed to our understanding of historical beginnings, both predating the sources discussed above. In the nineteenth century the reading of the Vedic corpus and subsequent philological studies led to a different reconstruction of the past, at variance with the traditional story. European scholars of Sanskrit had recognized that it was related in structure and sound to Greek and Latin. This led to the theory of a common ancestral language, Indo-European, used by the ancestors of people speaking these languages.

The focus of this research was on the Vedic corpus, the composition of which was earlier than that of the epics and *puranas,* and the language was a more archaic form of Sanskrit that is now called Old Indo-Aryan. This differentiated it from the later form of Sanskrit referred to as Classical Sanskrit. The *Vedas* were primarily manuals of rituals and commentaries on these, the narrative being incidental. Epic literature was the narrative of the society of heroes and the *Puranas* were sectarian literature of later times. Therefore the purpose of the epics, the *Puranas* and the *Vedas,* was different. Since the last were the earliest in time, Indian history was said to begin with the information that they contained. Unlike the *Puranas* and the epics, which have some explanation of the past, the Vedic corpus has little of this, but is a collection of compositions contemporary with the period from the mid-second millennium to the mid-first millennium B.C. The reconstruction was therefore based on the readings made by modern scholars of the evidence in the corpus.

Indo European and Indo-Aryan are language labels, but in the nineteenth century these were also incorrectly used as racial labels and this confusion persists. The correct usage should be 'Indo-European-speaking people' and 'Indo-Aryan-speaking people', but the shortened labels, Indo-European and Indo-Aryan or Aryan, are commonly used. Language is a cultural label and should not be confused with race, which, although also a social construct, claims that it has to do with biological descent. Indo-European is a reconstructed language, working back from cognate languages, and its speakers had central Asia as their original habitat. Gradually, over many centuries, they branched out and as pastoralists spread far afield in search of fresh pastures. They also worked as carriers of goods intended for exchange. Some migrated to Anatolia, others to Iran, and some among the latter, it is thought, migrated to India. In the texts composed by them, such as the *Avesta* in Iran and the *Rig-Veda* in India, they refer to themselves as *airya* and *arya,* hence the European term, Aryan. Vedic literature in the Indo-Aryan language has been studied intensively, as an early textual source of an Indo-European language which was concerned with rituals and their explanation, and was regarded as the most sacred. The beginnings of Indian history were associated with the coming of the 'Aryans', some time in the second millennium B.C.

But this picture of the past was again to be disturbed in the twentieth century. In the 1920s archaeology revealed the existence of an urban civilization, dating to a period prior to the *Rig-Veda,* in the north-west of India: the Indus civilization or the Harappa culture. This discovery took the formative period of civilization back to the third millennium B.C. Archaeology has provided evidence on the evolution of cultures from pre-Harappan societies, and this goes back still further in time. The Harappa culture provides no clues to the rule of Manus, nor does the Vedic corpus.

There are clearly many sources of information on the beginnings of Indian history. Archaeological evidence is chronologically more precise, but cannot be used to identify any culture as 'Aryan' since archaeology, in the absence of a script, cannot supply information on a language. Unfortunately, the Harappan script remains undeciphered. The theory of an Aryan invasion no longer has credence. The *Rig-Veda* refers to skirmishes between groups, some among those who identify themselves as *aryas* and some between the *aryas* and *dasas.* The more acceptable theory is that groups of Indo-Aryan speakers gradually migrated from the Indo-Iranian borderlands and Afghanistan to northern India, where they introduced the language. The impetus to migrate was a search for better pastures, for arable land and some advantage from an exchange of goods. The migrations were generally not disruptive of settlements and cultures. There is also the argument that these were dissident groups that had broken away from the speakers of Old Iranian, whose language and ideas came to be encapsulated in the *Avesta*. There is a significant reversal of meaning in concepts common to both the *Avesta* and the *Rig-Veda*.

There is a tendency among those who oppose the idea of Aryan speakers coming from outside India to equate invasion with migration. Historically the two are distinctly different processes in terms of what would have been the preconditions of either, such as the activities and organization involved, or the pattern of social and historical change that ensued. The migrant groups would have remained small as there is little evidence of the substantial cultural replacements associated with massive migrations. Migration raises different questions from those of invasion, relating to cultural interactions, linguistic changes and the defining of social status among both the host groups and those arriving.

The linguistic evidence remains firm. Indo-Aryan is of the Indo-European family of languages and there is a linguistic relationship with some ancient languages of west Asia and Iran, as well as some that took shape in Europe. Indo-Aryan is a cognate of Old Iranian, dating to the second millennium B.C., with which it has a close relationship. Indo-Aryan also incorporated elements of Dravidian and Munda, languages known only to the Indian subcontinent. The incorporation increases in the texts composed in locations eastwards into the Ganges Plain. This points to a considerable intermixing of the speakers of these languages.

The sequence of events seems to have been as follows. The cities of the Indus civilization had declined by the mid-second millennium B.C. and the economic and administrative system slowly petered out, the emphasis shifting to rural settlements. It was probably around this period that the Indo-Aryan speakers entered the north-west of India from the Indo-Iranian borderlands, migrating in small numbers through the passes in the north-western mountains to settle in northern India. Small-scale migrations have the advantage of not being dramatically disruptive and these could have started even earlier, although the cultural differences would have been registered only after the decline of the Harappan cities. Although archaeological confirmation of textual information is not possible, there are no strikingly large settlements in the area during this period. Textual sources suggest that initial settlements were in the valleys of the north-west and the plains of the Punjab, later followed by some groups moving to the Indo-Gangetic watershed. Such continuous small-scale migrations may have followed earlier pastoral circuits. The search was for pastures and some arable land, as they were mainly a cattle-keeping people. Myths in the *Avesta* refer to repeated migrations from lands in Iran to the Indus area, explaining these migrations as arising from a pressure on the land through an increase in human and animal numbers. The *Rig-Veda* suggests the close proximity of other peoples inhabiting the area.

During this period of the early first millennium the hymns of the *Rig-Veda,* composed in the previous centuries, were compiled in the form known to us today. The compilation is thought to be later than the composition, which adds to the problems of dating the hymns. Central to this compilation are what have been called the 'family books', said to have been among the earliest hymns, attributed to those belonging to the more respected families. They were claimed as inheritance by those who also claimed descent from the eponymous ancestor said to be the author of the book. Among the later commentaries on the *Rig-Veda,* the best known is that of Sayana, written in the fourteenth century A.D. and illuminating as a late perspective, but prior to modern analyses.

The Context of the *Rig-Veda*

The aim of this brief summary is to indicate the nature of the evidence from a variety of sources and organize it in a historical order. The diverse textual sources make it difficult to provide a neat reconstruction and there are inevitably loose ends. These are complicated further when attempts are made to correlate this evidence with non-textual sources.

The earliest dated evidence of a form of Indo-Aryan, which, although not identical to Rig-Vedic Sanskrit is nevertheless close to it, comes not from India but from northern Syria. The evidence is brief and scattered and consists of names and words that are in a form of Indo-Aryan. A treaty between the Hittites and the Mitannis dating to the fourteenth century B.C. calls upon certain gods as witnesses and among these are Indara/Indra, Mitras(il)/Mitra, Nasatianna/Nasatya, and Uruvanass(il)/Varuna, known to the *Rig-Veda* and the *Avesta*. Curiously, there is no reference to the dominant deities of the *Rig-Veda*—Agni and Soma. A text of a similar date on the training of horses includes some words that are a close variant of Indo-Aryan. The horse and chariot, introduced from central Asia, became common in west Asia in the second millennium B.C., suggesting a correlation between the arrival of horses and of Indo-Aryan speakers. The Kassite rulers of Babylon, who seem to have come from the Iranian plateau in the middle of the millennium, also mention gods, a few of whom have close parallels in Sanskrit, such as Surias and Maruttas. The Kassite language was not Indo-European despite some names sounding Indo-Aryan. The Indo-Aryan of west Asia is referred to as Proto-Indo-Aryan to differentiate it from Vedic Sanskrit and to indicate that it appears to be more archaic.

It would seem that sometime in the second millennium there were people in northern Syria who spoke a language that was Indo-Aryan in form, judging by what is referred to as the Hittite–Mitanni treaty of the fourteenth century B.C. It is not clear how this language reached the western end of west Asia when there is no archaeological or linguistic evidence of contact between north India and these areas in this period. One possibility is that the language originated in a region from where Indo-Aryan speakers could have travelled either westwards or to the south-east. This could have been north-eastern Iran, which would explain how people speaking an Indo-European language and using horses and chariots arrived in lands to the west. What is of historical interest is that, although the treaty suggests the military success of these people, Indo-Aryan nevertheless had a precarious presence in Syria and disappeared from this region after a while. Yet in India, where it arrived through migration, its presence came to be firmly established. Conquest, therefore, is not necessarily always the mechanism for the spread of a language. A more advanced technology, control over nodes of power and claims to ritual authority can be far more effective.

The connections between Iran and north India on the other hand are close. The language[s] of the *Avesta* and Indo-Aryan were cognates, descended from the same ancestral language. The date of the *Avesta*—the text of Zoroastrianism—has been controversial, but a mid-second millennium date is now being accepted. The linguistic relationship between the two includes not just words but also concepts. The interchangeability between 'h' and 's' is one of the differences, but there is a consistency in this change such as *haoma, daha, hepta hindu, Ahura* in Avestan, and *soma, dasa, sapta sindhu, asura* in Rig-Vedic Sanskrit. In terms of religious concepts the attributes of gods are often reversed. Thus Indra is demonic in the *Avesta,* as are the *daevas* (*devas* or gods in Sanskrit) and Ahura/*asura* emerges as the highest deity. This has led to the theory that originally the Old Iranian and Indo-Aryan speakers were a single group but dissensions led to their splitting up. It was then that the Indo-Aryan speakers living in the Indo-Iranian borderlands and the Haraxvati (Sarasvati) area of Afghanistan gradually migrated to the Indus plain, bringing with them their language, rituals and social customs, to settle as agro-pastoralists in the *sapta-sindhu* area, as described in the *Rig-Veda,* later merging with the local population.

This reconstruction tallies up to a point with the archaeological evidence. If the presence of Indo-Aryan speakers is indicated by the presence of the horse—which was central to both action and ritual in the *Rig-Veda*—then it dates to the early second millennium in the subcontinent, having been virtually absent in the Mature Harappan period. Some horse bones and terracotta representations of the later period have been found at sites adjoining the borderlands. The paucity of bones and representations points to its being an unfamiliar animal. Other items, small in number, turn up in excavations along the Indo-Iranian borderlands at sites that were entry-points to the Indus plains, which parallel those found in southern Afghanistan and north-eastern Iran. Among these areas is that of the Bactria Margiana Archaeological Complex (BMAC). Terracotta models of horses carrying riders sometimes with beaked faces, pottery recalling that of central Asia and Iran, compartmented seals, bronze dirks and axe-adzes hint at connections. These could be items of gift exchange limited to high-status families, but they suggest more than just accidental coming and going. The trickle of migration may have had its beginnings at this point but gained momentum later.

Evidence of Proto-Indo-Aryan in Syria has a bearing on the date of the *Rig-Veda.* If the Indo-Aryan of the Hittite–Mitanni treaty was more archaic than the Sanskrit of the *Rig-Veda,* the compositions of the latter would date to a period subsequent to the fourteenth century B.C. Even if they were of the same date, the language of the *Rig-Veda* would not be earlier than the second millennium B.C. Such a date would also corroborate its closeness to the language and concepts of the *Avesta.* The closeness gradually decreases as the location of Vedic Sanskrit shifts into the north Indian Plain. This date would also suit the composition of the *Brahmanas* as texts interpreting the ritual. The *Brahmanas* were post-Rig-Vedic, generally dated to the first millennium B.C., and revealed familiarity with the western and middle Ganges Plain, referring to migrations into this area.

Recently, it has been argued that the date of the *Rig-Veda* should be taken back to Harappan or even pre-Harappan times, and its authors equated with the creators of the Indus civilization. This would support the 'Aryan' authors of the *Rig-Veda* being indigenous to northern India, and also the Indo-Aryan language. By calling it the Indus-Sarasvati or Sarasvati civilization, the Vedic contribution is evoked—even if it is in fact absent.

This view overlooks the data from linguistics, and does not present an analytical understanding of the archaeological evidence. There are two aspects to this evidence: one is whether the artefacts and monuments of the Harappa culture are described in the *Rig-Veda;* the other is whether the concepts implicit in organizing the Harappan system of urban settlements find their counterpart in the *Rig-Veda.* Many scholars have described what they regard as the essential characteristics of Harappan urbanism, which they have found to be absent in the *Rig-Veda.* Among these may be listed cities with a grid pattern in their town plan, extensive mud-brick platforms as a base for large structures, monumental buildings, complex fortifications, elaborate drainage systems, the use of mud bricks and fired bricks in buildings, granaries or warehouses, a tank for rituals, and remains associated with extensive craft activity related to the manufacturing of copper ingots, etched carnelian beads, the cutting of steatite seals, terracotta female figurines thought to be goddesses, and suchlike.

The second aspect calls for a conceptual familiarity with the use of these objects and structures. The *Rig-Veda* lacks a sense of the civic life founded on the functioning of planned and fortified cities. It does not refer to non-kin labour, or even slave labour, or to such labour being organized for building urban structures. There are no references to different facets or items of an exchange system, such as centres of craft production, complex and graded weights and measures, forms of packaging and transportation, or priorities associated with categories of exchange. Rituals are not performed at permanent ritual locations such as water tanks or buildings. Terracotta figurines are alien and the fertility cult meets with strong disapproval. Fire altars as described in the corpus are of a shape and size not easily identifiable at Harappan sites as altars. There is no familiarity from mythology with the notion of an animal such as the unicorn, mythical as it was, nor even its supposed approximation in the rhinoceros, the most frequently depicted animal on the Harappan seals. The animal central to the *Rig-Veda,* the horse, is absent on Harappan seals. There is no mention of seals or a script in the *Rig-Veda*. Sculptured representations of the human body seem unknown. The geography of the *Rig-Veda* is limited to the northerly Indus Plain—the *sapta-sindhu* area—and is unfamiliar with lower Sind, Kutch and Gujarat, and with the ports and hinterlands along the Persian Gulf that were significant to Harappan maritime trade. . . .

Romila Thapar is Professor Emerita in History at Jawaharlal Nehru University, New Delhi. In 1983 she was elected General President of the Indian History Congress and in 1999 a Corresponding Fellow of the British Academy. She is the author of *Asoka and the Decline of the Mauryas, Ancient Indian Social History: Some Interpretations, History and Beyond, Sakuntala: Texts, Readings and Histories,* and *Cultural Pasts: Essays on Indian History.*

EXPLORING THE ISSUE

Was an Aryan Invasion Responsible for the Demise of the Indus Valley Civilization?

Critical Thinking and Reflection

1. Examine the evidence put forth by each of these historians. Based on this evidence, which of these windows into the past offers the more compelling argument. Critically discuss.
2. Research Hinduism, perhaps the world's oldest religion. Modern India is a majority Hindu nation. Critically explore what is at stake for modern Hindus in the outcome of this scholarly debate.
3. India claims that Hinduism was indigenous to the region. If evidence suggests that Hinduism was a transplant, there might be a political dimension to this issue. Analyze and critically discuss.
4. Examine references to Hindu sacred texts in both selections, looking for points of disagreement in interpretation. Which texts does each author explore? Critically discuss why the chosen texts support the author's thesis.
5. What interpretation might arise if an outside culture conquers an indigenous population? How might the interpretation be different if an outside culture, arriving peacefully, produces a fusion of the two cultures? Critically examine these two possibilities in the light of an indigenous national narrative about its own past.
6. Stanley Wolpert writes: "Devout Hindus believe the Aryans have always lived in India. . . . Historical scholarship and comparative linguistic studies of the past century and a half give us better reason to hypothesize, however, that Indo-Aryans were the easternmost wing of the once cohesive Indo-European-speaking tribes whose great dispersion from pastureland somewhere between the Caspian and Black Seas probably occurred around 20,000 B.C." What are the implications of these later studies?
7. What does historian Romila Thapar mean by this statement, referring to the Vedas, the earliest Hindu scriptures: "Had this been the only source available, the reconstruction of the beginnings of Indian history would have been relatively simple?"
8. Once you have discerned what the quotation above means, critically apply it to questions about India and Hinduism.

Is There Common Ground?

Since these two historians cite many of the same material and literary sources, what areas of agreement can you find in their citations? Both, for example, describe the existence of the Harappan cities, with their sophisticated examples of city planning and infrastructure. And, both cite the use of the pipal tree or its leaves as a symbol. Both look to religious and narrative sources. Both agree that Aryan and Dravidian peoples combined to shape the population of modern India.

Wolpert is a bit more secularly historical in his approach, though he cites a religious source. Thapar is a bit more interested in religious texts. And, she is a lot more objective in her use of these texts than some Hindu nationalists are. It is possible to disagree about whether or not an Aryan invasion caused the demise of the Indus Valley Civilization while agreeing about other related questions. As a student of history, it is important to make these distinctions.

Question: Can you find both points of agreement and the points of disagreement that remain?

Additional Resources

There are many sources that are useful to a study of Indus civilization. Gregory Possehl, ed., *Harappan Civilization: A Contemporary Perspective* (American Institute of Indian Studies, 1982) offers a series of essays on the subject, including one that compares the Indus demise with the Maya collapse. Possehl has also edited *Ancient Cities of the Indus* (Carolina Academic Press, 1979), another useful compilation. Archaeologist Jonathan Mark Kenoyer's *Ancient Cities of the Indus Valley Civilization* (Oxford University Press, 1999) contains much information along with many useful visuals. A summary article of his work can be found in "Birth of a Civilization," *Archaeology* (January/February, 1998).

Padma Manian, "Harappans and Aryans: Old and New Perspectives of Ancient Indian History," *The History Teacher* (November 1998), presents information as to how the questions raised in this issue are covered in the various history textbooks used in American colleges and universities. And Sudeshna Guha's "The Indus Civilization," *History Today* (October 2007) tells "how the interpretations of this civilization have shaped and been shaped by notions of an authentic 'Indian Civilization'."

Internet References . . .

Indus Valley Civilizations

Very comprehensive site for the world of ancient Indus civilization, including side shows, essays, resources, and much more; over 1,000 pages.

www.harappa.com/har/har0.html

Selected, Edited, and with Issue Framing Material by:
Helen Buss Mitchell, *Howard Community College*
and
Joseph R. Mitchell, *Howard Community College*

ISSUE

Was Sumerian Civilization Exclusively Male Dominated?

YES: Chester G. Starr, from *A History of the Ancient World* (Oxford University Press, 1965)

NO: Samuel Noah Kramer, from "Poets and Psalmists: Goddesses and Theologians," in Denise Schmandt-Besserat, ed. *The Legacy of Sumer* (Undena Publications, 1976)

Learning Outcomes

After reading this issue, you should be able to:

- Summarize the evidence about Sumerian civilization found on cylinder seals, in burial chambers, and in surviving texts.
- Summarize what we know about gender roles in ancient Sumer.
- Understand what surviving artifacts tell us about humans and about deities.
- Explain the connection between the gender of the gods/goddesses and gender roles among human males and females.

ISSUE SUMMARY

YES: Historian Chester G. Starr argues that Sumerian society was male dominated, from the gods to human priests and kings, and barely acknowledges the status of women in either the heavenly or the earthly realm.

NO: Museum Curator Samuel Noah Kramer who relies on much of the same data as Professor Starr, argues that powerful goddesses and earthly women played prominent roles in both cosmic and everyday lives.

This issue rests on a difference in interpretation rather than on a clearly stated topic debate. Each writer makes assumptions about what ancient Sumerian society was like and each finds evidence to support those assumptions. As you read these two selections, notice that both cite remarkably similar findings. The difference is that for Starr they are asides, whereas, for Kramer they are the focus. For centuries the story of life in the Fertile Crescent has been told as if only men were actors in the drama. If royal queens received splendid burials, does it make sense to refer to rulers exclusively as kings? If women in a particular culture exhibited what historians like to call agency, acting on their own behalf to shape their own lives, is it accurate to term that culture male dominated? Much will depend on interpretation, on whose perspective seems to you more accurate. Was Inanna a "fertility goddess" as Starr assumes or "Queen of Heaven" and goddess of everything as Kramer implies? Although Kramer's perspective is gaining acceptance, your textbook may continue to make Starr's assumptions.

Since the sophisticated civilization at Sumer is one of the earliest in human history, it has become a model for our understanding of human behavior. If men have always dominated women, then arguments that this arrangement is "natural" have greater strength. If, on the other hand, women played more active roles, then perhaps our understanding of what is by nature and what is by custom needs to be rethought. Virtually all of Kramer's evidence is present in Starr's selection. Is Starr correct to downplay or ignore most of it in favor of male-centered givens? As you read the YES selection, pay particular attention to every mention of women as a group and to particular royal and divine women. When you find these female characters more fully developed in the NO selection, ask yourself which viewpoint you question?

One of the dangers historians must constantly be aware of is called presentism. We all have a tendency to judge whatever we read about the past in terms of present values. If we assume that our ways of doing and being are best, we may judge the past in terms of what makes sense for us. Those who find it proper and even natural for men to dominate social, cultural, and religious life may assume that the past generated this pattern and be tempted to fit existing evidence into these assumptions. Those who question patriarchal dominance may be inclined to look for and find evidence of strong, contributing, and empowering women. The historian's task is to take the evidence on its own terms and let it tell its own story, whether or not that story meshes with the present one.

In 1970, virtually all world history books would have told the story of Sumer as Professor Starr has done. More than 40 years later, new understandings have led a growing number of scholars to take a fresh look at all of the past and question its archaeological and literary records, making as few assumptions as possible. Curator Kramer represents this new breed of scholars. He does not claim that women dominated Sumerian society, but he finds areas in which women seem to have held positions as exalted as those held by men and he presents female deities who refuse to be demoted. Their authority and enduring inspiration suggest that women were not seen as outsiders to power. Indeed, the idea of "sacred marriage" suggests that the vital acts of creation and sustenance flowed from a blending of male and female energies.

There seems to be a correlation between the perceived gender of the deity or deities and the status of women in any culture. In ancient Sumer, we find evidence of women high priestesses and one who achieved prominence as a poet. While Inanna, "the brave, crafty, ambitious, aggressive, desirable, loving and hating 'Queen of Heaven'" was glorified and exalted, women such as Enheduanna, the priestess/poet mentioned above played prominent roles in Sumer. Curator Kramer, in his selection, chronicles the demotion of Inanna with the arrival of Monotheism and the corresponding rapid decline in the fortunes of earthly women.

Because humans make assumptions about race and gender and then find evidence to support these assumptions, it is not surprising that Starr and Kramer reach different conclusions. Among Kramer's many books is *Sumerian Mythology: A Study of Spiritual and Literary Achievement in the Third Millennium B.C.* (Peter Smith Publishers, 1980). Sir Leonard Woolly discovered and excavated the Royal Cemetery of Ur; his *The Sumerians* (Oxford at the Clarendon Press, 1928, 1929) is a classic in the field. William W. Hallo, who participated with Kramer in the Invited Lectures that produced the book from which the NO selection is taken, is a prolific and compelling chronicler of this period. His recent *Origins: The Ancient Near Eastern Background of Some Modern Western Institutions* (E.J. Brill, 1996) contains three chapters concerning women—in law, in public life, and as authors.

Has patriarchy—the rule of society by men—always existed? Or, as historian Gerda Lerner argues in *The Creation of Patriarchy* (Oxford University Press, 1986), was this pattern created as a historical event? Erich Newman's *The Great Mother: An Analysis of the Archetype* (Princeton University Press, 1963) broke new ground in explaining the goddess archetype as did Elizabeth Gould Davis's *The First Sex* (Putnam, 1971), Merlin Stone's *When God Was a Woman* (Dorset Press, 1976), and Marija Gimbutus's *Goddesses and Gods of Old Europe* (University of California Press, 1982). *Engendering Archaeology: Women and Prehistory*, Joan M. Gero and Margaret W. Conkey, eds. (Basil Blackwell Ltd., 1991) examines the archaeological record for gender-based approaches and assumptions. In that work, see Susan Pollack's *Women in a Man's World: Images of Sumerian Women* and Pollack's *Ancient Mesopotamia: The Eden that Never Was* (Cambridge University Press, 1999).

Try to set aside your own assumptions about how women and men should behave and your own early twenty-first–century way of looking at the world. Try to see only the evidence as it has come down to us in cylinder seals, burial chambers, and texts. Based purely on what both writers agree is there, what conclusions can we draw about Sumerian society? Being able to critically evaluate what we learn permits us to make our own judgments and frees us from dependence on the theories of others.

YES 

Chester G. Starr

The First Civilization of Mesopotamia

The Mesopotamian Outlook

Sumerian civilization. The Sumerians, who were in the forefront of early Mesopotamian progress, are linguistically a puzzle, for their agglutinative, largely monosyllabic speech cannot be connected with any of the major groups of languages. By about 3500 B.C. they had begun to draw conventionalized pictograms (representations of physical objects) on clay tablets, found at Kish and Uruk, and perhaps on other, less enduring materials. Three hundred years later, about 3200, tablets show that the scribes of Sumer took a tremendous step, which we do not know ever to have occurred independently elsewhere; that is, they advanced to a mixture of ideograms (marks representing concepts such as "day") and phonograms (symbols expressing syllabic phonetic values, as we might draw a bee for the sound be). Since some symbols expressed more than 1 phonetic value and, on the other hand, 1 single sound could be expressed by up to 14 different marks, sometimes "determinatives" were prefixes to indicate the class to which the word in question belonged, as deity, bird, and so on. These elements came to be wedge-shaped marks impressed in the clay by a stylus; from the Latin word *cuneus* for wedge the Mesopotamian script is called "cuneiform."

From this stage onward cuneiform script could be employed to set down languages of any type; both Semitic dialects like Akkadian and Indo-European tongues like Hittite and Old Persian were so written. Due to the mixture of ideograms, syllabic phonograms, determinatives, and other complications the number of individual signs was much larger than in an alphabetic form of writing. The earliest Sumerian script had perhaps 2000 symbols, but eventually about 500-600 sufficed. Each of these, though considerably simplified over the years, remained so complicated that only professional scribes commonly wrote in the ancient Near East. Writing was an arcane mystery down to Greek times.

The earliest Sumerian tablets are very difficult to comprehend. Largely, though not entirely, they are temple accounts: "so many sheep, so many goats"; or "to so-and-so, beer and bread for one day." If we place them against the much larger bulk of written documents which had appeared by the end of the third millennium, it is nonetheless possible to gain precious light upon early Sumerian thought. The main characteristics of this outlook appeared very swiftly and were essentially fixed as the main lines of Mesopotamian civilization over the next 2500 years. Yet we can also observe that the structure of this outlook became ever more complicated and advanced. The "black-headed people," as the Sumerians called themselves, affected greatly their Semitic neighbors and followers, reaching on up through the Fertile Crescent, and were in turn influenced from the outside.

To a modern observer the pattern of thought which developed in third millennium Mesopotamia is marked by its formal, outwardly static, and religious qualities. In the Sumerian view their arts and crafts had been "revealed" to them by the gods above and were unchanging. Everything must have its name to assure its place in the universe, and one who knew the true name of something had a power over it. Among the earliest Sumerian documents are lists of stones, animals, plants, and the like, classified on their outward characteristics. Yet these lists, which students probably learned by heart, reflect the fact that men were deliberately analyzing and imposing abstract order upon the materials of nature. We must not make the mistake of underestimating the tremendous achievements of these first civilized thinkers merely because their approach was so different from our own; indeed, they created many of the basic tools of thought and concepts we take for granted.

It was now, for instance, necessary to count and to write down numbers; Mesopotamian arithmetic was based sometimes on units of 10, sometimes on units of 60. The latter style, which through its fractions gives us our division of the hour and of the circle, was eventually used especially in astronomy, where men charted the major constellations still marked on modern sky-charts. By the first millennium Mesopotamian scholars began a tradition of ever more refined, precise, and abstract thinking and evolved a concept of place-value notation which was the root of our number system. Civilization also required the measurement and weighing of quantities of grain and metals; the chief weight, a talent of 60 minas, remained the standard quantity on down through the Greek era. Geometry began in the measurement of fields and the requirements of building. The year was solar but was defined in 12 lunar months, with an intercalary month inserted about every 3 years, to fix the great religious festivals and so to regulate agricultural activity.

The arts also progressed. The use of mudbrick and baked brick produced heavy, massive architecture, in which true arches were developed. To cover the ugly brick walls the Sumerians decorated their temples with bands of colored clay cones rammed into the walls and semi-columns; painted frescoes appeared later.

The gods were now visualized in human shape and were represented in statues which are, as it were, the gods themselves; for any transcendental quality was lacking. In some temples there were placed before the gods statues of the rulers, commemorating their devout piety in an equally straightforward, factual, yet reverent manner. The technical problem that stone was hard to come by forced sculptors often to create seated figures and almost always to exaggerate the size of the head. Although some pieces are sharply conceived, they do not exhibit in general an intense interest in nature or a sense of human individuality. Equally significant are the many cylinder seals of men of property, carved with a representation of gods, imaginary animals, or myths. The demonic or bestial motifs that developed in this field were a rich repertoire of great influence on other Near Eastern and Greek art forms, but a modern rationalist will often feel disturbed by their suggestion that man did not yet recognize the distinctiveness of his own nature.

Early Mesopotamian religion. Man's failure fully to recognize himself is reflected in the religious aspect of the early Mesopotamian outlook. Sumerian civilization had a very strong religious imprint. Only in the confidence born of their common belief in divine support could these men have endured the hardships and unremitting toils necessary to assure a firm foothold in the valley. Their greatest building, the temples, are a mighty testimonial to a human ideal; the priests who clustered about these temples were so important that one may almost call an early Sumerian city-state a theocracy.

The character of this religious system becomes more apparent once there are written copies of Mesopotamian myths and artistic representations of the gods and heroes. To the inhabitants of Mesopotamia the gods were many, for they represented the forces which drove mankind; and in primitive thought these forces were many, distinct in origin. Yet the gods were grouped in a regular pantheon.

Highest was An, the divine force, which could be visualized in the overarching bowl of Heaven; his name meant "sky" or "shining." Then came Enlil, the active force of nature, who at times manifested himself in the raging storms of the plains, and at other times aided men. The goddess of earth was worshiped as Nin-khursag and under other names. Last of the four creator gods came Enki, the god of waters who fertilized the ground, and by extension became the patron of the skills of wisdom. To these were added 50 "great gods" who met in the assembly of the gods, the Annunaki; a host of other deities, demons, and the like also floated in the Mesopotamian spiritual world.

To the Sumerians their physical environment had come into being from a primordial chaos of water, whence the forces Tiamat and Abzu arose and, by processes of procreation, created the gods. Thereafter came the sky, the earth, and finally mankind. In the spring of each year occurred the greatest religious festival of the land, known as the Akitu in later Babylonia. This was the New Year's feast, an 11-day ceremony of gloom and purification and then of joy, which ended as the gods set the lots for mortal men during the coming year. On the fourth day of the festival the priests recited a myth of the creation called from its opening words *enuma elish:*

> When on high the heaven had not been named,
> Firm ground below had not been called by name . . .
> No reed hut had been matted, no marsh land had appeared.

Beside this ritual myth many other tales evolved to explain the nature of life. The underlying scheme of thought expressed therein postulated that the world was the product of conscious divine action for divine purposes; obvious, too, is the feeling that the world was all animate. Throughout ancient times, down to and past the rise of Christianity, mankind could not quite divest itself of the idea that trees, springs, and the like were endowed with human characteristics or were directed by manlike immortals. In Mesopotamia, as elsewhere, religion not only bound together society but also assured to man the fertility of his fields, his flocks, and himself. One of the greatest figures in Mesopotamian myth was the goddess of human fertility, Inanna (later Ishtar), who may in root have gone back to the Neolithic female figurines found in Halafian levels. Her descent to the underworld and then her return symbolized the renewal of agricultural life; her husband Dumuzi (later Tammuz), went permanently to the nether regions as a substitute for her. Each year he was mourned, and his marriage with Inanna was celebrated at the New Year's feast.

To modern men, who approach these early myths from a scientific point of view, the tales of the gods are neither sensible nor logical, and the view of life which they express in their repetitious verse is basically a primitive one of gross action and elemental passions. In explaining the nature of the universe men translated into divine terms their own earthly concepts of personal clash and procreation. Yet in early civilized societies these tales were so satisfying that people all over the Near East accepted them. Mesopotamian stories thus passed into the early chapters of the Book of Genesis, where they continued to answer men's curiosity about the Creation down to the past century.

Place of man. The gods, though human in appearance, paid little attention to mortal men as they drank and made merry, and also wrangled and abused each other in the divine assemblies. Men feared and honored the gods; each city-state was but the earthly domain of certain divine forces on high, for whose ease men toiled throughout their lives. Once dead, men and women could expect only to go to a shadowy, gray land of departed spirits. Such views befitted a land that had recently raised itself to the level of civilization by hard labor, where the climate was severe, where the dangers of flood and sudden disease were ever present, inexplicable, and incurable by human means.

Yet two further reflections may be made. In the first place, the spiritual world of early Mesopotamia was an orderly structure, within which men could operate in a rational fashion; the gods could be propitiated by their human servants through the creation of divine ceremonies. Again, mankind could not quite forget that *it* was the agent that built and tilled, even though human society was far from perfect. In part this hidden realization led to a nagging fear that men might be upsetting an order laid down by the gods. One myth thus depicted the gods, angered by the clamor of men, sending down the Flood; other myths seem akin to the Hebrew story of the Fall of Man from a primitive grace and leisure through his own unwillingness to be passive. In part, however, men were proud of their achievements. A prime reflection of this point of view is the myth of Gilgamesh.

The Gilgamesh epic. The tale of the hero Gilgamesh, two-thirds god in origin, had Sumerian roots but was more fully formulated into a continuous epic about 2000 B.C. Then it spread all over the Near East and long exercised men's imagination; one artistic symbol drawn from it, that of Gilgamesh strangling a lion, was handed down age after age until it appeared on medieval cathedrals in Western Europe.

Unlike the other myths, which were largely theological creations associated with certain rituals, this epic was centered on human figures. Essentially it was a mighty reflection on the nature of man, who strives and creates but in the end must die. Gilgamesh himself was a legendary king of Uruk, who built its great wall but treated his subjects so harshly that the gods created a wild man, Enkidu, to subdue him. Gilgamesh, wily as well as harsh, did not meet Enkidu head-on, but sent out a harlot, who by her arts tamed Enkidu—this taming we may perhaps take as an exemplification of the passage of mankind to civilization. "Become like a man," Enkidu put on clothing and went forth to protect the cattle against lions and wolves. The bulk of the epic then recounts the heroic adventures of Gilgamesh and Enkidu against various inhuman monsters:

> Who, my friends, [says Gilgamesh] is superior to death?
> Only the gods live forever under the sun.
> As for mankind, numbered are their days;
> Whatever they achieve is but the wind!

So, while they lived, let them at least make a name for themselves.

During the course of these exploits Enkidu offended the gods (especially Ishtar), and died after a long death-bed scene of recrimination against divine decrees. Gilgamesh first lamented, then set out to seek the plant of eternal life so that he might bring his friend back to life. Eventually Gilgamesh made his way to Ut-napishtim, the original Noah, who told him the story of the Flood and advised him how to get the miraculous plant under the sea. Although Gilgamesh succeeded in his quest, on his return journey he lost the plant to a snake. The dead, in sum, cannot be brought back to life.

When later we come to Greek civilization we shall meet another half divine hero, Achilles, who fought in the war against Troy and there lost his friend Patroclus; and at that point we shall be able to compare the essential qualities of two different civilizations, the Greek and the Mesopotamian, as reflected in their great epics, the tale of Gilgamesh and the *Iliad.* Here it may be observed that in the earlier tale the story is balder and has less artistic unity; it is more naive, far earthier (especially in the harlot scenes). Monsters are prominent in the plot of Gilgamesh's adventures, and the appeal is rather to emotion and passion than to reason, as is that of the *Iliad.*

In both epics the divine plane determines earthly events, though men have freedom to oppose the gods; but the heroes of the *Iliad* are more strongly characterized and far more optimistic. Mesopotamian pride in human achievements went hand in hand with fear for human audacity. Men must cling closely to their fellow men on earth and must appease the jealous gods carefully. The individualism of Homer's heroes, their ability to accept human fate while yet enjoying life, their passionate curiosity and delight in the physical world—these were qualities which did not exist in early, god-fearing Mesopotamia. Yet in saying so much, in an effort to relate the alien world of Gilgamesh to a world that most of us know far better, we must not depreciate the earlier epic too much. Poetically it was a magnificent creation, and psychologically it reflects a truly civilized meditation upon the qualities of mankind.

The Results of Civilization

Rise of classes (3000-2000 B.C.*).* That the early Mesopotamian outlook had at times a gloomy cast the modern historian can well understand. Not only did the fabrication of civilization itself impose terrific social burdens upon its human creators, but also the subsequent developments during the third millennium resulted in disturbing changes.

This evolution must be considered, if only briefly, in any sketch of early Mesopotamian civilization, for the structure of society had been greatly elaborated by the time of Hammurabi (1700); therewith, inevitably, the outlook of the Mesopotamian world was modified in important particulars. Although the documents available at the present time are not yet adequate to trace the political history of the third millennium in detail, it is amazing—and instructive—to see even dimly the rise of many critical problems which have been enduring issues in all subsequent civilized societies. Social classes, for example, became differentiated. Economic exploitation and social unrest inevitably followed hard upon this differentiation; law developed both to regulate social and economic relationships and to prevent undue oppression. Interstate warfare appeared and led to imperialism, which in turn produced military classes and bureaucratic systems to run the larger states born of conquest.

The first cities seem to have been masses of relatively undifferentiated fellow workers who were tightly grouped in an economic and spiritual unity. Separate classes, however, evolved rather quickly. Toward the top were the priests, who also worked in the early days but tended to become managers on behalf of the gods; the temples grew into powerful economic centers, which owned much of the land and absorbed a large part of the product in rents and temple dues. The records of Baba, divine consort of the main god of Lagash, show that her priests directed about one-sixth of the farm land of the city-state in the Early Dynastic period. Half of this domain was rented out to peasants, who paid their dues at the rate of one-third to one-sixth of the yield and also owed sums in silver, which they obtained by selling other parts of their produce in the city. The second half of her domain was cultivated by the labor of the peasants, organized in guilds under foremen. The goddess also controlled large flocks, shipping craft, fishermen, brewers, bakers, and spinners of wool; the growth in industrial production in Early Dynastic times, which was remarkable, was largely for purposes of cult as well as for military use and for the kings and their henchmen. The raw materials needed from outside Mesopotamia were obtained by merchants, who trafficked by sea, by river, and by land for stone, metals, wood incenses, and jewels.

Beside and above the priests rose the king or *lugal*. In later views kingship "was lowered from heaven by the gods" as a guarantee of earthly order. Palaces began to appear; the tomb of one queen of Ur, about 2500 B.C., astounded the modern world with its wealth of delicate jewelry, its harps, and the masses of sacrificed servants. To conclude that the kings and priests were simply parasites would be unjust, for these upper elements held together the state, harbored its reserves, and expanded its strength. Yet they did draw profit from their superior position, and the rest of society now fell into a dependent status.

One mark of this situation is the appearance of slavery. Some men were forced to sell themselves or their children into bondage through the workings of debt; others were captives, especially from the hilly country to the east. While the reduction of human beings to the legal level of chattels always has a distorting influence upon social relationships, morals, and general views of human nature, its effects must be assessed soberly. In the present case, the institution of slavery was but the extreme edge of the fact that the leisure of the upper classes and the great monuments of early times rested upon the forced labor of the multitude and otherwise would have been impossible. In other words, civilization was not lightly bought and did not directly benefit all men alike. Most of the labor force, however, in Mesopotamia as in other slave-holding societies of the ancient world consisted of technically free men. Slaves were rarely used in agriculture, the main occupation of mankind throughout the ancient world; rather, slaves lived in cities, where they were domestic servants, concubines, and artisans. As valuable pieces of capital, slaves were usually accorded a minimum standard of human needs, and at times were able to rise again into freedom through hard work. . . .

Conclusion. If we look back, rather than forward, the story of man's advance in Mesopotamia from the first Neolithic villages of the valley down to the age of Hammurabi must strike us as one of the most amazing achievements of mankind. Despite the difficulties of climate and terrain the settlers had harnessed their energies toward a remarkable physical progress, and the compact masses of population which now dotted lower Mesopotamia were far larger than had ever before been possible.

Chester G. Starr (1914–1999) was professor of history at the University of Michigan, Ann Arbor. He was the author of many books on the ancient world, including some focusing on Greek and Roman civilization.

Samuel Noah Kramer

Poets and Psalmists: Goddesses and Theologians

Introductory

Let us now turn . . . to an anthropological inquiry relating to the Sumerian counterpart of one of modern man's more disturbing social ills: the victimization of woman in a male-dominated society. At the *XVIII Rencontre assyriologique internationale* held in Munich in 1970, I read a paper entitled "Modern Social Problems in Ancient Sumer," that presented evidence in support of the thesis that Sumerian society, not unlike our own rather tormented society, had its deplorable failings and distressing shortcomings: it vaunted utopian ideals honored more in the breach than in observance; it yearned for peace but was constantly at war; it preferred such noble virtues as justice, equity and compassion, but abounded in injustice, inequality, and oppression; materialistic and shortsighted, it unbalanced the ecology essential to its economy; it was afflicted by a generation gap between parents and children and between teachers and students; it had its "drop-outs," "cop-outs," hippies and perverts.

This highly competitive, and in some ways hypocritical, unjust, oppressive, genocidal Sumerian society, resembled our own sick society in one other significant aspect—it was male dominated: men ran the government, managed the economy, administered the courts and schools, manipulated theology and ritual. It is not surprising to find therefore, that by and large, women were treated as second-class citizens without power, prestige, and status, although there are some indications that this was predominantly true only of later Sumerian society, from about 2000 B.C. on; in earlier days the Sumerian woman may have been man's equal socially and economically, at least among the ruling class. Moreover, in the religious sphere, the female deity was venerated and worshipped from earliest times to the very end of Sumer's existence; in spite of some manipulative favoritism on the part of the male theologians, God in Sumer never became all-male.

Woman in Early Sumer

We begin our inquiry with the little that is known about women's rights and status in early Sumer. Some time about 2350 B.C., a king by the name of Urukagina reigned for a brief period in Lagash, one of Sumer's important city-states. Many of his inscriptions were excavated by the French almost a century ago and have since been deciphered and translated. Among them is a "reform" document in which Urukagina purports to depict the evil "of former days," that is, of the times preceding his reign, as well as the measures he introduced to alleviate them. One of these reforms reads as follows: "The women of former days used to take two husbands, but the women of today (when they attempted to do this) were stoned with stones inscribed with their evil intent." To judge from this rather strident boast, women in pre-Urukagina days practiced polyandry, which hardly smacks of a male-dominated society.

Or, take the case of Baranamtarra, the wife of Urukagina's predecessor, Lugalanda. Quite a number of administrative documents concerned with this lady have been uncovered, and these indicate that she managed her own estates, and even sent diplomatic missions to her counterpart in neighboring city-states, without consulting her husband.

Even Urukagina who, because of his uptight reaction to polyandry, might perhaps be stigmatized as the first "sexist" known to history, was not all antifeminine. His wife Shagshag, for example, like her predecessor Baranamtarra, was the mistress of vast estates, and ran her affairs every bit her husband's equal. In fact Urukagina might well be acclaimed as the first known individual to favor "equal pay for equal work" regardless of sex. One of the remedial measures he proudly records in the above-mentioned reform document, concerns the bureaucratic gouging of the bereaved by officials in charge of a funeral. In pre-Urukagina days, reads the document, when a citizen was brought to rest "among the reeds of Enki," a cemetery that was deemed more desirable than an ordinary burial ground, there were on hand three male officials who received a considerable amount of beer, bread, and barley, as well as a bed and a chair, as compensation for their services. But Urukagina decreed that the food rations of the three male attendants be reduced considerably and that the furniture "bonus" be eliminated altogether. At the same time he ordered that a woman designated as *nindingir*, "Lady Divine," who formerly had received no remuneration, be given a headband and a *sila*-jar (about one-fifth of a gallon) of scented ointment as compensation for her services—a payment that compared not unfavorably with that received by her male colleagues.

Enheduanna: The First Woman Poet on Record

Nor was the *nin-dingir* the only priestess who played a significant role in the cult. A more prominent and important lady was the *en,* a Sumerian word that may be rendered "high priestess" as well as "high priest." According to Sumerian religious practice, the main temple in each large city had its *en* who was male if the deity worshipped in that temple was female, and was female if the deity worshipped there was male. Quite a number of these high-priestesses are known to us by name, beginning with about 2300 B.C., a generation or two after the days of Urukagina. The first of these is Enheduanna, the daughter of Sargon the Great, one of the first empire-builders of the ancient world, whom her father appointed to be high-priestess of great moon-god temple in the city of Ur. But not only was she the spiritual head of one of Sumer's largest temples, she was also a poet and author of renown. Quite recently it has been demonstrated that at least three poetic compositions—a collection of temple hymns and two hymnal prayers to the Goddess Inanna, are at least in part, the imaginative literary creation of this Enheduanna. Here, in Sumer, therefore, some 4300 years ago, it was possible for a woman, at least if she was a princess, to hold top rank among the literati of the land, and to be a spiritual leader of paramount importance.

Woman in Later Sumer

From the three centuries following the days of Enheduanna, little is known about Sumerian society and the status of woman. But from about 2000 B.C. there have been recovered legal documents and court decisions of diverse content, and from these we learn that the role of woman had deteriorated considerably, and that on the whole it was the male who ruled the roost. Marriage, for example, was theoretically monogamous, but the husband was permitted one or more concubines, while the wife had to stay faithful to her one and only spouse. To be sure, a married woman could own property and other possessions, could sometimes buy and sell without consulting her husband, and on rare occasions, could even set special conditions in her marriage contract. In case of divorce, however, the husband had very much the upper hand—he could divorce his wife virtually at will, although if he did so without good cause, he had to pay her as much as *mina* (about a pound) of silver, no mean sum in those days.

Female Deities: Victimization and Resentment

But it was not only on the human plane that women had lost some of their rights and prerogatives in the course of the centuries—it also happened on the divine plane. Some of the female deities that held top rank in the Sumerian pantheon, or close to it, were gradually forced down the hierarchical ladder by the male theologians who manipulated the order of the divinities in accordance with what may well have been their chauvinistic predilections. The goddesses, however, were no "pushovers"; more determined and aggressive than their human counterparts, they struggled to hold or regain at least part of their deprived supremacy to the very end of Sumer's existence. What is more, at least one of the goddesses, Inanna, "Queen of Heaven," continued to be predominant and preeminent to the very last, although the theologians ranked her only seventh in the divine hierarchy. The available texts are not explicit on the subject, but with a bit of between-the-lines reading and burrowing, it is possible to follow the struggling career of at least two important female deities, and to trace some of their ups and downs in myth and cult.

Nammu, Goddess of the Primeval Sea

The female deity that seems to have suffered the sharpest decline was Nammu, the goddess of the primeval sea who, according to several texts, was the creator of the universe and the mother of all the gods. By all genealogical rights, therefore, had the theologians played it fair, she should have had top billing in the pantheon. But in the god-lists where the deities are arranged in hierarchical order, she is rarely mentioned, and never at the head of the list. Moreover, her vast powers as goddess of the sea were turned over to the male deity Enki, who was designated by the theologians as the son of Nammu, in an apparent attempt to mitigate and justify this bit of priestly piracy. Even so, the king who founded the Third Dynasty of Ur, and ushered in a political and cultural Sumerian renaissance about 2050 B.C., chose as his royal name *Ur-Nammu,* "Servant of Nammu," which indicates that the goddess was still worshipped and adored by the mighty of the land.

Ki, Mother Earth

But it is Nammu's daughter Ki, "(Mother) Earth," whose gradual decline can be followed almost step by step with the help of the ancient texts. As noted above, the sea-goddess Nammu was conceived as the creator of the universe. Now the Sumerian word for universe is the compound *an-ki,* where an means both "heaven," and "(Father) Heaven," and ki means both "earth," and "(Mother) earth." It was the sexual union of Father Heaven with Mother Earth, that according to the Sumerian theologians, ushered in the birth of the gods unto their generations. The first to be born of this Heaven-Earth union, was the airgod Enlil, "Lord Air," and it was he who, by making use of his atmospheric power, succeeded in separating Heaven from Earth, thus preparing the way for the creation of vegetation and all living things including man. In view of these theological premises and postulates, the leading deities of the pantheon, once Nammu had been deprived of her supremacy, should have been ranked by the theologians in the order An (Heaven), Ki (Earth), and Enlil (Lord Air), and this may have been so in very early times. But by 2400 B.C., when the relevant inscriptional evidence first becomes available, we find the leading deities of the pantheon usually arranged in the order An (Heaven), Enlil (Lord Air), Ninhursag (Queen of the Mountain), and Enki (Lord of the Earth). What had evidently happened was, that the theologians, uncomfortable and unhappy with a female deity as the ruler of so important a cosmic entity as earth, had taken this power away from her and transferred it to the male deity Enlil who, as one poet puts it, "carried off the earth," after he had separated it from heaven. Moreover, after taking away from the goddess the rulership over the earth, the theologians also deprived her of the name "*Ki,* (Mother) Earth," since it no longer accorded with her reduced status. Instead they called her by one of her several epithets, Ninhursag, that means "Queen of the Mountain," and demoted her to third place in the pantheon.

But the worst was yet to come—even third place was deemed too high by male "chauvinistic" theologians, and she was finally reduced to fourth place, third going to Enki, "Lord of the Earth." This god's name was actually a misnomer, since he had charge only of the seas and rivers, and even this power, as noted earlier, he usurped from the Goddess Nammu. But the theologians of Eridu, a city not far from Ur, which was the God's main seat of worship, were consumed with ambition. As the name "Lord of the Earth" indicates, the devotees of this God were really out to topple the God Enlil who had become the ruler of the earth after he had separated it from heaven. To achieve their goal, they went so far as to have their God Enki confound the speech of man and turn it into a "babel" of tongues, in order to break up Enlil's universal sway over mankind that worshipped him "in one tongue." In spite of this, however, they failed to dethrone Enlil from second place, since his bailiwick was Nippur, Sumer's holy city, whose priests were too powerful to overcome. Disappointed and frustrated the Eridu theologians turned upon the female deity Ninhursag (originally named Ki) whose devotees were evidently too weak to prevent her victimization. And so, by 2000 B.C., when the pertinent texts become available once again, the order of the four leading deities of the pantheon is no longer An, Enlil, Ninhursag, Enki, but An, Enlil, Enki, and Ninhursag.

Still, as already noted, the Sumerian goddesses did not take male-domination "lying down," and not infrequently, according to the mythographers, they registered their resentment in no uncertain terms, and showed the male "victors" who was really "boss." As of today, for example, we have two myths in which Ninhursag and Enki are the main protagonists, and in both it is Ninhursag who dominates the action, with Enki "playing second fiddle."

The scene of one of these myths is Dilmun, the Sumerian "Paradise" land, where both Ninhursag and Enki are at home. Here, after considerable maneuvering, Ninhursag contrived to make eight different plants sprout. But when Enki sees them, they tempt his appetite, and he sends his vizier to pluck them and bring them to him. After which, he proceeds to eat them one at a time. This so enrages Ninhursag that she pronounces against him the "curse of death." And mighty male though he was, eight of his organs become sick, one for each of the plants he had eaten without permission from the goddess. The failing Enki would surely have died in due course, had not the goddess finally taken pity on him, and created eight special deities, each of whom healed one of Enki's ailing organs.

In the other available myth, we find Ninhursag and Enki acting as partners in the creation of man from the "clay that is over the Deep." In the course of a banquet of the gods, however, the two deities become tipsy, and the partnership turns into a competition. First Ninhursag fashions six malformed creatures whom Enki dutifully blesses and for whom he even finds useful "jobs" in spite of their handicaps. Then it was Enki's turn. But the creature he fashions displeased Ninhursag who proceeds to rebuke Enki bitterly for his clumsy effort, a reproach that the god accepts as his due, in language that is obsequious and flattering.

Prestigious Female Deities

Nor was Ninhursag the only female deity who, in spite of occasional victimization by the theologians, continued to be revered and adored in the land. There was Nidaba, the patroness of writing, learning, and accounting, whom the theologians provided with a husband by the name of Haia, who seemed to be no more than a shadowy reflection of the goddess. There was the goddess of medicine and healing who was worshipped in Lagash under the name of Bau, and in Isin under the name of Ninisinna. In Lagash, it is true, the theologians did succeed in making her husband Ningirsu paramount in cult and adoration. Even so, there are indications that originally Bau was of higher rank than her spouse. Moreover, when it came to the naming of their children, the people of Lagash preferred by far to include Bau rather than Ningirsu in the chosen theophoric name—clear evidence of the popularity of the goddess, no matter what the theological dogma. As for Ninisinna, it was she who was venerated as the heroic tutelary deity of Isin, while her husband Pabilsag is a far less impressive figure. Most interesting is the case of the Lagashite goddess Nanshe who was acclaimed and adored as Sumer's social conscience, and who was depicted as judging mankind every New Year. Her spouse Nindara, a far less significant figure, did not participate in this solemn and fateful procedure; it was her bailiff, the male deity Hendursagga, who carried out obediently and faithfully the verdict of his deeply revered mistress.

Inanna, "Queen of Heaven"

But the goddess that should be soothing balm to the resentful wounds of liberated women the world over, is the bright, shining Inanna, the brave, crafty, ambitious, aggressive, desirable, loving, hating "Queen of Heaven," whose powers and deeds were glorified and extolled throughout Sumer's existence in myth, epic, and hymn. No one, neither man nor god, dared oppose her, stand in her way, or say her nay. Early in her career, perhaps about 3000 B.C., she virtually took over the divine rulership of the important city, Erech, from the theoretically and theologically all powerful heaven-god An. In an effort to make her city Erech the center of civilized life, she braved a dangerous journey to the *Abzu,* "the Deep," where the cosmic and cultural divine laws were guarded by its King Enki. When this same Enki organized the universe and somehow failed to assign her the insignia and prerogatives she felt were her due, he had to defend himself apologetically and contritely against her angry complaint. When the rebellious highland, Ebih, failed to show her due honor, she virtually destroyed it with her fiery weapons, and brought it to its knees. Raped by the gardener Shukalletuda while sleeping wearily after a long cosmic journey under one of his shade-trees, she pursued him relentlessly and finally caught up with him and put him to death, but was gracious enough to console him with the promise to make his name endure in story and song.

The role that no doubt delighted Inannamost, one that guaranteed her the affection and veneration of every Sumerian heart, was that which she played in the New Year "Sacred Marriage" rite, that celebrated her sexual union with the King of Sumer in order to ensure the fertility of the soil and the fecundity of the womb. The first king whom the goddess selected as her mortal spouse was Dumuzi (Biblical Tammuz), who reigned early in the third millennium B.C. From then on, many, if not most of the rulers of Sumer, celebrated their marriage to the goddess as avatars, or incarnations of Dumuzi. Throughout the "Sacred Marriage" ceremony, it was the goddess who was the active, dominant protagonist; the king was but the passive, ecstatic recipient of the blessings of her womb and breasts, and of just a touch of her immortality. And when—so tell the mythographers—Dumuzi, with typical male arrogance, became weary of being subordinate to the goddess, and, in her absence, began to play high and mighty, she fastened upon him her "eye of death," and had him carried off to the Nether World. There he would have remained forever, had not his loving sister offered herself as his substitute, thus allowing him to return to earth for half the year.

Monotheism: Death-Knell of the Female Deity

So much for the Goddess Inanna, the feared and beloved "Holy Terror" of the ancients. The female deity, as is clear from what was said above, had her ups and downs in Sumerian religion, but she was never really licked or totally eclipsed by her male rivals. Even in much later days, when Sumer had become generally known as Babylonia, and the Sumerian language was superseded by the Semitic Akkadian, the poets continued to compose hymns and psalms to the female deities, and especially to the Goddess Inanna under her Semitic name Ishtar. The death-knell of the female deity in Near Eastern religious worship came with the birth of monotheism, and especially the Jahwistic monotheism propagated by the Hebrew prophets. For them, Jahweh was the one and only, omniscient, omnipotent and all-male—there was no room for any goddess no matter how minimal her power, or how irreproachable her conduct. Still, even in Jahwistic Judaism there are faint echoes of the female divinities of earlier days, and it is not altogether surprising to find that the Hebrew mystics, the Kabbalists, spoke of a feminine element in Jahweh designated as the "Shekinah," opposed to a masculine element designated as the "Holy One, Blessed Be He." And at least one passage in the renowned Kabbalistic book, the Zohar, states that Moses, the son of God, actually had intercourse with the "Shekinah,"—a distant but not so faint reminder of the "Sacred Marriage" between Dumuzi and Inanna, that provides us with one more example of the far, gossamer, reach of the "legacy of Sumer."

Samuel Noah Kramer (1897–1990) was a curator at the Museum of the University of Pennsylvania. He wrote and published widely on Sumerian texts and mythology.

EXPLORING THE ISSUE

Was Sumerian Civilization Exclusively Male Dominated?

Critical Thinking and Reflection

1. In this issue, the YES and NO selections cite the same evidence (in many cases) yet differ in their interpretations of the evidence. Find three examples of the same evidence interpreted differently and critically examine the differences.
2. Where we place our focus will determine what we see. What is central to one of these authors is often peripheral to the other. Find two examples that fit this pattern and critically analyze the differences in focus.
3. Historians must avoid "presentism"—judging the past, using the values and assumptions of the present. Write an analysis of how Starr and Kramer each "read" the evidence they find.
4. As new archaeological evidence is uncovered, we learn in a deeper way about the lives of people long dead. How can we take steps to see the evidence in the context in which it existed, rather than in our own context? Critically discuss and strategize.
5. From what you have learned in world history, is there a strong correlation between the gender of the deity and the lives of human beings who share or do not share the gender of the deity? Critically speculate about why this would be the case.
6. In the historical past, can you find evidence that when the deities change, there are corresponding changes in the human realm? Research how the lives of humans change as a result of our human understanding of the divine.
7. Samuel Noah Kramer writes: "Some of the female deities that held top rank in the Sumerian pantheon, or close to it, were gradually forced down the hierarchical ladder. . . . The goddesses, however, were no 'pushovers'; more determined and aggressive than their human counterparts, they struggled to hold or regain at least part of their deprived supremacy to the very end of Sumer's existence." Find two examples of this phenomenon.

Is There Common Ground?

Make a list of three factual statements about Sumerian civilization on which Charles Starr and Samuel Noah Kramer are in substantial agreement. Now, find three statements that indicate their areas of disagreement. Be a detective or an amateur anthropologist. Do some additional research and determine where you think the most accurate interpretation lies. Look at the evidence as containing "clues" to the mystery of this ancient world. How a detective assembles and interprets clues will lead to his/her particular theory about a crime. And, the same is true once the crime reaches the courtroom. The Prosecutor and the Defense Attorney will each present a coherent theory of what happened, based on a common core of evidence. The jury must decide which interpretation is more likely to be "true." This is also the task facing the historian.

Question: Apply what you have learned about forensics from television crime scene investigations to what historians and archaeologists call material culture—the matter that people and cultures leave behind. What clues do cylinder seals, burial chambers, and texts offer?

Additional Resources

For a look at assumptions challenged, students may enjoy Elaine Morgan's anthropological study *The Descent of Woman* (Bantam Paperback, 1972). Playing on the title of Charles Darwin's *The Descent of Man*, Morgan assumes that the mother/child dyad rather than the male/female pair bond is what evolution is based on and she reaches very different conclusions. What brought about the worldwide transition to patriarchy? Leonard Shlain's *The Alphabet versus The Goddess* (Viking/Penguin, 1998) claims that the widespread acquisition of alphabet literacy changes the way we perceive the world (through words instead of images) and rewires the brain, leading to the demise of Goddess worship, a plunge in women's status, and the advent of harsh patriarchy and misogyny.

Inanna's enduring fascination is captured in two recent books, both based on the poems dedicated to the goddess. Kim Echlin's *Inanna: From the Myths of Ancient Sumer* (Groundwood, 2003), which credits the priestess Enheduanna mentioned in the NO selection, explores the amorous and warlike aspects of the goddess and follows her descent into the underworld. In *Inanna: Queen of Heaven and Earth* (Point Foundation, 1992), storyteller and folklorist Diane Wolkstein has taken the goddess's words from "Inanna's scribe" (Samuel Noah Kramer) and, in her own words, "I have sung them as best I can."

Internet References . . .

Materials for the Study of Women and Gender in the Ancient World

Provides lists of website materials in areas such as bibliography, essays, and images; also contains a useful search engine.

www.stoa.org/diotima

Selected, Edited, and with Issue Framing Material by:
Helen Buss Mitchell, *Howard Community College*
and
Joseph R. Mitchell, *Howard Community College*

ISSUE

Did Egyptian Civilization Originate in Africa?

YES: Clinton Crawford, from *Origin and Development of the Ancient Egyptians* (Africa World Press, 1996)

NO: Kathryn A. Bard, from "Ancient Egyptians and the Issue of Race," in Mary R. Lefkowitz and Guy MacLean Rogers, eds., *Black Athena Revisited* (University of North Carolina Press, 1996)

Learning Outcomes

After reading this issue you should be able to:

- Describe the Afrocentric view of history and its challenge to the Eurocentric view of history.
- Understand the scholarly contribution of Caucasian scholar, Martin Bernal.
- Understand why the "blackness" of Ancient Egyptians is so hotly contested.

ISSUE SUMMARY

YES: Clinton Crawford, an assistant professor who specializes in African arts and languages as communications systems, argues that evidence from the fields of anthropology, history, linguistics, and archaeology prove that the ancient Egyptians and the culture they produced were of black African origin.

NO: Assistant professor of archaeology Kathryn A. Bard argues that although black African sources contributed to the history and culture of ancient Egypt, its civilization was basically multicultural in origin.

Africa, the continent that is considered by many to be the birthplace of humankind, has historically not been treated kindly by its global neighbors. Exploitation of every kind imaginable—culminating with the heinous Atlantic slave trade and resultant imperialism—has marked Africa's experience with the outside world. Western Europeans, in particular, developed theories to prove African inferiority in order to justify their barbaric actions. If Europeans brought civilization and Christianity to barbaric and heathen Africa, so the theory went, colonialism and even imperialism might be considered as gifts. Unfortunately, no field of academic endeavor escaped this prejudicial viewpoint, and by the nineteenth century pre-colonial Africa had been totally denied its history, and its culture had been dismissed as savage and primitive.

It is not surprising, therefore, that when most African countries gained independence after World War II, their intellectuals sought to reaffirm their continent's rich and glorious past, in order to eradicate the onus placed upon their homeland by Western historians and scientists. With assistance from African American scholars such as W.E.B. Du Bois, African historians—led by the Senegalese scientist and historian Cheikh Anta Diop—sought to write history from an African perspective in order to provide the continent with a positive account of its past. The Afrocentric view of history came of age during this time.

With recent archaeological discoveries suggesting that humankind originated in East Africa, it was natural for Africa's historians to explore the connections between black African and ancient Egyptian civilizations. Their findings seemed to confirm the interrelatedness of the two. Hence, these historians concluded that one of the oldest and most respected ancient civilizations was African in origin. Though undeniably part of the African continent geographically, Egypt had been separated from the rest of Africa culturally by what some have called an Orientalist mindset that classified Egypt as an Asiatic culture.

Which depiction of ancient Egypt is more historically accurate? Many scholars today maintain that ancient Egypt possessed a cosmopolitan, multicultural society, one that was influenced by all of its neighbors. While acknowledging the African influences on Egyptian civilization, these scholars hold that the claims of the Afrocentrists are too broad and sometimes historically inaccurate. In their opinion, to deny Egypt its multicultural past does a great disservice to all concerned parties, including Egyptians themselves.

Some Western scholars have brought recognition to the work of their African brethren, the most important being Martin Bernal and his two-volume work, *Black Athena: The Afroasiatic Roots of Classical Civilization* (Rutgers University Press, 1987, 1991). By referring to the Greek goddess of wisdom as "Black" in the book's title, Bernal was intimating a connectiveness between Greek and African civilizations, which he claims can be seen as emanating from Egypt. He also states that Asiatic forces, mainly Phoenician, also influenced the development of Greek civilization. Although the Egypt-as-African theory is not a major feature of *Black Athena*, Bernal's work does lend credibility to it in the following ways: (1) it exposes the scholarly classical community of the last 200 years as blatantly racist and antisemitic, thus incapable of seeing that Greek civilization may have been influenced by African and Asiatic sources; (2) it supports the idea that Egypt had strong African roots, which contributed to its civilization, and ultimately to Greece's.

Regarding the questions raised by Bernal and others, his opponents have stated that while every group has the right to seek the glories of its past, exaggerations and false claims benefit no one. Africans and African Americans, who have seen their past distorted beyond recognition, maintain that they are merely writing their own history to give credibility to what has been denied for centuries.

In the YES and NO selections, Clinton Crawford, using evidence from a variety of academic disciplines—history, linguistics, archaeology, anthropology, art—argues that ancient Egypt was indeed African in origin. Those who believe so, he states, "share a common ideological concern, namely that the social and political histories of the Egyptians be told truthfully." Kathryn A. Bard analyzes the same information and comes to a different conclusion—that ancient Egyptians were "North African peoples, distinct from sub-Saharan blacks" and anyone who claims that Egypt was a black or white society is promoting "a misconception with racial overtones that appeals to those who would rather increase than decrease the racial tensions that exist in modern society."

One of the difficulties one faces in judging the validity of the evidence presented in this issue is the number of academic disciplines with which they must be familiar. Some experience in linguistics, the study of languages, is very important as much of the proof offered stems from language analysis. Scientific knowledge is also necessary when analyzing information regarding skeletal remains, head shape, and melanin—an element that gives skin its color. Finally, since the subject is of ancient and even prehistoric times, familiarity with archaeology, anthropology, and related sciences would also be useful. Lack of such knowledge, common to most who come upon the Egypt-as-African question, makes an assessment of the evidence a difficult process.

Another problem is that so much of the debate regarding the origin of Egyptian civilization is influenced by today's volatile racial climate. Afrocentrists consider the view that Egyptian civilization had multicultural origins to be another attempt by Eurocentric scholars to "whitewash" African history. Those who oppose the Afrocentric view of the origins of Egyptian civilization maintain that they are merely stating the facts as they have been uncovered, and that no one benefits from a distortion of the historical record. Works useful to the Afrocentrist side begin with two books by Cheikh Anta Diop: *The African Origins of Civilization: Myth or Reality*? (Lawrence Hill Books, 1974) and *Civilization or Barbarism: An Authentic Anthropology* (Lawrence Hill Books, 1981).

For an Afrocentric viewpoint on the subject covered in this issue, see Ivan Van Sertima, ed., *Egypt: Child of Africa* (Transaction Press, 1994), which contains a series of essays on various phases of the subject. Professor Van Sertima's research also figures prominently in another issue in this volume: Was Mesoamerica's Olmec Civilization Influenced by African Sources? For works that dispute the Afrocentric view, see: Mary Lefkowitz, *Not Out of Africa: How Afrocentrism Became an Excuse to Teach Myth as History* (Basic Books, 1996); and Stephen Howe, *Afrocentrism: Mythical Pasts and Imagined Homes* (Verso Books, 1998).

Clinton Crawford

Origin and Development of the Ancient Egyptians

This [selection] discusses the origin, development, and interrelationship of the people and the culture of ancient Egypt. When people and their culture are viewed as reciprocal, we can understand more fully the evolution of a culture. Slowly but surely, American academia is beginning to admit the centrality of Egyptian civilization and its sub-Saharan antecedents to the history of the arts and sciences. It is impossible to reprise this debate in any detail here, but let us at least develop the outlines of the discourse. It is also imperative that ancient Egypt be understood as a Black civilization if it is to be a source of self-esteem for African-Americans.

Consider the following oft-cited remarks from Count C. F. Volney's *Ruins of Empire:*

> There [at Thebes, ancient metropolis of Upper Egypt], a people, now forgotten, discovered, while others were yet barbarians, the elements of the arts and science. A race of men now rejected for their *sable skin and frizzled hair*, founded on the study of the laws of nature, those civil and religious systems which still govern the universe. (Volney 1991: 16–17)

This eighteenth-century scholar was puzzled by characterizations of the "Negro" slaves of the western hemisphere because they looked very similar to the indigenous Africans he met in Egypt. Volney attempted to prove that the indigenous Africans in Egypt were similar to the American "Negro" slaves on the basis of his description of the Sphinx of Gizeh. He described the monument's facial characteristics—a common determinant of racial origin—as identical with all people of the Black races.

Similarly, a contemporary of Volney, Baron Denon (1798), also sought the identity of the ancient Egyptians through an examination of the Sphinx. He described the portraits he examined as having the indigenous African characteristics—broad noses, thick lips, and wooly hair. Denon argues that his drawings document an accurate appearance of the Sphinx's head before Napoleon's troops destroyed some of the evidence of its "Negroid looks" (ben-Jochannan, 1989, p. 14).

The list of historians and artists who affirm Volney's and Dennon's work is long. Among them are the German scholar and explorer Frobenius (1910), and Egyptian art historian Cyril Aldred (1956, 1961, 1962). On numerous occasions both scholars have made reference to the racial characteristics of the ancient Egyptians. Hopefully, Reba Ashton-Crawford's faithful rendering of the head of King Aha, or Narmer-Memes, together with the photograph of the Boston Museum of Fine Arts bust of Khafre, may help convert those who have been misled by the modern falsification that the makers of ancient Egypt were not Negroid and African.

Among other scholars on the long list, Cheikh Anta Diop, who is well known in the disciplines of history, egyptology, and anthropology, has advanced well-researched arguments in support of the position that the ancient Egyptians were Africoid and undoubtedly "black" in racial origin. Supporting Diop is Yosef ben-Jochannan, a renowned scholar of ancient and contemporary history and egyptology. Other supporters are Basil Davidson, Ivan Van Sertima, John Henrik Clarke, Chancellor Williams, Leonard Jefferies, Frank Snowden, and James Brunson.

Foremost, ben-Jochannan (1989) places the controversy in its historical context. Ben-Jochannan and Chancellor Williams (1976) argue that the ancient Egyptians were always referred to by the Greeks and Romans as people whose descendants came from the interior of Africa. He cites many examples from ancient texts which validate the point.

For example, Manetho (early and third century B.C.), a high priest of mixed Egyptian and Greek parentage, who wrote the first chronology of the Egyptian dynasties, testifies to the undisputed Negroid origin of the ancient Egyptians. Ben-Jochannan, as if unsatisfied with Manetho's accounts, recalls the many works of Herodotus which referred to the Egyptian as black. Herodotus observed that the probability of encountering men with black skin, woolly hair, without any other ethnic feature common of Negroes, is scientifically nil. To term such individuals as "whites" with black skin because of their fine features is no less absurd than the appellation "blacks" with white skin. If the absurdity of the latter is applied to three-fourths of the Europeans who lack Nordic features, then what can one conclude? Looking at these two appellations and their contradictions, one can conclude that a pseudo-scientific approach has given way to inaccurate generalization

(History of Herodotus, p. 115). This decree by Herodotus is but one of many such testimonies by the Greek "father of history," who made many pilgrimages to Egypt in the fifth century B.C.

Over the span of several centuries, from the fall of ancient Egypt to sometime in the 1800s, classical authors of antiquity [cited by Anta Diop (1974) and ben-Jochannan (1989)] had no difficulty classifying the physical characteristics of the ancient Egyptians. Diop commends Aristotle (389–332 B.C.), Lucan the Greek (125–190 A.D.), Aeschylus (525–456 B.C.), Strabo (58–25 A.D.), and Diodorus of Sicily (63–14 B.C.), among many others, for bearing out this evidence about the ancient Egyptians. Each of the ancient historians usually included a graphic description of the ancient Egyptians. For example, Diodorus of Sicily described the Egyptians as follows:

> The Ethiopians say that Egyptians are one of their colonies which was brought into Egypt by Osiris. . . . It is from them that the Egyptians have learned to honor kings and gods and bury them with such pomp; sculpture and writing were invented by the Ethiopians. (Anta Diop, 1974, pp. 1–2)

Diodorus' account supports Herodotus' statement. Diop employs Diodorus' account to illuminate at least two plausible implications: (1) that Ethiopia is an older civilization than Egypt; (2) that the Egyptians were a different race than the Ethiopians. Diodorus seriously discussed the possibility of considering the ancient Egyptians to be either close neighbors (separated by a physical barrier—a cataract) or actual descendants of Black Africans (Ethiopians). Herodotus, in Histories II (457–450 B.C.) had stated that the Colchians, Ethiopians, and Egyptians bore all of the Negroid racial characteristics of thick lips, broad nose, woolly hair, and dark complexion—a statement that parallels Diodorus' observations, documented many years later.

Despite the testimonies of the ancients, ben-Jochannan and Diop also sought new data to support their position. Ben-Jochannan uses many strategies to advance his claims. Conspicuously, some of the strategies included examining the names and terminologies which the African Egyptians used to describe themselves and their country. He also reviews the works of some of the modern-day scholars who have advanced the claim of an Indo-European/Caucasian genesis for the ancient Egyptians. Furthermore, to counter what he regards as a deliberate attempt to discredit the contributions of a great Black civilization, ben-Jochannan cites the findings from Ellio Smith's examination of mummies from the tombs of Egyptian Royalty (1912).

Ben-Jochannan argues that before the Greeks imposed the name *Egyptos* on the people of *Alke-bu-lan* (modern day Africa), the linguistic and papyrological evidence show that the Egyptians called their land *Kimit, Kham, Ham, Mizrain*, and *Ta-Merry*. It cannot be coincidental, according to ben-Jochannan, that the same words chosen to describe the empire of the ancient "Egyptians" also refer to the land and its people as "children of the sun." The fact remains, these people were of dark pigmentation. And it is no mistake that even the Greek word *Egyptos* means "land of the dark people."

In addition to his linguistic and papyrologic evidence, ben-Jochannan cites that the Nile Valley and (African) Great Lakes High Cultures, peopled by Blacks of Egypt and its close neighbor Nubia, had an organized system of education called the Mysteries System. . . . At the height of ancient Egyptian culture, the Grand Lodge of Alexandria was known as the world center of learning. Those foreign to ancient Egypt who did not attend the main educational center received training at the "established subordinate Lodges of the Osirica—which was centered in the Grand Lodge at Luxor, Nubia" (ben-Jochannan, 1989, p. xxv). This puts into a new perspective the well-known fact that the Greek philosophers Socrates, Aristotle, and Pythagoras all testified to the education they received from the Egyptians.

Having established the ancient Egyptian preference for how they wanted to be called and the consistent testimonies of other ancients, ben-Jochannan focuses primarily on several examples of the racist hypotheses which are still used in academic circles as authentic scholarship on Africa, especially as it relates to Egypt.

To expose some of the racist hypotheses, ben-Jochannan examines several attempts to undermine the Negroid origin of the ancient Egyptians. The most striking appeared in the January 9th, 1972 issue of *The New York Times* in a report by Donald Janson of his interview with archaeologist Ray Winfield Smith, of the Museum of the University of Pennsylvania. The article concerned a computer reconstruction of a bas-relief sculpture in which Queen Nefertiti is shown with the same pear-shaped, elongated torso used to characterize her husband, pharaoh Akhenaten, and all other persons during their reign. Their stylized portrayal represented the aesthetic choice of King Akhenaten and Queen Nefertiti's reign—a shift away from the conventional royal portrayal to a more naturalistic style. In apparent ignorance of the aesthetic shift of the eighteenth dynasty, Smith interpreted Akhenaten's "long, narrow face, hatchet chin, thick lips, thick thighs and spindly legs" as the manifestation of apparent glandular trouble associated with the syndrome of "a physical monstrosity" (p. 12), namely, "an extreme case of destructive periodontal disease—badly abscessed teeth which results in long narrow face, thick lips, and hatchet chin." Moreover, he insisted that the outstanding and intelligent achievements of Akhenaten's reign, particularly monotheism, cannot be attributed to him. Instead, Smith credited Nefertiti (who is generally perceived to be of European extraction) with the idea of monotheism, and with the change of aesthetic canons in art. Janson goes on to quote Smith's speculation that the abnormalities of Akhenaten are usually accompanied by sterility, so that Nefertiti's four daughters could not have been his. In his conclusion on Akhenaten, Smith compounded the pharaoh's plight by suggesting that Queen Nefertiti generally stood in her husband's shadow, an indication she had no need to embarrass him about his ineptness.

Winfield Smith's analysis of the Akhenaten bas-relief may not necessarily be racist, but rather one isolated incident plagued with errors. Ben-Jochannan, however, uses this article to illustrate the vicious, deliberate errors and the racism still leveled at people from Africa. He invites his readers to compare the facial characteristics of Akhenaten with those of all people indigenous to Africa and their descendants living in North America, the Caribbean, Brazil, and other parts of South America, and with the descriptions of the Egyptians by ancient Greek and Roman historians. Are we to understand that all those people who seem to fit Smith's description of Akhenaten were/are actually physically deformed?

In his quest to present further convincing evidence about the origin of the ancient Egyptians, ben-Jochannan uses some of the mummies presently on display at the Egyptian Museum in Cairo. These mummies represent many of the various facial types present in Egypt before and after the Dynastic periods. Referring to Smith's illustration, ben-Jochannan observes that most "reconstructions" of the ancient Egyptians we generally see are of the "C" type, which bears the facial characteristics of Europeans. Most people, however, if shown the majority of mummies and surviving sculpture in the round, would not have great difficulty deciding the racial origin of the ancient Egyptian. If ben-Jochannan has presented forceful and cogent evidence of the negroid origin of the ancient Egyptians, the findings presented in Anta Diop's great work, *African Origin of Civilization: Myth or Reality* (1974), are utterly convincing.

Like his contemporary ben-Jochannan, Diop presents evidence from the accounts of ancient Greeks and Romans. Beyond the ancients' testimonies, Diop employs several other approaches—linguistic, totemic, physical anthropology, microscopic analysis, osteological measurements, blood-group typing, cultural data, and the papyrus documents which illustrate how the Egyptians saw themselves. From the wealth of data Diop presents, I will focus on his scientific evidence, which has received the greatest attention from people in archaeology, anthropology, egyptology, history, and linguistics.

Diop (cited, Van Sertima, 1989) prefaces his argument by citing the theory of paleontologist Louis Leakey (cited, Diop, 1974), which has received general acceptance. Central to Leakey's theory is mankind's monogenetic and African origin. His evidence shows that man of 150,000 years ago was "morphologically identical with the man of today" and was "living in the regions of the Great Lakes of Africa, at the sources of the Nile and no where else" (p. 9). Justifying the morphological identity claim, Leakey advances two important points. First, it was out of pure necessity that the earliest men were "ethnically homogeneous and negroid" (p. 9). In defense of this assumption, Leakey uses Gloger's law, which posits that living organisms most likely adapt to their environment by developing characteristics peculiar to the given circumstances. In the case of human beings, Leakey insists, "warm blooded animals evolving in a warm humid climate will secrete black pigment (eumelanin)" (p. 9). Leaky implies that if mankind originated in the areas of the tropics, around the latitude of the Great Lakes of Africa, then logic would lead us to conclude that early man of this region had a dark pigmentation. Consequently, those who moved to other climatic regions must have adapted appropriately. Accordingly then, he argues that the "original stock" was split into different races, and this is one possible conclusion. To ensure that his hypothesis is taken seriously, Leakey points to the geographical constraints of early man, identifying the only two routes available to early man for migration to other continents—the Sahara and the Nile Valley.

To support his position about the African origin of the ancient Egyptians, Diop (1974) uses the historical background of the Nile Valley route and the peopling of that Valley by Negroid races. In substance, although the evidence provided by the physical anthropologists can be used to build "reliable and definitive truths, and sound scientific conclusions," the criteria used to supposedly finalize a solution of this problem are arbitrary, thus giving way to "scientific hair-splitting" (p. 129). He cites many studies which exemplify the hair splitting of the varying percentage of negroid presence in the Valley from the distant prehistoric ages to predynastic times. Diop examines one of the conclusions in Emile Massoulard's *Histoire et protohistoire d' Egypt* (1949). Massoulard states that the Negadah skulls are said to belong to a homogeneous group and therefore can provide sufficient data for a general conclusion about the racial origin. He cites that the dimensions of the skulls' total height, length, breadth of face, nasal capacity and so forth, approximate that of the present day negro. However, he insists that "the nasal breadth, height of orbit, length of palate and nasal index," seem similar to Germanic peoples. Generally, those who argue for the caucasian origin of the early Egyptians bypass the evidence which suggests negroid characteristics of predynastic Negadian people. Instead they focus almost exclusively on the few racial characteristics akin to the white races.

The other studies Diop cites include Thomson and Randall MacIver's 1949 study of skulls from El Amrah and Abydos, and Keith Falkenburger's recent study of 1,800 male skulls from the Egyptian populations ranging from predynastic to present day. Falkenburger's conclusions report 36 percent Negroid, 33 percent Mediterranean, 11 percent Cro-Magnoid, and 20 percent are estimated to be either Cro-Magnoid or Negroid. Falkenburger's percentage of Negroid skulls during the predynastic period of Egypt is higher than Thomson and Randall MacIver's findings of 25 percent men and 28 percent women.

Consequentially, Diop's analysis considers the discrepancies among the percentages of Negroid, Mediterranean,

Cro-magnoids, and cross-bred individuals. He draws our attention to what is, perhaps, the most salient of all the arguments put forth. Common to all these arguments is that all bodies of evidence converge at a point which shows that the Egyptian population in the predynastic epoch was Negroid. In view of the common and convincing evidence about the Negro origin of predynastic Egypt, those who insist on arguments that the Negro presence came later remain suspect (Diop, 1974, pp. 129–131).

To further reverse the present-day hypothesis of "White African/Egyptians," Diop employs the science of microscopic analysis of skin to accurately define ethnic affiliation. Since melanin (eumelanin), which determines color of pigmentation, is known to be virtually indestructible, and the scientific community widely agrees that the melanin in animal skin and fossils has survived for millions of years, Diop reasons that the skin of the Egyptian mummies (unparalleled specimens of embalming technique) are prime subjects for melanocyte analysis. Although melanin is mainly found in epidermis, it also penetrates the epidermis and lodges in the dermis. For example, the sample of mummies examined from the Marietta excavation in Egypt shows a higher level of melanin than in any "white skinned races" (p. 125). He assures us that if a similar analysis is done on the best preserved mummies in the Cairo Museum, the result will parallel his findings, proving that the ancient Egyptian belongs to the black races.

Osteological measurements were also a part of Diop's scientific analysis. In physical anthropology, the measurement of bones is a more accepted criterion than craniometry for accurately determining the distinctions of race. In other words, by means of osteological measurement one can differentiate the racial characteristics of a white and a black. Citing the study of the distinguished nineteenth-century German scientist Lepsius, Diop reconfirms that the ancient Egyptians belong to the black races, for, even though physical anthropology has progressed in its methodology, Lepsius' findings have not been invalidated by the new approaches. For example, his notation of some specific characteristics unique to the Egyptian skeleton still stands unchallenged. Lepsius contends that the bodily proportions, especially the short arms, are consistent with the negroid or negrito physical type.

Further, in his quest to provide more substantive evidence for the identity of the ancient Egyptians, Diop examines the etymology of the pharaonic language to see what they called themselves. Connected to the idea of self-description, Diop finds only one term that was designated for this purpose. That word was *kmt*, which literally translated means "the negroes." It is, according to Diop, the strongest term existing in pharaonic language to indicate blackness. Likewise, the character used to symbolize the word *kmt* in hieroglyph is "a length of wood charred at both ends" and not "crocodile scale" (as is commonly misinterpreted). Actually, the word *kmt* is etymologically related to the well-known word *Kamit*, which is common in modern anthropological literature. Diop cautions, however, against the manipulation of modern anthropological literature, which seeks to distort the meaning of the word *kmt* to have it imply "white." To guard against misinformation, he redirects our attention to the authenticity of the pharaonic mother tongue where the word *kmt* meant "coal black." (For an extensive discussion of the grammar of the pharaonic language see his *The African Origin of Civilization* [1974]). . . .

In divine epithets, according to Diop, "black" or "negro" was invariably used to identify the chief beneficent gods of Egypt. Thus, for example, *kmwr* means the "great Negro" (for Osiris). More importantly, *km* always precedes the names of the revered gods of Egypt: for example, Apis, Min Thot, Isis, Hathor, and Horus.

Many other scholars besides ben-Jochannan and Anta Diop who have succeeded in re-establishing the true origin of the ancient Egyptians also point out the African influence on the development of Greco-Roman civilization. Whereas it is not possible within the scope of this work to review many of those who have argued for the Negroid origin of the ancient Egyptians, I must not neglect to mention the challenging and thought-provoking work of Martin Bernal in *Black Athena* Volumes I and II (1987 and 1991, respectively). *Black Athena Volume I* is particularly important for establishing the racial origin of the ancient Egyptians and their contributions to a great civilization. Convinced by the archaeological findings for at least 7,000 years, he asserts that the Egyptian population comprised African, South-West Asian, and Mediterranean types. Furthermore, historically speaking, the farther south one moves along the Nile Valley, where the upper Egyptian Kingdoms had influence, "the darker and more negroid the population becomes" (p. 242). In fact, the darker and more negroid population is still dominant in these regions today.

Bernal's overall view of the ancient Egyptians is summarized in his introduction. He asserts that the Egyptian population was fundamentally African/ Black and that the African dominance was remarkable in the Old and Middle Kingdoms before the approximately 150 years of Hyksos reign, which notably was restricted to Lower Egypt. Supporting the claim of African dominance, Bernal joins Basil Davidson and James Brunson (cited, Van Sertima, 1989) in affirming that the most important and powerful dynasties were I–IV, VI, XI–XIII, XVII–XVIII, and XXV, and that the pharaohs of these dynasties were black (Bernal, 1987, p. 242).

Notwithstanding that Bernal devotes little time to the racial origin of the ancient Egyptians, he echoes the views of Diop, ben-Jochannan, and others with respect to what the ancients thought of the Egyptians. He professes that the ancient Greeks unanimously agreed upon the cultural supremacy of the Pharoanic civilization. Judging from how eloquently and respectfully the ancients wrote about the Egyptians, Bernal believes, if it were possible for the Greeks to review some of the modern arguments that deny the Black African origin of ancient Egypt, they would rebuke the absurdity of early nineteenth-century scholarship. Bernal enforces his position by recalling the fact that the Greeks of the Classical Age went to Egypt to learn philosophy, mathematics, history, and many more arts and sciences. In short, Egypt was the center of learning.

Closely associated with the modern distortion of the ancient Egyptian racial origin, Bernal argues, modern racism and slavery figured prominently in the modern debasement of the negroid presence in early Egyptian civilization. Bernal suggests that those people who imposed the most brutal form of human degradation upon African people through the slave trade employed a strategy which included "proving" that Blacks were biologically incapable of creating a civilization as magnificent as Egypt. By thus establishing the so-called "biological truth," the perpetrators of racism and "continental chauvinism" were able to discount the genius of Black Egyptians and replace it with an Indo-Asiatic, white model of civilization. The mission, then, of many nineteenth and twentieth-century historians was to maintain this status quo as "truth" despite many contradictions (Bernal, 1987, pp. 240–247).

The arguments presented here are a mere sampling of the voluminous body of findings that addresses the question of the racial origin of the ancient Egyptians. Ben-Jochannan, Anta Diop, Van Sertima, Bernal, and Williams are only a few of the modern scholars who have given credence to the testimonies of the ancients about the racial composition of the ancient Egyptians. The Greeks, in particular, maintained a reverence for the genius of the African civilization, Egypt, which was responsible for so many of their own cultural advancements.

By presenting convincing scientific evidence about the racial characteristics of the ancient Egyptians, Diop in particular helps write an important chapter in human history for the benefit of all people, especially downtrodden African peoples. The findings are overwhelmingly in favor of classifying the ancient Egyptians as belonging to the negro race.

Finally, in my arguments, I have used the work of contemporary observers—Volney, Denon, Aldred, ben-Jochannan, Chandler, Anta Diop, and museums with Egyptian art collections—who have presented written and photographic documentation about the physical characteristics of the ancient Egyptians. In every case that I have cited favoring the African/Negroid origin of the Egyptians, none of the sources sought to discount or discredit the importance of European civilization. In fact, the proponents of the African origin of Egyptian civilization share a common ideological concern, namely that the social and political histories of the Egyptians must be told truthfully. Those who are interested in having this truth told understand the need to recast Egypt into its rightful historical position. Diop and ben-Jochannan warn that the reestablishing of African history should not be used as a tool of divisiveness, but rather as a unifying force on behalf of all mankind.

This [selection] has addressed the reconsideration and accurate representation of the origin of the ancient Egyptians. In the discussion I have cited the findings of Yosef ben-Jochannan, Chiekh Anta Diop, and Martin Bernal. Generally speaking, the evidence of ancient Greek and Roman accounts affirms the African influence on ancient Egypt. In addition, scientific data from osteological measurement, eumelanin analysis, and cranium measurements independently support the argument that the ancient Egyptians were Black. As further evidence, the etymology of pharaonic language was examined to find out how the ancient Egyptians referred to themselves. Finally, photographic evidence of ancient Egyptian sculpture supplies mute yet eloquent testimony about the origin of the ancient Egyptians.

Clinton Crawford is an associate professor in the Department of Literature, Communications, and Philosophy at Medgar Evers College, City University of New York.

Kathryn A. Bard

Ancient Egyptians and the Issue of Race

Egypt straddles two major geographical regions: the continent of Africa and the Middle East. Because it was located on the African continent, ancient Egypt was an African civilization, though perhaps its African identity has been subtly minimized within the discipline of Near Eastern studies, which has its roots in European Orientalism of the nineteenth century. Many earlier European scholars working in Egypt, particularly during the days of the British empire, assumed that ancient history began with Egypt and Mesopotamia—in other words, that the earliest civilizations were Near Eastern ones, and ancient Egypt could be understood as such (and not as an African civilization). Some scholars, such as Sir Flinders Petrie (1899, 10) and Walter Emery (Emery 1967, 39), assumed that civilization was introduced into Egypt by an invading dynastic race from southwestern Asia, who replaced the prehistoric hunters and gatherers and early farmers living along the Nile—peoples much too primitive to "invent" civilization.

It is now known that as the land bridge between Asia and Africa, Egypt was the recipient of earlier technological developments in southwestern Asia, especially agriculture. The major cereal cultigens, emmer wheat and barley, as well as the domestic sheep/goat, are species not known in their wild form in Africa; they were domesticated much earlier, in southwestern Asia, and only later introduced into Egypt (Wetterstrom 1993, 200). There is no archaeological evidence, however, to suggest that a large-scale migration of peoples from southwestern Asia brought farming into Egypt, and the mechanisms by which domesticated cereals and perhaps the technology of farming were introduced into Egypt remain unclear. But recent research on the Predynastic period in Egypt (ca. 4000–3000 B.C.E.), including my excavations near Nag Hammadi in Upper Egypt, has shown that the cultural roots of Egyptian civilization are indeed indigenous (Hoffman, 1988, 47).

Less clear, however, has been the issue of race in ancient Egypt. The modern concept of race was unknown to the ancient Egyptians. Non-Egyptians were identified by their ethnic/tribal affiliations or by the region/country from which they came. Most physical anthropologists in the second half of this century do not believe that pure races ever existed, and they view the concept of "race" as a misleading one for their studies (Trigger 1978, 27). But a number of Afrocentrists have claimed that black civilization began with ancient Egypt. The very title of Martin Bernal's *Black Athena* alludes to the putative roots of Greek—and therefore Western civilization—as a black African civilization in Egypt.

Ancient Egyptians were Mediterranean peoples, neither Sub-Saharan blacks nor Caucasian whites but peoples whose skin was adapted for life in a subtropical desert environment. Ancient Egypt was a melting pot; peoples of different ethnic identities migrated into the Nile Valley at different times in its prehistory and history. The question of whether ancient Egyptians were black or white obscures their own identity as agricultural peoples of *Kmt*, as opposed to *dšrt*, the barren "Red Land" of the desert. *Kmt* means "Black Land," the fertile floodplain of the lower Nile Valley, where cereal crops grew in such abundance. It does not mean "Land of Blacks."

Egyptians were Egyptians, the people of *Kmt*. The name points to the importance of the Nile in their lives. Unlike that of other early riverine civilizations, the Egyptian floodplain required no fallow time, nor was salinization of soils a problem with irrigation agriculture (Butzer 1976, 90). The economic base of pharaonic civilization was provided by the incredibly rich potential of cereal agriculture in the Egyptian Nile Valley. Egyptians were the indigenous farmers of the lower Nile Valley, neither black nor white as races are conceived of today.

Just who the ancient Egyptians were can be addressed by several types of evidence: language, historical records, the material culture, and physical remains (usually skeletons from burials). Evidence may be used to study cultural and biological relationships between different groups as well as within groups. For the most part, analyses of the different types of evidence have to be pursued independently, using different data because of the very different variables of such data; only after that can relationships between the different data be studied—within a specific cultural context.

Looking first at the linguistic evidence, there is nothing that links Egypt to other areas in Africa except very generally. Egyptian, the language spoken by the ancient Egyptians and written on monuments in hieroglyphs, evolved over more than four thousand years, to be finally replaced by Arabic following the Arab invasion in the seventh century C.E. Egyptian is classified

From Kathryn A. Bard, "Ancient Egyptians and the Issue of Race," *Bostonia* (Summer 1992), as it appeared in Mary R. Lefkowitz and Guy MacLean Rogers, eds., *Black Athena Revisited* (University of North Carolina Press, 1996), pp. 103–111.

by linguists as one of the five main groups of what is called the Afro-Asiatic language family. The other languages in this family include the Semitic languages spoken in southwestern Asia (including modern Arabic and Hebrew); Berber, spoken by Berbers in North Africa to the west of the Nile; the Chadic languages, spoken in northern Central Africa in the vicinity of Lake Chad; and the Cushitic languages spoken in the Horn of Africa, such as Galla in eastern Ethiopia (and probably covering Omotic; cf. Greenberg 1955, 43). Egyptian is so distinctly different from these languages in its structure and vocabulary as to be classified by itself. But it is more closely related to other languages in the Afro-Asiatic family than to any Indo-European languages or to the Bantu languages spoken today in Sub-Saharan Africa. In the New Kingdom (ca. 1558–1085 B.C.E.), when Egypt had an empire in southwest Asia, more Semitic words appeared in what is called Late Egyptian, but this can be explained by increased interaction with Semitic-speaking peoples, and not with other Africans (although that too certainly occurred). The linguistic evidence, then, points to the relative isolation of speakers of Egyptian in relation to other languages spoken in Africa.

Another important type of evidence for the study of ancient populations is from the physical remains that have been preserved in Egyptian burials. D. E. Derry, who studied the physical remains of Old Kingdom elites buried at Giza (excavated in the first decade of this century by George Reisner of Harvard University), took skull measurements and concluded, like Petrie and Emery, that the pyramid builders were a dynastic race of invaders, probably from the East, "who were far removed from any negroid element" (1956, 81).

As practiced by Derry, however, craniometry is no longer considered a valid statistical means for evaluating genetic relationships of ancient populations. A more recent analysis of nonmetrical variations in skulls (Berry and Berry 1973) suggests that the Egyptian samples show genetic continuity from Predynastic times through the Old and Middle Kingdoms—over two thousand years—with a shift in the New Kingdom, when there were considerable infiltrations of new peoples into the Nile Valley. In this same study the Egyptian skulls were then analyzed with samples from the northern Sudan (the Neolithic site of Jebel Moya), West Africa (Ashanti), Palestine (the site of Lachish), and Turkey (Byzantine period). Not surprisingly, the Egyptian skulls were not very distinct from the Jebel Moya skulls but were much more distinct from all others, including those from West Africa. Such a study suggests closer genetic affinity between peoples in Egypt and the northern Sudan, which were close geographically and are known to have had considerable cultural contact throughout prehistory and pharaonic history. But the Egyptian and the Jebel Moya samples also seemed no more related to the samples from southwestern Asia in Palestine and Turkey than to modern (black) populations of West Africa (Berry and Berry 1973, 206).

Clearly more analyses of the physical remains of ancient Egyptians need to be done using current techniques, such as those Nancy Lovell at the University of Alberta is using in her work (see A. L. Johnson and N. Lovell 1994). Two problems, however, hinder such studies. First, graves in Egypt have been robbed since prehistoric times. Intact tombs, such as Tutankhamen's, are the great exception, and even his tomb had been penetrated twice in antiquity by robbers. Second, many skeletons excavated by earlier archaeologists working in Egypt were either not kept, or have been stored so poorly that today they are in very bad condition. The prehistoric burials that I excavated in 1978 at Naqada in Upper Egypt were sent off to storage in the basement of the Cairo Museum, never to be seen again. Even for the same age/sex group within a burial sample representing one small village community (in which there probably was some or even considerable intermarriage), there can be significant skeletal variability, and large samples need to be analyzed so that statistical findings will be valid. But nonskeletal features, which are the ones most frequently used to distinguish race today, have long since disappeared in the physical remains of burial—even when they have been mummified as in pharaonic Egypt (Trigger 1968, 11).

It is disturbing to me as an archaeologist that archaeological evidence—the artifacts, art and architecture of ancient Egypt—has been identified with race and racial issues. Racial issues, which in all fairness have arisen because of racial inequalities in the United States and elsewhere, have been imposed on the material remains of a culture even though these remains do not in themselves denote race. I am reminded of the excavation report of the Wellcome expedition at the site of Jebel Moya (Addison 1949). The English archaeologists who worked there in 1911–12 were certain that the advanced stone tools they excavated had to have been made by a prehistoric people who were white. This seems like a ridiculous conclusion today: stone tools thousands of years old cannot tell us the race of their makers any more than they can tell us what language their makers spoke.

The conventions of Egyptian art, as established by the beginning of the First Dynasty (ca. 3050 B.C.E.) do not represent humans as seen in perspective by the eye, but represent them in an analytic manner that transforms reality. The head, arms, and legs are drawn in profile; the torso is depicted frontally. Art may sometimes be grossly mannered and exaggerated, as it was during the reign of Akhenaten (ca. 1363–1347 B.C.E.) because of religious and cultural reforms conceptualized by that pharaoh. The conventions of Egyptian art were those of the crown and elites associated with the crown, and what is characteristic of Egyptian style in art for the most part represents a very small segment of the population.

Who and what were depicted on the walls of temples and tombs depended on Egyptian beliefs and ideology. Art was functional, and much of what is seen today in museums was created for the mortuary cult. Ancient

Egypt was a class-stratified society, and age and sex in art were differentiated by scale of figures, style of dress, and symbols of status or office, as well as by skin tone. Statues and reliefs of women were painted in lighter tones of yellow ochre-based paint; men were painted in darker tones of red ochre-based paint. This is not to suggest that all Egyptian men were darker than all Egyptian women, but rather that established artistic conventions served to convey such ideas as sex differentiation. Such conventions, however, were not hard and fast rules, and there are many known exceptions. For example, in the tomb of Queen Nefertari, Rameses II's chief wife, the queen's skin is painted a brown (red ochre) color in a scene where she is playing a board game, as a contrast to the solid background of yellow ochre paint.

Non-Egyptian Africans, as well as Asiatics, were usually depicted in representational art as distinctly different from Egyptians, especially in their clothing and hairstyles. In the well-known scenes from the Eighteenth Dynasty tomb of Rekmire, Asiatics, Cretans, and Nubians are painted in registers bringing tribute to the court of Tuthmoses III. The Nubians, from the Nile Valley south of the First Cataract at Aswan, are painted in darker skin tones than the Asiatics, and are depicted with more prognathous jaws than the Egyptians. Bringing exotic goods and pets that originated in regions south of Nubia, the Nubians also carry gold ingots shaped into large rings. Nubia had little agricultural potential compared to Egypt, but rich gold mines were located there in *wadis* to the east of the Nile. That in part explains why Egypt occupied Nubia and built forts and temple towns there in the Middle and New Kingdoms.

Nubians bearing gold ingots and exotic tribute in paintings from the tomb of Huy (Thebes, no. 40), dating to the time of Tutankhamen, wear long, pleated Egyptian robes, but their hairstyles and large earrings are distinctly non-Egyptian. They have neck markings that may represent scarification, a practice unknown in ancient Egypt, and their facial features may possibly be interpreted as prognathous. In one scene an elite Nubian woman is depicted standing in a cart drawn by oxen, something in which Egyptian women would never have ridden. The Nubian tribute-bearers are painted in two skin tones, black and dark brown. These tones do not necessarily represent actual skin tones in real life but may serve to distinguish each tribute-bearer from the next in a row in which the figures overlap. Alternatively, the brown-skinned people may be of Nubian origin, and the black-skinned ones may be from farther south (Trigger 1978, 33). The shading of skin tones in Egyptian tomb paintings, which varies considerably, may not be a certain criterion for distinguishing race. Specific symbols of ethnic identity can also vary.

Nor are black Africans depicted by standardized conventions. The scenes of Queen Hatshepsut's expedition to the land of Punt, from her Eighteenth Dynasty mortuary temple at Deir el-Bahri, show a land very different from Egypt. Punt is thought to have been located along and to the west of the Sudanese/Eritrean coast (Kitchen 1993). The houses of the Punt peoples were hemispherical and built on elevated posts, unlike the rectangular mudbrick houses of Egyptians. Punt was the source of incense, ivory, and ebony, and tribute-bearers are seen carrying these goods to the seafaring Egyptians. A grossly obese "queen" of Punt is very unlike the lithe Egyptian upper-class women shown in tombs of this period. The "king" of Punt, whom she follows, is depicted in an Egyptian loincloth, but with a long and very un-Egyptian beard.

Though some Egyptian details appear, the ethnographic details in the Punt expedition scenes portray a culture that is distinctly non-Egyptian. But what race the Punt peoples were cannot really be determined from these scenes. Egyptian artists or scribes who accompanied this expedition recorded very distinctive ethnographic details, but the Puntites' facial features look more Egyptian than "black." Identifying race in Egyptian representational art, again, is difficult to do—probably because race (as opposed to ethnic affiliation, that is, Egyptians versus all non-Egyptians) was not a criterion for differentiation used by the ancient Egyptians.

As enemies of Egypt—peoples who threatened the boundaries of Egypt's kingdom—Nubians and Asiatics were depicted generically on the walls of Egyptian temples in the New Kingdom. The enemies of Egypt were shown as bound captives, being vanquished by pharaoh. On Egyptian temples in Nubia, reliefs showing such scenes must have had as one of their purposes the intimidation of local people. It was the duty of the king to destroy Egypt's enemies, and this is what is symbolized on the handle of a cane and on a footstool from Tutankhamen's tomb, both carved with generic Asiatic and Nubian captives. The Nubians carved on these two artifacts have very different facial features from those of the bearded Asiatics, but the facial features of both types of foreigners differ from the sculpture of Tutankhamen in the tomb.

Given that conventions for differentiating ethnic identity varied, as did artistic conventions for skin tones, anomalies in Egyptian art cannot be used with any certainty for drawing inferences about the race of ancient Egyptians. A limestone female head found in Giza tomb 4440, dating to the Fourth Dynasty (ca. 2613–2494 B.C.E.), is described in the catalogue of the Museum of Fine Arts in Boston as "of negroid type with thick lips, wide nostrils, and full cheeks" (W. S. Smith 1960, 35). A limestone head representing the woman's husband, also from tomb 4440, is distinctly different in its facial features: "the aquiline type of face so characteristic of some of the members of the Cheops family" (Smith, 35). Neither of these heads is painted, so their skin tones are unknown. The genre (called "reserve heads"), known only from the Fourth Dynasty, suggests more individualistic portraits than are usual in Egyptian art, and this female head "of negroid type" is different from other known reserve heads. As the identity of the person represented is unknown, her place in Egyptian society cannot be ascertained—though she certainly was a woman of high position.

A sandstone statue of Mentuhotep II, the king who unified Egypt and founded the Middle Kingdom in the twenty-first century B.C.E., was found in a pit to the east of the king's mortuary complex at Deir el-Bahri. The king is shown wearing a white robe and the red crown of Lower Egypt—and his skin is painted black. But as with analogous cases noted above, paint applied to a statue offers no real indication of his actual skin color. Black-painted skin could be symbolic of something of which we are unaware four thousand years later.

Perhaps better known than the painted statue of Mentuhotep II are the two New Kingdom figures of Tutankhamen that Howard Carter found guarding the entrance to that king's burial chamber. The black, resin-covered skin on these two wooden figures is contrasted by their gold skirts, sandals, headdresses, and jewelry (Reeves 1990, 128). These two black renditions of the king contrast the lighter-toned paintings of him on the walls of the burial chamber, and with the colored inlay on the back of the famous golden throne. Other art in this tomb likewise depicts a young man with brown skin, in keeping with Egyptian artistic conventions. Far from suggesting that the king had black skin, the two guardian figures of Tutankhamen may appear black simply because resin was applied to the skin areas. It is possible, too, that the resin was originally lighter and became dark over time. Resin, a costly and exotic import in ancient Egypt, was a material befitting a king who was to go to the afterlife displaying all forms of worldly wealth.

The people who lived south of Egypt are also known from archaeological evidence excavated in Nubia. From the fourth millennium B.C.E., when complex society evolved in Egypt, there is evidence in Lower Nubia of what archaeologists call the A-Group culture: people who traded with the Egyptians for Egyptian craft goods found in their burials. But with the founding of the First Dynasty in Egypt, ca. 3050 B.C.E., the newly unified Egyptian state penetrated into Lower Nubia, probably by military campaigns, and the A-Group disappeared there. Who the A-Group were in terms of race cannot be ascertained from the artifacts in their graves, but their locally made grave goods demonstrate a different material culture from that of the Predynastic Egyptians (Trigger 1976, 33).

From the Old Kingdom (ca. 2686–2181 B.C.E.) there is some archaeological evidence of small-scale Egyptian settlements in Lower Nubia, but by the late Old Kingdom a group of indigenous peoples, known to archaeologists as the C-Group, moved into Nubia as Egyptian occupation ended. After Egypt was reunified during the Middle Kingdom (ca. 2040–1786 B.C.E.), large mud-brick forts were built along the Nile in the region of the Second Cataract (near the modern-day border of Egypt and the Sudan). But evidence of the C-Group in Lower Nubia is also known to date to the Middle Kingdom, and the C-Group culture actually survived the Egyptian withdrawal from Nubia at the collapse of the Middle Kingdom.

During the Middle Kingdom a powerful African polity arose whose capital was at Kerma near the Third Cataract in the Nile, in the northern Sudan. In Egyptian texts this culture is called "Kush." The eastern cemetery at Kerma was excavated by George Reisner, and artifacts from eight very large round tumuli are now in the Museum of Fine Arts in Boston (Reisner 1923a). These tumuli are of a different architecture than Egyptian tombs. Some of them, moreover, contained human sacrifices, not found in Egyptian burials (with the possible exception of the First Dynasty royal tombs at Abydos). A Swiss archaeologist currently excavating the town and cemetery at Kerma estimates that there are 30,000 to 40,000 burials (Bonnet 1992, 613). The sway of Kerma extended into Lower Nubia until the reunification of Egypt at the beginning of the New Kingdom.

With Egyptian control in the New Kingdom extending as far south as Gebel Barkal near the Fourth Cataract, where a temple to the god Amen was built, the Kerma kingdom came to an end. Egyptians restored the Middle Kingdom forts in Lower Nubia and built temple towns farther south. But after the collapse of the New Kingdom, ca. 1085 B.C.E., a new Kushite power eventually arose at Gebel Barkal, where the cult of Amen continued to be practiced. The earliest burials in the royal cemetery at el-Kurru near Gebel Barkal (see Dunham 1950), also excavated by George Reisner, date to around 850 B.C.E. A hundred years later the first Kushite garrisons were established in southern Egypt during the reign of the Kushite king Piye, who later established his rule over all of Egypt (Trigger 1976, 140, 145). The Twenty-fifth Dynasty (ca. 760–656 B.C.E.), whose kings were all Kushites, ruled in Egypt for about sixty years. The later kings of this dynasty were frequently at battle with the Assyrian army, which finally succeeded in ending Kushite control in Egypt. Piye built the first pyramid tomb at el-Kurru, whereas in Egypt pyramids as royal burial monuments had not been built for a thousand years. Later Kushite kings were mummified, according to Egyptian custom, and spread the cult of Amen throughout Nubia.

The archaeological evidence of African kingdoms south of Egypt, at Kerma and Gebel Barkal, suggests distinctly different cultures that came into contact with Egypt. During the Twenty-fifth Dynasty the polity centered at Gebel Barkal actually controlled Egypt for a period. Cultural connections, if any, between the earlier Kerma kingdom and the later kingdom centered farther up the Nile at Gebel Barkal are uncertain, but the well-preserved burials recently excavated at Kerma by Bonnet (1992) provide a new source of information about Nubian populations.

Presumably the Kushites buried at Kerma and later at el-Kurru were related to the Nubians depicted in New Kingdom tomb paintings, as opposed to blacks living farther south in Africa, but once again the evidence seems ambiguous. Skin color, which is considered a criterion for race, cannot be determined from skeletal remains, and the evidence of representational art is problematic. The archaeological evidence at Kerma and el-Kurru points to African cultures that were different from Egyptian culture but that were responsible nonetheless for major cultural achievements. The Kushite peoples were considered non-Egyptians by Egyptians—in other words, ethnically different—but how physically different they were has yet to be determined by physical anthropologists. In any event, they are certainly better candidates for "black" African kingdoms than is ancient Egypt.

Culturally and linguistically the ancient Egyptians were different from other peoples living outside the Nile Valley, as well as those farther south and east. From textual and representational evidence it may be shown that ancient Egyptians had a sense of ethnic identity—of being Egyptian, as opposed to non-Egyptian. Today in Africa there are many different ethnic groups speaking many different languages. With the exception of South Africa, identity in Africa today is not by race or, for the most part, by nation, but by ethnic or tribal affiliation, which often has a close association with a spoken language or dialect. Ancient Egypt was definitely the earliest African civilization and as such certainly had an influence not only on the other cultures that arose in the Near East, but also on the states that arose farther south in Africa—at Kerma, Gebel Barkal, and later at Meröe. The evidence cited here strongly suggests that the ancient Egyptians were North African peoples, distinct from Sub-Saharan blacks. But to state categorically that ancient Egypt was either a black—or a white—civilization is to promote a misconception with racist undertones that appeals to those who would like to increase rather than decrease the racial tensions that exist in modern society.

Kathryn A. Bard is an assistant professor of archaeology at Boston University. She received her PhD in Egyptian archaeology from the University of Toronto.

EXPLORING THE ISSUE

Did Egyptian Civilization Originate in Africa?

Critical Thinking and Reflection

1. Critically examine and analyze the YES selection evidence cited by Yosef ben-Jochannan in support of the Africanity of Egyptian Civilization. In what ways is the evidence convincing/unconvincing?
2. Which of the indicators in the YES selection, cited by Cheikh Anta Diop as evidence for "how Egyptians saw themselves," seems the most compelling? Critically discuss.
3. In the NO selection, several reasons are given for why art is not a reliable element in answering the question posed by this issue. Critically evaluate and discuss the reasons given.
4. Why does Kathryn Bard write: "It is disturbing to me as an archaeologist that archaeological evidence—the artifacts, art, and architecture of ancient Egypt—has been identified with race?" Critically evaluate and discuss this assertion.
5. What evidence/arguments does Bard present to support her claim that Egyptians had primarily an ethnic, rather than a racial, identity. Analyze this claim and critically discuss/debate it.
6. Critically debate the claim that racial issues in the contemporary United States have created/fueled the academic debate in this issue. What is the evidence in support of and in opposition to this claim? Which is more convincing?
7. How might Egypt's geographical position as "the land bridge between Asia and Africa" have added to confusion about Egypt's identity? Critically discuss.
8. Which of the academic fields cited in this issue—history, linguistics, archaeology, anthropology, art—offers the best "lens" through which to view this issue? Critically analyze the articles and support your choice of fields

Is There Common Ground?

This issue has become a hotbed of contentious debate. Each side in the debate has, at times, accused the other of an implied or overt racism. Perhaps we can seek the basis for common ground by defining our terms. There are a number of ways in which the word "African" might be used, in reference to ancient Egypt. One is geographical. Positioned as it is, Egypt is clearly part of the African continent. The next question might concern chromosomal analysis. How much DNA do Egyptians share with other Africans who live south of the Sahara desert? Historically, Egypt has been a major player on the world stage. Are the Pharaohs considered Africans in your World History text? Did the Romans Julius Caesar and Marc Antony regard Egypt as African when they came to woo Cleopatra? Perhaps the most relevant question is the one most difficult to answer: How did ancient Egyptians see themselves?

Additional Resources

Much of the recent debate on Egyptian origins has been fueled by Martin Bernal's two-volume *Black Athena*, documented in this issue's Issue Summary. An anthology of critical responses to Bernal's work is contained in Mary R. Lefkowitz and Guy MacLean Rogers, *Black Athena Revisited* (University of North Carolina Press, 1996). A response to this book is *Black Athena Writes Back: Martin Bernal Responds to His Critics* (Duke University Press, 2001). An attempt to evaluate both sides of this debate can be found in Jacques Berlinerblau, *Heresy in the University: The Black Athena Controversy and the Responsibilities of American Intellectuals* (Rutgers University Press, 1999). Two more recent works by Bernal, Volume III of *Black Athena* and *Debating Black Athena* are welcome additions to this ongoing debate. Finally, Stacy Schiff's very scholarly biography of Cleopatra, *Cleopatra: A Life* (Little, Brown and Company, 2010) offers an intense you-are-there feeling and cites many possible historical interpretations of a person about whom very little is definitively known. Cleopatra is revealed as a shrewd strategist and skilled negotiator. Her country was at the epicenter of the world and she did everything in her power to shape its ultimate destiny.

Internet References . . .

Afrocentrism

This website offers subheadings devoted to the theory of Afrocentrism, the Black Athena debate, a moderated discussion list, and a link to Paul Halsall's very extensive *Internet African History Sourcebook.*

www-sul.stanford.edu/depts/ssrg/africa/history/hisafrocen.html?pagewanted=all

Selected, Edited, and with Issue Framing Material by:
Helen Buss Mitchell, *Howard Community College*
and
Joseph R. Mitchell, *Howard Community College*

ISSUE

Were the Spartans Fighting for a Compromised View of Freedom at Thermopylae?

YES: Paul Cartledge, from "To Die For?" *History Today* (August 2002)

NO: Byron Farwell, from "The Spartan Way," *World and I* (March 1999)

Learning Outcomes

After reading this issue you should be able to:

- Describe the strategic significance of the Battle of Thermopylae.
- Differentiate among the Spartiates, the Perioikoi, and the Helots.
- Describe the personal characteristics and tactical goals of Xerxes, King of the Persians, and Leonidas, King of Sparta.

ISSUE SUMMARY

YES: Cambridge University Professor of Greek History Paul Cartledge argues that the Spartan notion of freedom was predicated on their enslavement of an underclass of Helots, thus creating a compromised view of freedom.

NO: Military historian Byron Farwell argues that there was a more complicated relationship between the Spartiates who enjoyed full citizenship and the Helots who fought beside them at Thermopylae.

When Xerxes, Great King of the Persians, undertook the conquest of the Greeks, this clash of civilizations focused in an epic battle at Thermopylae (the "hot gates"), a mountain pass near thermal spas that barred the Persian horde from Europe. This campaign was a return engagement for the Persians. Having been defeated by the Greeks at Marathon, a city 26 miles outside the city of Athens 10 years earlier (a runner covered the 26 miles and died after delivering the news of victory to the Athenians), the Persians had carefully assembled a massive fighting force and a strategy designed to conquer Europe and bring it within the scope and power of the Persian Empire. King Leonidas of Sparta commanded an advance force of, perhaps, 7,000 men, with an elite component that has come to be known as the 300 Spartans.

Each side saw the other as a hegemon, set on world domination. The Greek historian, Herodotus, quotes Xerxes as declaring, "Either our empire must pass under the dominion of the Greeks, or their land become the prey of the Persians; for there is no middle course left in this quarrel." Having repulsed Darius I, father of Xerxes, at Marathon, the Greeks were equally aware of this cultural conflict; and, they had no desire to be swallowed up by the Persian Empire. Both sides believed themselves to be fighting for freedom. To Xerxes and the Persians who were Zoroastrians (an early monotheism) the polytheistic Greeks, with their amoral gods, seemed spiritually inferior. The Greeks, for their part, saw the Persians as barbarians who did not share what they saw as the superior Greek culture.

Freedom was sacred to the Greeks. However, for the Spartans, freedom was quite a complex concept. In their highly stratified society, only the Spartiates, a military master race, had voting rights. A second class, the Perioikoi or Neighbors, were free men who fought alongside the Spartiates but had no voting rights. Most problematic were the Helots, a conquered indigenous population, who worked the farms the Spartiates owned but were forbidden to cultivate and fought alongside them when ordered to do so, but who had no rights at all. Freedom for the Spartans seemed to mean their own political freedom, as well as the continuing freedom to profit from the unfreedom of the Helots.

Before setting out to conquer Europe, Xerxes, a young man of 38, had two dreams/visions, in which a "tall and beautiful man" urged him on, threatening that if he faltered, "Thou art grown mighty and puissant in a short space, so likewise shalt thou within a little time be brought low indeed." Leonidas, past 60, recalled the prophecy of Apollo's priestess, the Oracle at Delphi, that "either Sparta would be destroyed by the barbarians or the king of Sparta would be destroyed" and elected to stand his ground with an elite force of Spartan fighters in a much-praised but suicidal engagement. Was the Spartan idea of freedom worth dying for or too compromised to remain a noble ideal? The YES selection explores the complications of Helot unfreedom. The NO selection introduces a more subtle relationship between Spartiates and Helots.

What does the word "freedom" mean to you? Is it possible or desirable to arrive at a universally accepted idea of what freedom means? There are, of course, parallels to the Greco-Persian Wars in the United States Civil War. Like the Spartans, the South was fighting to preserve a way of life that contained a complicated definition of freedom. In the twenty-first century, the West insists on a more comprehensive application of freedom. Freedom for all is the ideal at least, even if it is not always honored in practice. Is freedom divisible—open to some, closed to others?

To make the discussion more philosophical consider the question of "the price of freedom." Is it necessary that some people remain unfree in order to ensure the freedom of others? Novels such as *Brave New World* by Aldous Huxley examine the benefits and costs of a highly stratified society. In this fictional society, people are decanted with certain abilities and limitations. However, there is no crime, no unemployment, and no destructive competition. Is it necessary that some people be willing to spend their lives sweeping streets so that others can spend theirs making medical breakthroughs?

Plato's utopia, the *Republic*, has a three-tiered society. Producers and artisans, the lowest group, are permitted to keep the money they earn, as well as to marry and raise their own children. Soldiers live in communal barracks. Their needs are taken care of, but they receive no money and they neither marry nor have children. Even the Guardians, from whom the Philosopher King will be chosen, are barred from the cash economy. "Those who have cannot rule; those who rule cannot have," was Plato's succinct pronouncement. And, the state would raise promising toddlers from this group's eugenic matings for future roles in society. Some of these people might strike modern readers as quite unfree.

Paul Cartledge, author of the YES selection, is a recognized authority in the world of classics and ancient history. Author and editor of more than 30 books, his two most recent are *The Spartans: The World of the Warrior-Heroes of Ancient* Greece (The Overlook Press, 2002, 2003) and *Thermopylae: The Battle that Changed the World* (The Overlook Press, 2006). For a balanced examination of the Persians and the Greeks, see *Thermopylae: The Battle for the West by* Ernle Bradford (Da Capo Press, 1980). And, the first Greek historian, Herodotus, remains a fascinating chronicler of the outer events and inner landscapes of both Xerxes and Leonidas. Some of his writings may be found in Michael Grant's compilation *Readings in the Classical Historians* (Charles Scribner's Sons, 1992). And, Herodotus's *History* is available online at: http://classics.mit.edu/Herodotus/history.

The NO selection in this issue is a review of a historical novel, *Gates of Fire* by Steven Pressfield (Doubleday, 1998), which creates a fictional protagonist to embody a more nuanced relationship between Spartiates and Helots. Sometimes, heroic individuals turn out to have personal flaws. Often, historians are willing to overlook or minimize the character flaws of the individual because of the magnitude of what that person accomplished. Is the same true when we look at societies? Is it easier or more difficult, for example, to celebrate the many positive elements in antebellum U.S. culture, once we are reminded of the realities of the slavery system? In the case of this issue, do the "300 Spartans" take on a less heroic status once we know that only some of them were free? Or, might we find those who were unfree and yet fought a suicidal battle even more heroic? Are there ways in which a work of fiction is better able to offer us the subtleties that a more straightforward account might gloss over?

YES

Paul Cartledge

To Die For?

The events of September 11th, 2001, jolted many of us into rethinking what was distinctive and admirable—or at least defensible—about Western civilisation, values and culture. Some of us were provoked into wondering whether any definition of that civilisation and its cultural values would justify our dying for them, or even maybe killing for them. Those of us who are historians of ancient Greece wondered with especial intensity, since the world of ancient Greece is one of the principal taproots of Western civilisation. As J.S. Mill put it, the battle of Marathon fought in 490 BC between the Athenians with support from Plataea and the invading Persians was more important than the Battle of Hastings, even as an event in English history. So too, arguably, was the battle of Thermopylae of ten years later. Although this was a defeat for the small Spartan-led Greek force at the hands of the Persians, it was nonetheless glorious or culturally significant for that. Indeed, some would say that Thermopylae was Sparta's finest hour.

The Spartans were the Dorian inhabitants of a Greek city-state in the Peloponnese that for many centuries was one of the greatest of Greek powers. But who were they really, these Spartans? That question was supposedly asked in about 550 BC by the Persian Great King Cyrus, as reported by Herodotus. Three generations later, Cyrus's successor Xerxes found out all too painfully who they were, and what they were made of: a fighting machine strong enough, skilful enough and sufficiently iron-willed to repel his hordes from the attempt to incorporate the mainland Greeks in his oriental empire already stretching from the Aegean in the West to beyond the Hindu Kush. He discovered these things in person, at Thermopylae. Although this was formally a defeat for the Spartan forces under King Leonidas, the battle constituted a massive morale victory for the Greeks, and the following year the army Xerxes had left behind in Greece was decisively defeated in a pitched battle at Plataea, principally at the hands of the drilled and disciplined Spartan hoplite phalangites (heavy infantry) commanded by the Spartan regent Pausanias.

Thus, one not insignificant reason why today we should care who the ancient Spartans were is that they played a key role—some might say the key role—in defending Greece and so preserving a form of culture or civilisation that constitutes one of the chief roots of our own Western civilisation. That, at any rate, is certainly arguable. It helps to explain why 2002 might be called the Year of Sparta, rather as 2004 is to be the Year of Athens—and by extension of ancient Olympia and the Olympics.

This year there is a remarkable focus of academic and popular interest in the ancient Spartans. Two television series, one to be aired in over 50 countries on the History Channel, one on the UK's Channel 4; two discussion panels at international scholarly conferences, one to be held in the States (the Berkshire Women's History Conference), one in Scotland; and two international colloquia taking place in modern Sparta itself, one organised by Greek scholars, including members of the Greek Archaeological Service, the other by the British School at Athens (which has been involved with research in and on Sparta since 1906 and is currently seeking the funding to establish a research centre in the city). What can there possibly be still to talk about that merits focusing all this attention on ancient Sparta?

To begin with, Sparta, like some other ancient Greek cities or places, has left its mark on our consciousness by way of enriching English vocabulary. The island of Lesbos, for example, has given us 'lesbian', and Corinth 'corinthian'. But Sparta, prodigally, has given us not one but two English adjectives, and a noun besides: 'spartan', of course, 'laconic', and, less obviously, 'helot'.

To choose an illustration almost at random, a recent profile of the British Tory Party leader Iain Duncan Smith referred casually to his naval public school as 'spartan'—and aptly so, at least in so far as the British public school system, as invented virtually by Thomas Arnold of Rugby in the nineteenth century and continued by, say, Kurt Hahn's Gordonstoun in the twentieth, had been consciously modelled on an idea, or even a utopian vision, of ancient Sparta's military-style communal education.

The Spartan root of 'laconic' is not so immediately transparent, but it comes from one of the ancient adjectival forms derived from the name the Spartans more often called themselves by: Lacedaemonians. Diminutive but perfectly formed discourse can, according to Umberto Eco, be simply irresistible—and so it seemed to the Spartans, who perfected the curt, clipped, military mode of utterance, used in dispatches from the front or in snappy repartee to an insistent teacher, that we call laconic.

As for helot, the word is used to refer to a member of an especially deprived or exploited ethnic or economic underclass, and is a product of the dark underside of the Spartans' achievement. Other Greek cities, not least Athens, were dependent on unfree labour for creating and maintaining a politicised and cultured style of communal life.

But the slaves of the Athenians were a polyglot, heterogeneous bunch, mainly 'barbarians' or non-Greek foreigners, and they were mostly owned individually. The unfree subordinate population of Sparta, by contrast, was an entire Greek people, or perhaps two separate peoples united by a common yoke of servitude, whom they conquered during the eighth century and collectively labelled Helots. The word probably meant 'captives', and the Spartans treated them as prisoners of war whose death sentence they had suspended so as to make them work under constant threat of death, in order to provide the economic basis of the Spartan way of life.

These three words are a small token of the fact that English and indeed European or Western culture as a whole have been deeply marked by the Spartan image or myth, what the French scholar Francois Oilier neatly dubbed 'le mirage spartiate'. That phrase was coined in the 1930s, an era when Sparta—or rather ideas of how Sparta worked as a society—exercised a particular fascination for totalitarian or authoritarian rulers, most notoriously Hitler and pseudo-scholarly members of his entourage such as Alfred Rosenberg. Discipline, orderliness, soldierly hierarchy and subordination of individual endeavour to the overriding good of the state were among the Spartan virtues that most attracted them. . . .

Yet it is not only for what intellectuals or politicians have made of Sparta, through the centuries, that Sparta remains a choice subject of study. It is also for what the Spartans really did achieve, most conspicuously on the battlefields of 480–479. Had it not been for the Spartans' remarkably successful organisation of their society into a well-oiled military machine, and their diplomatic development of a rudimentary multi-state Greek alliance well before the Persians came to Greece, there would have been no core of leadership around which the Greek resistance could coalesce. Had it not been for the Spartans' suicidal but heroic stand at Thermopylae, which showed that the Persians could be resisted, it is unlikely that the small, wavering and uncohesive force of loyalist Greeks would have had the nerve to imagine that they might one day win. But for charismatic Spartan commanders of the character and calibre of Leonidas (r.490–480) and Pausanias (regent, 480–c.471), the Greek land forces would have been critically weakened.

Finally, had the loyalist Greeks lost in 480–479, and the Persians absorbed the Greeks of the mainland as well as of the islands and the western Asiatic seaboard into their farflung empire, the ensuing Greek civilisation would have been immeasurably different from and, most would say, inferior to what actually evolved in the fifth and fourth centuries.

What did the Spartans bring to the Greek cultural feast, beyond playing a vital role in winning the war that made it possible at all? Different interpreters might stress different aspects of the classical Greek cultural achievement, to emphasise either those aspects that they find most admirable and imitable or the ones that they consider to have been the most influential on subsequent cultures of the European or Western tradition. I would privilege three qualities or characteristics above all: a devotion to competition in all its forms almost for its own sake; a devotion to a concept and ideal of freedom; and a capacity for almost limitless self-criticism.

The first two might be found equally strongly in either of the two exemplars of ancient Greek civilisation, Sparta and Athens. The third, however, was a peculiarly Athenian cultural trait and not a Spartan one at all. Or so contemporary Athenians liked to think—and many have subsequently agreed. Demosthenes, for example, stated to an Athenian audience that it was forbidden to Spartans to criticise their laws, and there was undoubtedly no Spartan equivalent of either the tragic or the comic drama competitions which provided the Athenians with two annual state-sponsored opportunities for self-examination. On the other hand, the Spartans were not quite the unhesitatingly obedient automata of Athenian propaganda. On occasion grumbling might turn into open defiance of authority, both individually and collectively. Even Sparta's kings might be brought low, tried and fined—or, worse, exiled under sentence of death. It would be fairer and more accurate to say that the Spartans' culture was not one that favoured, let alone encouraged, open dissent or argument. . . .

As for the general Greek passion for freedom, it was said by Critias—an Athenian admirer, admittedly, who was also an extreme authoritarian thinker and politician, leader of the Thirty Tyrants regime (404–403)—that in Sparta there were to be found both the most free people in Greece, and the most unfree. By the most free he meant the Spartans themselves, or more precisely the Spartan master-class, who were freed by the compulsory labour of their enslaved workforce from the necessity of performing any productive labour apart from warfare. By the most unfree the author meant the Helots. These people were treated as a conquered population. They came to outnumber their Spartan masters manifold, and for that reason among others were constantly a source of fear, even terror, to them. In the 460s a massive Helot revolt, following a major earthquake that hit the town of Sparta directly, caused serious damage, psychological as well as political and economic. But the Spartans outmatched the Helots in terror in return. The first act of the Spartans' chief board of annual officials, the five Ephors, on taking office was to declare war in the name of the Spartan state on the Helots collectively, the enemy within. That meant that any killing of Helots by Spartan citizens, deliberate or otherwise, was officially sanctioned, even perhaps encouraged, and, crucially (the Spartans were hugely pious), was in religious terms free from ritual pollution.

The Helots, and the Spartans' severe treatment of them, at first puzzled and later disturbed the more sensitive Greek observers. Plato, for example, remarked that the helot system was the most controversial example of servitude in Greece. This controversy was heightened in Plato's lifetime, when, in the aftermath of a decisive defeat of Sparta by the Boeotians at Leuktra in 371, the larger portion of them, the Messenians, finally achieved their collective freedom and established themselves as free Greek citizens of the restored (as they saw it) free city of Messene. This autonomy was attained, moreover, after another collective revolt—something which slaves elsewhere in Greece could only dream of. . . .

Spartan girls, unlike Athenian girls, underwent a form of state education, separate from the boys but comparably rigorous and physical; this entitled them to equal food rations to enable them to develop physical strength, especially for eugenic reasons. Spartan wives and mothers were not shrinking violets. They openly berated and chastised any hint of cowardice in their sons. They wept tears of pain if their son or husband came back safe but defeated from battle, tears of joy if he died in a winning cause. The laconic admonition 'With your shield, or on it', meaning either come back alive and victorious or come back dead and victorious, was credited to the archetypal Spartan mother. They ritually humiliated men who were thought to have remained unmarried for too long, or showed signs of not wanting to get married at all. They inherited and owned property, including land, in their own right. They slept with men other than their husbands, and got away with it, indeed sometimes were actually encouraged to do so—by their husbands.

So independent-minded were they that Aristotle (admittedly not the most liberated of ancient Greeks in his outlook on women) believed that in Sparta the men, for all their prowess on the battlefield, actually were ruled at home by their women. In the second book of his *Politics* he devoted considerable space to the defects as he saw them of Lycurgus's arrangements, and no single factor did he reckon up more adversely than the excessively powerful position of the citizen women.

We should take at least some of this with a dose of salt. Our written sources are exclusively male and non-Spartan. Nevertheless, we may safely infer that Sparta was in vital respects seriously different, even alien, to the traditional Greek norms of political and social intercourse. That alone makes Sparta worth studying. Herodotus wrote that he agreed with the Theban poet Pindar that 'custom was king', in the sense that every human group believes that its own customs are not only better than those of others but absolutely the best possible. With Sparta, he was on to a winner. Here is an illustration from the seventh book of his *Histories*.

Shortly before Thermopylae, it was reported to Xerxes that the Spartans were combing and styling their long hair. He had been told, by an exiled Spartan former king in his entourage, that the Spartans feared the Law more even than his Persian subjects feared their Great King and that in obedience to their Law they would never flee in battle, no matter how greatly outnumbered, but stand firm either to conquer or to die. Xerxes had laughed, refusing to believe that men who coiffed their tresses before fighting would make serious opponents in the field. Yet events were soon to confirm the laconic statement reportedly made by the Spartan ex-king: 'This is their custom before risking their lives'.

Modern Sparta is a charming provincial capital; a few miles to the west, in the foothills of the Taygetos range, lie the ruins of Mistra, once capital of the Byzantine Despotate of the Morea. Here in the fifteenth century, as the Ottoman Turks prepared for their final assault on Constantinople, a monk, George Gemistos Plethon, sat composing Platonist nostrums for regulating the ideal state of human co-existence.

That utopianism seems a world away from the down-to-earth and brutally efficient society of ancient Sparta. And yet the ideal encapsulated in the myth of Thermopylae still resonates, if not always with the happiest of consequences. It is the concept that there are values that are worth dying for. Taken in a destructive direction, as by fundamentalist suicide-bombers, that notion can be wholly repellent. Developed in the direction taken by Lycurgus, however, it can generate ideals of communal co-operation and self-sacrifice that qualify properly and justly for the honorific label of utopia.

I end with one of Lycurgus's more long-lasting endeavours, his involvement—according to some sources—in the foundation of the Olympic Games (traditionally in 776 BC) and in the swearing of the first Olympic truce. That truce, partly religious and partly a pragmatic device to enable the Games to take place despite chronic inter-city warfare, is usually misunderstood. For once, though, a historical misunderstanding can be constructive today and in the future. Modern sport can too often be a form of war minus the shooting, as George Orwell put it. But it need not be so, and it is possible for individuals to go faster and higher and be stronger without provoking or exploiting international hatred. The modern Olympic movement, including the Olympic Truce organisation based at Olympia itself, offers a mental as well as material space for overcoming the sort of lethal differences that continue to divide peoples and cultures. For that ideal, we have to thank, in part at least, a Spartan.

Paul Cartledge is a professor of Greek history at Cambridge University and a fellow of Clare College. He is a world expert on Athens and Sparta in the Classical Age. He was chief historical consultant for the BBC TV series *The Greeks* and the series *The Spartans* presented by Bettany Hughes.

Byron Farwell

The Spartan Way

All were killed. No Spartan survived the final day of the Battle of Thermopylae. Deserted by their allies, even the Thespaseans, who had stood by the longest, the survivors of the three-hundred-man contingent sent by Sparta to face the massive invading army of Xerxes stood firm and fought. Each man knew his fate: death on this day in battle. No one lived to give an account of the slaughter and desperate valor of the final hours.

But what history cannot provide a skilled novelist can evoke, and there exists a rich historical background and much recent research on which to draw. In a new novel, *Gates of Fire,* Steven Pressfield has used both skillfully. His interest lies in the Spartan soldiers, their education, military training, and the army in which they served. To give his material a living voice, he has conjured up a survivor who lives long enough to bear witness and to describe the Spartan military system and the battle as it might have been. And it is here that the author falters. Characterization is not his strong point, but it hardly matters. His tale is an absorbing one.

Xeones, his protagonist, is a young man found on the field of battle grievously wounded and unconscious. He puzzled the Persians, for instead of the traditional felt cowl underneath his helmet he wore a dogskin cap of the sort worn by the Lakedaemonian helots (slaves), yet his shield and armor were fashioned of the finest bronze and etched with Hibernian cobalt. His crest denoted a full Spartiate, a Lakedaemonian of the upper class.

When he was able to speak, he continued to astonish, for he spoke in a compound of "the loftiest philosophical and literary language" and the "most crude gutter argot." He was brought on a stretcher before King Xerxes, son of Darius, commander of the Persian host, who was eager to learn what sort of men these were who before his eyes had slain some twenty thousand of his best warriors. What sort of system produced such men? Thus does the author set the stage for an account of the life of a young man who became a "squire of the heavy infantry, a servant of the battle train" in ancient Greece.

A Survivor's Story

Xeones was not born a Spartan. He was 10 when an Argive raiding party from a neighboring state killed his father and mother, destroyed their farm, and demolished their city-state. Together with a 13-year-old female cousin, Diomache, and Bruxieus, an ancient, educated, but near-blind family slave, he escaped into the hills. The trio managed to survive unharmed until Xeones, caught trying to steal a goose, was crucified by its enraged owners and left to die. He was rescued by Diomache, but his ordeal left him with permanently crippled hands, hands that could never hold a spear but could, he discovered, pull the string of a bow. This became his weapon, and Apollo became his god.

By their second summer in the mountains, Xeones and Diomache, aided by two puppies they found and trained, had become accomplished hunters and fledgling savages. Bruxieus' devoted attempts to educate and polish them had given them a smattering of philosophy and a nodding acquaintance with the poets, but their salvation, he was persuaded, lay in Athens, the only truly open city, center of freedom and culture, in Greece. Upon his death, in obedience to his wishes, they set out for the city. He was 12 and she 15. Full of hope, they told themselves that Diomache would soon find a husband and Xeones would easily find work as a sailor. But Athens was not the city of Bruxieus' dreams. Diomache became a prostitute and eventually a nun. Xeones was captured by the Spartans.

After an unhappy year in which he was cast among the helots, he was taken into the service of Alexandros, a scion of one of Sparta's noblest families and son of a polemarch, or war leader, who elevated him to the status of *parastates pais,* "a sort of sparring partner for the youths enrolled in the *agoge,* the notorious and pitiless thirteen-year training regimen which turned boys into Spartan warriors."

Eager to prove himself a warrior, Alexandros took Xeones as his squire and followed, without permission, an army sent to fight the Antirhionians. In the next five years the Spartans launched twenty-one campaigns against other Greeks, and Xeones fought in many of them.

He proved himself a disciplined warrior and was elevated to a position as squire to Dienekes, a Spartan hero. His social position was much changed. His Scythian bow was returned to him; he was later able to take a wife, by whom he sired a son and daughter, but the reader learns nothing of the domestic side of his life.

Nothing is told in a rush. Pressfield has obviously done his homework and moves effortlessly back and forth in time and place to flesh out Spartan life in peace and war.

The Persians Are Coming!

Xerxes, having succeeded to the Persian throne on the death of Darius, assembled a great host for the invasion of Greece. There was no secret about this and the Greeks trembled, but Sparta failed to convince all the disparate Greek states to unite and oppose him. A few allies were collected, however, and the Spartans were determined to display the mettle of their men.

The Peloponnese was separated from the rest of Greece by a narrow mountainous neck of land. A road ran through this rugged stretch, skirting the mountains and passing close to the sea. This passageway was called Thermopylae (hot gates), for there were spas there and the remains of three ancient gates. The Greeks decided to make their stand at the middle gate, known as the Phokian Wall.

Night had fallen when the Spartans and their allies reached the selected battlefield. Most of the local people, Phokians and Lokrians, had fled into the mountains. Stonemasons and engineers were summoned to construct a battle wall from the available stones. The engineers immediately fell to arguing about where and how it was to be built while the masons and soldiers stood idly by.

This impasse was solved by the Spartan battle king, Leonidas, a man well past 60, who simply picked up a boulder and put it in place. Then he set a second stone beside it and a third. Finally someone cried: "How long do you imbeciles intend to stand by gaping? Will you wait all night while the king builds the wall himself?" The men at once fell to. Nothing fancy. As Leonidas said: "A wall of stone will not preserve Hellas, but a wall of men."

Around midnight a few of the local people reappeared and were welcomed. One of them had actually seen the Persian host and told chilling tales of the magnitude of Xerxes' army, its vast quantities of supplies, and the skills of its warriors. He had seen the Persian archers practice; their arrows had blocked out the sun. Dienekes, who arrived to hear this, remarked coolly, "Good. Then we'll have our battle in the shade."

The Battle Begins

When the Persian advance guard of cavalry came into view, watch fires were set across the rocky plain in front of the wall. The area was soon blanketed with fire, smoke, and sea fog. Several days passed before the Persians could bring up their army and prepare for battle, time the Greeks used to advantage. In the evenings they sat about their fires talking of fear and of courage, that of both men and women. One spoke of a Spartan woman who on learning that all five of her sons had been killed in a single battle asked only who was victorious. Assured that the Spartans had triumphed, she walked away dry-eyed, saying only, "Then I am happy."

A Persian attempt to obtain an early surrender failed, the Spartans suggesting instead that the Persians surrender to them. It fell to the Thespaseans to repel the first Persian attack. When they fell back from exhaustion, "The Spartans came in frontally, eight deep at a double interval, allowing the Thespaseans to withdraw between the files."

The Persian shields proved too small and fragile to protect them, and their light spears and lances snapped and shivered against the heavy bronze shields of the Greeks. The Spartans struck overhand with their spears and the Persians fell in droves, valiant but ineffective. "The slaughter surpassed the mind's capacity to assimilate it," said Xeones. Although the squires worked furiously, hauling away the corpses, "the earth grew, not littered with enemy bodies, but piled with them. Stacked with them. Mounded with them." The Persians' supply of men seemed limitless, but at last they were driven from the field.

The last attack of the day was made by Xerxes' own household guards, picked champions of noble families, many of them the king's own kinsmen. Trained from birth "to draw the bow and speak the truth," they were called the Immortals. There were ten thousand of them, fresh and eager for battle against the now fewer than three thousand near-exhausted Greeks. Even this elite corps was beaten back as night fell. In more than seven hours of fighting, the Greeks had driven off four assaults.

The squires now tended to the wounds of their masters. Xeones bathed the face of Dienekes, who had lost an eye, "sliced through, leaving a ghoulish socket of tissue and blood." All night long the forges roared and smiths' hammers sounded throughout the Greek camps, as spears, swords, and shields were repaired for the next day's battle.

On the second day, the Persian weight of numbers took its toll. The Spartans and Thespaseans fought desperately to hold the wall, but by the day's end, their numbers further decreased by new casualties, they fell back, reeling from exhaustion. Astonishingly, with victory within their grasp, the Persians hesitated; a sense of terror seemed to seize them. Suddenly, a mighty bellow sounded from the heavens. Lightning bolts blazed across the sky, and a storm descended. Crying "Zeus Savior! Hellas and freedom!" Leonidas led the Greeks in a counterattack that sent their enemies flying.

Battle's End

With decisive victory an impossibility, Leonidas released all the surviving allies, and they wearily trudged homeward. The Spartans stayed. Even had they wanted to leave the field, this was made impossible, for a treacherous local Greek had led the Immortals through the mountains. After an all-night encirclement march, the Persians stationed themselves six miles to the rear. Then the surviving Spartans prepared to die fighting. Facing enemies to the front and rear, there was no question of the battle's outcome. Squires and helots were, with their families, manumitted by Leonidas, and those on the field were given the arms and panoply of the fallen. Thus Xeones, again a free man, was found in the attire of a full Spartan warrior.

"At last came the tide," said Xeones, "and within which one felt as a wave beneath the storming whims of the gods. . . . Chariots and Persian horsemen stampeded pell-mell into the Spartans." They died to the last man. Xeones lived only long enough to finish his tale.

The day the Spartans were defeated at Thermopylae was also the day that ended Xerxes' dreams of conquest, for the Persian fleet suffered a calamitous defeat in the Straits of Salamis, off Athens. Xerxes retreated to Asia, leaving behind an army of three hundred thousand to face the Greeks in the spring. Their defeat later on the plains of Plataea, primarily by the disciplined ranks of the full Spartan army, marked the end of Asian power in Greece and the beginning of the rebirth of Greek culture.

On the battlefield of Thermopylae a stone was raised, on which were carved the unforgettable words of the poet Simonides:

> Tell the Spartans, stranger passing by, that here obedient to their laws we lie.

Byron Farwell is a respected military historian and is the author of several books on nineteenth and early twentieth century British military colonialism, including *Eminent Victorian Soldiers, Prisoners of the Mahdi, Queen Victoria's Little Wars,* and *Mr. Kipling's Army.* He is also a contributing editor to *Military History and World War II.*

EXPLORING THE ISSUE

Were the Spartans Fighting for a Compromised View of Freedom at Thermopylae?

Critical Thinking and Reflection

1. Though the Greeks were defeated and slaughtered by the Persians at Thermopylae, that battle is sometimes called Sparta's finest hour. How might this be so? Critically discuss.
2. What was at stake for each side in the conflict? Did Xerxes and Leonidas each believe that there were no viable alternatives? Critically explain and discuss.
3. What was the status of the Helots in Sparta? How might this status have affected the Helots who fought and died at Sparta—either in life or in death? Critically analyze and examine this element of the battle.
4. If the Spartans were fighting for their freedom (against Xerxes and the Persians), yet only some Spartans were free, do you agree with the issue title that the Spartans were fighting for a compromised view of freedom at Thermopylae? Critically discuss.
5. What role do you think the personal ambitions and anxieties of Xerxes and Leonidas might have played in this battle? Critically discuss.
6. Did reading a scholarly review of the historical novel *Gates of Fire* (the literal meaning of Thermopylae) complicate your understanding of the Helots? Your view of what freedom meant to the Spartans? Critically discuss.
7. The recent film, *"300,"* brings Frank Miller's graphic novel to visual life on the screen. Do the computer-generated, nearly identical soldiers in the film underline the "unfreedom" and lack of individuality of the Helots? Critically discuss the role of film in enhancing historical analysis.

Is There Common Ground?

The "facts" about the Battle of Thermopylae are very well known and agreed upon. As you read through these two selections, make a list of at least three "factual" elements. Are they the most important or the most interesting element in this story? This issue asks us to go more deeply and consider the Spartan idea of freedom. In a sense, we might ask the same questions posed in this issue of Athenian society. Women were confined to the home after marriage and denied participation in the civic and political life of the city. So, when we read about Athenian Democracy, which half of the population are we going to consider? Spartan woman, ironically, had greater freedom in some areas than their Athenian counterparts. They were able to own property and make decisions about marriage that were denied to Athenian women. And, Athenians also had slaves.

Question: Maybe the question to ask about the Spartan concept of freedom is: Compared to whom? Research the Persian society that Xerxes left behind when he came to do battle with the Greeks. How free were the Persians?

Additional Resources

A fine biography of *Leonidas: Hero of Thermopylae* by Ian Macgregor Morris (Rosen Central, 2004) offers insights into the king who led the fight to the death. And, there are DVDs from The Teaching Company (2006) *Great Battles of the Ancient World,* as well as from A&E Home videos (2006) *Decisive Battles: The Ancient World.* Finally, of course, the film *"300"* is available now from Warner Home Video in a two-disc special edition. As you watch this film, ask yourself what point of view the director and cowriter Zack Snyder has taken in bringing Frank Miller's graphic novel *300* to the silver screen. The storyteller, who appears at the beginning, draws into his tale a group of Spartans the night before the battle? Is this device effective in increasing the viewer's empathy for the soldiers we know will die?

Internet References . . .

Thermopylae—300 Spartans

This site features links to the battle and other, related battles; warrior images; museum artifacts; and Greek archaeology, as well as scenes from the movie *"300."* "Questions & Answers" and "Thermopylae for Students" may be especially useful.

www.300spartanwarriors.com

Selected, Edited, and with Issue Framing Material by:
Helen Buss Mitchell, *Howard Community College*
and
Joseph R. Mitchell, *Howard Community College*

ISSUE

Should We Deny Alexander III His Title, "The Great"?

YES: Ian Worthington, from "How 'Great' Was Alexander?" *Ancient History Bulletin* (April–June 1999)

NO: Paul Cartledge, from "Alexander the Great: Hunting for a New Past?" *History Today* (July 2004)

Learning Outcomes

After reading this issue you should be able to:

- Summarize the military accomplishments and personal qualities of Alexander the Great.
- Summarize the criticisms made of Alexander's life and work.
- Understand why Alexander was called "The Great" during his lifetime.
- Understand the basis for denying him this title.

ISSUE SUMMARY

YES: Professor Ian Worthington argues that Alexander's actions were self-serving and eventually weakened his Macedonian homeland; therefore, he does not merit the historical reputation he has been given.

NO: Professor Paul Cartledge argues that we need to demythologize the reputation of Alexander, not deny him a claim to greatness.

From 431 to 404 B.C.E., the Greek city-states (*polei*) were destroying themselves in a needless but predictable series of wars that have become known as the Peloponnesian Wars. Chronicled by Thucydides, an eyewitness and participant, these wars showed the Greek states at their worst—selfish, contentious, avaricious, and power-hungry. The result was a series of conflicts in which one side, Sparta and its allies, was able to defeat its traditional enemy, Athens and its Delian League allies. Both sides suffered heavy losses and learned no lessons from the prolonged conflict. In their weakened, unenlightened state, they were easy prey to a strong, united Greek kingdom from the north—the Macedonians and their powerful king, Philip.

The Macedonians were considered barbarians by the Greek city-states of the south. However, they had unification and military prowess on their side, and soon all of Greece was under their control. Philip was deprived of his chance for a more exalted place in history when he was assassinated by a bodyguard, while attending a wedding festival in 336 B.C.E. He was succeeded by his son Alexander, then a young man of 19 years.

Alexander seemed to be destined for greatness. At an early age he displayed strong leadership and military skills, and to complement these, Philip hired the noted Greek philosopher, Aristotle, as a tutor to help develop Alexander's intellectual side. Although it is difficult to pinpoint specific contributions that Aristotle made to the development of his pupil, some general ones were a passion for Greek culture, a strong affinity for intellectual pursuits, and a keen interest in Greek literature and art.

Given the volatile nature of Macedonian politics and Alexander's lack of experience, accession to his father's crown was not guaranteed. But he did succeed, and within 14 years he conquered most of the then-known world. This earned him a place in history with the sobriquet—Alexander the Great.

Alexander's place in history was created immediately after his death. There were some who spoke of him as a divinity even while he was alive, and Alexander did nothing to discourage it. This glorification process continued through the next few centuries. The Romans, who featured likenesses of him in many of their art works, saw themselves in him as they began to follow in his footsteps, conquering much of the known world. The apex of his Roman reputation occurred when Plutarch (42–102 C.E.) wrote glowingly of him in his *Lives*, claiming that Alexander was descended from Hercules. A few of the historical figures who engaged in Alexandrine worship included Julius Caesar, Napoleon Bonaparte, and U.S. World War II General George Patton. Alexander's persona has also been featured in literary works by writers too numerous to mention.

What was the basis of Alexander's glowing historical reputation? Obviously, his conquests form its essence—but it is based on more than territorial accumulation. Some claim it is the story of the "philosopher-king," an intellectual leader who would attempt to create a cultural synthesis by fusing the best of East and West. Alexander's most ardent supporters applaud him for attempting to create a "one world" ideal and coming close to achieving it. Alexander's critics see a self-aggrandizing megalomaniac who ignored the human costs of his adventures and killed a senior cavalry commander and one of his most skilled and loyal supporters in a drunken rage. Most damning for the critics are Alexander's efforts to have himself worshiped as "divine."

For most of recorded history, humankind's story has been told through the words and deeds of its great men (and occasionally great women). This is known as the "heroic" approach to the study of history. In the first part of the twentieth century, this version of history dominated, and historical figures such as Alexander still received favorable press. But the repetitive violence of the twentieth century influenced people to interpret history in a less militaristic vein, and the positive assessment of Alexander the Great began to change. How much it will change remains to be seen.

Australian classicist Ian Worthington finds Alexander's claim to greatness undeserved due to the death and suffering caused by his military campaigns, and how much they weakened the Macedonian state at home. On the other hand, Cambridge Professor Paul Cartledge, though acknowledging Alexander's flaws, still finds some justification for calling him "the Great."

Someone once stated: "Pity the nation that has no heroes!" Someone else wryly replied: "Pity the nation that needs them!" To what extent have national desires throughout history created the aura of Alexander? How many historical figures were so inspired by his story that they sought to emulate it? And what were the results of such actions? Military historian John Keegan, in *The Mask of Command* (Jonathan Cape, 1987), contends that Alexander's ". . . dreadful legacy was to ennoble savagery in the name of glory and to leave a model of command that far too many men of ambition sought to act out in the centuries to come." But should Alexander be held responsible for the actions of those who have attempted to emulate him?

Also contributing to future analyses of Alexander might be a reaction against the experiences of many in what was the most violent century in the history of the world. The twentieth century saw two world wars and countless smaller ones. It had to create words such as *Holocaust* and *genocide* to describe some of the century's barbarities. It saw the names of Hitler, Stalin, and Mao Zedong become infamous for the millions of deaths they have caused, many in their own countries. Noted Holocaust historian Yehuda Bauer has summed up the world's propensity for violence and war—and its consequences: "Napoleon . . . won the Battle of Austerlitz—but was he there alone? Was he not helped a little bit by a few tens of thousands of soldiers whom he (and others) led into battle? How many soldiers were killed on both sides? And what about the civilians near the roads that the armies traveled on? What about the dead, the wounded, the raped, and the dispossessed? We teach our children about the greatness of the various Napoleons, Palmerstons, and Bismarcks as political or military leaders and thus sanitize history" (*Rethinking the Holocaust*, p. 40). Should Alexander's name be added to this list?

YES

Ian Worthington

How "Great" Was Alexander?

Why was Alexander III of Macedon called 'Great'? The answer seems relatively straightforward: from an early age he was an achiever, he conquered territories on a superhuman scale, he established an empire until his times unrivalled, and he died young, at the height of his power. Thus, at the youthful age of 20, in 336, he inherited the powerful empire of Macedon, which by then controlled Greece and had already started to make inroads into Asia. In 334 he invaded Persia, and within a decade he had defeated the Persians, subdued Egypt, and pushed on to Iran, Afghanistan and even India. As well as his vast conquests Alexander is credited with the spread of Greek culture and education in his empire, not to mention being responsible for the physical and cultural formation of the hellenistic kingdoms—some would argue that the hellenistic world was Alexander's legacy. He has also been viewed as a philosophical idealist, striving to create a unity of mankind by his so-called fusion of the races policy, in which he attempted to integrate Persians and Orientals into his administration and army. Thus, within a dozen years Alexander's empire stretched from Greece in the west to India in the far east, and he was even worshipped as a god by many of his subjects while still alive. On the basis of his military conquests contemporary historians, and especially those writing in Roman times, who measured success by the number of body-bags used, deemed him great.

However, does a man deserve to be called 'The Great' who was responsible for the deaths of tens of thousands of his own men and for the unnecessary wholesale slaughter of native peoples? How 'great' is a king who prefers constant warfare over consolidating conquered territories and long-term administration? Or who, through his own recklessness, often endangered his own life and the lives of his men? Or whose violent temper on occasion led him to murder his friends and who towards the end of his life was an alcoholic, paranoid, megalomaniac, who believed in his own divinity? These are questions posed by our standards of today of course, but nevertheless they are legitimate questions given the influence which Alexander has exerted throughout history—an influence which will no doubt continue.

The aims of this [selection] are to trace some reasons for questioning the greatness of Alexander as is reflected in his epithet, and to add potential evidence dealing with the attitude of the Macedonians, Alexander's own people, in their king's absence. It is important to stress that when evaluating Alexander it is essential to view the 'package' of king as a whole; i.e., as king, commander and statesman. All too often this is not the case. There is no question that Alexander was spectacularly successful in the military field, and had Alexander only been a general his epithet may well have been deserved. But he was not just a general; he was a king too, and hence military exploits form only a percentage of what Alexander did, or did not do—in other words, we must look at the 'package' of him as king as a whole. By its nature this [selection] is impressionistic, and it can only deal rapidly with selected examples from Alexander's reign and discuss points briefly. However, given the unequalled influence Alexander has played in cultures and history from the time of his death to today, it is important to stress that there is a chasm of a difference between the mythical Alexander, which for the most part we have today, and the historical.

Alexander died in 323, and over the course of time the mythical king and his exploits sprang into being. Alexander himself was not above embellishing his own life and achievements. He very likely told the court historian Callisthenes of Olynthus what to say about his victory over Darius III at the battle of Issus in 333, for example. Contemporary Attic oratory also exaggerated his achievements, and so within a generation of his death erroneous stories were already being told.

As time continued we move into the genre of pulp fiction. In the third or second century BC Alexander's exploits formed the plot of the story known as the *Alexander Romance*, which added significantly to the Alexander legend and had such a massive influence on many cultures into the Middle Ages. Given its life-span, deeds were attributed to Alexander which are unhistorical, such as his encounters with the tribe of headless men, his flying exploits in a basket borne by eagles, and the search for the Water of Life, which ended with his transformation into a mermaid. These stories became illustrative fodder for the various manuscripts of the *Alexander Romance*—one of the most popular episodes is Alexander's ascent to heaven, inspired by the myth of Bellerephon to fly to Mount Olympus on Pegasus, which is found in many Byzantine and later art-works, sculptures and paintings. As a result of the *Romance* Alexander astonishingly appears in the literature of other cultures: in Hebrew literature, for example, he was seen as a preacher and prophet, who even becomes converted to Christianity. In Persian literature he is the hero Sikandar, sent to punish the impure peoples. In the West he appears as a Frank, a Goth, a Russian and a Saxon.

Then there is Plutarch, writing in the late first and second century AD, who has probably done the most damage to our knowing the historical Alexander. In his treatise *On The Fortune or The Virtue of Alexander*, Plutarch was swayed (understandably) by the social background against which he was writing and especially by his own philosophical beliefs, and he portrayed Alexander as both an action man and a philosopher-king, whose mission was to impose Greek civilisation on the 'barbarian' Persians. Plutarch's work is essentially a rhetorical exercise, but as time continued the rhetorical aspects were disregarded in favour of a warrior-king who was more than the stuff legends were made of; this was a warrior who was seen to combine military success with wisdom and unification. And so Alexander emerges as the promoter of the brotherhood of man in Tarn's 1948 biography, which was greatly influenced by what Plutarch wrote.

The Alexander legend was a ready feeding ground for artists throughout the centuries as well. When Alexander invaded Persia in 334 he detoured to Troy to sacrifice at the tomb of his hero Achilles. This was a stirring story, which became a model for heroic piety in the Renaissance and later periods; thus, for example, we have Fontebasso's painting of Alexander's sacrifice at Achilles' tomb in the eighteenth century. In modern Greece Alexander became both an art-work and a symbol, as seen in the painting by Engonopoulos in 1977 of the face-less Alexander standing with his arm around the face-less Pavlos Melas, a modern hero of the struggle for Macedonian independence.

Thus, we can see how the historical Alexander has faded into the invincible general, the great leader, explorer and king, as time continued, especially in the Middle Ages with its world of chivalry, warriors and great battles: a superb context into which to fit Alexander, even if this meant distortion of the truth, and history subsumed to legend. Indeed, during the Middle Ages he was regarded as one of the four great kings of the ancient world. Let us now consider some specific aspects of Alexander's reign in support of this.

In 334 Alexander III left home for Asia, entrusting to Antipater as guardian . . . a stable—for a while—Greece and Macedon. The king also unilaterally made Antipater deputy hegemon in the League of Corinth. Alexander's 'mandate' or prime directive, as inherited from his father Philip II and endorsed by the League of Corinth, was to pursue his father's plan of punishing the Persians for their sacrilegious acts of 150 years ago and to 'liberate' (whatever that meant) the Greek cities of Asia Minor. In other words, a panhellenic mandate. After he had fulfilled it, people quite rightly would have expected him to return home. People were wrong: the king would soon disregard the prime directive for personal reasons, causing discontent amongst the army with him and also, even more ominously, with his countrymen back home.

We have a fair amount of information for events in mainland Greece, especially Athens, during the reign of Alexander, however events in Macedon in this period are undocumented and largely unknown. We certainly cannot say that there was a hiatus in Macedonian history, for Antipater kept Macedon powerful and united while Alexander was absent, so much so that there was economic growth, and education and military training, for example, remained at a high standard. However, appearance is not likely to reflect reality. Macedon in this period may well have been fraught with discontent, and it provides insights into the Macedonians' attitude to their king and he to them. At the same time a consideration of the Macedonian background also lends further weight to questioning the aptness of Alexander's title 'Great'.

Alexander's military successes throughout his reign were spectacular to a very large degree—and certainly manufactured by the king to be great—and we should expect his people back home to feel proud of their king at the head of his panhellenic mission of punishment and liberation, and to proclaim his victories to all and sundry. His deeds and the geographical extent of his conquests were certainly known for we have references to them in contemporary Attic oratory. However, the impression which strikes us about the Macedonians themselves is that Alexander was far from their idea of an ideal king. Why might they feel this way? In addressing this, we can begin with the vexed question of Macedonian manpower. Did Alexander's demands for reinforcements from the mainland seriously deplete the fighting strength of the army under Antipater? Did he make these demands regardless of the pressure under which he was putting Antipater and without regard for the lives of his people and the security of his kingdom from external threat? And if so, how did the people feel and how did they react? . . .

Alexander's generalship and actual military victories may be questioned in several key areas. For example, after the battle of Issus in 333 Darius fled towards Media, but Alexander pressed on to Egypt. He did not pursue Darius, as he surely ought to have done and thus consolidate his gains, especially when so far from home and with the mood of the locals so prone to fluctuation, but left him alone. He was more interested in what lay to the south: the riches of Babylon and then Susa, or as Arrian describes them the 'prizes of the war'. However, a war can hardly be seen as won if the opposing king and commander remains at large and has the potential to regroup. Alexander's action was lucky for Darius, then, as he was able to regroup his forces and bring Alexander to battle again almost two years later, at Gaugamela (331). It was not lucky for Alexander, though, and especially so for those men on both sides who fell needlessly that day in yet another battle.

We have also the various sieges which Alexander undertook and which were often lengthy, costly, and questionable. A case in point is that of Tyre in 332 as Alexander made his way to Egypt after his victory at Issus. In Phoenicia Byblos and Sidon surrendered to Alexander, as did the island town (as it was then) of Tyre until the king expressed his personal desire to sacrifice in the main temple there. Quite rightly considering his demand sacrilegious, the Tyrians resisted him and Alexander, his ego affronted and refusing to back down, laid siege to the town. The siege itself lasted several months, cost the king a fortune in money and manpower, and resulted in the slaughter of the male Tyrians and the selling of the Tyrian women and children into slavery. There is no question that control of Tyre was essential since Alexander could not afford a revolt of the Phoenician cities, given their traditional rivalries, as he pushed on to Egypt. Nor indeed, if we believe his speech at Arrian, could he allow Tyre independence with the Persian navy a threat and the Phoenician fleet the strongest contingent in it. However, there was no guarantee that the destruction of Tyre would result in the Phoencian fleet surrendering to him as he only seems to have *expected* it would. Moreover, laying siege to Tyre was not necessary: he could simply have left a garrison, for example, on the mainland opposite the town to keep it in check. Another option, given that the Tyrians had originally surrendered to him, would have been the diplomatic one: to recognise the impiety of his demand in their eyes and thus relinquish it, thereby continuing on his way speedily and with their goodwill. Ultimately no real gain came from his siege except to Alexander on a purely personal level again: his damaged ego had been repaired; the cost in time, manpower and reputation mattered little.

Alexander's great military victories over his Persian and Indian foes which have so long occupied a place in popular folklore and been much admired throughout the centuries are very likely to have been embellished and nothing like the popular conceptions of them. A case in point is the battle of Issus in 333. Darius threw victory away at that battle and he was, to put it bluntly, a mediocre commander—the battle might have been very different if Alexander had faced a more competent commander such as Memnon, for example. Alexander was lucky, but this does not come in the 'official' account we have of the battle, probably since he told Callisthenes, the court historian, what to write about it.

. . . [W]ord would filter through to the Macedonians back home. Alexander's growing orientalism, as seen in his apparent integration of foreigners into his administration and army, was a cause of great discontent as the traditional Macedonian warrior-king transformed himself into something akin to a sultan. He began to change his appearance, preferring a mixture of Persian and Macedonian clothing, despite the obvious displeasure of his troops, and he had also assumed the upright tiara, the symbol of Persian kingship. Some saw the writing on the wall and duly pandered to the king. Thus, Peucestas, the Macedonian satrap of Persis, was well rewarded by the king for adopting Persian dress and learning the Persian language. However, he was the only Macedonian to do so according to Arrian.

Significant also was Alexander's attempt to adopt the Persian custom of *proskynesis*—genuflection—at his court in Bactra in 327, and his expectation that his men would follow suit. *Proskynesis* was a social act which had long been practised by the Persians and involved prostrating oneself before the person of the king in an act of subservience, and thereby accepting his lordship. The custom however was regarded as tantamount to worship and thus sacrilegious to the Greeks—worship of a god or a dead hero was one thing, but worship of a person while still alive quite another. Callisthenes thwarted Alexander's attempt, something which the king never forgot and which would soon cost Callisthenes his life in sadistic circumstances.

Why Alexander tried to introduce *proskynesis* is unknown. Perhaps he was simply attempting to create a form of social protocol common to Macedonians, Greeks and Persians. However, he would have been well aware of the religious connotations associated with the act and hence its implications for his own being. It was plain stupidity on his part if he thought his men would embrace the custom with relish, and his action clearly shows that he had lost touch with his army and the religious beliefs on which he had been raised. Evidence for this may be seen in the motives for the Pages' Conspiracy, a serious attempt on Alexander's life, which occurred not long after Alexander tried to enforce *proskynesis* on all. A more likely explanation for the attempt to introduce *proskynesis* is that Alexander now thought of himself as divine, and thus *proskynesis* was a logical means of recognising his divine status in public by all men.

Indeed, Alexander's belief that he was divine impacts adversely on any evaluation of him. History is riddled with megalomaniacs who along the way suffered from divine pretensions, and the epithet 'Great' is not attached to them. Regardless of whether his father Philip II was worshipped as a god on his death, Alexander seems not to have been content with merely following in his footsteps but to believe in his own divine status while alive. . . .

Was Alexander using his own people for his own personal ends now? Philip II risked the lives of his men as well, but for his state's hegemonic position in international affairs, not for his own selfish reasons or a *pothos* which might well jeopardise that position of Macedon. Others saw the danger, even from early in his reign. Thus in 335, after the successful termination of the Greek revolt, which broke out on the death of Philip II, Diodorus says that Parmenion and Antipater urged Alexander not to become actively involved in Asia until he had produced a son and heir. Alexander opposed them for personal reasons: he could not procrastinate at home waiting for children to be born when the invasion of Asia had been endorsed by the League of Corinth! In the end, says Diodorus, he won them over. Then in 331 Darius III offered *inter alia* to abandon to Alexander all territories west of the Euphrates and to become the friend and ally of the king. Parmenion thought the Persian king's offer to be in the Macedonians' best interests, but Alexander refused to accept it (in a famous exchange in which Parmenion is alleged to have said that if he were Alexander he would accept the terms, and a displeased Alexander is alleged to have replied that if he were Parmenion he would, but instead he was Alexander). . . .

Alexander's autocratic nature and its adverse impact on his army have been illustrated many times, but it extended beyond the men with him to the Greeks back on the mainland. One example is his Exiles Decree of 324, which ordered all exiles to return to their native cities (excluding those under a religious curse and the Thebans). If any city was unwilling, then Antipater was empowered to use force against it. The context was no doubt to send home the large bands of mercenaries now wandering the empire and which posed no small military or political danger if any ambitious satrap [subordinate official] or general got his hands on them. The decree was technically illegal since it clearly flouted the autonomy of the Greek states, not to mention the principles of the League of Corinth, but Alexander cared little about *polis* autonomy or the feelings of the Greeks. Although the Athenians refused to receive back their exiles, resistance, to coin a phrase, was futile: Alexander was king, the Macedonians controlled Greece, and the final clause of the decree on coercing Greek cities would not be lost on them. The flurry of diplomatic activity to the king over the decree proves this, even though outright rebellion was not planned at that stage. His death altered the situation dramatically, and only one state, Tegea, actually implemented the decree.

There is no need to deal in great detail with the notion which originates in Plutarch's treatise on Alexander, and has found its way into some modern works (such as Tarn's biography), that Alexander pursued an actual policy to promote a unity of mankind. In other words, that Alexander is deserving of the title 'Great' for these ideological reasons. The belief is 'founded' on such factors as his integration of foreigners into his army and administration, the mass mixed marriage at Susa (324), and Alexander's prayer for concord amongst the races after the Opis mutiny (also 324). The belief is quite erroneous, and Alexander, as with everything else, was acting for purely political/military, not ideological, purposes. For one thing, it is important to note that in the army foreigners were not peppered consistently amongst existing units, and when this did happen the instances are very few and far between. Thus, a few Persians are found incorporated in the *agema* [the Royal squadron] of the Companion cavalry, and Persians and Macedonians served together in a phalanx at Babylon, but Alexander's motive in both cases was military.

While Alexander did use Persians and Orientals in his administration it was always Macedonians and Greeks who controlled the army and the treasury. For example, at Babylon Alexander appointed as satrap the Persian Mazaeus, who had been satrap of Syria under Darius and commander of the Persian right at the battle of Gaugamela. However, Apollodorus of Amphipolis and Agathon of Pydna controlled the garrison there and collected the taxes. In a nutshell, the natives had the local knowledge and the linguistic expertise. The conscious policy on the part of Alexander was to have the different races working together in order to make the local administration function as efficiently as possible, and had nothing to do with promoting racial equality.

Then there is the mass wedding at Susa, also in 324, at which Alexander and 91 members of his court married various Persian noble women in an elaborate wedding ceremony (conducted in Persian fashion too), which lasted for five days. The symbolism as far as a fusion of the races is concerned is obvious, but again too much has been made of this marriage: it is important to note that no Persian men were given honours at Alexander's court or in his military and administrative machinery. Moreover, no Macedonian or Greek women were brought out from the mainland to marry Persian noble men, which we would expect as part of a fusion 'policy'. A closer explanation to the truth is probably that Alexander could not afford these noble women to marry their own races and thus provide the potential for revolt, something mixed marriages with his own court might offset. That the marriages were forced onto his men is proved by the fact that all apart from Seleucus seem to have divorced their wives upon the king's death. Once again, however, Alexander seems to have ignored the displeasure of his men, ultimately at great cost to himself and his empire.

Finally, the great reconciliation banquet at Opis in 324 (after the second mutiny), in which Macedonian, Greek, Persian and Iranian sipped from the same cup, and Alexander significantly 'prayed for various blessings and especially that the Macedonians and Persians should enjoy harmony as partners in the government'. Yet, *inter alia* it is important to remember that Alexander had played on the hatred between the Macedonians and the Persians in ending the mutiny, and that the Macedonians were seated closest to him at the banquet, thereby emphasising their racial superiority and power. Moreover, we would expect a prayer to future concord after such a reconciliation since dissension in the ranks was the last thing Alexander needed given his plans for future conquest, which involved the invasion of Arabia in the near future! Thus, we may reject the notion of a 'brotherhood of mankind', and divorce it from any objective evaluation of Alexander.

In conclusion, the 'greatness' of Alexander III must be questioned, and the historical Alexander divorced from the mythical, despite the cost to the legend. There is no question that Alexander was the most powerful individual of his time, and we must recognise that. For sheer distance covered, places subdued, battle strategy, and breadth of vision he deserves praise. In just a decade he conquered the vast Persian empire that had been around for two centuries, and he amassed a fortune so vast that it is virtually impossible to comprehend. Alexander also improved the economy of his state (to an extent) and encouraged trade and commerce, especially by breaking down previously existing frontiers (of major importance in the hellenistic period), and an offshoot of his conquests was the gathering of information on the topography and geography of the regions to which he went, as well as new and exotic flora and fauna. However, at what cost? Was the wastage in human lives, the incalculable damage to foreign peoples, institutions, livelihoods, and lands, not to mention the continuation of the dynasty at home, the security of Macedon, the future of the empire, and the loyalty of the army worth it?

That Alexander did not endear himself to his own people and that they grew discontented with him, has significant implications for his ultimate objectives and how he saw himself. The move to establish a kingdom of Asia with a capital probably at Babylon is significant. Given his disregard of the feelings of his own people (as evidenced by his lack of interest in producing a legal and above-age heir to continue the dynasty and hegemonic position of Macedon), we can only surmise that his belief in his own divinity and his attempts to be recognised as a god while alive—including the attempt at *proskynesis*—are the keys to his actions and motives. As Fredricksmeyer has so persuasively argued, Alexander was out to distance himself as far as possible from the exploits and reputation of Philip II since his attitude to his father had turned from one of admiration and rivalry, from one warrior to another, to resentment. He strove to excel him at all costs and he could not handle praise of Philip. . . . Military conquest was one thing, but simple conquest was not enough: Alexander had to outdo Philip in other areas. Deification while alive was the most obvious way. Everything else became subordinated to Alexander's drive towards self-deification and then his eventual and genuine total belief in it.

Therefore, it is easy to see, on the one hand, why Alexander has been viewed as great, but also, on the other hand, why that greatness—and thus his epithet—must be questioned in the interests of historical accuracy.

Ian Worthington is professor of Greek history at the University of Missouri, Columbus. He is the author of *Alexander the Great: Man and God* (Pearson and Longman, 2003).

Paul Cartledge

NO

Alexander the Great: Hunting for a New Past?

Once upon a time, in the public square of the ancient city of Corinth, Alexander—already king of the Macedonians, but not yet 'the Great'—encountered the notoriously unconventional Diogenes the Cynic. Before he could engage the sage in any sort of philosophic dialogue, however, Diogenes curtly told him to go away, as he was blocking out the sunlight. First blood to Diogenes. Alexander, by no means unintelligent, was later questioned about the encounter, and is supposed to have responded: 'Had I not been Alexander, I should have wished to be Diogenes'.

Ben trovato, no doubt, though Alexander (356 BC to 323 BC) could of course afford to say that. He was Alexander, after all. Or rather: before all, before all else, and before all others. For Alexander personally embodied to the utmost degree the Homeric injunction 'always to be the best and excel all others' (in the words of E.V. Rieu's translation). Paradoxically, though, that is one of the very few things we can know for certain about Alexander the man (as opposed to Alexander the world conqueror). For the evidence for his personal life and inner motivation is not at all extensive or reliable. Nor are the available sources for his public career much better. Perhaps borrowing a leaf out of his tutor Aristotle's book, Alexander took unusual care to try to ensure that his deeds were reported and recorded. He also tried to make sure they were interpreted correctly among the various constituencies to which they were broadcast: Macedonians, Greeks, Persians and the countless other subjects of his vast empire. Yet no contemporary narrative account of his career exists, and what is generally reckoned to be the most persuasive of those that do survive was written by Arrian, a Greek from Asia Minor, well over four centuries after Alexander's premature death, aged thirty-two, at Babylon in 323 BC. This situation makes the search for the 'real' Alexander almost impossibly difficult.

For this reason, and because Alexander soon passed from the territory of factual history proper to the plane of myth and legend (thanks, not least, to his own self-propagandising efforts), the search for him has been likened to that for the historical Jesus. Much was written about both men, but practically nothing contemporary has survived, and very little indeed without a severely prejudiced axe to grind.

The risk, therefore, as well as the opportunity, is that we tend to create the Alexander of our dreams—or nightmares. There have been as many Alexanders as there have been students of Alexander.

My own version of him seeks to do some sort of justice to the many facets of this multi-talented individual. In my search for what made him 'tick', I draw, both literally and metaphorically, on the semantic field of the chase. Hunting wild game was not just an optional pastime in ancient Macedonia. It was integrated organically into the education and elevation of the aristocratic elite. It was therefore a relatively short step, I argue, for Alexander to go from hunting lot game to hunting for undying glory, and to aim to achieve that goal by trekking to the very ends of the earth and hunting down many thousands of human beings and wild animals en route.

Alexander's mother Olympias (after whom a reconstructed trireme commissioned in 1987 into the Hellenic navy is named) was a Greek princess from Epirus, in the northwest of the Greek peninsula. Her marriage to the far-from-monogamous Philip of Macedon was reportedly a love-match, although in this marriage as in his other six Philip was no doubt fighting his wars by matrimony, as an ancient biographer put it: using marriage alliance as a diplomatic tool. Not the least of his wars, though, was fought within the tempestuous marriage to Olympias. In one of the more remarkable moves of their incessant marital combat, the hyper-religiose Olympias ventured to claim that Alexander had been fathered by a snake—not a reference to her human husband, but to the Egyptian god Ammon (Amun) in disguise. Whatever his true paternity, Alexander was born in 356 BC at the Macedonian capital, Pella, about the time of the Olympic Games at which one of his father's racehorses carried off an olive crown.

Philip was not alone in finding the fiery Olympias difficult. Alexander once allegedly remarked that through her antics she made him pay a high rent for the nine months she had housed him in her womb. Indeed, he tried to distance himself so far from his natural mother that he had himself adopted symbolically by Queen Ada, the non-Greek ruler of Carla, the area around Halicarnassus (modern Bodrum in Turkey), and later formed a close, possibly even intimate, relationship with the mother of his defeated enemy, Great King Darius III of Persia. Yet it can be argued that, but for Olympias, Alexander would not have become king when he did: in 336 BC at the relatively early age of twenty, following Philip's assassination during the wedding celebrations for his and Olympias' other child, Cleopatra. And to Olympias, probably, is to be traced the streak of passionate mysticism that led Alexander to claim to be more than merely mortal, thanks to his supernatural birth as well as his superhuman achievements.

At a young age (perhaps even before his teens) Alexander is said to have singlehandedly tamed an unusually fiery and exorbitantly expensive Thessalian stallion called Bucephalas ('Ox-Head'—probably named for the shape of the white blaze on his muzzle). He rode Bucephalas both in war (for example, at the battle of Issus, 333 BC) and when indulging his insatiable passion for hunting wild animals in the rare intervals of rest between campaigning and marching.

Alexander was indeed almost inseparable from Bucephalas until the steed's death in Pakistan at the ripe age of around thirty. The Roman emperor Caligula later made one of his horses a consul of Rome; Shakespeare's Richard III would have given his kingdom for a horse; and Lt Col Rodolph de Salis of the Balaklava Light Brigade awarded a campaign medal to his charger Drummer Boy; but only Alexander founded a city in honour of his favourite mount and named it after him as a public memorial. The site of Bucephala has not, however, been identified.

Alexander was appointed regent of Macedon at the age of just sixteen, when father Philip was abroad on one of his many campaigns. The precocious Alexander seized—or created—the opportunity to wage war on a local non-Greek Thracian people and to establish a new city on the site of their former capital. That was not all. Philip had already founded two cities and named them after himself: Philippi (later celebrated for the Pauline epistle) and Philippopolis (modern Plovdiv in Bulgaria). Not to be outdone, Alexander named his new Thracian city after himself, Alexandroupolis—as it is still called. What the masterful Philip thought of his son's teenage presumption is not recorded.

In his formative years Alexander triumphantly passed two of the crucial tests of Macedonian manhood—hunting and killing a wild boar and a human enemy; 'being a man', in ancient Macedonia, had a more savage ring to it than the modern usage of the phrase might suggest. These feats of hunting prowess entitled Alexander to wear a distinctive kind of belt and to recline rather than sit during the symposia (drinking parties) that were a prominent feature of Macedonian court life. In most of Greece the consumption of alcohol at symposia was normally quite carefully regulated. But Macedonians—at least so it seemed to Greeks—drank to get drunk. One recent historian (J. Maxwell O'Brien) has followed the lead of Alexander's Greek critics and given this a modern 'scientific' spin, claiming that Alexander became a clinical alcoholic. This claim cannot be proven today, but there undoubtedly were episodes in which Alexander acted unfortunately when under the influence of alcohol—most disastrously in 328 BC, at Samarkand in central Asia, when in a drunken fit he killed 'Black' Cleitus, a senior cavalry commander who had been a personal companion since boyhood. His own early death, too, may well have been precipitated by unwisely immoderate consumption of alcohol.

From the age of thirteen to about sixteen Alexander was tutored at Mieza, away from the royal court, by Aristotle, the greatest intellectual of his day. But who influenced whom most, it would be hard to decide. Perhaps it was something of a dialogue of the deaf. Aristotle wrote at length about kingship in his treatise entitled *Politics*, and had some interesting things to say about a figure whom he called 'All-King', so wise and beneficent that his commands should unquestioningly be obeyed to the letter. But that figure, clearly, was a theoretical construct rather than an allusion to the living and breathing Alexander. On the other hand, Alexander shared his teacher's passion for Homer, treasuring a copy of the *Iliad* that Aristotle had personally annotated, and sending back botanical and other specimens from Asia to Aristotle's Lyceum institute for advanced study in Athens.

Aristotle is also said to have advised Alexander to treat all nonGreeks as slavish 'barbarians', advice which Alexander—to his credit—conspicuously did not follow. Indeed, he married, polygamously, three 'barbarians'—the daughter of a Sogdian warlord and two Persian royal women—and encouraged his closest companions to take foreign wives too. No doubt, as with Philip's marriages, these were predominantly motivated by realpolitik. It is notable that, unlike his father, Alexander married no Macedonian nor Greek woman. Moreover his marriages were designed to further a policy of orientalisation, the playing down of an exclusive Hellenism and the promotion of Graeco-oriental political and cultural mix.

The question of Alexander's sexuality—his predominant sexual orientation—has enlivened, or bedevilled, much Alexander scholarship. That he loved at least two men there can be little doubt. The first was the Macedonian noble Hephaestion, another friend from boyhood, whom he looked on—and may actually have referred to—as his alter ego. The Persian queen mother, it was said, once mistook the taller Hephaestion for Alexander, who graciously excused her blushes by murmuring that 'he too is Alexander'. Whether Alexander's relationship with the slightly older Hephaestion was ever of the sort that once dared not speak its name is not certain, but it is likely enough that it was. At any rate, Macedonian and Greek mores would have favoured an actively sexual component rather than inhibiting or censoring it. Like hunting, pederasty was thought to foster masculine, especially martial, bravery.

The other non-female beloved of Alexander's was named Bagoas. He was not just a 'barbarian' (Persian) but also a eunuch. There was a long Middle Eastern tradition of employing eunuchs as court officials, especially where a harem system was in place, as at the Achaemenid royal court (witness the Biblical book of Esther). Bagoas was not the first Persian court eunuch, either, to act as a power-broker between rival individuals and factions. A homonymous predecessor had done his murderous worst through the arts of poison, paving the way for Darius III's immediate predecessor to assume the Persian throne. The methods of Alexander's Bagoas were no less effective, if less violent, and Alexander's personal commitment to him seems to have attained levels of sexual intimacy that his Greek and Macedonian courtiers found embarrassing.

Yet in terms of his known activity, as opposed to his possible preferred orientation, Alexander was undoubtedly bisexual. He fathered at least one child, with his Sogdian wife Roxane. But perhaps sex as such did not hold as much attraction for him as other passions did (the Greek word eros could cover other strong desires too). Arrian, at least, thought that fighting and conquering gave him the same sort of thrills and satisfactions as sex did other men. By the age of twenty-six (in 330 BC) Alexander had conquered most of the known ancient world—that is, east of the Adriatic and as far east as modern Pakistan.

As a conqueror, Alexander is in a stratospheric league with Napoleon, Genghis Khan and few others. A combination of boldness of strategic invention, unshakeable personal courage, dashing leadership from the front, willingness to share the toughest rigours suffered by the ordinary soldiers, and a liberal dose of sheer good fortune ensured his stature as a great general. He was as magnificently successful in coping with the grim necessities and improvisatory diversions of sieges (as at Tyre in 332 BC) and guerrilla warfare as he was in executing theatrically staged set-piece pitched battles (the River Granicus in 334 BC, Gaugamela in 331 BC and River Hydaspes in 326 BC, as well as Issus). In terms of his prowess in military command he truly earned his title 'the Great'.

Alexander made it clear from early on that he intended to go to the outermost edge of the inhabited world, to what he conceived to be the girdling Ocean. For him, as for his latterday fictional avatar James Bond, the world was not enough. But in 326 BC his mainly Macedonian troops, on reaching the river Hyphasis (modern Beas in Pakistan), declared 'Not a step more!', and in 324 BC at Opis (near modern Baghdad) they again rejected his plans for permanent conquest, first of the Arabs and then, perhaps, the Carthaginians, and then . . . who knows? Those two mutinies prompted the adage that the only defeats Alexander suffered were at the hands of his own men, most of whom were most of the time fanatically loyal.

This is not to say that Alexander did not experience opposition to his person, his status or his inferred programmes and plans. On the contrary, his career as king opened in a flurry of accusation and counter-accusation (whole books have been written to exonerate him from the charge of patricideregicide). And it continued as it had begun, punctuated at regular intervals by plots, real or alleged, followed by exemplary treason trials and executions, or even straightforward assassinations of perceived rivals and enemies. His drunken manslaughter of 'Black' Cleitus was occasioned by taunts of tyrannical rule and excessive orientalism. The judicial murder of the cavalry commander Philotas and the consequent assassination of the latter's father Parmenion (Alexander's—and Philip's—premier general) were due more to concern for his personal authority and standing than to the need to extirpate genuine treachery. The execution of his official historian, the Callisthenes (a younger relative of Aristotle), followed a highly controversial attempt by Alexander to have himself kowtowed to in public in the Persian manner, to which Callisthenes had led the—all-too—successful Greek and Macedonian court opposition.

Not the least of the many extraordinary facts about Alexander is that both in his lifetime and after his death he was worshipped as a god, by Greeks and Macedonians as well as, for example, Egyptians (to whom he was Pharaoh). The episode that led to Callisthenes' death in 327 BC was connected to this fact. Greeks and Macedonians believed that formal obeisance should be paid only to gods. So the refusal of his Greek and Macedonian courtiers to pay it to Alexander implied that they, at any rate, did not believe he genuinely was a living god, at least not in the same sense as Zeus or Dionysus were. Alexander, regardless, did nothing to discourage the view that he really was divine. His claim to divine birth, not merely divine descent, was part of a total self-promotional package, which included the striking of silver medallions in India depicting him with the attributes of Zeus. Through sheer force of personality and magnitude of achievement he won over large numbers of ordinary Greeks and Macedonians to share this view of himself, and to act on it by devoting shrines to his cult.

The divine worship of a living ruler was one of his few unambiguous legacies. Another is his fame. That his legend has spread so far and so wide—from Iceland to China—since his death in 323 BC is due very largely to the Alexander Romance. This fabulous fiction took shape in Egypt, mostly some three or more centuries after Alexander's death. The text, originally in Greek, was disseminated in several languages, both Indo-European and Semitic, throughout the old Greco-Roman world and the newer Muslim-Arabic Middle East. Partly thanks to this work, Alexander became in various countries and times a hero, a quasi-holy man, a Christian saint, a new Achilles, a philosopher, a scientist, a prophet and a visionary. He has featured prominently in both the secular and the sacred visual art of numerous cultures.

Through his conquests Alexander ended the Achaemenid Persian empire that had been founded by Cyrus the Great more than two hundred years previously, in the mid-sixth century. He created the conditions for the development of new Graeco-Macedonian territorial kingdoms based on Macedonia, Syria and, most famously, Egypt—the Pharaoh Cleopatra, who committed suicide in 30 BC, was the last ruler of the Egyptian dynasty established by Alexander's boyhood companion and posthumous historian, Ptolemy son of Lagos (the Greek for 'hare'). Alexander is thus one of the few individuals in history who literally changed the world and was epoch-making.

But his achievement was also inchoate. Part of Alexander's enduring fascination, indeed, is that he died at the age of just thirty-two, at the height of his power and glory, with the world at his feet, full of plans, alleged or genuine. The new empire he had created was unlikely to have proved very lasting in any event. But it crumbled all the sooner once his centripetal force was removed. Perhaps the brute imperialism that was involved in its creation is not something to be mourned, but Alexander's apparently sincere notion of ethnic fusion, or at least co-operation, at the top of the administrative pyramid across cultural and political divides, is one surely to be welcomed—and maybe even imitated.

Alexander the Great remains, for many, an iconic figure in everyday life, prayed to by Greek fishermen, hymned by Turkish storytellers, and anathematised by Zoroastrian followers. If the modern secular equivalent of ancient divinity is to be featured as a brilliantly glowing star of the silver screen, it is apt that at least one more Alexander movie is in active production as I write. And this is to say nothing of the number of books about him, including novels and how-to business primers as well as ideally more reliable histories . . . The Alexander legend lives on. The hunt for a new Alexander is a vital part of living history today.

Paul Cartledge is a professor of Greek history at Cambridge University and a fellow of Clare College. He is a world expert on Athens and Sparta in the Classical Age. He was chief historical consultant for the BBC TV series *The Greeks* and the series *The Spartans* presented by Bettany Hughes.

EXPLORING THE ISSUE

Should We Deny Alexander III His Title, "The Great"?

Critical Thinking and Reflection

1. Examine Historian Ian Worthington's Statement: ". . . the greatness of Alexander must be questioned and the historical Alexander divorced from the mythical. . . ." What essential insight about historical figures is Worthington noting? Critically analyze and discuss.
2. Alexander's father, Phillip of Macedon, hired Aristotle to tutor his son. Aristotle had studied with Plato and Plato had studied with Socrates. So, King Phillip was consciously placing his son in an intellectual lineage that was illustrious. What evidence do we have that Alexander benefitted intellectually from this education? Critically discuss.
3. Examine Professor Paul Cartledge's statement that "In terms of his prowess in military command, he truly earned his title 'the Great'." Should extraordinary success in one arena be considered sufficient for deserving a reputation of "greatness?"
4. Philosopher King is Plato's term in the *Republic* for the benevolent dictator who would wisely rule his utopia. Research the meaning of this concept and critically apply it to an analysis of Alexander's kingship.
5. How would you go about separating what may, indeed, have been lofty ideals from their often-bloody and sometimes thoughtless implementation? Critically analyze and discuss this historian's dilemma.
6. Spend some time considering the evidence provided by each author. Then, conduct a debate: Should Alexander III be denied the title "the Great?"
7. What might be the evaluation written about Alexander by a soldier in one of his armies? After some research, undertake this evaluation, in the spirit of "History from the bottom up" (see Introduction).
8. What group of people in any society is in the best position to confer a term such as "the Great" on a leader. Critically analyze and discuss.

Is There Common Ground?

Summarize the points on which you believe the two writers would agree that contribute to Alexander III's being called "the Great." Then, summarize the points on which both writers are critical of Alexander. In the case of Alexander III, a significant challenge is separating myth from history. Alexander was certainly mythologized after his premature death. However, even during his lifetime, Alexander consciously set about constructing a heroic image for himself. Can a person be "great" as a military commander even if his campaigns cause a lot of death and destruction? Are those who praise Alexander legitimately able to ignore the dark side of his life and work because they see it as outweighed by his grand ideals and personal qualities? Every human being is a mixture of lofty and base qualities. How far should we go in minimizing the negatives in the lives of historical figures? Have a class discussion about the common ground you find in these two selections. Then, debate the issue Question. Much depends on whose point of view we take.

Question: An interesting exercise would be to write about Alexander III as his tutor, Aristotle; as King Darius III of Persia; as his mother, Olympias; as his horse, Bucephalas. Would any of these "voices" describe Alexander as "the Great"?

Additional Resources

As one can imagine, books about Alexander the Great are numerous. The late Ulrich Wilcken's classic biography, *Alexander the Great*, first published in 1931, has been reissued in 1997 (W.W. Norton). It contains a useful "Introduction to Alexander Studies" by Eugene N. Borza of Pennsylvania State University. Robin M. Fox, *The Search for Alexander* (Little, Brown & Company, 1980), was written for an accompanying television series, and contains some wonderful visual images, along with a highly readable and interesting text.

Other Alexander biographies that are worth reading are A.B. Bosworth, *Conquest and Empire: The Reign of Alexander the Great* (Cambridge University Press, 1993) and Peter Green, *Alexander of Macedon: A Historical Biography* (University of California Press, 1991). Michael Wood's *In the Footsteps of Alexander the Great* (University of California Press, 1997) is a book/television series that is worth recommending. Since the book contains the program narration, rent the videos and get the visual images along with the words. Ian Worthington has made two recent contributions to Alexandrine scholarship: *Alexander the Great: A Reader* (Routledge, 2003); and, *Alexander the Great: Man and God* (Pearson Longman, 2003).

Internet References . . .

Alexander the Great

A cradle-to-grave treatment of Alexander's life and accomplishments in small segments; includes some interesting visuals.

http://1stmuse.com/frames/project.html

Selected, Edited, and with Issue Framing Material by:
Helen Buss Mitchell, *Howard Community College*
and
Joseph R. Mitchell, *Howard Community College*

ISSUE

Did Christianity Liberate Women?

YES: Karen L. King, from "Women in Ancient Christianity: The New Discoveries," *Frontline Report* (April 6, 1998)

NO: Lisa Bellan-Boyer, from "Conspicuous in Their Absence: Women in Early Christianity," *Cross Currents* (Spring 2003)

Learning Outcomes

After reading this issue you should be able to:

- Describe conditions for women in the Greco-Roman world where Christianity went from persecution to the state religion of the Roman Empire.
- List and describe the roles open to women in early Christianity.
- Understand the process by which "books" were added to and subtracted from the canon of approved Christian scriptures.
- Understand how mimetic theory—that we become what we profess to hate—applies to early Christianity.

ISSUE SUMMARY

YES: Professor of New Testament Studies and the History of Ancient Christianity Karen L. King argues that evidence from biblical and other recently discovered ancient texts illuminates women's active participation in early Christianity—as disciples, apostles, prophets, preachers, and teachers.

NO: Art historian Lisa Bellan-Boyer argues that mimetic theory explains why women's richly diverse roles were severely circumscribed in the name of unity and in order to make the new religion of Christianity acceptable in the Greco-Roman world.

Have women been excluded from leadership roles in the Christian Church from the beginning? The ordination of women as ministers and priests during the twentieth century gives the impression that new ground is being broken by women who seek to lead congregations. Some believe that these women are carrying the movement for women's liberation in civil society inappropriately into churches and defying a 2,000-year tradition that has properly excluded them. Radical, however, means "from the roots" and a return to ancient sources may link modern claims with ancient practices.

It is deeply challenging to our modern notions of progress to think that, even by present standards, women may have been more "liberated" 2,000 years ago than they are today. Our greatest challenge might come from trying to imagine how early Christian women regarded their own status in what was frequently called the Jesus Movement. Did they feel liberated from the more patriarchal world of first century Palestinian Judaism and Hellenistic paganism? And, regardless of how they felt, does our assessment of their status merit claiming that Christianity liberated them?

The Jesus Movement began in Palestine. Jesus and all his original followers—women and men—were Jewish, and they never stopped thinking of themselves as Jewish. They continued to celebrate the High Holy days in autumn and Passover in spring, to go to the Temple, hear the scriptures read, and pray. What they added were two rituals shared by all Christians today—Baptism and the sharing of a Holy Meal. Living under Roman occupation, these early followers of Jesus had to keep a low profile. They met in one another's houses and traveled on foot from city to city, spreading the "good news" brought by Jesus. Wealthy women, often widows, offered their homes as meeting places, paid for the expenses of travel, and served as prophets, preachers, and presiders over rituals. A second chapter began when missionaries took the message to the Greco-Roman world. The new Christians were Gentiles, who did not share the Jewish heritage and long faith tradition of Jesus and his early followers. Many were slaves who thrilled to the message of equality under God.

Before the Christian Church became institutionalized and before a theology was clearly defined, early converts acted out of intense personal conviction and met informally to share their faith. Most "churches" (both Palestinian and Greco-Roman) were based in people's homes and it was likely this private dimension that made women's leadership possible. Gender conventions of the time, especially in the Greco-Roman world where Christianity grew rapidly, declared the public sphere male and confined the woman's sphere of influence to the home. An outcast sect because its followers refused to worship the Emperor, Christianity remained an underground religion until the early fourth century when Constantine, the Roman Emperor, forbade government persecution and, eventually, made Christianity the state religion.

Missionaries converted many Greeks to Christianity, resulting in more Gentile or non-Jewish Christians than Jewish Christians by the third century. The Greek-speaking world, where many of the women in these selections lived, was the first to accept Christianity in large numbers. If Christian women in both Jewish and Gentile environments during the early centuries enjoyed equality with men, what happened to create the climate of misogyny or hatred of women during later centuries?

In the sixth century a Christian Church Council at Macon actually debated whether or not women had souls. The question seemed to be whether women were made in the image and likeness of God, as men were, or merely in the image and not in the likeness. Women are still barred from the Roman Catholic priesthood, primarily using a theological argument introduced by Thomas Aquinas in the thirteenth century. He stated that women are inferior to men by nature and incapable of assuming leadership positions. If only males can "image" God to their congregations, women must be barred from the priesthood.

The Bible and many other sources provide evidence of women's active roles during the early years of what would later be called Christianity. Eusebius (263–339 C.E.), a Greek Christian and intimate friend of the Roman Emperor Constantine, wrote the only surviving comprehensive account of the first 300 years of Christian Church history. Sometimes called the Christian Herodotus, he certainly earned the title Father of Ecclesiastical (church) history. A translation of his work by G.A. Williamson *The History of the Church* (Dorset Press, 1984) is easy to obtain.

During the first centuries of Christianity, different schools of what would later become theology existed side by side. One of these was Gnosticism, a mystical worldview that predominated in Greece and Rome. Remarkable for its androgynous view of God as father and mother, Gnosticism was the first heresy condemned by the Christian Church because some of its views clashed with what had become orthodoxy. Four Gnostic Gospels, part of what scholars call the Nag Hammadi library, found in Egypt in the 1940s, are available in Marvin W. Meyer's translation in *The Secret Teachings of Jesus* (Vintage Books, 1986). Elaine Pagels, an authority in this field, has written a useful guide to Gnosticism in *The Gnostic Gospels* (Vintage Books, 1989). See also the PBS/Frontline website recommended for this issue.

A documentary sampling of writings about women, from ancient Greeks to modern Victorians, may be found in *Not in God's Image*, edited by Julia O'Faolain and Lauro Martines (Harper & Row, 1973). Including both religious and nonreligious writings, this book places Western attitudes toward women in a broader context. Karen Jo Torjesen's *When Women Were Priests* (Harper-San Francisco, 1995) highlights women as deacons, priests, prophets, and bishops and documents their later exclusion from many of these roles as the Christian Church joined the establishment and worship moved from private to public space.

Karen L. King, who teaches in the Divinity School at Harvard University, is widely regarded as a leading authority on women in ancient Christianity. Using both the scrolls included in the Bible and newly discovered texts from the same period, she reconstructs the enthusiastic and welcome participation of women in every aspect of the early Christian Church. Once Christianity moved from house churches to public meeting places and became the state religion of the Roman Empire, however, women's roles were restricted in a bid for legitimacy and in conformity with prevailing gender conventions.

Art historian Lisa Bellan-Boyer describes how the full and equal participation of early Christian women has been eclipsed by forcing them into a preexisting honor/shame system, based in Greco-Roman goddess attributes and social expectations. For example, the many Marys in the gospels were sorted into the one good Mary (the Mother of Jesus) and the one bad Mary (Mary Magdalene). The latter, a disciple, apostle, and missionary, has been merged and then identified with the repentant prostitute. According to Bellan-Boyer, we become what we profess to hate; and Christianity abandoned its radical beginnings in order to fit into an existing set of gender conventions. Women, Bellan-Boyer claims, were the sacrifice that got the early church to a state the victorious called "unity."

YES

Karen L. King

Women in Ancient Christianity: The New Discoveries

In the last twenty years, the history of women in ancient Christianity has been almost completely revised. As women historians entered the field in record numbers, they brought with them new questions, developed new methods, and sought for evidence of women's presence in neglected texts and exciting new findings. For example, only a few names of women were widely known: Mary, the mother of Jesus; Mary Magdalene, his disciple and the first witness to the resurrection; Mary and Martha, the sisters who offered him hospitality in Bethany. Now we are learning more of the many women who contributed to the formation of Christianity in its earliest years.

Perhaps most surprising, however, is that the stories of women we thought we knew well are changing in dramatic ways. Chief among these is Mary Magdalene, a woman infamous in Western Christianity as an adulteress and repentant whore. Discoveries of new texts from the dry sands of Egypt, along with sharpened critical insight, have now proven that this portrait of Mary is entirely inaccurate. She was indeed an influential figure, but as a prominent disciple and leader of one wing of the early Christian movement that promoted women's leadership.

Certainly, the New Testament Gospels, written toward the last quarter of the first century CE [Christian Era], acknowledge that women were among Jesus' earliest followers. From the beginning, Jewish women disciples, including Mary Magdalene, Joanna, and Susanna, had accompanied Jesus during his ministry and supported him out of their private means (Luke 8:1–3). He spoke to women both in public and private, and indeed he learned from them. According to one story, an unnamed Gentile woman taught Jesus that the ministry of God is not limited to particular groups and persons, but belongs to all who have faith (Mark 7:24–30; Matthew 15:21–28). A Jewish woman honored him with the extraordinary hospitality of washing his feet with perfume. Jesus was a frequent visitor at the home of Mary and Martha, and was in the habit of teaching and eating meals with women as well as men. When Jesus was arrested, women remained firm, even when his male disciples are said to have fled, and they accompanied him to the foot of the cross. It was women who were reported as the first witnesses to the resurrection, chief among them again Mary Magdalene. Although the details of these gospel stories may be questioned, in general they reflect the prominent historical roles women played in Jesus' ministry as disciples.

Women in the First Century of Christianity

After the death of Jesus, women continued to play prominent roles in the early movement. Some scholars have even suggested that the majority of Christians in the first century may have been women.

The letters of Paul—dated to the middle of the first century CE—and his casual greetings to acquaintances offer fascinating and solid information about many Jewish and Gentile women who were prominent in the movement. His letters provide vivid clues about the kind of activities in which women engaged more generally. He greets Prisca, Junia, Julia, and Nereus' sister, who worked and traveled as missionaries in pairs with their husbands or brothers (Romans 16:3, 7, 15). He tells us that Prisca and her husband risked their lives to save his. He praises Junia as a prominent apostle, who had been imprisoned for her labor. Mary and Persis are commended for their hard work (Romans 16:6, 12). Euodia and Syntyche are called his fellow-workers in the gospel (Philippians 4:2–3). Here is clear evidence of women apostles active in the earliest work of spreading the Christian message.

Paul's letters also offer some important glimpses into the inner workings of ancient Christian churches. These groups did not own church buildings but met in homes, no doubt due in part to the fact that Christianity was not legal in the Roman world of its day and in part because of the enormous expense to such fledgling societies. Such homes were a domain in which women played key roles. It is not surprising then to see women taking leadership roles in house churches. Paul tells of women who were the leaders of such house churches (Apphia in Philemon 2; Prisca in I Corinthians 16:19). This practice is confirmed by other texts that also mention women who headed churches in their homes, such as Lydia of Thyatira (Acts 16:15) and Nympha of Laodicea (Colossians 4:15). Women held offices and played significant roles in group worship. Paul, for example, greets a deacon named Phoebe (Romans 16:1) and assumes that women are praying and prophesying during worship (I Corinthians 11). As prophets, women's roles would have included not only ecstatic public speech, but preaching, teaching, leading prayer, and perhaps even performing the eucharist meal. (A later first century work, called the Didache, assumes that this duty fell regularly to Christian prophets.)

Mary Magdalene: A Truer Portrait

Later texts support these early portraits of women, both in exemplifying their prominence and confirming their leadership roles (Acts 17:4, 12). Certainly the most prominent among these in the ancient church was Mary Magdalene. A series of spectacular 19th and 20th century discoveries of Christian texts in Egypt dating to the second and third century have yielded a treasury of new information. It was already known from the New Testament gospels that Mary was a Jewish woman who followed Jesus of Nazareth. Apparently of independent means, she accompanied Jesus during his ministry and supported him out of her own resources (Mark 15:40–41; Matthew 27:55–56; Luke 8:1–3; John 19:25).

Although other information about her is more fantastic, she is repeatedly portrayed as a visionary and leader of the early movement.(Mark 16:1–9; Matthew 28:1–10; Luke 24:1–10; John 20:1, 11–18; Gospel of Peter). In the Gospel of John, the risen Jesus gives her special teaching and commissions her as an apostle to the apostles to bring them the good news. She obeys and is thus the first to announce the resurrection and to play the role of an apostle, although the term is not specifically used of her. Later tradition, however, will herald her as "the apostle to the apostles." The strength of this literary tradition makes it possible to suggest that historically Mary was a prophetic visionary and leader within one sector of the early Christian movement after the death of Jesus.

The newly discovered Egyptian writings elaborate this portrait of Mary as a favored disciple. Her role as "apostle to the apostles" is frequently explored, especially in considering her faith in contrast to that of the male disciples who refuse to believe her testimony. She is most often portrayed in texts that claim to record dialogues of Jesus with his disciples, both before and after the resurrection. In the Dialogue of the Savior, for example, Mary is named along with Judas (Thomas) and Matthew in the course of an extended dialogue with Jesus. During the discussion, Mary addresses several questions to the Savior as a representative of the disciples as a group. She thus appears as a prominent member of the disciple group and is the only woman named. Moreover, in response to a particularly insightful question, the Lord says of her, "You make clear the abundance of the revealer!" (140.17–19). At another point, after Mary has spoken, the narrator states, "She uttered this as a woman who had understood completely"(139.11–13). These affirmations make it clear that Mary is to be counted among the disciples who fully comprehended the Lord's teaching (142.11–13).

In another text, the Sophia of Jesus Christ, Mary also plays a clear role among those whom Jesus teaches. She is one of the seven women and twelve men gathered to hear the Savior after the resurrection, but before his ascension. Of these only five are named and speak, including Mary. At the end of his discourse, he tells them, "I have given you authority over all things as children of light," and they go forth in joy to preach the gospel. Here again Mary is included among those special disciples to whom Jesus entrusted his most elevated teaching, and she takes a role in the preaching of the gospel.

In the Gospel of Philip, Mary Magdalene is mentioned as one of three Marys "who always walked with the Lord" and as his companion (59.6–11). The work also says that Lord loved her more than all the disciples, and used to kiss her often (63.34–36). The importance of this portrayal is that yet again the work affirms the special relationship of Mary Magdalene to Jesus based on her spiritual perfection.

In the Pistis Sophia, Mary again is preeminent among the disciples, especially in the first three of the four books. She asks more questions than all the rest of the disciples together, and the Savior acknowledges that: "Your heart is directed to the Kingdom of Heaven more than all your brothers" (26:17–20). Indeed, Mary steps in when the other disciples are despairing in order to intercede for them to the Savior (218:10–219:2). Her complete spiritual comprehension is repeatedly stressed.

She is, however, most prominent in the early second century Gospel of Mary, which is ascribed pseudonymously to her. More than any other early Christian text, the Gospel of Mary presents an unflinchingly favorable portrait of Mary Magdalene as a woman leader among the disciples. The Lord himself says she is blessed for not wavering when he appears to her in a vision. When all the other disciples are weeping and frightened, she alone remains steadfast in her faith because she has grasped and appropriated the salvation offered in Jesus' teachings. Mary models the ideal disciple: she steps into the role of the Savior at his departure, comforts, and instructs the other disciples. Peter asks her to tell any words of the Savior which she might know but that the other disciples have not heard. His request acknowledges that Mary was preeminent among women in Jesus' esteem, and the question itself suggests that Jesus gave her private instruction. Mary agrees and gives an account of "secret" teaching she received from the Lord in a vision. The vision is given in the form of a dialogue between the Lord and Mary; it is an extensive account that takes up seven out of the eighteen pages of the work. At the conclusion of the work, Levi confirms that indeed the Saviour loved her more than the rest of the disciples (18.14–15). While her teachings do not go unchallenged, in the end the Gospel of Mary affirms both the truth of her teachings and her authority to teach the male disciples. She is portrayed as a prophetic visionary and as a leader among the disciples.

Other Christian Women

Other women appear in later literature as well. One of the most famous woman apostles was Thecla, a virgin-martyr converted by Paul. She cut her hair, donned men's clothing, and took up the duties of a missionary apostle. Threatened with rape, prostitution, and twice put in the ring as a martyr, she persevered in her faith and her chastity. Her lively and somewhat fabulous story is recorded in the second century Acts of Thecla. From very early, an order of women who were widows served formal roles of ministry in some churches (I Timothy 5:9–10). The most numerous clear cases of women's leadership, however, are offered by prophets: Mary Magdalene, the Corinthian women, Philip's daughters, Ammia of Philadelphia, Philumene, the visionary martyr Perpetua, Maximilla, Priscilla (Prisca), and Quintilla. There were many others whose names are lost to us. The African church father Tertullian, for example, describes an unnamed woman prophet in his congregation who not only had ecstatic visions during church services, but who also served as a counselor and healer (On the Soul 9.4). A remarkable collection of oracles from another unnamed woman prophet was discovered in Egypt in 1945. She speaks in the first person as the feminine voice of God: Thunder, Perfect Mind. The prophets Prisca and Quintilla inspired a Christian movement in second century Asia Minor (called the New Prophecy or Montanism) that spread around the Mediterranean and lasted for at least four centuries. Their oracles were collected and published, including the account of a vision in which Christ appeared to the prophet in the form of a woman and "put wisdom" in her (Epiphanius, Panarion 49.1). Montanist Christians ordained women as presbyters and bishops, and women held the title of prophet. The third century African bishop Cyprian also tells of an ecstatic woman prophet from Asia Minor who celebrated the eucharist and performed baptisms (Epistle 74.10). In the early second century, the Roman governor Pliny tells of two slave women he tortured who were deacons (Letter to Trajan 10.96). Other women were ordained as priests in fifth century Italy and Sicily (Gelasius, Epistle 14.26).

Women were also prominent as martyrs and suffered violently from torture and painful execution by wild animals and paid gladiators. In fact, the earliest writing definitely by a woman is the prison diary of Perpetua, a relatively wealthy matron and nursing mother who was put to death in Carthage at the beginning of the third century on the charge of being a Christian. In it, she records her testimony before the local Roman ruler and her defiance of her father's pleas that she recant. She tells of the support and fellowship among the confessors in prison, including other women. But above all, she records her prophetic visions. Through them, she was not merely reconciled passively to her fate, but claimed the power to define the meaning of her own death. In a situation where Romans sought to use their violence against her body as a witness to their power and justice, and where the Christian editor of her story sought to turn her death into a witness to the truth of Christianity, her own writing lets us see the human being caught up in these political struggles. She actively relinquishes her female roles as mother, daughter, and sister in favor of defining her identity solely in spiritual terms. However horrifying or heroic her behavior may seem, her brief diary offers an intimate look at one early Christian woman's spiritual journey.

Early Christian Women's Theology

Study of works by and about women is making it possible to begin to reconstruct some of the theological views of early Christian women. Although they are a diverse group, certain reoccurring elements appear to be common to women's theology-making. By placing the teaching of the Gospel of Mary side-by-side with the theology of the Corinthian women prophets, the Montanist women's oracles, Thunder Perfect Mind, and Perpetua's prison diary, it is possible to discern shared views about teaching and practice that may exemplify some of the contents of women's theology:

- Jesus was understood primarily as a teacher and mediator of wisdom rather than as ruler and judge.
- Theological reflection centered on the experience of the person of the risen Christ more than the crucified savior. Interestingly enough, this is true even in the case of the martyr Perpetua. One might expect her to identify with the suffering Christ, but it is the risen Christ she encounters in her vision.
- Direct access to God is possible for all through receiving the Spirit.
- In Christian community, the unity, power, and perfection of the Spirit are present now, not just in some future time.
- Those who are more spiritually advanced give what they have freely to all without claim to a fixed, hierarchical ordering of power.
- An ethics of freedom and spiritual development is emphasized over an ethics of order and control.
- A woman's identity and spirituality could be developed apart from her roles as wife and mother (or slave), whether she actually withdrew from those roles or not. Gender is itself contested as a "natural" category in the face of the power of God's Spirit at work in the community and the world. This meant that potentially women (and men) could exercise leadership on the basis of spiritual achievement apart from gender status and without conformity to established social gender roles.
- Overcoming social injustice and human suffering are seen to be integral to spiritual life.

Women were also actively engaged in reinterpreting the texts of their tradition. For example, another new text, the Hypostasis of the Archons, contains a retelling of the Genesis story ascribed to Eve's daughter Norea, in which her mother Eve appears as the instructor of Adam and his healer.

The new texts also contain an unexpected wealth of Christian imagination of the divine as feminine. The long version of the Apocryphon of John, for example, concludes with a hymn about the descent of divine Wisdom, a feminine figure here called the Pronoia of God. She enters into the lower world and the body in order to awaken the innermost spiritual being of the soul to the truth of its power and freedom, to awaken the spiritual power it needs to escape the counterfeit powers that enslave the soul in ignorance, poverty, and the drunken sleep of spiritual deadness, and to overcome illegitimate political and sexual domination. The oracle collection Thunder Perfect Mind also adds crucial evidence to women's prophetic theology-making. This prophet speaks powerfully to women, emphasizing the presence of women in her audience and insisting upon their identity with the feminine voice of the Divine. Her speech lets the hearers transverse the distance between political exploitation and empowerment, between the experience of degradation and the knowledge of infinite self-worth, between despair and peace. It overcomes the fragmentation of the self by naming it, cherishing it, insisting upon the multiplicity of self-hood and experience.

These elements may not be unique to women's religious thought or always result in women's leadership, but as a constellation they point toward one type of theologizing that was meaningful to some early Christian women, that had a place for women's legitimate exercise of leadership, and to whose construction women contributed. If we look to these elements, we are able to discern important contributions of women to early Christian theology and praxis. These elements also provide an important location for discussing some aspects of early Christian women's spiritual lives: their exercise of leadership, their ideals, their attraction to Christianity, and what gave meaning to their self-identity as Christians.

Undermining Women's Prominence

Women's prominence did not, however, go unchallenged. Every variety of ancient Christianity that advocated the legitimacy of women's leadership was eventually declared heretical, and evidence of women's early leadership roles was erased or suppressed.

This erasure has taken many forms. Collections of prophetic oracles were destroyed. Texts were changed. For example, at least one woman's place in history was obscured by turning her into a man! In Romans 16:7, the apostle Paul sends greetings to a woman named Junia. He says of her and her male partner Andronicus that they are "my kin and my fellow prisoners, prominent among the apostles and they were in Christ before me." Concluding that women could not be apostles, textual editors and translators transformed Junia into Junias, a man.

Or women's stories could be rewritten and alternative traditions could be invented. In the case of Mary Magdalene, starting in the fourth century, Christian theologians in the Latin West associated Mary Magdalene with the unnamed sinner who anointed Jesus' feet in Luke 7:36–50. The confusion began by conflating the account in John 12:1–8, in which Mary (of Bethany) anoints Jesus, with the anointing by the unnamed woman sinner in the accounts of Luke. Once this initial, erroneous identification was secured, Mary Magdalene could be associated with every unnamed sinful woman in the gospels, including the adulteress in John 8:1–11 and the Syro-phoenician woman with her five and more "husbands" in John 4:7–30. Mary the apostle, prophet, and teacher had become Mary the repentant whore. This fiction was invented at least in part to undermine her influence and with it the appeal to her apostolic authority to support women in roles of leadership.

Until recently the texts that survived have shown only the side that won. The new texts are therefore crucial in constructing a fuller and more accurate portrait. The Gospel of Mary, for example, argued that leadership should be based on spiritual maturity, regardless of whether one is male or female. This Gospel lets us hear an alternative voice to the one dominant in canonized works like I Timothy, which tried to silence women and insist that their salvation lies in bearing children. We can now hear the other side of the controversy over women's leadership and see what arguments were given in favor of it.

It needs to be emphasized that the formal elimination of women from official roles of institutional leadership did not eliminate women's actual presence and importance to the Christian tradition, although it certainly seriously damaged their capacity to contribute fully. What is remarkable is how much evidence has survived systematic attempts to erase women from history, and with them the warrants and models for women's leadership. The evidence presented here is but the tip of an iceberg.

Karen L. King is professor of New Testament Studies at the Harvard Divinity School. She is the editor of *Images of the Feminine in Gnosticism* (Trinity Press, 2000) and *Women and Goddess Traditions in Antiquity and Today* (Fortress Press, 1997).

Lisa Bellan-Boyer

Conspicuous in Their Absence: Women in Early Christianity

In recent decades, a great deal of work has been done to reconstruct our understanding of the ancient world and the early church, particularly in regard to the women who participated in early Christian communities. Enriched by interdisciplinary collaboration with cultural and social anthropologists, the findings of archeologists and the interpretations of art historians, we can visualize a fuller, more colorful picture of women's lives in the late Classical period than we have had available to us heretofore.

There was a much greater diversity of ministries available to early churchwomen than we have been led to think by the historiography of the past. It is now clear that the "open commensality" of Jesus was absolutely scandalous; the nearly infinite implications of women and men actually eating together are hard for modern people to grasp. Contemporary and interdisciplinary biblical scholarship has helped widen our knowledge of what open commensality meant in that social context. Psychology has brought some insight into the shadowy corners in the divided minds of the men of the early church, immersed in a deeply honor/shame-based culture and desiring social acceptability for the sake of church growth. Mimetic theory, as it has germinated following the work of Rene Girard, can provide some further tools to analyze and interweave the historical fragments in order to discern wider systemic patterns at work.

Other than the well-known statement of Caiaphas, in the Gospel of John's passion narrative, that "It is better for one man to die for the people than that the whole nation should perish" (John 11:50), there is no more concise formulation of the scapegoat mechanism in action than the sentence that is placed in the mouth of Simon Peter in the last part of the Gospel of Thomas: "Make Mary (Magdalene) leave us, for women are not worthy of life."

A close friend of mine, with a long record of church-based social activism, recently reminded me that: "The Orthodox are the Orthodox not because they are right, but because they won." My understanding of what Girard has brought to our ability to see into our cultural shadows makes it imperative that we look at history and myth, as written by those who won, with deep suspicion and an ever-present concern for what has been silenced and covered. This is the process of normalizing a view; relentlessly pursued by what Walter Wink calls "the domination system." I ask you to suspend what you think you may know about some cherished church traditions.

My approach uses both art history and mimetic theory, learned from the community of scholars working with tools uncovered by Rene Girard, to compose a picture of what happened during the long mystification and traditionalizing process. Art history can play an important part in helping clarify what affect the early church battles over dogma had on people and culture in the long centuries that followed. Simplistically depicted as a struggle of true-believing Orthodoxy over a bewildering assortment of heresies unhelpfully labeled "gnosticism," the history of the early church, as it is most commonly written, bears the perduring stain of mimetic rivalry.

I contend that women were the sacrifice that got the early church to a state that the victorious called "unity." This can be read in the surviving texts, both in and between the lines, and also in the visual tradition. Who is and is not present or absent in the icons, frescoes, woodcuts, and canvasses? What do these compositions say about their subjects as cultural objects? Given all the knowledge now available about the lives of women in the early church, who is conspicuous by their absence?

Contemporary scholars of the early Christian communities, such as Margaret MacDonald and Luise Schottroff, have offered practical and convincing circumstantial evidence for the robust presence and activity of women from all livelihoods and class levels in fostering the new religion. Women were often very successful as evangelists precisely because they could permeate barriers between the "inside" realm of women and the "outside" realm of men, either by the power-behind-authority of matriarchs in noble households (a la the present-day examples of Barbara and Laura Bush) or through the intermediary functions of craftswomen and tradeswomen who staffed the workshops associated with wealthy houses. Schottroff, in particular, has emphasized the stark necessity that women had to work alongside their husbands in trades and agriculture, and that there was no such thing as a stay-at-home farm wife or fish wife. Raw economics precluded such a luxury.

Women's tending of home and children was so much of an expectation that no special mention or commendation of it was thought of; and by the time of the Roman occupation of Palestine and the displacement of the peasantry off the land, the outside labor of women for supplementary income meant the difference between living or starving to death. So there were many peasant women working in the fields as hired laborers and shepherds, in workshops of all sorts, and as fisherwomen.

Women lived their lives in the tension between social standards that required women to stay indoors and hidden away as the coveted symbols of honor and shame-based cultural systems; and economic forces driving them out and into the fields and the streets of the city. Women in the Dustbowl era had to do sharecropping and migrant picking to secure their families' survival. In the Ellis Island immigration period, it was sweatshops and piece work at home in their tenement kitchen—all the while cooking meals, raising children, and caring for the sick and elderly. It was no different from the state of economic desperation so common to the majority of the women living in first- and second-century Palestine. Incorporating this understanding changes the way we exegete passages such as the Parable of the Lost Coin or the way we picture life on the shore of the Galilean Sea. This is fundamental to expanding our understanding of women in the time of Jesus.

Women could function as fluid intermediaries in part, because they "didn't count." As a consequence, they could escape notice, or "fly under the radar" in conducting house churches, catechizing converts in pagan households, seeing to the needs of prisoners, and acting as "look-outs." Margaret MacDonald's insightful mining of Greco-Roman records provides a vivid description of how valuable these ministries must have been in fostering the early church. The orders of widows provided the believing community with a safety net that was even commended by Christianity's pagan critics: well-off widows took in poor widows, who looked after orphans, thus forming viable and sustaining "family."

The patronage of wealthy widows accounts for much travel under sponsorship for both female and male evangelists, as for other types of emissaries, and it is well known that travel was extremely important in nurturing the early church. The Deacon, Phoebe, is one example of a traveling woman, and the Ethiopian eunuch traveling as the emissary of Candace are some examples from canonical texts. Mary Magdalene, the "Apostle to the Apostles" and John the Evangelist are said, in Eastern Church tradition, to have traveled together as partner-evangelists.

This may have been a model of partnership ministry that was not uncommon in the early church, and might well account for Paul's reference to "sister-wives" in First Corinthians. It would have been a very effective model in that time and place, as well as many others: the men more able, in terms of social acceptability, to speak in public places and proselytize on the streets, and the women able to go places denied to the men: in the confines of private, family space, and in the workshops and warehouses of those who supplied the material needs of large households.

Roman critics slandered early Christians by spreading rumors having to do with this cult of wicked, home-wrecking women under the spell of evil men: they will insinuate themselves inside your honorable household and subvert it, with their sexual immorality, hysteria, witchcraft, incest, and cannibalism. Later, orthodox churchmen concerned with fostering church growth and assimilation used these very same languages of contagion and scandal about fellow Christians in putting down the groups of heretics and "Gnostics" in which women played significant roles, controlling and subduing the "house churches" in the process. The perennial reappearance of these coded attributes of sin and scandal should sound a bell for those with an ear for the mimetic processes at work, as they lead up to acts of sacrificial violence.

In both the first and second centuries, the radical hospitality and table culture of the house churches, following the example of Jesus, was an invitation to scandal: Uncovered women, eating and talking with men—teaching men! They could be nothing else but prostitutes and courtesans. Celibate women—in particular—were thought of as sexual deviants and outlaws, because of their defiance of the enforced convention. They rebelled against the state, which imposed strict marriage and childbearing requirements on women, backed up by severe punishments written into the Roman law codes. The very existence of Christian women who had deliberately chosen a life of celibacy posed an embarrassment to the honor of the law-abiding, paternalistic Roman household. It is instructive to recall a twentieth-century example of similar marriage and childbearing requirements for women: Nazi Germany.

"Holy in body and spirit," they challenged the cultural structures of the honor/shame system, which MacDonald has succinctly described with the sentence: "Men defend honor, women embody shame." Sadly, it is not hard to find this system hard at work in our own historical period, fuelling millions of episodes of domestic violence, perhaps most dramatically illustrated by the prevalence of "honor killings" in the Middle East.

The Pastoral Epistles, especially 1st and 2nd Timothy and Titus, reveal the ambivalent position of celibate women in the church community. Paul and his followers endorsed celibacy, but this led to many dilemmas of practical theology: believing women married to pagan husbands, the legally mandated remarriage of young widows (under sixty), Christian women who defied their paterfamilias by refusing arranged marriages to pagans, etc. As the ideal of celibacy placed into practice began to impact public opinion about Christians, churchmen revealed what Luise Schottroff calls a "divided mind" toward women who embraced celibacy as a way to an independent, spiritually free way of life. This "divided mind" is evident in the second-century text: The Acts of Paul and Thecla, sometimes known as just The Acts of Paul. Hmm. . . .

Thecla becomes a follower of Paul after hearing him preaching outside her window, where she is transfixed by his words. Leaving family and fiance, she becomes active in a house church and lives under the protection of the wealthy widow, Tryphaena. She travels and evangelizes, eventually becoming a spiritual teacher in her own right, independent of Paul. As a result of this boldly public ministry, several attempts are made to kill her. Celibate Thecla is accused of sorcery and adultery. In an echo of Peter's denial, Paul stands weakly by as Thecla is stripped in public. Accused of being shameless, she is ritually shamed. As she is traveling with Paul in Antioch, a Syrian named Alexander sexually assaults her, but she escapes and causes him to be ridiculed. For this mortal blow to his honor, she is sent to the beasts in the arena.

Why has Thecla disappeared? Saint Thecla was removed from the Vatican's list of official Saints in the 1960s, when St. Christopher and many others were also removed. There is a continuing tradition about her in the Eastern Churches, though it is but a glimmer.

Looking at Church hagiographies about early Christian female martyrs shows that conflicted, ambivalent thinking about their sister Christians continued in the minds and hearts of the Christian men who set down their stories.

The medieval repression of the Beguines is only one later example of how this ambivalence carried on. In the hagiographies, female saints who resisted the patronal systems of Mediterranean household law by clinging to celibacy and dying as martyrs are generally depicted in the most passive, meek, and mild terms—like sacrificial lambs. Their roll call is a long one: St. Ursula and the 11,000 Virgins, St. Barbara, St. Catherine, St. Agatha, St. Lucia, et al.

Women of the early church who were known to not be purely virginal were even more problematic to the honorable status of the men in the community. Female slaves were expected to be sexually available to their owners, and former slaves came with this in their (often immediate) past. How did the church's valuation of celibacy work for them? How easy for them to declare themselves a "born-again virgin by choice" in the wording of today's faith-based sexual abstinence for teens movement? That female slaves were active participants in church communities, and even bore some leadership authority is attested to by the correspondence of Pliny the Younger to the Emperor Trajan, circa 112 C.E., in which he reports on the torture of two female slaves (ancilla) who are called deacons (ministra). Pliny states that these two deacons had been turned in by an informant. MacDonald posits the likelihood that they either annoyed the pagan patriarch of the household they belonged to and were simply dumped on Pliny, or sacrificed in order to deflect suspicion from a Christian master or mistress.

All the major objections against "Gnostic" groups mimicked pagan criticisms of early Christians, and included all the major headings from the list of archaic accusations familiar to mimetic theorists. As orthodox doctrine developed in the Byzantine era, it distinguished itself from the horde of heretics by claiming that their theology was more incarnational, thereby affirming the true humanity of Christ. While the centuries wore on, however, Greco-Roman goddess attributes and social conventions migrated onto churchwomen to reflect social systems of honor/shame, "good girl/bad girl" dualities. This was calcified into the culture of the Roman Church by Pope Gregory (for whom the chant form is named) in the sixth century, in a famous series of sermons that merely made official what had been a popular trend for some time.

This was to conflate all the women who supported and participated in the life and ministry of Jesus into as few women as possible, making the many Marys into one honorable Mary and one Mary who bore the mark of shame. Mary, the Mother of Jesus, like her son, become less and less Jewish and more and more divinized. She became increasingly separated from all other women, "blessed among women" so as to become ostracized from them, or they from her. One can never be as good as the Blessed Virgin Mary, no matter how unassailable one's bodily purity may be or how selfless a mother. You could be "as good" as Mary Magdalene, though.

Mary Magdalene's reputation as a prostitute, however undeserved, clings to her today, despite having been officially rescinded by the Vatican in 1969 and thoroughly deconstructed by New Testament scholars and historians of church art such as Jane Schaberg and Susan Haskins. The stain of a reputation is a hard thing to lose even now—clearly impossible for the women who embodied the shame and honor of their house church communities. By the Medieval period, Magdalene Houses all over Western Europe provided the public with a steady supply of designated penitents who enacted the community's shame, functioning as female versions of the Spanish colonial orders of Penitente. Interestingly, while the Beguinage where independent communities of women lived and worked were violently suppressed, the Magdalene Houses for public penitents were officially fostered and supported.[1]

The casting of Mary Magdalene as a prostitute happened concurrently with the development of the Cult of the Virgin Mary, and this is no coincidence at all. Gradually, pagan goddess attributes sorted themselves out between the "good" girl and the "bad" girl with astonishing continuity: portraits of Mary, the Mother of Jesus, were decorated with starry crowns and crescent moons, attributes of the ever-virgin Athena/Diana. Pomegranates and vineyards, attributes of Demeter and Persephone and the Syrian Mother Goddess, become associated with Mary Magdalene. Many of the clues to this syncretic divination process have their roots and ruins at Ephesus, the great temple city dedicated to the Mother Goddess centuries before the Greek conquest. A city that was, of course, a center of Paul's ministry. It is said, in the Eastern Church's tradition, to be a place where Mary, the Mother of Jesus spent time in her later years. It is also the place where Mary Magdalene is said to have been buried.

White doves were an attribute of the Syrian Mother Goddess, and of Venus to the Romans. So familiar to Christians as the symbol of the Holy Spirit: in the classical period, white doves were strongly associated with this then-ancient Temple at Ephesus. Demolished in the Byzantine era, the great columns of the Temple to the Mother

Goddess at Ephesus were transported to Constantinople by Justinian to become the great columns in the Cathedral of Hagia Sophia, or Holy Wisdom. They are still there today.

Between the time when Christianity became a state-sponsored religion and the period of the schism between the Eastern and Roman Churches, the Cult of the Virgin gradually crystallized into its own form of inherently anti-incarnational "Gnostic" heresies, and the process of "becoming what you profess to hate," a basic principle of mimetic theory, had come full circle. The "law of anti-idolatry" spoken of so eloquently by Sandor Goodhart calls us to unpack this history, to look at what kinds of sacrifices women and their friends have had to make in order for the domination system to ensure that the repetitive duality of who can wear the white dress and who must wear the red dress will be preserved.

Theologies of Mary's immaculate conception and emphases on "pure vessel" and "ever virgin" language about her isolates and denatures her in a way not far distant from the kind of Goddess who is spawned from the forehead of her Father. Because this "blessed among women" is said in legends to have visited Mount Athos in Greece, for centuries the Orthodox monasteries there have dedicated themselves to barring female humans and domestic animals from the place of pilgrimage, calling this an honor to Mary. Of course, the monks have no way of preventing Holy Sophia from sending female flora and fauna there, anyway. And a question, for me, hangs in the air: Wouldn't this way of being "honored" make a real flesh-and-blood Mary feel lonely? When she had her important news to tell, the Mary of the text sought out the company of other women—her cousin, Elizabeth, and the circle of women that were certainly a big part of her cousin's village life.

"Pure vessel" theology has been the subject of long dispute between the Eastern and Roman Churches, and then the Roman Church and the Protestant Reformers and secular Enlightenment. These rivalries reached a climax in the middle of the nineteenth century with the declaration of the Doctrine of the Immaculate Conception and were closely tied to the declaration of the Doctrine of Papal Infallibility. These are intimately related to the idea of Mary as a cosmic "Beatrix Mundi," of which John Paul II is so fond. What does it mean for a Church hierarchy that refuses to even consider the ordination of women, to call Mary "The Queen of Priests" in the ordination liturgy?

It is critically important to pay attention to language about the Church, who genders it, and how it is done. Hearing Cardinals talk about how the Church is working to uphold Her honor is quite instructive in this era of sexual scandal.

The "true-believing" (as the term "orthodox" is commonly translated) leadership of the Church became what they professed to hate. This can be detected in the phenomenon of "reversing the text." This is something the early Church "fathers" accused opposing groups of doing on a regular basis—turning a text inside out and standing it on its head so that it means the opposite of what it says, solely for the evil purpose of spreading chaos and confusion.

As concerns the place of women in the faith community, two texts come immediately to mind as nominations for orthodoxy's "text reversal." First is Matthew 23:9, where Jesus says: "Call no man on earth your father, for you have one Father who is in Heaven." Structuring that title as a necessary resume requirement for Churchly office has proven to be a reversal of this instruction from Jesus, turning away from his radical re-visioning of what it could mean to be family to one another, and back toward the old paternalistic domination system of the pagan world.

The second text is the frequently ignored (excluded from the common lectionary) passage in Luke 11:27, a scene which also appears in the Gospel of Thomas 79:1–2. When Jesus is on the street, a woman calls out to him: "Blessed is the womb that bore you and the breasts that nursed you!" He answers: "Blessed rather are those who hear the word of God and obey it!" Beyond virginity, honor/shame based patriarchal systems value women primarily for their fertility, especially for being "fruitful" in bearing strong sons. I read this text as a rebuke of the woman for her admiration (envy'?) of Mary as a particularly blessed mother. Jesus tells her that is not what it's about: in the realm of God, biology is not destiny.

The missing pieces of history surrounding the family life of this woman of first-century Palestine (and all the other women of her era); and the structures of the sacred that have been erected to fill those pieces still have power to provoke the honor/shame reflex today. Lest you doubt this, I remind you of Mayor Giuliani's rage at the Brooklyn Museum over the Chris Ofili painting/collage of the Madonna, adorned with pictures clipped from pornographic magazines and elephant dung.

The overarching cultural motifs clarified by mimetic theory are evident in this history. It is a history in which real women lived out their lives in social systems where their roles were largely circumscribed, as symbols of family honor and social acceptability. Their passion and commitment still shine through, if we will not neglect to keep their lamps faithfully filled. In their time, the women of the early church were sacrificial victims to a rivalry over honor and "true belief." Let them now be inspired and inspiring "Sheroes for Christ"—models of resistance and reform.

Note

1. On Sunday, January 19, 2003, ABC "World News Tonight" aired a segment on the Magdalene Houses of Ireland. Terry Moran, the anchor introduces the segment by relating how this has become yet another variety of scandal in the Roman Catholic Church, and with a few phrases about the history of the Magdalene House system. The news writers for the network provided him with this sentence:

"These workhouses in Ireland were named after Mary Magdalene, who is identified as a repentant prostitute in the Gospel of Saint Luke."(?!) The broadcast went on to talk about the recent coverage of this story on BBC-TV, and shows clips from a BBC docudrama about the Magdalene Houses, titled: "Sinners." Operated as profit-making convent laundries, they were actually prisons, dumping places for "wayward" girls and unwed mothers, some of whom spent their entire lives in these dismal places. Told that they must remain there to "wash away their sins," the girls and women were called by numbers, not names. Hilary Brown, the correspondent reporting from County Cork, interviewed two of the surviving witnesses to the cruelties of the Magdalene Houses, Sadie Williams and Mary Norris, who have campaigned for a memorial to the women who died in the Magdalene House system, known as the "Irish Gulag." The last Magdalene House was closed seven years ago, in 1996. There was at least one in every city in Ireland.

Lisa Bellan-Boyer combines theological and biblical studies with interests in art history and psychology in her interdisciplinary and intercultural work. She is a researcher on the staff of the Newark, New Jersey, Museum.

EXPLORING THE ISSUE

Did Christianity Liberate Women?

Critical Thinking and Reflection

1. What sources does Karen L. King cite to support her argument that Christianity liberated women? Once you have identified the sources, critically discuss the evidence they offer.
2. What evidence does Lisa Bellan-Boyer provide to explain why women's roles within the Christian Church were severely circumscribed? Critically discuss this evidence.
3. How might the different centuries each writer chooses to focus on account for their different findings? Analyze what we know about gender roles and the social structure in each time and place that provides the context for one of these selections.
4. What are the key elements in Karen L. King's summary of "Early Christian Women's Theology?" How are these principles similar to and different from the "official" Christian theology of today? How might we account for the differences, then and now? Critically examine both the content and context that shaped these early theological principles.
5. What does Karen L. King mean when she writes: "What is remarkable is how much evidence has survived systematic attempts to erase women from history?" Analyze what evidence has survived as well as the systematic attempts to erase women from history.
6. What does Lisa Bellan-Boyer mean when she writes: "The 'true-believing' (as the term 'orthodox' is commonly translated) leadership of the Church became what they professed to hate?"
7. Research mimetic theory and critically analyze Bellan-Boyer's application of it to this question. How does it explain the contraction of women's roles described in the NO selection?
8. Both writers speak about the conflation of women named Mary into one "good" and one "bad" Mary. Despite corrections made by Christian church officials, these errors persist. What are the costs of intentionally misunderstanding the role of Mary Magdalene, the apostle, prophet, and teacher? Critically discuss.

Is There Common Ground?

If we read these two authors sequentially, we have a comprehensive look at the first four centuries of Christianity. The YES selection celebrates the roles filled by women in a community of fervent believers, during the early years. The NO selection, by contrast, chronicles the circumscribing of women's richly diverse roles, as the institutional Christian Church sought acceptance in the Greco-Roman world. Gender conventions were firmly in place in the Greco-Roman world, with public space being assigned to men and private space declared the domain of women. During the centuries of persecution, fervent Christians met in secret, and women were able to be full participants in the life of the church. Once persecution ended, however, and Christianity became not only acceptable but, eventually, the official religion of the Roman Empire, an institution was created and public worship spaces called basilicas were built. Eager to gain acceptance in the Greco-Roman world, the Christian Church conformed to the existing gender system, gradually diminishing the public and even the private roles of women.

What can we learn from this radical change? One current secular parallel might be the Occupy Movement. Leaderless and radically democratic, this phenomenon exists as a "people's movement." What do you think would happen if Occupy became an official political party or set up a suite of offices in New York or Washington? A single spokesperson would be required to "speak" for the group. Formal positions would have to be taken, printed, and distributed. Money would have to be raised. An organizational chart would have to be developed.

Question: What would remain of the original impulse that brought many thousands to the street? And, does this "thought experiment" help us better understand the centuries of early Christianity?

Additional Resources

During the Patristic Age, holy women paid a high price for their piety, energy, and talent. Gilian Close captures this time in *This Female Man of God: Women and Spiritual Power in the Patristic Age, AD 350–450* (Routledge, 1995). Women were "the Devil's gateway," so anyone holy enough to be an exemplar of the faith could not actually *be* a woman. Being holy, these women were judged to be clearly and self-evidently male. Feminine spirituality as a concept had no credibility. *Adam's Fractured Rib* (Fortress Press, 1970) by Margaret Sittler Ermarth explores some sources of the fear and hatred of women. Former Boston College theologian Mary Daly in *The Church and the Second Sex* (Beacon Press, 1985) follows up on Simone de Beauvoir's feminist classic *The Second Sex* by documenting sexism in Christian Church history and the "otherness" of women.

Internet References . . .

From Jesus to Christ: The First Christians

Based on a six-part PBS/FRONTLINE series, one of which is devoted to "The Roles for Women," this site contains the raising of important questions on the subject, which are subsequently answered by a noted expert in the field.

www.pbs.org/wgbh/pages/frontline/shows/religion/first/roles.html

Selected, Edited, and with Issue Framing Material by:
Helen Buss Mitchell, *Howard Community College*
and
Joseph R. Mitchell, *Howard Community College*

ISSUE

Were Internal Factors Responsible for the Fall of the Roman Empire?

YES: Adrian Goldsworthy, from *How Rome Fell: Death of a Superpower* (Yale University Press, 2009)

NO: Peter Heather, from "The Huns and the End of the Roman Empire in Western Europe," *English Historical Review* (February 1995)

Learning Outcomes

After reading this issue you should be able to:

- List internal factors that contributed to the fall of the Roman Empire.
- List external factors that contributed to the fall of the Roman Empire.
- Explain how the fall of Rome provided a transition from the Greco-Roman classical era to the Middle Ages in the Western world.

ISSUE SUMMARY

YES: Historian Adrian Goldsworthy argues that internal military and political conditions were responsible for the fall of the Roman Empire.

NO: Professor of history Peter Heather argues that the invasion of the Huns forced other Germanic tribes to seek safety within the confines of the Roman Empire and ultimately threaten it, thus permitting the invasion of the Huns to indirectly bring about the fall of the Roman Empire.

Periodization (see Introduction) illuminates the past by delineating significant changes in humanity's progress from one time period to another. The European Enlightenment which marks the transition from the medieval to the modern world, is one such example. The decline and fall of the Roman Empire is another, because it notes the end of the Greco-Roman classical era and the beginning of the Middle Ages. Greek and Roman cultures provided Western civilization with some of its greatest historical and cultural endowments. Thus, the demise of these cultures continues to interest Western historians.

Not until the Italian Renaissance, with its renewed interest in classical antiquity, did the fall of Rome, along with its antecedent causes, earn an official place in the world of scholarship. Humanist scholar Francesco Petrarca (Petrarch) (1304–1374) blamed internal problems for the empire's demise. In the next century, however, Niccolo Machiavelli (1469–1527), perhaps the first modern political scientist, blamed the constant attacks of neighboring barbarians, which eventually wore down the empire and caused its collapse.

Modern historical scholarship on the fall of Rome began with Edward Gibbon (1737–1794), who injected another variable into the mix. In his multivolume work *The Decline and Fall of the Roman Empire* (first published between 1776 and 1782), Gibbon stated that the rise of Christianity may have played a significant role in Rome's collapse. Because he was a product of Europe's Enlightenment era and shared its skepticism regarding the effects of organized religion on a civilization's progress, many modern historians consider his focus on Christianity to be overemphasized. In general, he took a more fatalistic approach to the empire's demise, stating, that "the decline of Rome was the natural and inevitable effect of immoderate greatness."

More recently, countless reasons have been given for Rome's fall: the disintegration of the imperial economy, agricultural problems caused by climatic changes, manpower shortages due to lead poisoning from the empire's water pipes, destruction of the leadership class through imperial executions and civil wars, racial mixing that diluted the old Roman stock, the drain of gold and silver, widespread slavery that made the rich richer and the poor poorer, and a class war waged by peasant soldiers against the ruling class. This list is not complete, but it does testify to the interest historians have taken in the fall of Rome.

The Roman Empire of the fourth century was huge. Its empire extended completely around the Mediterranean Sea, though modern Ireland and Scotland remained "barbarian," uncivilized from the Roman point of view. With their genius for administration and infrastructure, the Romans had been an important power for more than 1,000 years. Roads radiated out to distant lands and Roman law reached even further. Of course, an extended empire also meant a vast frontier to defend. In the fourth century, the Roman Empire had divided into eastern and western capitals—Constantinople in the east shared control with Rome in the west. Increasingly the two sectors were divided by language—Latin in the west; Greek in the east—and resources. Gradually, the east became more populous and wealthy, with stronger emperors and a well-equipped army and navy. The rise of Christianity and Islam, growing decadence, lead in the water conduits, as well as fiscal and military challenges probably combined to weaken the western empire. Though the date of 476 is often given as marking the "fall" of the Roman Empire, many scholars believe the process of decline might have lasted a century.

While acknowledging the probability of multiple causation in most historical events, twenty-first-century historians continue to debate the reasons for Rome's demise by analyzing and evaluating the effects of internal and external forces. By applying the Roman experience to the rise and fall of other civilizations—past and present—contemporary historians continue to revitalize the debate.

Our two historians reflect this internal/external dialogue. Peter Heather stresses the role of the barbarians in the empire's downfall, but offers a different spin. The fourth century C.E. invasion of Europe by the Huns was key to the fall of the Roman Empire, in his view, because it forced Germanic tribes to seek safety within the empire's boundaries where they developed a sense of unity that ultimately gave them the power to supplant it. Adrian Goldsworthy states that political and military problems within the empire, including civil wars and corrupt emperors, were responsible for the empire's demise.

Most historians studying the fall of Rome agree that neither internal nor external forces can be ignored, yet many continue to produce works that emphasize one side or the other of the debate. E.A. Thompson, *Romans and Barbarians: The Decline of the Western Empire* (University of Wisconsin Press, 2002, reprint) has been a standard source on the external forces side for decades. Arthur Ferrill's *The Fall of Rome: The Military Explanation* (Thames & Hudson, 1986) is another account of the role played by the barbarians in Rome's collapse. Hugh Elton, *Warfare in the Roman Empire, AD 350–425* (Oxford University Press,1998) brings the subject up to date. In *Warfare in the Western World* (Salamander Press, 1998), John Warry surveys the role of wars and their effects on Greco-Roman civilization, titling a concluding chapter, "The Coming of the Barbarians." Derek Williams in *Romans and Barbarians: Four Views from the Empire's Edge, First Century AD* (St. Martin's Press, 1998), and Thomas S. Burns, *Rome and the Barbarians, 100 BC–AD 400* (Johns Hopkins University Press, 2003) offer two more contemporary updates. Finally, Peter Heather's *The Fall of the Roman Empire: A New History of Rome and the Barbarians* (Oxford University Press, 2006) elaborates on the ideas expressed in the YES selection.

A.H.M. Jones's *The Decline of the Western World* (Oxford University Press, 1964) and Peter Brown's *The World of Late Antiquity* (Thames & Hudson, 1971) are classics on the internal factors side of the debate. Averil Cameron, *The Later Roman Empire: AD 284–430* (Harvard University Press, 1993) surveys the centuries before the empire's fall. Geza Alfoldy's *The Social History of Rome* (Johns Hopkins University Press, 1988) is a short but well-packed volume on Rome's social history that sets the stage for the fall of Rome. Jaroslav Pelikan, *The Excellent Empire: The Fall of Rome and the Triumph of the Church* (Harper & Row, 1987) gives a religious spin to the question.

YES

Adrian Goldsworthy

How Rome Fell: Death of a Superpower

It will be enough for me, however, if these words of mine are judged useful by those who want to understand clearly the events which happened in the past and which will (human nature being what it is), at some time or other and in much the same ways, be repeated in the future.'—*Thucydides, writing at the very end of the fifth century* B.C.

The Western Roman Empire ceased to exist in the fifth century. Even those scholars who talk of transformation admit this simple fact. The Eastern Roman Empire lasted for another thousand years until it was overrun by the Turks. Even at its height it could never hope to dominate the world. It was a power, rather than a superpower. The sixth century demonstrated that it lacked the capacity to recapture the lost western provinces. In the seventh century the Arab conquests stripped it of even more territory. It continued to exist as just one amongst many powers in the known world, and some of these were geographically larger and both militarily and financially stronger. Even so, none could be said to have replaced the Roman Empire or matched its former size and power.

None of this happened quickly, but viewed in the long term it cannot be seen as anything other than decline and—in the case of the Western Empire—fall. It was a long process and no single event, lost war or decision can be said to have caused it. The basic question remains of why this occurred, and whether the most important cause was internal problems or external threats. Throughout their history the Romans had always fought a lot of wars against very varied opponents. They had suffered some serious defeats, but had always recovered. There was never any question that such defeats could cause the collapse of the empire. Yet this did happen in the west in the fifth century and therefore we must ask whether the threats faced by the Late Roman Empire were greater than those of earlier periods. This in turn raises two basic possibilities. Either one or more individual enemy was more formidable, or there were simply so many simultaneous threats that the empire could not cope.

It is usually asserted that the Sassanid Persians were far more formidable than the Parthians, or indeed any enemy the Romans had faced for centuries. They certainly won more victories over the Romans than the Parthians. On the other hand, the levels of Persian aggression varied enormously and there were long periods of peace. Some Persian kings needed the wealth and glory offered by a successful war with Rome. Usually this was necessary to secure their own hold on power. The largest Roman armies of the period were those sent east to face the Persians and massive resources were expended on frontier fortifications. Having said that, only border territory was ever actually lost to Persia and even this was on a fairly modest scale. The idea that from its first appearance in the third century Persia was an especially deadly opponent—even a rival superpower—remains firmly entrenched in the minds of scholars. It is a belief that is very hard to reconcile with the evidence, but this does not mean that it will not continue to be asserted.

Groups from the tribal peoples of Europe eventually took control of the Western Empire. However, it is extremely difficult to see major change in the military efficiency of the tribal peoples of Europe from Julius Caesar's day to that of Stilicho's or Aetius'. To some degree larger tribal confederations appeared, but we should never exaggerate the degree of unity. It is convenient to talk of *the* Franks or *the* Goths, in spite of the fact that these remained divided into many separate and sometimes mutually hostile tribes. At no stage before the creation of the barbarian kingdoms inside the provinces was there a single king of all the Franks or any other people. Attila united both his own people and allied and subject races to a remarkable degree. Yet, once again, he was unable to take much territory from the Romans and was essentially a raider and extortionist on a grand scale. Other powerful barbarian leaders had emerged in the past and, like Attila, they had proved unable to pass on their power to a successor. The Huns were a frightening enemy, but it is worth remembering that their power had been broken before the final collapse of the Western Empire and that they had anyway devoted most of their attentions to the Eastern Empire.

There is no good case for claiming that the enemies of the Late Roman Empire were simply more formidable than those of earlier periods. This also makes it harder to argue that the Roman Empire had to adapt in the third century to face new and more dangerous threats, most of all the Sassanid 'superpower'. Does this mean that it was the sheer quantity rather than the scale of individual threats that was the problem? There certainly do seem to have been more major wars in the third and subsequent centuries than in the early Principate. In particular, raiding by barbarian groups in Europe is much more prominent in our sources. Such predatory attacks, often on a small scale, were not new. In the past they had always increased in scale and frequency whenever the frontier defences were perceived to be weak. An impression of vulnerability encouraged attacks and this makes it hard to judge whether an increase in raids and invasions was the consequence of a rise in barbarian numbers and strength or a result of Roman weakness. It is clear that all of Rome's enemies, including the Persians, exploited the empire's frequent internal disputes and civil wars.

There may be other reasons for Roman weakness and we need to consider these. Unfortunately, for so many of the theories about long-term problems we lack the basic information either to confirm or deny them. There are no good figures for the population of the empire at any period and, therefore, we cannot say with any certainty that this was in long-term decline. Similarly, we must study the economy without any adequate statistics. It seems more than probable that levels of trade and prosperity fell from the end of the second century onwards and never again achieved the levels of the early Principate. However, sources at best hint at such trends, and some scholars will interpret these glimpses of the past in radically different ways. The same is true of the traditional picture of a Late Roman world where the burden of tax was oppressive and fell disproportionately heavily on the poor, who were already oppressed by their rich landlords. Land fell out of cultivation and the rural population was reduced to the level of serfs. None of this is implausible, but that is also true of other models and it is impossible to prove any of them. Far more data—the bulk of which must come from archaeology if it can ever be found—is needed before we can speak with some confidence on these topics. The same is true of claims about climate change and other wider problems.

The type of evidence we have, as well as the interests of scholars, has meant that a good deal of the work on Late Antiquity has focused on economy and society, law and government, intellectual life, culture and religion. Studies tend to concentrate on broad themes and inevitably this emphasises continuity rather than change. By comparison, narrative history has all too often been neglected and certainly has made only a minor contribution to most scholars' mental picture of the period. There are exceptions and study of the frontier relations and foreign wars has often been more traditional in style, since a narrative or chronological element is obviously essential. At the same time civil wars and internal conflict have not received such detailed and coherent treatment. This is odd, for these are the one aspect of the empire's internal problems for which we have considerable evidence.

It is worth once again emphasising that from 217 down to the collapse of the Western Empire there were only a handful of periods as long as ten years when a civil war did not break out. Some of these conflicts were very brief and some were confined to a small region—the usurpers who were proclaimed and then suppressed, or rejected and murdered by their own men after a reign lasting just a few weeks. Challenges for imperial power were sometimes resolved without serious fighting. On the other hand, some conflicts were fought on a very large scale and lasted for years. It is easy to remember Constantine as the great emperor who united the entire empire under his control, but we should not forget that he was a usurper who fought or prepared for civil wars for the first half of his reign.

Civil war and challenges to the imperial throne were common occurrences. Every adult emperor from Septimius Severus onwards experienced at least one such conflict during their lifetime. Usurpers never wanted to destroy or change the empire. These were not conflicts about ideology, but purely for political power. A small minority of the losers in these wars were allowed to keep their lives, although only a tiny handful were permitted to continue in a public career. In the vast majority of cases such conflicts only ended with the death of one of the rivals. Usurpers were the most direct and personal threat faced by any emperor and tended to be treated accordingly. It was normal for an emperor to abandon a war against a foreign enemy to deal with a Roman rival.

Usurpers did not act alone. They needed supporters and the most important of these expected rewards including promotion and riches if the rebellion was successful. If a usurper was suppressed, then many of his backers were likely to suffer with him. Punishment was often extended to their families, especially those holding any office or whose wealth made them appealing targets for informers. In this way even a localised rebellion could mean life, death, imprisonment or ruin to people in distant provinces who had not been involved in it in any direct way. This was a world of patronage, where the powerful exerted themselves to secure benefits for relatives and friends. Such webs of favour and gratitude could become very dangerous for all concerned at times of internal conflict.

All usurpers needed military backing to succeed. Emperors from Augustus onwards tried to keep their soldiers loyal through solemn oaths and regular donatives. On the whole, the army tended to stay loyal to an established dynasty unless the emperor seriously alienated them. Few usurpers could count on similar loyalty. Losses were considerable in some civil wars, as the army wasted its strength fighting against itself. Soldiers fighting an internal struggle could not simultaneously operate on one of the frontiers. Time and again substantial parts of the army were drawn away and Roman military dominance across its borders reduced or utterly shattered. Successive civil wars dislocated the army's administrative and logistical structures, its training patterns, recruitment and also its discipline, which suffered whenever licence was given in an effort to win loyalty. Ordinary soldiers could usually expect to change sides to join the victors after a failed rebellion. This was not so easy for more senior officers.

Each civil war cost the empire. Anything gained by the winning side inevitably had to be taken from other Romans and a prolonged campaign was likely to involve widespread destruction within the provinces where fighting occurred. Almost as important as the physical price of civil war was its impact on attitudes and behaviour from the emperor down. Personal survival became the first objective of every emperor and shaped all of their decisions and the very structure of the empire. In the quest to protect themselves successive emperors gradually reshaped the empire itself and, ironically enough, often made themselves more rather than less vulnerable.

The biggest change was the marginalisation of the senatorial class in the third century and, along with them, the city of Rome as a real rather than merely spiritual capital of the empire. Senators—and most of all a handful of distinguished men and those trusted with senior provincial commands—were for a long time the only possible rivals for imperial power. At first the major military provinces were divided up so that no one man commanded too large an army. By the end of the third century senators had virtually ceased to hold military rank of any kind. They had also all but ceased to become emperor.

Emperors could now come from a far wider section of the empire's population. Any connection with the imperial family—even spurious claims to be the illegitimate son of an emperor—was sufficient to make a claim. In the past Rome's emperors had had to be wary of only a small number of senators, men who were known to them personally and whose careers meant that they spent many years in and around Rome. Now a rival could be almost anyone. They did not need political connections or family reputation, simply the ability to persuade some troops to back them. Many emperors were equestrians, and almost all were army officers or imperial officials.

The trend towards smaller provinces continued. In addition, military and civil power were made separate. This helped to protect an emperor against challengers, but made it far harder to get things done. In particular, it was very difficult to raise and supply a large enough army to deal with a serious problem on the frontiers. From the emperor's point of view this was comforting, since the same army could easily have been turned against him by a rival. At times extraordinary commands were created so that one commander could deal with a problem, but emperors had to be wary of offering such power to a potential usurper. More often emperors chose to go themselves and take personal command of a campaign. From the middle of the third century onwards Roman emperors spent much of their time performing tasks that would once have been dealt with by an imperial legate. Again, it is worth emphasising that it was not the scale of the problems that had increased, but the ability of the empire to employ its resources to deal with them.

An emperor could not be everywhere at once. If he was unwilling to trust anyone else with sufficient power to deal with a distant problem, then it would simply not be dealt with at all. Time and again this sense of neglect by central government prompted a region to rebel and proclaim its own emperor. One solution was to have more than one emperor. The tetrarchic system is often praised, but its success was always limited and no one was able to repeat the dominance of Diocletian for any great length of time. In a way, the acceptance that more than one emperor would exist offered usurpers the prospect of advancing to supreme power in stages. It also tended to encourage regionalism as separate military and civil hierarchies developed in different parts of the empire. Each group was naturally inclined to give priority to its own aims and problems, and often proved reluctant to assist other parts of the empire.

Emperors had always travelled in some state, surrounded by members of their household, bureaucrats and guards. This increased massively in scale during the third century. All wanted to have sizeable military forces under their direct control. If the field armies were intended to perform a strategic role, then this was first and foremost to guard against Roman rivals. Emperors surrounded themselves with more and more attendants and personal bodyguards, and made court ceremonies? increasingly elaborate. In part this was to dignify and secure the rule of men who had often seized power in brutal fashion comparatively recently. It was also intended to protect the emperor's person. Assassination was less common in the fourth century than the third. At the same time all of this tended to isolate the emperor. It made it harder for him to know personally even his more senior officials and commanders, let alone the vastly inflated number of bureaucrats who now worked in the imperial administration. Control over the activities of the men who represented imperial authority throughout the provinces was extremely limited.

All emperors lived with the fear of usurpation. It shaped their behaviour and also that of all of the officials and officers who served under them. A career in the imperial service offered the prospect of legal privileges and wealth, gathered both through pay and, even more, from bribes and payments for services. The most successful achieved very high rank with all the patronage and influence this brought. A small minority were even able to reach imperial rank. However, alongside the advantages came serious risks. Any suspicion that an individual was plotting against the emperor was likely to be punished severely. The same was true of anybody associated with a failed usurper or their supporters. In a system where careers were routinely advanced by personal recommendation, such networks of patronage inevitably put many individuals in danger. Personal survival and personal success and profit were the foremost aims of most officials.

The imperial bureaucracy in the Late Roman Empire was certainly far larger than in the first and second centuries. The army mayor may not have been bigger, but certainly consisted of far more small, independent units. Size on its own does not mean that either of these institutions was more efficient. There were far more administrators than could readily be supervised, especially since they formed part of a bureaucracy that was both divided and confused in its structure. The imperial administration raised funds and resources to support both itself and the army. Such short-term expedients as debasing the coinage suggest that at times this supply proved inadequate. However, on the whole the system seems to have functioned in the third and fourth centuries, at the very least to a minimal necessary level. It still left plenty of room for inefficiency and corruption, and such wastage may well have been on a massive scale. Most individual members of the bureaucracy did their job well enough to keep the system functioning and prevent their peculation becoming too blatant. Some may genuinely have been both honest and competent.

Civil wars were most common in the third century, but remained frequent afterwards. The state developed in ways intended to protect emperors from internal rivals, but singularly failed to do so. Personal survival had always been an important concern for all emperors since the creation of the Principate. Augustus had fought his way to power through a series of civil wars. Assassination plots and open rebellion were threats faced by each of Rome's rulers from the very beginning. Augustus was a monarch, but created a system in which his power was carefully veiled. Since he was not formally a king, there was no clear institution to arrange the succession. Some have seen this as a fatal flaw in the system of the Principate—effectively, an accident waiting to happen. Others would go further and see the Augustan system as a 'millstone', revered by tradition that prevented proper reform of the empire in the third and fourth centuries.

This cannot explain the quite staggering difference berween the Principate and the Late Roman Empire. There was civil war for a year after the death of Nero in 68 and another longer conflict after Pertinax was murdered in 193. Claudius, Domitian and Marcus Aurelius each faced a challenge from a rebellious governor, although all of these revolts swiftly collapsed. Assassination plots and attempted coups at Rome were a little more common, although some of these may have been imagined by nervous emperors or invented by their ruthless subordinates. The early Principate was not wholly free from the reality or threat of internal conflict, but for more than two hundred years it still suffered only rarely from these. This is also in marked contrast to the last half-century of the Republic. If the system created by Augustus was so seriously flawed, then only remarkable luck could explain this. With Gibbon, we might stop 'inquiring *why* the Roman empire was destroyed', and instead 'be surprised that it lasted so long'.

It stretches credibility to see two centuries of largely unbroken internal peace as a mere fluke, especially when they were followed by a longer period when civil war was so very frequent. It is true that each fresh bout of internal conflict weakened imperial authority and the institutions of the state and therefore made future usurpations and rebellions more likely. Yet, once again, it cannot have been solely chance that such a cycle did not develop earlier. In the third century the empire largely lost the Republican façade so carefully constructed by Augustus. He and his successors ruled through the Senate. As a body this had no real political independence, but sensible emperors took care to respect its dignity. More importantly, they employed senators in virtually all important posts, effectively ruling the empire through them.

It may seem odd in this day and age to praise a system based on an aristocratic elite, consisting of men who were amateurs in the modern sense. Yet the system had many advantages in the Roman context. It provided a manageable group of senior soldiers and administrators—an emperor could know all of these men and their families. Only a minority were potential rivals and these could be closely observed. Public life remained focused on the fixed location of Rome itself, making it easier to sense the mood of the aristocracy. Emperors in the first and second centuries were able to trust selected senators to control substantial armies and large provinces. Only rarely—usually during times of major conflict with Parthia—was it necessary to appoint a commander to control more than one province and this did not automatically lead to an attempt at usurpation. In the first and second centuries emperors were able to delegate and did not feel obliged to direct campaigns in person. Rome was the centre of the empire in more than just a spiritual sense. We do not need to idealise the senatorial legates of the early period. Some were incompetent, a few untrustworthy and probably quite a lot were more or less corrupt. In all these respects they seem at the very least no worse than the senior officials of the Late Roman Empire. Politically, the small senatorial class was simply easier for an emperor to control. Reliance on the Senate was a Republican tradition, but actually made sound sense.

The governments of ancient states had limited ambitions and did not concern themselves with major programmes of health, education or the detailed day to day regulation of markets, industry and agriculture. For all its size and sophistication, the Roman Empire was not fundamentally different in this respect. It raised revenue and other resources and made use of these in a range of ways. The army was the biggest single cost, but there was also the maintenance of many buildings, some ports and a vast road network, as well as the subsidised or free doles of food to the population of Rome and later Constantinople. None of these duties of the empire ground to a halt in the third or fourth century. However, this does not mean that they were functioning well.

The Roman Empire did not fall quickly, but to use this as proof that its institutions were essentially sound is deeply misguided. The empire was huge and faced no serious competitors. Persia was the strongest neighbour, but there was never a prospect of a Persian army reaching the Tiber. Rome was massive, heavily populated and rich. This remained true even if the population and economy were in decline. It had a transport system of all-weather roads and busy commercial routes by river, canal and sea on a scale unmatched again in Europe until recent centuries. Although we may note the difficulties emperors had in making their will felt in distant provinces, their capacity to do this at all was still far greater than the leaders of any other people. The Roman army was a large, sophisticated, permanent and professional force backed by an extensive logistical system. Like the empire itself, it was different from anything else in existence in the known world. The Romans possessed many great advantages over all of their competitors. None of these rivals had the power to push the empire over in the third or fourth centuries. The empire was huge and did not need to operate at the highest levels of efficiency to succeed. It possessed massively greater resources, technological and other advantages. There was also the probability that somewhere along the line some officers and officials would do their job at least moderately well. This meant that the Romans were likely to prevail in the long run. None of its enemies were capable of inflicting more than a limited defeat on the Romans.

None of this meant that the cost of repeated civil war was not felt. It is not difficult to make the case that the majority of emperors in the first and second centuries had the wider good of the empire as their main ambition. All were concerned with personal survival, but this had not become the overwhelming priority it would be for their successors in later eras. That is not to say that the later emperors were more selfish, but simply that they could never be as secure. Many may have had the best of intentions to rule well, but the government of the empire became first and foremost about keeping the emperor in power—and at lower levels, about the individual advantage of bureaucrats and officers.

The Late Roman Empire was not designed to be an efficient government, but to keep the emperor in power and to benefit the members of the administration. Many of these could enjoy highly successful careers by the standards of the day without ever being effective in the role that they were theoretically supposed to perform. Sheer size prevented rapid collapse or catastrophe. Its weakness was not obvious, but this only meant that collapse could come in sudden, dramatic stages, such as the loss of the African provinces to the Vandals. Gradually, the empire's institutions rotted and became less and less capable of dealing with any crisis, but still did not face serious competition. Lost wars were damaging, but the damage was not fatal to the empire itself. As an example, from 376–382 the Romans could not lose the war against the Goths, but they still struggled to win it. Even defeats at the hands of the Persians did not deprive the empire of major or essential resources.

The Roman Empire continued for a very long time. Successive blows knocked away sections of it, as attackers uncovered its weaknesses. Yet at times the empire could still be formidable and did not simply collapse. Perhaps we should imagine the Late Roman Empire as a retired athlete, whose body has declined from neglect and an unhealthy lifestyle. At times the muscles will still function well and with the memory of former skill and training. Yet, as the neglect continues, the body becomes less and less capable of resisting disease or recovering from injury. Over the years the person would grow weaker and weaker, and in the end could easily succumb to disease. Long decline was the fate of the Roman Empire. In the end, it may well have been 'murdered' by barbarian invaders, but these struck at a body made vulnerable by prolonged decay.

Adrian Goldsworthy is a British historian, specializing in the military history of the Greek and especially Roman periods. His many books include *The Roman Army at War: 100 BC to AD 200*, *In the Name of Rome: The Men Who Won the Roman Empire,* and *The Punic Wars.*

Peter Heather

The Huns and the End of the Roman Empire in Western Europe

Based on the Mediterranean, the Roman Empire forged Europe as far as the rivers Rhine and Danube—and, for lengthy periods, extensive lands beyond those boundaries—together with North Africa and much of the Near East into a unitary state which lasted for the best part of 400 years. The protracted negotiations required to bring just some of this area together in the European Community put the success of this Empire into perspective. Yet since the publication of Gibbon's masterpiece (and long before), its very success has served only to stimulate interest in why it ended, 'blame' being firmly placed on everything from an excess of Christian piety to the effect of lead water pipes. The aim of this paper is to reconsider some of the processes and events which underlay the disappearance of the western half of the Roman Empire in the fifth century AD. This was an area encompassing essentially modern Britain, France, Benelux, Italy, Austria, Hungary, the Iberian Peninsula, and North Africa as far east as Libya, whose fragmentation culminated in the deposition of Romulus Augustulus on or around 4 September 476. That groups of outsiders—so-called 'barbarians'—played an important role in all this has never been doubted. A full understanding of the barbarians' involvement in a whole sequence of events, taking the best part of a hundred years, lends, however, an unrecognized coherence to the story of western imperial collapse.

There are two main reasons why this coherence has not been highlighted before. First, most of the main barbarian groups which were later to establish successor states to the Roman Empire in western Europe, had crossed the frontier by about AD 410, yet the last western Roman emperor was not deposed until 476, some sixty-five years later. I will argue, however, that the initial invasions must not be separated from the full working-out of their social and political consequences. Not just the invasions themselves need to be examined, but also the longer-term reactions to them of the Roman population of western Europe, and especially its landowning elites. While the western Empire did not die quickly or easily, a direct line of historical cause and effect nonetheless runs from the barbarian invasions of the late fourth and early fifth centuries to the deposition of Romulus Augustulus. The second reason lies in modern understandings of what caused the different groups of outsiders to cross into the Empire in the first place. These population movements did not happen all at once, but were stretched out over about thirty-five years, c. 376–410. Here again, however, a close re-examination of the evidence reveals that the years of invasion represent no more than different phases of a single crisis. In particular, the two main phases of population movement—c. 376–86 and 405–8—were directly caused by the intrusion of Hunnic power into the fringes of Europe.

The Huns were very much a new factor in the European strategic balance of power in the late fourth century. A group of Eurasian nomads, they moved west, sometime after AD 350, along the northern coast of the Black Sea, the western edge of the great Eurasian Steppe Illiterate, and not even leaving a second-hand account of their origins and history in any Graeco-Roman source, they remain deeply mysterious. Opinions differ even over their linguistic affiliation, but the best guess would seem to be that the Huns were the first group of Turkic, as opposed to Iranian, nomads to have intruded into Europe. Whatever the answer to that question, the first half of this study will reconsider their impact upon the largely Germanic groups of central and eastern Europe which had previously been the main focus of Roman foreign policy on Rhine and Danube.

This fundamental change in the nature of political activity from regimes independent of the immigrant groups to regimes which included them—a direct result of the disappearance of the Huns as an outside 'force—had important consequences. No group of supporters was ready (nor previously had any of the more traditional power-blocks ever been ready) to back a regime without some kind of pay-off. One effect of including immigrants in governing coalitions, therefore, was to increase the numbers of those expecting rewards, most obviously involvement in the running of the Empire. Burgundian kings took Roman titles, for instance, while the Visigoth Theoderic II attempted to order affairs in Spain. The Vandals' intervention in Italy in 455 should likewise be read as an attempt to stake their claim in the new political order. That they sacked the city of Rome has naturally received most attention; but Geiseric, the Vandal leader, also took back to North Africa with him Eudoxia and Eudocia—respectively wife and daughter of Valentinian III—and married the

From *English Historical Review,* vol. 110, no. 435, February 1995.

daughter to his son and heir Huneric. The two had been betrothed but not married under the treaty of 442, yet in 455 Petronius Maximus married her to his son, the Caesar Palladius. Thus Geiseric intervened in Italy at least partly out of fear that a match which should have cemented the Vandals' status within the western Empire was not going to take place. Subsequent years, similarly, saw Geiseric forward the imperial claims of Olybrius who married Placidia, the younger daughter of Valentinian, and was thus his relative by marriage.

Involvement in imperial affairs carried great prestige, and had been sought, as we have seen, since the time of Alaric and Athaulf. The western Empire only had this prestige, however, because it was, and was perceived to be, the most powerful institution of the contemporary world. Prestige certainly incorporates abstract qualities, but the attraction of the living Empire for immigrant leaders was firmly based upon its military might and overall wealth. They wished to avoid potentially dangerous military confrontations with it, while its wealth, when distributed as patronage, could greatly strengthen a leader's position. By the 450s, however, the real power behind the western imperial facade was already ebbing away. As we have seen, Britain, parts of Gaul and Spain (at different times), and above all North Africa had removed themselves or been removed from central imperial control. The rewards—money or land, such wealth being the basis of power—which were given after 454 to new allies from among the barbarian immigrants therefore only depleted further an already shrunken base.

Take, for example, Avitus. Under him, the Goths were sent to Spain to bring the Suevi to heel. Unlike the 410s, however, Theoderic II's troops seem to have operated by themselves, and according to Hydatius' account basically ransacked northern Spain, including loyal Hispano-Romans, for all the wealth they could muster. This benefited the Goths, but not the Roman state; there is no indication that Roman administration and taxation were restored. Likewise the Burgundians: after participating in Spain, they received new and better lands in Savoy, which, an enigmatic chronicle entry tells us, they divided with local senators. Another prosperous agricultural area no longer formed part of central imperial resources.

After 454, there thus built up a vicious circle within the western Empire, with too many groups squabbling over a shrinking financial base. In political terms, this meant that there were always enough groups left out in the cold, after any division of the spoils, which wanted to undermine the prevailing political configuration. Moreover, with every change of regime, there had to be further gifts to conciliate supporters anew. Having been granted a free hand in Spain under Avitus, the Goths then received the city of Narbonne and its territory (especially, one supposes, its tax revenues) as the price of their support for Libius Severus, Majorian's successor, in the early 460s. Even worse, this concentration on the internal relations of the established power-blocks allowed the rise of other more peripheral forces, which would previously have been suppressed, and whose activities took still more territory out of central control. Particularly ominous in this respect was the expansion of the Armoricans, and, above all, the Franks in northern Gaul from the 460s, as increasingly independent leaders gathered around themselves ever larger power-bases.

There were only two possible ways to break the circle. Either the number of political players had to be reduced, or the centre's financial base had to expand. This clarifies the logic behind the policies pursued by the only effective western regimes put together after the death of Aetius: those of Majorian (457–61) and Anthemius (467–72). Majorian's regime combined the sufferance of all the western army groups with the support of Italian aristocrats and a careful courting of the Gauls who had previously backed Avitus. He also won at least the temporary acquiescence of the Goths and Burgundians, and Constantinople seems eventually to have recognized him. Anthemius was son-in-law of the former eastern Emperor Marcian, and came to Italy with an army and a blessing from the reigning eastern Emperor, Leo. His leading general was Marcellinus, commander in Dalmatia; Ricimer accepted him in Italy (they forged a marriage alliance); Gallic landowners were again carefully courted; and, at the start of his reign at least, the major immigrant groups deferred to him. The central policy of both these regimes was to reconquer Vandal Africa, Majorian making his bid in 460, Anthemius in 468. Victory in either of these wars would have renewed imperial prestige, but, more important, would have removed from the political game one of its major players, and, perhaps above all, restored to the rump western Empire the richest of its original territories.

Both Vandal expeditions failed, and as a result both regimes fell apart. But what if either had succeeded? Particularly in 468, a really major expedition was put together and the later success of Belisarius shows that reconquering North Africa was not inherently impossible. There was, so to speak, a window of opportunity. Buoyed up by victory and the promise of African revenues, a victorious western emperor could certainly have re-established his political hold on the landowners of southern Gaul and Spain, many of whom would have instinctively supported an imperial revival. Sidonius, and the other Gallic aristocrats who organized resistance to Euric, for instance, would have been only too happy to reassert ties to the centre. Burgundians, Goths, and Suevi would have had to be faced in due course, but victory would have considerably extended the active life of the western Empire. The failure of the expeditions foreclosed the possibility of escaping the cycle of decline. With the number of players increasing rather than diminishing, as the Franks in particular grew in importance, and with the Empire's financial base in decline, the idea of empire quickly became meaningless, since the centre no longer controlled anything anyone wanted. In consequence, the late 460s and 470s saw one group after another coming to the realization that the western Empire was no longer a prize worth fighting for. It must have been an extraordinary moment, in fact, when it dawned on the leaders of individual interest groups, and upon members of local Roman landowning elites, that, after hundreds of years of existence, the Roman state in western Europe was now an anachronism.

The first to grasp the point seems to have been Euric the Visigoth. After the Vandals defeated Anthemius, he quickly launched a series of wars which, by 475, had brought under his control much of Gaul and Spain. There is a striking description of his decision to launch these campaigns in the Getica of Jordanes:

> Becoming aware of the frequent changes of [western] Roman Emperor, Euric, King of the Visigoths, pressed forward to seize Gaul on his own authority.

This extract captures rather well what it must have been like suddenly to realize that the time had come to pursue one's own aims with total independence. The correspondence of Sidonius Apollinaris likewise shows members of the Roman landowning elite of southern Gaul transferring their allegiance piecemeal to Euric's colours at much the same time: some had taken stock of the terminal decline of the Empire as early as the 460s; others, like Sidonius himself, did not accept the situation until the mid-470s. Euric's lead was followed at different times by the other interested parties.

The eastern Empire, for instance, abandoned any hope in the west when it made peace with the Vandals, probably in 474. As we have seen, Constantinople had previously viewed North Africa as the means of reinvigorating the western Empire. Making peace with the Vandals was thus a move of huge significance, signalling the end of attempts to sustain the west; diplomatic recognition as western emperor was subsequently granted to Julius Nepos, but he never received any practical assistance. That the western Empire had ceased to mean anything dawned on the Burgundians at more or less the same time. Gundobad, one of the heirs to the throne, played a major role in central politics in the early 470s; a close ally of Ricimer, he helped him defeat Anthemius, supported the subsequent regime of Olybrius, and, after Ricimer's death, even persuaded Glycerius to accept the throne in 473. Sometime in 473 or 474, however, he 'suddenly' (as one chronicler put it) left Rome. Possibly this was due to his father's death, or perhaps he just gave up the struggle; either way, he never bothered to return. Events at home were now much more important than those at the centre, which now, of course, was the centre no longer.

The army of Dalmatia made one final attempt to sponsor a regime when Julius Nepos marched into Italy in 474, but one year later he left again—definitively—in the face of the hostility of Orestes and the army of Italy. Fittingly, it was the army of Italy which was the last to give up. In 475, its commander Orestes proclaimed his son Romulus Emperor, but within a year lost control of his soldiers. Not surprisingly, given all the resources which had by now been seized by others, it was shortage of money which caused the unrest. Odovacar was able, therefore, to organize a putsch, murder Orestes, and depose Romulus Augustulus. He then sent an embassy to Constantinople which did no more than state the obvious: there was no longer any need for an emperor in the west. With this act, the Roman Empire in western Europe ceased to exist.

That the Huns and other outside, 'barbarian', groups were a fundamental cause of western imperial collapse is not a novel conclusion. The real contribution of this paper to scholarly debate, outside matters of detail, lies in three main lines of argument. First, the invasions of 376 and 405–8 were not unconnected events, but two particular moments of crisis generated by a single strategic revolution: the emergence of Hunnic power on the fringes of Europe. This was not a sudden event, but a protracted process, and the movements of the Huns provide a real unity and coherence to thirty-five years of instability and periodic invasion along Rome's European frontiers in the later fourth and early fifth centuries.

Second, while some sixty-five years separate the deposition of Romulus Augustulus from these invasions, they are, nonetheless, intimately linked. The regular crises for the Empire in intervening years represent no more than the slow working-out of the full political consequences of the invasions, with the events of 476 marking the culmination of the process whereby the after-effects of invasion steadily eroded the power of the western Roman state. The loss of territory to the invaders—sometimes sanctioned by treaty, sometimes not—meant a loss of revenue, and a consequent loss of power. As the state lost power, and was perceived to have done so, local Roman landowning elites came to the realization that their interests would best be served by making political accommodations with the outsiders, or, in a minority of cases, by taking independent responsibility for their own defence. Given that the Empire had existed for four hundred years, and that the east continued to prop up the west, it is not surprising that these processes of political erosion, and of psychological adjustment to the fact of erosion, took between two and three generations in the old Empire's heartlands of southern Gaul, Italy, and Spain (even if elites in other areas, such as Britain, were rather quicker off the mark). Despite the time-lag, the well-documented nature of these processes substantiates a very direct link between the period of the invasions and the collapse of the Empire. There was no separate additional crisis. Simply, the overwhelming consequences of the arrival, inside the body politic of the western Roman state, of new military forces, with independent political agendas, took time to exert their full effect.

A third line of argument has concerned the paradoxical role of the Huns in these revolutionary events. In the era of Attila, Hunnic armies surged across Europe from the Iron Gates of the Danube towards the walls of

Constantinople, the outskirts of Paris, and Rome itself. But Attila's decade of glory was no more than a sideshow in the drama of western collapse. The Huns' indirect impact upon the Roman Empire in previous generations, when the insecurity they generated in central and eastern Europe forced Goths, Vandals, Alans, Suevi, Burgundians across the frontier, was of much greater historical importance than Attila's momentary ferocities. Indeed, the Huns had even sustained the western Empire down to c. 440, and in many ways their second greatest contribution to imperial collapse was, as we have seen, themselves to disappear suddenly as a political force after 453, leaving the west bereft of outside military assistance.

I would like to finish by trying to place these lines of argument in broader historical perspective. Taken together, they indicate firmly, of course, that it was a foreign policy crisis which brought down the western Empire, and thus cast further fuel on long-raging fires of debate over whether it was internal or external factors which caused the fall of Rome. Indeed, there exists a vast secondary literature—what Peter Brown once labelled the 'sacred rhetoric'—which would argue precisely the opposite, seeing internal social, economic, and psychological developments as fully explaining imperial collapse. According to this view, the balance of power on the frontier was broken by progressive Roman enfeeblement, rather than by developments in areas beyond Rome's control.

Transformations within the Roman world must obviously be taken into account when we look at the ability of outside groups to create increasing mayhem inside its borders. Despite possible appearances, the argument of this paper is itself very far from monocausal, since internal and external factors obviously interrelate. On a very basic level, the economic, demographic and other resources of a society fundamentally explain its success or failure in the face of outside threat. If the Empire had a sufficiently large and wealthy population, it would have been able to resist even the new forces unleashed by the Huns. More particularly, as we have seen, the appearance of barbarian powers actually within the Empire's borders, in the fifth century, opened up a pre-existing fault line in the relationship between imperial centre and local Roman landowning elites. The centre relied on a mixture of constraint and reward to focus the loyalties of landowners, some of them many hundreds of miles distant, upon the Empire. The new barbarian powers of the fifth century undermined the ability of the Empire to prop up the position of its local supporters, to reward them, or even to constrain their loyalty. The Empire thus fell apart as local landowners found alternative methods to guarantee their elite status, making accommodations with the new powers in the land.

Even so, it remains very much to the point to ask a hypothetical question. What would have happened had barbarians not invaded the Empire en masse in the face of the Hunnic threat? Despite continued attempts of late to stress the importance of internal factors, there is still not the slightest sign that the Empire would have collapsed under its own weight. Indeed, a great body of recent (and not so recent) research in two separate areas would collectively support the contention of this paper, derived from a close examination of the sequence of events, that it was developments beyond, rather than within, the imperial frontier which upset the prevailing balance between Rome and its neighbours. There is no space here to deal with either fully, but brief summaries can at least set an agenda for further debate.

First, there have been substantial reappraisals of different aspects of the later Roman Empire, whose cumulative effect, to my mind, has been to overturn the 'sacred rhetoric'. The fourth-century Empire was not socially rigid, economically stagnant, culturally dead, or politically dislocated to an obviously greater degree than earlier Roman societies. Much, of course, was problematic about the late Roman world, but perfect societies exist only in historians' imaginations. Recent studies have revealed that there was no fundamental dislocation in the rural economy, the power-house of the Empire; that trade was flourishing in a far from demonetarized economy; and that local elites were participating in imperial structures in unprecedented numbers. Traditional classicists' prejudice has also given way—in some cases, at least—to a fuller appreciation of the cultural dynamism generated by the incorporation of Christianity within the existing political and social edifice.

On a second front, archaeological investigations have also revealed a total transformation in the nature of Germanic societies in the first three centuries or so AD. Causes are still a matter for debate, but agricultural output and economic sophistication both grew exponentially, generating in their wake profound social change. In particular, differentiation in status and wealth expanded markedly, creating much more pronounced social hierarchies. All this is consonant with the literary evidence, which shows the existence of much larger political entities and of real dynasties among at least some Germanic groups of the fourth century. Demonstrably true of Goths on the Danube, it also seems to be the case with the Franks and Alamanni of the Rhine frontier. Fourth-century Alamannic society threw up a succession of leaders with pre-eminent power—Chnodomarius, Vadomarius, and Macrianus being described as such by Ammianus—and Roman policy was precisely directed towards containing the threat they posed: kidnapping them at banquets being a preferred approach. These new, larger entities, as might be expected, acted more assertively towards the Roman state. In the aftermath of a Roman civil war, for instance, Chnodomarius actually attempted to annex Roman territory (and was matched in this by some Prankish groups), and the later 360s and early 370s saw both Alamannic and Gothic groups demand (and succeed in establishing) less subservient diplomatic relationships.

Taken together, these entirely separate areas of research suggest that any substantial change in the strategic balance of power was prompted by the growing strength and cohesion of Germanic groups, not the enfeeblement of the Roman Empire. Even so, the effects of those changes should not be overstated. Germanic groups were stronger in the fourth century; but when it came to direct confrontation, the Roman Empire was still overwhelmingly victorious in the vast majority of cases. And this, perhaps, finally allows us to bring the role of the Huns in the destruction of the western Empire into clear focus. Individually, the new Germanic powers were still no match for the Roman state in the fourth century. By themselves, they could generate some adjustment in relations along the frontiers, but were not about to pull the Empire apart. The most important effect of the Huns, therefore, was to make sufficient numbers of these new Germanic powers, which were not themselves politically united, act in a sufficiently similar way at broadly the same time. If ambition had prompted just one new dynast to invade the Empire on his own, his fate would have been the same as that of Chnodomarius, crushed by Julian at Strasbourg (or, indeed, of Radagaisus). The Huns, however, induced too many of these more substantial groups to cross the frontier in too short a space of time for the Roman state to be able to deal with them effectively. The balance of power on the frontier was already swinging away from the Empire, but only within a limited arc. By creating an accidental unity of purpose among Rome's neighbours, the Huns shattered frontier security, and set in motion processes which generated—out of unprecedented combinations of outside military power and existing local Roman elites—a new political order in western Europe.

Peter Heather teaches history at Worcester College, University of Oxford. He is the author of *The Fall of the Roman Empire: A New History of Rome and the Barbarians* (Oxford, 2005).

EXPLORING THE ISSUE

Were Internal Factors Responsible for the Fall of the Roman Empire?

Critical Thinking and Reflection

1. Examine the arguments given by both the internal and external selections in the Fall of the Roman Empire debate. Which selection presents the stronger argument? Critically discuss.
2. Do you think the Roman Empire could have fallen if only one of the factors mentioned in the selections was present? Defend your position either in a written statement or oral debate.
3. Develop a list of past empires that have fallen. Which ones come closest to the Roman Empire model? Critically analyze and respond.
4. Imagine that you were an adviser to the Roman Emperor. Develop a plan that would save the Empire from falling? Critically reflect and respond.
5. Investigate the theory put forth by the eighteenth century historian Edward Gibbon that the rise of Christianity may have played a role in Rome's demise. Critically analyze whether Gibbon presents a credible argument?
6. Historians today are beginning to compare the conditions that caused Rome's fall with conditions currently existing in the United States and its declining position as a world power. Critically examine this thesis and either defend or refute its claims.
7. Develop a blueprint for a contemporary empire that would last forever. Could this ever exist? Why or why not?

Is There Common Ground?

Since the internal/external theories are both recognized by all scholars, the question seems to be which elements had the greater effect on the Fall of Rome. Carefully read the claims in both the YES selection and the NO selection, looking for shared assumptions. What tips each author in one direction or the other? Another factor that should be considered is that in some instances, an empire has more control over its internal factors than it has over the external forces that may threaten it. On balance, do you see Rome being more threatened by internal or external factors?

A recent article by Bryan Ward-Perkins, "The End of the Roman Empire: Did it Collapse or Was it Transformed?" *History Today* (June 2005), presents two views. One summarizes the work of Peter Brown, who describes a period he names "Late Antiquity" that stretches from the third to the eighth century and that is characterized by "lively and positive developments"—a continuity argument. The other view reflects Bryan Ward-Perkins's own work and reaffirms the decline of "economic activity and the high living standards" of the Roman Empire—a discontinuity argument.

Perhaps, what is most remarkable is the length of time that, despite its many internal and external challenges, the Roman Empire endured.

Question: An equally relevant line of inquiry might be: What factors allowed this empire to exist and prosper for as long as it did? Perhaps common ground may be found in resolving this question.

Additional Resources

Both historians who contributed to this issue have written books on the subject: Adrian Goldworthy, *How Rome Fell: Death of a Superpower* (Yale University Press, 2009) and Peter Heather, *The Fall of the Roman Empire* (Macmillan, 2005). Both are contemporary and readable. Also an article in the English journal *History Today* by Bryan Ward-Perkins "The End of the Roman Empire: Did It Collapse or Was It Transformed? (June 2005) adds an interesting twist to the subject.

Despite its age, one should not ignore Gibbon's classic, *The History of the Decline and Fall of the Roman Empire*, recently reissued. Its lasting value is more evident today when scholars and politicians are currently debating the pros and cons of the "New American Empire."

There has been renewed interest in the role of the barbarians in this period. Many historians are now willing to credit them with helping to establish the Middle Ages, viewing that era as emerging from Greco-Roman, Christian, and barbarian influences. Perhaps it's time to put the term "barbarians" to rest. For more information on the barbarians and their contributions, see, Peter S. Wells, *The Barbarians Speak: How the Conquered Peoples Shaped the Roman Empire* (Princeton University Press, 1999), and, Richard Fletcher, *The Barbarian Conversion: From Paganism to Christianity* (Henry Holt and Company, 1997).

Internet References . . .

The Illustrated History of the Roman Empire

A multifaceted site that contains valuable information, some of it visual, on the Roman Empire in general and its decline and fall in particular.

www.roman-empire.net/

Unit II

UNIT

The Medieval/Renaissance Worlds

In this unit we find the world's civilizations building upon what the ancients created, struggling to survive in some cases and moving in new directions in other cases. During the Byzantine Empire of the sixth century, Justinian and Theodora ruled as Augusti. We have much evidence of their official history in the laws they instituted, the wars they fought, and the churches, convents, and monasteries they built. Surprisingly, a palace insider named Procopius was also writing a Secret History *that he planned to publish after the death of the sovereigns. Unfortunately for him, he died first. However, both his official accounts and his* Secret History *survive. How can we sort truth from bias?*

The Crusades took Christian knights to Jerusalem in what some are now calling a Holy War to reclaim the sacred sites of Christianity from the Muslims. We look at the motivations of these knights, what they hoped to gain, and how they conducted their crusades. And, we explore how contact with the Golden Age of learning in the Muslim world affected Europe. Did the return of Plato and Aristotle's writings, along with new scientific discoveries and new institutions, seed in Europe a rebirth of its own culture? With the explosion of creativity that we call the Renaissance, did highborn women experience a "rebirth" along with men, or were the freedoms they had enjoyed during the Middle Ages restricted?

After centuries of success, the Maya civilization in Mesoamerica collapsed. Was the environment no longer able to sustain it? Did wars overextend the available resources? On the steppes of Central Asia, a poor, fatherless boy rose to become the ruler of an empire. A revisionist historian takes a fresh look at the progressive ideas of Genghis Khan. Zen Buddhism came to Japan and mingled with the long history of the Samurai warrior and its Bushido Code of honor and service. China undertook extensive maritime adventures that paralleled those of Christopher Columbus, before abruptly halting them and turning inward. Why? We explore possible explanations.

Selected, Edited, and with Issue Framing Material by:
Helen Buss Mitchell, *Howard Community College*
and
Joseph R. Mitchell, *Howard Community College*

ISSUE

Did the Byzantine Empire Benefit from the Rule of Justinian and Theodora?

YES: Paolo Cesaretti, from *Theodora: Empress of Byzantium*, trans. Rosanna M. Giammanco Frongia (Transworld Publishers, 2002)

NO: Procopius, from *Procopius of Caesarea: The Secret History*, trans. Richard Atwater (P. Covici and Covici Friede, 1927)

Learning Outcomes

After reading this issue you should be able to:

- Understand the evolution of Constantinople (now Istanbul) as a fortress city that straddles Europe and Asia.
- Describe the personal and political partnership of Justinian and Theodora who referred to themselves as Augusti (plural of Augustus and modeled on titles in the Roman Empire).
- Explain the difficulty of finding the "truth" in Procopius's two historical accounts—one public, the other secret.

ISSUE SUMMARY

YES: Professor of Byzantine Studies, Paolo Cesaretti, argues for a balanced view of the accomplishments of Justinian and Theodora in the Byzantine Empire of the sixth century.

NO: Procopius, a contemporary of the Byzantine rulers, argues in a "secret history" that their rule was marked by personal and administrative failings.

Accurate and reliable historical accounts depend on good sources. In this issue we confront the dilemma posed by an "insider's" account that was kept secret by its author and that contrasts sharply with published historical accounts by the same author. Which more accurately reflects reality—the open or the secret history of the Byzantine Empire, both written by Procopius?

The Roman Emperor Constantine had established an eastern capital on the strait of Bosporus, where Europe and Asia meet, in 330. Endowed with his name, Constantinople was a fortress city, built to repel attacks from land and sea. After the fall of Rome and the elevation of a Germanic ruler in 476, power within the empire shifted to the eastern capital, which had been built on the ancient Greek city of Byzantium. The Byzantine emperors claimed succession from their counterparts in ancient Rome, and their Christian Empire preserved both the brilliance of Greek culture and the administrative genius of the Romans.

Justinian, who had been groomed by his uncle Justin I, became emperor in 527. He codified the laws of ancient Rome, preserving principles of reason and justice. However, he did press Justin to amend the law forbidding a patrician to marry an actress, when he fell in love with Theodora, a former actress who would become the empress. Byzantine emperors claimed divine right of sovereignty, and the emperor had a quasi-priestly role in some religious services. Justinian and Theodora used the ancient Roman term, referring to themselves as Augusti (plural of Augustus), the absolute rulers of Byzantium.

Under the leadership of his able general Belisarius, Justinian reclaimed North Africa from the Vandals, part of southern Spain from the Visigoths, and most of Italy from the Ostrogoths. Procopius was advisor to Belisarius, accompanying the general on many military campaigns. His eight-volume *History of the Wars* is ambitious, adopting a sophisticated tone of impartiality and hinting at criticisms of the royal sovereigns. A later commentary *On the Buildings* was filled with praise for the emperor, as builder of magnificent sacred and secular edifices.

The *Secret History*, begun at the same time as his published works (in the 550s), was intended by Procopius to be published after the death of Justinian. Unfortunately for Procopius, he predeceased his emperor. The *Secret History* purports to be the history of "what really happened," and Procopius fears that disparities between this work and the public ones might cause future generations to "think me a writer of fiction." Both the Augusti are portrayed in the *Secret History* as ambitious, cruel, arrogant, and two-faced. He presents "evidence" that both were "fiends" in the literal sense of demonically driven. Little wonder then that he feared discovery of this work would merit him "a most horrible death."

Whatever else it might be, the rule of Justinian and Theodora is also a love story. From her humble and unsavory beginnings, Theodora rose to become the partner of her husband Justinian, during one of the most interesting chapters in the history of the Byzantine Empire. Procopius's *Secret History* is available in English translation on the Internet, as are his published works on the wars and buildings. All were written after Theodora's death in 548.

Even to Procopius's jaundiced eye, she was beautiful and clever. When Belisarius took back Italy, a western capital was established at Ravenna, in northeastern Italy. In the church of San Vitale, built during the sixth century, mosaics of Justinian and his entourage cover the left wall of the sanctuary, while mosaics of Theodora and her attendants cover the right. Each appears to be offering the priest one of the elements that will be used in the mass—the bread and the wine. What this church (one of many that the Augusti built) reveals most clearly is their full partnership as rulers of an empire. Most histories of Western art will have photos of these magnificent purple, green, and gold portraits, created from drawings the royal couple posed for in Constantinople.

Omitted from this issue, but very prominent during the age of Justinian and Theodora was the Monophysite Controversy. In the early centuries of Christianity, councils met at Nicea and Chalcedon to establish the doctrine of the Trinity (that God is three persons in one nature or essence) and that Jesus had a dual nature—fully God and fully human. These became the doctrinal positions of the Christian Church.

Theodora, like many people of her time and place, followed the Monophysites who contended that Jesus had a single, divine nature. Justinian held the Orthodox dual-nature position most of his life, but converted to Monophysitism, long after Theodora's death and shortly before his own. Each of the Augusti built churches and established monasteries and convents for followers of their version of Christianity. Neither appeared to pressure the other to change—a further example of a very egalitarian marriage. For more on this controversy, see W.H.C. Frend, *The Rise of the Monophysite Movement: Chapters in the History of the Church in the Fifth and Sixth Centuries* (Cambridge University Press, 1972).

Virtually all biographies of Justinian and Theodora, as well as histories of the Byzantine Empire of this period, have relied on Procopius's "secret" first-hand account, at least since 1623 when it was found in the Vatican Library and published for the first time. Professor Cesaretti quotes extensively from Procopius, although he offers a balanced portrayal of both Justinian and Theodora.

And, Procopius is the source for Theodora's dramatic speech, during the Nika rebellion. As events unfold in the Hippodrome, where the Blue and Green factions contend in chariot races, imagine 100,000 people engrossed in, sometimes, 24 races in a single day, interspersed with wild animal acts. Theodora's father had been a bear trainer and her early life in the theater was probably by necessity rather than choice. Even the children of her family had to work in order to put food on the family table.

As you read these two accounts, one of the most basic questions to ask yourself is this: Is it ever possible to have an "unbiased" historical account? Perhaps, we might begin with the areas in which even Procopius is willing to praise the Augusti. Magnificent churches, for example, remain as testimony to their vision and commitment to faith. And, there are other sources that describe aspects of the reign of Justinian and Theodora.

Would we be willing to have future generations rely on tabloid journalism or gossip columnists for the "truth" about famous people? Do multiple biographies increase our chances of discerning what actually occurred and who the biographical subjects actually were during their lifetimes? Procopius is a primary source. To what extent is he a trustworthy one?

YES

Paolo Cesaretti

Theodora: Empress of Byzantium

Like every great story, the events of the Nika rebellion have been told an infinite number of times; each retelling prompts new interpretations and debates. . . . The Nika rebellion actually sprung from the grass roots of society, and it was prompted not by nostalgia for the past but by present needs; as was always the case in Constantinople, the truth was a complex mosaic of elements.

Some dignitaries of the empire had already likened Justinian to a sea monster that sucked up water and money. Others criticized his policies regarding the many nomadic tribes that moved along the dangerous borders of the empire from the Danube to Arabia: he had purchased their nonbelligerence at too high a price, they said. Even Khosrow I, the new king of Persia, demanded gold before he would consider the possibility of peace along the eastern frontier. In addition, the emperor's imitation of God did not seem to be particularly welcome "in the high heavens." The tragic Antioch earthquake of 526 was followed by a second one in 528. In 530, yet another earthquake had shaken Antioch's historical rival, Laodikeia, one of the best ports of the Levant and the capital of the new province of Theodorias (recently established in honor of Theodora Augusta).

The two sovereigns had dug deep into the imperial coffers to help with post-earthquake reconstruction, displaying dedication and generosity, but their actions had not served to dispel concerns and suspicions aroused by the behavior of some of their closest collaborators. It was rumored, for example, that the jurist Tribonian, who supervised the great project of rewriting the body of laws and was quaestor of the sacred palace (a sort of minister of justice), "was always ready to sell justice for gain." The perception of judicial disarray enraged the masses, who were already bitter about John the Cappadocian's fiscal policies. Capping a swift series of promotions, John had become praetorian prefect of the East, the most influential of ministers. Justinian relied heavily on his skills, and for ten years, from 531 to 541, John exerted great power throughout the empire.

John the Cappadocian did not have a classical education, but he knew accounting very well. Justinian expected him to generate the income, or the savings, which he needed to pursue his "Great Idea" of renewal and restoration, and John met his expectations. He made sure that fiscal laws were obeyed. He supervised the landowners, the merchants, and the shopkeepers. Revenues were routed directly to him by his inspectors, instead of passing through the provincial élites, the curiae, as they once had. John the Cappadocian was pivotal in the process of centralization required by Justinian's plan. A manager with a sharp eye for cutting costs, John reduced and even eliminated part of the postal service, which is the essential glue of any polity. The post had been among the empire's traditional glories—one of the services that set the Roman civilized world "of the thousand cities" apart from the "barbarian" no-man's-lands.

. . . The public post not only guaranteed speedy communications, but also affected the supply of all kinds of raw materials and staples. The results of its elimination were disastrous for rural industry, a productive base that contributed food and tax revenue to the empire. The owners of large estates, who had been accustomed to "sell[ing] their excess crops," now saw "their crops rotting on their hands and going to waste." The small landowners bore the brunt of the new situation, since they supplied the city markets. Unable to afford the cost of private transportation, the farmers (both men and women) trudged along the roads of the empire carrying their crops on their backs. . . . Overcome by fatigue, many lay down and died on the road. Others abandoned their crops and moved to the city, trusting in some form of Providence, whether divine or imperial.

When the food supply is irregular, life gets harder in a capital over-crowded with mouths to feed. Besides, hungry people talk. . . . And so before long John the Cappadocian was being blamed on moral and Christian grounds, instead of being judged simply by bureaucratic or political criteria. It was rumored that he was an evil man who kept Roman citizens in secret chambers, forcing them to pay taxes he claimed were overdue by threatening them with the same humiliating torture inflicted on slaves or highway robbers. All this, to channel money into Justinian's coffers. Or was it for personal gain?—some swore that John embezzled most of the taxes that the citizens believed they were contributing to the welfare of the empire.

The slanderous rumors intensified: John was getting rich; John was a drunk; John had an infamous retinue of jesters and prostitutes both male and female; he was a heathen who pretended to say Christian prayers while actually reciting magical pagan formulas. The rumors and accusations were not so different from those that once circulated about Theodora. In time, John and the empress would grow to be enemies, but they were both victims (for different reasons) of hostile preconceptions among those who considered themselves decent and upright citizens.

Because the factions were so active in the Hippodrome, that place became a natural sounding board for economic and political tensions. After the violent urban riots of 523–24, after Justinian's arbitrary protection of the Blue radical fringe, the Greens had even chanted:

> Would that Sabbatius [Justinian's father] had never been born! That he might not have a murderer [Justinian] for a son!

The year 532 began with new trouble between the Blues and the Greens. Now focused on military issues in the west, Justinian ordered that the situation be brought under control with the same measures he had used in 524 against *his* Blues; such measures were now to be applied impartially to the extremists of both factions. Eudaemon, the city prefect, ordered the militia to arrest anyone engaged in violence, no matter what faction they belonged to. The Greens saw this as a continuation of the unjustified persecution of their group, while the Blues felt betrayed by their longtime patron, especially when they heard that the investigations and arrests were culminating in death sentences for members of *both* factions. Four rebel leaders, both Green and Blue, were sentenced to be hanged.

The scaffold where the sentences were carried out was in Sykae (Galata), beyond the Golden Horn, in a square near one of the many monasteries where religious men tried to merge heavenly and earthly life through prayer and exercise, without meddling in politics. Tensions were running high, and the hangman's hand was unsteady: two of the prisoners, one Blue and one Green, survived the first attempt. The noose was wound more tightly, but the two men fell from the scaffold still alive. Shouting, the public proclaimed it a miracle, a sign of God's favor.

With the help of the nearby monks, the two prisoners were ferried over to the city and brought to a church that had the right of asylum. Eudaemon stationed a circle of militiamen around the edifice, while the crowd demanded freedom for the two men who had been saved by the hand of God. It was Saturday, January 10, 532.

A few days later, Tuesday, January 13, was a day for the emperor to preside over chariot races at the Hippodrome. Both factions took the floor: the spokesman for the Greens talked with devout respect, but the Blues' spokesman had a more colloquial tone. They both asked for pardons, but Justinian rejected their pleas with the customary arrogance of the potentate who receives a supplication. He may have wanted to show how firm he was, but his stubbornness seemed unjustified and arrogant more than authoritative.

After twenty-two chariot races, the short winter day was coming to a close. It was then that an unheard-of, new shout rose from the Hippodrome crowd:

> Long live the benevolent Greens and Blues!

It was shocking to hear the two names pronounced together: never before had one faction recognized the other's "benevolence" or humanity (*philanthropia*). Indeed, this virtue had always been considered a uniquely imperial prerogative. So here was a brand-new situation: the established power no longer appeared to be completely sacred.

For their part, the emperors of the past had always set the factions against each other so as to avoid potentially threatening coalitions. They simply applied the divide-and-conquer strategy learned from that ancient Roman culture whose glory Justinian sought to renew. But now events were conspiring against him. His great vision of the Mediterranean scenario had neglected some essential elements of the urban scene right under his nose. Meanwhile, the Greens and Blues were setting aside their reciprocal hostility and turning jointly against the palace. Maybe it was good medicine for healing the "disease of the soul" that affected them.

Justinian's ears ("donkey ears," according to his critics) heard the acclamation that was being shouted over and over, louder and louder. It rose like thunder, shouted by tens of thousands of voices. The emperor, the "Chosen One," could not bear it. He left the Kathisma and retreated to the sacred palace, the glorious public institution that was also his personal haven.

Now a new shout was heard in the Hippodrome, terrifying in its brevity:

> *Nika! Nika! Nika!*

"May you win! May you win! May you win!" *Nika* was the Greek version of the Latin *Tu vincas,* the cheer from the crowds that usually greeted the Augustus in his role as military chief. The crowd's change of language signaled a change in meaning. The phrase no longer exhorted the emperor to prevail over an enemy; now one faction was exhorting the other, one citizen wishing another, "may *you* be victorious!" Thus, the emperor was no longer "benevolent" and "humane" or "victorious." Strengthened by its size and its everyday language, the crowd had seized those prerogatives for itself, without any partisan distinctions. Being able to speak out meant being able to act.

The emperor did not lower himself to a verbal confrontation, for it would have meant recognizing the opposing party. Just as Asterius gave no answer when the little girls pleaded with him in the Kynêgion years before, the prefect Eudaemon, who was in charge of public order, gave no answer to the crowds that flocked to his palace to hear the fate of the two men who had survived the hanging. His refusal was the legendary straw that broke the camel's back. The crowd went on a rampage: it killed soldiers and officers, set fire to the prefecture, and threw open the jail doors. The factions joined against one common enemy, one oppressor: Eudaemon. (Ironically, the Greek root of his name refers to happiness.)

Then the crowd attacked the doors of the sacred palace. The elegant and decorative guards were not warriors: they put up no opposition. The crowd set fire to the palace vestibule (the Chalkê), to the senate building, and to the basilica of the Holy wisdom (Hagia Sophia). These were some of the most distinctive building of Constantine's city: the palatial symbol of power; the home of the senate that had raised up the second Rome to equal the first; and the church that kept the city under God's protection were all lost in a single night of fire. . . .

On Sunday, January 18, the emperor made an appearance in the imperial box at the Hippodrome. In his hands he reportedly carried the Gospel, and in his mind must have been two political, personal precedents. The first was from the time of the civilian uprising against Anastasius. In response to his critics, Anastasius had provocatively appeared in public without the imperial crown and invited the arena to choose a new monarch. Taken by surprise, the crowd did nothing but reconfirm his position and their trust in him. The second precedent was from Easter 527, when for the first time Justinian had blessed the crowd as the Augustus.

As he had done on that occasion, he now assumed a priestly role. Then he made himself into a sacrificial lamb, saying, "I forgive you the offense you have committed against me. I shall order no arrests as long as calm returns. You are not to blame for what happened. I am, for my sins." . . . [T]he Christian reference to his sins backfired, for the crowd grasped his weakness. . . . The jeering grew, and the emperor began descending the stairs of the Kathisma. The doors closed behind him, hiding him again in the protective shell of his palace. Instead of a possible arbiter and moderator in the dispute between ministers and factions, he had become an enemy, the greatest enemy. . . .

The right gesture might be taken as a sign, so Justinian's secret council considered all kinds of possible actions. A "true Roman male" in ancient times—even someone as abominable as Nero—would have killed himself to save his honor, but suicide was an unsuitable choice for a Christian. Flight seemed to be the only option left. The southern coast of the Black Sea (or Pontos Euxeinos) offered a safe haven, with lands and palaces still faithful to the crown. This would be a good temporary solution, a fine place from which to later recapture the city. But Justinian knew his ancient history, and he knew that such a solution was rarely successful.

Like a great ship, the *restitutio* seemed to have run aground even before setting sail; the restoration seemed to be sunk, and it looked as if the Augusti would never reach their glorious destination. But a real boat was at the palace quay, waiting to take the sovereigns on a far shorter crossing, to safety.

At this point—according to Procopius, who probably got an eyewitness account from Belisarius—Theodora stepped in. Her speech to the emperor's secret council is the longest one of hers ever recorded, and while her biographer may have polished it and added erudite allusions to suit his rhetorical purpose, it remains unique. It may not reflect the actual form of speech, but it testifies to Theodora's intentions and her logical argument. She took the floor before the highest dignitaries of the empire and said:

> As to the belief that a woman ought not to be daring among men or to assert herself boldly among those who are holding back from fear, I consider that the present crisis most certainly does not permit us to discuss whether the matter should be regarded in this or in some other way.
>
> For in the case of those whose interests have come into the greatest danger nothing else seems best except to settle the issue immediately before them in the best possible way.
>
> My opinion then is that the present time, above all others, is inopportune for flight, even though it bring safety.
>
> For while it is impossible for a man who has seen the light not also to die, for one who has been an emperor it is unendurable to be a fugitive. May I never be separated from this purple, and may I not live that day on which those who meet me shall not address me as mistress.
>
> If, now, it is your wish to save yourself, O Emperor, there is no difficulty. For we have much money, and there is the sea, here the boats. However, consider whether it will not come about after you have been saved that you would gladly exchange that safety for death.
>
> For as for myself, I approve a certain ancient saying that royalty is a good burial-shroud.

She was not speaking in abstractions, in general statements for the whole group; she spoke to Justinian, her preferred interlocutor. She looked only into the eyes of God's "Chosen One." The other characters had suddenly fallen to the back of the stage; they were mere extras, and the close-up was now on the two rulers.

They were separated from the group, and Theodora—in a move worthy of an Attic tragedy—separated her destiny from that of the emperor. The emperor could save himself if he chose: there was no dearth of money, the sea was open, the ships were ready to welcome whoever wanted to flee. But Theodora saw flight not as salvation but as a "second death," in the words of the Gospel—a fate even worse than death.

She was accustomed to defying the world's customs and conventions: she would not run. Should Justinian choose to retreat, she would not share his fate; he would prove himself unworthy of the throne. In spite of his ego, his studies of antiquity, even his concept of messianic power, he might choose to flee, doing something that no Roman emperor had ever considered suitable or possible. *She* would remain faithful to her purple. She would carry on the traditions of antiquity, in the present, in her deeds—not just in words, not just in plans for the future. She would do so by resisting, even dying, because there was no life without the purple cloak of power. To avoid being separated from her purple, Theodora was saying, she was even willing to lose Justinian and marry death instead, to choose the purple over the man who had granted it to her.

Belisarius entered the Hippodrome from the western gate, which had direct access to the Blues's section; Mundus and his men used the entrance ominously called the "Deadman's Gate." The large crowd assembled in the huge arena was armed with only primitive weapons and it could not resist the two select corps of military professionals. A ferocious slaughter ensued; this was perhaps the bloodiest Sunday of the first Christian millennium.

The palace guard, which had been hesitating between the rebels and the legitimate ruler, opened the doors of the imperial gallery and easily captured the frightened Hypatius and his followers, including his brother Pompeius. There was no resistance.

The uprising was defined as a crime of high treason, which was punished by beheading. The rebels were immediately led before the emperor. Hypatius told Justinian that he had given him proof in writing of his fealty.

"Your message never reached us," was the answer.

He added that he had been forced to act under duress.

"But you did not have to wait such a long time to show your loyalty to the emperor."

At this point Hypatius began begging for his life.

Since the two men knew each other well, the emperor was inclined to spare Hypatius in a generous act of clemency. Justinian may have thought about all the Christian blood had already been shed that day; he may have considered the lofty concept of "benevolence" that the rebels had wanted to grab away from the emperor. And, of course, he may have recalled the recent blame over his treatment of Vitalian. He was not eager to hear the same accusations again in the future.

Just as in the previous council, when debating between resistance and fight, the emperor's thinking was worlds away from the blunt realism of the daughter of the Hippodrome. She knew the arena habitat all too well. Theodora knew that a wounded beast has to be killed immediately.

Letting the two brothers live would be seen as proof of weakness, she argued; it would undermine the continuity of power, dim the splendor of the emperor's majesty, and rekindle the conspiracies. A few hours earlier, the emperor had appeared before the rebels with the Gospels in his hand–and what had been the result? Theodora insisted that the law be applied. She disregarded her family ties to Hypatius and Pompeius (through her daughter, who had married into the house of Anastasius). Theodora put aside her private life and reacted to public events. And in one stroke she implicitly shifted Justinian's personal, private position: from that moment on, he had to acknowledge that *he* owed his purple to *her.*

Like a meridian, Easter Day, 542, marked fifteen years of Justinian and Theodora's reign. They must have reviewed a list of their accomplishments and of the other initiatives still in the planning stage or already under construction, from the most remote borders of the empire to the heart of Constantinople. After the destruction wrought by the Nika rebellion, they had completely rebuilt Constantinople in just ten years, transforming it from a city of late antiquity into an imperial capital. A jewel of the Byzantine age, it was to be admired by medieval visitors from both West and East (the Slavs called it Tsargrad), raided by invaders in the second millennium (the Crusaders first, then the Ottoman Turks), and celebrated by poets such as W. B. Yeats. All of this made Constantinople a universal city of the soul. None of this would have transpired without Theodora's unforgettable speech on that bloody Sunday in 532, in the midst of the raging rebellion.

The emperors' architectural and urban planning policy did not aim to revive the art of previous centuries. Constantine's and Theodosius's achievements inspired Justinian's politics, but their art and architecture did not inspire his. The Augusti leaned toward the new and the grandiose, fusing classical elements with oriental seduction, three-dimensional naturalism with geometric abstraction, urban tradition with Christian touches; they even indulged in personal whims. They rediscovered the daring, insouciant, lighthearted quality that had blessed their early years together, the boldness of those intricate laws that seemed to be written for everyone but were really conceived only for the two of them. They were inimitable. There were no other comparable patrons of art and architecture until the Renaissance.

After the Nika—which was a political phenomenon that impacted the urban fabric—Justinian and Theodora focused on secular architecture, starting with a redefinition of the facade of power: the facade of the palace. They totally redesigned the vestibule, the Chalkê or "bronze house" (a little building with a golden bronze roof). From the palace, the Chalkê opened onto the imperial square (the Augustaeum), with access to the basilica of the Holy Wisdom—the celebrated Hagia Sophia. The Chalkê was the visual threshold of power, its projection upon the city. After the fires of the rebellion, Justinian and Theodora set out to make the new incarnation of the Chalkê more splendid and precious. So the interior of the new dome was decorated with mosaics celebrating Belisarius's victories over the Vandals and the Goths. Nearby were the baths of Zeuxippus and the Senate palace; they were also destroyed in the flames of 532. Now they were rebuilt "in more beautiful form" than before.

But the emperor and empress did not stop here. They had inherited a complex metropolis with an urban administration and police force of more than a thousand men. This required premises for the supply and management of food staples and the channeling of water through aqueducts that still astonish us fifteen hundred years later. Like the ancient provincial benefactors of the earliest pagan tradition (the "Euergeti"), the two emperors undertook other initiatives "for the welfare of their subjects." Some, like the hospitals and almshouses, were Christian institutions; but the porticoed streets, roads, and cisterns were secular public works that stand to this day as masterpieces of ancient architecture (the Basilike Cistern is one shining example). The rulers who commissioned them, and the skilled engineers and architects, both knew how to "enhance the monumental significance even of those buildings that had a purely functional purpose." Edward Gibbon was wrong to disparage this period: it was not a time dominated simply "by the darkest shadows of shame." . . .

The Augusti intended the church of the Holy Apostles to be their final resting place; they poured their deepest feelings into the church of Saints Sergius and Bacchus; but their pride and joy—especially the emperor's—was the Holy Wisdom. Fifteen hundred years after it was built, after acting as a mosque and then a museum, it is still among the most famous and admired buildings in the world—though, paradoxically, it is famous for what it was *not* meant to be: an architectural space, a temple of light, the final wonder of Christian antiquity.

Medieval visitors might have come closest to the spirit of the place since they recognized Constantinople as the Mother of all cities. Admiring the Holy Wisdom, they found renewed faith in Paradise; they were surrounded by objects, colors, visions, and scents (lost to us now) that they perceived as promises and prefigurations. If the city rebuilt by the emperor and the empress in the light of Christianity was a sacred shell, then the Holy Wisdom was its pearl. It was the most visible, most flaunted treasure of Justinian and Theodora.

The two rulers used the Holy Wisdom to express their power fully. They were not building but *re*building a city that had risen against them. They wanted the result to be a total redemption, a gesture of great daring that would fully display their personal and institutional arrogance. Perhaps because of this, there is no great church less mystical than the Holy Wisdom. It was not meant to be the church of a monastic order or a district or a guild, nor was it built by an individual suppliant. It was the basilica where the emperor of Constantinople, the thirteenth apostle, the Viceroy of Christ on Earth, the highest, noblest man of all, attended sacred ceremonies. In the symmetrical, inverted projection of roles between imperial Constantinople and papal Rome, the only worthy comparison is the basilica of Saint Peter's at the time of the universalist popes of the Renaissance.

Paolo Cesaretti is professor of Byzantine studies at the University of Chieti, Italy, and the author of many books on Byzantine art and architecture.

Procopius

Procopius of Caesarea: The Secret History

Character and Appearance of Justinian

As soon as he took over the rule from his uncle, his measure was to spend the public money without restraint, now that he had control of it. He gave much of it to the Huns who, from time to time, entered the state; and in consequence the Roman provinces were subject to constant incursions, for these barbarians, having once tasted Roman wealth, never forgot the road that led to it. And he threw much money into the sea in the form of moles, as if to master the eternal roaring of the breakers. For he jealously hurled stone breakwaters far out from the mainland against the onset of the sea, as if by the power of wealth he could outmatch the might of ocean.

He gathered to himself the private estates of Roman citizens from all over the Empire: some by accusing their possessors of crimes of which they were innocent, others by juggling their owners' words into the semblance of a gift to him of their property. And many, caught in the act of murder and other crimes, turned their possessions over to him and thus escaped the penalty for their sins.

Others, fraudulently disputing title to lands happening to adjoin their own, when they saw they had no chance of getting the best of the argument, with the law against them, gave him their equity in the claim so as to be released from court. Thus, by a gesture that cost him nothing, they gained his favor and were able illegally to get the better of their opponents.

I think this is as good a time as any to describe the personal appearance of the man. Now in physique he was neither tall nor short, but of average height; not thin, but moderately plump; his face was round, and not bad looking, for he had good color, even when he fasted for two days. To make a long description short, he much resembled Domitian, Vespasian's son. He was the one whom the Romans so hated that even tearing him into pieces did not satisfy their wrath against him. . . .

Now such was Justinian in appearance; but his character was something I could not fully describe. For he was at once villainous and amenable; as people say colloquially, a moron. He was never truthful with anyone, but always guileful in what he said and did, yet easily hoodwinked by any who wanted to deceive him. His nature was an unnatural mixture of folly and wickedness. What in olden times a peripatetic philosopher said was also true of him, that opposite qualities combine in a man as in the mixing of colors. I will try to portray him, however, insofar as I can fathom his complexity.

This Emperor, then, was deceitful, devious, false, hypocritical, two-faced, cruel, skilled in dissembling his thought, never moved to tears by either joy or pain, though he could summon them artfully at will when the occasion demanded, a liar always, not only offhand, but in writing, and when he swore sacred oaths to his subjects in their very hearing. Then he would immediately break his agreements and pledges, like the vilest of slaves, whom indeed only the fear of torture drives to confess their perjury. A faithless friend, he was a treacherous enemy, insane for murder and plunder, quarrelsome and revolutionary, easily led to anything evil, but never willing to listen to good counsel, quick to plan mischief and carry it out, but finding even the hearing of anything good distasteful to his ears.

How could anyone put Justinian's ways into words? These and many even worse vices were disclosed in him as in no other mortal nature seemed to have taken the wickedness of all other men combined and planted it in this man's soul. And besides this, he was too prone to listen to accusations; and too quick to punish. For he decided such cases without full examination, naming the punishment when he had heard only the accuser's side of the matter. Without hesitation he wrote decrees for the plundering of countries, sacking of cities, and slavery of whole nations, for no cause whatever. So that if one wished to take all the calamities which had befallen the Romans before this time and weigh them against his crimes, I think it would be found that more men had been murdered by this single man than in all previous history.

He had no scruples about appropriating other people's property, and did not even think any excuse necessary, legal or illegal, for confiscating what did not belong to him. And when it was his, he was more than ready to squander it in insane display, or give it as an unnecessary bribe to the barbarians. In short, he neither held on to any money himself nor let anyone else keep any: as if his reason were not avarice, but jealousy of those who had riches. Driving all wealth from the country of the Romans in this manner, he became the cause of universal poverty.

Now this was the character of Justinian, so far as I can portray it.

From *Secret History,* 1927. (Chicago: Covici Friede, 1927; reprinted at University of Michigan Press, 1961).

How Theodora, Most Depraved of All Courtesans, Won His Love

He took a wife: and in what manner she was born and bred, and, wedded to this man, tore up the Roman Empire by the very roots, I shall now relate.

Acacius was the keeper of wild beasts used in the amphitheater in Constantinople; he belonged to the Green faction and was nicknamed the Bearkeeper. This man, during the rule of Anastasius, fell sick and died, leaving three daughters named Comito, Theodora and Anastasia: of whom the eldest was not yet seven years old. His widow took a second husband, who with her undertook to keep up Acacius's family and profession. But Asterius, the dancing master of the Greens, on being bribed by another removed this office from them and assigned it to the man who gave him the money. For the dancing masters had the power of distributing such positions as they wished.

When this woman saw the populace assembled in the amphitheater, she placed laurel wreaths on her daughters' heads and in their hands, and sent them out to sit on the ground in the attitude of suppliants. The Greens eyed this mute appeal with indifference; but the Blues were moved to bestow on the children an equal office, since their own animal-keeper had just died.

When these children reached the age of girlhood, their mother put them on the local stage, for they were fair to look upon. . . .

. . . Now Theodora was still too young to know the normal relation of man with maid, but consented to the unnatural violence of villainous slaves who, following their masters to the theater, employed their leisure in this infamous manner. And for some time in a brothel she suffered such misuse.

But as soon as she arrived at the age of youth, and was now ready for the world, her mother put her on the stage. Forthwith, she became a courtesan, and such as the ancient Greeks used to call a common one, at that: for she was not a flute or harp player, nor was she even trained to dance, but only gave her youth to anyone she met, in utter abandonment. Her general favors included, of course, the actors in the theater; and in their productions she took part in the low comedy scenes. For she was very funny and a good mimic, and immediately became popular in this art. There was no shame in the girl, and no one ever saw her dismayed: no role was too scandalous for her to accept without a blush. . . .

Thus was this woman born and bred, and her name was a byword beyond that of other common wenches on the tongues of all men.

But when she came back to Constantinople, Justinian fell violently in love with her. At first he kept her only as a mistress, though he raised her to patrician rank. Through him Theodora was able immediately to acquire an unholy power and exceedingly great riches. She seemed to him the sweetest thing in the world, and like all lovers, he desired to please his charmer with every possible favor and requite her with all his wealth. The extravagance added fuel to the flames of passion. With her now to help spend his money he plundered the people more than ever, not only in the capital, but throughout the Roman Empire. As both of them had for a long time been of the Blue party, they gave this faction almost complete control of the affairs of state. . . .

How Justinian Created a New Law Permitting Him to Marry a Courtesan

Now as long as the former Empress was alive, Justinian was unable to find a way to make Theodora his wedded wife. In this one matter she opposed him as in nothing else. . . . But finally her death removed this obstacle to Justinian's desire.

Justin, doting and utterly senile, was now the laughing stock of his subjects . . . but Justinian they all served with considerable awe. His hand was in everything, and his passion for turmoil created universal consternation.

It was then that he undertook to complete his marriage with Theodora. But as it was impossible for a man of senatorial rank to make a courtesan his wife, this being forbidden by ancient law, he made the Emperor nullify this ordinance by creating a new one, permitting him to wed Theodora, and consequently making it possible for anyone else to marry a courtesan. Immediately after this he seized the power of the Emperor, veiling his usurpation with a transparent pretext: for he was proclaimed colleague of his uncle as Emperor of the Romans by the questionable legality of an election inspired by terror.

So Justinian and Theodora ascended the imperial throne three days before Easter, a time, indeed, when even making visits or greeting one's friends is forbidden. And not many days later Justin died of an illness, after a reign of nine years. Justinian was now sole monarch, together, of course, with Theodora.

Thus it was that Theodora, though born and brought up as I have related, rose to royal dignity over all obstacles. For no thought of shame came to Justinian in marrying her, though he might have taken his pick of the noblest born, most highly educated, most modest, carefully nurtured, virtuous and beautiful virgins of all the ladies in the whole Roman Empire: a maiden, as they say, with upstanding breasts. Instead, he preferred to make his own what had been common to all men, alike, careless of all her revealed history, took in wedlock a woman who was not only guilty of every other contamination but boasted of her many abortions.

I need hardly mention any other proof of the character of this man: for all the perversity of his soul was completely displayed in this union; which alone was ample interpreter, witness, and historian of his shamelessness. For when a man once disregards the disgrace of his actions and is willing to brave the contempt of society, no path of lawlessness is thereafter taboo to him; but with unflinching countenance he advances, easily and without a scruple, to acts of the deepest infamy.

However, not a single member of even the Senate, seeing this disgrace befalling the State, dared to complain or forbid the event; but all of them bowed down before her as if she were a goddess. Nor was there a priest who showed any resentment, but all hastened to greet her as Highness. And the populace who had seen her before on the stage, directly raised its hands to proclaim itself her slave in fact and in name. Nor did any soldier grumble at being ordered to risk the perils of war for the benefit of Theodora: nor was there any man on earth who ventured to oppose her.

Confronted with this disgrace, they all yielded, I suppose, to necessity, for it was as if Fate were giving proof of its power to control mortal affairs as malignantly as it pleases: showing that its decrees need not always be according to reason or human propriety. Thus does Destiny sometimes raise mortals suddenly to lofty heights in defiance of reason, in challenge to all outcries of injustice; but admits no obstacle, urging on his favorites to the appointed goal without let or hindrance. But as this is the will of God, so let it befall and be written.

Now Theodora was fair of face and of a very graceful, though small, person; her complexion was moderately colorful, if somewhat pale; and her eyes were dazzling and vivacious. All eternity would not be long enough to allow one to tell her escapades while she was on the stage, but the few details I have mentioned above should be sufficient to demonstrate the woman's character to future generations.

What she and her husband did together must now be briefly described: for neither did anything without the consent of the other. For some time it was generally supposed they were totally different in mind and action; but later it was revealed that their apparent disagreement had been arranged so that their subjects might not unanimously revolt against them, but instead be divided in opinion.

Thus they split the Christians into two parties, each pretending to take the part of one side, thus confusing both, as I shall soon show; and then they ruined both political factions. Theodora feigned to support the Blues with all her power, encouraging them to take the offensive against the opposing party and perform the most outrageous deeds of violence; while Justinian, affecting to be vexed and secretly jealous of her, also pretended he could not openly oppose her orders. And thus they gave the impression often that they were acting in opposition. Then he would rule that the Blues must be punished for their crimes, and she would angrily complain that against her will she was defeated by her husband. However, the Blue partisans, as I have said, seemed cautious, for they did not violate their neighbors as much as they might have done.

And in legal disputes each of the two would pretend to favor one of the litigants, and compel the man with the worse case to win: and so they robbed both disputants of most of the property at issue.

In the same way, the Emperor, taking many persons into his intimacy, gave them offices by power of which they could defraud the State to the limits of their ambition. And as soon as they had collected enough plunder, they would fall out of favor with Theodora, and straightway be ruined. At first he would affect great sympathy in their behalf, but soon he would somehow lose his confidence in them, and an air of doubt would darken his zeal in their behalf. Then Theodora would use them shamefully, while he, unconscious as it were of what was being done to them, confiscated their properties and boldly enjoyed their wealth. By such well-planned hypocrisies they confused the public and, pretending to be at variance with each other, were able to establish a firm and mutual tyranny.

How the Defender of the Faith Ruined His Subjects

As soon as Justinian came into power he turned everything upside down. Whatever had been before by law, he now introduced into the government, while he revoked all established customs: as if he had been given the robes of an Emperor on the condition he would turn everything topsy-turvy. Existing offices he abolished, and invented new ones for the management of public affairs. He did the same thing to the laws and to the regulations of the army; and his reason was not any improvement of justice or any advantage, but simply that everything might be new and named after himself. And whatever was beyond his power to abolish, he renamed after himself anyway.

Of the plundering of property or the murder of men, no weariness ever overtook him. As soon as he had looted all the houses of the wealthy, he looked around for others; meanwhile throwing away the spoils of his previous robberies in subsidies to barbarians or senseless building extravagances. And when he had ruined perhaps myriads in this mad looting, he immediately sat down to plan how he could do likewise to others in even greater number.

As the Romans were now at peace with all the world and he had no other means of satisfying his lust for slaughter, he set the barbarians all to fighting each other. And for no reason at all he sent for the Hun chieftains, and with idiotic magnanimity gave them large sums of money, alleging he did this to secure their friendship. This, as I have said, he had also done in Justin's time. These Huns, as soon as they had got this money, sent it together with their soldiers to others of their chieftains, with the word to make inroads into the land of the Emperor: so that they might collect further tribute from him, to buy them off in a second peace. Thus the Huns enslaved the Roman Empire, and were paid by the Emperor to keep on doing it.

This encouraged still others of them to rob the poor Romans; and after their pillaging, they too were further rewarded by the gracious Emperor. In this way all the Huns, for when it was not one tribe of them it was another, continuously overran and laid waste the Empire. For the barbarians were led by many different chieftains, and the war, thanks to Justinian's senseless generosity, was thus endlessly protracted. Consequently no place, mountain or cave, or any other spot in Roman territory, during this time remained uninjured; and many regions were pillaged more than five times. . . .

Proving That Justinian and Theodora Were Actually Fiends in Human Form

Now the wealth of those in Constantinople and each other city who were considered second in prosperity only to members of the Senate was brutally confiscated, in the ways I have described, by Justinian and Theodora. But how they were able to rob even the Senate of all its property I shall now reveal.

There was in Constantinople a man by the name of Zeno, grandson of that Anthamius who had formerly been Emperor of the West. This man they appointed, with malice aforethought, Governor of Egypt, and commanded his immediate departure. But he delayed his voyage long enough to load his ship with his most valuable effects; for he had a countless amount of silver and gold plate inlaid with pearls, emeralds and other such precious stones. Whereupon they bribed some of his most trusted servants to remove these valuables from the ship as fast as they could carry them, set fire to the interior of the vessel, and inform Zeno that his ship had burst into flames of spontaneous combustion, with the loss of all his property. Later, when Zeno died suddenly, they took possession of his estate immediately as his legal heirs; for they produced a will which, it is whispered, he did not really make.

In the same manner they made themselves heirs of Tatian, Demosthenes, and Hilara, who were foremost in the Roman Senate. And others' estates they obtained by counterfeited letters instead of wills. . . .

I could hardly catalogue all the other people whose estates these two chose to inherit. However, up to the time when the insurrection named Nika took place, they seized rich men's properties one at a time; but when that happened, as I have told elsewhere, they sequestrated at one swoop the estates of nearly all the members of the Senate. On everything movable and on the fairest of the lands they laid their hands and kept what they wanted; but whatever was unproductive of more than the bitter and heavy taxes, they gave back to the previous owners with a philanthropic gesture. Consequently these unfortunates, oppressed by the tax collectors and eaten up by the never-ceasing interest on their debts, found life a burden compared to which death were preferable.

Wherefore to me, and many others of us, these two seemed not to be human beings, but veritable demons, and what the poets call vampires: who laid their heads together to see how they could most easily and quickly destroy the race and deeds of men; and assuming human bodies, became man-demons, and so convulsed the world. And one could find evidence of this in many things, but especially in the superhuman power with which they worked their will.

For when one examines closely, there is a clear difference between what is human and what is supernatural. There have been many enough men, during the whole course of history, who by chance or by nature have inspired great fear, ruining cities or countries or whatever else fell into their power; but to destroy all men and bring calamity on the whole inhabited earth remained for these two to accomplish, whom Fate aided in their schemes of corrupting all mankind. For by earthquakes, pestilences, and floods of river waters at this time came further ruin, as I shall presently show. Thus not by human, but by some other kind of power they accomplished their dreadful designs. . . .

Deceptive Affability and Piety of a Tyrant

Justinian, while otherwise of such character as I have shown, did make himself easy of access and affable to his visitors; nobody of all those who sought audience with him was ever denied: even those who confronted him improperly or noisily never made him angry. On the other hand, he never blushed at the murders he committed. Thus he never revealed a sign of wrath or irritation at any offender, but with a gentle countenance and unruffled brow gave the order to destroy myriads of innocent men, to sack cities, to confiscate any amount of properties.

One would think from this manner that the man had the mind of a lamb. If, however, anyone tried to propitiate him and in suppliance beg him to forgive his victims, he would grin like a wild beast, and woe betide those who saw his teeth thus bared!

The priests he permitted fearlessly to outrage their neighbors, and even took sympathetic pleasure in their robberies, fancying he was thus sharing their divine piety when he judged such cases, he thought he was doing the holy thing when he gave the decision to the priest and let him go free with his ill-gotten booty: justice, in his mind, meant the priests' getting the better of their opponents. When he himself thus illegally got possession of estates of people alive or dead, he would straightway make them over to one of the churches, gilding his violence with the color of piety—and so that his victims could not possibly get their property back. Furthermore he committed an inconceivable number of murders for the same cause: for in his zeal to gather all men into one Christian doctrine, he recklessly killed all who dissented, and this too he did in the name of piety. For he did not call it homicide, when those who perished happened to be of a belief that was different from his own.

So quenchless was his thirst for human blood; and with his wife, intent on this end, he neglected no possible excuse for slaughter. For these two were almost twins in their desires, though they pretended to differ: they were both scoundrels, however they affected to oppose each other, and thus destroyed their subjects. The man was lighter in character than a cloud of dust, and could be led to do anything any man wished him to do, so long as the matter did not require philanthropy or generosity. Flattery he swallowed whole, and his courtiers had no difficulty in persuading him that he was destined to rise as high as the sun and walk upon the clouds. . . .

There remained, while he ruled the Romans, no sure faith in God, no hope in religion, no defense in law, no security in business, no trust in a contract. When his officials were given any affair to handle for him, if they killed many of their victims and robbed the rest, they were looked upon by the Emperor with high favor, and given honorable mention for carrying out so perfectly his instructions. But if they showed any mercy and then returned to him, he frowned and was thenceforth their enemy.

Despising their qualms as old-fashioned, he called them no more to his service. Consequently many were eager to show him how wicked they were, even when they were really nothing of the sort. He made frequent promises, guaranteed with a sworn oath or by a written confirmation; and then purposely forgot them directly, thinking this summary negligence added to his importance. And Justinian acted thus not only to his subjects, but to many of the enemy, as I have already said.

He was untiring; and hardly slept at all, generally speaking; he had no appetite for food or drink, but picking up a morsel with the tips of his fingers, tasted it and left the table, as if eating were a duty imposed upon him by nature and of no more interest than a courier takes in delivering a letter. Indeed, he would often go without food for two days and nights, especially when the time before the festival called Easter enjoins such fasting. Then, as I have said, he often went without food for two days, living only on a little water and a few wild herbs, sleeping perhaps a single hour, and then spending the rest of the time walking up and down.

If, mark you, he had spent these periods in good works, matters might have been considerably alleviated. Instead, he devoted the full strength of his nature to the ruin of the Romans, and succeeded in razing the state to its foundation. For his constant wakefulness, his privations and his labors were undergone for no other reason than to contrive each day ever more exaggerated calamities for his people. For he was, as I said, unusually keen at inventing and quick at accomplishing unholy acts, so that even the good in him transpired to be answerable for the downfall of his subjects.

Procopius was a historian during the reign of Justinian and Theodora.

EXPLORING THE ISSUE

Did the Byzantine Empire Benefit from the Rule of Justinian and Theodora?

Critical Thinking and Reflection

1. Examine the evidence provided in the selections of the challenges faced by Justinian and Theodora in the early 530s. Was it predictable that the events and decisions of this time would lead to a crisis? Critically discuss.
2. What were the issues in the Nika Rebellion, and what was Justinian's proposed course of action? In your view, what would have been the consequences if Justinian had followed this course? Critically analyze.
3. Keeping in mind the joint rulership of Justinian and Theodora, analyze her speech at the height of the crisis (from Procopius's account). Was it the crucial element in resolving the crisis? Critically discuss/debate this question.
4. What does Professor Paolo Cesaretti mean when he writes: ". . . As was always the case in Constantinople, the truth was a complex mosaic of elements." Analyze and critically discuss. Is this true in every time and place?
5. What is Procopius implying when he writes of Theodora: "Thus was this woman born and bred; and her name was a byword beyond that of other common wenches on the tongues of all men." Is this a credible charge, given that Theodora was the co-ruler of Byzantium? Critically analyze and discuss/debate this question.
6. Critically examine the chapter titles in Procopius's "secret" history. What do they reveal about his biases? Analyze and critically discuss.
7. How do most historians minimize potential biases in their accounts? List and discuss specific strategies.

Is There Common Ground?

Procopius's public and secret histories are the most frequently cited sources for the reign of Justinian and Theodora. The few words of praise he offers the Emperor and Empress are probably credible. And, his references to public acts and building projects are supported by documentation in other sources. Common ground, in this case, would have to be sought by sifting and comparing all available accounts.

Procopius is like the modern person who writes an "unauthorized biography" of a famous subject. Sometimes, today, the claims of such a biographer are challenged and sources disputed. However, in the case of Justinian and Theodora, most other voices from that time and place are silent. Then, as now, many people seem to enjoy gossip and relish in hearing stories that place well-known people in a bad light.

Question: Since other "voices" are absent, what alternative evidence might one consult to make a judgment about the reign of Justinian and Theodora? What remains from their time as rulers of Byzantium that might also speak to the question of this issue?

Additional Resources

In addition to the excellent biography of Theodora that forms the YES selection, see also James Allan Evans, *The Emperor Justinian and the Byzantine Empire* (Greenwood Press, 2005) and *The Empress Theodora: Partner of Justinian* (University of Texas Press, 2002). On the magnificent structures, especially the churches of Hagia Sophia (Holy Wisdom), the Basilica of the Holy Apostles, and the church of Saints Sergius and Bacchus, see Cyril Mango, *Byzantine Architecture* (Faber & Faber, 1986).

Finally, Judy Chicago chose Theodora as one of the women to occupy a seat at "The Dinner Party," her massive art installation, in the form of an equilateral triangle, featuring 39 women omitted from history. In storage for decades, "The Dinner Party" has been bought and donated to The Brooklyn Museum, where it is now on permanent display. Theodora's biography and a photo of her magnificent purple, green, and gold mosaic-like porcelain plate can be found in Judy Chicago, *The Dinner Party* (Penguin Books, 1986).

Internet References . . .

The Reign of Justinian and Theodora

From Vasilief's *A History of the Byzantine Empire: Justinian the Great and His Successors (518–610)*. This site gives context and background, taking on directly the role and goals of Procopius.

www.ellopos.net/elpenor/vasilief/justinian-theodora.asp

Selected, Edited, and with Issue Framing Material by:
Helen Buss Mitchell, *Howard Community College*
and
Joseph R. Mitchell, *Howard Community College*

ISSUE

Did Environmental Factors Cause the Collapse of Maya Civilization?

YES: David Drew, from *The Lost Chronicles of the Maya Kings* (University of California Press, 1999)

NO: Payson D. Sheets, from "Warfare in Ancient Mesoamerica: A Summary View," in M. Katherine Brown and Travis W. Stanton, eds., *Ancient Mesoamerican Warfare* (AltaMira Press, 2003)

Learning Outcomes

After reading this issue you should be able to:

- Detail the accomplishments of the Maya civilization before European conquest.
- Describe internal and external pressures on the Maya during the period covered by this issue.
- Summarize the state of Mesoamerican warfare during this period.

ISSUE SUMMARY

YES: Writer and documentary presenter David Drew argues that environmental factors and their effects on Maya civilization were primarily responsible for its collapse.

NO: Anthropology professor Payson D. Sheets argues that military expansion was a potential cause of the Maya collapse.

A notable civilization from long ago wrote in hieroglyphs, developed an accurate calendar, built pyramid-like structures to honor its gods, practiced polytheism with gods represented by animal imagery, and advanced in areas such as mathematics and astronomy. These characteristics could be used to describe the ancient Egyptians. But here they are used to describe the Mayas of Mesoamerica, who established a New World civilization a millennium before the arrival of Europeans. Though this civilization had flourished for millennia, even before the Spanish invasion, this Amerindian civilization was already in a state of decline when *conquistadors* arrived.

What has never been lost is a sense of the holiness of the Earth. Deep underground, priests still pray to the Earth, the ancestors, the ancient kings of Maya, chanting from the preconquest creation book, the *Popul Vuh*: ". . . holy earth, heart of earth, giver of life, give us children, keep them on your green road and let there be continuity within." Daykeepers are guardians of the Mayan calendar of 260 days, based on what the Quiche Maya believe is the gestation period of the human baby in the womb. In their sacred book of origins, we read that ". . . humankind was given memory to count the days, to be bearers of respect for its divinity, to keep the rituals which connect humanity, nature and the heavens. . . ." There have been four Suns or long epochs, each ending with the completion of a cycle. And, each has been followed by the beginning of a new cycle.

The Spanish *conquistadors*, following in Christopher Columbus's footsteps, subdued all of Mesoamerica in the sixteenth century and completely destroyed what remained of the Maya civilization. The result of these Spanish conquests, aided by uncontrolled ecological growth that covered what remained, was the total disappearance of this once highly advanced civilization. It would remain obscured until it was rediscovered in the nineteenth century by explorers seeking to find the lost civilization of the ancient Mayas.

Within the last century, work by archaeologists, linguists, and scientists has not only exposed what remains of the Maya grandeur but, by deciphering their language, has uncovered the secrets of their advanced civilization. The continuing discoveries have inspired regular reassessments of earlier theories. It was once thought, for example, that Mayas were peaceful people, with little interest in war as a means to achieving ends. Recent linguistic decipherments now tell us that this was not true. As far as the Mayas are concerned, however, today's theory is only as good as the latest archaeological discovery or linguistic decipherment, both ongoing processes.

In studying the decline of civilizations, it is generally easy to see that, in most instances, a combination of internal and external factors is responsible for their demise. This is certainly true for the Mayas. Both Drew and Sheets would agree that there is no single explanation for the Maya collapse; the question seems to be: Which set of factors was more responsible for the demise? Complicating the search for answers to the Maya collapse are the regional and individual differences that existed within the myriad of city-states that provided the civilization with its political base. It should be noted that the reasons for their collapse could also differ due to regional or local conditions. Today's research seems to bear out the legitimacy of this dichotomy.

Studying the reasons for the Maya collapse offers an opportunity to compare/contrast it with other civilizations that experienced a similar rise/decline/fall trajectory. In Norman Yoffee and George L. Cowgill, eds., *The Collapse of Ancient States and Civilizations* (University of Arizona Press, 1988), the rise and fall of Mesopotamia, Rome, and Ancient China are compared with those of the Mayas. Can what is learned from such comparisons offer any clues regarding the possible future collapse of contemporary nation-states, including our own? This question has been raised by several scholars, including Jared Diamond, author of *Collapse: How Societies Choose to Fail or Succeed* (Viking Penguin, 2005).

In spite of the wealth of information about the Mayas we now possess, there are still questions that have not been definitively answered. One of the most important questions is, What caused the decline of Maya civilization? Maya scholars have developed many theories regarding its decline, using the best evidence available to them at the time. However, because additional data continues to be found and additional theories continue to be proposed, consensus has not yet been reached.

This issue seeks to explore the two major theories involving the Mayan decline: (1) It occurred due to internal political, social, and environmental factors that the Mayas could not or would not control; (2) The demise was brought about by factors caused by excessive militarism, which first resulted in territorial expansion and later in weakness and eventual decline. Complicating the search for answers to the cause(s) of the Maya demise, are the local/regional differences present in the Maya city-states. Were factors that were present in the Northern Lowlands states also present in their Southern counterparts? And, what about their Highland counterparts? Could different conditions and circumstances in each area have produced a variety of factors that combined to bring about the eventual collapse of the entire Maya civilization? And, within a region, can we be sure that the factors that led to one city-state's demise were also responsible for the collapse of others? The possibility exists that each political entity may have had its own unique set of circumstances which contributed to its particular decline and fall.

In spite of these intrinsic difficulties, Maya scholars continue to explore potential reasons for the full civilization's collapse. Both the "internal conditions" and "outside forces" theories are considered by David Drew and Payson D. Sheets. In the selections that follow, Drew considers internal stresses—overpopulation, agricultural scarcities, disease, natural disasters—to be the major factors responsible for the collapse of the Maya city-states. Sheets represents those scholars emphasizing the warlike nature of the Mayas and the effects this characteristic may have had on the Maya collapse. Future archaeological work in Central America is likely to shed more light on the reasons for the Maya decline.

YES

David Drew

The Lost Chronicles of the Maya Kings

The Maya Collapse

For the early explorers, the enigma of their downfall was perhaps the greatest of the Maya mysteries. The builders of the magnificent cities seemed to have vanished without trace. John Lloyd Stephens saw the 'shattered bark' of Maya civilization left adrift in the jungle, her crew perished and 'none left to tell what caused her destruction'. When had the forests engulfed the temples and pyramids and how had such glory come to pass away? A century later the first question was answered, although it only served to deepen the mystery surrounding the second. As men such as Sylvanus Morley assiduously tracked down dated inscriptions in the forests and excavations proceeded at some of the major sites, it became clear that dynastic role at individual Maya cities had come to an abrupt halt during the course of the ninth century, now known as the 'Terminal Classic' period, No more monuments with dated inscriptions were set up and the construction of palaces and temples ceased. Yet this was more than the end of kings. For evidence was to accumulate that most of the major cities in the Southern Lowlands were abandoned, their populations never to return, Classic Maya civilization had folded utterly and the signs were that this 'Collapse', as it came to be called, had been a disaster of such a magnitude that it had little precedent in world history. . . .

Half a century ago a range of explanations had already been offered to account for what had happened, including plague, agricultural failure, earthquake, invasion from beyond the boundaries of the Maya world and peasant revolt. Today scholars shy away from presenting the fall of the Classic Maya as a tidy sequence of any single root cause and effect. For if factors can be identified which may ultimately have served to trigger the collapse of particular cities, these only operated because of deep-seated structural problems within the fabric of Maya society. In a pattern of cyclical inevitability that the Maya themselves would have understood, any civilization tends to accumulate imbalances and tensions within the very system that has created its success. The Maya were no exception, for centuries of growth produced intolerable strains which in the end proved socially and politically explosive. Yet if one had to select a fundamental 'cause', it must have lain in the glaring imbalance between the burgeoning Maya population and the productive capacity of their agriculture. . . .

If the evidence suggests that populations were increasing rapidly and that most available land was turned over to agriculture, the other element in the equation, the question of how much food the land could have produced, is of course impossible to answer. We now have an impressionistic picture of the range of Maya adaptations. We know that their agriculture was considerably more intensive than once thought, but any more precise understanding of the nature and effectiveness of cultivation across the Southern Lowlands will elude scholars for many years to come. Much as with population estimates, the evidence to date is limited and comes from scattered studies that have covered in detail only a tiny fraction of the region. And what they do reveal is great variability, that topography, differing soil fertility and localized weather patterns would have rendered conditions for agriculture very different from one area to another. There seems little doubt, however, that the land must have been under tremendous pressure. Over much of the region slash-and-burn agriculture would still have been the mainstay of the farming regime. Farmers who practise the same system today testify that even where a regular period of fallow is maintained, soils will naturally decline over the years in fertility and crop yields. The responsible farmer will see that from time to time fields are rested for longer periods. But with more and more mouths to feed and nowhere to move to, no other lands to till, this may have been impossible at the end of the Late Classic. Indeed many believe that the reverse was increasingly the case, that they would have been forced to shorten the period of fallow on already tired fields. This would have been an extremely risky strategy, courting disaster for short-term ends.

The increasing dearth of forest would have had a profound impact, firstly in encouraging soil erosion. But trees were also vital for so many aspects of life. Originally, of course, there would have been quite enough to go round and large areas of forest would have formed buffer zones between territories. Tracts of jungle must have been safeguarded and harvested as a renewable resource. But by the end of the eighth century one can well imagine strategic decisions being made to fell many of the remaining areas of virgin forest. The Maya were without doubt responsible farmers, with two thousand years' experience of conjuring harvests of maize from sparse tropical soils. They must have been aware of the impact they were having on their environment. But they could no longer afford to be enlightened guardians of forest and field. The picture that emerges is of the environment progressively degraded, of Maya agriculture reaching the very limits of its capacity and being unable to feed populations adequately. The key evidence comes from the bones of Maya people throughout the region. Studies from sites such as Tikal, Altar de Sacrificios and La Milpa tell the same story of an increasingly unhealthy and stressed population. Skeletons had shrunk, the life expectancy of children was beginning to decrease rapidly and disease was commonplace in a manner not observed in the more robust bones of earlier centuries. On the whole, kings and nobility continued to live well and remain healthy, but this would not be the case for long.

Another variable that has to be considered in the overall picture is that of climate change. Over the centuries the climate and patterns of rainfall in the Maya lowlands have been inherently unstable. Modern statistics reveal that rainfall varies considerably in quantity from year to year. Localized droughts are common and when the rains do come they can appear with extraordinary violence in the form of hurricanes that sweep in from the Caribbean. In 1961, for example, Hurricane Hattie wrecked Belize City and then headed inland to bring havoc to much of the Petén. At the time of writing, much of Nicaragua, Honduras and the Caribbean coast of Guatemala is still recovering from the devastating effects of Hurricane Mitch. Spanish accounts of the conquest period speak of an equally unpredictable climate and, in the northern Yucatán in particular, the common occurrence of drought. Diego de Landa was struck by this in talking to local people and records that in 1535, there was a terrible drought when 'such a famine fell upon them that they were reduced to eating the bark of trees . . . nothing green was left'. Such uncertainties undoubtedly preoccupied the Prehispanic Maya and underlined the need, revealed in the codices, for effective divination and the right ritual action to be taken, in the way of suitable offerings for the gods, to avert such calamities.

Given the seemingly precarious situation at the end of the Late Classic, short-term changes in weather patterns or sudden natural disasters could have proved catastrophic in a way that they would not have done in previous centuries. There is now evidence that they may have been confronted by problems of a different order entirely. As we know to our cost today, the removal of large areas of tropical forest does not simply degrade the soil but also adversely affects the climate. Any more localized changes of this kind in the Southern Lowlands may be difficult to detect since, as Don Rice points out in his survey of the eighth century Maya environment, both human impact and climate change leave traces—in the pollen record, for example—which are very difficult to tell apart. But in northern Yucatán, at some distance from the great Classic cities to the south, the analysis of sediments from the remote Lake Chichancanab has suggested that a period of consistent dryness set in throughout the Maya area between 750 and 800 and may have lasted for two centuries. There is some evidence for longer term shifts or cycles of climate change in earlier periods . . . . notably dry episode may have contributed to the downfall of The Late Preclassic city or El Mirador. But that which began in the later eighth century appears to have been the most severe in the Maya region for thousands of years and could have brought prolonged droughts of a kind that the Maya would never have experienced before. Thus to people living on the edge, this may have acted as the final blow which led to social breakdown and disaster.

The exact circumstances and the pattern of events at each of the major cities as they fell apart undoubtedly differed from place to place. The wealth of archaeological and epigraphic evidence from Copán and its region makes it the only example to date where it is possible to reconstruct plausibly and in some detail the end of a Classic Maya city. After its foundation by Yax K'uk Mo in 426, the city and royal dynasty at Copán flourished. To begin with it was a small centre amidst rich farmland overlooking the river. The abundance and increased prosperity amply justified the king's role as leader of his society. The 'semi-divine' authority, the lavish display and the trappings of Copán's kings increased. It was all a great success and the city attracted more and more people to it, even from as far away as central Honduras. But, as the population grew, the urban nucleus expanded over the most fertile bottomland into a continuous, densely packed residential mass. Gradually there became less and less good land available for cultivation and they began to farm the slopes of the surrounding hills, all the while making sizeable inroads into the local forest cover. Eventually the hills, too, were dotted with groups of houses and trackways, much as they are today, and as the eighth century wore on, Copán's farmers were forced to till the very poorest soils around the hilltops. Finally, by the end of the century, deforestation, soil erosion and dramatically falling crop yields meant that the valley could no longer feed itself. For a time, perhaps the city was able to depend for food upon tribute in kind from the satellite communities that it dominated. But they, too, would have been feeling the strain, with little surplus to spare, and have been increasingly disinclined to support the demands of the centre. . . .

The end of dynastic rule at Copán is signalled by two most unusual monuments. The first is an unprepossessing, damaged stela of curiously rounded, columnar form known as Stela. It depicts the standing figure of the already dead Yax Pac descending into the jaws of the Underworld. On the back of the stone is a short inscription which has so far proved impossible to decipher in its entirety. But, following an abbreviated date which almost certainly corresponds to 820, the second glyph block features the verb *hom,* which David Stuarr has interpreted as to 'dismantle' or 'destroy'. The next glyph includes the word for 'founder' as it appears in the inscription on top of Altar Q, where it refers to the foundation of the Copán royal line some 400 years earlier by Yax K'uk Mo. On Stela 11 this reference to the founder is coupled with the suffix *nah* meaning 'house'. Put together, what this would mean is 'the founder's house is destroyed', in other words the dynasty which began with Yax K'uk Mo had come to an end. If the interpretation is correct, this inscription is unique in actually announcing the termination of a royal line. It is an extraordinary and quite uncharacteristic admission of failure. . . .

There is no means of knowing what happened to the members of the royal family, although there is evidence that the residential compound of Yax Pac and his line may have been destroyed at about this time. Somewhat later, William Fash suggests, his tomb may have been looted and his funerary temple ransacked. There is no sign, however, of any major upheaval or of what might be termed a popular uprising. Fash believes that the political endgame at Copán amounted to a nobles' revolt. Perhaps it was a takeover by the heads of those non-royal lineages who commanded popular support in the countryside and could distance themselves from the perceived failures of the ruling family. For the houses of these lineages continued to be occupied and indeed were added to over the following century. Thus at Copán rule by a single king seems to have devolved to that of the group. These leading families evidently attempted to stay on and revive the valley's fortunes. But after a century or so, perhaps because of renewed infighting and the continuing decline of agriculture, they appear to have drifted away to smaller, still fertile areas of land in the surrounding hills. At least here, on the less crowded fringes of the Maya world, they had somewhere to go. They reverted, it seems, to a simpler, decentralized way of life, of the kind that had existed before the onset of dynastic rule. Between about 1000 and 1200, the population of Copán fell away rapidly. From the evidence of their rubbish dumps and burials, small groups continued to inhabit parts of the city, but after this time the valley was largely abandoned.

The uniquely detailed picture that emerges from Copán offers a model of how some of the principal elements in the process of Maya 'Collapse' fitted together. Deterioration of the environment and the failure of agriculture imposed intolerable strains on the political system, which finally came apart and led to the toppling of royal scapegoats. In essence this pattern must have been repeated in many other cities, though elsewhere, where kingdoms jostled more densely together, the drift towards failure was more chaotic and more violent. Along the Usumacinta and Pasión rivers, and in the heartland region of the Petén and adjacent areas, the old system of alliances formed around Tikal and Calakmul had broken down by the middle of the eighth century. It is obvious enough today that the only thing which might have enabled the Classic Maya to surmount their problems was political unity and co-operation. This was clearly impossible. Under pressure the political system atomized, reverted to type, with each one of a host of now antagonistic city-states looking to its own interests in what became a struggle for survival. For in many areas, especially those away from the major rivers or lakes, the strain on the environment and the decline of agriculture was in all probability much greater than that visible at Copán. The only option that would keep kings in power and feed their populations was to take land and desperately scarce resources from others. Inscriptions suggest that the incidence of warfare and, most would conclude, its intensity, increased markedly during the latter part of the eighth century. The pattern may have been set with the destruction of Dos Pilas and the conflagration in the Petexbatún area that began in the 760s. This was all-out, brutal war that laid waste the whole region. Along the Usumacinta the last texts that survive from the major cities all speak of warfare, and at some of them there are signs of destruction. Buildings were burnt and monuments defaced at Piedras Negras, and at Yaxchilán archaeologists have recently discovered that a section of the city known as the 'Little Acropolis' was fortified with hastily erected walls, and projectile points covered the ground that Yaxchilán, like Dos Pilas, may finally have fallen in war. . . .

David Drew, an award-winning archaeology writer and presenter of television documentaries, is also a Fellow of the Royal Geographical Society and the Royal Anthropological Society.

Payson D. Sheets

Warfare in Ancient Mesoamerica: A Summary View

This [article] focuses on warfare in ancient Mesoamerica rather than violence or conflict. The latter two may occur on the interpersonal or interfamilial level and often do not preserve well archaeologically. However, warfare as a socially sanctioned and planned aggressive activity can be preserved reasonably well, especially in a society with considerable architecture as well as writing and art in various media. The objective of this [article] is to briefly consider the history of Mesoamerican warfare . . . and to comment on current status of Mesoamerican warfare in general. It is refreshing for me to summarize and comment on a book on Mesoamerican warfare not written by the traditional "big gun" distinguished scholars but by the next generation of archaeologists exploring the nature and implications of war with new data and ideas.

Overview of Mesoamerican Warfare Studies

The first European contact with a New World civilization was in war, as the Spanish and their Tlaxcalan and other allies conquered the Aztec capital Tenochtitlán. As the Spanish expanded their contacts and attempted to establish control in the sixteenth century, they chronicled warfare and sacrifice throughout Mesoamerica. Despite Spanish documentation of Contact period indigenous warfare, scholars in the early and middle part of the twentieth century often depicted ancient civilizations as peaceful. As scholars have depicted societies as bellicose or peaceful or as they have explored the reasons for warfare, they often have revealed more about their own assumptions and desires than the subject matter under study.

As reflected in this volume, Mesoamerican scholars in recent years have recognized the abundant and wide range of material correlates that warfare has left in the archaeological record. Those material correlates range from the instruments of warfare and fortifications through artistic depictions to textual statements of warfare and its consequences. Certainly, warfare was initiated as a means to capture sacrificial victims for largely religious purposes on occasion, but even then can this be divorced from a function of bolstering political authority? As the evidence for warfare in Mesoamerica accumulates, we must also consider that warfare was an integral component to the emergence of middle range and complex societies throughout the Formative, Classic, and Postclassic.

Warfare in pre-Columbian Oaxaca has been studied for more than half a century, beginning with Caso at Monte Albán. Marcus and Flannery have broadened and deepened our understanding of conflict within and surrounding the Oaxaca Valley, including some evidence of warfare prior to the founding of Monte Albán about 500 B.C. Redmond and Spencer convincingly documented the conquest of the Cuicatlan Canada north of the Oaxaca Valley by Monte Albán. However, as Joyce argues in this volume the claims of militarism from Monte Albán may have been exaggerated. He searched the lower Verde Valley for evidence of Monte Albán conquest in the Late Formative and found little. Ironically, he did find evidence for a strong presence of a different foreign polity a few centuries later that could have had military aspects. Teotihuacan entered the area in a major way in the Early Classic, as evidenced by the lower Verde area having the highest percentage of green Pachuca obsidian of any area outside the Basin of Mexico, along with some settlement shifts to defensible locations and some ceramic changes. Judging from present evidence, if this area had been conquered, it was more likely by Teotihuacan than Monte Albán.

These issues in Oaxaca are exemplary of deeper questions in Mesoamerican archaeology. Often we ask, Was the expansion of society X of an economic nature, or was it theocratic, or was it political? The issues are often simplified to a prime motivator for expansion that can focus on mercantile objectives versus religious conversion or conquest and domination. However, what many of these essays indicate to me is that our Western categories may be useful for initial heuristic purposes but may be misleading if they are allowed to stand unchallenged in the final analysis. Most expansions involved what we would categorize as economic, political, and religious phenomena in deeply intertwined manners.

The recognition of the centrality of warfare to the Classic Maya has been a long time coming. Thompson, the great mid-twentieth-century Mayanist, did acknowledge that warfare existed, but he emphasized warfare in Postclassic and historic times. In his magnum opus *The Rise and Fall of Maya Civilization* (1st ed. 1954, 2nd ed. 1966), he argued that all Mesoamerican warfare originated in the need to obtain captives for the sacrifices needed to nurture the deities. He viewed the Mexicans as more warlike than the Maya, a trend that culminated with the Aztecs.

Thompson did refer to the jaguar and eagle as war gods, which was a step toward the current recognition of the two warrior orders, of eagle and jaguar knights, that were at Teotihuacan and were adopted by the Maya at Tikal and other areas. They become common in the Late Classic (at Bonampak) and Epiclassic (at Cacaxtla) as well as the Early Postclassic (at Tula) . . . and Late Postclassic (at Tenochtitlén). In Aztec mythology, the opposition of jaguar and eagle knights represented the earth and the sky and thus femaleness and maleness. Not only did the warrior orders operate in military campaigns, but they figured prominently in public performances while presenting their captive victims to ensure the proper working of the cosmos.

As early as 1940, Means perceived a fundamental difference between Andean and Middle American warfare. He saw Inka warfare directed toward conquest and acculturation, to bring other peoples into Inka civilization. In contrast, he, like Thompson, viewed Middle American warfare as oriented toward capturing opposing warriors to sacrifice them to provide sustenance for their deities. I believe the fact that it is the only reference to warfare in the Maya area in the index of that entire synthesis volume *The Maya and Their Neighbors* indicates how unimportant warfare was considered by the principal scholars of those decades.

One discovery that made scholars rethink the "peaceful Maya" were the huge ditch-and-parapet fortifications constructed in the Late Formative by Tikal to protect them from Uaxactún. After Tikal apparently conquered Uaxactún, the earthworks no longer served any purpose, and they fell into disrepair. The discovery a decade later of defensive fortifications around Becán indicated the threat of warfare was more widespread among the Maya. More recently, Demarest and Inomata have shown the intensity and social consequences of warfare in the Petexbatun region that led to the end of civilization as the Classic Maya knew it in that area.

Artistic evidence of warfare has also accumulated in the nineteenth and twentieth centuries, as stela scenes and painted evidence from ceramics and murals have become available and are better understood. Hieroglyphic evidence has accumulated more in the "punctuated equilibrium" model rather than a "uniformitarian" accumulation. Throughout most of the past two centuries, epigraphic evidence of warfare grew very slowly, but that changed dramatically with the decipherment of the "shell/star" hieroglyph for warfare and the linking of it with the Venus cycle, captives, and Tlaloc-Venus warfare and numerous hieroglyphic decipherments, particularly in the southern Maya lowlands.

Warfare was woven deeply into the social fabric of most Formative and all Classic and Postclassic Mesoamerican civilizations. It appears that all levels of those societies, from commoners to elites, believed that sacrifice was essential for the proper functioning of the cosmos. Based on the core belief that one does not receive something for nothing, people would offer sacrifices in various forms to receive rain, a good crop harvest, a propitious marriage, recovery from disease, or other anxious need. The sacrifice could take the form of bloodletting, sacrificing food or drink, or the sacrifice of a person. Sacrifice of a person captured in warfare became very common in the Classic and Post-classic. Sacrifice in general and human sacrifice in particular probably had deep roots in the Formative period, with origins possibly in the Archaic or earlier, but it is not until the Late Formative that sacrifice is commonly preserved in the archaeological record.

Evidence of Warfare in Mesoamerica

One of the advantages of studying Mesoamerican warfare is that a wider range of phenomena is available to the scholar than in other pre-Columbian culture area of the New World. I note a dozen of them here with the objective of encouraging future scholars to spread a wide net in their studies.

Fortifications. Site fortification is prima facie evidence of fear of attack, and in many cases one can identify from whom that fear developed. The Tikal ditch-and-embankment built in fear of Uaxactún is a good example. As that feature seems to have no other function than defense, it is unusually unequivocal evidence. In contrast, the apparent fortifications of sites such as Becán, Cacaxtla, Xochicalco, and Monte Albán could also have had residential and/or agricultural functions.

Art and iconography. The prominent display of trophy heads in skull racks or display of them in sculpture or other forms of art are generally the result of opposing warriors being captured in battle and brought into the victorious settlement for sacrifice. The five-point star is now widely recognized as indicating Venus and the need to capture victims for sacrifice in the Classic and Postclassic of Mesoamerica. Headrick provides a good example of the iconography of aggression.

Weapons. The discovery of weapons of war in sites and the depiction of war weapons in art are reasonably reliable indicators of warfare. McCafferty notes a large number of dart points associated with Structure 1 at Cholula that, combined with other evidence, indicates warfare activity. However, the presence of items that *could* be used in war does not mean that they *were* used in war because such implements can be used in hunting or in art as mythology or as symbolic of hunting, war, aggression, or defense. A technology that could have been used in war but evidently was much more important in hunting is illustrated by the bow and arrow coming into ancient El Salvador in the Terminal Classic (ca. A.D. 800). The evidence is the ubiquity of the small projectile points made from snapped prismatic blade sections. They must be arrow points, as they are too small and fragile to be atlatl dart points or spear points. They commonly are found in the most mountainous of terrain, far from any human settlements, and evidently were used for hunting, particularly of deer. The rarity of other indicators for warfare in pre-Columbian El Salvador further substantiates the argument that these artifacts were not used for intraspecies purposes.

The weapons depicted in sculptures, such as the atlatls and darts in the hands of the atlantid figures at Tula, are unequivocal. Equally convincing are the weapons depicted in aggressive murals at Chichén Itzá and other Classic and Postclassic sites. In addition to bows and arrows and atlatls and darts, spears and clubs were used in war. The latter, resembling a baseball bat but with obsidian or occasionally chert prismatic blade segments inserted longitudinally, must have had a horrific impact, as the lithics shattered on impact, macerating tissue and causing massive hemorrhaging. Such a club is illustrated on Stela 5 at Uaxactún. These clubs with lithic inserts would be useful only in warfare and not in hunting or other uses. As LeBlanc notes, the sling is useful to herding peoples and as an implement of war. It is also useful to agriculturalists to discourage herbivory by birds in maize fields.

Epigraphy. It has taken Mayanists a long time to get past their suspicions about the possible reliability of the written record of the Classic period. We all learned at an early age what liars the Aztecs were, deliberately rewriting their history for self-aggrandizement to look eminently civilized in the finest aggressive Mesoamerican sense. Fortunately, it turns out that the Maya texts are generally reliable. Thus, the Maya text describing a battle, a capture, or a decapitation should be taken seriously. The texts are often limited to the victor proclaiming the outcome, with no details about the scale of battle, the reasons for it, and the planning for it.

Osteology. Skeletal analyses can divulge evidence of trauma. An occasional broken bone is not reliable evidence of warfare, but a high frequency of parry fractures in the radius and ulna of young adult males is a good indicator. Skull fracture patterns can also be evidence of warfare, as can simultaneous multiple burials. Decapitations can be indirect indications, after a captive was hauled into the victorious polity and sacrificed.

Artifacts. Warfare, especially toward the severe end of the spectrum, can result in abrupt changes in artifact or architectural styles or frequencies. However, it is risky to argue in the other direction, of artifactual changes indicating warfare in the absence of supporting data, as so many ecologic, economic, religious, demographic, social, adaptive, or political phenomena can also spread or suppress artifact and technologies.

Assimilation or elimination. Warfare can cause a functioning polity to disappear rapidly, but so can other factors. A sudden change in upper-level administration, as apparently occurred in the Early Classic period in Uaxactún, can be evidence of a conquest.

Language and cognition. The terms and concepts used by a society at the time when warfare is being studied or perhaps later among members of the same ethnic-linguistic group can provide extraordinary insight into warfare. This category provides a hearty dose of *their* view, of the emic perspective. Many other indicators here discussed are our interpretive impositions on the archaeological record, with all the dangers inherent in that. Those dangers include the fact that so often we see what we are trained to see and want to see in the archaeological record. Thus, their cognitive categories act as an antidote to exclusively relying on our etic categories. At least knowing their categories helps us be aware of our projecting our own biases onto the archaeological record. . . .

(T)he Classic Maya had four distinct linguistic categories of warfare. *Chu-c'ah,* or "capture," warfare involves the planning of a battle, a successful encounter with the opposition, and the capture of at least one opposing warrior. Both sides could win, each by capturing someone from the other side. The capture of a person can symbolically extend to the defeat of the opposing polity, but this obviously is not a defeat in warfare as conceptualized in the modem Western world. A *ch'ak,* or "axe," event is similar to the capture event, but the person captured is an elite. The capture of 18 Rabbit from Copan by Quirigua and his subsequent decapitation is the best-known example. A *hubi,* or "destruction," is of greater societal consequence and is more similar to warfare as practiced by modern "civilizations." The most severe form of warfare was the "shell-star" battle, where a polity can conquer and assimilate another, resulting in the long-term or even permanent suppression of political and economic independence. Certainly an important endeavor by Maya archaeologists would be to identify the material correlates of each of these emic types of warfare and see how they change through time or vary among contemporary polities.

Ethnohistory and history. The Spanish in the sixteenth century recorded warfare throughout Mesoamerica. Their recording of chronic warfare among pre-Columbian societies should be taken with a grain of salt. For instance, the Aztec claims of their military struggles with Tlaxcala seem exaggerated, and I suspect the Aztecs completely surrounded Tlaxcala with conquered peoples and maintained Tlaxcala as a convenient nearby hunting preserve where their youths could prove themselves in battle and bring captives back to Tenochtitlán. I would not call Tlaxcala an independent polity. And it was to the advantage of the Mexican warrior who brought back a Tlaxcalan captive to believe and act as if he was obtained from an enemy warring state rather than from a hunting preserve. If this interpretation is correct, the Tlaxcalans were subjugated more profoundly by their being maintained as a hunting preserve than were many societies that were militarily conquered by the Aztec war machine and only loosely assimilated into their empire. McCafferty's chapter further underscores the inconsistencies of the ethnohistoric record and illustrates the need for archaeological evidence in conjunction with the written record to provide a more complete picture.

Oral history, mythology, and religion. Sources such as the Chilam Balam, Popol Vuh, Mixtec codices, and the Florentine Codex provide insights on competition, sacrifice, and warfare.

Settlement patterns. The finding of contested zones, of "no-man's-lands" between polities, can be indications of protracted hostilities. They can occur between states, between city states, or between chiefdoms, as illustrated by the uninhabited zones between the Barriles chiefdoms in western Panama.

Desecratory termination rituals. Several chapters in this volume make significant progress in identifying deposits that may often represent the result of warfare in the deliberate termination of buildings and the supernatural powers in them, as different from dedicatory and reverential termination rituals. One key difference is the scale and intensity of architectural destruction, and the term *desecration* is appropriate here. And it is important to note that if these identifications are correct, Brown and Garber . . . have moved the earliest identification of warfare in the Maya area into the Middle Formative period. Their estimated date of about 650 B.C. is slightly earlier than the time that Marcus and Flannery see the earliest warfare in the Oaxaca Valley. The differences between dedication, desecration, and reverential termination rituals are subtle, yet they are of great importance and deserve considerable research attention to improve our understanding of warfare.

Several studies in this volume successfully combine several lines of evidence to better illuminate our understanding of ancient Mesoamerican warfare. In particular, Freidel and colleagues, provide an excellent example of how to closely examine epigraphic, architectural, sculptural, artistic, and artifactual evidence to distinguish conquest of one polity by another versus internal strife and usurpation of power. These authors suggest that the Maya rules of dynastic succession at Tikal were magically manipulated by Nuun Yax Ain (Curl-Snout), who took the Tikal throne from Toh-Chak-Ich'ak (Great-Jaguar-Paw) with the assistance of Siyah K'ak' (Smoking Frog). They suggest that Nuun Yax Ain performed magical rituals that legitimated his place in the Tikal dynastic sequence. What actually happened at Tikal, two-thirds of the way through the fourth century, is far from being well understood. However, I am optimistic that by conjoining multiple lines of evidence and analyzing them carefully, Mayanists might convince even a jury in Los Angeles.

It is instructive to review the history of studies of Mesoamerican warfare to see the changes in assumptions and understandings as twentieth-century archaeologists have explored the topic. One of the most important recent changes is the combination of field archaeology with epigraphy and iconography, which has combined emic with etic approaches. I believe one area that needs further development is for archaeologists to move beyond the assumption that warfare occurred just on the battlefield at a distance from the city. I suggest that at the first stages of preparation for warfare, the action in fact did occur at a distance (such as setting the field of battle with the battle standards). I suspect a participant in the battle might emphasize the more important battle was occurring in the supernatural realm. And the end of the battle is not the end of the story. Perhaps we can learn more about Mesoamerican warfare by studying the next steps, of bringing the captives back, of creation of "stage space" in which to reenact battles, in which the captives shed blood and lose their lives in order that the cosmos may continue functioning. The Western view of war emphasizes the field of battle, body counts, and equipment destroyed, but to understand Mesoamericans we must also emphasize the public performances within the city before and especially after the battle was completed. Mesoamerican city planning not only took into account the cardinal-cosmological directions but also built stage space in overt ways to render visible and audible the enactments of battles and communications with the supernatural realm. Maya stage space in their cities certainly was not a proscenium stage.

Warfare should not be seen as a monolithic repetitive entity among Mesoamerican societies. Rather, warfare varied considerably, depending on factors such as the degree of political centralization, presence or absence of competitive nearby polities, demographic and ecologic processes, ritualization of warfare, resource unpredictability, and economic and technological changes. Hassig deals with some of these factors, and I anticipate that future warfare research will both broaden and deepen them. Are there correlations between the degree of political centralization and the nature of warfare? In a general sense, there is a relationship, as both of the most highly urbanized and centralized civilizations, Teotihuacan and the Aztecs, waged war with standing armies against external polities. Hassig characterizes Teotihuacan and the Aztecs as meritocratic states with some social mobility for individuals based on their military successes. Both states were relatively innovative in military techniques and technology, and both developed large standing armies that expanded over much of Mesoamerica, but neither society lasted for a long time. In contrast, the Maya waged aristocratic wars, were more conservative, avoided having large standing armies of commoners, and as a result were less expansionistic and in the long run more stable. I believe that we can include the Olmec with the Maya in these characteristics. Additionally, I believe that the Zapotecs more closely resemble the Maya than the Basin of Mexico states. Occasional incorporations of the Basin of Mexico style of dispersed leadership occurred in the Maya area in the very Late Classic at Seibal and at about the same time at Chichén Itzá. I believe that Hassig underestimates the degree to which religion permeated Mesoamerican warfare, particularly in those societies that waged aristocratic wars, but his distinctions are significant and bear further scrutiny. That Teotihuacan and, to a lesser degree, the Aztecs avoided the cult of the king and avoided prominent public depictions of supreme rulers is an important symptom of the significant differences in internal organizational principles among Mesoamerican states.

Conclusions

Many scholars have studied warfare in Mesoamerica. In retrospect, the way research questions have been phrased has often overly focused the domain under consideration. The scholars who argue about what was the "real" nature of war among Mesoamerican societies may have prematurely limited their answers because in the two societies where war is better understood, the Aztec and the Maya, there were quite different kinds of warfare practiced, with markedly different tactics and societal implications. Thus, the scholars who argue that one kind of war is the "true" warfare can be as correct as the scholars who argue a different kind of war is the "true" form. Thus, we need not a leveling of the playing field but rather an acknowledged broadening of the playing field.

It is my opinion that the debate over whether warfare in Mesoamerican societies was motivated primarily by political, economic, religious, or demographic-ecologic factors is healthy and eminently worthwhile. And I am confident that the debate will go on indefinitely because thorough and precise knowledge of the cause(s) of warfare is not attainable. Even under the ideal circumstances for warfare scholarship, having unrestricted access to a recent and historically documented war and to participants in that war, it is not possible to accurately know the role of all factors. The factors vary with different participants in the war and even with a particular participant over time. But that is not cause for pallo-despair, as debate and skepticism can stimulate better scholarship to move us slightly closer to understanding the behaviors and beliefs of warfare, some of the instigating pressures, and occasionally something about the motivations of ancient wars.

I also look forward to Mesoamerican archaeologists incorporating the research of cultural anthropologists. For instance, Ember and Ember "conducted a detailed multivariate study of 186 preindustrial societies to explore the reasons why they went to war. The Embers found that the single highest predictor of warfare is a society's fear of resource unpredictability, often due to apparently capricious natural disasters that destroy food resources. Predictable, chronic natural disasters, such as long-term drought, are less causative of warfare. Unless a society is already greatly stressed, it can accommodate to a long-term drought by such means as intensifying water control. I suspect that the migration of the Anasazi from the Mesa Verde region to the middle Rio Grande was such an accommodation to the long drought of the late thirteenth century in the Southwest. The fear of future sustenance loss or loss of other resources rather than actual deprivation seems to be the strongest motivator for warfare according to the Embers. The second-strongest predictor, about half as strong as resource unpredictability, is a society socializing their members for mistrust of the "other." These two strongest factors certainly are far from being mutually exclusive, and when a society fears an unpredictable nature and foments distrust and hatred for "outside" societies, warfare is a common result. Although many societies in their sample are not state level, these results are intriguing and eminently researchable among Mesoamerican societies from the Formative through the Postclassic. I look forward to explorations to see how fear of an unpredictable nature and fear of others may have underlain Mesoamerican warfare and how a range of coping mechanisms ranging from extending water control through fortifications to developing supernatural access may have been involved.

Payson D. Sheets, professor of history at the University of Colorado, has worked at several Mesoamerican archaeological sites.

EXPLORING THE ISSUE

Did Environmental Factors Cause the Collapse of Maya Civilization?

Critical Thinking and Reflection

1. Are there characteristics of Maya civilization as a whole that seem to suggest its flexibility and ability to endure internal and external challenges? What are they? Critically discuss their strengths and, perhaps undetected, weaknesses.
2. Are there characteristics of Maya civilization as a whole that seem to suggest its vulnerabilities, even if these vulnerabilities might not have been apparent at the time covered by this issue? What are they? Critically discuss these vulnerabilities, as well as the factors that mitigated their effects for a while.
3. Examine the evidence offered by writer David Drew in support of environmental causes for the Maya collapse. Is this evidence persuasive? Critically discuss.
4. Evaluate the review Payson D. Sheets provides of Mesoamerican warfare studies. What evidence does he cite? Is it persuasive? Critically discuss.
5. What does David Drew mean when he writes: "Yet if one had to select a fundamental 'cause,' it must have lain in the glaring imbalance between the burgeoning Maya population and the productive capacity of their agriculture . . .?" Analyze and critically discuss.
6. Payson D. Sheets indicates his pleasure in reviewing a book on Mesoamerican warfare that contains "new data and ideas." What are some of these new data and new ideas? How do they contribute to our understanding of the questions raised in this issue? Critically analyze and discuss.
7. At the end of his review, Professor Sheets offers a possible psychological explanation—"fear of an unpredictable nature and fear of others." In your view, might these fears underlie all warfare? Analyze and critically discuss.

Is There Common Ground?

In this issue both writers acknowledge multiple factors that might have caused the Maya collapse. Make a comprehensive list, based on your reading of both selections. Then, divide the list into two sections—one that applies to the entire civilization and another that applies only or mainly to one or more of the city-states.

Question: Would you be able to build a case that all of these factors, in one way or another, played a role in the Maya collapse? Or, are you more convinced that the civilization collapsed piece by piece. The common ground will be found in agreement between authors on the points that support your thesis.

Additional Resources

There are many highly recommendable books on the Mayas. Some of the recent additions to the field of Mayanology are: David Webster, *The Fall of the Ancient Maya: Solving the Mystery of the Maya Collapse* (Thames and Hudson, 2002); David Drew, *The Lost Chronicles of the Maya Kings* (University of California Press, 1999); and Arthur A. Demarest, *Ancient Maya: The Rise and Fall of a Rainforest Civilization* (Cambridge University Press, 2004). Several anthologies offer new insights into the Maya collapse: Arthur A. Demarest, Prudence M. Rice, and Don S. Rice, eds., *The Terminal Classic in the Maya Lowlands Collapse, Transition, and Transformation* (University of Oklahoma Press, 2003); and M. Katherine Brown and Travis W. Stanton, eds., *Ancient Mesoamerican Warfare* (AltaMira Press, 2003). Recently the role of drought in the Maya collapse has been emphasized by some. For information, consult Richardson Benedict Gill, *The Great Maya Droughts: Water, Life, and Death* (University of New Mexico Press, 2001).

Internet References . . .

Lost King of the Maya

Site based on a 2001 PBS special, which contains a guided tour of important Maya sites, a historical account of their first discovery, a map of the Maya world, an exercise in reading Maya hieroglyphs, and a list of related resources.

www.pbs.org/wgbh/nova/maya/

Selected, Edited, and with Issue Framing Material by:
Helen Buss Mitchell, *Howard Community College*
and
Joseph R. Mitchell, *Howard Community College*

ISSUE

Could the Crusades Be Considered a Christian Holy War?

YES: Arthur Jones, from "Memories of Crusades Live on in Today's War," *National Catholic Reporter* (vol. 38, no. 1, p. 1, October 26, 2001)

NO: Jonathan Phillips, from "Who Were the First Crusaders?" *History Today* (vol. 47, no. 3, p. 16, March 1997)

Learning Outcomes

After reading this issue you should be able to:

- Describe the goals and purposes of the Crusades from the perspective of Christian Church leaders.
- Create your own definition for what might qualify as a "holy war."
- List and describe the reasons given by individuals for undertaking a Crusade.
- Describe the spread of Islam from the seventh to the eleventh centuries.

ISSUE SUMMARY

YES: Editor-at-Large Arthur Jones argues that the Crusades could be called a Christian Holy War and finds resonances of that long-ago conflict in today's Muslim–Christian conflicts.

NO: Lecturer in Medieval History Jonathan Phillips argues that motivations for the Crusades included religious fervor, the desire for wealth, and a family history of pilgrimage, not holy war.

Arthur Jones begins his selection with President Bush's inadvertent use of the word "crusade" on September 16, 2001 ("This crusade, this war on terrorism, is going to take a long time.")—a word Jones claims echoed into Muslim memories of centuries of Christian incursions. Point of view is pivotal. Christians might view the Crusades as a noble effort to reclaim the central sites of their faith, or as an unfortunate but long forgotten chapter in world history. Muslims, by contrast, may have fresh memories of "the holy religious war of the Christians" and their own "war against the cross" that began in the eleventh century and continues today.

Christianity began as a persecuted sect in the Roman Empire that took seriously its founder's injunction to "turn the other cheek" and repay evil with good. Early Christians would have no part of war. But by the fourth century, Constantine, the Holy Roman Emperor, had won battles with the cross on his shield and made Christianity the official faith of the empire. And, in the fifth century, Augustine had articulated a Just War Theory for Christianity. Even against this background, however, papally sanctioned violence was something new, Jones suggests.

Muhammad's revelation from God ignited a fervor on the Arabian Peninsula that swept across north Africa and into Christian Europe, beginning in the seventh century. By 750 it had spread throughout the Byzantine Empire. At least in part, Jones argues, the Crusades can be viewed as a Christian counteroffensive, designed to take back their conquered territories and reclaim the Holy Land, the site of Jesus's ministry, death, burial, and resurrection.

Muslims regard both Jews and Christians as People of the Book, praise their prophets—Abraham, Moses, and Jesus—and have historically permitted them to worship freely in Muslim territories. The higher head tax Jews and Christians had to pay in Muslim-controlled lands was another disincentive to convert them. So, in the Fertile Crescent, Muslims and Christians had lived together for centuries before the First Crusade—in mutual toleration, if not friendship. One key to the ferocity of the First Crusade is its point of origin. Most Frankish knights would have had no contact with Islam. However, their epic poem "The Song of Roland" changed the "enemy" that defeated Charlemagne's rearguard in the Pyrenees from the Basques, who were the actual victors, into the "treacherous" Muslims of Spain.

Jonathan Phillips situates the Crusades within the social, intellectual, religious, economic, and psychological realities of late eleventh-century Europe, which he calls "one of the most guilt-ridden societies in history." People, he argues, would have had many reasons for joining a crusade—the promise of salvation, the lure of wealth, and family traditions of pilgrimage. And, Pope Urban II's original goal was a very specific one—to assist the Byzantine Emperor Alexius in his struggle against the Seljuk Turks of Asia Minor. These motivations, Phillips contends, are sufficient to account for the 60,000 who joined the First Crusade. It is not necessary to posit the rallying point of a "holy war" as motivation.

Fulcher of Chartres, the priest-chaplain of the First Crusade, described "a new path to heaven" and said confidently that those who undertook this "holy war" would experience "forgiveness of sins." Those who quest for God—in the eleventh century or the twenty-first—believe they will be blessed. During the Seventh Crusade, led by St. Louis, King of France, Yves le Breton reported encountering an old woman who wandered the streets with a dish of fire in her right hand and a bowl of water in her left hand. With the fire, she explained, she would burn up Paradise, until there was nothing left of it, and, with the water, she would put out the fires of Hell, until nothing remained of them. "Because," she said, "I want no one to do good in order to receive the reward of Paradise, or from fear of Hell; but solely out of love for God."

With the emergence of Islamic revivalism in the modern world, the historical relationships between the West and the Muslim world have attained a renewed level of interest. The relevance of the Crusades to this contemporary situation provides some food for thought. The Islamic world has always viewed the Crusades as an invasion of its territory by a foreign power; it appears the West has not viewed them in the same light. An interesting question with contemporary applicability is: To what extent can the Crusades be viewed as a Christian *jihad* (Holy War)? As the West responds to Islamic-inspired terrorism today with shock and outrage, is it not possible that a millennium ago, Middle Eastern Muslims responded in the same manner to the European crusaders?

Both struggles spring, at least in part from religious motivation. Christian crusaders believed they were fighting a just war in the service of God; securing indulgences for services rendered; and the ultimate prize, gaining the right to eternal salvation. With a slight change in language, we hear the same promises in Islamic revivalism—fighting the infidels in the name of Allah; participating in a fierce struggle between the forces of good and evil; and ultimately acquiring a special place in heaven as martyrs of the faith. Failure to hear these resonances might prevent us from learning a lesson from history.

For general sources on the Crusades, start with Steven Runciman's three-volume work *A History of the Crusades*, 4th ed. (Cambridge University Press, 1954). Jonathan Riley-Smith's *The First Crusaders, 1095–1131* (Cambridge University Press, 1997) represents current scholarship. Smith states that the Crusades "drew on the tradition of Pilgrimage to Jerusalem . . . and pious violence" as motivating forces. He also points out that many of the Crusaders from the times he researched came from the same families and clans, and concludes that the sustenance they received from these ties helped make the Crusades possible. A readable, popular account of the Crusades, which features many interesting illustrations and useful maps, is W.B. Bartlett, *God Wills It: An Illustrated History of the Crusades* (Oxford University Press, 1999). Another good general source is Thomas F. Madden, *A Concise History of the Crusades* (Roman & Littlefield, 1999).

Editor-at-Large Arthur Jones presents a case for calling the Crusades a Christian holy war and finds resonances of that long-ago conflict in today's Muslim–Christian conflicts. Lecturer in Medieval History Jonathan Phillips finds motivations for the Crusades in religious fervor, the desire for wealth, and a family history of pilgrimage, not in holy war.

YES

Arthur Jones

Memories of Crusades Live on in Today's War

Crusade!

On Sept. 16, the word shot around the Islamic world. And shocked it. President George W. Bush thought he'd used the term innocently enough. On that Sunday, walking from his helicopter to the White House, he said of U.S. retaliation to the Sept. 11 attacks, "this crusade, this war on terrorism, is going to take a long time."

As the Muslim uproar swelled, Bush quickly apologized. But damage had been done. The BBC, for example, in its Persian and Uzbeck broadcast news services, had translated Bush's remark in the way the Islamic world understands it, as "the war of those signed with the cross," and "the holy, religious war of the Christians." (In Islam's many national languages, from Arabic to Farsi to Urdu, the Muslims call their defense against the crusaders, "the war against the cross.")

Only a minority of Muslims actually believe America had declared a "holy war" against them, cautions Paul E. Chevedden of the University of California, Los Angeles. And Georgetown University's Zahid H. Bukhari, speaking of both Muslims and Westerners, said, "Certain lobbies, certain people, do use the word [crusade] to project what is happening because they have their own agendas to present. They like the terminology and can be more effective because of it."

To Muslims, whose memory of historic grievances may be sharper than that of most Christians, the concept of a "holy war" has implications lost in history's mists. To some millions of Muslims within the Islamic world, crusade still means centuries of bloody Western Christian incursions fought over the Holy Land. Those memories are like ghosts dancing to the U.S. drums of war.

NCR talked to historians of religion and those engaged in Muslim-Christian dialogue and, as the globe's sole superpower searches for one man among the rocks and caves of Islamic Afghanistan, learned lessons for today from the history of the medieval crusades. From today's perspective, there are some surprises, some odd similarities and parallels.

Christians did indeed at one time have their "holy wars," accompanied by language that could have come from bin Laden himself.

The historical record tells us that Fulcher of Chartres (1058–1130), priest-chaplain on the First Crusade, wrote in his eyewitness account that this Crusade was a *novum salutis genus,* "a new path to Heaven." Those Christians who followed this "holy war" path would, wrote Fulcher, experience "full and complete satisfaction" and "forgiveness of sins."

A World Bursting Apart

To Chevedden, however, who is an associate at UCLA's Gustav E. von Grunebaum Center for Near Eastern Studies, the Crusades have to be understood as part of tremendous geo-political, socio-economic and religious shifts underway at the time. "The Mediterranean world of the 11th century was changing in a remarkable manner; it was witnessing the birth of a new world. The Crusades were the product of the sudden and all-transforming change that produced Western European civilization. An old world burst apart, and a new one took its place."

Bukhari, director and principal co-investigator for Georgetown's Muslims in the American Public Square project, and Fr. James Fredericks of Loyola Marymount theology department, see similar shifts underway today. Bukhari explained that during a period of great transformation "the Crusades were a clash of religions. In the transformations of modern times, we have a clash of civilizations. To some extent there is the same connotation, the whole West as a symbol of Christianity, the entire Muslim world as the symbol of Islam."

But what must be taken into account, he said, is the evolution underway. One aspect of that, he said, is "the evolving debate within Islam about living according to Islamic beliefs, to divine guidance. The notion of how to do that has been evolving since World War II, which triggered the end of colonialism. Among Muslim countries and the Muslim world (which includes those Muslims who live as minorities in non-Muslim countries), there is a debate over issues of democracy, civil rights, human rights, the role of women and living with people of other faiths."

And that debate, he said, "will be violent in some places, look absurd in others, be serious in others, but evolve ultimately, hopefully, in a positive direction."

Bukhari, a Pakistani who has lived in the West for 17 years, said that when "looked at in the time period of 30 to 40 years, things are going very much in a positive direction. Especially with those Muslims living in Western societies. But we are talking only about 30 to 40 years. What evolution will the next 30 to 40 years bring?"

Fredericks, a priest of the San Francisco archdiocese whose field is comparative religion, comments, "We

Americans are so concerned with the violent [Islamic] fringe, we miss what's going on at a deeper level."

To Fredericks, the geo-politic transformations Islam is signaling are enormous. This is a huge, huge topic. First, Christianity and Islam—you cannot say it about Judaism—are religions that have been at the foundations of empires. Further, Christianity and Islam are the bases of entire cultural outlooks.

Christian nations today are, by and large, secular societies, in which Protestantism was able to adjust more quickly than Roman Catholicism. "Christianity has made its peace—an uneasy truce—with secular culture. Christianity," he continued, "has grudgingly yielded its place at the center of culture. It isn't that anymore."

The peace isn't total, and opposition to the peace does not just come from Christian reactionaries, traditionalists and conservatives. "We see opposition," he said, "not just from the new religious right, though in the culture wars they get all the publicity, but in the theology of liberation. The theology of liberation also says that religious voices, religious values, need to be very public realities at the center of culture.

"The other thing—and it's such a complicated picture," he said, "there is something in the very character of Christianity that resists privatization. Christianity wants to be a very public religion. So when Christianity becomes a private religion, it is in a rather anomalous situation."

The same statement, he said, can be made about Islam. "Islam wants to be a very public force, a very public reality." Islam wants of its very character to be the basis of society. It always has.

"From the beginnings of Islam," said Fredericks, "submitting to Islam meant renouncing one culture that was sinful and violent and discriminatory and based on petty racial and ethnic rivalries, and recognizing there is this universal humanity, universal morality. A powerful conversion takes place from an immoral society to a moral society." In fact, he said, submission—submission to Allah—is what Islam means.

For Islam to accept a privatized place within secular society "is very, very difficult. We in the West tend to presume that this is an inevitable process. I think that's naive."

Fredericks argues that because Christians "slowly and begrudgingly, and with a great deal of violence" more or less worked out a modus vivendi with the secular nation, Muslims will not necessarily follow suit.

"Why should we presume that that's normative?" he asked.

"Alternative Modernities"

Speaking to Bukhari's point about Islam in the recent post-colonial period, Fredericks talked of "alternative modernities," of Islamic states developing in unique and non-Western ways.

He uses Indonesia, the largest of all Islamic nations, as an example. "If one allows, and it is controversial to do so, that Indonesia's Sukarno [1949–1967] and Suharto [1967–1998] regimes were aftermaths connected to Dutch colonialism, then what we're hearing from Indonesia's Muslims today is, 'We want to be a nation. We don't want to go back to the Middle Ages. And—the West doesn't get this—we want to be a modern nation. We just don't want to be modern the way you're modern. We think that's sick.' "

Think of such a development, says Fredericks, in terms "of 'religious nationalism' as an alternative to Western secularism. Islam saying our religious nationalism is a way of being a modern, national state: Economically competitive, a state able to provide basic social services to its population. We want to be a success. But secularism—with all the immorality that comes with it—isn't going to cut it for us. We're not that kind of people. We want to be an Islamic state."

What the world may be witnessing, contends Fredericks, is not just a violent fringe but manifestations of religious nationalism that from Egypt to Iran to Indonesia "may have more in common with the theology of liberation than we've recognized. Both are a critique of Western secular, capitalist, consumerist, materialist, globalist secularism. And that's something we ought to pay attention to and be respectful of." Like Islam, liberation theology seeks to put Christian values, such as a preferential option for the poor, at the center of culture.

Scott Bartchy, director of the Center for the Study of Religion at UCLA, said Americans need to understand that at the deepest level they have been moving away from cultural values built around honor—shame—still the dominant framework for values around much of the world. In contrast, the United States "has an achievement-guilt culture focused almost entirely on the individual," he said.

"Certainly we have very little sense of honor," he said. "Most Americans will say honor is nice, but give me the check instead. And if we had any shame, we wouldn't have had the last 20 years of U.S. politics."

Bartchy said that in Germany in the 1970s, Chancellor Willi Brandt resigned as a matter of honor when an East German mole penetrated West Germany's security services. In Japan, "CEOs or government officers caught in whatever, resign." By contrast, he said, "in America if you get caught out, you back and fill. You don't resign, you just tough it out."

The 80 percent of the world living with honor-shame values have strict gender divisions and roles, systems that generate enormous competition among the males, and a sense of bonding within the family. "Islam," he said, "has created a sense of what anthropologists call 'fictive' and I choose to call 'surrogate' kinship: It goes beyond the family to create a sense of brotherhood. It's no accident that the extremist group in Egypt is the 'Brotherhood.' "

In many ways, said Bartchy, "Islam, for all the way it looks, is still kind of a thin overlay of ancient tribal cultures." For example, nothing in the Quran or the Islamic tradition supports honor killing of women, yet in some countries women are killed if they have been raped, he said. "If the father isn't strong enough, the brothers are supposed to go out there and kill that woman. And if they can kill her in public it's even better, because that at least eliminates the shame from the family."

The only groups in the United States that live up to these strong honor-shame codes, Bartchy said, are inner-city gangs and the Mafia. They cannot allow themselves or their family to be "dissed, or shamed." Every time they step over the threshold, they are in competition with the world outside. "From the time you're 3 years old until you die, you do and say those things that will bring honor back to your family."

Which, in part, said Bartchy, explains Osama bin Laden's popularity in Afghanistan. "Whatever else he was doing," he said, "Osama was accumulating an enormous amount of honor. Spending his own wealth initially on the widows and orphans of the mujahideen—an enormous contrast to what the royal elites back home in Saudi Arabia were doing."

In bin Laden's eyes, said Bartchy, these Saudis were not sharing, and Islam requires it. As bin Laden and those sympathetic to him looked at the United States, "they saw the ever-increasing gap between the elite—the enormously rich—and the Americans at the bottom. Then Osama and his allies looked at the Saudi leadership doing the same and reasoned: 'How did Saudis learn that those values are OK? Because they looked to the West.'" (Bartchy left unanswered the next question: "How did the West learn that those values are OK?")

"Basically," he said, "what Muslims in the Near East want is the same things we want. Even the most conservative bring their kids to the United States to be educated. What they can't understand is how we say we're so strong for democracy and participation and yet we continue to prop up regimes in their part of the world they regard as terribly oppressive and corrupt."

At home what bothers Bartchy is the tone of the American popular response, even among his students. They believe, he said, "the only way to look at us is as the victims. We can do anything we damn well please overseas, and that should never have any effect on what comes down."

What the Peeves Really Are

Bush used the word crusade and apologized. He warned against racism and bigotry, and visited with Muslims at Islamic centers. Sound moves?

If Bush wants support, to prove he's not against Islam "the first place you start is at home," said Yvonne Haddad, professor of the history of Islam and Christian-Muslim relations at Georgetown University. "And his rhetoric—in the speech to Congress, listening to it as an American, I was impressed. Listening with the other ear, as Muslims overseas would hear it, it was awful: he talked about 'us' and 'them,' you're either with us or against us. He showed no reflection on what the issues, the peeves, really are."

And some of those peeves can be seen as related to the Crusades. Israel occupies the same geographic area the Crusades were about, she said. "Therefore anybody who supports Israel's policies is perceived as continuing the Crusades."

And a thousand years after the first one, the Crusades remain a source of contention.

Pressures That Led to an Empire-wide Movement

The Nine Crusades, which took place in the 11th, 12th and 13th centuries, were a counteroffensive by Christians against Muslims occupying the Holy Land.

Was the Islamic threat real? "You betcha," said Professor Paul E. Chevedden. "Islamic conquest had taken from Christendom its choicest province—Syria, Egypt, North Africa and Iberia [Spain and Portugal]."

Islam pushed its way north into Italy until it captured Monte Cassino, St. Benedict's monastery, then moved into eastern Switzerland. On the Great St. Bernard Pass, Muslims even captured the abbot of Cluny, France.

The Crusades, in response, were applications of Roman Catholicism's "just war" tradition, said Chevedden of UCLA's Gustav E. von Grunebaum Center for Near Eastern Studies. Islam had the Holy Land, and the pope wanted it back.

A grave pitfall for today, insists Chevedden, would be to view the Crusades in isolation from the world-transforming events in the Mediterranean and in western Asia at the turn of the second millennium. Those events included pressures from expanding populations, rapidly developing urbanism, intellectual and technological inquiries and advances, plus rising commerce pushing into new areas.

The clash between Christendom and Islam was a 1,000-year struggle, the most protracted conflict in human history. What should not be overlooked, Chevedden said, is that, for the most part, Islam, rather than Christianity, was in the ascendancy.

Scott Bartchy, director of UCLA's Center for the Study of Religion, though well aware of what Islam gave to the West during those 1,000 years, looks at the early heritage of both Christianity and Islam from the perspective of violence/non-violence.

During the first 250 to 300 years of Christianity, it was initially persecuted, then scapegoated through four more tense periods, as it became an empire-wide movement. "Never," emphasized Bartchy, "never once during this period is anybody killed in the name of Jesus. The Christians are not a guerrilla band, they are not social bandits. They stay in the urban environment, gain a reputation not only for helping their own widows and orphans, but others' as well. Not only burying their own dead but—a major deal at that time—other people's as well. They never become violent."

Bartchy called it "remarkable" that Jesus' nonviolence had taken "such a hold" across those early centuries. It was Emperor Constantine's adopting Christianity as the Roman Empire's religion in the fourth century that "wrecked things. He never got it," said Bartchy. "He puts the Chi-Rho symbol on Roman shields, and for the first time Christians start killing people in the name of Jesus."

Bartchy contrasts that Jesus with Islam's Muhammad who, in the early seventh century, "goes into Medina and in effect becomes the civil authority. Functionally he's an innovator, a Jesus of Nazareth and a Constantine, all rolled into one."

Bartchy said Muhammad "never ever renounces violence, and for all the fine things in the Islamic tradition, there's never been any serious commitment to nonviolence. In a war, if you follow the prophet, you shouldn't hurt women or children. Or trees. Quite charming that. And the violence should be defensive."

Bartchy said that after the Crusades the Near Eastern Islamic world felt itself transgressed upon, "and there's a certain victim mentality." Culturally, he said, Muslims saved much from the Greek philosophers that the West later appropriated. Technologically Islam held its own, even into the 16th and 17th centuries. "But then the West got the technological edge in military stuff and began pushing," said Bartchy, "and the Muslims again get into the mentality of being victims."

Consequently, Bartchy summarized, today "some of the more extreme people have given themselves permission to do almost anything in the name of defense. And that's what we see."

The Crusades were religious, political and economic. The First Millennium had just ended, the 11th century was the setting of an enormous spiritual revival. For centuries, with the Holy Land under benign Islamic rule, pilgrims traveled together to Jerusalem under arms to protect themselves from robbers. Confessors in that era regularly gave pilgrimages as a penance, so ensuring the safety of pilgrims was one element of the Crusades.

Other elements included merchants in Italian cities wanting Eastern trading outlets and the ambitions of chivalrous knights—high-born youths looking for action and conquest.

There also was a shift within Islam precipitating the Crusades. The more restrictive Turkish Muslims had taken over the Holy Land, and the pope, disenchanted with the warring European nobles' inability to form a coalition to battle Islam, brought his own unifying authority to bear.

The scene was set, and all the elements combined in the urge to free the Holy Land from Islam. Thus nine Crusades, each generally less successful than the one before it.

Crusaders Went from Victory to Disaster

In box scores, there were nine Crusades between 1095 and 1272. The outcome was Crusaders 2, Muslims 5, plus two negotiated ties. And the Muslims remained in control.

The Crusades (1095–1272) got their name from the crosses Pope Urban II distributed in 1095 after he called on the factious European kings and princes to band together and recover the Holy Sepulcher from the Muslim Seljuk Turks.

They agreed. It would be the first of nine crusades.

Even as the potential First Crusaders were looking into strategy and logistics, peasants in France heard the papal call. Less worried than their leaders about tactics and supplies, several thousand started marching. They resupplied themselves by sacking Belgrade. German peasants set out and financed themselves by attacking Jews.

At Constantinople, what was left of these ragtag bands joined forces, sailed to Jerusalem, dispersed the Turks and declared a victory.

The European nobility finally set off, led by Raymond IV of Toulouse and Bishop Ademar. The First Crusade (1096–99) took Nicea, Antioch and consolidated Western control over what they now called the Latin Kingdom of Jerusalem, with Godfrey of Bouillon as ruler.

The Muslims retaliated. The Second Crusade (1147–49) failed to recapture cities taken by the Turks; the Third Crusade (1189–91) failed to retake Jerusalem, which was back in Muslim hands. But Saladin decreed Christians could have access to the Holy Sepulcher.

The Fourth Crusade (1220–04) got bogged down in the more profitable venture of fighting Venice, sacking Constantinople, crushing the Byzantine Empire and establishing the Latin Empire of Constantinople.

Quite disastrous was the 1202 Children's Crusade, led by two young peasants. Stephen in France and Nicolas in Germany led several thousand children out of their homelands and into starvation and disease, and into the arms of adults who sold them into slavery and other fates worse than death.

The second longest crusade, the Fifth Crusade (1218–21) was an unsuccessful war against Egypt, and the Sixth Crusade (1228–29), which eschewed military arms, was led by Holy Roman Emperor Frederick II who negotiated a degree of Christian control over the holy sites.

France's Louis IX led the next two crusades, the Seventh (1248–50) and Eighth (1270), with no noticeable gains. Louis died in North Africa, and the Eighth Crusade was called off. The English launched the Ninth Crusade (1271–72) under Prince Edward. It changed nothing, though the prince later became King Edward I.

Arthur Jones is editor-at-large for *The National Catholic* Reporter.

Jonathan Phillips

Who Were the First Crusaders?

Who were the people who answered Urban II's call to crusade between 1096 and 1099? Jonathan Phillips investigates their origins and motives.

The canons of the council summarised the offer made by Urban II as he launched the First Crusade:

> Whoever, for devotion alone, not to gain honour or money, goes to Jerusalem to liberate the Church of God can substitute this journey for all penance.

In other words, if people fought God's enemies on earth and completed a pilgrimage to the Holy Land, their actions would receive a spiritual reward of remarkable magnitude. Urban blended the familiar ideas of pilgrimage and penance with the more radical notion of papally-sanctioned violence to produce what a contemporary writer described as "a new means of attaining salvation." He followed the speech at Clermont with an extensive preaching tour through France and by the dispatch of letters and legations elsewhere in Europe.

The response to his appeal was remarkable, and in total almost 60,000 people set out for the Holy Land. The population of Europe at the end of the eleventh century is estimated to have been around 20 million, so clearly the vast majority of people chose to remain in the West. If, however, one adds contact through ties of family and friendship then it is clear that the crusade touched the lives of millions.

Fulcher of Chartres, a participant in the crusade, wrote that people "of any and every occupation" took the cross. He also commented "whoever heard of such a mixture of languages in one army, since there were French, Flemings, Frisians, Gauls, Allobroges [Savoyards], Lotharingians, Allemani [South Germans and Swiss], Bavarians, Normans, English, Scots, Aquitainians, Italians, Danes, Apulians, Iberians, Bretons, Greeks and Armenians." Representatives of the last two groups probably joined the expedition en route, but the remainder had been attracted by Urban's initial call to arms. The crusade therefore appealed to people from almost every level of society right across Christian Europe. The purpose here is to give some insight into who the First Crusaders were, to explain why they took the cross, and to understand the importance of identifying those who took part in the expedition.

The reasons for such a wide-ranging response are complex. Our distance from events and the nature of the surviving evidence mean that we can never achieve a perfect insight into a crusader's mind. We should not necessarily look for a single motive in determining an individual's desire to take the cross, although certain themes emerge more clearly than others. An understanding of the actions of each crusader must be grounded in the cultural, political and economic context of the time.

Spiritual concerns were a prominent factor governing people's lives in the late eleventh century. It was an intensely religious age; pilgrimage and monastic life flourished, and donations to ecclesiastical institutions were increasingly commonplace. Christian Europe was also one of the most guilt-ridden societies in history. Sin was ubiquitous in everyday life and the images of fire and torture so frequently depicted on churches reinforced the fear of eternal damnation. The need for all people—whether rich or poor, nobles or labourers—to atone for their actions helps to explain the level of enthusiasm for the First Crusade and also the crusaders' determination to fulfil their vows by completing the journey to Jerusalem.

The pope's original conception of the crusade was for a compact contingent of knights to assist Emperor Alexius of Byzantium in his struggle against the Seljuk Turks of Asia Minor before marching on to the Holy Land. His appeal was directed, therefore, towards the knightly classes of his native France, a region of weak central authority and endemic lawlessness which was often initiated by the knights themselves. The crusade may have been one way to channel this violence elsewhere as well as giving the knights an opportunity of salvation. The knights responded in large numbers and formed the backbone of the Christian army.

As we have seen, however, Urban's offer was so attractive that almost all elements of society were represented on the crusade. The most notable exception to this was the absence of any kings. Urban regarded the crusade as a papally-directed enterprise and had not explicitly invited the secular monarchs to become involved. In any case, Philip I of France was excommunicated on account of an adulterous relationship with the Countess of Anjou; Henry IV of Germany was the papacy's principal opponent in a bitter struggle concerning the supremacy of lay versus sacral power (known as the Investiture Contest), and William Rufus was too entangled in the government of England to be particularly interested. It was not until the crusade of Sigurd of Norway (1107–10), that a king participated in a campaign in the Holy Land, although it should be noted that the rulers of Spain had long been involved in the Reconquista, their own struggle against the Muslims.

While the non-participation of kings may be regarded as part of Urban's design, the pope had not anticipated that his call would appeal to monks. He wrote "we do not want those who have abandoned the world and vowed themselves to spiritual warfare either to bear arms or to go on this journey; we go so far as to forbid them to do so." Other churchmen such as priests and clerks, were permitted to join as long as they secured the permission of their bishop, and in any case, some religious officials were needed to administer to the crusaders' spiritual needs during the course of the expedition. Urban's message also struck a deep chord with the wider populace, including women, children, the old, the infirm and the poor. Clearly these groups would hinder the progress of an army because they had to be fed and protected. The pope tried to limit their involvement by requiring people to consult their parish priests before taking their vows, but this measure failed and the crusade set out accompanied by many noncombatants. In the course of the crusade the majority of this anonymous mass perished through starvation or disease, deserted, or were enslaved.

It is among the members of the noble and knightly classes that we can begin to pinpoint the individuals who took the cross. In part this is because, as men of standing, their deeds feature in the narrative accounts of the crusade. Some, such as the southern Italian knight, Hugh the Beserk, are mentioned on only one occasion for an act of particular bravery: in this case because Hugh had single-handedly defended a tower for an entire day against Turkish attacks during the siege of Antioch. For the leaders of the major contingents, however, there is a much fuller picture, particularly when their force happens to have included a chronicler. The anonymous author of the Gesta Francorum, for example, was a member of Bohemond of Taranto's army, and Raymond of Aguilers was the chaplain to Raymond of Saint-Gilles, the Count of Toulouse. The latter writer noted "It seems too tiresome to write of each journey . . . so we have taken care to write of the Count of Saint-Gilles without bothering with the others." In the case of Hugh of Vermandois, younger brother of Philip I of France, there is much less information because, as far as we are aware, no member of his contingent wrote an account of the crusade.

While narrative works provide the majority of our material they are not the only source of information for the crusade. In recent years the use of charters has enhanced our understanding of the motivation, financing and family networks of the crusaders. It is the nature of eleventh-century charters which holds the key to this. Charters from later periods tend to convey only a bare minimum of information, such as names, places, dates, and the exact subject of the transaction. Some charters from the time of the First Crusade, however, provide more of a clue to the hopes and fears of individual crusaders, as well as basic factual information.

Crusading was extremely expensive. To equip oneself with chainmail, horses and supplies would cost a great deal—some estimates suggest over four years' annual income. However, the recent experience of the Norman Conquest, for example, would have given people some idea of the resources needed to fight a large-scale and lengthy military expedition. In order to finance the crusade it was often necessary to mortgage or sell lands and rights to the church. The records of these transactions give further indication as to who took part and how they raised money for the journey. Incidentally, the issue of cost is another reason why the old cliche of crusaders being freebooting younger sons is deeply suspect, simply because such men would have been unable to afford to set out in the first instance.

In fact, largely through the use of charters, all sorts of combinations of family members can be found on the crusade. For example, Hugh of Merysur-Seine mortgaged lands at Rosnay to the abbey of Molesme in order to pay for both his own and his brother's journey. Jonathan Riley-Smith has traced the remarkable involvement of the Montlhery clan. One member, Miles of Bray, was accompanied on the First Crusade by his son, Guy, his brother-in-law, Walter of St. Valery, and two of Walter's sons; his nephew, Baldwin (later Baldwin II of Jerusalem), and two other nephews—Humberge of Le Puiset and Everard III of Le Puiset—were amongst members of the network to take the cross in 1095–96.

Some crusader families had an existing tradition of pilgrimage to the Holy Land which may have formed a further reason for their taking the cross. For example, both the great-grandfather and the grandfather of the First Crusader, Adhemar III of Limoges, had been to Jerusalem in the course of the eleventh century. The influence of pilgrimage is a theme more thoroughly explored in the work of Marcus Bull.

Although the religious motivation of the First Crusaders should be emphasised, it would be naive to argue that other interests were absent. When a noble embarked upon the crusade it was inevitable that he would be accompanied by his household retainers. He would have to provide support for his knights, squires and servants. All were an integral part of a medieval army and, because of this, ties of allegiance and loyalty should be advanced as a further reason for taking the cross, even though such a commitment was, in theory, a strictly voluntary exercise. The desire for land was a further motive, but it did not apply to all the crusaders. Many charters contain clauses detailing financial arrangements that would come into force only if the crusader died during the expedition. Such measures suggest that the participants were well aware of the dangers of the crusade, but hoped to return home once the vow was completed. Two brothers, Bernard and Odo, entered into an agreement with the abbey of Cluny:

> For the remission of our sins, setting out with all the others on the journey to Jerusalem, we have made over for 100 solidi . . . a manor known as Busart. We are making this on the condition that

> if, on the pilgrimage that we are undertaking, we may die, the manor may remain in perpetuity under the control of . . . the monastery of Cluny. But if we may return . . . we may keep it in our lifetime, but after our death it may not come into the possession of our heirs . . . but will pass to Cluny.

The fact that the Crusader States were seriously undermanned throughout their existence also indicates that relatively few crusaders chose to remain in the Levant and become settlers. Some men, however, were explicit in their intention never to return to the West and clearly planned to carve out new territories for themselves in the East. Raymond of Saint-Gilles was rumoured to be one such person. The French knight Achard of Montmerle might also have been planning to stay in the Holy Land. The charter detailing his agreement with the abbey of Cluny includes the clause "if I die, or if I choose to remain in those lands [the Levant] . . ." shows at least an awareness of the possibility of settling in the East, a course of action which would presumably necessitate the taking of land.

The need to repay debts incurred in paying for the expedition, coupled with poor economic conditions—a series of droughts and bad harvests had marked the early 1090s—suggests that the desire for money may have been a priority for the crusaders. Perhaps the search for salvation and the wish for financial gain seem too mutually exclusive in our eyes. One has only to think of TV evangelism to shudder at the potential for abuse in this connection, yet it is not improbable or contradictory that pious men took the cross also hoping to improve their financial and material prospects. There must also have been crusaders for whom the wish to accumulate wealth predominated. The sources indicate that such people must have been gravely disappointed. There is remarkably little evidence of people returning from the crusade with newfound riches. One rare example is reported by Abbot Suger of Saint Denis. He wrote that Count Guy of Rochefort "returned from the expedition to Jerusalem renowned and rich," an ironic reversal of Urban II's injunction against crusaders seeking honour or money.

People certainly brought back relics from the Holy Land. Lord Riou of Loheac, for example, acquired a fragment of the True Cross and bequeathed it to his local church when he died in 1101. But the experience of the First Crusade does not suggest that it was the route to easy profit. None-the-less, the narrative sources contain frequent reports of the crusaders seeking booty. After the siege of Ma'arrat an Nu'man (December 1098) Muslim graves were dug up and the bodies slit open to check if any treasure had been swallowed. Acts of a similarly brutal nature were repeated elsewhere. The most likely explanation for this behaviour is that substantial sums of money were required to keep the expedition going.

The duration and rigour of the campaign exhausted the resources of the vast majority. Crusaders endured terrible suffering during the march across Asia Minor and at the siege of Antioch (October 1097–June 1098). Food prices became grossly inflated and losses of horses and equipment were enormous. It is an important distinction, therefore, that acts of greed were usually initiated in response to the need to survive, rather than the long-term motivation to accumulate treasure. For those interested solely in money, the cost of warfare and the duration of the expedition meant that the depredation of land closer to home had to be a safer option than going on crusade. If some had set out hoping to acquire untold riches it seems that the hardships of the expedition soon deterred them because throughout the course of the crusade a stream of deserters left the main army unable to endure the experience.

News of the expedition to Jerusalem spread rapidly across Northern and Central Europe and also down through Italy and to Sicily. The pope accepted the reality of the situation and began to dispatch letters of instruction and encouragement to these areas. The only region where he actively discouraged recruitment was the Iberian peninsula because he did not want people distracted from the "reconquista," although we know that some Spanish crusaders ignored him and travelled to Jerusalem. When the forces of the First Crusade began to assemble in 1096 the racial mix of the armies is an impressive testimony to the power of Urban's appeal. Another indication of the range of participants involved is provided by Raymond of Aguilers. He relates that in the Provencal contingent alone no less than seven different currencies were in circulation. He mentioned the use of coins from Lucca, Chartres, Le Mans, Melgueil, Le Puy, Valence and Poitou. Currency from the first five places have been discovered in a single collection at Antioch and tentatively associated with the siege that took place there.

Because almost every region of Latin Christendom was represented on the First Crusade difficulties emerged in communication and leadership. Problems also arose on account of hostility between regional contingents of the army. An episode related by Ralph of Caen—a visitor to the Levant soon after the First Crusade—serves to illustrate the tensions that sometimes broke out in the course of the campaign. As morale sagged during the siege of Antioch, gangs of northern and southern French grouped up on linguistic lines to forage for supplies. They assaulted or freed their captives according to the language they spoke, while those responding in tongues other than Occitan or a northern French dialect were spared as neutrals.

In the course of the crusade and afterwards, the Franks (as they were known collectively) established a series of states in the Levant. During the early years of settlement the polyglot nature of the crusader army was, to some extent, distilled. In some states the origins of the dominant Latin Christian element reflected the ancestry of the particular leader who had based himself there. Bohemond of Taranto's principality of Antioch had a strong contingent of Normans from Southern Italy. Similarly, because it was Raymond of Saint-Gilles who had set up the county of Tripoli, the area had a Provencal influence. The kingdom of Jerusalem, in consequence of its spiritual importance, attracted sellers from a wider number of regions and represented, therefore, a more diverse grouping.

The creation of the Frankish states, each with its own character and links to the West, as well as the over-arching bond of Latin Christianity, meant that strong ties existed between the settlers and their co-religionists in Europe. As the Muslim jihad gathered momentum in the course of the twelfth century, the Franks in the East needed military and financial help. It is interesting to note that traditions of crusading and ties of kinship between those in the Holy Land and the West were two ideas that the settlers emphasised in their attempts to secure support.

Pope Eugenius III drew attention to the concept of crusading ancestory in Quantum Praedecessores his appeal for the Second Crusade (1145–49). He wrote:

> It will be seen as a great token of nobility and uprightness if those things acquired by the efforts of the fathers are vigorously defended by you, their good sons. But if, God forbid, it comes to pass differently, then the bravery of the fathers will have proved to be diminished in the sons. We impress upon you . . . to defend in this way the Eastern Church, which was freed from their [the Muslims'] tyranny, as we have said before by the spilling of your fathers' blood.

In effect this amounted to an appeal to those families with traditions of crusading. The counts of Flanders were a group particularly receptive to such a message. They also had close family ties with the settlers. When Count Thierry took the cross in 1146 he was perpetuating a well-established line of involvement with the Holy Land. His grandfather, Robert I, had mounted a large-scale pilgrimage to Jerusalem in 1087–90. His uncle, Count Robert II, was one of the leading figures on the First Crusade. His cousin, Count Charles the Good, had visited Jerusalem around 1107, and was probably offered the throne of the kingdom of Jerusalem in 1123–24. In 1134 Thierry gained close links with the house of Jerusalem through his marriage to Sibylla of Anjou, a daughter of King Fulk. Thierry had also journeyed to the Holy Land in 1139 and seems to have planned another trip in 1142 only to turn back at an early stage.

An awareness of the identity of the First Crusaders reveals the impact of Pope Urban's call on the people of Europe in 1095–96. But answering the question "Who were the First Crusaders?" can tell us more. We are able to use the answer to start following traditions of crusading and the creation of family ties between the Levant and the West and from this information we have a better understanding of the nature of Latin settlement in the East and the subsequent history of the crusades.

Jonathan Phillips is lecturer in medieval history at Royal Holloway University of London and the author of *Defenders of the Holy Land: Relations between the Latin East and the West,* 1119–1187.

EXPLORING THE ISSUE

Could the Crusades Be Considered a Christian Holy War?

Critical Thinking and Reflection

1. Research the reasons for the First Crusade. Do you find these justifications to be well-thought-out and carefully considered? Critically discuss the implications of calling the First Crusade.
2. Research the role of the Christian Church in offering indulgences, including forgiveness of sins, as a recompense for undertaking a crusade. Are there any higher stakes? Critically discuss.
3. Examine Arthur Jones's assertion that Christianity and Islam are religions that have been at the foundations of empires and are the bases of entire cultural outlooks. What implications flow from these historical realities? Critically discuss.
4. Examine the inherent conflict between the Western acceptance of a secular society and the Muslim commitment to living in an Islamic state. What implications flow from these historical realities? Critically discuss.
5. What are the implications for this issue of Arthur Jones's statement: "The clash between Christendom and Islam was a 1,000-year struggle . . . for the most part, Islam, rather than Christianity, was in the ascendency."? How, for examples, did Muslims treat Christians when they (Muslims) controlled Jerusalem? And, what was the Christian posture toward Muslims in similar circumstances?
6. Jonathan Phillips writes: "We should not necessarily look for a single motive in determining an individual's desire to take the cross [go on Crusade]." What does he see as the primary motives? Critically examine these motives.
7. When we sharpen our focus to the level of the individual, complexity emerges. With a wider lens, we might see entire civilizations and religions in conflict. Critically discuss these differences in perspective.

Is There Common Ground?

In any war, the goals of the nation or the overarching power that declares it might be shared imperfectly or not at all by the foot soldiers. While Pope Urban II called the First Crusade to reclaim the Holy Land from the Muslims who had captured it, individual crusaders might have been thinking of their individual salvation, their debts, a family history of pilgrimage, or many other complex reasons for participation.

Common ground is increasingly possible to find if we move our lens of focus in and out, allowing both the grand aims of the Pope and the particular reasons for the crusaders to both be true. A related question, however, involves the goals of the papacy. From that perspective, might we be more likely to admit the possibility that a kind of "holy war" was being declared on Muslims by the head of the Christian Church?

Question: In the light of current events, how "fresh" or how "stale" are these ancient memories?

Additional Resources

For an Arab perspective on the Crusades, see Amin Maalouf, *The Crusades Through Arab Eyes* (Schocken Books, 1985), and Carole Hillenbrand, *The Crusades: Islamic Perspectives* (Routledge, 2000), as well as Francesco Gabrieli, ed., *Arab Historians of the Crusades* (University of California Press, 1984). Karen Armstrong's *Holy War: The Crusades and their Impact on Today's World* (Anchor Books, 2001) is a Western source that speaks of the Crusades in an objective and critical manner, especially their links with contemporary conflicts among Muslims, Christians, and Jews in the Middle East.

The Crusades had a decidedly martial component. However, they were also part of a long tradition of pilgrimage. Chaucer's *Canterbury Tales* capture the stories told by pilgrims on their way to and from Canterbury Cathedral in England in early spring. Perhaps the best known pilgrimage is the *Camino*, or Way—a 500-mile walk across northern Spain from the Pyrenees to the Church of Santiago de Compostella in the northeastern corner. In a recent film, "*The Way*," Martin Sheen, carries the ashes of his son on the *Camino*. The film is directed by Sheen's son, Emilio Estevez, who plays the son in flashbacks and "appearances."

Internet References . . .

The Christian Crusades

This site explores the history and legacy of the crusades. Links to other websites include: Islam's Stake: Why Jerusalem was Central to Muhammad by Karen Armstrong and Judaism's Stake: The Mysteries of Solomon's Temple by David Van Biema.

http://gbgm-umc.org/umw/bible/crusades.stm

Selected, Edited, and with Issue Framing Material by:
Helen Buss Mitchell, *Howard Community College*
and
Joseph R. Mitchell, *Howard Community College*

Was Mongol Leader Genghis Khan an Enlightened Ruler?

YES: Jack Weatherford, from *Genghis Khan and the Making of the Modern World* (Crown Publishers, 2004)

NO: Mike Edwards, from "Genghis Khan," *National Geographic* (December 1996)

Learning Outcomes

After reading this issue you should be able to:

- Define "Revisionist History."
- Understand how a powerful ruler might be both brutal and enlightened.
- Understand the key features of Genghis Khan's Mongol Empire.
- Understand the key features of a nomadic culture.

ISSUE SUMMARY

YES: Anthropology professor Jack Weatherford argues that despite the Mongol's reputation for barbarity, Genghis Khan was in many ways an enlightened and benevolent ruler.

NO: Journalist and writer Mike Edwards counters that although Genghis Khan did have an enlightened side, the barbarity of his conquests overwhelms any good that he may have accomplished.

The mention of Genghis Khan and the Mongols conjures up negative images of bloodshed and violence, conquests and slavery, barbarism and depravity. Descending from a nomadic tribe from present-day northern Mongolia, he united the local tribes, formed them into the world's finest military force, and conquered an empire whose size was unparalled in history. In the thirteenth century, people spoke of him in the same manner as fourth century people did of Attila the Hun, another conqueror from the east, who earned the sobriquet "The Scourge of God."

However, circa 1395, English writer Geoffrey Chaucer—in his now famous *Canterbury Tales*—used the following words to describe Genghis Khan and his place in history:

> This noble king was called Genghis Khan,
> Who in his time was of so great renown
> That there was nowhere in no region
> So excellent a lord in all things.

Quite complimentary words coming from a European writer describing a leader of the Mongols, whose empire once extended to China and India, and included all of the Middle East, Russia, and a good portion of eastern Europe. Genghis Khan ("Strong Ruler," "Oceanic Ruler,"—in other words "Ruler of the World") also threatened the very fabric of western European civilization. Yet Chaucer chose to write about him, only about a century after his death, in a most laudatory manner.

What emerges from these two perspectives are two Genghis Khans, one earning praise, the other denunciation. Everyone agrees that he was powerful. The Kalmyk people who live today at the northwest corner of the Caspian Sea trace their bloodline to Genghis Khan, whom they call "Shaker of the Universe."

Genghis Khan's birth name was Temujin, and he was born circa 1165 in what is today northern Mongolia, a member of the Mongol tribe. It was an area that experienced constant intertribal warfare within a harsh physical environment. When he was a young boy, his father Yesugei was poisoned by another tribe, the Tatars, which left Temujin's life, as well as those of his mother and full- and half-brothers, in precarious straits. At a young age, he found the woman he would love all his life and a blood brother whom he would later kill as a threat to his power. He endured serious hardships and constant danger before organizing first his own Mongol tribe, and then uniting all of the other nomadic tribes under his leadership. In 1206, he was proclaimed "Great Khan."

Possessing charismatic leadership skills and sound military strategy and tactics, he set out to extend his empire's boundaries. China finally fell in 1215, with the emperor forced to pay a huge tribute to the Mongols in exchange for peace and security. Later, the Islamic kingdom of Khwarazm was conquered and by 1221, Genghis Khan's empire extended to the Indus River in India. At the same time, Mongol forces were expanding into Russia, which eventually came under their domination, but Genghis Khan would not live to see this, as he died peacefully in 1227 in his Mongolian homeland. Under the leadership of his sons and successors, the Mongol Empire would continue to grow until internal dissension and historical circumstances would cause its fragmentation and demise.

History has not been kind to Genghis Khan. In many books the violence and bloodshed he and his followers caused seem to take center stage. Lost among tales of brutality, however, are the genuine reforms he initiated, and the ways in which he may have wittingly or unwittingly shaped the course of Western history. Some now credit him with establishing the rule of law, supporting religious freedom, initiating the creation of public schools, and making free trade possible. Many of these eventually became hallmarks of the Western world. This issue seeks to balance the two views of Genghis Khan. First, anthropologist Jack Weatherford presents a revisionist view, which credits him with being an important but controversial force in world history. Journalist Mike Edwards then states that although Genghis Khan had his positive side, the level of violence and bloodshed for which he was responsible must always temper his positive accomplishments.

No one occupies a higher place in Mongolian history than Genghis Khan. It is with him that their history began. He continued to be a most revered character down to the twentieth century. In the 1930s, when Communist interests from Russia took control of Mongolia, they tried to stamp out all positive influences on Mongolian culture, including the beatific memory of Genghis Khan. The culture was ruthlessly suppressed, and those who promoted it were imprisoned or murdered. It is estimated that more than 30,000 people lost their lives in these "purges." Today, with the end of monolithic communism, the Mongolian people are free to promote their own culture, and Genghis Khan has reassumed his exalted place in Mongolian history.

Like many heroes, he is lauded for rising from harsh and unpromising beginnings. After his father was poisoned, Temujin's mother and her sons were expelled from their tribe and left on the steppes to die. They scrounged for food, eating roots, rodents, and fish. Having met the love of his life, Temujin organized a raid to free her, making her in Jack Weatherford's memorable phrase "the grandmother of kings." Loyalty figured prominently . . . except when it no longer did. To Borte/Borje he gave his heart. However, when his blood brother later threatened his rule, the ties of blood were broken. The Great Khan, as a mature leader, seemed to have an extraordinarily wide view of the world, creating an empire in which the humblest slave could rise to the rank of army commander if he showed the requisite skill and bravery. He forbade the kidnapping of women, perhaps remembering his wife's early trauma, and he also forbade the killing of priests, monks, nuns, mullahs, and other holy people. Though he was said to worship the sky, Genghis Khan guaranteed religious freedom for Buddhists, Muslims, Christians, and Hindus. And, even enemy envoys and ambassadors were safe within his territory.

YES

Jack Weatherford

Genghis Khan and the Making of the Modern World

. . . Fate did not hand Genghis Khan his destiny; he made it for himself. It seemed highly unlikely that he would ever have enough horses to create a Spirit Banner, much less that he might follow it across the world. The boy who became Genghis Khan grew up in a world of excessive tribal violence including murder, kidnapping, and enslavement. As the son in an outcast family left to die on the steppes, he probably encountered no more than a few hundred people in his entire childhood, and he received no formal education. From this harsh setting, he learned, in dreadful detail, the full range of human emotion: desire, ambition, and cruelty. While still a child he killed his older half brother, was captured and enslaved by a rival clan, and managed to escape from his captors.

Under such horrific conditions, the boy showed an instinct for survival and self-preservation, but he showed little promise of the achievements he would one day make. As a child, he feared dogs and he cried easily. His younger brother was stronger than he was and a better archer and wrestler; his half brother bossed him around and picked on him. Yet from these degraded circumstances of hunger, humiliation, kidnapping, and slavery, he began the long climb to power. Before reaching puberty, he had already formed the two most important relationships of his life. He swore eternal friendship and allegiance to a slightly older boy who became the closest friend of his youth but turned into the most dedicated enemy of his adulthood, and he found the girl whom he would love forever and whom he made the mother of emperors. The dual capacity for friendship and enmity forged in Genghis Khan's youth endured throughout his life and became the defining trait of his character. The tormenting questions of love and paternity that arose beneath a shared blanket or in the flickering firelight of the family hearth became projected onto the larger stage of world history. His personal goals, desires, and fears engulfed the world.

Year by year, he gradually defeated everyone more powerful than he was, until he had conquered every tribe on the Mongolian steppe. At the age of fifty, when most great conquerors had already put their fighting days behind them, Genghis Khan's Spirit Banner beckoned him out of his remote homeland to confront the armies of the civilized people who had harassed and enslaved the nomadic tribes for centuries. In the remaining years of life, he followed that Spirit Banner to repeated victory across the Gobi and the Yellow River into the kingdoms of China, through the central Asian lands of the Turks and the Persians, and across the mountains of Afghanistan to the Indus River.

In conquest after conquest, the Mongol army transformed warfare into an intercontinental affair fought on multiple fronts stretching across thousands of miles. Genghis Khan's innovative fighting techniques made the heavily armored knights of medieval Europe obsolete, replacing them with disciplined cavalry moving in coordinated units. Rather than relying on defensive fortifications, he made brilliant use of speed and surprise on the battlefield, as well as perfecting siege warfare to such a degree that he ended the era of walled cities. Genghis Khan taught his people not only to fight across incredible distances but to sustain their campaign over years, decades, and, eventually, more than three generations of constant fighting.

In twenty-five years, the Mongol army subjugated more lands and people than the Romans had conquered in four hundred years. Genghis Khan, together with his sons and grandsons, conquered the most densely populated civilizations of the thirteenth century. Whether measured by the total number of people defeated, the sum of the countries annexed, or by the total area occupied, Genghis Khan conquered more than twice as much as any other man in history. The hooves of the Mongol warriors' horses splashed in the waters of every river and lake from the Pacific Ocean to the Mediterranean Sea. At its zenith, the empire covered between 11 and 12 million contiguous square miles, an area about the size of the African continent and considerably larger than North America, including the United States, Canada, Mexico, Central America, and the islands of the Caribbean combined. It stretched from the snowy tundra of Siberia to the hot plains of India, from the rice paddies of Vietnam to the wheat fields of Hungary, and from Korea to the Balkans. The majority of people today live in countries conquered by the Mongols; on the modern map, Genghis Kahn's conquests include thirty countries with well over 3 billion people. The most astonishing aspect of this achievement is that the entire Mongol tribe under him numbered around a million, smaller than the workforce of some modern corporations. From this million, he recruited his army, which was comprised of no more than one hundred thousand warriors—a group that could comfortably fit into the larger sports stadiums of the modern era.

In American terms, the accomplishment of Genghis Khan might be understood if the United States, instead of being created by a group of educated merchants or wealthy planters, had been founded by one of its illiterate slaves, who, by the sheer force of personality, charisma, and determination, liberated America from foreign rule, united the people, created an alphabet, wrote the constitution, established universal religious freedom, invented a new system of warfare, marched an army from Canada to Brazil, and opened roads of commerce in a free-trade zone that stretched across the continents. On every level and from any perspective, the scale and scope of Genghis Khan's accomplishments challenge the limits of imagination and tax the resources of scholarly explanation.

As Genghis Khan's cavalry charged across the thirteenth century, he redrew the boundaries of the world. His architecture was not in stone but in nations. Unsatisfied with the vast number of little kingdoms, Genghis Khan consolidated smaller countries into larger ones. In eastern Europe, the Mongols united a dozen Slavic principalities and cities into one large Russian state. In eastern Asia, over a span of three generations, they created the country of China by weaving together the remnants of the Sung dynasty in the south with the lands of the lurched in Manchuria, Tibet in the west, the Tangut Kingdom adjacent to the Gobi, and the Uighur lands of eastern Turkistan. As the Mongols expanded their rule, they created countries such as Korea and India that have survived to modern times in approximately the same borders fashioned by their Mongol conquerors.

Genghis Khan's empire connected and amalgamated the many civilizations around him into a new world order. At the time of his birth in 1162, the Old World consisted of a series of regional civilizations each of which could claim virtually no knowledge of any civilization beyond its closest neighbor. No one in China had heard of Europe, and no one in Europe had heard of China, and, so far as is known, no person had made the journey from one to the other. By the time of his death in 1227, he had connected them with diplomatic and commercial contacts that still remain unbroken.

As he smashed the feudal system of aristocratic privilege and birth, he built a new and unique system based on individual merit, loyalty, and achievement. He took the disjointed and languorous trading towns along the Silk Route and organized them into history's largest free-trade zone. He lowered taxes for everyone, and abolished them altogether for doctors, teachers, priests, and educational institutions. He established a regular census and created the first international postal system. His was not an empire that hoarded wealth and treasure; instead, he widely distributed the goods acquired in combat so that they could make their way back into commercial circulation. He created an international law and recognized the ultimate supreme law of the Eternal Blue Sky over all people. At a time when most rulers considered themselves to be above the law, Genghis Khan insisted on laws holding rulers as equally accountable as the lowest herder. He granted religious freedom within his realms, though he demanded total loyalty from conquered subjects of all religions. He insisted on the rule of law and abolished torture, but he mounted major campaigns to seek out and kill raiding bandits and terrorist assassins. He refused to hold hostages and, instead, instituted the novel practice of granting diplomatic immunity for all ambassadors and envoys, including those from hostile nations with whom he was at war.

Genghis Khan left his empire with such a firm foundation that it continued growing for another 150 years. Then, in the centuries that followed its collapse, his descendants continued to rule a variety of smaller empires and large countries, from Russia, Turkey, and India to China and Persia. They held an eclectic assortment of titles, including khan, emperor, sultan, king, shah, emir, and the Dalai Lama. Vestiges of his empire remained under the rule of his descendants for seven centuries. As the Moghuls, some of them reigned in India until 1857, when the British drove out Emperor Bahadur Shah II and chopped off the heads of two of his sons and his grandson. Genghis Khan's last ruling descendant, Alim Khan, emir of Bukhara, remained in power in Uzbekistan until deposed in 1920 by the rising tide of Soviet revolution. . . .

Most leaders, whether kings or presidents, grew up inside the institutions of some type of state. Their accomplishments usually involved the reorganization or revitalization of those institutions and the state that housed them. Genghis Khan, however, consciously set out to create a state and to establish all the institutions necessary for it on a new basis, part of which he borrowed from prior tribes and part of which he invented. For his nation-state to survive, he needed to build strong institutions, and for Genghis Khan this began with the army that brought him to power; he made it even stronger and more central to government. Under Genghis Khan, cowherds, shepherds, and camel boys advanced to become generals and rode at the front of armies of a thousand or ten thousand warriors. Every healthy male aged fifteen to seventy was an active member of the army. Just as he had done when first elected tribal khan, he appointed his most loyal followers as the heads of groups of one thousand soldiers and their households, and his oldest followers, such as Boorchu, took charge of units of ten thousand. He rewarded men who came from lowly black-boned lineages and placed them in the highest positions based on their achievements and proven loyalty to him on and off the battlefield. Compared with the units of ten thousand that he gave to his loyal friends, those assigned to the control of members of his own family were more meager—five thousand each to his mother, his youngest brother, and his two youngest sons, Ogodei and Tolui. With only eight thousand for Chaghatai and nine thousand for Jochi, even his two eldest sons did not receive a full *tumen* of ten thousand. Genghis Khan appointed trusted friends of his own to oversee the administration for several family members, particularly for his mother, youngest brother, and Chaghatai. He explained the need for such overseers by stating that Chaghatai was "obstinate and has a petty, narrow mind." He warned the advisers to "stay beside him morning and evening to advise him."

In order to maintain peace in this large and ethnically diverse set of tribes that he had forged into one nation, he quickly proclaimed new laws to suppress the traditional causes of tribal feuding and war. The Great Law of Genghis Khan differed from that of other lawgivers in history. He did not base his law on divine revelation from God; nor did he derive it from an ancient code of any sedentary civilization. He consolidated it from the customs and traditions of the herding tribes as maintained over centuries; yet he readily abolished old practices when they hindered the functioning of his new society. He allowed groups to follow traditional law in their area, so long as it did not conflict with the Great Law, which functioned as a supreme law or a common law over everyone.

The Great Law, however, did not represent a single codification of the law so much as an ongoing body of legal work that he continued to develop throughout the remaining two decades of his life. Genghis Khan's law did not delve into all aspects of daily life; instead, he used it to regulate the most troublesome aspects. As long as men kidnapped women, there would be feuding on the steppes. Genghis Khan's first new law reportedly forbade the kidnapping of women, almost certainly a reaction to the kidnapping of his wife Borte. The persistent potential for strife originating in such kidnappings still plagued Genghis Khan within his own family in the uncertainty of whether his eldest son had been fathered by him or by Borte's kidnapper, and the uncertainty would cause increasingly more severe problems as Genghis Khan grew older.

Concomitant with an end to kidnapping, he forbade the abduction and enslavement of any Mongol. From his own capture and enslavement by the Tayichiud, he knew the individual and personal anguish of being abducted and forced to work as a slave, but he also recognized how detrimental the practice was to the entire social fabric and what strong animosities and violence it perpetrated throughout the tribes of the steppe.

Genghis Khan sought to remove every source of internal dissension within the ranks of his followers. Based upon his own experiences over the disruptions that surrounded questions of the legitimacy of children, he declared all children legitimate, whether born to a wife or a concubine. Because haggling over the value of a wife as though she were a camel could provoke lingering dissension among his men, he forbade the selling of women into marriage. For the same reasons, he outlawed adultery, an act that the Mongols' defined differently than most people. It did not include sexual relations between a woman and her husband's close relatives, nor those between a man and female servants or the wives of other men in his household. In keeping with Genghis Khan's dictum that matters of the *ger* should be decided within the *ger* and matters of the steppe decided on the steppe, adultery applied to relations between married people of separate households. As long as it did not cause a public strife between families, it did not rank as a crime.

Theft of animals had always been considered wrong, but it had been commonplace in the raiding culture of the steppes, and had also been the cause of lingering animosity and discord. Perhaps remembering the great harm caused to his family when their eight geldings were stolen, Genghis Khan made animal rustling a capital offense. Additionally, he required anyone finding a lost animal to return it to the rightful owner. For this purpose, he instituted a massive lost-and-found system that continued to grow as his empire spread. Any person who found such goods, money, or animals and did not turn them in to the appropriate supervisor would be treated as a thief; the penalty for theft was execution.

Aside from fighting over lost animals, the steppe people argued frequently over hunting rights for wild animals. Genghis Khan codified existing ideals by forbidding the hunting of animals between March and October during the breeding time. By protecting the animals in the summer, Genghis Khan also provided a safety net for the winter, and hunters had to limit their kill to what they needed for food and no more. The law also specified how animals should be hunted as well as the manner of butchering, so as to waste nothing.

In addition to sex, property, and food, Genghis Khan recognized the disruptive potential of competing religions. In one form or another, virtually every religion from Buddhism to Christianity and Manichaeanism to Islam had found converts among the steppe people, and almost all of them claimed not only to be the true religion but the only one. In probably the first law of its kind anywhere in the world, Genghis Khan decreed complete and total religious freedom for everyone. Although he continued to worship the spirits of his homeland, he did not permit them to be used as a national cult.

To promote all religions, Genghis Khan exempted religious leaders and their property from taxation and from all types of public service. To promote related professions, he later extended the same tax exemptions to a range of professionals who provided essential public services, including undertakers, doctors, lawyers, teachers, and scholars.

Genghis Khan made a number of laws designed specifically to prevent fighting over the office of khan. According to his law, the khan must always be elected by a *khuriltai*. He made it a capital offense for any member of his family to claim the office without election. To prevent rival candidates from killing each other, he ordered that the death penalty would be applied to members of his family only through a *khuriltai* of the whole family and not through any individual member. In so doing, he outlawed the very means that he himself had used to begin his rise to power—killing his half brother.

Mongol law, as codified by Genghis Khan, recognized group responsibility and group guilt. The solitary individual had no legal existence outside the context of the family and the larger units to which it belonged; therefore, the family carried the responsibility of ensuring the correct behavior of its members. A crime by one could bring punishment to all. Similarly, a tribe or a squad of soldiers bore the same liability for one another's actions, and thereby the entire nation, not just the army or just the civil administration, bore responsibility for upholding and enforcing the law. To be a just Mongol, one had to live in a just community.

Enforcement of the law and the responsibility to abide by it began at the highest level, with the khan himself. In this manner, Genghis Khan had proclaimed the supremacy of the rule of law over any individual, even the sovereign. By subjugating the ruler to the law, he achieved something that no other civilization had yet accomplished. Unlike many civilizations—and most particularly western Europe, where monarchs ruled by the will of God and reigned above the law—Genghis Khan made it clear that his Great Law applied as strictly to the rulers as to everyone else. His descendants proved able to abide by this rule for only about fifty years after his death before they discarded it.

To run the empire in general, but most specifically to record the many new laws and to administer them over the vast stretches of land now under his control, Genghis Khan ordered the adoption of a writing system. Although writing had been introduced to the steppes many centuries earlier by Muslim merchants and itinerant Christian monks, few of the native people learned the skill, even those among the most sophisticated tribes of Tatars, Naiman, and Kereyid; and so far as is known, no Mongol had learned it. In his conquest of the Naiman in 1204, Genghis Khan discovered that Tayang Khan kept a scribe who wrote down his pronouncements and then embossed them with an official state seal. The scribe came from the Uighur people, who had originated on the Mongol steppe, but in the ninth century had migrated to the oases of what is now the Xinjiang region of western China. The Uighur language was closely related and proved relatively easy to adapt for writing in the Mongolian language. Derived from the Syriac alphabet used by the missionary monks who brought Christianity to the steppe tribes, the writing was made from letters rather than characters, but it flowed vertically down the page in columns, like Chinese.

To keep track of his laws, Genghis Khan created the position of supreme judge for his adopted brother Shigi-Khutukhu, the Tatar boy with the golden earrings and nose ring whom he had found and given to his mother to raise. Genghis Khan charged him to "punish the thieves and put right the lies," as well as to keep a record of his decisions on white paper bound in blue books, the sacred color of the Eternal Sky. This close association between writing and the keeping of the law in Genghis Khan's administration probably accounts for why the Mongolian word for book, *nom*, was derived from the Greek *nomos*, meaning "law." In the Mongol world of the thirteenth century, the law and the written word were one and the same.

In maintaining loyalty and cohesion in the vast apparatus of his state, Genghis Khan innovated on an ancient political practice of hostage taking. He demanded that each of the commanders of the units of one thousand and ten thousand send their own sons and their sons' best friends to him personally to make his own unit. Instead of threatening to kill them if their relatives misbehaved, Genghis Khan introduced a far more effective strategy. Genghis Khan trained the would-be hostages as administrators and kept them as a ready reserve to replace any ineffective or disloyal official. The threat of such potential replacement probably did much more to ensure loyalty in the field than the threat that the relative might be killed. Genghis Khan thus changed the status of hostages, transforming them into an integral part of his government that gave almost every family a direct and personal connection to the imperial court.

Genghis Khan divided the elite unit into the day guard and the night guard. As the name indicated, they formed a permanent watch over him and his encampment, but they functioned as much more than a bodyguard. They controlled the boys and girls who worked in the court, and they organized the herders of the different animals. They oversaw the movement of the camp, together with all the weapons and accoutrements of the state: banners, pikes, and drums. They also controlled the cooking vessels and the slaughter of animals, and they ensured the proper distribution of meat and dairy products. The guard helped to adjudicate legal hearings, carry out punishments, and generally enforce the law. Because they controlled the entrance to and egress from the royal tents, they formed the basis of government administration.

All members of Genghis Khan's own regiment held the rank of elder brother to the other nine units of ten thousand, and therefore they could issue orders to any of them and expect to be obeyed without question. Unlike other armies in which each individual held a rank, in the Mongol army, the entire unit held a rank. The lowest-ranking man in Genghis Khan's *tumen* of ten thousand outranked the highest-ranking men of the other *tumen*. In turn, within each *tumen*, every member of the commander's unit of one thousand outranked every man in the other nine units of one thousand.

To facilitate communication so that the orders got to the intended recipient, Genghis Khan relied on a system of fast riders known as arrow messengers. The military supplied the riders, but the local people supplied the stations. The postal service ranked alongside the military in importance for the Mongols, and individual Mongols were allowed to serve in it in lieu of regular military service. Depending on local terrain, the stations were set approximately twenty miles apart, and each station required about twenty-five families to maintain and operate it. Although the stations were open for public use, much of the information on the individual stations and the total number at any given time remained a carefully guarded secret, and therefore the information has not survived. Some idea of its expanse can be derived from the eighteenth century, however, when the system still operated and required approximately sixty-four stations to cross Mongolia from the Altai Mountains in the west to the entrance through the Great Wall into China in the east.

Genghis Khan adapted a variety of older methods of communication over shorter distances, such as the use of torches, whistling arrows, smoke, flares, and flags, for even more rapid transmission of information during maneuvers, hunts, and military movements. The herders had earlier developed a complicated system of arm signals that could be used long after individuals had passed out of hearing range, and under Genghis Khan these, too, were built upon to make an ever more elaborate system of rapid and efficient communication for use in battle or troop maneuvers. . . .

The Eternal Spirit of Genghis Khan

Genghis Khan's was the last great tribal empire of world history. He was the heir of ten thousand years of war between the nomadic tribes and the civilized world, the ancient struggle of the hunter and herder against the farmer. It was a history as old as the story of the Bedouin tribes that followed Muhammad to smash the pagan idolatry of the city, of the Roman campaigns against the Huns, of the Greeks against the wandering Scythians, of the city dwellers of Egypt and Persia who preyed on the wandering tribes of Hebrew herders, and, ultimately, of Cain, the tiller, who slew his brother Abel, the herder.

The clash between the nomadic and urban cultures did not end with Genghis Khan, but it would never again reach the level to which he brought it. Civilization pushed the tribal people toward the ever more distant edges of the world. Chiefs such as Sitting Bull and Crazy Horse of the Lakota Sioux, Red Eagle of the Muskogee, Tecumseh of the Shawnee, and Shaka Zulu of South Africa valiantly but vainly continued the quest of Genghis Khan over the coming centuries. Without knowing anything about the Mongols or Genghis Khan, these other chiefs faced the same struggles and fought the same battles across Africa and throughout the Americas, but history had moved beyond them. In the end, sedentary civilization won the long world war; the future belonged to the civilized children of Cain, who eternally encroached upon the open lands of the tribes.

Although he arose out of the ancient tribal past, Genghis Khan shaped the modern world of commerce, communication, and large secular states more than any other individual. He was the thoroughly modern man in his mobilized and professional warfare and in his commitment to global commerce and the rule of international secular law. What began as a war of extinction between the nomad and the farmer ended as a Mongol amalgamation of cultures. His vision matured as he aged and as he experienced different ways of life. He worked to create something new and better for his people. The Mongol armies destroyed the uniqueness of the civilizations around them by shattering the protective walls that isolated one civilization from another and by knotting the cultures together.

The great actors of history cannot be neatly tucked between the covers of a book and filed away like so many pressed botanical specimens. Their actions cannot be explained according to a specific timetable like the coming and going of so many trains. Although scholars may designate the beginning and ending of an era with exact precision, great historical events, particularly those that erupt suddenly and violently, build up slowly, and, once having begun, never end. Their effects linger long after the action faded from view. Like the tingling vibrations of a bell that we can still sense well after it has stopped ringing, Genghis Khan has long passed from the scene, but his influence continues to reverberate through our time. . . .

Jack Weatherford is professor of history at Macalaster College in Minnesota and the author of *A History of Money* (Three Rivers Press, 1998).

Mike Edwards

Genghis Khan

In the northwest wall of old Samarkand stood a gate through which caravans embarked on the Silk Road. It was by that entrance, or the rubble of it, that I walked in. Through this same gate in 1220 rode Genghis Khan, who was about to ravage one of Central Asia's greatest cities.

Samarkand's population, by a modern estimate, was 200,000 or more. Its artisans produced saddles, copper lamps, and silver lame. An aqueduct sluiced water across the arid steppe, making gardens bloom. There is only grass now, nibbled to the nub by goats. I see bits of porcelain and an occasional brick—nothing more. The remains of workshops, palaces, and all else lie beneath wind-heaped ridges and hillocks.

Samarkand, Bukhara, Urgench, Balkh, Merv, Nishapur, Herat, Ghazni: One after another the cities of Central Asia toppled before the horsemen bursting from the steppe of Mongolia. Rarely had the world witnessed such a whirlwind of destruction.

Nor had an empire existed so vast as Genghis's sons and grandsons would establish—to be exceeded, in fact, only by the British Empire of the 19th century. In 1280 Mongol rule stretched from the Yellow Sea to the Mediterranean. Almost as quickly as the empire rose, however, it began to fracture into independent fiefdoms, such as the Golden Horde in Russia, a remnant of which hung on until 1502. . . .

The question usually asked about the Mongols is: Were they merely pillagers and killers? Not in Mongolian eyes. To Mongolia, Genghis was George Washington, first ruler of united Mongolia. And in China his grandson Kublai is likewise admired as a unifier. Also, to their credit, the Mongols were more tolerant of other religions than many regimes today. In Genghis's own clan were Buddhists, Muslims, and Christians, as well as worshipers (as Genghis was) of Tengri, the ruler of heaven. To be sure, mosques and temples were burned in besieged cities, but it was not Mongol policy to punish people for their faith.

Nevertheless, the Mongols killed ruthlessly—opposing armies as well as hapless noncombatants—and subjugated millions as they pursued the dream of empire. The 13th century was one of the most war torn in history, probably exceeded in cruelty only by our own. Crusaders marched in the Holy Land, Chinese dynasties fought one another, and several wars scourged Central Asia before Genghis invaded. Thus Genghis was a man of his time—only more so.

Yet some cities that offered no resistance escaped with payment of a tribute and with looting by the army—standard practices. Many rulers chose to collaborate. From their kingdoms the Mongols drew not only taxes but also troops; thus the Mongol army that sacked Baghdad in 1258 included Georgians, Armenians, and Persians.

Several cities that felt the Mongol fury thrived in what today is Uzbekistan, one of the five Central Asian nations that calved from the collapsing Soviet Union in 1991. In Uzbekistan, for instance, there is Samarkand, and as I stood upon the ruins and looked out on the tawny steppe, it was not hard for me to imagine Genghis's cavalry approaching—"more numerous than ants or locusts," more than "the sand of the desert or drops of rain."

This florid arithmetic is from the pen of a Persian historian, Ala-ad-Din Ata-Malik Juvaini, who wrote his *History of the World-Conqueror* as a Mongol civil servant. As I roamed the places of Mongol destruction, Juvaini was my loquacious informant. Historians consider his book an important account of Genghis's campaigns, but he was writing in part to please his masters, and, like other chroniclers of the time, he never met a fact that couldn't be hyperbolized. So modern historians fall back often on such words as "perhaps."

At Samarkand, however, the Mongols must indeed have seemed as thick as locusts. There were perhaps (see what I mean?) 80,000 riders, trailed by a great herd of spare mounts. And in front they drove thousands of civilians, a human shield.

Samarkand was the capital of Shah Muhammad of the Khwarizm empire, which sprawled westward to the Caspian Sea and included parts of what are today Afghanistan and Iran. Muhammad had invited disaster by slaying a Mongol ambassador and a caravan of traders. Juvaini says Muhammad had 110,000 troops in Samarkand and that when Genghis appeared, Muhammad speedily decamped with many of his men. After only a day's fighting the city's nobles opened the gates, praying for mercy.

"But there were soldiers who did not want to surrender," Yuri Buryakov, an Uzbek archaeologist who is an authority on Samarkand's fate, told me. "About a thousand took refuge in the mosque. They thought they would be protected by Allah. They thought the Mongols wouldn't dare kill them there. But to the Mongols it didn't make any difference. They would kill anywhere."

The mosque was huge. Excavating its site in the 1980s, Buryakov found the remains of carved wood partitions and clay walls measuring 161 by 87 yards. "The Mongols shot flaming arrows. Maybe they hurled vessels of oil—Genghis had mangonels [catapults]. When we excavated, we found burned bones."

The city walls were leveled, as was the fortress that crowned the city core. Down too came the aqueduct, says Juvaini, and Samarkand's soldiers and citizens took "a sip at the cup of destruction." Buryakov estimates the dead at 100,000.

In time another Samarkand arose; I gazed at its domes from the ruins. This is the city of another formidable conqueror, Timur, or Tamer-lane, a Turkic warrior who built a new empire in the 1300s, after the Mongol collapse.

Near those domes, coals glowed and hammers clanged. I approached Makhmud Dzhurayev, who is so proud of his forged axheads that he stamps them with his initials. "How would you like to go live in Mongolia?" I asked.

"Mongolia?" he stammered.

Then I explained. "If the Mongols captured Samarkand today, you might be taken to Mongolia because you have a skill."

Makhmud recovered. "Let it be the United States," he said. "Or Japan—I'd like to learn to make samurai swords."

Smiths, weavers, falconers, scribes, physicians: Juvaini says the Mongols marched 30,000 skilled men from Samarkand to toil in less developed Mongolia. With them, no doubt, went thousands of their women and children. . . .

When Temujin is born, in the 1160s, Mongolia is a realm of perhaps 30 nomadic tribes, with a total population between 1.5 million and 3 million. Roughly half are Turkic-speaking peoples who predate the Mongols themselves. From this same territory an even earlier people, the Xiongnu, raided China for centuries; they may have been the same people as the Huns, who scourged Europe in the fourth and fifth centuries.

The *Secret History* offers a wealth of detail on Temujin's rise to power. At first, life is difficult. When Temujin is nine, his father, Yisugei, a minor chieftain, is poisoned by Tatar tribesmen. It is revenge, for Yisugei once robbed them. To survive, Temujin and his brothers catch fish and snare marmots, and their mother gathers berries.

As a young man he makes allies. One is Jamuqa, who becomes his *anda*, or blood brother. Another is Toghril, a leader of the Kereyit tribe. When the Merkit tribe kidnaps Temujin's teenage bride, Borte, in a raid, these friends muster warriors to rescue her.

In manhood Temujin gradually brings several tribes under his control by conquest or bestowal of booty. Defeating the Tatars, who killed his father, he is merciless. All but the smallest males are killed; children and women are enslaved. The Tatar tribe ceases to be. (In Europe, however, a variation of the name, "Tartars," was for centuries used to refer to the Mongols.)

Alliances shift. Temujin's friends Jamuqa and Toghril oppose his growing power. Temujin crushes Toghril's army in a fierce three-day clash. Then, in 1205, he defeats the Naiman, his last powerful enemy tribe. With them is Jamuqa, who is captured. "Let me die quickly," he asks. Temujin grants his blood brother's wish.

In 1206, at a *kuriltai*, or great assembly, Temujin is enthroned as Genghis Khan—"strong ruler" or perhaps "oceanic ruler," hence ruler of the world. He is about 40. . . .

The Mongol army was on the move soon after Genghis became great khan. Genghis's first campaign beyond Mongolia was in 1209 against the kingdom of Xi Xia. Its capital, Ningxia, stood at the site of the modern Chinese city of Yinchuan, and to reach it, the Mongols had to cross the harsh Gobi desert. Such travel was no great obstacle to nomads who, in a pinch, subsisted on mare's milk and blood drawn from a slit in a horse's hide.

Ruled by the Tanguts, a Tibetan people, Xi Xia produced fine cloth. More important, in Professor Rossabi's mind, it controlled oases along the Silk Road and exacted heavy taxes from Mongol caravans.

The army that Genghis led south already was being molded into the disciplined force that would ride into Europe and deep into China. He organized his troops on a decimal system: the squad (*arvan*) of 10 and company (*zuun*) of 100 up to the division (*tumen*) of 10,000. Moreover, he erased tribal hierarchies. Kereyits, Merkits, and others were scattered among various units, and command went to proven campaigners, not tribal chiefs.

Genghis also created a 10,000-man personal guard and kept hostages from powerful families. The possibility of a revolt obviously worried him. In fact, Larry Moses believes, Genghis attacked Xi Xia in part because some of his tribal enemies had fled there.

Xi Xia had a population of perhaps five million and a large army that seems not to have been well led. When Genghis came against the enemy in a mountain pass and could not break through, he feigned withdrawal, a favorite Mongol trick. The Xi Xia army came out in pursuit. Suddenly the Mongols turned, raining arrows and capturing the Xi Xia commander. Emperor Xiangzong sought peace in 1210, offering tribute and a daughter to marry Genghis. Xi Xia was now regarded as a vassal.

Inevitably the Mongols turned covetous eyes upon the kingdom east of Xi Xia. It had at least 20 million people and was vastly richer. Time and again this part of what is now China (unified in 1279 under Genghis's grandson Kublai) had yielded to raiders such treasures as jade, silk, and gold Buddhas.

In Genghis's era the north China cornucopia was ruled by people known as the Jurchen, who called their dynasty Jin ("golden"). Like dynasties before, the Jin bestowed tribute on the nomads and traded luxury goods, grain, and implements for their animals and hides. Terms were generous. "It was a kind of bribe," explains Rossabi, "to keep the nomads from attacking."

But this largesse was drying up, for the Jin had fallen on hard times. Moreover, there were political problems. Native Chinese resented the Jurchen overlords. Disloyalty troubled the army. Genghis knew these things from merchants and defecting Jin civil servants. He knew too that much of the huge Jin army—600,000 or more troops—was tied down on the regime's southern flank, after years of war with the Song dynasty. Thus Genghis took aim at a hobbled regime. In fact, nearly all his victim states were crippled by internal dissent or other problems.

In 1211 the army set out, 70,000 strong. The Great Wall as we know it did not exist, though lesser walls did. Genghis easily broke through them; Chinese texts say dispirited frontier troops even went over to him.

But many battles lay ahead. Elite troops of Genghis's enemy waited in the Juyong Pass to intercept the Mongols, who were heading to the capital, Zhongdu, buried today beneath sprawling Beijing. One of Genghis's trusted generals, Jebe, who was nicknamed "Arrow," caught the defenders off guard by using the feigned retreat trick.

Genghis did not march immediately on Zhongdu. His horsemen were superb with the bow, able to shoot forward or backward at full gallop, but he lacked the means to attack Zhongdu's 40-foot walls. Instead, Genghis sent his troops to ravage the heartland; the booty would keep them content.

When at last he surrounded the capital in 1214, his arsenal included Chinese bombardiers and mangonels powered by plunging weights that could hurl hundred-pound stones against walls and gates. These were not needed, however. Beset with internal problems, Jin Emperor Xuanzong offered gold, silver, and other treasure if the Mongols would withdraw. Genghis was presented with a Jin princess—yet another wife (he would have six Mongol wives and many others from foreign conquests). She came with 500 servants.

Alas for the Jin, they hadn't seen the last of the Mongols. When the emperor moved his capital south to Kaifeng, distancing himself from this barbarous foe, Genghis suspected him of regrouping to attack. Or perhaps that was just Genghis's excuse. The Mongols stormed back in 1215 to starve Zhongdu into submission, then to sack and massacre. Genghis carried off a hoard of imperial treasure. Years later a traveler, seeing a white hill, was told it was the bones of Zhongdu's inhabitants.

The Mongols had overrun a territory about the size of New York State. Envoys from Korea arrived, offering to pay tribute; they knew the fate of Zhongdu. Genghis expected north China to pay as well, but he seems not to have considered attaching it to Mongolia.

Returning to Mongolia, as he always did after a campaign, Genghis began to think of building a capital. From Xi Xia he had claimed 30,000 artisans, some of whom may have helped raise his citadel, Karakorum, where trade routes intersected on the Mongolian grassland.

Perhaps Genghis intended Karakorum to become a monumental city such as those he had seen that were built by the Chinese and the Xi Xia Tan-guts. It never achieved such greatness, although it had huge palaces for the ruler and his kinsmen as well as a treasury, a mosque, a Buddhist temple, and probably a Christian church. Chinese invaders destroyed the city in 1388.

Ever the borrower, Genghis had co-opted a scholar in China to advise him on building a government. Uygurs were recruited as accountants and scribes. Soon a school was turning out Mongol administrators, who swelled the small bureaucracy of tax collectors and record keepers.

Meanwhile, Genghis was troubled by events in Kara-Khitai, at Mongolia's western edge. Kuchlug, a renegade prince of the Naiman, the formidable tribe that Genghis had defeated in Mongolia, had seized power in that kingdom. And Kuchlug was gathering other allies. Did he plan to attack Genghis? Jebe attacked in 1218 with 20,000 horsemen.

Most of the people of Kara-Khitai were Muslims. Kuchlug had forbidden them to worship and had even crucified an imam. So when Jebe appeared at the walls of Kashgar, where Kuchlug was sojourning, there was rejoicing—a rare reception for the dreaded Mongols. Kuchlug was beheaded, and Genghis took the friendly people of Kara-Khitai under his wing.

Now that his realm touched the Khwarizm empire, Genghis sent an array of gifts to Shah Muhammad at Samarkand: jade, ivory, gold, cloaks of white camel wool. Genghis also proposed trade and sent out a caravan of 450 merchants. They only reached Utrar at the eastern edge of Muhammad's realm, where the governor, suspecting that they were spies (some probably were) seized and executed them. Juvaini says Muhammad approved this. In any case, he soon made a worse mistake.

When Genghis sent an ambassador to demand that the shah hand over Utrar's governor for punishment, Muhammad killed the envoy and sent his head to Genghis. "The Mongols believed in the absolute inviolability of ambassadors," Morris Rossabi points out. "To harm them was a heinous crime." Hence the terrible Mongol campaign in Central Asia was punitive— with, we can assume, the added incentive of great booty.

No doubt Muhammad felt secure. His army, it is said, numbered 400,000, but many were of uncertain loyalty. Nor did Muhammad enjoy the fealty of his heavily taxed subjects. Again it was a crippled regime that braced for a Mongol onslaught.

Genghis's army never exceeded 110,000 men, modern historians say. Before attacking Khwarizm, he requested soldiers from Xi Xia, his supposed vassal. Back came a tart reply: If Genghis did not have enough troops, he had no business being khan. That insult would be avenged too.

Though outnumbered, Genghis boldly split his forces as he advanced in 1219. One column besieged Utrar, another attacked farther south. Genghis rode west to Bukhara. Muhammad froze; he had no strategy to counter envelopment, other than to keep his troops hunkered down in his cities. At Utrar a garrison of several thousand held out for a month or longer, as boulders whistled from Mongol mangonels and rooftops were bombed with flaming naphtha—probably a stubborn-burning mixture of sulfur, niter, and petroleum. Inalchug, the governor who had slain Genghis's traders, fought to the end, flinging bricks from the top of his fortress. The victors leveled the citadel and the city walls. Utrar's artisans would now ply their skills for Mongol benefit. . . .

The Mongol hordes rampaged on, toppling Urgench, a great Silk Road city on the Amu Darya south of the Aral Sea, after a fierce battle; 100,000 defenders were said to have been slain. The Mongols diverted the river to flood the city's remains.

They moved south to the city of Merv, in present-day Turkmenistan. In its rubble a Muslim holy man and his helpers spent 13 days counting corpses, according to Juvaini, who says they tallied 1.3 million—"taking into account only those that were plain to see." Balkh, in Afghanistan, fabled "Mother of Cities," surrendered. Its citizens were massacred anyway—"divided up according to the usual custom into hundreds and thousands to be put to the sword."

Several Muslims wrote accounts of the butchery in these Islamic cities, and their reputed tolls are invariably enormous. In Nishapur, one said, the Mongols killed even the dogs and cats. Perhaps the chroniclers' fealty to their boastful Mongol employers led to exaggeration. Large though these cities were, no one today thinks they had populations of such magnitude. And did the Mongols really line up and slaughter civilians? "I can't believe they would have wasted time doing that," Larry Moses told me. "The Mongols pretty much annihilated the armies they came against, and a lot of civilians were marched in front of the army as cannon fodder, but I don't think civilians were simply wiped out. The Mongols needed people to move their packtrains and siege weapons." . . .

Of all the enemies that Genghis faced, only Jalal ad-Din won his admiration. While Jalal's father, Shah Muhammad, fled ignominiously, Jalal rode south into Afghanistan and gathered troops.

Genghis sent one of his lieutenants after him. Suddenly Jalal turned and dealt his pursuers a stinging defeat. Now the great khan took charge, pinning the Khwarizm heir against the Indus River in what is now Pakistan. Jalal led charge after fearless charge. Unable to break the Mongol grasp, he at last leaped into the river and swam away. Genghis forbade his archers to shoot. "Such a son," he exclaimed, "must a father have!"

As for Muhammad, Jebe and another Mongol general, Subedei, chased him through Iran to the Caspian Sea, where, exhausted, he died of pleurisy. All the finery of his rule had been lost; he was buried in the rags of a servant.

The Mongols always benefited from superior generalship. Commanders were audacious, knowing they could depend on their well-disciplined troops. Among those entrusted with command were Genghis's sons Jochi, Chaghatai, Ogodei, and Tolui, all born to his first wife, Borte. But the most important leaders were Genghis's comrades from the tribal wars, and among these Jebe and Subedei were peerless.

Reaching the Caspian, this intrepid pair wondered what lay beyond. Europe was as unknown to them as Mongolia to Europeans. With 20,000 men, they embarked on a reconnaissance in force. They vanquished two armies in Georgia and, crossing the Caucasus Mountains in winter, defeated a coalition of Turkic tribes on the Russian steppe. As they plundered the countryside, alarm spread through the Russian principalities—not yet united—of Kiev, Chernigov, Galicia, Rostov, and Suzdal. The princes assembled an army of 80,000 that challenged the Mongols on the Kalka River in 1223.

Mongol archers rode before the enemy, filling the air with arrows. Some of the princes charged hastily, only to see the archers vanish into smoke as the Mongols lit fires of dung and naphtha. They blundered on to discover that the smoke hid not lightly armored archers but cavalrymen brandishing lance and sword and mace. Parts of the Russian force turned in confusion, colliding with other units, and then a rout began.

In the flush of victory Jebe and Subedei dined atop a large wooden box. Inside it three captured Russian princes were suffocating, a means of death apparently chosen because in Mongol tradition the blood of a respected warrior should not be spilled on the ground in execution. It is doubtful that the princes appreciated the courtesy.

Jebe and Subedei swept east to the Volga, fought two more battles, and finally rejoined Genghis on the Central Asian steppe. Living off the land, acquiring fresh horses by conquest, vanquishing every opposing army, they rode 8,000 miles, circling the Caspian in one of the greatest cavalry exploits of all time.

Behind, they left a populace fearful and confused. "Unknown tribes came, whom no one exactly knows . . . nor whence they came out, nor what their language is, nor of what race they are," wrote a monk in the principality of Novgorod. To their sorrow, the Russians would soon learn all.

Turning for home at last, the Mongols extracted incalculable wealth from Central Asia. Warriors blazed with gold chains and jewels, and their horses were laden with bolts of silk and bags of coins. Several of the ravaged cities never recovered their former glory. Some historians say that the Mongol depredations strangled development for centuries.

Genghis had not forgotten that the ruler of Xi Xia had refused to supply troops for the western Asia campaign. Moreover, while Genghis was away fighting, Xi Xia had tried to wriggle free of Mongol control. In 1226 the khan led his army south from Mongolia once more. . . .

Xi Xia was long referred to as the "mysterious kingdom." In the past hundred years research has revealed that it had its own written language and produced fine silk scrolls and statuary.

Several versions exist of Genghis's second Xi Xia campaign. I heard one of these from Zhong Kan, emeritus director of the Yinchuan museum. A diminutive whirlwind, he flung his arms for emphasis while speaking, puffing cigarettes all the while.

We were walking on the bank of a wide canal running from the Yellow River, and with a windmill gesture toward the swiftly flowing water, he said, "It is very old. It was here before Genghis's time."

"And there"—he swung his arms away—"was the city wall. Just 500 yards away. When the Mongols could not get in the city, they came here"—the arms brought me back to the canal—"and broke the dike." Zhong believes the flood undermined the wall, or threatened to, and compelled Xi Xia to surrender.

It may have been the Yellow River, not the canal, that the Mongols unleashed, although that seems unlikely to Zhong Kan: The river is 28 miles from the city. Or perhaps Xi Xia surrendered after its army was defeated in fierce battles outside the walls.

Whatever happened, Genghis Khan was dying.

The *Secret History* says that as the Xi Xia campaign began, Genghis went hunting for wild asses. When his mount shied, he fell, "his body being in great pain." Another account says Genghis was ill—perhaps with typhus.

He already had chosen his successor, Ogodei, third son by his first wife. Juvaini says Genghis considered Ogodei wise and valorous; he was also a lover of strong drink and good times.

From his deathbed Genghis ordered the extermination of the Xi Xia people. His army is said to have killed "mothers and fathers down to the offspring of their offspring." Some were merely enslaved instead; still, the destruction of kingdom and people was wholesale, which is why Xi Xia lapsed into a historical blur.

In August 1227, somewhere south of Yinchuan, Genghis died. He was probably 60. Accounts say his body was borne to Mongolia for burial near a mountain called Burkhan Khaldun. Forty "moonlike virgins" and 40 horses were killed and buried with him, as if for his pleasure in the next world. To discourage grave robbers, a thousand horsemen are said to have trampled the site until it could not be found. It eludes searchers still.

Genghis was, wrote one of the Persian historians, "possessed of great energy, discernment, genius, and understanding, awe-inspiring, a butcher, just, resolute, an overthrower of enemies, intrepid, sanguinary, and cruel." A more comprehensive epitaph could not be written, except to add that he bequeathed to his clan a unified Mongolia and the most powerful army in the world.

His sons and grandsons would send that army surging anew into Russia and China, and even farther, while Mongolia creased the firmament of nations like a shooting star. Awash in power and wealth, the Mongols would find they had only one dangerous foe: one another.

Mike Edwards writes for *National Geographic* magazine, and his work has been featured in its historically based articles.

EXPLORING THE ISSUE

Was Mongol Leader Genghis Khan an Enlightened Ruler?

Critical Thinking and Reflection

1. Jack Weatherford writes: ". . . fate did not hand Genghis Khan his destiny; he made it for himself." Critically discuss both parts of this assertion.
2. How significant to Weatherford's thesis is the claim that Genghis Khan "insisted on laws holding rulers as equally accountable as the lowest herder."? Critically discuss the implications of this statement.
3. In what specific ways did the Great Law of Genghis Khan differ from those of other lawgivers in history?
4. In what specific ways was Genghis Khan "the thoroughly modern man"?
5. How does Mike Edwards support his claim that "the Mongols always benefitted from superior generalship"? Based on what you now know about Mongol society, what is the significance of this claim?
6. When you read Mike Edwards's accounts of ruthless military campaigns, are you able to reconcile these with the more "enlightened" side of Genghis Khan that Jack Weatherford emphasizes? Having read both selections, do the "two sides of Genghis Khan" seem less incompatible? Or more so? Critically discuss.
7. Do you find it significant that Genghis Khan ordered the extermination of the Xi Xia people from his death-bed? What offence had they committed? Critically discuss this "crime and punishment."

Is There Common Ground?

Both selections agree on the early life of Temujin, the future Genghis Khan. He was only nine when he lost his father, a catastrophic loss that also included the loss of his tribe. There is strong accord on the qualities the young Temujin cultivated—survival and self-preservation, friendship and enmity. And, both authors are awed by his three-decade rise to world prominence. Perhaps, like all of us, and certainly like all famous people, Genghis Khan is at the mercy of which of his deeds are most noted and remembered. As a remarkably complex person, he cannot be summarized under only one set of characteristics. Without his military conquests, would we have remembered him only as a footnote—an enlightened ruler? As an exercise, you might want to read a laudatory biography of a famous, living person, and then follow this by reading a "tell all" or "unauthorized biography." Perhaps both kinds of biographies could be written about any person, depending on where the biographer shined his or her light of research.

Additional Resources

For general information on Genghis Khan and the Mongols, consult: David Morgan, *The Mongols* (Blackwell Publishers, 1990); J.J. Saunders, *The History of the Mongol Conquests* (University of Pennsylvania Press, 2001); and, Reuven Amitai-Preiss and David O. Morgan, eds., *The Mongol Empire and Its Legacy* (Brill Academic Publishers, 1999). For sources concentrating on Genghis Khan's life and accomplishments, consult: Paul Ratchnevsky, *Genghis Khan, His Life and Legacy* (Blackwell Publishers, 1993 reprint); Jean-Paul Roux, *Genghis Khan and the Mongol Empire* (Harry N. Abrams, 2003); and Nicolai Trubetzkoy, *The Legacy of Genghis Khan* (Michigan Slavic Publications, 1991).

There are two contemporary accounts of Genghis Khan's life and work that are worth consulting: Ata-Malik Juvaini, *Genghis Khan: The History of the World Conqueror* (University of Washington Press, 1997), written by a noted Persian scholar; and, *Secret History of the Mongols: The Origin of Genghis Khan*, Paul Kahn and Frances Woodman Cleaves (Cheng & Tsui, 1999, expanded edition), a book begun shortly after Genghis Khan's death, written to preserve his place in history. Though somewhat shrouded in myth and memory, it does contain valuable information on his early life. Another issue in this volume offers the same public history/secret history accounts of the lives and reign of Justinian and Theodora of the Byzantine Empire.

Internet References . . .

The Mongols in World History

This comprehensive site provides much information on the Mongols and their impact on history. Some of the components are visual. Major areas include: The Mongol Conquests, Key Figures in Mongol History, and The Mongol's Mark on Global History.

http://afe.easia.columbia.edu/mongols

Selected, Edited, and with Issue Framing Material by:
Helen Buss Mitchell, *Howard Community College*
and
Joseph R. Mitchell, *Howard Community College*

ISSUE

Was Zen Buddhism the Primary Influence on the Japanese Samurai?

YES: Winston L. King, from *Zen and the Way of the Sword: Arming the Samurai Psyche* (Oxford University Press, 1993)

NO: Fred Stern, from "Samurai: A Thousand Years of Warriors," *World and I* (January 2010)

Learning Outcomes

After reading this issue you should be able to:

- Explain the history of Zen Buddhism and the warrior tradition in Japan.
- Understand how the samurai tradition developed.
- Describe the key features of the Bushido Code.

ISSUE SUMMARY

YES: Religious scholar Winston L. King argues that the monk Eisai introduced Zen to the Hojo samurai lords of Japan who recognized its affinity with the warrior's profession and character.

NO: Poet and art critic Fred Stern argues that the primary influence on the samurai was the historical warrior tradition in Japan, especially the Bushido Code of honor, loyalty, and self-sacrifice.

The word Zen means meditation. From India, Buddhist meditation masters brought their method of practice first to China (where it was known as Ch'an) and in the seventh century to Japan, where the school of Buddhism known as Zen flourished beginning during the twelfth and thirteenth centuries. What Western thinkers call truth and salvation lay within the person, according to Zen Masters, not in sacred texts, rituals, or doctrines. The realization of satori, or enlightenment, was a visceral rather than an intellectual experience and it could be achieved existentially, through a life of action.

From the time of the Hojo regent Hojo Tokiyori (1227–1263) Zen and the samurai class became closely allied. However, Buddhism and its Zen offshoot was not the only religious alternative in Japan. The influences of Confucianism, imported from China, and Shinto, the indigenous faith of Japan, were both significant. Like the Chinese, who found themselves Confucian on state occasions, Taoist in matters of health, and Buddhist at the time of death, Japanese people did not feel these religious traditions were mutually exclusive.

The warrior class that developed in Japan between the ninth and twelfth centuries and supported the shogunates that ruled Japan prior to the nineteenth-century Meiji Restoration was also called bushi, and the code by which they lived and died became known as bushido—the way of the warrior. As skilled fighting men, the samurai were, above all, loyal to the emperor, to an overlord or daimyo, and to other samurai of higher rank. Skilled in swordsmanship, horsemanship, and hand-to-hand combat, many were often also adept at painting, calligraphy, and poetry. They lived spartan lives marked by honor, pride, patriotism, and honesty. Prepared at any moment to lay down their lives for their lord, the samurai preferred ritual suicide (known as seppuku or hara-kiri, meaning disembowelment) to capture in battle or to dishonor. Later scholars have found elements of Buddhism, Confucianism, and Shinto in the Bushido Code and disagree about which influence predominated.

From Shinto comes reverence for the Emperor as a God-like father of the nation. Out of this loyalty to the Imperial family flows an intense patriotism as well as the promise that to die for one's country in battle is to become God-like oneself. This absolute fidelity of the samurai may be seen continuing into the modern era. Kamikaze pilots and suicide torpedoists who willingly sacrificed their lives for the success of the nation and to honor the Emperor during World War II were following their own version of the Bushido Code.

Confucianism draws attention to the Five Constant Relationships—between parent and child, husband and wife, older and younger sibling, older and younger friend, and ruler and subject—as models for achieving harmony with the Way of Heaven. To know one's place, to do one's duty, to honor those above and act kindly toward those below, this was the way to live a life of balance, to serve the common good, and to please the ancestors. Samurai loyalty to emperor and overlord may be understood within this context of properly lived human relationships.

Buddhism focuses on how to become enlightened—to see things as they actually are—and, thus, escape the continual round of birth/death/rebirth known as samsara. Zen Buddhism emphasizes meditation as a path to true seeing, into the heart of the cosmos and into the Buddha-nature that is within all things. It makes no hard distinctions between sacred and secular, understanding that the way of enlightenment involves the reconciliation of all apparent opposites. Once these artificial distinctions collapse, a genuine experience of things as they are becomes possible.

Each lifetime arises out of the karma of previous lifetimes. Whatever the person desires, whatever the person does not yet understand, these are the karmic predispositions that travel from birth to birth and govern the agenda of a present lifetime. So, despite the Buddhist prohibition against killing (not only other humans but all living things endowed with Buddha-nature), a samurai might see himself as destined by karma to live a warrior's life. As you read the following selections, decide for yourself which influence—Zen Buddhism or the Bushido Warrior Code—predominated in forming the inner life of the samurai warrior.

Because it insists on "no reliance on words or concepts," Zen is difficult to approach by way of printed texts. However, *Zen Flesh, Zen Bones: A Collection of Zen and Pre-Zen Writings*, compiled by Paul Reps (Doubleday, 1989) introduces us to monks who drop sacred texts into the fire, spend years facing walls in silent meditation, and even cut off their own arms to show zeal. This brings us closer to what in Zen might have touched the heart of a samurai.

Two other classics are Miyamoto Musashi's *A Book of Five Rings* (The Overlook Press, 1974) and Yamamoto Tsunetomo's *Hagakure: The Book of the Samurai* (Kodansha International, 1983), both easily accessible. Musashi's guide to strategy was based on kendo or sword fighting but is consulted by business people who find the challenges faced and the tactics needed today little changed in 350 years. *Hagakure's* central contention is that bushido is a way of dying and that only a samurai prepared to die at any moment can be totally faithful to his lord.

Finally, Akira Kurosawa's 1954 film *The Seven Samurai* has inspired hundreds of imitators. Seven ronin (freelance samurai, not in service to a feudal lord) are called upon to aid villagers at an isolated outpost who are beleaguered by invading bandits. The honor code of the samurai is a key theme in this classic film as well as in one of its most popular descendants John Sturges's *The Magnificent Seven*, and also in Ed Zwick's 2003 epic *The Last Samurai*. Hired by the Emperor to train Japan's first modern army, Captain Nathan Algren (Tom Cruise) is captured and won over by a band of samurai warriors. For classroom and library, Films for the Humanities & Sciences offers *Samurai Japan* [ISBN 0-7365-0642-X].

YES

Winston L. King

The Japanese Warrior Adopts Zen

Zen Buddhism first became an important factor in the training and life of the Japanese warrior class in the thirteenth century. During the late-twelfth-century struggle of the Genji and Heike clans, Jōdo (Pure Land) Buddhism—in which Amida and his infinite mercy and forgiveness were paramount—was perhaps the soldier's favorite religious loyalty, especially in the hour of death. But with the coming of the Hōjō regency to power, Zen Buddhism increasingly took the leading role.

Eisai: "Founder" of Zen

Eisai (1141–1215) is the first name to reckon with in this Zen ascendancy. Sometimes he is called the founder of Zen Buddhism in Japan. This is not strictly true. The Zen practice of meditation, imported from China (where it was known as Ch'an), had been practiced in Japan since the seventh century, where it was considered one of several types of Buddhist spiritual training and given a home at Enryakuji by Tendai Buddhism.

The situation is rather that Eisai (also called Yōsai), a Tendai monk at Enryakuji, attempted to give Zen a more independent status than Enryakuji leaders were willing to allow it. Eisai, wishing to study with some of the masters of the more venerable Chinese tradition, made two trips to China to "renew" and deepen his understanding of Buddhism, and there he came into contact with the respected masters of the independent Ch'an (Zen) school. At the end of his second visit, from 1187 to 1191, he was given ordination as a Rinzai Zen master, and on his return to Japan he sought to establish a temple in Kyoto in which specific Zen training and meditation—of course, Zen means just that, "meditation"—would be given a central place. To the day of his death, Eisai still considered himself to be a Tendai monk. But Enryakuji would have nothing to do with his "new" Tendai Buddhism and frustrated his efforts. Eisai then journeyed to the shogunal headquarters in Kamakura, where he gained the favor of the widow of the first shogun, Minamoto Yoritomo; Eisai was installed as the head of a newly built temple at her behest. Somewhat later he returned to Kyoto by invitation and spent his last years there as an honored monk-teacher.

Rather curiously, Eisai has been memorialized in a very concrete way: the drinking of tea, bitter green tea *(matcha)* that is "brewed" by stirring the powdered tea leaves into boiling hot water in a tea bowl and whipping it to a froth with a special "feathered bamboo" whisk. He held it to be ideal for keeping the meditator awake and good for the health in general. Later, tea drinking was made into a ritualized fine art with skilled tea masters being much sought after and munificently rewarded by such as Toyotomi Hideyoshi, Tokugawa Ieyasu's predecessor in military and political power. Sometimes the tea drinking was a lavish and ostentatious ceremony—as with Hideyoshi, who used it as a means of political maneuver and dominance. In other versions, the emphasis was on perfect (highly polished) simplicity and "naturalness," as befitting its Zen origins. In modern Japan, there are both the genuinely simple-natural drinking of tea in the Zen monastery and an assiduously cultivated commercialized form carried on by modern tea masters.

To return to Eisai: His accomplishments on behalf of Zen were two. First, though he himself remained a Tendai-Zennist, his special emphasis on Zen practice as a somewhat distinctive and independent religious discipline began the process of establishing Zen as a separate sect. Thus his "new" Zen Buddhism became a part of what is known as the Kamakura period populist Buddhism, which brought Buddhism out of its high-class elitism into the life of the common people. His "companions" in this were Hōnen and Shinran, who taught the sufficiency for salvation of the repetition (in faith) of Amida Buddha's name, and Nichiren, who proclaimed the full efficacy of the Lotus Sutra's name as a mantric chant.

The second accomplishment of Eisai was his bringing of Zen practice in its own independent right to the attention of the new lords of Japan, the Hōjō regency samurai government. It was their interest in Zen, their perception of it as congenial to the warrior's profession and character, that brought Zen and the samurai together. However, even though the Hōjō regents gave Zen a friendly interest and preferential treatment, it was some time before Zen freed itself completely from the Tendai qualifications and Shingon esoteric practices imposed on it by Eisai and came to be defined by its own specific genius and quality. This was accomplished by various of Eisai's disciples and by Dōgen (1200–1253), who also studied Ch'an in China from 1223 to 1228 and returned to Japan to found a competing school of Zen, the Sotō. There was also a continuing stream of Ch'an masters from the mainland who forwarded the process of developing the distinctive independent character of Zen teaching and practice.

Zen as the Warrior's Religion

The fourth Hōjō regent, Hōjō Tokiyori (1227–1263), nearly fifty years after Eisai's death, was the first to give more than a merely general official friendliness to Zen; he became personally interested in Zen practice and was certified by a Chinese master as having attained to enlightenment. From this time on, Zen and the new warrior-masters of Japan were closely related to each other; this personal interest and discipleship carried on over to the Ashikaga shoguns who governed Japan—or the greater part of it—from 1333 to 1573 and who moved the shogunal headquarters from Kamakura back to Kyoto.

Thus it was that from Tokiyori onward, Zen was the unofficial-official religion of the rulers and ruling class. As a matter of course, Zen prospered as sect and institution. The later Hōjō regents, particularly several of the Ashikaga shoguns, were generous patrons of Zen. By the time of Soseki Musō (1275–1351), the most prominent Zen monk of his time, and nearly a century after Eisai, Zen had grown into a nationwide establishment—courtesy of the Hōjō regents and the shogunate. Zen temples were constructed in all the prefectures. The Five Mountain *(gozan)* system of precedence was established, by which five large temples around Kyoto, with Nanzenji at their head, and another five in Kamakura (one of them Eisai's special temple) were given first-rank status. A second-level class (subordinate to the first class), consisting of some sixty temples, was also established. Finally, there were some two hundred local temples scattered through most of Japan. Again, be it repeated, to this establishment the shogunal authorities gave their full backing and support.

And not only did the Zen sect prosper in terms of the favor of high officials, but also among the rank-and-file samurai themselves. It seems that from the beginning of Zen's "new" presence, its meditation and discipline commended themselves to the samurai, of both high and low rank. One samurai vassal counseled his son, "The duty of a warrior like that of a monk, is to obey orders. . . . He must consider his life not his own but a gift offered to his lord." Indeed, the samurai so "adopted" Zen, for practice in meditation and as a Buddhism suited to them, that it became a proverb in the Kamakura era that "Tendai is for the imperial court, Shingon for the nobility, Zen for the warrior class, and Pure Land for the masses."

But the alliance between the Ashikaga shogunate, now settled in Kyoto, led to far more than the nationwide founding of Zen temples. With Ashikaga Takauji, the first of the Ashikaga shoguns, Zen priests became the official advisers to the shogunate. Because Zen monks were the leading scholars of the day, and numbers of them had been to the Chinese mainland, their advisory role had a great influence on many aspects of official policy and national life. Many of them were traveled men of the world whose ordination as Buddhist monks gave them a high social standing and did not exclude them from the world or from taking part in secular life. (It may be remarked in passing that Zen draws no sharp line between the "sacred" and the "secular"; to the enlightened person, the two are one—it is the inner-personal quality of life that is the domain of virtue and holiness. The Buddha-nature is in everything without essential distinction.) Hence they rendered important diplomatic services, were often negotiators with mainland Chinese officials and other foreigners, and were sent as shogunal emissaries. The Shōkokuji Zen temple in Kyoto was the government's operative foreign-relations center for a considerable period of time.

There was another important aspect of Zen influence, one whose marks still remain in the Japanese cultural and artistic tradition. As Heinrich Dumoulin observes: It was the Zen monk-scholar-artist who opened the world of "*haute* culture" to the warrior clans. The Hōjō regency in Kamakura kept its deliberate distance from the Kyoto court circles—the better to keep its political power intact and to avoid the enervating, effeminizing influence of the imperial and aristocratic circles. The rough, stern warrior clans of the north and east disdained and distrusted the soft and cultured life as corruptive of the more stalwart virtues. But this attitude changed with the passing years, especially under the Ashikaga regime when the shogunate moved its headquarters to Kyoto. The warrior leaders found themselves hungry for the literacy and aesthetic attainments they came in contact with in Kyoto. Zen monks as chosen advisers to the shogunate—disciplined in living, skillful in language and a new style of painting, some of them writers, poets, and men of the world as well as redoubtable warriors—thus became tutors to the warrior-class leaders and influential in setting new cultural styles.

So, too, the influence of Zen, direct and indirect, on the art of the day was substantial. There was painting, for example. Zen set a new style of direct, spontaneous, and spare "painting." Zen artist-monks disdained the colorful and decorative for the most part and opted for *sumie* (India ink drawings), also called *suiboku* ("water and ink" creations). There were self-portraits (almost caricatures, designed to express one's personal essence), persons, animals, birds, vegetation, as well as calligraphy. Much of it was a sheerly black-on-white style of instant art—jet-black indelible ink on porous white paper. Such work required complete poise and decisiveness, for the first stroke was also the last; there could be no patching, no alteration. Its production was fully visceral, a disciplined spontaneity. The starkly simple result admirably expressed the Zen "view" of life.

There was also the Noh play, not originated but strongly influenced by Zen in the days of the Ashikaga Shogun Yoshimitsu (1368–1394), who took a strong personal interest in Noh development. Again, as with sumie, the sparse action and enigmatic, suggestive symbolism suited the Zen genius, even though the themes of the plays were Shintoist and Amidist. Yoshimitsu also built the famous "worldly" Golden Pavilion (Kinkakuji); his successor, two generations later, Shogun Ashikaga Yoshimasa, built the Silver Pavilion (Ginkakuji) in 1473 into which to retire for a Zen meditator's life.

Despite all the personal and official favor shown to Zen by individual regents and shoguns and the semiofficializing of Zen as the government's religion, Zen as a sect avoided the political embroilments that were characteristic of the Nara and Enryakuji temples and the Pure Land Ikkō sect. Zen monks counseled shogunal officials and, as already observed, acted as government representatives in international affairs. But there was never a Zen lobbying group at head shogunal quarters or Zen groups or temples maneuvering to gain power at the expense of competitors.

If we ask why this should be the case, three possible factors may be mentioned. The first and most obvious is: Why *should* Zen enter the always dangerous field of religious–political intrigue? It was already the personal practice of several shoguns; within a hundred years after Eisai, its temples had been established throughout Japan, and Zen had been adopted by the shogunal government as a near-official religion; its monks were advisers to the shoguns, and the samurai looked on it as their special religious faith. Besides this, in Zen's heyday of cultural popularity, Zen scholar-monks set the tone and the pace of new cultural styles. What more was there to ask for? What need to intrigue at court?

Another factor of at least some importance in this connection was what might be called Zen anti-institutionalism. In religious terms, Zen was a rejection of many creedal and ritual elements of the Buddhist tradition embodied in most of the other sects; this allowed considerable freedom of action and practice on its part. On the sectarian-institutional level, Zen favored individual rather than factional or organizational action. Some of the leading Zen monasteries were physically large—the Hōjō regents and Ashikaga shoguns had been generous in their support of the Zen "establishment." Despite this, the relationships between Zen and the government, as well as with other groups, tended to be on the level of the personal—influential individuals rather than organizational muscle-flexing. Thus no given Zen temple—paralleling Enryakuji of the Tendai, Kōya-san of the Shingon, or the great fortress-temple of the Pure Land Honganji near Osaka—ever became a powerful and belligerent institution seeking to gain political advantages.

The third factor to be noted is only partially explanatory of this situation. The great sectarian temples that were now and again embroiled in conflict with the civilian government—the Nara sects, Enryakuji, and Kōya-san—had been established centuries before Zen came on to the scene as a sect; and in those centuries they had accumulated their great estates, their vested interests, and their armies of soldier-monks. Thus Zen missed out on this enfeudalizing of the religious establishment and the politicizing of its role. Of course, it must be said that so, too, had the Honganji Jōdo Shinshu (Pure Land) sect, for the Pure Land sects were established at roughly the same time as Zen, in the thirteenth century. Yet Honganji Buddhism gave birth to Ikkō militancy. In any case, Zen's nonpolitical character saved it from the bloody purges that Oda Nobunaga inflicted on Enryakuji and the Ikkō barons in the sixteenth century.

There is another aspect of the religious and political situation that is of importance here: the historical framework of the relation of both Shinto and Buddhism to the state. Shinto, as Japan's first and basic religion, had the emperor as its high priest; as guardian of the Three Sacred Treasures and performer of annual fertility-prosperity rituals, his first concern and main function were the preservation of his people in safety and prosperity. Therefore, in times of crisis, such as the Mongolian invasions in the late thirteenth century, Shinto priests assiduously prayed to the gods and believed that they had responded by sending the gales *(kami kaze)* that had wrecked the Mongol fleets.

But it must also be recollected that Buddhism was first brought into Japan in the sixth century primarily as a more potent means to the same end—preservation of the nation. All the Buddhist sects—with the possible partial exception of the Pure Land—well understood this to be their role in times of crisis. When the Mongols attacked, Buddhist clergy joined their sutra chanting to the ritual efforts of the Shinto priests to bring victory—and were rewarded accordingly. Clans often endowed their local Buddhist monasteries and temples to provide prayers in times of crisis or sickness. And with the transformation of Hachiman, the Shinto god of war, into a bodhisattva [a being whose actions promote unity or harmony; one who vows to postpone one's own enlightenment in order to help all sentient beings realize liberation] of high rank. Buddhist warriors could pray to him for victory as well as Shintoists could. Nor did Zen totally escape this influence. It is significant that Eisai entitled his first major writing *Treatise on the Spread of Zen for the Protection of the Nation.*

As an inevitable and natural result, the nonviolent message of Buddhism was qualified, modified, or overlaid by duty to clan lord, so that Buddhist warriors fought other Buddhist warriors to the death, it is to be presumed with only minor twinges of conscience. Of course, this is not unique to Buddhism. After the officialization of Christianity in Europe by the emperor Constantine in 330 C.E. [Christian Era], the followers of the Prince of Peace not only launched massive crusades against the infidel Muslims, but also fought one another savagely over the truth of their differing doctrines.

It should be said in all fairness that many Buddhist warriors did retire to monasteries, in their later years usually, to pursue their spiritual welfare and in some measure atone for their un-Buddhist conduct in killing their fellow men. But there was an inbuilt factor in Buddhism itself that worked against the teaching that all life, especially human life, is sacred. This was the Buddhist teaching of karmic destiny. For instance, some of the warriors portrayed in the *Heike Monogatari* (Tale of the Heike) lamented the fact, at reflective moments or when they had committed some militarily necessary cruelty, that they had been born into a warrior family and thus must carry on with a warrior's bloody career. And free as Zen may have been in some respects from the bonds of the Buddhist tradition, it was not free from the bonds of the teaching of karma.

To this must be added a peculiarly Japanese factor: the strong sense of family loyalty and tradition, especially in the upper classes. Reflecting the Chinese reverence for ancestors, the family—and its role, occupation, business—is a "sacred" inheritance, entailing the son's—especially the eldest son's—following in his father's footsteps. (One contemporary Shinto priest proudly notes that he is the twenty-eighth in the family who has occupied the headship of a particular shrine.) When this is added to, or is seen as the vehicle of, karmic predetermination, the individual is required, even fated, to accept the role that has been given him—for instance, as a samurai whose destined duty was to be a fighting, life-destroying "Buddhist."

For all its freedom from some of the liabilities of the other sects and despite its emphasis on individual freedom and opposition to institutional bonds, Zen did not escape these doctrinal and historical influences. When it was becoming a distinct and independent sect in the thirteenth century, the institutional format of religion in the service of the state and of warlike sects and monk-warriors had been long set. What could be more natural under the circumstances than for Zen monks, favorites of the Hōjō regents and their successors, the Ashikaga shoguns, and as valued spiritual tutors of the fighting forces, to put themselves completely at the service of the state.

Although he belonged to a subsequent period when Zen no longer occupied its privileged and somewhat exclusive position in government circles, Sūden (Den-chōrō, d. 1633) beautifully illustrates the qualities, accomplishments, and diverse roles characteristic of talented Zen monks. He was head of two Kyoto Zen temples, Konchi-in and, the most prestigious temple of all, Nanzenji, to whose restoration he devoted two years. Then in 1608, Tokugawa Ieyasu called Sūden into the service of the shogunate. (He had previously served as a field secretary in Ieyasu's campaigns.) Sūden handled all documents dealing with foreign relations and was placed in general charge of the Tokugawa religious policy—continuing in that post for another seventeen years after Ieyasu's death—working for the regulation and subordination of Buddhist sects to government control and for the exclusion of Christianity.

In his earlier years, just before he entered a monastery on his father's death, he had fought in his father's forces, taking the heads of three enemies as trophies. Hence Ieyasu allowed the temple built at his own place of retirement in Sumpu for Sūden, to display three black stars on its banner in honor of Sūden's prowess as a warrior. Thus was Sūden the warrior, "executive secretary" in the field to the man who became Japan's de facto ruler in 1600, then his "secretary of state" and the director of religious affairs for the shogunate—all the while presumably retaining his standing as a Zen monk. One is reminded of some of medieval Europe's priest-statesmen such as Armand-Jean Cardinal Richelieu.

In the light of these intimate connections between Zen and the ruling warrior class and also the apparent great popularity of Zen meditation among the rank-and-file samurai, especially during the warring centuries (1200-1600), it is necessary to know something of the samurai class to which Zen would prove of such value in their mode of life. That is, their use of Zen in their martial calling can make sense only if something of their history; their weapons—especially the sword—and their manner of using them; their hopes, fears, and ideals; their social role; and their conceptions of themselves and their "calling" are also known to us.

Winston L. King is Professor Emeritus at Vanderbilt University. A long-time writer on religion, he is the author of a number of books on Buddhism in Asia.

Fred Stern

Samurai: A Thousand Years of Warriors

They dominated Japanese history for the better part of a thousand years. And although the samurai—the elite military class of Japan which originated in the late 8th Century—were transformed into primarily political and cultural entities by events of the 19th Century, their exploits on the battlefield, their Zen philosophy and stoicism which inspired great bravery, even their beautifully crafted accoutrements of war continue to excite and exert outsize influence in Japan and beyond.

Origin and Evolving Roles of Samurai

Japan is a relatively small island nation, and the limits of its land mass are exaggerated by its mountainous terrain. The result is a country of great beauty but of limited arable land, i.e., land suitable for farming. Therein lies the underlying reason for the rise of a Japanese military class, the samurai. As the eminent British Field Marshall Viscount Montgomery of El Alamein, second in command under General Dwight Eisenhower in World War II, noted about the origin of the samurai in his fascinating History of Warfare: "The Japanese archipelago stretches for over 1,000 miles, but a great part of the land is mountainous and infertile, and the high incidence of war can largely be attributed to competition for the sparse areas of good rice land."

Early in the 8th Century, a system of "shoens," roughly the equivalent of European medieval manors, evolved in Japan, and remained for centuries. With good land so scarce and so valuable, it is not surprising that these large landowners sought to protect their crops and their holdings. To keep intruders away they hired armed guards, many of whom had previously policed the imperial cities or had some military background. They were called "samurai," a word that probably had its roots in a term meaning "to serve."

Most of the samurai's military actions were domestic in nature, civil wars of varying size and duration, fought primarily for the protection of their lords and their property. In this role, the samurai became very powerful, and on a grander scale, they even decided who would be Japan's ruling families.

But during two foreign invasions of Japan, the samurai were drawn into battles beyond domestic squabbles and land or power grabs. This time they were fighting foreign armies, and the outcome of these wars would determine their islands' future. These were the Mongol invasions, launched by Mongol fleets from Korean coasts. The period of the invasions and the unrest which followed lasted from 1274 to 1281 AD. The first invasion was said to involve some 900 ships and more than 30,000 assorted Mongolian troops and their satellites—Koreans, Chinese, and other outsiders who greatly outnumbered the defending samurai. The aggression proved unsuccessful largely because of hurricane force winds which came to the aid of the samurai. The second Mongol invasion was said to fail because of the emperor's prayers, although no doubt fierce storms, a fortified coastal wall that the Japanese had constructed after the first invasion, and of course the brave and determined samurai, again vastly outnumbered, also played critical roles.

The Mongol invasions forced disparate groups of samurai who had heretofore fought among themselves, to unite and face a common enemy. Thus the Kamakura Period (1192–1332) became a pivotal era in Japanese history. Additionally, this was the time that the position of shogun was established. The shogun was the highest ranking samurai warrior in the land, and from that time on shoguns assumed the top governmental post, essentially running the government and making administrative appointments. They ruled from the city of Edo, now called Tokyo, while the emperors were based in Kyoto which was technically speaking the Japanese capital at that time.

The Muramachi Period which followed (1333–1573) brought 250 turbulent years. It is easy to compare this period to the middle ages in Europe where many small armies were engaged in perpetual and counterproductive fighting. During this period the samurai were in great demand and had no trouble finding willing employers.

A consolidation of the Japanese government which had been divided between Edo and Kyoto, took place in the next period, the Azuchi-Momoyama years (1573–1603). Brief though this period was, it was during this time that the foundation for a caste system was set. The samurai had a choice between settling on estates and castles, or continuing life as warriors.

The Edo Epoch (1603–1868) saw the final establishment of a societal hierarchy. By imperial decree, the samurai were placed at the very top of society, just after the lords (daimyos) whom they served, followed by farmers, artisans, and merchants. This era proved to be a relatively peaceful one, and it was during this time that some of the most spectacular art used by the samurai was created.

It may seem strange that the great age of the samurai came to an end about the same time that a fleet commanded by an American commodore, Mathew Perry, steamed into Edo Bay, the harbor of Tokyo in 1853. Commodore Perry gave an ultimatum to the Japanese emperor demanding the opening of Japan to Western trade. The emperor did not immediately accede but the die was cast: Japan would end centuries of isolation and become an international presence.

For the samurai class, the transition away from the military which had begun earlier during the Edo Epoch accelerated. Now, with "the opening" of Japan, there would be a greatly expanded need for administrators, government officials, scholars, and the like, and the samurai, an amazing 1.9 million men by that time, stepped in to fill these positions, all the while retaining their elevated status. Descendants of the samurai warriors continued in these important roles for many years and into the next century.

Samurai Art and Arms

Throughout their thousand-year history, the samurai valued quality in both the efficiency and the design of their weapons. Often, samurai armaments—although deadly in their function—were quite beautiful. Careful observation of these objects opens a window on more than simply samurai philosophy, warfare, and other activities. They help us learn and appreciate much about Japan including its history, culture, and technological development.

The Metropolitan Museum of Art in New York City recently mounted an extensive exhibition of samurai armor, swords, and art. Ten years in the making, the exhibit is probably the most complete show of its kind ever presented.

More than 200 objects were put on display, although some are so old and now so fragile, they can be displayed for only a limited period of time, requiring rotation during the exhibit. Many of them have been designated Japanese "national treasures" an important honor, and most have never been seen before in the West.

In addition to exquisite armor, swords, sword fittings, archery, and other equipment, there are banners, accessories, and fantastic helmets. The exploits of the samurai throughout the centuries are also captured on screens and scrolls detailing battles that often involved many thousands of foot soldiers and samurai mounted on horseback. Amazingly several of the objects shown in these old screens and scrolls have been preserved and are on display, right alongside their graphic depictions.

Frankly a fully clothed samurai had something of the appearance of a character from a Gilbert and Sullivan operetta. But samurai armor functioned exceptionally well, despite its unusual appearance. If you compare samurai battle outfits to the armor worn by medieval knights, which you may be accustomed to seeing in film and books, you will note obvious physical differences which point to differing purposes. The armor of the medieval knight was more defensive, mainly meant to protect, whereas the samurai armor enabled the warrior to take the offense, with protection taking only a secondary consideration.

First of all, consider the material. Medieval knights wore [steel-plated] armor. Great in combat providing you had a crane-like contraption to position your armored knight on his horse. The steel while serving a protective function could also immobilize a knight and render him helpless. The samurai, on the other hand, valued mobility, especially in the early years when most fought on foot. Accordingly, they chose leather construction which was tough enough to protect against the weapon of the day, the arrow. The leather was sewn together in small strips, allowing maximum flexibility for the warrior who often fought on or along steep inclines, without compromising protection. In all its bright colors, there was no attempt at camouflage; the intention was to frighten, not hide. His armor was a samurai's major expense.

As Japanese weaponry advanced, and deadly swords came into use for man-to-man combat, the samurai used a type of modified steel armor which retained maximal flexibility due to unique construction techniques. And the samurai continued to favor color. Whereas the appearance of the medieval knight, at least color-wise was quite dull, the samurai could not select more colorful attire.

Another difference in the accoutrements of the European versus Japanese warriors was the helmet. The medieval knight had a closed helmet with a slot he could open so he could see what he was doing or where he was going. The samurai helmet, on the other hand, presented a ferocious face to frighten opponents and often also featured surprising horns or antlers. Outsized helmets indicated rank. Late in samurai history, after guns and gunpowder had arrived in Japan, horns or antlers or other tall appendages on top of these helmets helped soldiers identify their military leaders above a haze of gun smoke.

Over the centuries, the weapons of the samurai continued to improve in their deadly efficiency. Early on the samurai were proficient in bow and arrow. After [steel making] and blade making were perfected, the Japanese warriors combined the use of arrows shot from horseback, then coming in with long swords for final combat. Daily training was used to assure maximal results. The samurai valued their horses in battle, and paid attention to outfitting them, much as medieval knights did. During the relatively peaceful Edo Epoch, a saddle and stirrups were created for one of the most famous of the samurai, Toyotomi Hideyoshi. Together with intricate, opulent sword mountings using gold, lacquer, and silk, these objects from the period survive today and are on view in the Met Museum exhibition.

The long sword was eventually replaced by a curved or slung sword (tachi) in the 11th Century. The slung or curved sword allowed for quick withdrawal of the blade once it came into play. Many of the samurai wore two swords: a swung blade and a shorter dagger type sword that was put to good use.

Two groups of artisans were responsible for these weapons. First were the blade makers. They used only the finest of steels, and their procedures and steel selection were part of a proud tradition that went through generations of individual families. The second group was the steel polishers who were responsible for the tempering line or pattern along the blade. The pattern of the ground, polished blade was considered a form of art, and some blades became so famous that they have names and can easily be recognized by connoisseurs.

In the final century of their existence the samurai imported Western style guns, and used them effectively.

Why did the samurai fight so bravely? Part of the answer rests with a code, the "Bushido" or "way of the warrior" which they followed assiduously. As the historian Arthur May Knapp describes it, "The samurai had behind him a thousand years of training in the law, obedience, duty and self-sacrifice." This was indoctrination that had begun at birth. It was a doctrine reinforced by the teachings of Zen Buddhism which trained the warrior to be blind to the dangers of the battlefield and, often unlike the medieval knight, to not think in terms of self-preservation. The samurai did not accept defeat and invariably took his own life when defeated or when he considered himself as having failed in his endeavors.

Was it merely a coincidence that the prestigious Japanese military class, the samurai, and the prestigious knights of Europe emerged and became a potent force during their regions' middle ages? True, they had important differences. Most obviously, the samurai both gained and retained power and influence for many more centuries than their European counterpart. And we also know that the knight originated at the royal courts of Europe and was granted his station and rights at the discretion of the ruler, whereas the samurai practiced a form of self-creation. Self-sacrifice was probably more deeply ingrained in the samurai, self-preservation perhaps more common among the knights. And chivalry—the deference paid to women—was an important aspect of medieval knighthood, but seemed largely absent from the samurai culture.

But the two groups of warriors had much in common: their role in protecting a feudal system; their loyalty to their lord or emperor; their commitment to a higher philosophy; the value they placed on bravery in battle and on military victory; their tournaments and acceptance of violence toward opponents. The era of knighthood and of the samurai both ended with the disappearance of feudalism in their respective continents, and with the coalescing of small governorships into larger nations. But their deeds and the legends surrounding them continue to inspire and intrigue both East and West.

Fred Stern is a poet and writer on the arts.

EXPLORING THE ISSUE

Was Zen Buddhism the Primary Influence on the Japanese Samurai?

Critical Thinking and Reflection

1. Briefly describe the religious traditions of Japan—the indigenous Shinto and the imported Confucianism and Zen Buddhism.
2. Critically analyze the samurai tradition that developed in Japan between the ninth and twelfth centuries, drawing on evidence provided by both the YES and NO selections.
3. How did the character and role of the samurai support the shoguns that ruled Japan? Critically discuss.
4. Analyze the Bushido Code and its role in the life and death of a samurai. Critically discuss the skills and virtues a samurai was expected to embody.
5. Critically analyze the evidence offered by each side. Which side seems more convincing? Critically discuss why you believe this to be the case.
6. What conflicts might exist between Zen Buddhism and the Bushido Code? Critically discuss.
7. On what basis does Winston L. King argue that Zen Buddhism played a significant role in the samurai tradition? Be specific in providing evidence.
8. On what basis does Fred Stern argue that the warrior tradition in Japan can account for the rise of the samurai? Be specific in providing evidence.

Is There Common Ground?

Both authors in this issue agree that Zen Buddhism and the Bushido Code were allied. The history of Japan and the influence of Zen Buddhism on the shoguns and daimyo form one thread in this narrative. The other thread is the long history of a proud warrior tradition that lasted, in Fred Stern's words, for a thousand years. The samurai, in this issue, are at the intersection of these two threads.

Our task is to examine the evidence provided by each writer and assign weight to both Zen Buddhism and the warrior tradition. Depending on how convincing each author is, we might be pulled in one direction or another. Each selection in this issue also introduces other issues. The roles of Confucianism (imported from China) and Shinto (the religion of national patriotism that is indigenous to Japan) expand the religious context. And, the scarcity of arable land made protection of landholdings essential. Would you add either or both of these factors as significant influences on the samurai tradition?

Sometimes what seems a powerful influence in one historical time period fades to a minor influence in the minds of later historians. A culture dominated by religion would be likely to look for a religious explanation when examining an earlier time and place. And, a culture engaged in war would be predisposed to seeing historical events through that lens. Our task is to avoid the error known as presentism, as much as possible. We are best able to understand the past if we can put the values and priorities of the present aside and take the past on its own terms.

Question: To the extent possible enter the mind of a samurai. Which factor seems more compelling to you: Zen Buddhism or the long warrior tradition? Are you able to choose one over the other or must you insist that a combination of factors informs your personal life and the tradition to which you belong?

Additional Resources

In *The Modern Samurai Society: Duty and Dependence in Contemporary Japan* (Amacom, 1982), Mitsuyuki Masatsugu traces the evolution of the loyal samurai warrior of the past into the devoted samurai executive of today. A similar aim motivates Eiko Ikegami's *The Taming of the Samurai: Honorific Individualism and the Making of Modern Japan* (Harvard University Press, 1995). However, she roots Japan's tradition of competitive individualism in samurai honor consciousness. Which qualities in the samurai tradition made this transition from warrior to bureaucrat possible? Haru Matsukata Reischauer's *Samurai and Silk: A Japanese and American Heritage* (Harvard University Press, 1986) honors her two grandfathers—one a provincial samurai who became a founding father of the Meiji government, and the other from a wealthy peasant family who almost singlehandedly developed the silk trade with America.

Internet References . . .

Bushido: The Way of the Warrior

A site with brief but useful information on the samurai, including their creed, Bushido, and other websites related to the subject.

http://mcel.pacificu.edu/as/students/bushido/bindex.html

Selected, Edited, and with Issue Framing Material by:
Helen Buss Mitchell, *Howard Community College*
and
Joseph R. Mitchell, *Howard Community College*

ISSUE

Did Women and Men Benefit Equally from the Renaissance?

YES: Margaret L. King, from *Women of the Renaissance* (The University of Chicago Press, 1991)

NO: Joan Kelly-Gadol, from "Did Women Have a Renaissance?" in Renate Bridenthal, Claudia Koonz, and Susan Stuard, eds., *Becoming Visible: Women in European History*, 2nd ed. (Houghton Mifflin Company, 1987)

Learning Outcomes

After reading this issue you should be able to:

- Understand the concept of periodization, the chunking of history into coherent periods of experience, such as Middle Ages, Renaissance, etc.
- Determine what changed and what remained the same, as the Middle Ages gave way to the Renaissance.
- Describe the lives of high-born women during both these periods.

ISSUE SUMMARY

YES: Historian Margaret L. King surveys Renaissance women in domestic, religious, and learned settings and argues that reflected in their lives was a new consciousness of themselves as women, as intelligent seekers of a new way of being in the world.

NO: Historian Joan Kelly-Gadol argues from her work as a Renaissance scholar that well-born women seemed to have enjoyed greater advantages during the Middle Ages and experienced a relative loss of position and power during the Renaissance.

In 1974 Joan Kelly-Gadol published a pathbreaking essay that challenged traditional historical periodization for women (see Introduction). Before that, virtually every publication on the Renaissance proclaimed it to be a great leap forward for everyone, a time when new ideas were widely discussed and the old strictures of the Middle Ages were thrown off. The difficulty for Kelly-Gadol was that her own work on women during the medieval and Renaissance periods told a different story. She was one of the first to raise this troubling question: Are the turning points in history the same for women as they are for men? Kelly-Gadol found that well-born women lived in a relatively free environment during the Middle Ages. The courtly love tradition allowed powerful, property-owning women to satisfy their own sexual and emotional needs. With the arrival of the Renaissance, however, the courtly love tradition was defined by powerful male princes who found it desirable for women to be passive and chaste in order to serve the needs of the rising bourgeoisie.

The field of women's history has a history of its own. Beginning with the pioneering work of historians such as Mary Ritter Beard, *Woman as Force in History: A Study in Traditions and Realities* (Collier Books, 1946), scholars first engaged in what Gerda Lerner has called "compensatory history"—compensating for past omissions by researching and writing about the "great women" of history. In a second phase, women's history moved to "contributory history." Looking past the great women, historians took all the traditional categories of standard male history and found women who filled them—women who spent their lives as intellectuals, soldiers, politicians, and scientists. The current phase of women's history parallels more general trends in social history, concentrating on the ordinary people who lived during historical epochs. In this more mature phase, the emphasis is on women's culture—how women saw the world from within their own systems and ways of doing things. If Beard was doing compensatory history, Kelly-Gadol might be said to have been engaging in contributory history. The women she wrote about led lives similar to those of men in their class during the Middle Ages, but Kelly-Gadol contends that they had a different experience during the Renaissance—a contraction of their sphere of influence and a loss of freedom in the expression of their sexual and emotional needs. For the first time, a sexual double standard appeared—men could engage in extramarital liaisons, whereas, women must remain chaste.

One caution to keep in mind is that people are not aware of the times in which they live in terms of the historical periods that scholars later use for identification. People of the past, like people today, are more concerned with their personal lives and fortunes than with historical trends. Periodization, or marking of turning points in the past, can be useful. It can help us identify broad trends and forks in the road as we explore the past. What women's history has taught us, however, is that looking at the experiences of men may or may not tell us what the experiences of women were like during the same time periods.

Mary Beard's book and the field of women's history that it inspired made possible the work of later scholars such as Joan Kelly-Gadol. Beard had challenged traditional notions about the role of women in history; Kelly-Gadol challenged history itself. Margaret L. King's study, from which the first selection is taken, confronts Kelly-Gadol's question directly and explores it in the light of all we now know about the richly diverse lives of women who lived during the Renaissance.

Once we begin to consider the experiences of women in history as separate from those of men, we meet a new set of challenges. Women are not a universal category and their experiences throughout history are as varied as their race, social class, ethnicity, religion, sexual orientation, and a host of other categories make them. In recent years historians have begun to consider the ways in which women's historical experience is more or less the same (with regard to childbirth, access or lack of access to birth control, and female sexuality, for example) and the ways in which one woman's experience differs radically from another's (because of racial, class, or a host of other differences).

The periodization question remains a fascinating one. Following Kelly-Gadol, other scholars began to look at other historical periods, using women's experiences as a starting point. In *Becoming Visible* (from which Kelly-Gadol's selection was excerpted) William Monter asks: Was There a Reformation for Women? For a fuller explanation of the differences among compensatory, contributory, and other approaches, see Gerda Lerner's essay "Placing Women in History" in *Major Problems in Women's History*, 2nd ed., edited by Mary Beth Norton and Ruth Alexander (D.C. Heath, 1996). This collection also contains Gisela Bock's "Challenging Dichotomies in Women's History" and "Afro-American Women in History" by Evelyn Brooks Higginbotham, which questions the concept of a universal womanhood by exploring the varying experiences of African American women.

For a Marxist analysis of women in history, see Juliet Mitchell's "Four Structures in a Complex Unity" in *Woman's Estate* (Pantheon Books, 1971). Mitchell argues that production, reproduction, sexuality, and the socialization of children must all be transformed together if the liberation of women is to be achieved; otherwise, progress in one area can be offset by reinforcement in another. This issue compares the lives of high-born women before and after the Renaissance. From an economic perspective, of course, the lives of wealthy women and wealthy men are radically different from the lives of poor women and poor men. What this issue highlights is the assumption that within a social class the experience of men is normative—that is, it represents the experience of both sexes. As we understand more about the potential differences in women's and men's historical experiences—even within the same social class—we must always remember to ask ourselves: Which woman are we talking about when we make historical generalizations?

YES 

Margaret L. King

Virgo et Virago: Women and High Culture

Women of Might, Power, and Influence

On the stake that supported the burning corpse of the peasant Joan of Arc, who had donned armor and rallied a king, a placard bore the names that the people of the Renaissance gave to the women they hated: heretic, liar, sorceress. The mystery of that hatred has preoccupied the many tellers of the tale of the life of this patron saint of France. Their answers cannot be recounted here, but without simplifying too much they can be summed up in this way: she was hated because she did what men did, and triumphantly. The men who planted stakes over the face of Europe would not tolerate such a transgression of the order they imagined to be natural. In the age of emblems, Joan of Arc is an emblem of the Renaissance women who attempted to partake in the civilization of the Renaissance: not as bearers of children or worshippers of God, but as forgers of its cultural forms. These women did not share her fate, but a few of them understood it.

Foremost among these women, in the records that that age has left us, are those who had no choice about the role they played. Like Joan, they bore arms, or wielded powers still more formidable. They were the queens and female rulers who ruled as the surrogates of their absent husbands, dead fathers, and immature sons. Extraordinary in their personal strengths and achievements, they have left no residue: their capital passed through the male line of descent and not to female heirs—at least not in the centuries of which we speak. But as women who held command, even if briefly and without issue, they deserve our attention.

In Italy later in the same century that Joan illumined with her strength, Caterina Sforza posed a more traditional but still boldly independent figure. The illegitimate granddaughter of Francesco Sforza, who was in turn the illegitimate usurper of the dynasty of the Visconti in Milan, Caterina was propelled into the political maelstrom of quattro-cento Italy by her marriage to Girolamo Riario, nephew of Pope Sixtus IV. After her husband's assassination in 1488, she fiercely defended her family's interests and the cities of Imola and Forli. Greatly outnumbered by her besiegers, she defended Forli against the enemy who held her six children hostage. Twelve years later, she again commanded the defense of those same walls, was defeated, possibly raped, and was brought captive to Rome by Cesare Borgia.

While Sforza, like Joan of Arc, assumed a military role, she secured no power; few women, even of the most exalted noble and royal families, ever did. Two major exceptions were the Italian-born Catherine de'Medici, who as the widow of France's King Henri II was the regent for his successors, François II and Charles IX, and Elizabeth, daughter of the Tudor king of England. Both molded a Renaissance identity for a female sovereign that expressed the ambiguity of their roles. The former adopted for herself the emblem of Artemisia (the type of armed-and-chaste maiden to be considered at greater length below), who was known for her dutiful remembrance of her predeceased husband, Mausolus. Wielding this device, Catherine de'Medici could both act assertively and demonstrate piety to the male rulers between whom she transmitted power. The more independent and bolder Elizabeth was a master builder of her public image and presented herself to her subjects in a variety of feminine identities: Astraea, Deborah, Diana. At the same time, to win support in moments of crisis for the unprecedented phenomenon of a female monarch, she projected androgynous images of her role (man-woman, queen-king, mother-son), and haughtily referred to herself as "prince," with the body of a woman and heart of a king. She defied the identification of her sex with instability and incompetence. In 1601, the elderly Elizabeth asked Parliament in her Golden Speech: "Shall I ascribe anything to myself and my sexly weakness? I were not worthy to live then"; "my sex," she said a few weeks before her death, "cannot diminish my prestige." Had she married, she might have borne an heir. But had she married, she would have fallen under the influence of a male consort. Instead, a complete dyad in herself, she took no husband and declared herself married to England. Her heroic virginity, more in the pattern of the great saints than of a modern woman, set her apart from the other women of her realm who continued to marry and dwell within the family. Her sexual nature was exceptional, just as her kingly authority was anomalous. In and of herself, she insisted on her right to rule, and was the only woman to hold sovereign power during the Renaissance.

Much of the culture of the late sixteenth-century Tudor court revolved around this manlike virgin whose name still identifies it: Elizabethan. Subtly, the poets, playwrights, and scholars of the age commented on the prodigy among them. Foremost among these commentators was William Shakespeare; in the androgynous heroines of his comedies can be found versions of the monarch, sharp-witted and exalted beyond nature. These female characters, played by boys dressed as women who often dressed as boys to create beings of thoroughly confused sexuality, charmed and entranced like the queen herself. The Shakespearean genius also understood how deeply the phenomenon of a queen-king violated the natural order. In the seemingly lighthearted "Midsummer Night's Dream" he spoke about the abnormality of a political order ruled by a woman when the Amazon Hippolyta was wedded at the last to the lawful male wielder of power. Like Joan of Arc, Elizabeth was perceived (and perceived herself) as an Amazon, and deep in the consciousness of the age she dominated was the discomfiture caused by an armed maiden, a rational female, an emotional force unlimited by natural order.

The phenomenon of enthroned women like Catherine and Elizabeth provoked controversy about the legitimacy of female rule. No one was more outspoken than the Presbyterian John Knox, who charged in his *First Blast of the Trumpet Against the Monstrous Regiment of Women* of 1558 that "it is more than a monster in nature that a woman shall reign and have empire above man." "To promote a woman to bear rule, above any realm, nation, or city, is repugnant to nature, contumely to God, . . . and, finally, it is the subversion of good order, of all equity and justice." When a woman rules, the blind lead the sighted, the sick the robust, "the foolish, mad and frenetic" the discreet and sober. "For their sight in civil regiment is but blindness, their counsel foolishment, and judgment frenzy." Woman's attempt to rule is an act of treason: "For that woman reigneth above man, she hath obteined it by treason and conspiracy committed against God. . . . [Men] must study to repress her inordinate pride and tyranny to the uttermost of their power." God could occasionally choose a woman to rule, John Aylmer wrote a year later, refuting Knox; but most women were "fond, folish, wanton flibbergibbes, tatlers, triflers, wavering witles, without counsell, feable, careless, rashe proude," and so on.

Most defenders of female rule in the sixteenth century could not transcend the problem of gender. While Knox was driven to fury by the accession of Mary Tudor to power, the behavior of her successor Elizabeth the Great enraged the French Catholic political theorist Jean Bodin. In the sixth book of his *Six Books of the Republic*, Bodin explored thoroughly the emotional dimension of female rule. A woman's sexual nature would surely, he claimed, interfere with her effectiveness as ruler. As Giovanni Correr, the Venetian ambassador to France, said of another Queen Mary, the unfortunate monarch of Scotland, "to govern states is not the business of women." Other Venetian ambassadors to the court of Elizabeth's successors were more impressed: that queen by her exceptional wisdom and skill had "advanced the female condition itself," and "overcome the distinction of sexes." Male observers thus viewed the sex of the female monarch as an impediment to rule or considered it obliterated, overlooking it altogether, as though the woman was no woman. Spenser simply made his monarch an exception to the otherwise universal rule of female subordination: "vertuous women" know, he wrote, that they are born "to base humilitie," unless God intervenes to raise them "to lawful soveraintie" (*Faerie Queene* 5.5.25).

Although this problem was agonizing for the few women who ruled, there were only a handful who had to face it: it was rare for a woman to inherit power as did these English queens. It required, in fact, the timely death of all power-eligible males. Most women in the ruling classes did not rule, but only shared some of the prerogatives of sovereignty. In the vibrant artistic and intellectual climate of the Renaissance, particularly in Italy, this meant that they exercised the power of patronage. Women who did not rule or direct with their armies the forces of destruction could wield their authority and wealth to shape thought and culture.

Wherever courts existed as centers of wealth, artistic activity, and discourse, opportunities abounded for intelligent women to perform in the role of patroness of the arts and culture. In France, Anne of Brittany, Queen of Charles VIII, commissioned the translation of Boccaccio's *Concerning Famous Women (De claris mulieribus)*, and filled her court with educated women and discussions of platonic love. The same king's sister-in-law Louise of Savoy tutored the future king François I and his sister, Marguerite, according to the principles of Italian humanism. The latter—Marguerite d'Angoulê me, later of Navarre—was the director of cultural matters at her brother's royal court and the protector of a circle of learned men. Influenced by the evangelism of Lefèvre d'Etaples and Guillaume Budé, guided in matters of spirit by the bishop Guillaume Briçonnet, she was at the center of currents of protoreform. An original thinker herself, her collection of stories, the *Heptaméron*, raised questions about the troubled roles of women in a man's world. From this court circle of active patronesses and educators there derived other women of some power and influence: among them the Calvinist Jeanne d'Albret, Marguerite's daughter and the mother of the future king Henry IV, a valiant fighter for her family and religion; and Renée, the heir of Louis XII who was bypassed in favor of her male cousin François I and made wife instead to the Duke of Ferrara, who chose as a companion for her own daughter the adolescent Italian humanist Olimpia Morata.

In Spain the formidable Isabella guided religious reform and intellectual life, while in England, her learned daughter Catherine of Aragon, King Henry VIII's first queen, was surrounded by the leading humanists of the era. It was for her that Erasmus wrote his *Institution of Christian Matrimony (Christiani matrimonii institutio)* and Juan Luis Vives his *Instruction of a Christian Woman (Institutio foeminae christianae)* and other works. She sought

Vives as a tutor for her own daughter, the future queen Mary Tudor. A generation earlier, the proto-figure of the royal patroness and learned woman in England was Margaret Beaufort, Countess of Richmond, already noted as the mother of that country's first Tudor monarch. At the courts of Edward IV and Richard III, she had surrounded herself with minstrels and learned men, supported the art of printing (then in its early stages), endowed professorships of divinity at Oxford and Cambridge (where she founded two colleges), supervised the education of her son and grandchildren, and herself translated from the Latin the devotional *The Mirror of Gold of the Sinful Soul.*

In Italy, where courts and cities and talented men clustered, opportunities abounded for the cultivated woman to help shape the culture of the Renaissance. Notable among such patronesses was Isabella d'Este, daughter of the rulers of Ferrara, sister of Beatrice, who was to play a similar but paler role in Milan, and of Alfonso, Ferrante, Ippolito, and Sigismondo, whom she was to rival in fame. Trained by Battista Guarini, the pedagogue son of the great humanist Guarino Veronese, she had mastered Greek and Latin, the signs of serious scholarship, alongside such skills as lute-playing, dance, and witty conversation. Married to the ruler of Mantua, she presided at that court over festivities and performances, artists, musicians and scholars, libraries filled with elegant volumes; she lived surrounded everywhere by statues, ornate boxes, clocks, marbles, lutes, dishes, gowns, playing cards decorated with paintings, jewels, and gold. Ariosto, Bernardo da Bibbiena, and Gian Giorgio Trissino were among those she favored. She studied maps and astrology and had frequent chats with the ducal librarian, Pellegrino Prisciano. Her *Studiolo* and *Grotta*, brilliantly ornamented rooms in the ducal palace, were her glorious monuments. For these and other projects, she designed the allegorical schemes, consulting with her humanist advisers. Ruling briefly when her husband was taken captive during the wars that shook Italy after the invasion of the forces of France, Spain, and Empire, she was repaid with anger for her bold assumption of authority. Her great capacity was left to express itself in patronage.

Also dislodged from the limited tenure of sovereignty was the wealthy Venetian noblewoman Caterina Cornaro. Born to an ancient Venetian noble family with interests in the eastern Mediterranean—her own mother was from a Greek royal family—Cornaro was married in 1472, at age eighteen, to the King of Cyprus, James II. Her city was concerned with her royal marriage from the start: the island of Cyprus was strategically important, and the Serenissima was jealous of its citizens' involvement in consequential foreign affairs. Venetian concern was justified, for Cornaro became queen of Cyprus a year later, after her husband's sudden death, and held unstable sway, racked by conspiracies, for sixteen years. When Cornaro was tempted by a marriage into the Neapolitan royal house, Venice exerted its authority mightily to force her to abdicate the Cypriot throne. A Neapolitan connection would have meant the alienation of Cyprus from Venetian control. The legate dispatched to the island and charged to persuade her to step down was none other than her brother. He came with offers of an annual salary of 8,000 ducats and a small fiefdom on the Venetian terra firma: she would win fame for herself, he promised, and be known forever as Queen of Cyprus, if she donated her husband's island to her *patria.* Thus compensated by fame and wealth, Cornaro left her rich island kingdom for the miniature one at Asolo. In that court she reigned as queen over a coterie of *letterati*: not the least of them Pietro Bembo, who memorialized the activities over which Cornaro presided in the Arcadian dialogue *Gli Asolani.* Published in 1505 by Aldo Manuzio in Venice, ten years after the conversations that sparked Bembo's imagination had taken place, it circulated in twenty-two editions, Italian as well as Spanish and French. Perhaps more significantly, it influenced the even more famous and complex dialogue of Baldassare Castiglione, commemorating a court presided over by another patroness of letters.

Cornaro's court as described by Bembo prefigures the one in Urbino which Castiglione described. There two women—the Duchess, Elisabetta Gonzaga, and her companion, Emilia Pia—guided and inspired the discussions of proper behavior for both sexes that made up the age's principal handbook of aristocratic values, circulated in some hundred editions and translated into all the major vernaculars: *The Book of the Courtier (Il libro del cortigiano).* For both sexes, that behavior is sharply defined by the phenomenon of the court: men were not to be too boisterous; women were to be occasions of beauty and delight. No court "however great, can have adornment or splendor or gaiety in it without ladies"; in the same way, no courtier can "be graceful or pleasing or brave, or do any gallant deed of chivalry, unless he is moved by the society and by the love and charm of ladies." "Who learns to dance gracefully for any reason except to please women? Who devotes himself to the sweetness of music for any other reason? Who attempts to compose verses . . . unless to express sentiments inspired by women?"

The virtues that women had to possess to inspire these male achievements were manifold. The courtly lady shares some virtues possessed also by the gentleman—she should be well born, naturally graceful, well mannered, clever, prudent, and capable—but also others which are distinctively hers. If married, she should be a good manager of her husband's "property and house and children," and possess "all qualities that are requisite in a good mother." Beauty is a necessity for her, though not for her male counterpart: "for truly that woman lacks much who lacks beauty." Above all, she must be charming: "she will be able to entertain graciously every kind of man with agreeable and comely conversation suited to the time and place and to the station of the person with whom she speaks, joining to serene and modest manners, and to that comeliness that ought to inform all her actions, a quick vivacity of spirit whereby she will show herself a stranger to all boorishness; but with such a kind manner as to cause her to be thought no less chaste, prudent, and gentle than she is agreeable, witty, and discreet." The qualities the court lady possesses are distinct from those of the courtier she is set to amuse: "above all . . . in her ways, manners, words, gestures, and bearing, a woman ought to be very unlike a man; for just as he must show a certain solid and sturdy manliness, so it is seemly for a woman to have a soft and delicate tenderness, with an air of womanly sweetness in her every movement, which, in her going and staying, and in whatever she says, shall always make her appear the woman without any resemblance to a man." Unlike the queen who bears the power and the glory of the males who otherwise occupy her throne, according to Giuliano de' Medici, Castiglione's spokesman by no means hostile to the female sex, the aristocratic lady must be taught to be something other than a man. The same was true of her humbler counterpart in the bourgeois or artisan classes. . . .

A final question remains—the one implied in the title of a work aiming to describe "Women of the Renaissance." Was there a Renaissance for women? Joan Kelly wrote boldly in 1977 that there was not: "at least, not during the Renaissance." At the time, her insight was powerful. For she was the first historian to point unremittingly to the dismal realities of women's lives in the Renaissance centuries. Within the family, they were subject to fathers and husbands and their surrogates in modes that did not relent before the end of Renaissance centuries. They bore special burdens of economic hardship, which limited their dowries and determined their destinies if they were of the elite, or which condemned them (much as it condemned their brothers) to lives of servitude if they were not. Within the church, they were powerless as well. In Roman Catholic countries, those women who chose or were consigned to the religious life were increasingly enclosed, scrutinized, and constrained. In Protestant countries, they were denied the option of convent or anchorage and placed under the spiritual supervision of the same men who decided their social destiny. In both settings, they could seize, at their peril, the option of nonconformity: they could be heretics, prophets, sectaries, or witches. In the world of learning, women remained suspect throughout the period. They snatched an education, in a few cases, from affectionate fathers, brothers, uncles, and grandfathers. But if they wrote, they were declared to be unwomanly; and if they wrote very well, they were labeled Amazons, fearsome and unnatural beings. This does not look like a Renaissance, a rebirth into a new life, but a continuation and in some ways an intensification of the disabilities and prejudices inherited from the Middle Ages and from antiquity.

Yet an argument can be made to the contrary, and has been, for instance, by the splendid historian of Italian society, David Herlihy. Woman's charismatic role, her astonishing success as intermediary with the divine, rooted in her female role as mother projected on a cosmic scale, gave her special prominence precisely in the Renaissance centuries. As it did, in the case of a few exceptional women. One might wonder if the far greater numbers of those who burned and suffered the torments of the torture chamber might overshadow the figures of spiritual prominence; or if the ordinary suffering of the great mass of women overshadows them, for though these women were subject to the same harsh austerities as men of the age, they were deprived, unlike men, of all autonomy. Nevertheless, Herlihy's suggestion is persuasive. Something changed during the Renaissance in women's sense of themselves, even if very little changed or changed for the better in their social condition. That change did have its roots in the spiritual experience of women, and it culminates in the consciousness put into words by the first feminists of the Renaissance. Not monsters, not defects in nature, but the intelligent seekers of a new way, these women wielded the picks of their understanding to build a better city for ladies.

Margaret L. King is a history professor at the Graduate Center of the City University of New York. She has written extensively on the subjects of women, humanism and the Renaissance.

Joan Kelly-Gadol

Did Women Have a Renaissance?

One of the tasks of women's history is to call into question accepted schemes of periodization. To take the emancipation of women as a vantage point is to discover that events that further the historical development of men, liberating them from natural, social, or ideological constraints, have quite different, even opposite, effects upon women. The Renaissance is a good case in point. Italy was well in advance of the rest of Europe from roughly 1350 to 1530 because of its early consolidation of genuine states, the mercantile and manufacturing economy that supported them, and its working out of postfeudal and even postguild social relations. These developments reorganized Italian society along modern lines and opened the possibilities for the social and cultural expression for which the age is known. Yet precisely these developments affected women adversely, so much so that there was no renaissance for women—at least, not during the Renaissance. The state, early capitalism, and the social relations formed by them impinged on the lives of Renaissance women in different ways according to their different positions in society. But the startling fact is that women as a group, especially among the classes that dominated Italian urban life, experienced a contradiction of social and personal options that men of their classes either did not, as was the case with the bourgeoisie, or did not experience as markedly, as was the case with the nobility.

Before demonstrating this point, which contradicts the widely held notion of the equality of Renaissance women with men, we need to consider how to establish, let alone measure, loss or gain with respect to the liberty of women. I found the following criteria most useful for gauging the relative contraction (or expansion) of the powers of Renaissance women and for determining the quality of their historical experience: 1) the regulation of *female sexuality* as compared with male sexuality; 2) women's *economic* and *political roles*, that is, the kind of work they performed as compared with men, and their access to property, political power, and the education or training necessary for work, property, and power; 3) the *cultural roles* of women in shaping the outlook of their society, and access to the education and/or institutions necessary for this; 4) *ideology* about women, in particular the sex-role system displayed or advocated in the symbolic products of the society, its art, literature, and philosophy. Two points should be made about this ideological index. One is its rich inferential value. The literature, art, and philosophy of a society, which give us direct knowledge of the attitudes of the dominant sector of that society toward women, also yield indirect knowledge about our other criteria: namely, the sexual, economic, political, and cultural activities of women. Insofar as images of women relate to what really goes on, we can infer from them something about that social reality. But, second, the relations between the ideology of sex roles and the reality we want to get at are complex and difficult to establish. Such views may be prescriptive rather than descriptive; they may describe a situation that no longer prevails; or they may use the relation of the sexes symbolically and not refer primarily to women and sex roles at all. Hence, to assess the historical significance of changes in sex-role conception, we must bring such changes into connection with all we know about general developments in the society at large.

This essay examines changes in sex-role conception, particularly with respect to sexuality, for what they tell us about Renaissance society and women's place in it. At first glance, Renaissance thought presents a problem in this regard because it cannot be simply categorized. Ideas about the relation of the sexes range from a relatively complementary sense of sex roles in literature dealing with courtly manners, love, and education, to patriarchal conceptions in writings on marriage and the family, to a fairly equal presentation of sex roles in early Utopian social theory. Such diversity need not baffle the attempt to reconstruct a history of sex-role conceptions, however, and to relate its course to the actual situation of women. Toward this end, one needs to sort out this material in terms of the social groups to which it responds: to courtly society in the first case, the nobility of the petty despotic states of Italy; to the patrician bourgeoisie in the second, particularly of republics such as Florence. In the third case, the relatively equal position accorded women in Utopian thought (and in those lower-class movements of the radical Reformation analogous to it) results from a larger critique of early modern society and all the relations of domination that flow from private ownership and control of property. Once distinguished, each of these groups of sources tells the same story. Each discloses in its own way certain new constraints suffered by Renaissance women as the family and political life were restructured in the great transition from medieval feudal society to the early modern state. The sources that represent the interests of the nobility and the bourgeoisie point to this fact by a telling, double index. Almost all such works—with certain notable exceptions, such as Boccaccio and Ariosto—establish chastity as the female norm and restructure the relation of the sexes to one of female dependency and male domination.

The bourgeois writings on education, domestic life, and society constitute the extreme in this denial of women's independence. Suffice it to say that they sharply distinguish an inferior domestic realm of women from the superior public realm of men, achieving a veritable "renaissance" of the outlook and practices of classical Athens, with its domestic imprisonment of citizen wives. The courtly Renaissance literature we will consider was more gracious. But even here, by analyzing a few of the representative works of this genre, we find a new repression of the noblewoman's affective experience, in contrast to the latitude afforded her by medieval literature, and some of the social and cultural reasons for it. Dante and Castiglione, who continued a literary tradition that began with the courtly love literature of eleventh- and twelfth-century Provence, transformed medieval conceptions of love and nobility. In the love ideal they formed, we can discern the inferior position the Renaissance noblewoman held in the relation of the sexes by comparison with her male counterpart and with her medieval predecessor as well.

Love and the Medieval Lady

Medieval courtly love, closely bound to the dominant values of feudalism and the Church, allowed in a special way for the expression of sexual love by women. Of course, only aristocratic women gained their sexual and affective rights thereby. If a knight wanted a peasant girl, the twelfth-century theorist of *The Art of Courtly Love,* Andreas Capellanus, encouraged him "not [to] hesitate to take what you seek and to embrace her by force." Toward the lady, however, "a true lover considers nothing good except what he thinks will please his beloved"; for if courtly love were to define itself as a noble phenomenon, it had to attribute an essential freedom to the relation between lovers. Hence, it metaphorically extended the social relation of vassalage to the love relationship, a "conceit" that Maurice Valency rightly called "the shaping principle of the whole design" of courtly love.

Of the two dominant sets of dependent social relations formed by feudalism—*les liens de d´ependence,* as Marc Bloch called them—vassalage, the military relation of knight to lord, distinguished itself (in its early days) by being freely entered into. At a time when everyone was somebody's "man," the right to freely enter a relation of service characterized aristocratic bonds, whereas hereditability marked the servile work relation of serf to lord. Thus, in medieval romances, a parley typically followed a declaration of love until love freely proffered was freely returned. A kiss (like the kiss of homage) sealed the pledge, rings were exchanged, and the knight entered the love service of his lady. Representing love along the lines of vassalage had several liberating implications for aristocratic women. Most fundamental, ideas of homage and mutuality entered the notion of heterosexual relations along with the idea of freedom. As symbolized on shields and other illustrations that place the knight in the ritual attitude of commendation, kneeling before his lady with his hands folded between hers, homage signified male service, not domination or subordination of the lady, and it signified fidelity, constancy in that service. "A lady must honor her lover as a friend, not as a master," wrote Marie de Ventadour, a female troubadour or *trobairitz.* At the same time, homage entailed a reciprocity of rights and obligations, a service on the lady's part as well. In one of Marie de France's romances, a knight is about to be judged by the barons of King Arthur's court when his lady rides to the castle to give him "succor" and pleads successfully for him, as any overlord might. Mutuality, or complementarity, marks the relation the lady entered into with her *ami* (the favored name for "lover" and, significantly, a synonym for "vassal").

This relation between knight and lady was very much at variance with the patriarchal family relations obtaining in that same level of society. Aware of its incompatibility with prevailing family and marital relations, the celebrants of courtly love kept love detached from marriage. "We dare not oppose the opinion of the Countess of Champagne who rules that love can exert no power between husband and wife," Andreas Capellanus wrote (p. 175). But in opting for a free and reciprocal heterosexual relation outside marriage, the poets and theorists of courtly love ignored the almost universal demand of patriarchal society for female chastity, in the sense of the woman's strict bondage to the marital bed. The reasons why they did so, and even the fact that they did so, have long been disputed, but the ideas and values that justify this kind of adulterous love are plain. Marriage, as a relation arranged by others, carried the taint of social necessity for the aristocracy. And if the feudality denigrated marriage by disdaining obligatory service, the Church did so by regarding it not as a "religious" state, but an inferior one that responded to natural necessity. Moreover, Christianity positively fostered the ideal of courtly love at a deep level of feeling. The courtly relation between lovers took vassalage as its structural model, but its passion was nourished by Christianity's exaltation of love.

Christianity had accomplished its elevation of love by purging it of sexuality, and in this respect, by recombining the two, courtly love clearly departed from Christian teaching. The toleration of adultery it fostered thereby was in itself not so grievous. The feudality disregarded any number of church rulings that affected their interests, such as prohibitions of tournaments and repudiation of spouses (divorce) and remarriage. Moreover, adultery hardly needed the sanction of courtly love, which, if anything, acted rather as a restraining force by binding sexuality (except in marriage) to love. Lancelot, in Chrétien de Troyes's twelfth-century romance, lies in bed with a lovely woman because of a promise he has made, but "not once does he look at her, nor show her any courtesy. Why not? Because his heart does not go out to her. . . . The knight has only one heart, and this one is no longer really his, but has been entrusted to someone else, so that he cannot bestow it elsewhere." Actually, Lancelot's chastity represented more of a threat to Christian doctrine than the fact that his passion (for Guinevere) was adulterous, because his attitudes justified sexual love. Sexuality could only be "mere sexuality" for the medieval Church, to be consecrated and directed toward procreation by Christian marriage. Love, on the other hand, defined as passion for the good, perfects the individual; hence love, according to Thomas Aquinas, properly directs itself toward God. Like the churchman, Lancelot spurned mere sexuality—but for the sake of sexual love. He defied Christian *teaching* by reattaching love to sex; and experiencing his love as a devout vocation, as a passion, he found himself in utter accord with Christian *feeling*. . . .

The Renaissance Lady: Politics and Culture

In his handbook for the nobility, Baldassare Castiglione's description of the lady of the court makes [the] difference in sex roles quite clear. On the one hand, the Renaissance lady appears as the equivalent of the courtier. She has the same virtues of mind as he, and her education is symmetrical with his. She learns everything—well, almost everything—he does: "knowledge of letters, of music, of painting, and . . . how to dance and how to be festive." Culture is an accomplishment for noblewoman and man alike, used to charm others as much as to develop the self. But for the woman, charm had become the primary occupation and aim. Whereas the courtier's chief task is defined as the profession of arms, "in a Lady who lives at court a certain pleasing affability is becoming above all else, whereby she will be able to entertain graciously every kind of man" (p. 207).

. . . The Renaissance lady is not desired, not loved for herself. Rendered passive and chaste, she merely mediates the courtier's safe transcendence of an otherwise demeaning necessity. On the plane of symbolism, Castiglione thus had the courtier dominate both her and the prince; and on the plane of reality, he indirectly acknowledged the courtier's actual domination of the lady by having him adopt "woman's ways" in his relations to the prince. Castiglione had to defend against effeminacy in the courtier, both the charge of it (p. 92) and the actuality of faces "soft and feminine as many attempt to have who not only curl their hair and pluck their eyebrows, but preen themselves . . . and appear so tender and languid . . . and utter their words so limply" (p. 36). Yet the close-fitting costume of the Renaissance nobleman displayed the courtier exactly as Castiglione would have him, "well built and shapely of limb" (p. 36). His clothes set off his grace, as did his nonchalant ease, the new manner of those "who seem in words, laughter, in posture not to care" (p. 44). To be attractive, accomplished, and seem not to care; to charm and do so coolly—how concerned with impression, how masked the true self. And how manipulative: petitioning his lord, the courtier knows to be "discreet in choosing the occasion, and will ask things that are proper and reasonable; and he will so frame his request, omitting those parts that he knows can cause displeasure, and will skillfully make easy the difficult points so that his lord will always grant it" (p. 111). In short, how like a woman—or a dependent, for that is the root of the simile.

The accommodation of the sixteenth- and seventeenth-century courtier to the ways and dress of women in no way bespeaks a greater parity between them. It reflects, rather, that general restructuring of social relations that entailed for the Renaissance noblewoman a greater dependency upon men as feudal independence and reciprocity yielded to the state. In this new situation, the entire nobility suffered a loss. Hence, the courtier's posture of dependency, his concern with the pleasing impression, his resolve "to perceive what his prince likes, and . . . to bend himself to this" (pp. 110–111). But as the state overrode aristocratic power, the lady suffered a double loss. Deprived of the possibility of independent power that the combined interests of kinship and feudalism guaranteed some women in the Middle Ages, and that the states of early modern Europe would preserve in part, the Italian noblewoman in particular entered a relation of almost universal dependence upon her family and her husband. And she experienced this dependency at the same time as she lost her commanding position with respect to the secular culture of her society.

Hence, the love theory of the Italian courts developed in ways as indifferent to the interests of women as the courtier, in his self-sufficiency, was indifferent as a lover. It accepted, as medieval courtly love did not, the double standard. It bound the lady to chastity, to the merely procreative sex of political marriage, just as her weighty and costly costume came to conceal and constrain her body while it displayed her husband's noble rank. Indeed, the person of the woman became so inconsequential to this love relation that one doubted whether she could love at all. The question that emerges at the end of *The Courtier* as to "whether or not women are as capable of divine love as men" (p. 350) belongs to a love theory structured by mediation rather than mutuality. Woman's beauty inspired love but the lover, the agent, was man. And the question stands unresolved at the end of *The Courtier*—because at heart the spokesmen for Renaissance love were not really concerned about women or love at all.

Where courtly love had used the social relation of vassalage to work out a genuine concern with sexual love, Castiglione's thought moved in exactly the opposite direction. He allegorized love as fully as Dante did, using the relation of the sexes to symbolize the new political order. In this, his love theory reflects the social realities of the Renaissance. The denial of the right and power of women to love, the transformation of women into passive "others" who serve, fits the self-image of the courtier, the one Castiglione sought to remedy. The symbolic relation of the sexes thus mirrors the new social relations of the state, much as courtly love displayed the feudal relations of reciprocal personal dependence. But Renaissance love reflects, as well, the actual condition of dependency suffered by noblewomen as the state arose. If the courtier who charms the prince bears the same relation to him as the lady bears to the courtier, it is because Castiglione understood the relation of the sexes in the same terms that he used to describe the political relation: that is, as a relation between servant and lord. The nobleman suffered this relation in the public domain only. The lady, denied access to a freely chosen, mutually satisfying love relation, suffered it in the personal domain as well. Moreover, Castiglione's theory, unlike the courtly love it superseded, subordinated love itself to the public concerns of the Renaissance nobleman. He set forth the relation of the sexes as one of dependency and domination, but he did so in order to express and deal with the political relation and its problems. The personal values of love, which the entire feudality once prized, were henceforth increasingly left to the lady. The courtier formed his primary bond with the modern prince.

In sum, a new division between personal and public life made itself felt as the state came to organize Renaissance society, and with that division the modern relation of the sexes made its appearance, even among the Renaissance nobility. Noblewomen, too, were increasingly removed from public concerns—economic, political, and cultural—and although they did not disappear into a private realm of family and domestic concerns as fully as their sisters in the patrician bourgeoisie, their loss of public power made itself felt in new constraints placed upon their personal as well as their social lives. Renaissance ideas on love and manners, more classical than medieval, and almost exclusively a male product, expressed this new subordination of women to the interests of husbands and male-dominated kin groups and served to justify the removal of women from an "unladylike" position of power and erotic independence. All the advances of Renaissance Italy, its protocapitalist economy, its states, and its humanistic culture, worked to mold the noblewoman into an aesthetic object: decorous, chaste, and doubly dependent—on her husband as well as the prince.

Joan Kelly-Gadol (1928–1982) was a Renaissance scholar and theorist in women's history. Her works include *Leon Battista Alberti: Universal Man of the Early Renaissance* (University of Chicago Press, 1969).

EXPLORING THE ISSUE

Did Women and Men Benefit Equally from the Renaissance?

Critical Thinking and Reflection

1. What are the key characteristics your history text assigns to the Renaissance? Do the examples in the text concern men or assume the subjects are men? If the evidence is drawn exclusively from the experiences of one gender, is it historically accurate to generalize from this experience to all people? Critically discuss.
2. On what basis does historian Margaret L. King argue that the women she studied developed a new consciousness of themselves as women and as intelligent seekers of a new way of being in the world? Critically evaluate this evidence.
3. On what basis does historian Joan Kelly-Gadol determine that the women she studied had enjoyed greater advantages during the Middle Ages? Critically evaluate this evidence.
4. Critically examine the evidence about the lives of women provided in these two selections; then construct an argument for continuity (that things remained basically similar) between the Middle Ages and the Renaissance (for these women).
5. Critically examine the evidence about the lives of women provided in these two selections; then construct an argument for discontinuity (that things basically changed) between the Middle Ages and the Renaissance (for these women).
6. Did you find both areas of continuity and areas of discontinuity? What are the challenges for the historian in the light of varying experiences for women and men and uneven experiences even within one gender? Critically discuss.
7. Based on all you now know, give your own answer to this question: Did women and men have different experiences when the Middle Ages gave way to the Renaissance? Critically debate this question.

Is There Common Ground?

Despite the constriction of personal freedom that Kelly-Godol finds, there is a case to be made, as Margaret L. King does, that women had a new personal experience of themselves and their possibilities as human beings. This might form the basis for common ground. Humans are complex creatures who do not lead lives of seamless experience. A person could achieve financial success and experience the breakup of a long-term relationship. Would that person be more happy than unhappy? Perhaps more accurately, we could say that person was happy in one area and unhappy in another.

Another area of potential common ground concerns the economic status of the women studied in this issue. Even as they experienced a contraction of personal freedom, in Kelly-Godol's selection, they remained wealthy, being able to enjoy leisure time and have their material needs and wants satisfied. Further, only leisured women, such as those studied by Margaret L. King, would have had the luxury to contemplate themselves as beings with new possibilities.

Question: Do only the wealthy—what historians sometimes call the "leisured class"—have the time (free from the labor required to survive) to contemplate the emergence of new human possibilities?

Additional Resources

Picturing Women in Renaissance and Baroque Italy, Geraldine A. Johnson and Sara F. Matthews Grieco, eds. (Cambridge University Press, 1997) offers a collection of essays, exploring women as producers, sponsors, and subjects of art—conflicting images of women suggest a lack of fixed gender roles. Catherine King's *Renaissance Women Patrons: Wives and Widows in Italy, c.1300–c.1550* (Manchester University Press, 1998) explores women's artistic patronage during a time when artistic patronage was taken seriously. And, finally, *Birth of the Chess Queen* by Stanford gender scholar Marilyn Yalom (Harper Collins, 2004) contends that the arrival of the queen (to replace a weak vizier who could move only one square diagonally per turn) was linked with the rising status of women in medieval Europe.

Internet References . . .

Biographies of Notable Medieval and Renaissance Women

Contains biographical sketches of many notable women who lived during the Middle Ages and Renaissance periods. Each one provides valuable links to more information one each subject, as well as for the Renaissance in general. Click on "Medieval Women's History."

http://womenshistory.about.com/library/biblio_list_medieval.htm

Selected, Edited, and with Issue Framing Material by:
Helen Buss Mitchell, *Howard Community College*
and
Joseph R. Mitchell, *Howard Community College*

ISSUE

Did China's Worldview Cause the Abrupt End of Its Voyages of Exploration?

YES: Nicholas D. Kristof, from "1492: The Prequel," *The New York Times Magazine* (June 6, 1999)

NO: Bruce Swanson, from *Eighth Voyage of the Dragon: A History of China's Quest for Seapower* (Naval Institute Press, 1982)

Learning Outcomes

After reading this issue you should be able to:

- Define "worldview" and outline key components of China's worldview during this period.
- Understand the life and times of Zheng He, sometimes called "the Chinese Columbus."
- Describe the extent of China's voyages of exploration.

ISSUE SUMMARY

YES: Journalist Nicholas D. Kristof argues that China's worldview, shaped by centuries of philosophical and cultural conditioning, was responsible for its decision to cease its maritime ventures during the Ming dynasty.

NO: Naval historian Bruce Swanson acknowledges that China's worldview played a role in its decision to cease its maritime programs, but argues that there were other more practical considerations that were responsible for that decision.

Few historical figures of the last 500 years can match the name recognition of Christopher Columbus, whose voyages and their results forever altered the course of history. But what about Zheng He? Does his name have the same evocative power as Columbus's? Probably not, and yet in the same century, Zheng He led more and longer naval expeditions, commanded larger ships and more men, and was, within the Asian world, as popular and noteworthy as Columbus. An interesting historical lesson, replete with "what might have been's," can be learned from the life and career of the "Chinese Columbus."

Zheng He's life is in itself an interesting story. Born to Muslim parents living in China, he was a young boy when he was captured by the Chinese army, and eventually castrated, a common practice for prisoners of war at that time. Soon after, he came into the service of a Chinese royal prince Zhu Di, 1 of 26 sons of the Chinese emperor, whom he served with honor and distinction. As a result of an internal power struggle, Prince Zhu Di seized the royal throne from his nephew, and became the Ming dynasty's Emperor Yongle, who would rule China from 1402 to 1424. Zheng He played a significant role in this chain of events, and would soon be rewarded for his meritorious service.

China's new emperor was an ambitious man who set out to establish his legacy as one of China's greatest rulers. As a means to achieve this exalted status, he emphasized the importance of China's need to reestablish its role in the commercial and maritime affairs of Asia. When it was time to select someone to command this project, the new emperor selected Zheng He. For more than two decades, Zheng He ran China's maritime operations for his emperor, and his plan included seven major voyages. In the process, "Admiral Zheng visited 37 countries, traveled around the tip of Africa into the Atlantic Ocean and commanded a single fleet whose numbers surpassed the combined fleets of all of Europe. Between 1405 and 1433, at least 317 ships and 37,000 men were under his command" ("Admiral Zheng's Fleet": www.oceansonline.com/zheng.htm).

China's dominance of Asian waters brought the anticipated fame, wealth, and glory to Emperor Yongle and his eunuch admiral. However, when the former died suddenly in 1424, his successor decided to de-emphasize China's international maritime policies, and ordered plans already underway for Zheng He's seventh voyage to be halted. This proved to be a temporary setback when a new emperor, interested in reviving Yongle's maritime policies, ordered Zheng He's seventh voyage to proceed at once.

It would, however, prove to be China's last government-sponsored maritime venture.

Zheng He died in 1433, and, soon afterward, China began to lose interest in overseas exploration, and eventually scrapped its maritime projects. This would have grave consequences for China, when later in the century, European countries began to send ships into Asian waters. What began as an exploration, eventually turned into domination, conquest, colonization, and imperialism—with dire consequences for China and the rest of Asia. Much of what follows is historical speculation, but one wonders what would have occurred if those first Western explorers who rounded Africa and headed toward Asia ran into a strong maritime force the size of Admiral Zheng's? And, if China had continued to support its maritime ventures after his death, perhaps history would have had to credit one of his successors with the discovery of the "New World."

There are numerous reasons given for China's retreat from maritime excellence. Some state that a Ming court conflict between eunuchs and Confucian scholars, traditional rivals in court politics, occurred, and the latter eventually won by depicting China's maritime expeditions as costly, eunuch-induced extravagances, and not in China's best long range interests. Others stress a series of other factors, including: (1) fear of future Mongol invasions; (2) population shifts away from coastal provinces, (3) a desire to promote internal trade efforts; (4) the high cost of supporting the maritime ventures, including the money spent to prevent piracy and the profits lost to it; and (5) the corruption which emanated from the costly maritime programs.

Zheng He was a eunuch. The role of court eunuchs in Chinese history has been a turbulent one; sometimes they are portrayed as loyal civil servants, other times as despised outcasts. No one however can question their staying power, as during the reign of Pu Yi (1903–1912), who would be China's last emperor, they were still a troublesome court presence. In Bernardo Bertolucci's Academy Award-winning film *The Last Emperor* eunuchs are portrayed as having a corrupting influence on the court and they are eventually banned from the "Forbidden City." Although historically they were far from angelic, they have sometimes been blamed for conditions and events that were not of their making. Shih-Shan Henry Tsai attempts to correct the myths and stereotypes regarding eunuchs in his *The Eunuchs in the Ming Dynasty* (State University of New York Press, 1996), which provides a badly needed fresh look at the eunuchs in the period covered by this issue.

Much of any standard world history textbook in North America will be devoted to Western dominance over the past half millennium. Between 1500 and 2000, the economic, political, and cultural story in your text probably favors the West and highlights its many innovations and accomplishments. It is not accidental that 1500 marks the rough beginning of Europe's Age of Discovery (one of the turning points in the periodization of history—see Introduction). After reading this issue, one is left to wonder whether this Western dominance would have been possible if a strong Chinese naval presence had existed. Perhaps the course of world history would have been altered. No colonialism; no imperialism! Perhaps we would all be speaking Chinese.

In our selections, long-time journalist specializing in Asian affairs Nicholas D. Kristof argues that China gave up on its maritime efforts because they contradicted the worldview that China had cultivated for thousands of years. Naval historian Bruce Swanson states that this was only one of many factors responsible for China's retreat from naval supremacy.

YES

Nicholas D. Kristof

1492: The Prequel

For most of the last several thousand years, it would have seemed far likelier that Chinese or Indians, not Europeans, would dominate the world by the year 2000, and that America and Australia would be settled by Chinese rather than by the inhabitants of a backward island called Britain. The reversal of fortunes of East and West strikes me as the biggest news story of the millennium, and one of its most unexpected as well.

As a resident of Asia for most of the past 13 years, I've been searching for an explanation. It has always seemed to me that the turning point came in the early 1400s, when Admiral Zheng He sailed from China to conquer the world. Zheng He (pronounced jung huh) was an improbable commander of a great Chinese fleet, in that he was a Muslim from a rebel family and had been seized by the Chinese Army when he was still a boy. Like many other prisoners of the time, he was castrated—his sexual organs completely hacked off, a process that killed many of those who suffered it. But he was a brilliant and tenacious boy who grew up to be physically imposing. A natural leader, he had the good fortune to be assigned, as a houseboy, to the household of a great prince, Zhu Di.

In time, the prince and Zheng He grew close, and they conspired to overthrow the prince's nephew, the Emperor of China. With Zheng He as one of the prince's military commanders, the revolt succeeded and the prince became China's Yongle Emperor. One of the emperor's first acts (after torturing to death those who had opposed him) was to reward Zheng He with the command of a great fleet that was to sail off and assert China's pre-eminence in the world.

Between 1405 and 1433, Zheng He led seven major expeditions, commanding the largest armada the world would see for the next five centuries. Not until World War I did the West mount anything comparable. Zheng He's fleet included 28,000 sailors on 300 ships, the longest of which were 400 feet. By comparison, Columbus in 1492 had 90 sailors on three ships, the biggest of which was 85 feet long. Zheng He's ships also had advanced design elements that would not be introduced in Europe for another 350 years, including balanced rudders and watertight bulwark compartments.

The sophistication of Zheng He's fleet underscores just how far ahead of the West the East once was. Indeed, except for the period of the Roman Empire, China had been wealthier, more advanced and more cosmopolitan than any place in Europe for several thousand years. Hangzhou, for example, had a population in excess of a million during the time it was China's capital (in the 12th century), and records suggest that as early as the 7th century, the city of Guangzhou had 200,000 foreign residents: Arabs, Persians, Malays, Indians, Africans and Turks. By contrast, the largest city in Europe in 1400 was probably Paris, with a total population of slightly more than 100,000.

A half-century before Columbus, Zheng He had reached East Africa and learned about Europe from Arab traders. The Chinese could easily have continued around the Cape of Good Hope and established direct trade with Europe. But as they saw it, Europe was a backward region, and China had little interest in the wool, beads and wine Europe had to trade. Africa had what China wanted—ivory, medicines, spices, exotic woods, even specimens of native wildlife.

In Zheng He's time, China and India together accounted for more than half of the world's gross national product, as they have for most of human history. Even as recently as 1820, China accounted for 29 percent of the global economy and India another 16 percent, according to the calculations of Angus Maddison, a leading British economic historian.

Asia's retreat into relative isolation after the expeditions of Zheng He amounted to a catastrophic missed opportunity, one that laid the groundwork for the rise of Europe and, eventually, America. Westerners often attribute their economic advantage today to the intelligence, democratic habits or hard work of their forebears, but a more important reason may well have been the folly of 15th-century Chinese rulers. That is why I came to be fascinated with Zheng He and set out earlier this year to retrace his journeys. I wanted to see what legacy, if any, remained of his achievement, and to figure out why his travels did not remake the world in the way that Columbus's did.

Zheng He lived in Nanjing, the old capital, where I arrived one day in February. Nanjing is a grimy metropolis on the Yangtze River in the heart of China. It has been five centuries since Zheng He's death, and his marks on the city have grown faint. The shipyards that built his fleet are still busy, and the courtyard of what had been his splendid 72-room mansion is now the Zheng He Memorial Park, where children roller-skate and old couples totter around for exercise. But though the park has a small Zheng He museum, it was closed—for renovation, a caretaker told me, though he knew of no plans to reopen it. . . .

The absence of impressive monuments to Zheng He in China today should probably come as no surprise, since his achievement was ultimately renounced. Curiously, it is not in China but in Indonesia where his memory has been most actively kept alive. Zheng He's expeditions led directly to the wave of Chinese immigration to Southeast Asia, and in some countries he is regarded today as a deity. In the Indonesia city of Semarang, for example, there is a large temple honoring Zheng He, located near a cave where he once nursed a sick friend. Indonesians still pray to Zheng He for a cure or good luck.

Not so in his native land. Zheng He was viewed with deep suspicion by China's traditional elite, the Confucian scholars, who made sure to destroy the archives of his journey. Even so, it is possible to learn something about his story from Chinese sources—from imperial archives and even the memoirs of crewmen. The historical record makes clear, for example, that it was not some sudden impulse of extroversion that led to Zheng He's achievement. It grew, rather, out of a long sailing tradition. Chinese accounts suggest that in the fifth century, a Chinese monk sailed to a mysterious "far east country" that sounds very much like Mayan Mexico, and Mayan art at that time suddenly began to include Buddhist symbols. By the 13th century, Chinese ships regularly traveled to India and occasionally to East Africa.

Zheng He's armada was far grander, of course, than anything that came before. His grandest vessels were the "treasure ships," 400 feet long and 160 feet wide, with nine masts raising red silk sails to the wind, as well as multiple decks and luxury cabins with balconies. His armada included supply ships to carry horses, troop transports, warships, patrol boats and as many as 20 tankers to carry fresh water. The full contingent of 28,000 crew members included interpreters for Arabic and other languages, astrologers to forecast the weather, astronomers to study the stars, pharmacologists to collect medicinal plants, ship-repair specialists, doctors and even two protocol officers to help organize official receptions.

In the aftermath of such an incredible undertaking, you somehow expect to find a deeper mark on Chinese history, a greater legacy. But perhaps the faintness of Zheng He's trace in contemporary China is itself a lesson. In the end, an explorer makes history but does not necessarily change it, for his impact depends less on the trail he blazes than on the willingness of others to follow. The daring of a great expedition ultimately is hostage to the national will of those who remain behind. . . .

The disappearance of a great Chinese fleet from a great Indian port symbolized one of history's biggest lost opportunities—Asia's failure to dominate the second half of this millennium. So how did this happen? While Zheng He was crossing the Indian Ocean, the Confucian scholar-officials who dominated the upper echelons of the Chinese Government were at political war with the eunuchs, a group they regarded as corrupt and immoral. The eunuchs' role at court involved looking after the concubines, but they also served as palace administrators, often doling out contracts in exchange for kickbacks. Partly as a result of their legendary greed, they promoted commerce. Unlike the scholars—who owed their position to their mastery of 2,000-year-old texts—the eunuchs, lacking any such roots in a classical past, were sometimes outward-looking and progressive. Indeed, one can argue that it was the virtuous, incorruptible scholars who in the mid-15th century set China on its disastrous course.

After the Yongle Emperor died in 1424, China endured a series of brutal power struggles; a successor emperor died under suspicious circumstances and ultimately the scholars emerged triumphant. They ended the voyages of Zheng He's successors, halted construction of new ships and imposed curbs on private shipping. To prevent any backsliding, they destroyed Zheng He's sailing records and, with the backing of the new emperor, set about dismantling China's navy.

By 1500 the Government had made it a capital offense to build a boat with more than two masts, and in 1525 the Government ordered the destruction of all ocean-going ships. The greatest navy in history, which a century earlier had 3,500 ships (by comparison, the United States Navy today has 324), had been extinguished, and China set a course for itself that would lead to poverty, defeat and decline.

Still, it was not the outcome of a single power struggle in the 1440's that cost China its worldly influence. Historians offer a host of reasons for why Asia eventually lost its way economically and was late to industrialize; two and a half reasons seem most convincing.

The first is that Asia was simply not greedy enough. The dominant social ethos in ancient China was Confucianism and in India it was caste, with the result that the elites in both nations looked down their noses at business. Ancient China cared about many things—prestige, honor, culture, arts, education, ancestors, religion, filial piety—but making money came far down the list. Confucius had specifically declared that it was wrong for a man to make a distant voyage while his parents were alive, and he had condemned profit as the concern of "a little man." As it was, Zheng He's ships were built on such a grand scale and carried such lavish gifts to foreign leaders that the voyages were not the huge money spinners they could have been.

In contrast to Asia, Europe was consumed with greed. Portugal led the age of discovery in the 15th century largely because it wanted spices, a precious commodity; it was the hope of profits that drove its ships steadily farther down the African coast and eventually around the Horn to Asia. The profits of this trade could be vast: Magellan's crew once sold a cargo of 26 tons of cloves for 10,000 times the cost.

A second reason for Asia's economic stagnation is more difficult to articulate but has to do with what might be called a culture of complacency. China and India shared a tendency to look inward, a devotion to past ideals and methods, a respect for authority and a suspicion of new ideas. David S. Landes, a Harvard economist, has written of ancient China's "intellectual xenophobia"; the former Indian Prime Minister Jawaharlal Nehru referred to the "petrification of classes" and the "static nature" of Indian society. These are all different ways of describing the same economic and intellectual complacency.

Chinese elites regarded their country as the "Middle Kingdom" and believed they had nothing to learn from barbarians abroad. India exhibited much of the same self-satisfaction. "Indians didn't go to Portugal not because they couldn't but because they didn't want to," mused M. P. Sridharan, a historian, as we sat talking on the porch of his home in Calicut.

The 15th-century Portuguese were the opposite. Because of its coastline and fishing industry, Portugal always looked to the sea, yet rivalries with Spain and other countries shut it out of the Mediterranean trade. So the only way for Portugal to get at the wealth of the East was by conquering the oceans.

The half reason is simply that China was a single nation while Europe was many. When the Confucian scholars reasserted control in Beijing and banned shipping, their policy mistake condemned all of China. In contrast, European countries committed economic suicide selectively. So when Portugal slipped into a quasi-Chinese mind-set in the 16th century, slaughtering Jews and burning heretics and driving astronomers and scientists abroad, Holland and England were free to take up the slack. . . .

If ancient China had been greedier and more outward-looking, if other traders had followed in Zheng He's wake and then continued on, Asia might well have dominated Africa and even Europe. Chinese might have settled in not only Malaysia and Singapore, but also in East Africa, the Pacific Islands, even in America. Perhaps the Famao [a clan of people who live in Pate, an island off the coast of Africa, and who are rumored to be descendents of Chinese shipwreck survivors from countless generations ago] show us what the mestizos [racially mixed people] of such a world might have looked liked, the children of a hybrid culture that was never born. What I'd glimpsed in Pate was the high-water mark of an Asian push that simply stopped—not for want of ships or know-how, but strictly for want of national will.

All this might seem fanciful, and yet in Zheng He's time the prospect of a New World settled by the Spanish or English would have seemed infinitely more remote than a New World made by the Chinese. How different would history have been had Zheng He continued on to America? The mind rebels; the ramifications are almost too overwhelming to contemplate. So consider just one: this [selection] would have been published in Chinese.

Nicholas D. Kristof is a journalist, specializing in Asian affairs. He is co-author, with his wife Sheryl Wudunn, of *China Wakes* (Vintage Books, 1995).

Bruce Swanson

Continental and Maritime Ideologies in Conflict: The Ming Dynasty

In 1405, China's progressive attitude toward exploitation of the sea culminated in a series of naval expeditions into the South China Sea and the Indian Ocean. The latter expeditions included visits to Ceylon, India, the Persian Gulf, and Africa. These spectacular voyages, in fact, proved that China was the supreme world seapower whose shipbuilding techniques and navigational abilities were unmatched by any other nation.

But China's prominence as the world's greatest naval and maritime power was short-lived. The last of seven expeditions ended in 1433; never again were naval expeditions attempted by emperors. As a result, it is tempting to dismiss these voyages as a temporary aberration of the Chinese emperor who sponsored them. To do so, however, would be to ignore the ineluctable influence of the maritime spirit on China, particularly the growing awareness of the potential of seapower to expand and control the tribute system. At the same time, the subsequent cessation of the voyages clearly highlights the equally strong force of continentalism among members of the imperial court as they attempted to steer China away from maritime pursuits.

Early Ming Strategic Considerations

Before discussing the voyages and their itineraries, it is important to examine certain factors that reflected China's continuing struggle between supporters of continentalism on the one hand and the maritime ideology on the other.

The First Ming Emperor

The first Ming emperor, Zhu Yuanzhang, was an orphaned peasant from the riverine area near Nanjing. As a child, he had been taken in by Buddhist monks and educated in a monastery. Upon leaving the monastery, he was unable to gain employment and was soon begging for a living. At the age of twenty-five, the vagrant joined a rebel band that fought government soldiers for over a decade in the central China river valleys. Warfare finally wore down the Mongol-backed local forces and the entire Yangzi Valley came under rebel control. In due course, Zhu assumed leadership of the rebels and defeated the government forces. He then established his capital at Nanjing in 1356. Twelve years later, after taking his rebel army north and capturing Beijing from the Mongols, Zhu founded the Chinese Ming dynasty.

Although Zhu, being from a riverine area, had presumably come into contact with many men who had knowledge of the sea, his initial concerns lay in consolidating Chinese rule and making China's borders and strategic cities safe from Mongol invasion. Accordingly, he took several actions that temporarily stifled maritime activities.

Walls, Canals, and Coastal Defense

With the Mongols only recently defeated, Zhu set about improving city defenses. For example, he directed the construction of a protective wall some 20 miles in length around Nanjing. The barrier was 60 feet high and nearly impenetrable by a force armed with the weapons of the time.

On the coast, Zhu faced the problem of piracy by Japanese and Chinese freebooters, which had increased alarmingly. He ordered that Chinese not be permitted to go overseas—those who violated his edict would be executed as traitors. In 1374 Zhu backed up his decree by abolishing the superintendencies of merchant ships at the ports of Ningbo, Quanzhou, and Guangzhou. Next, he strengthened coastal defenses by constructing forts; in the four-year period from 1383 to 1387, more than one hundred thirty forts were built in the Zhejiang-Fujian coastal zones. In Zhejiang alone, more than fifty-eight thousand troops were conscripted to man the provincial coastal forts.

Zhu also directed the Board of Works to undertake extensive reconstruction of the canal system, which had been damaged by flood and warfare. One of the long-term projects called for enlarging the Grand Canal, which upon completion was to replace the pirate-plagued sea route. The latter route had been reopened earlier when civil strife closed down the canal.

The Tribute System

The first Ming emperor wasted little time before trying to reestablish the tributary system. He ordered missions to proceed to peripheral states such as Japan, Annam,

Champa, and Korea, where it was proclaimed that all who wished to enter into relations with China must acknowledge the suzerainty of the new emperor. Very soon some of these states sent reciprocal missions to Peking where Zhu received their kowtows acknowledging him as the Son of Heaven. These missions also served other purposes, such as providing the new Chinese dynasty with information on the current situations in border areas. . . .

The Mongol-Muslim Alliance

The first Ming emperor also had to deal with the continuing threat posed by the retreating Mongols. It took Zhu's armies until 1382 to drive remaining Mongol military units from Yunnan in southwest China. Moreover, during the next twenty years, periodic "mopping-up" operations continued beyond the Great Wall in northeast China and in Korea as well.

For the Ming government, the biggest threat lay westward. A Turkic nomad and Muslim named Timur, or Tamerlane, was conquering the entire central Asian region from Siberia to the Mediterranean and southward to the Indian Ocean. Included in the ranks of his fierce Muslim cavalry were remnants of the retreating Mongol armies.

According to an official Ming history, Zhu was anxious to bring Timur into the tribute system. He sent several small missions on the overland caravan route to seek out the Muslim leader. The Chinese apparently were unaware of just how paltry their offer of suzerainty appeared to the ferocious Timur. The Muslims, in fact, scorned the Chinese. "Because they believe [that] our people [are] wild and boorish, they do not hope for politeness, nor respect, nor honor, nor law from us; and apart from their own realms they do not know of a city [anywhere] in the world."

In 1394, after only a quarter century of Ming rule, an incident occurred that would seriously jeopardize the Chinese dynasty. At that time, Zhu received what he thought was a tribute mission from Timur that delivered a letter acknowledging the Chinese emperor as the ruler of all mankind. The letter, forged by an ambitious merchant or court official, led Zhu to send a return mission to central Asia in appreciation of Timur's vassalage. In 1395, when the Chinese embassy reached Timur and delivered Zhu's note, the Muslim leader became so enraged that he advised his staff to prepare for an invasion of China to bring down the Chinese "infidels." He took the Chinese mission hostage. By 1404 his plans were nearly complete, and he had massed two-hundred thousand Muslim and Mongol cavalrymen in the Pamirs, near modern-day Afghanistan.

Fortunately for the Chinese, Timur died in 1405, following an all-night drinking bout. On his deathbed he reportedly "expressed his regret in having neglected the conquest of such infidel countries as China and drawn his sword against Muslim armies." Two more years passed before the Chinese heard from the freed hostages that Timur had died.

Foreign Policy Under the Second Ming Emperor

While Timur was preparing to invade China, the death of Zhu Yuanzhang in 1398 produced another period of civil war lasting until 1403. Succeeding Zhu was his grandson, a young boy whose court remained in Nanjing. In the north, however, Zhu's fourth son, Chengzu, decided to overthrow his nephew from the southern capital. As the military commander responsible for anti-Mongol operations in the Peking area, he controlled some of the best troops in China. His ultimate success came in 1403, when he defeated the Nanjing forces loyal to his father and assumed the throne with the name Yongle, meaning "perpetual happiness."

Clearly, Yongle's ambition and leadership ability forecast a dynamic reign. As with his father before him, one of Yongle's primary objectives was to establish his sovereignty throughout the tribute system by reinstilling the belief among all foreign states that China was supreme. In order to persuade the tributaries, however, Yongle had to work out a strategy that would both gain respect for Chinese power and enrich the imperial treasuries.

He dealt with Japan first. In 1403 the superintendencies of merchant shipping were reopened and new hostels were built to house Japanese tributary missions coming by sea. A system was devised whereby legitimate Japanese merchants were given trading passports that could be checked by Chinese authorities on each visit. In this way pirates could be identified, while honest Japanese and Chinese businessmen were free to carry on lucrative trade.

In Annam Yongle faced a critical problem. In 1400, while he was fighting to usurp the throne from his nephew, events there were coming to a head. Hanoi had fallen to Champa and the Annamese Tran dynasty was destroyed. The South China Sea was now in the hands of Cham and rebel Annamese pirates, and Chinese merchant shipping, both official and unofficial, was seriously disrupted. In 1406 Yongle decided to attack across the land border in order to pacify the two warring states and then reestablish Annam as a Chinese province. Hanoi was captured in 1406, but the Chinese armies soon bogged down in Annamese cities awaiting reinforcements and supplies. Before long nearly ninety thousand Chinese troops were in Annam attempting to control the countryside through a costly sinicization program.

Problems in inner Asia were developing concurrently with the Annam invasion. Word of the Muslim conquests in central Asia had reached Yongle, but the distance and harsh nature of that western area precluded the dispatch of a large army to confront Timur. Caution got the better of Yongle. He elected to send a small fact-finding mission to Timur in 1402 to inquire why the Muslim leader, since 1395, had failed to pay tribute. In a move that suggested that Yongle would settle for political equality with remote central Asia, he approved the construction of a Muslim mosque in Peking. This may have been done to induce the warring Muslims to keep open the silk route connecting western China with the cities of the Timurid empire (these included Gilgit and Herat, located in modern-day Pakistan and Afghanistan, respectively).

With the silk route used only sporadically, the wealthy classes, the court, and the treasury had become heavily dependent upon southern maritime trade for the import of precious stones, fragrant woods, spices, and rare objects. To ensure the safety of Chinese traders on the sea and the uninterrupted flow of luxury items, it was essential that Yongle build a navy that would convince the ocean states of China's "world supremacy." He devised a forceful plan calling for the aggressive use of seapower to underline Chinese suzerainty over the peripheral southern ocean states. Since the first expedition was to sail all the way to the Muslim states of Aden, Mecca, Djofar, and Hormuz, Yongle likely concluded that the voyages would also be useful in countering Timur's influence in that area.

The Ming Ships and Expeditions

In 1403, a year of momentous decisions, Yongle directed Chinese shipyards in Fujian to undertake an aggressive shipbuilding effort that would result in the construction of more than two thousand large seagoing vessels over the next sixteen years.

The *baochuan*, or treasure ships, were the largest vessels constructed by the Chinese. Their size has been the subject of many arguments among scholars. Ming histories record that the treasure-ships were 440 feet long and 180 feet wide (an unlikely construction ratio of 5:2). At best, this configuration is an exaggeration, for such broad-beamed vessels would be unresponsive even under moderate sea conditions. In fact, acceptance of these figures degrades the reputation of Chinese shipbuilders of the period, who would have recognized that such vessels were impractical to build. Until research proves otherwise, it is this writer's opinion that the largest vessels were shaped much like the three largest junks, of which records are available. These, the Jiangsu trader, the Beizhili trader, and the Fuzhou pole junk, were built on a proportion of about 6.4:1—much closer to the modern naval architecture ratio of 9:1. The former was about 170 feet long and had five masts, while the latter two had lengths of 180 feet with a beam of 28 feet. It may be significant that Fujian shipyards were give the first-order calling for the construction of 137 ships, since these were the yards that probably developed the technique for building the Fuzhou pole junk. . . .

Zheng He

In addition to overseeing the construction of the Ming fleet, Yongle selected the senior officers who were to lead the expeditions. For overall commander the emperor picked a Muslim eunuch named Zheng He, who had been in his service since 1382. As a small boy, Zheng He had been taken prisoner in Yunnan during the final rout of the Mongols.

Following his capture, Zheng He, by custom, was castrated and subsequently made an officer in Yongle's army, where he distinguished himself during the successful usurpation campaign of 1403. For his loyal service, Zheng He, at age thirty-three, was made a grand eunuch and appointed superintendent of the Office of Eunuchs. His military prowess, along with his knowledge of Turku languages and Islam, made Zheng He the ideal choice for senior admiral of the Ming fleet. He was given the name Sanbao Taijian, meaning "three-jewelled eunuch."

During his voyages, Zheng He was accompanied by other Chinese Muslims, including one named Ma Huan, who came from the Hangzhou Bay area. Ma was knowledgeable in matters of the sea and in the Arabic and Persian languages. His chief distinction, however, was the account of three voyages he made with Zheng He.

From Ma Huan we learn that Zheng He's general procedure was to bring the fleet together in late spring near modern-day Shanghai, where a series of briefings and religious ceremonies was conducted. Once prayers had been offered, and the fleet had been organized and briefed, it sailed leisurely on a four- to eight-week "shakedown cruise" to an anchorage at the mouth of the Min River in Fujian Province. There the ships would carry out further intensive training throughout the late summer and early fall. Finally, in December or January, they would set sail during the favorable monsoon.

The Sea Routes

The sea routes followed by Ming naval captains had been known and used for several centuries. Since the Song dynasty, in fact, the routes had been systematized into two major sea lanes: the East Sea Route and the West Sea Route. Each was subdivided into a major and minor route. For example, the major East Sea Route extended to northern Borneo and the Philippines. The minor West Sea Route encompassed ports in Sumatra and the Malay Peninsula. The major West Sea Route was that route taken to the Indian Ocean via the Malacca Strait.

Following the period of intensive training, the fleet wound its way through the Taiwan Strait and sailed directly into the South China Sea, where land falls were made on Hainan Island and the Xisha Islands (Paracel Islands). From the Xishas the fleet turned westward and made for an anchorage at modern-day Qui Nhon on the Champa (southern Vietnam) coast. The total time of the Fujian-Champa transit was about ten days. Once there, provisions were taken aboard and the crews had "liberty" and "swim call." From Qui Nhon the fleet sailed southward toward the west coast of Borneo, making land falls on the various islands in the southern portion of the South China Sea.

After rounding Borneo, the ships entered the Java Sea and sailed to Sarabaja in Java. At this port Chinese crews were again rested for several months, until about July, when the period of favorable winds occurred. They then sailed through the Malacca Strait via Palembang and thence westward to Sri Lanka. From Sri Lanka the ships made their way to Calicut on the Indian coast, where the fleet was divided into smaller "task forces." Some went to Chittagong in modern-day Bangladesh; others went to Hormuz, Aden, and Jidda; and some visited the African coast near the mouth of the Red Sea. Hormuz usually was reached in January of the first year, and the Chinese returned to Malacca by March. They remained in Malacca only briefly, sailing northward to the Yangzi River by July of the second year. . . .

The Decline of Maritime Spirit in the Ming

During the Ming expeditions, a number of political, military, social, and economic factors acted to slow and then finally halt the policies that had promoted maritime experimentation and growth.

The Grand Canal

One of the first indications of China's impending maritime collapse occurred when the Grand Canal was reopened in 1411, making it again possible to ship grain via the inland route. This event marked another closing of the coastal maritime route, and many personnel of the coastal fleets were reassigned to work on the canal. In 1415 the government officially banned grain transport by sea and authorized the construction of three thousand shallow-draft canal barges. This diversion of manpower and shipbuilding expertise was soon felt in the maritime industries. Oceangoing ship construction lagged and was halted altogether by Yongle's successor in 1436. At the same time, regulations were issued that reassigned the men of the Indian Ocean expeditionary force to canal duties as stevedores.

Population Shifts

Significantly, the conclusion of Ming voyages caused a shift of population away from the sea coast that, from 1437 to 1491, resulted in a loss of eight million people in the three principal coastal provinces of Zhejiang, Fujian, and Guangdong. Meanwhile, inland areas such as Yunnan and Hebei gained four million in population. Many coastal inhabitants also emigrated to southeast Asia.

Warfare and Border Pressure

During the fifteenth century China suffered several serious military setbacks along its land borders that deflected interest in maritime expeditions. In 1418 Annam, tiring of the Chinese presence, launched a war of independence. In a way similar to recent United States efforts, the Chinese tried to carry the fight for some nine years, but Annamese guerrilla tactics eventually prevailed. In 1420 the Ming navy lost a battle on the Red River; in 1427 the Chinese emperor finally grew weary of increased war costs and evacuated nearly one hundred thousand Chinese soldiers from Annam. Chinese suzerainty was maintained, however.

In the north, China faced a graver threat in the form of continued Mongol raids along the entire length of the Great Wall. In 1421, in an effort to counter the resurgent Mongols, Yongle moved the capital from Nanjing to Beijing. Troops were shifted from the seacoast to shore up the northern capital's defenses, which lay less than 100 miles from one of the strategic northern passes that intersected the Great Wall. Despite these precautions, the Chinese emperor was captured in 1449, and the Ming court was forced to resurrect its continental defense strategy completely. These policies did little to diminish the northern nomad threat, however; the critical northern frontier remained under nomad pressure for the next three hundred years. Martial law was periodically imposed, and senior military officials spent their careers defending the north rather than performing naval and coastal defense duties.

Corruption in Government

Politics within the Ming court also began to turn attention away from the sea, as eunuchs and Chinese bureaucrats vied for power. The praise and favors lavished on palace eunuchs in the early Ming period eventually led to their complete domination of governmental affairs. By the middle of the fifteenth century, the first in a series of eunuch strongmen ascended to power. Very quickly they set about sealing their hold over the most important government agencies, taking control of the army, the police, and finance ministries. When opposed, the eunuchs often resorted to terrorist tactics, arresting and executing those that dared question their authority. Many became quite corrupt, employing ships and crews to transport ill-gotten goods and transferring soldiers to palace construction work.

By 1480 the political intrigues had increased to such an extent that when a powerful eunuch initiated a request to prepare another series of maritime expeditions in emulation of Zheng He, he was greeted by fierce opposition within the ranks of government bureaucrats. Jealous officials within the Board of War conspired to have records of the Indian Ocean voyages destroyed, so as to frustrate any attempt to imitate the early Ming expeditions.

Piracy

As officials became more absorbed in intrigues at court, they too tended toward corruption, which carried over to coastal trade. Unscrupulous merchants regained control as the government's monopoly on foreign trade was relinquished, and smuggling and piracy flourished. The Ming histories record that "the powerful families of Fujian and Zhejiang traded with the Japanese pirates. Their associates at court protected them and carried out their bidding. . . . Palace attendants outfitted merchant ships and the criminal elements of the coast abetted them in making profit." In fact, while Zheng He and his companions were conducting their voyages, Japanese pirates successfully carried out five major incursions against the Chinese mainland. In 1419 the northern coastguard fleets were helpless in preventing a sizeable force of several thousand pirates from landing on the Liaodong Peninsula. It required a well-trained force of Chinese army troops to subdue the pirates. As an example of the magnitude of this action, the Chinese army commander captured 857 pirates alive and beheaded another 742.

Although Japanese piracy continued to plague the Chinese, it ceased in 1466 when Japan fell into civil war. By 1523, however, Japanese and Chinese raiders were again launching attacks along the coast. Ningbo was burned in that year, and in 1552 a flotilla sailed up the Yangzi, sacking cities without opposition. Natives of the coast fled further inland to escape the ravages of these attacks. In 1555 Nanjing came under seige and the port of Quanzhou in Fujian was plundered. In an attempt to stop these raids, Ming provincial administrators resorted to the Tang dynasty's practice of constructing beacon stations to give advance warnings of pirates. By 1562, 711 beacon stations lined the coast from Jiangsu to Guangdong. By 1563 the army had to be used to combat the sea rovers, who controlled nearly all of the Fujian coast.

Scholarship and Neo-Confucianism

Finally, a version of neo-Confucianism developed that was markedly idealistic and influenced by Buddhism, resulting in a loss of interest in geomancy and maritime expansion. As early as 1426, a minister memorialized the court, stating the following:

> Arms are the instruments of evil which the sage does not use unless he must. The noble rulers and wise ministers of old did not dissipate the strength of the people by deeds of arm. This was a farsighted policy. . . . Your minister hopes that your majesty . . . would not indulge in military pursuits nor glorify the sending of expeditions to distant countries. Abandon the barren lands abroad and give the people of China a respite so that they could devote themselves to husbandry and to the schools. Thus, there would be no wars and suffering on the frontier and no murmuring in the villages, the commanders would not seek fame and the soldiers would not sacrifice their lives abroad, the people from afar would voluntarily submit and distant lands would come into our fold, and our dynasty would last for ten thousand generations.

Such statements helped check Chinese maritime pursuits and force China to restore continentalist policies. Scholars who devoted their lives to the classics were again revered, while the military class was looked upon with great suspicion by the gentry and officials.

By the early fifteenth century, regulations were again in force that made it a capital offense to build a seagoing junk with more than two masts. By 1525 an imperial edict authorized coastal officials to destroy all ships of this kind and place the crews under arrest.

The timing of Chinese maritime decline could not have been worse, for it coincided with European maritime expansion into Asia. The Portuguese arrived in 1516, and although they were expelled in 1521, their exodus was short-lived. They returned and established settlements in Xiamen in 1544 and Macao in 1535. The Spanish occupied the Philippines in 1564 and established trade relations with China shortly thereafter. Then, in the seventeenth century, the Dutch arrived in Asia just as the Ming dynasty was being conquered by the Manchu cavalry that overran Beijing in 1644. Thus was the stage set for the last foreign imperial rulers in China—the Qing.

Bruce Swanson was a well-known authority of Chinese maritime affairs. He has written articles on the subject and was a regular participant in conferences related to the maritime environment in China.

EXPLORING THE ISSUE

Did China's Worldview Cause the Abrupt End of Its Voyages of Exploration?

Critical Thinking and Reflection

1. How does the Chinese worldview of the late 1400s differ from the European worldview of the same period? Both parts of the world were dominated by monarchs. And, both were involved in voyages of discovery and exploration. Are the views of these two regions more similar or more different? Critically discuss.
2. Does Zheng He meet the definition of a "Great Man" in the historical sense of having dominated an age in a particular part of the world? Like Western military heroes, such as Alexander the Great and Napoleon Bonaparte, Zheng He brought commercial and maritime dominance to China. Unlike his Western counterparts, however, Zheng He served an emperor. Critically analyze his role in terms of the Great Man theory of history.
3. How was Zheng He similar to and different from Christopher Columbus, with whom he is often compared? How was his nation similar to and how was it different from Columbus's? Critically analyze and debate/discuss.
4. What do you think Nicholas D. Kristof means when he writes: ". . . an explorer makes history but does not necessarily change it, for his impact depends less on the trail he blazes than on the willingness of others to follow?" Critically analyze and discuss this claim.
5. What are the implications of Bruce Swanson's statement that "The timing of Chinese maritime decline could not have been worse, for it coincided with European maritime expansion into Asia?" Critically analyze and discuss.
6. Would Europe's Age of Exploration have been possible if China had continued its maritime adventures? What might this have meant for the Americas? Critically research, analyze, and debate this question.
7. The United States, like China, has undergone periods of isolationism. Based on what you know about U.S. history, speculate about the reasons that might have led China to withdraw from world affairs.

Is There Common Ground?

Both writers mention China's brief period of maritime supremacy, and both mention multiple factors to account for the abrupt end of China's Voyages of Exploration. Based on what you have read, can the story of China's radical inward turn be told without including the prominent role played by Zheng He? Was he, perhaps, perceived to be irreplaceable in skill and loyalty? Although each writer tips his interpretation in one direction or another, both acknowledge a number of factors that might account for a dramatic change in China's goals.

As a way toward establishing common ground, it might be useful to list the factors mentioned by both writers that explain China's change in policy. Are there areas of agreement? What are the areas of disagreement?

Question: How significant is it that only after many centuries have elapsed are we able to sort out which factor might be the dominant one?

Additional Resources

For other works on the subject, see Shi-Shah Henry Tsai, *Perpetual Happiness: The Ming Emperor Yongle* (University of Washington Press, 2001) which provides a fresh look at the man responsible for Ming China's maritime activities; Timothy Brook, *The Confusions of Pleasure: Commerce and Culture in Ming China* (University of California Press, 1999) is more useful for general information on Chinese society during the Ming dynasty than specific information of Zheng He and his voyages. An ancillary work, *Chinese Maps: Images of 'All Under Heaven'* by Richard J. Smith provides background to China's worldview and its development and displays the advanced Chinese map work completed during China's maritime voyages.

A decade ago, Gavin Menzies's *1421: The Year China Discovered America* (William Morrow, 2003) was published. It extended the breadth of China's maritime efforts by claiming that it was the Chinese who discovered America during the Ming era. However, most who reviewed the book found it long on claims and short on documentation.

Finally, two important reference works on Ming China, both edited by Frederick W. Mote and Denis Twitchett are: *The Cambridge History of China: The Ming Dynasty, 1368–1644, Part I* (Cambridge University Press, 1988); and *The*

Cambridge History of China: The Ming Dynasty, 1368–1644, Part II (Cambridge University Press, 1998.

The relatively recent publication dates on many of these books, and the presence of numerous websites containing information about Zheng He, show the timeliness of the subject and give hope that more information and scholarship on a neglected figure in Chinese and world history will be forthcoming.

Internet References . . .

The Great Chinese Mariner Zheng He

This brief site contains an account of Zheng He's travels, a map depicting one of his voyages, and several other useful visuals. What is more important is other links which provide useful information on the great Chinese admiral.

www.chinapage.com/zhenghe.html

Unit III

UNIT

The Premodern World

As China ended its Age of Exploration, Europe's continued, and a "new" North American continent became populated with Europeans. Knowing all we now know about the results of this influx, how can we fairly evaluate the effects of Christopher Columbus's voyages on subsequent world history? A Reformation within Christianity broke apart a powerful medieval synthesis and facilitated the development of national states. Subsequent religious wars pitted Protestants and Catholics against each other for two centuries. How would we go about evaluating whether the Reformation improved the lives of European Christians?

During the age of Shakespeare and beyond, a woman ruled England, challenging gender expectations and expressing what we might now call androgynous behavior—as a comrade to military troops and as a skilled diplomat. However, in a baffling period in European history, many thousands of women were tortured and killed, having been found guilty of witchcraft. Often these witch hunts occurred in the most literate countries. How can we explain this?

Perhaps surprisingly, this was also the time of the Scientific Revolution. Studying the entire scope of world history might help us understand how the barbarity of witch hunts and the rationality of the scientific method could emerge more or less together. Are there parallels in our own experience? Accounts of the Age of Enlightenment usually place its origins in France. However, there were Enlightenment "projects" in many regions, including England where the Glorious Revolution had brought about a bloodless coup that instituted democracy. Is it possible that a British Enlightenment led the way?

Selected, Edited, and with Issue Framing Material by:
Helen Buss Mitchell, *Howard Community College*
and
Joseph R. Mitchell, *Howard Community College*

ISSUE

Is Christopher Columbus's Reputation as a Positive Force in World History Still Merited?

YES: Robert Royal, from "Columbus and the Beginning of the New World," *First Things: A Monthly Journal of Religion and Public Life* (May 1999)

NO: Gabriel Garcia Marquez, from "For a Country Within Reach of the Children," *Americas Magazine* (November/December 1997)

Learning Outcomes

After reading this issue you should be able to:

- Explain the reasons for reassessing Columbus's reputation over the last two centuries.
- Describe internal and external pressures on Europe, during the 1400s.
- Recount what we know of Columbus's personal qualities.
- Describe European attitudes toward the new Peoples of the Americas.

ISSUE SUMMARY

YES: Robert Royal argues that, although there were negative effects that emanated from Columbus's New World discoveries, they continue to "remind us of the glorious and ultimately providential destiny of the ongoing global journey that began in the fifteenth century."

NO: Nobel laureate Gabriel Garcia Marquez argues that Columbus's voyages had a negative effect on the Americas, much of which is still felt today.

In October 1998, a *New York Times* article covered a dispute between Hispanic-Americans and Italian-Americans with regard to which ethnic group should play the more important role in the organization of New York's Columbus Day Parade. While both groups had legitimate claims to the Columbus legacy (after all, Columbus was a Genoese Italian, but he did his most important work for the Spanish nation), the dispute must have drawn an ironic response from those who had witnessed the revisionist bashing that the "Admiral of the Ocean Sea" had received in recent years.

In the five centuries since "Columbus sailed the ocean blue," his historical reputation and the evaluation of the significance of his accomplishments have both undergone a series of metamorphoses. In the distant past, the small and eclectic cadre of Columbus critics would number French essayist, Michel Montaigne; English writer Samuel Johnson; French philosopher, Jean-Jacques Rousseau; and French historian and philosopher, Abbe Guillaume Reynal, some of whom believed that the world would have been better off without the admiral's discoveries.

Only in the last two centuries has Columbus's stock risen in the theater of public opinion and historical significance. There were many reasons for this change including: (1) the United States acting as a model for democratic government in a nineteenth/twentieth-century world living under monarchial/autocratic rule; (2) the part played by the United States in the Allied victory during World War I, which ended the German, Austrian, Ottoman, and Russian Empires and brought a greater level of democracy to many parts of Europe; and (3) the role assumed by the United States in saving Europe and the world from the specter of fascist militarism during World War II. All these events affected the reversal of Columbus's historical fortunes, as many wondered what the world would have become if the United States had not been there to provide inspiration and assistance in these times of need. Thus, some of the credit our nation accrued was passed on to Columbus, whose work had made our nation possible. Samuel Eliot Morison's 1940 book, *Admiral of the Ocean Sea*, marked the apex of this laudatory view of Columbus and his accomplishments.

Historians and publishers have long loved anniversaries and, especially, the attention and publicity they generate. Next to a millennial celebration, none may be more significant than a quincentennial one. Thus, on the 500th anniversary of Columbus's first voyage, the requisite number of tomes on Columbus and his accomplishments were made ready for an eager market. But the world of 1992 was different from the world of Morison's *Admiral of the Ocean Sea*, and the historical profession had changed along with it.

The end-of-the-millennium generation of historians treated Columbus differently than had their immediate predecessors. Operating from a different world view, many of them had come to see Columbus as a flawed figure directly or indirectly responsible for the horrors of the transatlantic slave trade, the annihilation of Native American civilizations through cruelty and disease, and the ecological destruction of a continental paradise.

A number of recently published books about Christopher Columbus opened a national dialogue on the subject. The national Columbus exhibition in Washington, DC was received with skepticism by some and quiet reverence by others. While some participated in the national Columbus Day celebration on October 12, 1992, others declared it a day of mourning in honor of those who had lost their lives as a result of Columbus's enterprises. A cultural hornet's nest was unleashed, and any who entered into the Columbus fray had to have the thickest of skin.

Fortunately, as is usually the case, the passage of time has had a moderating effect. Other anniversaries have taken center stage, and we will have to wait until the year 2092 for the next major Columbus debate. For now, we have the opportunity—with cooler heads and calmer temperaments—to examine the Columbus legacy.

Pouring through the many Columbus-oriented works that were products of the quincentennial anniversary is likely to leave one bewildered and perplexed. One wonders how writers can take the same neutral, factual information and use it to arrive at diametrically opposed conclusions concerning Columbus and his place in history. Of course, as is usual in historical matters, a historian's life experiences and the perspective derived from them are important determinants in the process of wringing conclusions from the historical data.

It is worth noting that when the Columbus "iconography" was established in the West, the perspective on civilization was a decidedly Eurocentric one. As a result, many potentially negative voices were either muted or silenced. As Western history became more "inclusionary" and a multicultural view of history made its way into the public consciousness, these dissenting voices have begun to be heard. They have produced an alternative interpretation of Columbus's voyages and their impact on history that is radically different from the one reached by their predecessors. What the future trajectory of Columbus historiography will be like remains unclear.

One important question germane to the Columbus debate is: To what extent can he be held personally responsible for the transatlantic slave trade, the annihilation of Native American populations, the ecological destruction of the Western Hemisphere, and other evils that were committed long after his death? Even if we subscribe to the Great Man theory of history, is it reasonable to assign blame to the "Great Man" for all seen and unforeseen consequences of his actions. Critics might emphatically say that we should. If the hero deserves the credit, he also deserves the blame. When we look at history "from the bottom up," we are likely to find a different historical experience than the one enjoyed by the Great Man. Over this century, a consensus assessment of Columbus's role in world history needs to explore answers to the basic question posed by this issue.

The writers whose voices inform this issue are both passionate. Robert Royal, while admitting negative possibilities, stresses the positive elements that came from Columbus's discoveries. Gabriel Garcia Marquez finds no positive results from Columbus's voyages of "discovery" and emphasizes their unmitigatedly negative impact on the New World and its peoples.

Robert Royal

Columbus and the Beginning of the New World

. . . The world we know began in the fifteenth century. Not the world of course in the sense of human life or human civilizations, which had already existed for millennia, but the world as a concrete reality in which all parts of the globe had come into contact with one another and begun to recognize themselves as part of a single human race—a process still underway. The spherical globe we had known about since the classical world; in the Middle Ages, readers of Dante took it for granted. Yet it was only because of a small expedition by a few men driven by a mishmash of personal ambition, religious motives, and the desire for profit that an old mathematical calculation was turned into a new human fact. Or as a historian sixty years later accurately characterized the discovery of the New World, it was "the greatest event since the creation of the world (excluding the incarnation and death of Him who created it)."

In our own confused way, we continue to pay homage to that achievement. In 1999, NASA will put a satellite into an orbit a little less than a million miles out into space in what is called L-l, the libration point where the gravity of the earth and the sun exactly balance one another. Equipped with a telescopic lens and video camera, it will provide a twenty-four-hour-a-day image of the surface of the earth. Not surprisingly, one of the enthusiasts behind the project is Al Gore, probably the most environmentally agitated public figure alive. But in spite of the damage that Gore and many others believe we humans have inflicted on the planet since our first large steps in exploring it, and despite the laments of multiculturalists about Europe's rise to world dominance, the new satellite will be called Triana, after Rodrigo de Triana, who first spotted lights on land from the deck of the Pinta during the first voyage of Columbus.

Perhaps the name is only a bow to growing Hispanic influence in the United States; perhaps it hints that we would like to think of ourselves as equally on the verge of another great age of discovery. But whatever our sense of the future, the Columbus discoveries and the European intellectual and religious developments that lay behind them are today at best taken for granted, at worst viewed as the beginning of a sinister Western hegemony over man and nature. The last five centuries, of course, offer the usual human spectacle of great glories mixed with grim atrocities. But we cannot evaluate the voyages of discovery properly—much less the fifteenth-century culture from which they sprang—without gratitude for what they achieved or understanding of their human dimensions. In the fifteenth century, the discoveries were rightly regarded as close to a miracle, especially given the way the century had begun.

The early 1400s were marked by profound religious, political, economic, and even environmental turmoil. At one point in the first decade of the century, there were simultaneously three claimants to the papal throne and three to the crown of the Holy Roman Empire. And the large-scale institutional crises were only a small part of the story. Europe was still suffering from the devastation wrought at the height of the Black Death over half a century earlier and in smaller waves thereafter. Overall, something like 40 percent of the population disappeared in the mid-fourteenth century, in some regions even more. Land lay fallow for lack of workers, villages were deserted, poverty spread. As many modern environmentalists have devoutly wished, nature took its vengeance as human population decreased. Wolves multiplied and returned, even appearing in capital cities. Human predators—in the form of brigands—made travel unsafe over wide areas. The consequences of the retreat of civilization spurred Henry V, fabled victor of Agincourt, to offer rewards for the elimination of both types of pests. Though the beauty of landscapes emerged as never before in contemporary painting and literature, it was not a century that indulged itself in easy sentimentality about the goodness of unimproved nature, human or otherwise. On the contrary, natural hardships spurred the fifteenth century to nearly unparalleled achievements.

But if the internal situation were not enough, Europe was also being squeezed by forces from outside. In 1453, the Ottoman Turks finally succeeded in taking Byzantium. Turkish troops had already been fighting as far into the Balkans as Belgrade a few years earlier. Otranto, in the heel of Italy, fell to them in 1480 for a time. We might have expected the Christian powers to lay aside rivalries momentarily and defend themselves from an alien culture and religion. But the main Atlantic nation-states—England, France, and Spain—were still only beginning to take shape. The rest of Western Europe was broken, despite the theoretical claims of the emperor, into a crazy quilt of competing small powers. So no coordinated effort occurred, though Plus II and other popes called for a crusade. Plus even wrote to Sultan Muhammad II, conqueror of Constantinople, inviting him to convert to Christianity. Whether this letter was intended seriously or as a mere pretext for further action, it failed. Neither "European" nor "Christian" interests were sufficiently united to galvanize the effort. The Pope died in 1464 at the eastern Italian port of Ancona waiting for his people to rally behind him.

A crusade to retake the Holy Land was sometimes a mere pipe dream, sometimes a serious proposal during the course of the century. Ferdinand of Spain listened frequently to such plans, but refrained from doing much. (Machiavelli praises him in The Prince as one of those rulers who shrewdly take pains to appear good without necessarily being so.) Charles VIII of France invaded Italy in 1494 but also had in mind an attempt to retake Constantinople and restore the Eastern Christian Empire. Earlier, Henry V, on his way to Agincourt, proclaimed his intentions not only to assume the French throne but to "build again the walls of Jerusalem." Western Europe had a persistent if vague sense of responsibility to defend Christianity from Islamic military threats and a deeper need to recover the parts of Christendom lost to Muslim conquest, even if the good intentions were thwarted by intra-European distractions.

Had Islam continued its advance, much of Europe might have then resembled the cultures we now associate with the Middle East. The Americas might have been largely Muslim countries as opposed to largely Christian ones. Islam was more advanced than Europe in 1492, but in the paradoxical ways of culture, its very superiority contributed to its being surpassed. Muslims do not seem to have taken much interest in Western technical developments in navigation, and even well-placed countries like Morocco were never moved to brave the high seas in search of new lands. European technological innovation and military advances may have been born of necessity, given the superiority of outside cultures and the conflicts and rivalries among European nations.

This reminds us of something often overlooked in most contemporary historical surveys. The "Eurocentric" forces, of which we now hear so much criticism, were actually something quite different in the fifteenth century. What we today call "Europeans" thought of themselves as part of Christendom, and a Christendom, as we shall serf, that desperately needed to return to some of its founding truths. Similarly, they did not regard themselves as the bearers of the highest culture. Ancient Greece and Rome, they knew, had lived at a higher level, which is why the Renaissance felt the need to recover and imitate classical models. The fabled wealth of the distant Orient and the clearly superior civilization of nearby Islam did not allow Christendom to think itself culturally advanced or, more significantly, to turn in on itself, as self-satisfied empires of the time such as China did. Contemporary European maps—the ones all the early mariners consulted in the Age of Discovery—bear witness to their central belief: Jerusalem, not Europe, was the center of the world.

But this very sense of threat and inferiority, combined with the unsettled social diversity of Europe at the time, gave Europeans a rich and dynamic restlessness. Not surprisingly, the rise towards a renewed Europe began in the places least affected by the population implosion and, therefore, more prosperous: what we today call the Low Countries and, above all, Northern Italy. Renascences, as Erwin Panofsky demonstrated a few decades ago, had been occurring in Europe since the twelfth century. But the one that took place in Northern Italy in the fifteenth century—the one we call the Renaissance—produced multiple and wide-ranging consequences.

Pius II was in many ways emblematic of the mid-century. A cultivated humanist born in Siena in 1405 with the imposing name Aeneas Sylvius Piccolomini, he initially came under the spell of St. Bernardino, who preached a strictly observant reformed Franciscan life (of which more anon). But he shortly became attracted to the exciting life of the Renaissance Italian humanists, which is to say libertinism and literary pursuits. He shifted parties among papal contenders, pursuing his own ambitions for many years, wrote a popular history (Historia rerum ubique gestarum) that gathered together wide-ranging facts and fictions about foreign lands, and even became imperial poet and secretary to the Holy Roman Emperor Frederick III. But compared with the squabbling popes and anti-popes who preceded him and the colorful escapades of the Borgias, Pius had his virtues. He was learned and hard-working, enjoyed nature, sought reform, and could have made a difference in Europe had his office enjoyed the respect it once had and was to have again later. The religious renaissance, however, like the cultural, scientific, and artistic one with which we are more familiar, had to come from other sources.

Renaissance achievements found multiple and overlapping uses in a Europe in ferment. The geometry developed by the Florentine Paolo Toscanelli allowed Filippo Brunelleschi, over the objections of a commission of Florentine experts, to dare construction of the unsupported dome that crowns the magnificent Florentine Duomo. Just a few decades later, an intellectually curious Genoese mariner corresponded with Toscanelli in preparation for his attempts to convince another panel of experts in Spain that it was possible to sail west to the Indies (no serious thinker at the time, by the way, believed the earth was flat). His figures were wrong; the distance was greater than he claimed. The experts—and perhaps Columbus himself—knew it. But it was an age when for various reasons people had the faith to attempt things beyond what was previously thought possible. It is worth looking closely at some of those reasons.

Much has recently been written, for example, claiming that the Christian dimension of Columbus' personality was merely a cover for greed and ambition. These alleged traits are then read as a metaphor for a hypocritical European expansion under the cover of religion. Hypocrites certainly existed in the fifteenth century, as they do today. But real history—as opposed to anachronistic morality tales—is always more complex than the simple motives we project back onto figures quite different from ourselves. Like the Italian humanists, who are often wrongly portrayed as modern unbelieving intellectuals, Columbus combined his faith with new knowledge and new interests. But that did not make his faith any less real. He wanted that Renaissance ideal, glory: in this case, that of an unprecedented voyage. He drove hard bargains with Ferdinand and Isabella to secure the financial benefits of his discoveries for himself and his descendants. (The Muslim conquests and consequent monopolies over Eastern trade routes made the European search for alternate routes all the more necessary and profitable.) Yet when all the mundane reasons have been listed, the spiritual dimension of the project remains in ways that are quite unexpected.

In the preface to his Libro de las profecias (Book of Prophecies), an anthology of prophetic texts that he compiled near the end of his life, Columbus relates to Ferdinand and Isabella how, long before he ever approached them, he had become convinced that the westward voyage was not merely possible but his own personal vocation:

> During this time, I searched out and studied all kinds of texts: geographies, histories, chronologies, philosoph[ies], and other subjects. With a hand that could be felt, the Lord opened my mind to the fact that it would be possible to sail from here to the Indies, and He opened my will to desire to accomplish this project. This was the fire that burned within me when I came to visit your Highnesses.

Of course, the reading alone suggests we are dealing with an unusual kind of sailor, one who, like the humanists of his day, has engaged in sifting and comparing ancient and modern knowledge for new purposes. There is some irony, then, in the fact that he claims that God intended to produce a milagro ebidentisimo ("highly visible miracle") in this enterprise by using an uneducated man: "For the execution of the journey to the Indies, I was not aided by intelligence, by mathematics, or by maps. It was simply the fulfillment of what Isaiah had prophesied."

Columbus clearly employed considerable intelligence, mathematical skill, and geographical knowledge in planning his route. He also knew from much experience at sea that winds in the Atlantic nearer the equator would carry him west, those to be found more to the north would take him east, back to Europe. And he was alert to other environmental signs. Late in the first voyage he turned south to follow a flock of birds that he rightly assumed were headed towards land. Without this chance or providential fact, he probably would have come ashore somewhere between Virginia and Florida instead of the Caribbean, with doubtless immensely different effects on subsequent world history.

Despite all the knowledge, abstract and practical, that Columbus brought to bear on his task, the religious intuitions he describes may strike us as bordering on delusion, on a par with the equally unexpected mystical speculations of the mathematician Pascal, or Newton's commentaries on the prophecies in the Book of Daniel. But anyone familiar with how prophecies have functioned throughout history knows they often work themselves out in ways their authors never envisioned. In Columbus' case, we may wish to avoid judging too quickly the "hand that could be felt" and other evidence that at times he seems to have heard something like divine locutions. They may have been delusions, intuitions, or something else moving in the depths of human history.

Far from being a later and idealized reinterpretation of his own past, Columbus' remarks are confirmed by a curious source. Recent scholars have discovered notes in Columbus' own hand dated 1481, over a decade before his first voyage, in the back of a copy of Aeneas Sylvius Piccolomini's (the later Pius II) Historia rerum ubique gestarum. There Columbus compiles a shorter list of prophecies from various sources which, it now seems perfectly clear, guided his whole life project. . . .

Much of this real history has been obscured for a long time by persons who found it expedient to use Columbus as a symbolic figure. For most older Americans, he was presented as a heroic proto-American, combating the obscurantism of reactionary Spanish Catholics who thought he would sail off the end of the flat earth. (As we have seen, neither Columbus nor his intellectual critics believed in such absurdities.) In that reading, he became a forerunner of American Protestantism, modern science, and capitalist enterprise. It is no great loss that we have discarded that historical illusion.

Columbus also did service as an ethnic hero for Catholics, mostly Irish and Italian, during the large waves of immigration at the end of the nineteenth and beginning of the twentieth century. There was less harm here, because he was a true hero. Enthusiasm grew so heated that on the four hundredth anniversary of his voyage in 1892 efforts were made to have him canonized. But Leo XIII, fully aware of Columbus' irregular marital situation (for reasons of inheritance he never married the woman he lived with after his wife died), contented himself with praising his human virtues: "For the exploit is in itself the highest and grandest which any age has ever seen accomplished by man; and he who achieved it, for the greatness of mind and heart, can be compared to but few in the history of humanity."

In recent years, of course, Columbus' standing as hero has come under severe assault. He and the culture he represented have been castigated for initiating the modern cultural dominance of Europe and every subsequent world evil: colonialism, slavery, cultural imperialism, environmental damage, and religious bigotry. There is a kernel of truth in these charges, but obviously to equate a single individual or a complex entity like a culture with what are currently judged to be the negative dimensions of the emergence of an interconnected human world is to do great historical injustice to both individuals and ideas.

Europeans, for example, had an ambivalent stance towards the new peoples they encountered. On the one hand, there arose almost instantaneously the beginnings of the "noble savage" myth, which had a varied career in the hands of writers like Thomas More, Montaigne, and Rousseau. On the other hand, actual experience of the new cultures revealed peoples who displayed much savagery and sometimes little nobility.

Columbus himself adhered to one side or the other in this culture war at different times in his life. In one of his first communications with the Spanish monarchs after the discovery, he described the Tainos of the Caribbean in glowing terms:

> I see and know that these people have no religion whatever, nor are they idolaters, but rather they are very meek and know no evil. They do not kill or capture others and are without weapons. They are so timid that a hundred of them flee from one of us, even if we are teasing. They are very trusting; they believe there is a God in Heaven, and they firmly believe that we come from Heaven. They learn very quickly any prayer we tell them to say, and they make the sign of the cross. Therefore Your Highnesses must resolve to make them Christians.

As the self-contradictions of this passage suggest, Columbus was under the spell of one current in European mythology that believed such "uncivilized" peoples to be somehow closer to the conditions of the Garden of Eden than those enmeshed in the conflicts of "civilization."

In fact, the Tainos themselves were enmeshed in the tribal raiding, slavery, and cannibalism that existed in the Caribbean long before any European arrived (the word "cannibal" is a corruption of the native term for the fierce Caribs who eventually gave their name to the whole region). Columbus was for a while on surprisingly good terms with his Tainos, who in turn used the Spaniards to their advantage against their enemies. But the distance between the cultures was great, and, with the arrival of less-than-ideal explorers in subsequent voyages, the situation took a bad turn. Towards the end of his third voyage, Columbus wrote to complain about criticism of his governorship over both natives and Spaniards:

> At home they judge me as a governor sent to Sicily or to a city or two under settled government and where the laws can be fully maintained, without fear of all being lost. . . . I ought to be judged as a captain who went from Spain to the Indies to conquer a people, warlike and numerous, and with customs and beliefs very different from ours.

Columbus had discovered that the Indians were real flesh-and-blood human beings, with the same mix of good and evil that everywhere constitutes the human condition.

Today, the usual way of characterizing the behavior of the Europeans at this early stage is to fault them for not having the kind of sensitivity to the Other that a modern anthropologist or ethnologist would bring to such situations. Overlooked in this condemnation is the fact that it was precisely out of these tumultuous conflicts that the West began to learn how to understand different cultures as objectively as possible in their own terms. Columbus himself astutely noted differences between the various subgroupings of Tainos as well as their distinctiveness from other tribes. And even when he was driven to harsh action—against both Indians and Spaniards—it was not out of mere desire for power. Bartolome de las Casas, the well-known defender of the Indians, notes the "sweetness and benignity" of the admiral's character and, even while condemning what actually occurred, remarks, "Truly I would not dare blame the admiral's intentions, for I knew him well and I know his intentions were good." Las Casas attributes Columbus' shortcomings not to malign intent but to ignorance concerning how to handle an unprecedented situation.

This raises the question of larger intentions and the world impact of fifteenth-century European culture. The atrocities committed by Spain, England, Holland, and other European powers as they spread out over the globe in ensuing centuries are clear enough. No one today defends them. Less known, however, are the currents within that culture that have led to the very universal principles by which, in retrospect, we criticize that behavior today. For instance, not only Las Casas, but a weighty array of other religious thinkers began trying to specify what European moral obligations were to the new peoples.

Las Casas, who was the bishop of Chiapas, Mexico, where relations between mostly native populations and the central government remain dicey even today, bent over backwards to understand local practices. He once even described human sacrifices as reflecting an authentic piety and said that "even if cruel [they] were meticulous, delicate, and exquisite," a view that some of his critics have remarked exhibits a certain coldness towards the victims. Other missionaries learned native languages and recorded native beliefs. The information coming from the New World stimulated Francisco de la Vitoria, a Dominican theologian at the University of Salamanca in Spain, to develop principles of natural law that, in standard histories, are rightly given credit as the origin of modern international law. To read Vitoria on the Indies is to encounter an atmosphere closer to the UN Universal Declaration of Human Rights than to sinister Eurocentrism.

Las Casas and Vitoria influenced Pope Paul III to make a remarkable statement in his 1536 encyclical Sublimis Deus:

> Indians and all other people who may later be discovered by the Christians are by no means to be deprived of their liberty or the possession of their property, even though they be outside the faith of Jesus Christ. . . . Should the contrary happen it shall be null and of no effect. . . . By virtue of our apostolic authority we declare . . . that the said Indians and other peoples should be converted to the faith of Jesus Christ by preaching the word of God and by the example of good and holy living.

The Spanish crown itself had moral qualms about the conquest. Besides passing various laws trying to eliminate atrocities, it took a step unmatched before or since by any expanding empire: it called a halt to the process while theologians examined the question. In the middle of the sixteenth century, Charles V ordered a theological commission to debate the issue at the monastery of Valladolid. Las Casas defended the Indians. Juan Gines de Sepulveda, the greatest authority on Aristotle at the time, argued that Indians were slaves by nature and thus rightly subject to Spanish conquest. Though the commission never arrived at a clear vote and the Spanish settlers were soon back to their old ways, Las Casas' views were clearly superior and eventually prevailed.

Conquest aside, the question of even peaceful evangelizing remains very much with us. Today, most people, even Christians, believe it somehow improper to evangelize. The injunction to preach the gospel to all nations, so dear to Columbus' heart, seems an embarrassment, not least because of the ways the command has been misused. But some of the earlier missionaries tried a kind of inculturation that recognized what was good in the native practices and tried to build a symbolic bridge between them and the Christian faith. The Franciscans in New Spain and the Jesuits in Canada, for example, tried this approach. Not a few of them found martyrdom.

Many contemporary believers do not think that there was much need to evangelize. This usually arises out of the assumption that native religions are valid in their own way. It will not do, however, given the anthropological evidence, to make facile assumptions that all spiritual practices are on an equal plane. The early explorers who encountered them did not think so, and neither should we. For example, the Mexican novelist Carlos Fuentes, no special friend of Christianity or the Spanish conquest, in the very act of admiring the richness of Aztec culture, characterizes the Aztec gods as "a whole pantheon of fear." Fuentes deplores the way that missionaries often collaborated with unjust appropriation of native land, but on a theological level notes the epochal shift in native cultures thanks to Christian influence: "One can only imagine the astonishment of the hundreds and thousands of Indians who asked for baptism as they came to realize that they were being asked to adore a god who sacrificed himself for men instead of asking men to sacrifice themselves to gods, as the Aztec religion demanded."

This Copernican Revolution in religious thought has changed religious practice around the world since it was first proclaimed in Palestine two millennia ago, yet is all but invisible to modern critics of evangelization. Any of us, transported to the Aztec capital Tenochtitlan or to many other places around the world before the influence of Christianity and Europe, would react the way the conquistadors did—with rage and horror. We might not feel much different about some of the ways that Europeans, imitating Islamic practice, evangelized at times by the sword and perpetrated grave injustices around the world. But it is reductionist in the extreme to regard evangelization simply as imperialism. The usual uncritical way in which we are urged to respect the values of other cultures has only the merest grain of truth buried beneath what is otherwise religious indifferentism.

For all our sense of superiority to this now half-millennium-old story, we still face some of the same questions that emerged in the fifteenth century. We still have not found an adequate way to do justice to the claims of both universal principle and particular communities. We have what Vaclav Havel has called a "thin veneer of global civilization" mostly consisting of CNN, Coca Cola, blue jeans, rock music, and perhaps the beginning glimmer of something approaching a global agreement on how we should treat one another and the planet.

But that minimal unity conceals deeper conflicts involving not only resistance to superficiality but the survival of particular communities of meaning. We say, for example, that we have an equal respect for all cultures—until we come up against religious castes and sexism, clitorectomies and deliberate persecution. Then we believe that universal principles may take precedence. But whose universal principles? A Malaysian prime minister has lately instructed us that, contrary to international assumptions, "Western values are Western values: Asian values are universal values." It may take another five hundred years to decide whether that is so, or whether the opposition it assumes between East and West will persist.

All of this may seem a long way from the fifteenth century. But it is not mere historical fantasy to see in that beginning some of the global issues that are now inescapably on the agenda for the new millennium. Christianity and Islam, the two major proselytizing faiths in the world, are still seeking a modus vivendi. The global culture initiated by Columbus will always be inescapably European in origin and, probably, in basic shape. We chose long ago not to stay quietly at home and build the otherwise quite wonderful contraptions called cuckoo clocks. That decision brought (and brings) many challenges, but the very struggle should remind us of the glorious and ultimately providential destiny of the ongoing global journey that began in the fifteenth century.

Robert Royal is vice president of the Ethics and Public Policy in Washington, DC and the author of *The Virgin and the Dynamo: Use and Abuse of Religion in the Environmental Debate* (Eerdmans, 1999).

Gabriel Garcia Marquez

For a Country Within Reach of the Children

Christopher Columbus, with the authorization of a letter from the Spanish monarchs to the emperor of China, had discovered this paradise through a geographical error that changed the course of history. On the eve of his arrival, even before he heard the wings of the first birds in the darkness at sea, Columbus detected the scent of flowers on the wind coming off the land, and it seemed the sweetest thing in the world to him. He wrote in his shipboard diary that they were met on the beach by natives as naked as the day they were born, handsome, gentle, and so innocent they traded all they had for strings of colored beads and tin trinkets. But his heart almost burst from his chest when he discovered that their noserings were made of gold, and their bracelets, necklaces, earrings, and anklets; that they had gold bells to play with, and some sheathed their private parts in gold. Those splendid ornaments, and not their human values, condemned the natives to their roles as protagonists in the second Genesis which began that day. Many of them died not knowing where the invaders had come from. Many of the invaders died not knowing where they were. Five centuries later the descendants of both still do not know who we are.

It was a more discovered world than anyone believed at the time. The Incas had a well-organized, legendary state with ten million inhabitants and monumental cities built on the Andean peaks to touch the sun god. To the amazement of European mathematicians, they had masterful systems of numeration and computation, archives and records for general use, and an unremitting veneration for public works, whose masterpiece was the garden of the imperial palace with its life-size trees and animals, all of gold and silver. The Aztecs and Mayas molded their historical consciousness into sacred pyramids among active volcanoes, and they had clairvoyant emperors, celebrated astronomers, and skilled artisans who overlooked the industrial uses of the wheel but utilized it in children's toys.

At the juncture of the two great oceans lay a territory of forty thousand square leagues, barely glimpsed by Columbus on his fourth voyage although today it bears his name: Colombia. For some ten thousand years it had been inhabited by scattered communities with different languages, distinct cultures, and their own well-defined identities. They had no notion of the state or of political cohesion but had discovered the political miracle of living as equals despite their differences. They possessed ancient systems of science and education, and a rich cosmology linked to brilliant metalwork and inspired pottery. In their creative maturity, they had aspired to incorporate art into daily life—perhaps the supreme destiny of the arts—and achieved their goal with remarkable success, in household utensils as well as in the way they lived. For them, gold and precious gems did not have exchange value but cosmological and artistic power, although the Spaniards viewed them with Western eyes: more than enough gold and gems to leave the alchemists idle and pave the streets of heaven with pieces of four. This was the motive and force behind the Conquest and the Colonization, and the real origin of what we are. A century went by before the Spaniards shaped the colonial state with one name, one language, one god, and the same borders and political division into twelve provinces that it has today. Which gave rise, for the first time, to the notion of a centralized, bureaucratic nation, creating out of colonial lethargy the illusion of national unity. Sheer illusion in a society that was an obscurantist model of racial discrimination and larval violence beneath the cloak of the Holy Office. The cruelty of the conquistadors, and the unknown diseases they brought with them, reduced the three or four million Indians encountered by the Spaniards to no more than a million. But the racial mixing known as mestizaje had already become a demographic force that could not be contained. The thousands of African slaves brought here against their will for barbaric labor in mines and on plantations contributed a third notable element to the criollo crucible, with new rituals of imagination and memory and other, distant gods. But the Laws of the Indies imposed millimetric standards of segregation according to the degree of white blood in each race: several categories of mestizos, black slaves, free blacks, varying classifications of mulattoes. It became possible to distinguish as many as eighteen different degrees of mestizos, and the white Spaniards even set their own children apart, calling them criollo whites. Mestizos were not permitted to fill certain high positions in government, to hold other public offices, or to enroll in secondary schools and seminaries. Blacks lacked everything, even a soul; they did not have the right to enter heaven or hell, and their blood was deemed impure until distilled by four generations of whites. Because of how difficult it was to determine the intricate demarcation lines between races, and given the very nature of the social dynamic that created mestizaje, such laws could not be enforced with too much rigor, yet racial tensions and violence increased. Until just a few years ago the children of unmarried couples were still not admitted to secondary schools in Colombia. Blacks have achieved legal equality but still suffer many forms of discrimination in addition to the ones peculiar to poverty.

The generation that won independence lost the first opportunity to eradicate this deplorable legacy. The group of young romantics inspired by the enlightenment of the French Revolution established a well-intentioned modern republic but could not eliminate these vestiges of colonialism. Even they were not free of its evil influence. At the age of thirty-five, Simon Bolivar ordered the execution of eight hundred Spanish prisoners, even those lying wounded in a hospital. Francisco de Paula Santander was twenty-eight when he gave the order to shoot thirty-eight Spaniards, including their commanding officer, who had been captured at the Battle of Boyaca. In an indirect way, some of the virtuous aims of the republic fostered new social tensions between poor and rich, laborers and artisans, and other marginal groups. The savage civil wars of the nineteenth century were an outgrowth of these inequalities, as were the countless political upheavals that have left a trail of blood throughout our history. Two innate abilities have helped U.S. to elude our calamitous fate, to compensate for the gaps in our cultural and social circumstances and carry on a fumbling search for our identity. One is a talent for creativity, the supreme expression of human intelligence. The other is a fierce commitment to self-improvement. Enhanced by an almost supernatural shrewdness, and as likely to be used for good as for evil, they were a providential resource employed by the Indians against the Spaniards from the very day they landed. To get rid of Columbus they sent him from island to island, always on to the next island, to find a king covered in gold who never existed. They deceived the conquistadors, already beguiled by novels of chivalry, with descriptions of fantastic cities built of pure gold, right there, on the other side of the hill. They led them astray with the tale of a mythical El Dorado who covered his body with gold dust once a year and plunged into his sacred lagoon. Three masterpieces of a national epic, used by the Indians as an instrument of survival. Perhaps another of the pre-Columbian talents that we have inherited is an extraordinary flexibility in adapting without delay to any environment and learning with ease the most dissimilar trades: fakirs in India, camel drivers in the Sahara, English teachers in New York.

On the other hand, a trait that may come from the Spanish side is our congenital status as immigrants with a spirit of adventure that seeks out risks rather than avoiding them. Of the five million or so Colombians who live abroad, the immense majority left to seek their fortune with nothing but their temerity, and today they are everywhere, for good reasons or bad, for better or worse, but never unnoticed. The distinguishing Colombian trait in world folklore is that they never let themselves die of hunger. Even more striking is that the farther away they are from Colombia, the more Colombian they become.

This is true. They have assimilated the customs and languages of others and made them their own but have never been able to shake the ashes of nostalgia from their hearts, and they miss no opportunity to express this with every kind of patriotic ceremony, exalting all that they long for in the distant homeland, even its defects.

In the most unexpected countries you can turn the corner and find a living replica of any spot in Colombia: the square, its dusty trees still hung with paper garlands from the last Friday night party; the little restaurant named for an unforgotten town, with the heartbreaking aromas of Mama's kitchen; the July 20 school next to the August 7 tavern that plays music for crying over the sweetheart who never was.

The paradox is that, like their forebears, these nostalgic conquistadors were born in a country of closed doors. The liberators tried to open them to fresh winds out of England and France—the legal and ethical theories of Bentham, the education of Lancaster, the study of languages, the popularization of arts and sciences—in order to eradicate the vices of a Spain more Catholic than the Pope and still wary after the financial harassment of the Jews and eight hundred years of Muslim occupation. The nineteenth century radicals, and then the Generation of the Centenary, proposed the same idea with policies of massive immigration aimed at enriching the culture of mestizaje, but all of them were frustrated by our almost theological fear of foreign devils. Even today we have no idea how much we depend on the vast world we know nothing about. We are conscious of our ills but have exhausted ourselves struggling against the symptoms while the causes go on forever. An indulgent version of our history, meant to hide more than it clarifies, has been written for us and made official; in its original sins are perpetuated, battles are won that never were fought, and glories we never deserved are sanctified. In short, we indulge ourselves with the delusion that although history may not resemble the Colombia we live in, one day Colombia will resemble her written history.

In similar fashion, our conformist, repressive education seems designed to force children to adapt to a country that never took them into account, rather than placing the country within their reach and allowing them to transform and enlarge it. The same kind of thoughtlessness inhibits their innate creativity and intuition, thwarts their imaginations and precocious insights, their wisdom of the heart, until children forget what they doubtless knew at birth: that reality does not end where textbooks say it does; that their conception of the world is more attuned to nature than any adult's; that life would be longer and happier if all people could do the work they like and only the work they like.

These intersecting destinies have forged a dense, indecipherable nation where improbability is the only measure of reality. Our banner is excess. Excess in everything:

in good and evil, in love and hate, in the jubilation of victory and the bitterness of defeat. We are as passionate when we destroy idols as when we create them.

We are intuitive people, immediate and spontaneous autodidacts, and pitiless workers, but the mere idea of easy money drives us wild. In our hearts we harbor equal amounts of political rancor and historical amnesia. In sports a spectacular win or defeat can cost as many lives as a disastrous plane crash. For the same reason we are a sentimental society where action takes precedence over reflection, impulsiveness over reason, human warmth over prudence. We have an almost irrational love of life but kill one another in our passion to live. The perpetrator of the most terrible crimes is betrayed by his sentimentality. In other words, the most heartless Colombian is betrayed by his heart.

For we are two countries: one on paper and the other in reality. We are precursors of the sciences in America but still take a medieval view of scientists as hermetic wizards, although few things in daily life are not scientific miracles. Justice and impunity cohabit inside each of us in the most arbitrary way; we are fanatical legalists but carry in our souls a sharp-witted lawyer skilled at sidestepping laws without breaking them, or breaking them without being caught. We adore dogs, carpet the world with roses, are overwhelmed by love of country, but we ignore the disappearance of six animal species each hour of the day and night because of criminal depredations in the rain forest, and have ourselves destroyed beyond recall one of the planet's great rivers. We grow indignant at the nation's negative image abroad but do not dare admit that often the reality is worse. We are capable of the noblest acts and the most despicable ones, of sublime poems and demented murders, of celebratory funerals and deadly debauchery. Not because some of us are good and others evil, but because all of us share in the two extremes. In the worst case—and may God keep us from it—we are all capable of anything.

Perhaps deeper reflection would allow us to determine to what extent our character comes from our still being essentially the same clannish, formalistic, introverted society that we were in colonial times. Perhaps calmer reflection would allow us to discover that our historical violence is the force left over from our eternal war against adversity. Perhaps we are perverted by a system that encourages us to live as if we were rich while forty percent of the population exists in abject poverty, that fosters in us an elusive, instantaneous notion of happiness: we always want a little more of what we already have, more and more of what once seemed impossible, much more of what the law allows, and we obtain it however we can, even if that means breaking the law. Realizing that no government can satisfy these desires, we have become disbelieving, non-participatory, ungovernable, and characterized by a solitary individualism that leads all of us to think we depend only on ourselves. More than enough reason to go on asking ourselves who we are and by which face we wish to be known in the third millennium.

GABRIEL GARCIA MARQUEZ, Nobel Laureate in literature, is the author of many novels, among them *One Hundred Years of Solitude* and *Love in the Time of Cholera,* and is a Columbian.

EXPLORING THE ISSUE

Is Christopher Columbus's Reputation as a Positive Force in World History Still Merited?

Critical Thinking and Reflection

1. What does Robert Royal mean when he writes: ". . . the world we know began in the Fifteenth Century?" Analyze and critically discuss.
2. Recounting Columbus's first contact with the "natives," Gabriel Garcia Marquez writes: "Those splendid ornaments, and not their human values, condemned the natives to their roles as protagonists in the second Genesis which began that day." What does he mean? Critically discuss.
3. Evaluate the global culture Columbus's voyages initiated in the fifteenth century. What implications flow from the expansion of the "known world" these voyages made possible. Research and debate this question.
4. Analyze the transition from a Eurocentric to a more inclusionary and multicultural view of history that has taken place among the past generation of historians. What are the implications of having potentially many points of view? Critically discuss.
5. Based on what you have read, is it fair to hold Columbus personally responsible for the transatlantic slave trade, the annihilation of Native American populations, and the ecological destruction of large portions of the Western Hemisphere? Make both the positive and negative arguments.
6. Would Europe have been better off had it followed China's example and closed down its voyages of exploration in the fifteenth century (see Issue Was Zen Buddhism the Primary Influence on the Japanese Samurai?). Critically analyze and discuss.
7. Would the Americas have been better off if Columbus had not "discovered" them in the fifteenth century? Eventually, some nation would have found its way to this great land mass. Construct several counterfactual scenarios, imagining alternative voyages of discovery.

Is There Common Ground?

Though the YES selection and the NO selection have different points of view—European and Mesoamerican—they both admire the spirit of adventure that Columbus's voyages represent. Do you believe the forces that inspire exploration create dynamic cultures that are more likely to prosper? If so, is the prosperity worth the harm to "native" populations? Robert Royal, while acknowledging negatives, finds these voyages of discovery to be one of what are sometimes called the "hinges of history," swinging the future in a different direction. Gabriel Garcia Marquez might agree that this age of discovery was a "hinge of history." However, he would see it swinging in a dramatically different direction.

As an exercise in exploring point of view, describe Columbus's voyages from the decades-later point of view of a sailor on one of his sailing vessels; then, describe them from the point of view of one of the "natives" on the beach. At "first contact," much was yet to unfold. Were there other significant choices along the way that might have changed the course of history? What if Europe had not had a fierce appetite for gold? What if the Spanish monarchs, like their counterparts in China, had decided to withdraw funding for future voyages of exploration?

Question: Do you think there were many decision points along the way that might have spared the Americas some of the worst of foreign exploitation and imperialism?

Additional Resources

The post-quincentennial Columbus years have produced a large volume of works on the subject of voyages of exploration. Some of those on the negative side of the admiral's contributions to world history include Basil Davidson, *The Search for Africa: History, Culture, Politics* (Random House, 1994)—that contains a chapter entitled "The Curse of Columbus"—which blames him for the horrors of the transatlantic slave trade. David Stannard, *American Holocaust: Columbus and the Conquest of the New World* (Oxford University Press, 1992) goes so far as to hold Columbus responsible for the genocidal acts committed against Native American populations. Kirkpatrick Sale's *The Conquest of Paradise: Christopher Columbus and the Columbian Legacy*.(Penguin Books, 1991) takes a more philosophical approach, but still considers Columbus's legacy to be a negative one, especially as far as the environment is concerned.

Columbus has not been without support. The late Italian historian Paolo Emilio Taviani (1913–2001), in *Columbus: The Great Adventure: His Life, His Times, and His Voyages* (Orion Books, 1991) makes a passionate plea for history to view the positive side of the Columbus legacy. Several articles do the same, including: Robert Royal, "Columbus as a Dead White Male: The Ideological Underpinnings of the Controversy over 1492," *The World and I* (December 1991); Dinesh D'Sousa, "The Crimes of Christopher Columbus," *First Things* (November 1995); and Michael Marshall, "Columbus and the Age of Exploration," *The World and I* (November 1999).

Internet References . . .

Columbus and the Age of Discovery

This university-run website includes a "computerized informational retrieval system" which contains 1,100 text articles related to Christopher Columbus.

http://muweb.millersville.edu

Selected, Edited, and with Issue Framing Material by:
Helen Buss Mitchell, *Howard Community College*
and
Joseph R. Mitchell, *Howard Community College*

ISSUE

Was Gender a Major Issue in Queen Elizabeth I of England's Reign?

YES: Retha Warnicke, from "Elizabeth I: Gender, Religion and Politics," *History Review* (September 2007)

NO: Susan Doran, from "Elizabeth I: Gender, Power & Politics," *History Today* (May 2003)

Learning Outcomes

After reading this issue you should be able to:

- Recount the accomplishments of Elizabeth I during her long reign.
- Explain the criticisms made of her style and decision making.
- Describe some of the challenges of being one of England's first woman monarchs.
- Define the key features of patriarchy and gender roles.

ISSUE SUMMARY

YES: Professor and author Retha Warnicke argues that gender was a major issue in Elizabeth I's reign.

NO: Lecturer and author Susan Doran argues that Elizabeth I's gender had less impact on her reign than is generally assumed.

As we begin our exploration of the role of gender during the reign of Queen Elizabeth I, let's take a look at the context in which she lived and reigned. Elizabethan society was strongly patriarchal, meaning that in ordinary worldly affairs men ruled. Women were regarded as "the weaker sex," not just in terms of physical strength, but also emotionally. The common assumption was that women needed direction from men. If they were married, their husband was expected to look after them. If they were single, then their father, brother, or another male relative was expected to take care of them and direct their lives.

Marriage and motherhood were considered a woman's primary, if not exclusive, occupations. Children were seen as blessings from God, and Tudor women took great pride in being mothers. On average, a woman gave birth to a child every two years during their two or three decades of fertility; however many babies and young children died in childhood. Although many women in this period were, like the Queen, highly educated, their education came by way of private tutors. Women were barred from schools and universities, as well as from the professions of law, medicine, and politics.

No wonder Elizabeth was constantly pressured to marry and bear an heir. She was clearly not conforming to gender expectations. However, she was well aware that marriage and motherhood would compromise or destroy her autonomy and her royal power. Her strategy was to assume an androgynous gender role that included both masculine and feminine elements. In her famous speech to the troops who had gathered at Tilbury for the landing of the Spanish Armada, Queen Elizabeth played both gender roles: "I know I have the body but of a weak and feeble woman; but I have the heart and stomach of a king, and of a king of England too . . . I myself will take up arms, I myself will be your general, judge, and rewarder of every one of your virtues in the field."

William Shakespeare, who was fortunate to have the Queen as a patron, gave his audiences strong female characters. Like Elizabeth, the heroines of his romantic comedies—Beatrice in *Much Ado About Nothing*, Rosalind in *As You Like It*, and Viola in *Twelfth Night*—reflect this blend of femininity and masculinity. Although they are at times bound by the gender conventions of the day, they are also very self-aware; they speak up and move around in the world, often in the woods rather than in their fathers' or husbands' houses. Ironically, women were not allowed to act on the public stage. Acting was considered dishonorable for women and in Shakespeare's plays the roles of women were often played by young boys. A 2002 poll conducted by the British Broadcasting Corporation (BBC) selected Queen Elizabeth I (1558–1603) as England's most admired monarch. Three years earlier, in an issue which surveyed the last millennium, *Time* magazine selected her as the sixteenth century's "Person of the Century." Long a popular subject for historians, novelists, poets, filmmakers, and television series producers, the Queen's media accolades should have surprised no one. But, was all this attention deserved?

Elizabeth was the daughter of King Henry VIII and Anne Boleyn, a woman the king eventually had executed for treason. Her childhood and formative years were filled with isolation, uncertainty, and fear. And when her half sister Mary Tudor attempted to recreate England as a Catholic state (her father had made it into a Protestant one) there was great danger that Elizabeth would be murdered to prevent her from succeeding to the throne.

But succeed she did and for 45 years she steered the English ship-of-state through the turbulent waters of national politics, religious divisiveness, political intrigues, and international diplomacy. When she was finished she had survived the court plots and cabals that threatened her reign, going so far as to execute those whom she viewed as dangerous to her and to the state. She firmly established the Church of England as the national church, navigating through opposition from Catholics, and some Protestants, who felt the English church was not Protestant enough. When one of the English Church cardinals disagreed with her, she had him dismissed. Finally, she masterfully protected English interests throughout the world, using force only when absolutely necessary. If there was any doubt about recognizing England as a European power, the defeat of the Spanish Armada in 1588 settled that. She also was responsible for the development of English sea power which led to the development of colonies; the British Empire was a product of these endeavors.

But Elizabeth was far from perfect. One historian referred to her as a bully and a show-off, and there were many complaints, especially during her later years, due to her indecisiveness in dealing with problems and implementing policies. Could these criticisms have originated as complaints by male counselors about a queen to whom they may have felt superior?

Elizabeth accomplished all she did as a female operating in a patriarchal world. England had never had such a strong woman monarch, and if fate had made this a necessity, both political advisors and church leaders expected her to heed their sage advice and turn it into policy. Much of Elizabeth's time and energy was spent finding a consensus to implement her policies and not those of her counselors. Her ability to do that may have been her most outstanding accomplishment.

She also chose not to marry, for fear that a husband might inhibit her ability to rule. Although constantly urged by counselors to wed, she never did, choosing instead to devote all her energies to England and its people (and to retain her freedom).

The role gender played in Elizabeth's rule frames this issue. Examining the leading political and religious issues of the day, Retha Warnicke finds that gender was a major factor in Elizabeth's reign. Examining the same issues, Susan Doran argues that gender had less impact on her rule than is generally assumed.

YES 

Retha Warnicke

Elizabeth I: Gender, Religion and Politics

A Patriarchal Society

In 1558, when Elizabeth I became the third queen regnant of the British Isles, the prevailing models for her reign were not propitious. The first queen regnant, Mary Stewart, who succeeded to the Scottish throne in 1542, had faced three rebellions directed against her husbands, who were expected by her subjects to control her realm. Indeed in 1561 Elizabeth had to send an envoy to France to inform Mary, whose first husband, Francis II, had recently died, that her French marriage had led to the Lords of the Congregation's successful revolution in Scotland. Mary Tudor, the second queen regnant, who reigned from 1553 to 1558, also offered a poor marital example. Choosing to wed Philip of Spain, Mary had to squash armed challenges to her authority by rebels concerned about Spanish influence. Addressing this issue in 1554, Parliament found it necessary to enact a statute establishing that queens regnant possessed sovereign powers.

In general females, whether married or single, were viewed as emotional and libidinous, incapable of autonomous political action and biologically inferior to males. Single women—without husbands to advise them and manage their affairs—were looked upon with suspicion and were expected to live under the supervision of male relatives or guardians. That Elizabeth's Church of England joined the Protestant confession, which championed women's vocation as marriage, caused the status of the already marginalised single woman to begin to decline even further.

It was in this patriarchal atmosphere that Elizabeth succeeded to the throne. Clearly, her royal status exempted her from many female handicaps, but she had to govern a realm in which crown and church office-holders were mostly male and to negotiate the prevailing view that monarchs ought to be kings. In 1565 Sir Thomas Smith, equating the reign of a female ruler to that of a king in his minority, stated it was understood that the counsel of wise men would 'supply' her 'defaults'. Some writers argued that because a woman was incapable of controlling her appetites, she was more likely, as queen, to become a tyrant than was a king.

Two recent books have raised questions about whether it mattered that Elizabeth was a female rather than a male ruler. In 1999 Anne McLaren identified Protestants in both England and Scotland, who, seeing that they were to be governed by queens regnant, expected the women not only to listen to their Protestant male councillors' advice but also to heed it. By contrast, in 2005, Natalie Mears denied the existence of any overwhelming evidence proving Elizabeth's councillors treated her differently from a male ruler. Although admitting that she found some gendered criticisms of Elizabeth, Mears dismissed them as infrequent or occasional. Gender was not the major issue; religion was.

The Church

It seems appropriate to look at a few of Elizabeth's problems to determine whether her gender figured in her relationship with her councillors. In 1559, when she summoned Parliament, the most pressing issue was the religious settlement. The Church had gone through several changes since Henry VIII had become the Supreme Head of the Church. In his son Edward VI's reign, the royal headship continued and parliaments authorised English prayer books and denied Christ's bodily presence in the Eucharist. Following Mary Tudor's accession, her parliaments revoked these statutes, restoring papal allegiance and the Catholic mass. These various statutes reflected the monarchs' personal beliefs.

From the passage of the Acts of Uniformity and Supremacy in 1559, writers have questioned the nature of Elizabeth's faith. Although recognising that her denial of papal power meant she adhered to some kind of Protestantism, they believed the compromises leading to those statutes' enactment made it unlikely they wholly mirrored her beliefs. That the statutes authorised an English prayer book displeased not only the Catholics, who preferred the Latin mass, but also some Protestants, who thought the reformed service contained too much ritual, such as the sign of the cross in christenings. Mostly Protestants did agree with the Catholics, however, that a woman should not possess the Church's headship.

Since women were allowed neither to deliver the sacraments nor to preach and were expected to remain silent in their parish churches, how then could the queen become the head of the Church? Elizabeth's legislators set out to ensure she would have no sacerdotal function, but since someone had to select the ecclesiastics and monitor the Church's general well-being, they agreed to place her in charge, settling on the title of Supreme Governor instead of the headship.

As Protestants sometimes associated the headship with the papacy, they found attractive the alternative status of governor, and Elizabeth, who on some religious issues, such as her hostility to clerical marriage, was more conservative than many of her ministers, seemed content with the lesser title. Mostly, it made no difference to her exercise of administrative powers, but some of her councillors remained uneasy with her meddling in religious matters. In 1560, Robert Jones wrote to Sir Nicholas Throckmorton, the English ambassador to France, about a recent conversation with Sir William Cecil. The latter had criticised Jones for revealing to Elizabeth the ambassador's views on the Council of Trent. Cecil had admonished Jones for telling the queen 'a matter of such weight, being too much, he said, for a woman's knowledge'.

In addition, preachers, even at court, gave sermons in which they claimed to be messengers sent by God to remind Elizabeth of her Christian obligations. The Scottish minister John Knox is well known for lecturing, like an Old Testament Prophet, to Mary Stewart at Edinburgh about court frivolities, but English preachers also warned Elizabeth that God could send ambassadors to punish monarchs in defiance of His law. Especially were they contemptuous of her mild nature, characterising her as a sheep and demanding she aggressively pursue military endeavors, thereby denouncing qualities contemporaries identified as feminine.

Elizabeth's disagreements with her first two archbishops of Canterbury, Matthew Parker and Edmund Grindal, and other ecclesiastics are well known. She expected them to enforce, on their own authority and not hers, laws they disliked, such as requiring clerics to wear vestments reminiscent to some of Catholic uniforms. A dispute over prophesyings with Grindal is especially noteworthy. Ministers seeking further reform wanted to develop a preaching clergy and began scheduling meetings, called prophesyings, to offer instruction in sermon-giving and in Biblical exegesis. After learning that some disaffected preachers were using them to promote beliefs contrary to Church doctrine, Elizabeth denounced the prophesyings as subversions of the ecclesiastical hierarchy. Disagreeing with her, Grindal viewed them, if properly managed, as useful methods for continuing Church reform. When the frustrated queen demanded he suppress the prophesyings in 1577, he refused. He informed her in a letter that she should take advice from her bishops, since bishops had judged Roman emperors, not emperors the bishops. He continued: 'Remember Madam, that you are a mortal creature', and 'although ye are a mighty prince . . . he which dwelleth in heaven is mightier'. While conceding she was a mighty prince, Grindal addressed her as Madam, not as Your Majesty. Ignoring the pleas of her privy councillors, Elizabeth suspended him from office.

Marriage

Another troubling issue was the possibility of Elizabeth's marriage. Her councillors agreed she should seek a husband but, as she explained to Parliament in 1559, when she was 25 years old, it would suffice her to have engraved on her tombstone that she had lived and died a virgin. She promised that if God determined she should wed, she would take care to choose a spouse who would not prejudice her realm. In 1566, seven years later, she was still assuring Parliament that although she was personally not inclined to marry, she would do so:

> I will marry as soon as I can conveniently, if God take not him away with whom I mind to marry, or myself, or else some other great let [hindrance] happen. And I hope to have children; otherwise, I would never marry.

Her speeches troubled her subjects because, despite some of her well-known courtships, she did not aggressively move to complete arrangements with a suitor. After her sister's accession, although also denying she wished to take a husband, Mary had quickly chosen Philip of Spain and ordered her councillors to negotiate their marriage treaty.

The problem was as Hugh Latimer had explained it in a sermon at Edward VI's court. If the king were succeeded by one of his half-sisters and she married a foreigner, England's diplomacy would be tied to his native land. After Mary wed Philip and agreed to join Spain in the French war in which Calais was lost, some critics blamed his influence. The assumption was that a wife, even a queen regnant, would relinquish her authority to her husband. By contrast, a king who wed a foreigner could easily reject the alliance underpinning their marriage because he remained in control of his realm. In 1516, in *The Education of a Christian Prince,* Erasmus warned against these unions since they often fostered warfare rather than peace—his example was the union of Margaret Tudor and James IV, which did not prevent James from invading England and meeting death at Flodden Field in 1513.

To return to Latimer's sermon, if one of Edward's half-sisters wed a subject, he would almost certainly foster discord in the realm by favouring his allies. Norman Jones has argued that when rumors spread in 1560 about Elizabeth's possible marriage to Lord Robert Dudley, his powers at court were greatly strengthened against his rival, William Cecil. Jones concluded about queens regnant: 'Any man to whom they were attracted acquired through the possibility of marriage inordinate power in the realm; the sort of power no mistress could ever achieve, since men were allowed to be out in the world.' In other words, men could more easily than women promote their political agendas.

Her rumoured relationship with Dudley caused Elizabeth other problems. While without worrying about blemishing their honour, kings could beget illegitimate children, queens regnant could not take lovers without besmirching their reputations and becoming the subject of gossip and innuendo. In France, in late 1560, Ambassador Throckmorton was so incensed by the rumours circulating about Elizabeth's affection for Dudley that he sent a messenger to warn her bluntly she was gravely damaging her honour. Elizabeth's father had ennobled his illegitimate son as duke of Richmond, and courted his next wife before beheading or divorcing the wife he already had, without eliciting such disapproval from his courtiers.

Elizabeth decided never to marry, of course, and scholars are still debating when she first arrived at that conclusion. Some claim it was in 1559 when she informed her Parliament she preferred the single life. Others think she seriously entered into courtships until 1582, the year the one with Francis, duke of Anjou, ended. Contemporaries also held opinions about her intentions. In March 1564 Elizabeth's Scottish ambassador, Thomas Randolph, expressed the fear to Cecil that she had decided not to marry, and later that year Sir James Melville, a Scottish ambassador in England, opined she would not take a husband because she wanted to be both king and queen.

It is likely that her decision not to marry was for political rather than personal reasons. As a single woman, she would not have to allow a husband access to her apartments, thus avoiding any possible duplication of the Scottish queen's experience. Because Mary Stewart had refused to relinquish regal powers to her second husband, Lord Henry Darnley, he invited assassins into her supper room in 1566 to imprison her and kill her allegedly influential secretary. Remaining unwed, Elizabeth could also avoid the seemingly inevitable rebellions against a queen regnant's authority when she chose a husband.

Mary Queen of Scots

Another of Elizabeth's problems was how to treat her Scottish cousin. After James Hepburn, earl of Bothwell, seized and raped Mary in 1567, she wed him, the usual reaction of abducted early-modern heiresses. Some of her subjects, appalled by Bothwell's advancement, imprisoned her and forced her to abdicate in favour of her son, James. When she escaped in 1568 and her army met defeat on the battlefield, she fled to England. Although officially failing to declare Mary guilty of a crime, Elizabeth imprisoned her Catholic cousin, while permitting her young son, James, guided by his Protestant regent, James, earl of Moray, to continue as king of Scotland.

Subsequently, Mary became involved in various conspiracies to escape captivity.

As McLaren pointed out, Elizabeth's Protestant advisors expected her to seek and heed their advice. Nowhere is this more evident than in issues concerning the Scottish queen. In 1568 Sir Francis Knollys, Elizabeth's maternal cousin by marriage and the treasurer of the chamber (later of the household), became Mary's custodian. He was surprised to hear a suggestion of Mary's agent, John Leslie, bishop of Ross, apparently with Elizabeth's approval, for Mary's joint governance of Scotland with James. Knollys wrote to Elizabeth that he was astonished she had let her judgement be ruled by the 'affections and passions' dominating her thoughts and warned her to consult with her faithful councillors, whose opinion should be given the most weight in treating these difficult matters. He reminded Elizabeth of her duty to support James's Protestant regent and speculated that Mary would be too stubborn to move to her next designated residence if Elizabeth appeared too tender and soft, qualities his contemporaries identified as feminine. Early the next year, after learning about Elizabeth's dealings with Alvarez de Toledo, duke of Alva, regent of the Netherlands and Mary's ally, Knollys explained to his queen that she should turn those difficult foreign policy matters over to her council resident for resolution and warned that her councillors could not govern England unless she accepted their advice.

Meanwhile, the imprisoned Mary agreed to wed Thomas, fourth duke of Norfolk, as part of a plot calling for her recognition as Elizabeth's heir. In northern England in 1569, Charles Neville, sixth earl of Westmorland, and Henry Percy, eighth earl of Northumberland, fomented an unsuccessful rebellion, later called the Northern Rising, denouncing Protestantism and supporting Mary's English claims. Upon learning that the rebellion was suppressed, Elizabeth, concerned about military expenses, dismissed most of the troops raised to combat the rebels. In response, her maternal cousin, Henry Carey, first Lord Hunsdon and governor of Berwick, wrote angrily to her, surmising that she must have been bewitched and asserting her need to seek counsel from her trusted friends.

This plain speaking was most evident in these relatives' correspondence, but others could also be blunt. In 1571 Cecil, then ennobled as Lord Burghley, discovered evidence of the Ridolfi Plot, proposing Catholic armies invade England and release the Scottish queen. This plot included Mary's marriage to Norfolk, who planned to rule England with her. Norfolk was condemned as a traitor in January 1572 and beheaded in June; the Parliament demanding his execution also called for Mary's death. One of its members, Thomas Digges, warned that Elizabeth's faithful subjects would withdraw their allegiance from her if she failed to heed their request to condemn Mary for her crimes.

Until 1586 Elizabeth ignored her legislators' and councillors' demands that she have Mary tried for treason. In July of that year, a letter Anthony Babington wrote to Mary, promising to obtain troops to free her and then to send six men to assassinate Elizabeth, was intercepted by a spy of her secretary, Sir Francis Walsingham. It was read, copied, and sent on to Mary. In her intercepted, ciphered response to Babington, which no longer exists, Mary allegedly placed Elizabeth's assassination before her own release from prison. Yet this change in Babington's proposed sequence is not credible since Mary had long feared that if Elizabeth died first, even of natural causes, then her English custodian would kill his captive. All historians agree Walsingham's secretary recopied her ciphered letter and added a postscript, requesting the names of the six assassins. His recopied version, not Mary's original, went to Babington. It is likely Walsingham's secretary added references in it to Elizabeth's assassination, thereby creating the sequence Mary would have rejected. Probably, in her original response, she discussed only the part of Babington's plot that involved her release, leaving Elizabeth's death for others to arrange.

Walsingham carefully nurtured the conspiracy, waiting to arrest Babington until after Mary responded to his letter. Walsingham's motive was to force Elizabeth's hand, since he concluded that the only way to persuade her to heed her councillors' advice was to make it appear Mary had agreed to her English cousin's assassination. The reason Elizabeth was reluctant to approve regicide was that she, like other rulers, believed that monarchs were God's lieutenants on earth with special destinies to fulfill and were responsible only to God for their actions. A monarch's public execution would challenge the validity of the political hierarchy and make other sovereigns' lives vulnerable at a time when Protestant preachers were warning that God would send ambassadors to punish monarchs who disobeyed His law, as they defined it. Meanwhile, Elizabeth justified her leniency on the basis that she followed a woman's code of honour emphasising mercy rather than justice.

Calling Mary a murderess, Elizabeth appointed a commission to try her. After her conviction, Parliament asked Elizabeth twice for Mary's execution, agreeing with the commissioners' recommendation of the death penalty for her. As is well known, Elizabeth reluctantly signed the death warrant; the privy council ordered it delivered without her knowledge, and Mary was beheaded. Would Elizabeth's father have delayed so long? Probably not, and some of Elizabeth's councillors believed she was too soft, that is feminine, in matters concerning her cousin.

Afterwards, Burghley began to worry about Elizabeth's willingness to wield her regal powers. Paul E. J. Hammer has pointed out that, as a female monarch, Elizabeth's ongoing 'great fear' was that her greatest male subjects would unite against her and attempt to control crown policies, as they actually did when engineering Mary's execution. Elizabeth responded to their success in 1587, according to Burghley, with threats to use her prerogative to execute those involved in her cousin's death. In a letter to an anonymous correspondent, Burghley made the following gendered statement about Elizabeth's decision to seek legal advice concerning her prerogative:

> I would be loath to see a woman of such wisdom as she is, to be wrongly advised, for fear, and men shall be otherwise punished than law may warrant, with an opinion gotten from the judges that her prerogative is above the law.

As in Grindal's letter, Burghley referred to her as a woman, albeit a wise one, and not as the queen.

The Role of Gender

By the end of Elizabeth's reign, had her success as queen regnant significantly changed the cultural attitudes about a woman ruler? The answer is no, since her status was viewed as an exception to the appropriate practice. Later, after the Stuart succession, some writers did recall her governance with nostalgia. In the mid-1590s, however, as most historians agree, the factional politics emerging at the aged queen's court somewhat decreased her powers. One of the factions was led by Robert Devereux, second earl of Essex, and the other by Burghley, who had gained a dominant political position, and by his son Robert Cecil, who is well known for describing Elizabeth as 'more than a man and in truth somewhat less than a woman'. Hammer has argued that the two factions were struggling for control of crown policies, as well as patronage. Angered by Elizabeth's habit of delaying difficult decisions, as well as by Burghley's dominance, Essex referred privately to her as the 'Juno to his Aeneas', meaning she 'embodied a perverse female opposition' to him, the popular military leader. Essex also was willing 'to act behind her back', a defiance leading to his execution in 1601. After Elizabeth's death, the reformed preacher Henry Hooke welcomed James I as king with the comment: the 'elect might hope that what was not possible for a woman to effect, a man should be both able and industrious to perform'.

These incidents indicate that gender was a major issue in Elizabeth's reign. Most of her councillors were not as directly critical as her relatives, Knollys and Hunsdon, but many, like Essex, demonstrated impatience with the aged queen's governance. It is also true that the myriad problems arising from religious controversies, Elizabeth's single status, Mary Stewart's captivity and factional politics were extremely difficult to resolve. For the most part, the queen's tactic of delaying decisions about them was probably politically wiser than accepting her male councillors' 'solutions'.

Retha Warnicke is an expert on gender issues in the Early Modern Period (1400–1700) and the author of numerous articles. Her books include *The Marrying of Anne of Cleves: Royal Protocol in Tudor England* (Cambridge, 2000) and *Mary, Queen of Scots* (Routledge, 2006).

Susan Doran

Elizabeth I: Gender, Power & Politics

Judging from the results of last year's BBC television poll of Great Britons, Elizabeth I is the best known and most admired English monarch, at least among those members of the public who decided to vote. Given her high profile in films and biographies, the Queen's relative success in the poll is perhaps unsurprising, especially as her life was so full of incident and drama. The evidence suggests, however, that it was specifically Elizabeth's ability as a woman to exercise power successfully in a man's world that earned her the votes and commanded the respect of today's viewers; she scored highest on her bravery and leadership qualities, while the comments of her supporters, as reported on the BBC website, emphasised her difficulties as a female ruler and her role as 'the ultimate British feminist icon'.

Recent academic opinion is usually less kind to Elizabeth. Christopher Haigh has described her as a bully and a showoff, while Susan Brigden seems to share the Elizabethan Council's irritation with their Queen's indecision, prevarications and sometimes faulty judgement. Nonetheless, whatever their views about the character of the Queen, many historians today share the preoccupation with Elizabeth's gender; they tend to stress the problems she faced as a female ruler in the patriarchal sixteenth century and the ways she attempted to circumvent them. I would suggest, however, that these difficulties have been overstated and that Elizabeth's methods of negotiating her gender have been partially misunderstood.

Of course, there is no question that early-modern society was deeply patriarchal in its structure and attitudes. Male primogeniture governed most property arrangements as well as the laws of succession to the crown. In theory, at least, women were not expected to assert any independent authority but were deemed subservient to male relatives whether fathers, brothers or husbands. The Scottish Calvinist preacher John Knox (c.1513–72) famously railed against female monarchy as an abomination in his *The First Blast of the Trumpet against the Monstrous Regiment of Women,* a work written in 1558 to contest Catholic Mary I's right to be queen. Yet, despite patriarchal attitudes, female rule was no great novelty in the sixteenth century; not only had women inherited the thrones of Castile, Scotland and England before Elizabeth's accession, but more importantly they had also been selected to act as regents in Spain, Scotland, the Netherlands and France during the absences of their monarchs. Furthermore, Knox's views were extreme and reiterated by only a handful of other Protestants.

In fact, at the time of Elizabeth's accession, barely a murmur was heard querying the legitimacy of female rule. Catholics at home and abroad presumably did not think to use Knoxian-style arguments to challenge Elizabeth's right to the throne, because their claimant, Mary, Queen of Scots, was also a woman. In general, the prevailing sentiment within England in mid-November 1558 was not concern at the accession of another queen of England, but rather relief that Mary Tudor's reign—marked by harvest failure, epidemics and military humiliation—was now over, and that Elizabeth's succession was smooth and for all practical purposes undisputed without military intervention from France, Scotland or Spain. Protestants were obviously delighted by the new regime: Thomas Becon, who in 1553 had bemoaned the accession of a female ruler as God's punishment towards a 'people unworthy to have lawful, natural and meet governors', now accepted with joy Elizabeth as:

> . . . a most worthy patroness of all true religion and of learning, a most noble defender of all godly-disposed people [and] a noble conqueror of antichrist.

With Elizabeth on the throne, Knox himself hurriedly backtracked, even though he never actually recanted his earlier opinions. Other Protestant theologians, though, explicitly endorsed Elizabeth's right to rule and openly rejected Knox's arguments. In a letter to William Cecil in 1559, John Calvin (1509–64) reasoned that female rule was acceptable in countries where it had been established by law or custom and, furthermore, asserted that in exceptional circumstances God deliberately chose to channel His authority through women rulers, witness the Judge Deborah and prophetess Huldah in the Hebrew Bible. Possibly because Knox's views were not widely held, only two English writers felt impelled during the first years of Elizabeth's reign to write tracts refuting his *First Blast,* and only the work of one of them—John Aylmer's *Harborowe for faithfull and true subiectes*—was published (in 1559). In England, it seems, the monarchy was excluded from patriarchal assumptions and a female monarch was given rights by God which permitted her to rule over men.

Elizabeth justified her right to rule on the non-gendered grounds of the laws of inheritance, her father's will and the 1544 Act of Succession. At the same time, like her grandfather, Henry VII, and half-sister, Mary, she emphasised the role of God in preserving her from danger and placing her on the throne; during the Coronation procession of January 1559 she not only allowed herself to be identified with Deborah, the instrument of Divine Providence, but also compared herself to Daniel, who had been saved from the lion's den. Throughout the reign, Elizabeth claimed the same prerogatives as her male predecessors, adopted the same visual imagery and mottos on her coinage, and participated in traditional royal rituals, adapting them where necessary to suit a female monarch. Thus, on Maundy Thursday she washed the feet of poor women (instead of men) as part of the Easter ceremonies; on the feast of St George, her ladies-in-waiting joined her in the Great Procession with the Knights of the Garter; and she sometimes chose to wear a magnificent gown rather than the customary martial attire. In the 1570s after the papal bull of excommunication, she decided to use the ancient form of royal magic and touch for the King's Evil (to cure the disease of scrofula) in order to emphasise her God-given sovereignty.

Despite the general acceptance of a woman's right to rule, there was at the outset of the reign some uncertainty about the extent to which Elizabeth would exercise power. Aylmer had assumed that the government would be in her name and on her behalf but executed by her Council and Parliament. Her first principal secretary, William Cecil, had initially presumed that the queen would leave the cut and thrust of decision-making to her most important councillors, particularly over areas of policy which fell within the male preserve of diplomacy and international affairs. But Elizabeth immediately made it absolutely clear that she intended to rule in deed as well as in name. She put her stamp on the membership of the Council by appointing several of her relatives and loyal friends, as well as associates of Cecil. Although she agreed to a change in title from Supreme Head to Supreme Governor of the Church of England, she made sure that the new settlement of religion reflected her own religious preferences as much (or more) than those of Protestant theologians or trusted ministers. Those royal injunctions of 1559 which ordered wafers to be used for communion, insisted on clerical dress, and safeguarded church music in cathedrals, were the product of her own desires, and indeed were anathema to most of her advisers. Similarly, royal proclamations of 1560 and 1561 designed to prevent further outbursts of iconoclasm, particularly those which threatened funeral monuments, were the work of her hand.

As time went on, Elizabeth continued to exercise power and to take the final decisions on policy. It was the Queen who prevented influential councillors and members of parliament from passing legislation in the 1560s and 1570s which would have excluded Mary, Queen of Scots, from the throne. Without Elizabeth's protection after 1569, moreover, Mary might well have knelt at the scaffold years before her execution in 1587.

As far as foreign policy is concerned, Elizabeth usually put her weight behind those more cautious councillors who wanted to avoid outright war with Spain during the 1570s and early 1580s and who preferred to follow a policy of giving underhand aid to Protestants abroad while outwardly posing as a mediator in the struggle between Philip II of Spain and his rebellious subjects in the Netherlands. In consequence, despite considerable pressure from Walsingham, Leicester and other zealous Protestants, Elizabeth's government did not send troops to fight against Spain until late 1585.

In religious matters it was largely owing to Elizabeth that the English Church remained only 'halfly' reformed, and that moderate liturgical changes proposed by her bishops and backed by Archbishop Matthew Parker failed to pass through convocation in 1563 and Parliament in 1566. Had a more radical and less assertive monarch been sitting on the throne, a very different Church of England would have emerged in the second half of the sixteenth century.

Baffled by the Queen's failure to see the wisdom of their advice, Elizabeth's advisers often expressed their frustration in the gendered, sometimes misogynistic language of their day. Thus, they would criticise the Queen's feminine irresolution, female fickleness and womanly compassion towards papists and traitors. Nonetheless, their concern was more about what they saw as the Queen's mistaken policies and refusal to listen to good sense than about the inappropriateness of a woman taking decisions. Until at least the mid-1580s their frustration was a measure of Elizabeth's independence and their failure to persuade or browbeat her into following their own particular line of policy.

Elizabeth's independence was made more palatable to her councillors by the style of her leadership. But whether or not the qualities she exhibited in managing her male advisers can be labelled 'feminine' is a moot point, and writers today should really stop making simplistic assertions that Elizabeth capitalised on her 'feminine characteristics' to secure obedience and achieve her goals in statecraft. Like her father, Elizabeth displayed a mixture of radiating charm and unpredictable rages; like him, too, she demanded to be the centre of attention and enjoyed the flattery of courtiers (even if she had the intelligence to see through it). Unlike Henry VIII, though, she was immensely loyal to those she trusted, and men soon realised that they could present her with unwelcome advice without risking their necks. Her frequent refusal to be proactive or pinned down to a particular line of action may have infuriated them, yet this flexibility and apparent indecisiveness always left open the possibility that she might rethink her position and change her mind. Consequently, until the later 1590s, when Elizabeth's skills of political management were waning, there was no need for anyone in the Council or at court to feel permanently excluded from power or entirely cut off from influencing the Queen, unless he unwisely overstepped the mark by questioning her authority.

Historians and literary critics have also suggested that Elizabeth dealt with the problems of her gender by adopting strategies that turned her into the iconic Virgin

Queen: first by deciding to remain unwed and second by fashioning herself into the Virgin Mary for propaganda purposes. Each of these propositions present problems of interpretation. As far as Elizabeth's marriage is concerned, it has become almost a cliché that the Queen was determined to stay single so that she could rule as well as reign. Elizabeth, it is said, had learned this maxim from the sad experiences of Mary, who had allowed political power to slip into the hands of her husband, Philip of Spain, thereby dragging England into the disastrous Habsburg wars against France which resulted in the loss of Calais. Yet there is little evidence that Elizabeth rejected the idea of marriage as a deliberate act of will. On the contrary, far from being totally committed to the single life, Elizabeth on two occasions signalled that she wanted to marry a particular suitor. In 1560 she gave every appearance of being in love with Lord Robert Dudley; in 1579 she demonstrated a strong inclination to wed the French duke, Francis of Anjou. In both instances, however, the fierce opposition to her choice of husband, expressed in Council, at court and in the country at large, led Elizabeth to conclude that she would lose the support of influential subjects and create grave political difficulties if she went ahead with the match. In the case of Dudley, Cecil and other royal servants warned her that marriage to him would seriously damage her reputation and might even imperil her seat on the throne. They were probably right; the widespread rumours that Elizabeth had been involved in an adulterous relationship with her favourite and had conspired with him to murder his wife could only be allayed if she distanced herself from him. As for Anjou, most English Protestants abhorred his religion, disliked his French blood, and believed that Elizabeth's marriage to him would bring the wrath of God down on England. Once again, Elizabeth demonstrated political sense in ultimately rejecting his suit.

Despite the hostility targeted at Dudley and Anjou, Elizabeth was under intense pressure from her councillors and Parliament to end uncertainties about the succession by marrying and giving birth to an heir. Cecil, who had spearheaded the campaign against the Dudley match, found what he thought was a far better marital candidate in the Archduke Charles of Austria, a younger son of the Holy Roman Emperor Ferdinand. The Archduke, argued Cecil, was suitable in terms of his age, lineage and reputation, and would bring England an advantageous diplomatic alliance with the Habsburgs. In his enthusiasm for the match, Cecil persuaded himself that Charles's religion (he was a Catholic) would not prove a barrier to it. Elizabeth, though, was less keen on the Archduke. With Dudley out of the running she preferred to remain single, and besides she had heard unfounded rumours that Charles was deformed. Nonetheless, she found it impossible to withstand the pressure from all sides to marry; after all, the public image she had cultivated was that of a queen devoted to the interests of her subjects, even to the point of self-sacrifice. She therefore could hardly seem to be putting her personal preferences above the dynastic needs of her country. Consequently, in 1564 Elizabeth agreed to open discussions with the Austrians and soon afterwards she authorised envoys and councillors to negotiate a matrimonial treaty. From the start, however, Elizabeth insisted that the marriage had to be on her terms, terms which denied the Archduke any political power in England and compelled him to accompany her to Protestant church services and to forgo a public mass. It should not be thought that Elizabeth stipulated these conditions in order to sabotage the negotiations; Cecil and other supporters of the match also required them as safeguards for England's political interests. Although the Austrians eventually agreed to the articles which excluded Charles from any role in government, the Archduke demanded access to the mass, if only a private one to be held in his own apartment. On this issue the negotiations broke down, for Elizabeth refused to permit any compromise over religion. No doubt she was heartily relieved to have found a get-out clause, but her decision was supported by a number of her councillors as well as her divines and London preachers. Thus, in the end it was the religious question and not gender concerns that caused the collapse of the Archduke Charles matrimonial suit.

The image of Elizabeth as the Virgin Queen was not evident early in the reign, when Elizabeth's hold on power was arguably the least secure, nor was it she herself who first devised the image. The language and iconography of perpetual and powerful virginity first made their appearance during the Anjou matrimonial negotiations of 1578–81 as part of the weaponry employed against the match by its opponents. Thereafter, the figure of Elizabeth as the Virgin Queen gained currency as a courtly fashion with an intent both to flatter, and also in many cases (including that of Edmund Spenser's *Faerie Queene*) to criticise the Queen. Courtiers and poets were the main creators of the image, though certainly Elizabeth helped to promote it in her entertainments at court (such as the 'Four Foster Children of Desire') and in the miniatures she commissioned, where she was portrayed as the goddess Diana or Cynthia. Whenever Elizabeth was depicted or addressed as the Virgin Queen, it is very rare indeed to see any unambiguous allusions to the Virgin Mary. Far more common are the direct iconographic or poetic references to the classical goddesses Diana, Cynthia and Astraea or to Petrarch's chaste maidens, Laura and Tuccia. For all these reasons, there seems to be no case for claiming that Elizabeth appropriated the cult of the Virgin Mary as a strategy to secure acceptance as a female ruler.

Why did representations of Elizabeth as a Virgin Queen become so pervasive in poetry and portraiture during the 1590s? One strong possibility is that this mode of representation was thought a safe and effective way of depicting an elderly woman as a credible military and political leader of a country at war. Elizabeth's impenetrable physical body was a natural metaphor for the impregnable body politic withstanding invasion from a foreign king. At the same time, symbolic associations with the moon-goddesses, Diana, Phoebe and Cynthia, signified both England's sea-power and the Queen's immutability and continuing potency, despite her advancing age.

Arguably, Elizabeth experienced her greatest difficulties with her gender during the last fifteen years of her life, just when the image of her as the allpowerful Virgin Queen was taking hold. Until then, the gendered outbursts of courtiers and councillors had barely affected the tone of political life, as outward deference and respect continued to be shown to the Queen. During the 1570s, moreover, Elizabeth and her courtiers had engaged in chivalric and Renaissance courtly love conventions, made popular through Petrarch's poetry, and had absorbed Castiglione's *Il Cortegiano* (published in English in 1561 and Latin in 1571) as a working model for their behaviour at court. In consequence, Elizabeth's favourites had attended devotedly upon her and courted her with their love-poetry, elegies of praise, fine dancing and skill at the tilt. Christopher Hatton was one of the most successful of the exponents of the courtier's craft, earning his reward in lucrative grants of land and promotion to high office.

During the 1590s, however, disillusionment with Elizabeth's reign appears to have become entrenched, while misogynistic complaints about female rule became more outspoken. Robert Devereux, 2nd Earl of Essex (1566–1601), and other young male courtiers balked at playing the role of ardent and adoring suitors to an ageing and imperious queen. Military men held the monarch's gender responsible for a lack of energy and boldness in the prosecution of the war against Spain. Essex spoke for many of them when he complained in 1597 to a French envoy:

> They laboured under two things at this Court, delay and inconstancy, which proceeded chiefly from the sex of the queen.

At the same time, the presence of an adult male king, James VI of Scotland, waiting to inherit the throne made many of Elizabeth's courtiers impatient to see the end of female rule. John Harington, for example, mused that:

> . . . whensoever God shall call [Queen Elizabeth], I perceive we are not like to be governed by a lady shut up in a chamber from all her subjects and most of her servants, and seen seld but on holidays . . . but by a man of spirit and learning, of able body, of understanding mind.

With a male monarch on the throne, thought Harington, the privy chamber would again be staffed by men, and male courtiers would no longer be denied opportunities for intimacy and advancement.

Undoubtedly, Elizabeth's authority was affected by this new attitude at court. Once out of England, her military commanders flagrantly disobeyed royal instructions. During the Rouen campaign of 1591, for example, Essex conferred no fewer than twenty-four knighthoods in defiance of the Queen's express instructions. More seriously, during the Cadiz campaign of 1596 he planned to seize a base in Spain in total contradiction of Elizabeth's orders, and was only thwarted in his design by his co-commander, Lord Admiral Howard. Part of the problem was that Elizabeth was at a disadvantage in not being able to go in person to the battlefield. As an unmarried queen, moreover, she could not even call on her husband to act as a figurehead in her place, as had her sister Mary at St Quentin. But age was another factor. In the 1590s Elizabeth was old enough to be the grandmother of the new generation of courtiers, many of whom found her out of touch with their culture and aspirations. Their declining respect for their queen was demonstrated in the many sexual scandals that disrupted the court in the 1590s. Not only were a significant number of male courtiers prepared to flout Elizabeth's authority by embarking on illicit sexual relationships with maids of honour, but also every elopement and pregnancy that occurred was a stark reminder of 'her own physical and political sterility'. Nonetheless, despite her age, Elizabeth could on occasions impress observers with her majesty and intelligence: in 1596 her impromptu speech in Latin reprimanding a Polish ambassador who had offended her, so delighted English listeners that it was published; in 1601 her 'Golden Speech' which silenced complaining members of parliament was similarly printed and distributed to the wider populace.

All in all, Elizabeth's gender had less impact on political life than is generally assumed. The key political issues of the day were those that had dominated earlier reigns: religion, the succession and international affairs. While Elizabeth had her own style of leadership, she worked within the same institutional structures and adopted the same royal conventions as earlier monarchs. Even Elizabeth's image was not so very different from that of her male predecessors and contemporary kings; like them she emphasised her regality, religion and role as carer of her people. The part that Elizabeth's conservatism and reliance on tradition played in making female rule acceptable to male subjects should not be forgotten; she provoked no fears that the social and gender hierarchy would be subverted by female monarchy. In this sense, Elizabeth was no feminist icon. Her reign did however demonstrate that a woman could be an exceptionally successful ruler even in dangerous times. In this sense, she was!

Susan Doran is a British historian whose primary studies surround the reign of Elizabeth I, in particular the theme of marriage and succession. She has published and edited 16 books, most notably *Elizabeth I and Religion,* 1558–1603, *Monarchy and Matrimony,* and *Queen Elizabeth I,* part of the British Library's Historic Lives series.

EXPLORING THE ISSUE

Was Gender a Major Issue in Queen Elizabeth I of England's Reign?

Critical Thinking and Reflection

1. Critically examine the gender system during the Elizabethan era. In what ways was Queen Elizabeth able to ignore traditional gender expectations during her reign? In what ways was she forced to negotiate the gender system? Critically analyze and discuss.
2. In your view, were the strong and androgynous heroines of Shakespeare's plays primarily a reflection of the powerful female monarch or were they primarily a support to his patron as she attempted an androgynous approach? Critically research, analyze, and discuss.
3. After reading both selections, how important do you believe Elizabeth's decision not to marry was to her long-term success as a woman ruling in a patriarchal society? Critically analyze and discuss.
4. How might a marriage have compromised Elizabeth's reign? Imagine several scenarios in which the hereditary Queen married and/or produced a male heir to the throne; then, critically apply these counterfactuals to Queen Elizabeth's historical context.
5. What does Retha Warnicke mean when she writes: "By the end of Elizabeth's reign, had her success as Queen Regnant significantly changed the cultural attitude about a woman ruler? The answer is No, since her status was viewed as an exception to the appropriate practice." Critically discuss why you think this could be so?
6. What is the significance of the following statement by Susan Doran: "The part that Elizabeth's conservatism and reliance on tradition played in making female rule acceptable to male subjects should not be forgotten. She provoked no fears that the social and gender hierarchy would be subverted by female monarchs"? Critically discuss.
7. Does having a female ruler or a female president challenge accepted gender stereotypes? Research, analyze, and critically discuss/debate.

Is There Common Ground?

Both authors agree that Elizabeth I of England was a great monarch, deserving all the historical praise and respect she has received. They also agree that being a woman ruling within a patriarchal political system caused many problems for her, most of which she was able to overcome.

The differences expressed in the selections come from what each chooses to emphasize. Warnicke opts to accentuate the patriarchal system and how it made Elizabeth's reign a difficult one. Doran emphasizes Elizabeth's ability to work within the patriarchy to achieve her desired results. She also finds the patriarchy less burdensome to Elizabeth than Warnicke does.

Another difference between Warnicke and Doran is how each views gender as a factor during Elizabeth's rule. Doran finds that the problems Elizabeth faced—religion, the succession, and international affairs—were no different from those that faced her male and female predecessors, and she contends that solutions to them superseded gender. Warnicke emphasizes the political factionalism that existed and how conflicts developed due to gender issues perceived by some of Elizabeth's counselors.

Question: Which elements of the gender system that we explore in this issue remain today and might confront a woman who is a candidate for president of the United States?

Additional Resources

Needless to say, Elizabeth I has been the subject of countless books. Among the noted biographies, three stand out: Alison Weir, *The Life of Elizabeth I* (Ballantine Books, 1999); Anne Somerset, *Elizabeth I* (Anchor Books, 2003); and Christopher Hibbert, *The Virgin Queen: Elizabeth, Genius of the Golden Age* (Da Capo Press, 1992).

Books on the Elizabethan Era which explore the subjects contained in this issue include: Anne McLaren, *Political Culture in the Reign of Elizabeth* (Cambridge University Press, 1999); Natalie Mears, *Queenship and Political Discourse in the Elizabethan Era* (Cambridge University Press, 2005); and Susan Doran and Thomas Freeman, eds., *The Myth of Elizabeth I* (Palgrave, Macmillan, 2003).

Elizabeth has also been the subject of several motion pictures starring leading actresses. Helen Mirren, *Elizabeth I* (2006) and Cate Blanchett, *Elizabeth: The Golden Age* (2007). Finally, a 1972 BBC six-part series *Elizabeth R* (1972) has been reissued on DVD. It offers an interesting and accurate account of Elizabeth's life and work.

Internet References . . .

Queen Elizabeth I

This site features many links to the life, lifestyle, family tree, rule, and power of Elizabeth I. The times are included, with links to Court Life, Elizabethan Europe, and the Tudors. Excellent bibliography.

www.elizabethi.org/us

Selected, Edited, and with Issue Framing Material by:
Helen Buss Mitchell, *Howard Community College*
and
Joseph R. Mitchell, *Howard Community College*

ISSUE

Did Martin Luther's Reforms Improve the Lives of European Christians?

YES: Robert Kolb, from *Martin Luther as Prophet, Teacher, Hero* (Baker Books, 1999)

NO: Hans Küng, from *Martin Luther: Return to the Gospel as the Classical Instance of a Paradigm Shift* (Continuum, 1996)

Learning Outcomes

After reading this issue you should be able to:

- Define and explain the Protestant Reformation, inaugurated by Martin Luther.
- Define and explain the religious wars of the sixteenth and seventeenth centuries in Europe and their roots in strongly held theological differences.
- Define and explain the phenomenon known as a "paradigm shift."

ISSUE SUMMARY

YES: Religion and History Professor Robert Kolb argues that Martin Luther was seen as a prophetic teacher and hero whose life brought hope, divine blessing, and needed correctives to the Christian church.

NO: Theologian and Emeritus Theology Professor Hans Küng argues that Martin Luther was the inaugurator of a paradigm shift and the unwitting creator of both bloody religious wars and an unhealthy subservience by ordinary Christians to local rulers in worldly matters.

When Martin Luther was born in 1483, his father Hans hoped the boy would become a lawyer. Instead, a mystical experience during a thunderstorm led Martin to enter religious life as an Augustinian monk. Scrupulous in observing his religious duties, young Martin became increasingly aware of his own sinfulness and increasingly fearful of divine justice. He came to believe that "fallen" humans, on their own, can never do anything to merit salvation; instead, it is the grace of God alone that "justifies" them.

Sent by his order to teach philosophy at the University of Wittenberg, Luther was appalled at the selling of indulgences (pardon for sin) and denounced the practice, along with other abuses, in 95 theses of protest, addressed to the Archbishop of Mainz in 1517. The invention of the printing press spread his ideas throughout the German states and beyond. Summoned to appear before the Imperial Diet at Worms in 1521, Luther clung to his beliefs, displeasing the emperor and earning himself a condemnation. Hidden by his patron, the Elector Frederick of Saxony, Luther translated the Bible into German, unaware, for the moment, that he had launched a radical, religious revolution.

Eager for reform rather than revolution, Luther sought to modify what he regarded as abuses within the Christian Church. His idealistic intention was to strip the "modern" church of power and corruption and return it to its roots—the pristine days of early Christianity. Certainly he had no intention of founding a new religion. This theological conservatism was matched by his opposition to the Peasants' Revolt of 1524–1525. Siding emphatically with the forces of law and order, Luther urged the princes to put down the rebellion and safeguard the God-given social order. In many ways, he was a reluctant revolutionary.

Lutherans, as they called themselves against Luther's wishes, gathered to read the scriptures in their own language, sing, pray, and listen to a sermon being preached. A widespread anticlerical feeling inspired many to challenge the wealth and influence of what was increasingly seen as an Italian church. Luther's religious alternative was also attractive to those whose feeling of national pride in the semiautonomous German states led them increasingly to resent pronouncements from Rome. Violent conflict between Protestant Princes and Imperial Catholic forces broke out during Luther's lifetime and people were instructed to follow the religion of their local prince—Lutheran or Catholic.

Luther had married a former nun Katherine von Bora and fathered a number of children. Living a family life, like those in his congregation, rather than observing the Catholic requirement for celibacy, Luther must have seemed in some ways much more approachable. Insisting on "the priesthood of all believers," Luther urged his followers to read the scriptures for themselves and find the truth within them. As the tide of Reformation spread to Switzerland, England, and beyond, however, thousands died, and Christianity became increasingly fragmented. At the time of Luther's death in 1546, much of Western Europe was in the process of dissolving centuries-old ties that had bound people and nations into a spiritual and temporal unity called Christendom.

If we admit that reform was needed, the next question becomes: was the reform movement initiated by Luther worth the theological, political, and, especially, the human cost? For religious historian Bernard M. G. Reardon, Luther was a man completely in sync with his time. Although he remained very medieval and unmodern—untouched by the new humanism of people such as the Dutch thinker Erasmus of Rotterdam—Luther was filled with the dynamism that sprang from his spiritual conviction. Believing himself divinely called to a holy mission, Luther was able to inspire others to an intense, personal relationship with the God of history and the redeemer of human frailty and despair.

For centuries after his death, Luther was either effusively praised or roundly condemned. Evangelicals extolled his reforms, whereas Catholics vilified him for destroying the unity that had been Christianity. As passions have cooled and an ecumenical spirit has taken the place of religious bickering, we are beginning to see more balanced accounts of Luther's life and work that credit him with bringing about needed reforms while acknowledging his personal and professional failings.

A good place to begin understanding this complex reformer is with Roland Bainton's much acclaimed biography *Here I Stand: A Life of Martin Luther* (Abingdon,1950). Bainton also profiles Katherine von Bora and other women in *Women of the Reformation in Germany and Italy* (Augsburg, 1971). Jonathan W. Zophy's *A Short History of Renaissance and Reformation Europe: Dances over Fire and Water*, 2nd ed., covers cultural, economic, religious, political, and social developments and includes gender as a significant subject for historical analysis.

Psychologist Erik Erikson wrote a now controversial Freudian interpretation of Luther's motivations *Young Man Luther: A Study in Psychoanalysis and History* (W.W. Norton and Company, 1958). Other biographies include Heiko Oberman's *Luther: Man Between God and the Devil* (Yale University Press, 1989) and Eric Gritsch's *Martin—God's Court Jester: Luther in Retrospect* (Fortress Press, 1983). The latter reflects Luther's name for himself—the sometimes-mocked instrument of God's will on earth—and contains an excellent historiographical chapter "God's Jester Before the Court of History." Perhaps the most respected work is a three-volume biography titled *Martin Luther* by Martin Brecht, translated by James L. Schaaf (Fortress Press, 1985).

Religion and History Professor Robert Kolb contends that Martin Luther was seen as a prophetic teacher and hero whose life brought hope, divine blessing, and needed correctives to the Christian church. Theologian and Emeritus Theology Professor Hans Küng views Martin Luther as the inaugurator of a paradigm shift and as the unwitting creator of both bloody religious wars and an unhealthy subservience by ordinary Christians to local rulers in worldly matters. Is it possible that challenges brought by Erasmus might have brought about a less traumatic, if slower, path to eventual reform that would have left Christianity intact and spared the suffering and death endured by hundreds of thousands. Could Europeans have been spared the bloodshed of the religious wars and bequeathed a more serene history for all of us?

YES

Robert Kolb

Martin Luther as Prophet, Teacher, Hero

Introduction

In an attack published in 1529, Johannes Cochlaeus, Martin Luther's fierce foe and first biographer, characterized the Reformer as having seven heads. Throughout the almost five centuries since then, Luther has been depicted by friend and foe alike as having many more than seven faces. The image makers of his own age began immediately to project into public view a picture which reflected their experience of Luther. Their successors have taken the raw material of his life and thought and cast it into forms which would serve their own purposes—with varying degrees of historical accuracy. Few public figures have enjoyed and suffered the process of publicity as has Martin Luther.

Most ages seize historical personalities as clay from which they mold icons of mythical proportions to embody their values and aspirations. Into the apocalyptically charged atmosphere of late medieval Germany stumbled Martin Luther, whose career coincided with the invention of the medium of print. At the outset of his career, historical and religious conditions, medium, and man came together in a unique manner to begin fashioning a public persona which soon loomed larger than life over the German and western European ecclesiastical landscape. Read in the streets of towns and discussed in the taverns of villages, his own publications and the representations of his thought and person by other pamphleteers produced a cultural paragon which his followers in the sixteenth century put to use in several ways.

In the conclusion to his pioneering assessment of the changing views about the Reformer from Wittenberg, Horst Stephan observed that new images of Luther are always "born out of a new encounter with the testimony of the original image, and they are reflections of his form in water of different depths and different hues." To a degree perhaps unique in the history of the church since the apostolic age, the image of this single person, Martin Luther, has directly shaped the institutions and life of a large body of Christendom. He has influenced his followers both as churchman and as teacher of the church. Calvinist churches, of course, look to John Calvin as model and magister for their ecclesiastical life. John Wesley exercises a continuing role in the Methodist churches. To a far greater extent, however, Lutheran churches have found in Luther not only a teacher but also a prophetic hero and authority. Heinrich Bornkamm's observation extends beyond the borders of the German cultural realm which he was sketching: "Every presentation and assessment of Luther and the Reformation means a critical engagement with the foundations of our more recent history. Like no other historical figure, that of Luther always compels anew a comprehensive reflection on the religious, spiritual, and political problems of our lives."

Since Stephan's study others have examined the interpretation of Luther's thought and work both within and outside Lutheranism. None of these, however, has focused in detail on the ways in which Luther's image and thought shaped Lutheran thinking and action during the century following his appearance on the stage of Western history. From the very beginning Luther's students and friends regarded him as a figure of more than normal proportions. Some saw him as an illustrious hero of the faith. Others regarded him as a powerful doctor of the church in line with Moses, Paul, and Augustine. Many also regarded him as a unique servant of God, a prophet and the eschatological angel who is depicted in Revelation 14 as the bearer of the gospel in the last days and whose authority could be put to use in governing and guiding the church, particularly in the adjudication of disputes over the proper and correct understanding of biblical teaching.

Without taking into account the conceptual framework of biblical humanism on the one hand, and that of late medieval apocalyptic on the other, such images seem strange to us moderns. Within the context of Luther's time, however, they provided vehicles by which people could make sense of Luther's impact on their lives and his role on the stage of human history. With such images of Luther in mind his followers set about to reshape the institutions and ideas which held their world together.

This inquiry will review how Luther's message and his career reshaped sixteenth-century German Lutherans' views of God and human history. Three conceptions of the Reformer emerge, reflecting a variety of needs in his society, which was organized around religious ideas and ecclesiastical institutions and practices. Although all three of these conceptions appeared in the first few years of public comment on Luther, they developed in different ways as the years passed. Their influence can best be presented through a chronological tracking of their evolution as exhibited in representative writings from the pens of his disciples. To be sure, historians' analyses always oversimplify: the categories are not so distinct and discrete that they can be neatly separated from each other.

Thus our discussion of each motif will reveal aspects of the others.

First, for some of his followers during the subsequent decades, the Reformer functioned as a prophet who replaced popes and councils as the adjudicating or secondary authority (interpreting the primary authority, Scripture) in the life of the church. Like almost every age, the late Middle Ages were a period of crisis, and people were rethinking questions of authority in various aspects of life. Within the church Luther's challenge to the medieval papacy heightened the crisis by confirming doubts about the old religious system. Although Luther and his adherents did not discard the ancient fathers of the church nor disregard their usefulness, they did affirm the primacy of biblical authority; for them Scripture was the sole primary source of truth. The church, however, always needs a more elaborate system of determining the meaning of the biblical message; and the tradition, in the hands of popes, bishops, and councils, could no longer suffice to adjudicate differences in interpretation of the Scripture. To replace the medieval authorities who had interpreted biblical dicta regarding truth and life, Luther emerged as a prophet of God in whose words a secondary level of doctrinal authority could be found. Those who believed that this Wittenberg professor was God's special agent—a voice of divine judgment upon the corruption of the old system—were able to ascribe such authority to him without difficulty. When the living myth had disappeared into his tomb, and could no longer adjudicate disputes by composing letters or formal faculty opinions, his writings—widely available in print—were used as a secondary authority by some of his disciples.

Second, over the years Luther functioned as a prophetic teacher whose exposition of the biblical message supported and guided the biblical exposition of his followers. Luther based his perception of life and truth upon his conviction that God has spoken reality into existence and shaped human life through his world. Teaching—the content of the Word—thus was paramount in Luther's conception of the way in which God came to people in the sixteenth century and functioned as their God. While the Reformer was still alive and writing, his vast literary output enabled him to influence a broad circle of readers and of nonreaders who heard his ideas from them. When he died, his adherents continued to learn and to teach others through the published corpus of his thought. In elaborating Luther's role as teacher, we must pay attention to the ways in which his writings were reproduced and used in the Lutheran churches of Germany after his death. For his heirs not only reprinted his complete corpus and individual treatises in it; they also repackaged and organized Luther's thought topically for handy reference in the pastor's library. In this manner Luther continued his teaching activity after his death through citations, reprintings, and the organizing of his thought for consumption in a new era.

Third, for his German followers Luther remained above all a prophetic hero whom God had chosen as a special instrument for the liberation of his church—and of the German people—from papal oppression and deceit. As a heroic prophet, Luther symbolized the divine Word which brought God's judgment upon the old papal system, and he embodied the hopes of the people and the comfort of the gospel which brought new heavenly blessings upon the faithful children of God. In their troubled times his followers saw in Martin Luther the assurance that God would judge their enemies and intervene eschatologically on their behalf with the salvation he had promised. . . .

Conclusion

Theander Luther

Five hundred years after his birth Martin Luther continues to engage and fascinate those who encounter him. The testimony of his biography and his writings continues to cast "reflections of his form in water of different depths and hues," as Horst Stephan commented nearly a century ago. Modern scholars have formed their own judgments of Luther and have put his thoughts to their own use on bases different from those that motivated his contemporaries. Apt is Mark Edwards's observation that twentieth-century accounts often give a false representation of sixteenth-century perceptions, "not because the historian knows too little but because the historian knows too much." This is the case because historians have a view "from above"—a more comprehensive view of Luther's context, of his impact, even of the corpus of his writings—a view which none of Luther's contemporaries, nor Luther himself, could have had. For instance, as Edwards observes, "we forget that, except perhaps for a few of Luther's students, no contemporary read Luther's works in light of his pre-Reformation lectures on Psalms, Galatians, and Romans." In fact, the few who had read manuscript notes on these lectures preferred his later works, which more reflected what they had heard from him.

On the other hand, when modern historians come to what Luther wrote and wrought, they do not bring the yearnings and longings shaped by the spirit of medieval apocalyptic nor the humanistic adventure of return to the sources. Instead, we bring our own conceptual framework and our own questions and goals to the texts and story of Martin Luther. Further, it is impossible to return to the pristine sources of the 1510s, 1520s, and 1530s uninfluenced by the interpretations of Luther forged by his students and contemporaries and those who followed them in the succeeding two generations.

From the perspective of the sixteenth century, Luther had seven heads or more. To a remarkable if not unique degree this monk and professor became a fixation for foes and friends alike. Whatever the reasons (as assessed by twentieth-century scholars) may have been, this widespread fixation developed less on the strength of political power or economic resources or social status than on the strength of his ideas and through the public presentation and projection of these ideas. His disciples perceived him to be an authoritative prophet or an insightful teacher or a national and cultural hero, or one who combined two or all of these roles.

As Luther's supporters praised him by recounting his heroic deeds or by repeating his insightful instruction or by putting his image and ideas to use in the life of church and society, they inevitably cast the raw material of his life into forms dictated by the challenges and concerns of their own times. Around 1520 a host of images were marshaled to describe this prophetic figure. In the first decade of his emergence in public he was seen as an authority for determining the proper exposition of biblical truth, the new teacher of the church for the last times, and a hero who would end papal tyranny. All three representations of the Wittenberg professor continued to be in vogue throughout his life and in the years immediately after his death. Gradually, however, his role as adjudicatory authority, which was transferred from his person to his writings, appeared ever less able to serve effectively as a means of deciding and defining public teaching. The national hero he remained, ever more simplified and stylized but not less important because of that, particularly as the shadow of the Counter-Reformation grew heavier over evangelical Germany. His role as teacher continued as well, albeit in limited and adapted form. Changing times meant changing use of the individual who had been thought to personify the message of God and to satisfy the longings of the people.

Not all of Luther's followers put him to use as a substitute for popes and councils, as a secondary authority who could adjudicate disputes over the gospel and the practice of the church. Many did, for the church always needs such a secondary authority. The conviction that the papacy was Antichrist and that councils and the Fathers were fallible produced a crisis of authority in the churches of the Reformation. Among Luther's followers biblical authority prevailed unchallenged as the primary authority for determining truth in the presentation of the gospel. The Fathers and councils had also schooled the thinking of the Wittenberg disciples, although they reckoned with the possibility of errors in patristic and conciliar writings and thus dismissed them as secondary authorities. Accordingly, some certain standard for adjudication of disputes over the interpretation of the biblical message was needed.

Luther's prophet-like appearance on the late medieval scene and his own dynamic concept of the Word of God—as it is repeated in the mouths of living speakers of the biblical message—prompted his contemporaries to attribute adjudicatory authority to him. Medieval apocalyptic hopes and humanist convictions regarding the power of effective oral communication combined with his own understanding of the power of God in the living voice of the gospel to create a belief that he was a special tool of God. As such, it was believed, he spoke God's word of condemnation against the deceiving tyrants of the papal system and announced God's word of grace and mercy in Jesus Christ, and he did so with an authority which he had received along with the gift of clear interpretation of the biblical message. But even while he lived, appeals to his authority were restricted to those circles that accepted him as God's authoritative prophet for the latter day. Furthermore, once he died and could no longer directly apply God's Word to current situations, and the church had to rely on the written works he had left behind, it ceased to be practical—and possible—to regard him as a secondary, adjudicatory authority in the church. The written corpus was too bulky. It contained contradictions. It became politically delicate to emphasize Luther so strongly.

The negative side of Luther's proclamation—in defense of the gospel and in opposition to papal oppression—had made him a hero of Herculean proportions to his contemporaries around 1520; and a hero for nation and people, for freedom and humanity, he remained, particularly as the Roman Catholic prelates and princes became increasingly aggressive and the political tensions within the empire mounted—culminating in the Thirty Years' War. In the following centuries, pressed into a variety of images and forms by the governments of divine-right monarchies and by fans of the Enlightenment, by theologians of diverse perspectives and by politicians of various ideologies, Luther's persona continued to prove itself a useful symbol—a hero of one kind or another—even when his authority and indeed his theology were rejected by his partisans. More often than not, misunderstanding of the hero—occasionally perhaps deliberate, often innocent—separated the historical figure of the Reformer from the Luther myths created ever anew for some purpose or another.

Luther has found enduring use as a teacher of the church as well. To a remarkable extent his thought continued to determine the agenda of theological discussion in many parts of Christendom in succeeding generations. Those who claimed his name could not escape addressing the emphases of his theology—justification, the Word of God as means of grace, the authority of Scripture, the nature and effect of the sacraments, to name but a few of his doctrinal accents. Nonetheless, from the beginning his followers' understanding of his teaching was influenced by the medieval heritage which continued to echo through the minds of his contemporaries, by the agenda of polemic set by his foes as well as his friends, by their individual pastoral or professorial concerns, and by the method and theology of his Wittenberg colleague Philip Melanchthon. Melanchthon's practice of theology schematized the thinking of students into the forms dictated by the loci method, and they could recognize no alternative to placing Luther's thought into these Melanchthonian forms.

The dogmatic tradition which ran from Melanchthon through Martin Chemnitz's commentary on his *Loci communes theologici* to Johann Gerhard and the dogmatic works of Lutheran orthodoxy became the standard expression of what Lutherans believed and taught. Other sources may have shaped preaching, catechetical instruction, and pastoral care, but the conceptual framework into which graduates of Lutheran theological faculties placed materials from

Luther's pen and the pens of other theologians came from the Melanchthonian dogmatic tradition. Modern scholars may express chagrin or regret over this fact; indeed, they may find Luther more refreshing or relevant than the works of his followers. But his epigones did fulfil the calling of all theologians: they applied the biblical message and the tradition of their church to the lives of their parishioners in their own generation. And however they may have adapted Luther, they adopted what they understood the heart of his message to be, even if from later perspectives they may have sacrificed too much of its peculiar insights.

. . . [T]hat the hero Luther could be honored and celebrated by being cited in formulaic ways made it unnecessary for young pastors to read his writings and glean the fullness of his unique exposition of the biblical message. The dynamic of his homiletical teaching was placed into forms which limited the ways in which Luther could continue to teach his church. The sermonic ways in which he treated and conveyed the biblical message were set aside. The full scope of his teaching was channeled for the usage of a new day.

Indeed, Luther's teaching for the early sixteenth century needed to be reshaped and readdressed to changing patterns of church life and new issues as well as old. In the course of that inevitable process the vigor and vitality of the prophetic teacher were tamed even as the content of his teaching was preserved within the forms which his followers found useful for conveying his message in their generations. At the outset of the seventeenth century Luther continued to teach, particularly through the most practical of his writings: the postils and the commentaries which could aid preaching, his catechisms, his devotional meditations. His followers regarded him as the greatest of their teachers even if they received his teaching through a grid constructed by others, above all Philip Melanchthon. Luther's prophetic authority as a substitute for popes and councils in adjudicating disputes over the biblical message had waned. Although its memory echoed through certain expressions of praise during the closing decades of the sixteenth century and the opening years of the seventeenth, the Book of Concord had become the secondary authority for a majority of Lutheran churches. The authority of Luther's person, and then the corpus of his writings, had been replaced by the authority of his church's confessional documents. Even those images which had given substance to the claim for his authority—above all, angel of the apocalypse and prophet—were by the end of the sixteenth century no longer used as grounds on which to justify his adjudication of doctrinal differences or to define public teaching, but were used instead to focus attention on his heroic deeds of resistance to papal oppression, deeds out of which the new and final revelation of the gospel had appeared.

Nonetheless, the vibrant interest in Luther's person and career, as well as the availability of much of the corpus of his writings, ensured that his voice continued to inform and form the faith and the life of the people of his church. Even though the extravagant appraisal of his contemporaries had been tamed, for most Lutherans of the early modern period this prophet and teacher loomed over their lives as a unique hero of the faith and of God's Word.

Robert Kolb is assistant professor of religion and history at Concordia College. He has written extensively on religious subjects, including Lutheran Church history and popular Christianity.

Hans Küng

Martin Luther: Return to the Gospel as the Classical Instance of a Paradigm Shift

Why There Was a Lutheran Reformation

Hardly a single one of Luther's reform concerns was new. But the time had not been ripe for them. Now the moment had come, and it needed only religious genius to bring these concerns together, put them into words and embody them personally. Martin Luther was the man of the moment.

What had been the preparation for the new paradigm shift in world history immediately before the Reformation? Briefly:

- the collapse of papal rule of the world, the split in the church between East and West, then the twofold, later threefold, papacy in Avignon, Rome and Pisa along with the rise of the nation states of France, England and Spain;
- the lack of success by the reform councils (Constance, Basal, Florence, Lateran) in 'reforming the church, head and members';
- the replacement of the natural economy by a money economy, the invention of printing and the widespread desire for education and Bibles;
- the absolutist centralism of the Curia, its immorality, its uncontrollable financial policy and its stubborn resistance to reform, and finally the trade in indulgences for rebuilding St Peter's, which was regarded in Germany as the pinnacle of curial exploitation.

However, even north of the Alps, as a result of the Roman system, some of the abuses were quite blatant:

- the retrograde state of church institutions: the ban on levying interest, the church's freedom from taxation and its own jurisdiction, the clerical monopoly of schools, the furthering of beggary, too many church festivals;
- the way in which church and theology were overgrown with canon law;
- the growing self-awareness of university sciences (Paris!) as a critical authority over against the church;
- the tremendous secularization even of the rich prince bishops and monasteries; the abuses caused by the pressure towards celibacy; the proletariat, which comprised far too many uneducated and poor people;
- the radical critics of the church: Wycliffe, Hus, Marsilius, Ockham and the Humanists;
- finally a terrifying superstition among the people, a religious nervousness which often took enthusiastic-apocalyptic forms, an externalized liturgy and legalized popular piety, a hatred of work-shy monks and clerics, a malaise among the educated people in the cities and despair among the exploited peasants in Germany. . . . All in all this was an abysmal crisis for mediaeval theology, church and society, coupled with an inability to cope with it.

So everything was ready for an epoch-making paradigm shift, but there was need of someone to present the new candidate for a paradigm credibly. And this was done by a single monk, in the epoch-making prophetic figure of Martin Luther, who was born on 10 November 1483 in Eisleben in Thuringia. Although as a young monk and doctor of theology Luther certainly did not understand himself primarily as a prophet but as a teacher of the church, intuitively and inspirationally he was able to meet the tremendous religious longing of the late Middle Ages. He purged the strong positive forces in mysticism, and also in nominalism and popular piety, confidently centred all the frustrated reform movements in his brilliant personality, which was stamped with a deep faith, and expressed his concerns with unprecedented eloquence. Without Martin Luther there would have been no Reformation in Germany!

The Basic Question: How Is One Justified Before God?

But when did things get this far? As a result of acute fear of death during a violent thunderstorm and constant anxiety about not being able to stand in the final judgment before Christ, at the age of twenty-two, in 1505, Luther had entered a monastery against the will of his father (who was a miner and smelter by trade). But when did the Augustinian monk who loyally obeyed the rules and was concerned for righteousness by works become the ardent Reformer of 'faith alone'? Historians argue over the precise point in time of the 'breakthrough to the Reformation'.

Be this as it may, there is no disputing the fact that Martin Luther, who had a very similar scholastic training in philosophy and theology to Thomas Aquinas, was in deep crisis over his life. Being a monk had not solved any of his problems, but had accentuated many of them. For the works of monastic piety like choral prayer, mass, fasting, penitence, penance to which Luther submitted himself with great earnestness as an Augustine eremite could not settle for him the questions of his personal salvation and damnation. In a sudden intuitive experience of the gracious righteousness of God (if we follow the 'great testimony' of 1545), but presumably in a somewhat longer process (if we look at his earlier works more closely), in his crisis of conscience a new understanding of the justification of the sinner had dawned on Luther. Whenever precisely the 'breakthrough to the Reformation' took place (more recent scholarship is predominantly for a 'late dating' to the first half of 1518), the 'shift to the Reformation' happens here.

So the starting point of Luther's reforming concern was not any abuses in the church, not even the question of the church, but the question of salvation: how do human beings stand before God? How does God deal with human beings? How can human beings be certain of their salvation by God? How can sinful human beings put right their relationship with the just God? When are they justified by God? Luther found the answer above all in Paul's Letter to the Romans: human beings cannot stand justified by God, be justified by God, through their own efforts—despite all piety. It is God himself, as a gracious God, who pronounces the sinner righteous, without any merits, in his free grace. This is a grace which human beings may confidently grasp only in faith. For Luther, of the three theological virtues faith is the most important: in faith, unrighteous sinful human beings receive God's righteousness.

That was the decisive theological factor. But there was a second one: starting from a new understanding of the event of justification Luther hit upon a new understanding of the church. This was a radical criticism of a secularized and legalized church which had deviated from the teaching and praxis of the gospel, and of its sacraments, ministries and traditions. But in this criticism had not Luther broken completely with the Catholic tradition? With his understanding of justification was he not *a priori* un-Catholic? To answer this question, for all the discontinuity one must also see the great continuity between Luther and the theology which preceded him. . . .

Where Luther Can Be Said to Be Right

Does Luther have the New Testament behind him in his basic approach? I can venture an answer which is based on my previous works in the sphere of the doctrine of justification. In his basic statements on the event of justification, with the 'through grace alone', 'through faith alone', the 'at the same time righteous and a sinner', Luther has the New Testament behind him, and especially Paul, who is decisively involved in the doctrine of justification. I shall demonstrate this simply through the key words:

- 'Justification' according to the New Testament is not in fact a process of supernatural origin which is understood physiologically and which takes place in the human subject, but is the verdict of God in which God does not impute their sin to the godless but declares them righteous in Christ and precisely in so doing makes them really righteous.
- 'Grace' according to the New Testament is not a quality or disposition of the soul, not a series of different quasi-physical supernatural entities which are successively poured into the substance and faculties of the soul, but is God's living favour and homage, his personal conduct as made manifest in Jesus Christ, which precisely in this way determines and changes people.
- 'Faith' according to the New Testament is not an intellectualist holding truths to be true but the trusting surrender of the whole person to God, who does not justify anyone through his or her grace on the basis of moral achievements but on the basis of faith alone, so that this faith can be shown in works of love. Human beings are justified and yet always at the same time (*simul*) sinners who constantly need forgiveness afresh, who are only on the way to perfection. . . .

The Problematical Results of the Lutheran Reformation

The Lutheran movement developed a great dynamic and was able to spread powerfully not only in Germany but beyond, in Lithuania, Sweden, Finland, Denmark and Norway. Parallel to the events in Germany, in Switzerland, which had already begun to detach itself from the empire since the middle of the fifteenth century, an independent, more radical form of Reformation had been established by Ulrich Zwingli and later Jean Calvin which, with its understanding of the church, was to make more of an impact than Lutheranism in both the old world and the new. But it was Luther himself at any rate who in the 1520s and 1530s succeeded in establishing the Reformation movement within Germany.

Indeed, Germany had split into two confessional camps. And in view of the threat to the empire from the Turks, who in 1526 had defeated the Hungarians at Mohács and in 1529 had advanced as far as Vienna, Luther had even asked which was more dangerous for Christianity, the power of the papacy or the power of Islam; he saw both as religions of works and the law. At the end of his life Luther saw the future of the Reformation churches in far less rosy terms than in the year of the great breakthrough. Indeed in the last years of his life, although he was indefatigably active to the end, Luther became increasingly subject, on top of apocalyptic anxieties about the end of the world and illnesses, to depression, melancholy, manic depressions and spiritual temptations. And the reasons for this growing pessimism about the world and human beings were real—not just psychological and medical. He was not spared great disappointments.

First, the original Reformation enthusiasm soon ran out of steam. Congregational life often fell short of it; many who were not ready for the 'freedom of a Christian' also lost all church support with the collapse of the Roman system. And even in the Lutheran camp, many people asked whether men and women had really become so much better as a result of the Reformation. Nor can one overlook an impoverishment in the arts—other than music.

Secondly, the Reformation was coming up against growing political resistance. After the inconsequential Augsburg Reichstag of 1530 (the emperor had 'rejected' the conciliatory 'Augsburg Confession' which Melanchthon had the main part in drafting), in the 1530s the Reformation was able at first not only to consolidate itself in the former territories, but also to extend to further areas, from Württemberg to Brandenburg. But in the 1540s the emperor Charles V, overburdened in foreign politics and at home constantly intent on mediation, had been able to end the wars with Turkey and France. Since the Lutherans had refused to take part in the Council of Trent (because it was under papal leadership: Luther's work *Against the Papacy in Rome, Founded by the Devil*, 1545), the emperor finally felt strong enough to enter into military conflict with the powerful Schmalkald League of Protestants. Moreover the Protestant powers were defeated in these first wars of religion (the Schmalkald wars, 1546/47), and the complete restoration of Roman Catholic conditions (with concessions only over the marriage of priests and the chalice for the laity) seemed only a matter of time. It was only a change of sides by the defeated Moritz of Saxony—he had made a secret alliance with France, forced the emperor to flee through a surprise attack in Innsbruck in 1522, and so also provoked the interruption of the Council of Trent—which saved Protestantism from disaster. The confessional division of Germany between the territories of the old faith and those of the 'Augsburg Confession' was finally sealed by the religious peace of Augsburg in 1555. Since then what prevailed was not religious freedom, but the principle *cuius regio, eius religio*, i.e., religion went with the region. Anyone who did not belong to either of the 'religions' was excluded from the peace.

Moreover, the Protestant camp itself was unable to preserve unity. At a very early stage Protestantism in Germany split into a 'left wing' and a 'right wing' of the Reformation.

The Split in the Reformation

Luther had roused the spirits, but there were some that he would only get rid of by force. These were the spirits of enthusiasm, which while certainly feeding on mediaeval roots, were remarkably encouraged by Luther's emergence. A great many individual interests and individual revolts began to spread under the cloak of Luther's name, and soon Luther found himself confronted with a second, 'left-wing' front. Indeed Luther's opponents on the left (enthusiastic turmoil, riots and an iconoclastic movement as early as 1522 in his own city of Wittenberg!) were soon at least as dangerous for his enterprise of Reformation as his right-wing opponents, the traditionalists orientated on Rome. If the 'papists' appealed to the Roman system, the 'enthusiasts' practised an often fanatical religious subjectivism and enthusiasm which appealed to the direct personal experience of revelation and the spirit ('inner voice', 'inner light'). Their first agitator and Luther's most important rival, the pastor Thomas Münzer, combined Reformation ideas with ideas of social revolution: the implementation of the Reformation by force, if need be with no heed to existing law, and the establishment of the thousand-year kingdom of Christ on earth!

But Luther—who politically was evidently trapped in a view 'from above' and has been vigorously criticized for that from Thomas Münzer through Friedrich Engels to Ernst Bloch—was not prepared to draw such radical social conclusions from his radical demand for the freedom of the Christian and to support with corresponding clarity the legitimate demands of the peasants (whose independence was manifestly threatened and increasingly exploited) against princes and the nobility. Despite all the reprehensible outbursts, were not the demands of the peasants also quite reasonable and justified? Or was it all just a misunderstanding, indeed a misuse, of the gospel? Luther, too, could not deny the economic and legal distress of the peasants.

But a plan for reform would by no means *a priori* have been an illusion. Why not? Because the democratic order of the Swiss confederacy, for the peasants of southern Germany the ideal for a new order, could have been a quite viable model. However, all this was alien to Luther, trapped in his Thuringian perspective and now with his conservative tendencies confirmed. Horrified by news of the atrocities in the peasant revolts, he fatally took the side of the authorities and justified the brutal suppression of the peasants.

The Freedom of the Church?

As well as the left-wing Reformation there was the right wing. And here we must note that the ideal of the free Christian church, which Luther had enthusiastically depicted for his contemporaries in his programmatic writings, was not realized in the German empire. Granted, countless churches were liberated by Luther from the domination of secularized bishops who were hostile to reform, and above all from 'captivity' by the Roman Curia, from its absolutist desire to rule and its financial exploitation. But what was the result?

In principle Luther had advocated the doctrine of state and church as the 'two realms'. But at the same time, in view of all the difficulties with Rome on the one hand

and with enthusiasts and rebels on the other, he assigned to the local rulers (and not all of them were like Frederick 'the Wise') the duty of protecting the church and maintaining order in it. As the Catholic bishops in the Lutheran sphere had mostly left, the princes were to take on the role of 'emergency bishops'. But the 'emergency bishops' very soon became 'summepiscopi' who attributed quasi-episcopal authority to themselves. And the people's Reformation now in various respects became a princes' Reformation.

In short, the Lutheran churches which had been freed from the 'Babylonian captivity' quickly found themselves in almost complete and often no less oppressive dependence on their own rulers, with all their lawyers and church administrative organs (consistories). The princes who even before the Reformation had worked against peasants and citizens for the internal unification of their territories (which had often been thrown together haphazardly) and a coherent league of subjects had become excessively powerful as a result of the secularization of church land and the withdrawal of the church. The local ruler finally became something like a pope in his own territory.

No, the Lutheran Reformation did not directly prepare the way (as is so often claimed in Protestant church historiography) for the modern world, freedom of religion and the French revolution (a further epoch-making paradigm shift would be necessary for this), but first of all for princely absolutism and despotism. So in general, in Lutheran Germany—with Calvin, things went otherwise—what was realized was not the free Christian church but the rule of the church by princes, which is questionable for Christians; this was finally to come to a well-deserved end in Germany only with the revolution after the First World War. But even in the time of National Socialism, the resistance of the Lutheran churches to a totalitarian regime of terror like that of Hitler was decisively weakened by the doctrine of two realms, by the subordination of the churches to state authority which had been customary since Luther, and the emphasis on the obedience of the citizen in worldly matters. It can only be mentioned in passing here that in the sermons before his death Martin Luther had spoken in such an ugly and un-Christian way against the Jews that the National Socialists did not find it difficult to cite him as a key witness for their hatred of Jews and their antisemitic agitation. But these were not Luther's last words, nor should they be mine.

I would like to close with three great statements which are utterly characteristic of Luther.

First, the dialectical conclusion of his work 'The Freedom of a Christian': 'We conclude, therefore, that a Christian lives not in himself, but in Christ and in his neighbour. Otherwise he is not a Christian. He lives in Christ through faith, in his neighbour through love. By faith he is caught up beyond himself into God. By love he descends beneath himself into his neighbour. Yet he always remains in God and in his love . . . As you see, it is a spiritual and true freedom and makes our hearts free from all sins, laws and commands. It is more excellent than all other liberty which is external, as heaven is more excellent than earth. May Christ give us liberty both to understand and to preserve.'

Then Luther's summary plea before the emperor and the Reichstag at Worms: 'Unless I am convinced by the testimony of the Scriptures or by clear reason (for I do not trust either in the Pope or in councils alone, since it is well known that they have often erred and contradicted themselves), I am bound by the Scriptures I have quoted and as my conscience is captive to the Word of God, I cannot and I will not retract anything, since it is neither safe nor right to go against the conscience. God help me. Amen.'

And finally, the last thing that Luther wrote: 'Nobody can understand Virgil in his *Eclogues* and *Georgics* unless he has first been a shepherd or a farmer for five years. Nobody understands Cicero in his letters unless he has been engaged in public affairs of some consequence for twenty years. Let nobody suppose that he has tasted the Holy Scriptures sufficiently unless he has ruled over the churches with the prophets for a hundred years. Therefore there is something wonderful, first, about John the Baptist; second, about Christ; third, about the apostle. "Lay not your hand on this divine Aeneid, but bow before it, adore its every trace." We are beggars. That is true.'

Hans Küng, a Swiss Roman Catholic theologian, is professor emeritus at Tubingen University in Germany and the author of dozens of influential books.

EXPLORING THE ISSUE

Did Martin Luther's Reforms Improve the Lives of European Christians?

Critical Thinking and Reflection

1. After reading both selections, critically analyze the contrasting portraits of the reformer, Martin Luther. How might we explain these variations? Critically discuss.
2. Can the same qualities that help a person successfully inaugurate change become liabilities in the aftermath and implementation of the great change? Critically discuss how this might be the case.
3. In what way might the "Law of Unintended Consequences" be used to explain the reading by Hans Küng? Is some sort of "blowback" inevitable following any large shift? Critically discuss.
4. The Reformation occurred at a time when National States were being created in Europe. Do you see these two developments—religious reform and political change—reinforcing each other or competing? Critically discuss on what basis you made your decision.
5. Research this fracturing of the unity that was once Christendom. What positive outcomes and what negative outcomes would you cite? Analyze and critically discuss.
6. How did Luther's doctrine of church and state as two realms lead to the subordination of churches to their local princes? Critically analyze the implications of this doctrine in the political realm.

Is There Common Ground?

Knowing that you and other human beings are a mixture of virtues and vices or positive and negative qualities, is it possible that both portraits of Martin Luther are correct in different circumstances? A complex person who saw himself on a mission might fail to anticipate all the consequences of his reforms. Should he, nonetheless be held accountable for them? Did Luther remain a prophetic teacher and hero after the break with Rome or did his roles necessarily change? How would you reconcile these two portraits of Martin Luther? Might one portrait be more accurate from within the emerging Protestant branch of community and the other portrait be more accurate from within the Roman Catholic community, from which reformers such as Luther split?

Perhaps the most significant question is: Which European Christians do we mean? During this time period, when a monarch or local prince followed a different branch of Christianity than some of the people, the people were required to change their religion. Sometimes, there was a seesaw effect, especially in England where Protestant monarch followed Catholic monarch, followed Protestant monarch, at a dizzying rate.

Question: Many European Christians were, no doubt, confused and some were probably angry at the rate and scope of change. If we read the selections with this in mind, is it easier or more difficult to find common ground between the authors?

Additional Resources

For background in the times that produced Luther and the other reformers, *The European Reformation*, by Vivian Green, another of the Sutton Pocket Histories (Sutton Publishing Limited, 1998), offers a helpful timeline of dates and suggestions for further reading. An opening chapter on "The Medieval Background" sets the context for Luther, Zwingli, The English Reformation, and Calvin, explained in later chapters. A massive collection of Luther's writings is available in the 55-volume *Luther's Works*, edited by Helmut Lehman and Jaroslav Pelikan (Concordia and Fortress Presses, 1955–1975).

Context for the German political situation may be found in *The German Peasant War_1525*, Bob Scribner and Gerhard Benecke, eds. (Humanities Press, 1991), which has an excellent collection of well-introduced primary source materials. Finally, an informative chapter on "The Peasants' War" may be found in a larger and very useful work *The Holy Roman Empire: A Dictionary Handbook*, Jonathan W. Zophy, ed. (Greenwood Press, 1980).

Internet References . . .

Selected Works of Martin Luther (1483–1546)

From the "Project Wittenberg Website," this site features primary source materials on all of Luther's major works, including the famous 95 Theses.

www.iclnet.org/pub/resources/text/wittenberg/wittenberg-luther.html

Selected, Edited, and with Issue Framing Material by:
Helen Buss Mitchell, *Howard Community College*
and
Joseph R. Mitchell, *Howard Community College*

ISSUE

Were European Witch Hunts Misogynistic in Nature?

YES: Anne Llewellyn Barstow, from "On Studying Witchcraft as Women's History," *Journal of Feminist Studies in Religion* (Fall 1988)

NO: Robert W. Thurston, from "The World, the Flesh and the Devil," *History Today* (November 2006)

Learning Outcomes

After reading this issue you should be able to:

- Describe what happened in Europe between 1400 and 1700 that focused on witchcraft.
- Understand the worldview and culture of this time period.
- Describe the religious wars.
- Describe the growth of national states.

ISSUE SUMMARY

YES: History Professor Anne Llewellyn Barstow claims that the European witch hunt movement made women its primary victims, and was used as an attempt to control their lives and behavior.

NO: History Professor Robert W. Thurston argues that fear of heresy, rather than misogyny, accounts for the witch craze of 1400–1700.

Virgins and whores, goddesses and devils, mystics and conjurers—women have sometimes been perceived as "troublesome creatures." Their very existence has even been seen as a threat to human society, especially with regard to their sexuality. This has resulted in repeated attempts on the part of the patriarchal system, which has so dominated the course of history, to control women's lives. Sometimes this system has resulted in second-class status, shattered dreams, and crushed spirits for women; other times the treatment of women was downright misogynistic. The witch hunt craze of early modern Europe is described by some historians as an example of the latter.

Although belief in witches and witchcraft dates back to recorded history's earliest days, the persecution of those accused reached its apex in Europe's early modern period, especially in the sixteenth and seventeenth centuries. In the northern, western, and central parts of the continent, witch trials became a frightening reality, as thousands were tried and many were executed for supposed evil doings and "pacts with the devil." Although exact figures are not known, a moderate estimate of 200,000 tried with half of those executed, has been offered by Anne Llewellyn Barstow. And certainly germane to this issue is the fact that 80 percent of both groups—those brought to trial and those executed—were women.

What factors caused this wave of witch hysteria? First of all, the Protestant Reformation had created a religious uncertainty that gave the witch hunts a *raison d'être*. Protestants and Catholics battled for the hearts, minds, and souls of Europe's populace, and religious wars became the order of the day. *Malleus Maleficarum* (A Hammer of Witches) written by Heinrich Kramer and James Springer, two Dominican priests, attests to the volatile anxiety-ridden religious mood of the day. Published in 1487, it describes in graphic detail, the evil committed by witches, instructions on how to thwart their powers, tortures to elicit confessions, and guidance in how to punish them, all in gruesome detail. With this mindset firmly in place, the witch hunts were a predictable outcome.

In the political realm, with the growth of national states in Europe and their creation of divine right monarchies, political orthodoxy became as important as religious orthodoxy. Both had to be enforced to keep the dynastic ship afloat. Those who deviated had to pay the price. Social factors also entered into the witch craze fray. Tensions between and among classes permeated the era and led to violent behavior usually geared to keeping the lower classes subjugated. If women had any idea of using these conditions to assert themselves, the trials and resultant executions served as brutal reminders of the power of the status quo and the lengths to which those in power would go to maintain societal control.

Of course, one cannot escape the one constant of the multicentury witch hunt: most of the victims were women. But was gender the only factor in determining the outcome of the witch hunts? Were women singled out for prosecution solely on the basis of their sex? Or were there other factors—political, economic, social, legal, or local—that influenced the witch hunts. These questions had been raised in the historical debates of previous generations, but interest was renewed in the 1960s, presumably due to the increased attention given to women's studies. This included the study of violence against women, which has reached epic proportions in the contemporary world. Were there signs of such actions against women in the past? Was the witch craze just one extreme example of a pattern of violence against women?

A seminal article by Hugh Trevor-Roper entitled "The European Witchcraze of the Sixteenth and Seventeenth Centuries," *Encounter* (May and June 1967), later republished in *The European Witchcraze in the Sixteenth and Seventeenth Centuries, and Other Essays* (Harper Torchbooks, 1969) got the historical process started. Still, it was not until recent times that the idea of the witch hunts as exemplary of misogyny or hatred of women reached center stage. Since that time, it has been impossible to remove the gender factor from any witchcraft studies.

The two selections in the issue represent the best in recent witchcraft scholarship. Anne Llewellyn Barstow makes a persuasive case for gender as the key factor in determining witch hunt outcomes. She sees this as part of a long struggle to "keep women down." Robert W. Thornton focuses, instead, on demonology, finding fear of heresy, rather than misogyny, at the root of this multicentury obsession.

Violence against women, which is considered by many to be epidemic in this generation, has caused a reassessment of misogyny. Domestic violence, spousal abuse, sexual assault, rape, and sexual harassment, have occupied recent headlines and created an acute awareness of the potential for violence faced by all women. In seeking the roots of such violent behavior, a search for historical antecedents is a logical place to start. Renewed interest in the witch hunt phenomenon has enlivened interest in the subject of violence against women, a unique synthesis of two subjects with such far-reaching results.

Despite a plethora of available information and data, we are no closer today to definitive answers to some of the major questions involving early modern Europe's witch hunt experiences. For example, were the witch hunts a centralized movement initiated by society's "power elite"; or did local variables play a more important role in their development and outcomes? If women's sexuality were a major force in the witch craze phenomenon, who introduced it into the public record, and why? If fear of heresy were the chief impetus for this movement, why did it last for more than three centuries? And if women were viewed as "creatures of God," how could the executions of witches be accompanied by such sadistic tortures? Was there another lesson being taught here?

In the generation-long historiography of the European witch craze, Hugh Trevor-Roper's essay mentioned earlier is a good place to start. William Monter's *Witchcraft in France and Switzerland: The Borderlands* (Cornell University Press, 1969); and *Ritual, Myth, and Magic in Early Modern Europe* (Ohio University Press, 1984), along with his many articles, are important contributions to the study of the witch hunts. Brian P. Levack's *The Witch-Hunt in Early Modern Europe* (Addison-Wesley, 1995) provides a thorough, textbook-like coverage of the subject. Anne Llewellyn Barstow's *Witchcraft: A New History of European Witch Hunts* (HarperCollins, 1994) is a recent assessment of the relationship between the witch hunts and gender. An alternative companion piece would be Robin Brigg's recent book *Witches and Neighbors: The Social and Cultural Context of European Witchcraft* (Penguin Books, 1998).

YES

Anne Llewellyn Barstow

On Studying Witchcraft as Women's History

On average, witchcraft, the ultimate in human evil, was sex-related to women in much the same proportion as sanctity, the ultimate in human good, was sex-related to men.

— Christina Larner, *Witchcraft and Religion*

After years of being relegated to folkloric and esoteric studies, European witchcraft is beginning to emerge as an important chapter in early modern history. In particular, the persecutions of the sixteenth and seventeenth centuries have become the subject of scholarly attention. One might assume that the persecutions have been seen as an integral part of women's history, but that is not the case. The witch craze has been interpreted by most historians as *not* a matter of gender.

Given that over 80 percent of the victims were women, this is a surprising and, I believe, a disturbing conclusion. I will therefore examine what difference it makes when one subjects this material to the insights of women's history.

Historians have in fact interpreted the witch-craze as the result of religious upheaval, of the growth of the nation-state, of the isolation of mountain folk—of anything, in short, rather than of what women were doing or were perceived as being. When one focuses on the roles women played in early modern society, and how those roles changed in the sixteenth century, a different picture emerges. This approach enables one to see that women had served as healers, midwives, and counsellors, using an age-old combination of experience ("common sense") and magical techniques to cure and advise. Long respected for these skills, they began to be attacked for them at the end of the Middle Ages. Further, one must ask the economic question: How were women coping with the increasing gap between poor and rich that emerged in the sixteenth century? When one sees how women's basic options narrowed, then one is ready to ask about other changes in sixteenth-century society that affected them, such as legal shifts.

One must remember that European women *as a group* were first subject to criminal persecutions on witchcraft charges. Having been kept out of the courts because they were seen by law as minors, women suddenly were held legally responsible for their actions, once witch allegations were made. Seen as a group of independent adults, women thus entered European legal history by being accused of witchcraft. And those accusations were heavily negative about female sexuality: women were blamed for preventing conception, causing miscarriage, abortion, and stillbirth, making men impotent, seducing men, having sex with the devil, giving birth to demons. Underlying these charges lay the fact that women healers were the authorities on sexuality, which led to a deadly professional rivalry between folk healers and priests and university-trained doctors. Added to this rivalry was the conviction that women were more strongly sexed than men, which led to deep-seated fears in some males.

I believe that the sudden rise in prosecutions for witchcraft that began in Europe c. 1560 was related in part to attempts to take away women's control of their sexual and reproductive lives. This fitted into the strongly patriarchal concept of family for which the sixteenth century is known, and into the attack by doctors on midwives and folk healers, and by Reformers, both Catholic and Protestant, on traditional sexual mores.

Although men could be arraigned on the charge of witchcraft, and were prosecuted in small numbers, the craze was aimed mostly at women: 80 percent of the accused and 85 percent of those executed were female. Men were associated with witchcraft chiefly because they were related to women who were already suspect or because they had committed other crimes. And yet, although men "qualified," women were overwhelmingly singled out. The extent of the attack on women becomes clear when we recall that 92 percent of the accused in the English county of Essex were women, and that all but two of the female inhabitants of Langendorf in the Rhineland were arrested. In twelfth-century Kiev when periodic fears of witchcraft arose, all of the old women of the area were seized and subjected to the ordeal by cold water (thrown, bound hand and foot, into the Dnieper River). Christina Larner, the analyst of Scottish witchcraft, observed that there were periods "when no mature woman in Fife or East Lothian can have felt free from the fear of accusation." Given these cases, we see that the notorious examples of the two German villages left with only one female inhabitant apiece and of Rheinback, where one person, most often female, out of every two families was put to death, are not unbelievable. Christina Larner put the question precisely when she asked, "Was witch-hunting also woman-hunting?"

Despite such evidence, historians have for the most part not dealt with the persecutions as an attack on women. And yet the first major research published on witchcraft, the documents book and analysis brought out by Joseph Hansen at the turn of the century, had offered a promising beginning. Hansen recognized that women had been singled out as victims, and he gathered some of the more misogynist materials to illustrate this discrimination. Hansen's insights were not entirely lost on Wallace Notestein, who in 1911 devoted one paragraph of his study of English witchcraft to the subject. Observing that about six times as many women were indicted as men, he concluded that "this was to be expected." Implying that by nature women would be suspected of witchcraft, Notestein left it at that.

Hansen's insights had no further influence on research for the next half century. While the issue of gender virtually dropped out of the discussions, what remained was a disturbing glimpse of how historians saw women in history. L'Estrange Ewen's first analysis of the English Home Counties trials, for example, provided plenty of information about misogyny in the courts, but he did not mention women as a category at all. Four years later, however, while publishing further trial documentation, he briefly stated his thoughts about the victims:

> That many of the condemned women, although innocent of witchcraft, were really undesirable neighbours cannot be doubted. Mental institutes not being features of the social life, numbers of melancholics were at large, others again, mentally sound, ranked as thieves, cozeners, whores, blasphemers, blackmailers, abortionists, perhaps even poisoners. Mentally degraded, they allowed vermin and domestic animals to suck or lick their blood, although many of such recorded practices can have been nothing more than misunderstanding or hallucination.

Not only condescending to the victims, Ewen went on to libel them:

> At heart they were murderers, and morally as guilty as cutthroat or poisoner. But their confessions are not greatly to be relied upon, obtained as they were by deceit and duress, and, it may be supported, sometimes coloured by vanity.

Although he conceded that "occasionally the witches did possess abnormal power," he had little awareness of the positive role they had filled in premodern society as healers and diviners; instead, he perpetuated the worst of the "hag" stereotype about these women.

In disparaging the very nature of women, writers such as Ewen had of course a long tradition to draw on. In the 1480s when Kramer and Sprenger, authors of the witch-hunters manual, *Malleus Maleficarum*, described women as liars, unfaithful, immoderate, sexually insatiable, and downright evil, they quoted at length from biblical, classical, and medieval sources. As Barbara Walker observes, "From Terrible Crone to castrating witch was not a large step. . . . She had many guises: she-demon, witch, sorceress, succubus, Hag." The witch-hunters of the sixteenth century had models of castrating, death-dealing female types with which to demonize their own women, and many twentieth-century historiographers of the witch-craze have not demythologized their own attitudes toward the women they write about.

In the same category is Julio Caro Baroja's brief mention, at the end of his 1965 book on Basque witchcraft, of the sick, "slightly mad, weird" old women who are his typical witches. Seeing them as pathetic outsiders "with an overdeveloped sense of their own importance," he concluded that "a woman usually becomes a witch after the initial failure of her life as a woman, after frustrated or illegitimate love affairs have left her with a sense of impotence or disgrace," and he regretted that "those unfortunate sick people" were put to death because their type of neurosis was not understood. I conclude from this that it is just as well that most historians did not attempt a gender analysis before we had the insights of women's history to guide us.

The 1967 essay which launched the recent revival of witchcraft studies, H. R. Trevor-Roper's "European Witch-Craze of the Sixteenth and Seventeenth Centuries," while utterly deficient in gender analysis, sheds some light on how historians were missing the point. While making an important analysis of how social tension was generated "by unassimilable social groups," he had a logical opening to discuss women and why some of them were seen as unassimilable. But he could not seem to think of "women" as a group, as a societal category. Sixty pages later, at the end of the essay, he finally identified the victims, calling them "hysterical women in a harsh rural world or in artificial communities—in ill-regulated nunneries . . . or in special regions like the Pays de Labourd, where . . . the fishermen's wives were left deserted for months." Again, we find the theory of the sexually deprived female. But for most of his essay, the victims have no identity. Trevor-Roper understood the dynamics of the medieval persecution of heretics, Jews, and Moors, and realized that the witch-craze was also a persecution of "unassimilable" groups—but thinking of women as either hysterical or as sex-starved individuals, he could not draw any conclusions about them as a group.

Trevor-Roper's controversial essay inspired a series of archival studies of witch trials, written in order to refute him but all showing their debt to him nonetheless. Alan Macfarlane's careful analysis of the Essex trials confirmed that 92 percent of the victims there were women, an extraordinarily high percentage, but he concluded that "there is no evidence that hostility between the sexes lay behind their prosecutions." Keith Thomas in his influential study of English folk religion concurred with Macfarlane. While denying that either misogyny or psychological factors mattered, he made the useful point that economic and social considerations are valid, because women "were the most dependent members of the community, and thus the most vulnerable to accusation." He also pointed out that charges of female sexual irregularities—illegitimacy, promiscuity, sexual voracity—figured in the trials, but he seemed not to realize that these are the stuff of which misogyny is made.

Both Macfarlane and Thomas said that the question of why women are singled out must be looked into—but neither of them did so. Succeeding works documented a vast amount of woman-hatred, making it all the more surprising that scholars still did not see gender as the central issue. Erik Midelfort's research on southwestern Germany is a case in point. While analyzing massive witch panics such as Wiesensteig where sixty-three women were burned to death, and Quedlinburg, where 133 witches, mostly female, were executed in one day, Midelfort suggested that "women seemed . . . to provoke somehow an intense misogyny at times" and asked that we study "why that group *attracted to itself* the scapegoating mechanism." Not content with blaming the victims, Midelfort went on to deny that there had been a particular tradition of misogyny in the sixteenth century. Complaining that this alleged tradition had been documented "only in literary sources," he overlooked the fact that his own material was primary proof for it.

By this time in the development of witchcraft studies, a pattern of denial is clear. Historians were denying that misogyny and patriarchy are valid historical categories and were refusing to treat women as a recognizable historical group. Reading these works is like reading accounts of the Nazi holocaust in which everyone agrees that the majority of victims were Jewish, but no one mentions anti-Semitism or the history of violent persecution against Jews, implying that it was "natural" for Jews to be victims. Without mention of a tradition of oppression of women, the implication for the sixteenth century is that of course women would be attacked—and that it must somehow have been their fault. This is what historians conclude when they have no awareness of traditional misogyny or traditional oppression of women.

In 1948 in the work of the researcher of northern French witchcraft, Emile Brouette, misogyny was finally related again to the persecutions. Even if one believes that it is possible to be antifeminist without burning witches, he maintained, still it is theologically only one step from scorning a woman to believing that she is a servant of the devil. This perception was rejected by Brouette's successor there in witchcraft studies, Fr. Pierre Villette, who insisted that it was "psychologie féminine" and that alone which explained the large numbers of female victims; in other words, women do threaten men and drive them to attack. Villette even excused the virulent misogyny of the authors of the *Malleus Maleficarum*, in light of this frightening "female psychology."

Working twenty years later in the same northern French area as Villette had covered in the 1950s, Robert Muchembled drew quite different conclusions. Ascribing the preponderance of female victims (82 percent) partly to traditional misogyny, literary as well as theological, lay as well as clerical, Muchembled moved the argument along by tying female oppression to the general sexual repression of the two Reformations. His proofs were the increased punishment for prenuptial pregnancy, bastardy, and adultery, with heavier penalties against women than men. He also documented the intrusion of the state into village life, which brought elite fantasies about witches and an impersonal bureaucratic form of justice that seriously disturbed traditional village relationships. As society became more repressive, the charges against alleged witches became wilder: while some of the accused had had reputations for lasciviousness, even women with good names were now accused of having sex with the devil or keeping a demon lover. Muchembled was right to broaden the scope and to see that the witch-hunt involved persecuting women for their sexuality.

The years after 1972, when Midelfort's work was published, show a change in scholars' interpretations of this evidence, a change which must be credited to the nascent movement for women's history. Midelfort himself took a different position nine years later, claiming that "one cannot begin to understand the European witch-hunt without recognizing that it displayed a burst of misogyny without parallel in Western history," and he even suggested that future research should investigate the fantasies of the bishops and university professors who presided over the German trials. This indicates a more sympathetic approach, one perhaps influenced by the work in women's history accomplished in the intervening decade.

In a general interpretation of early witchcraft up to 1500, Jeffrey Burton Russell made a major attempt to place women at the center of the problem. Russell understood one role of medieval women, namely their leadership in heretical groups; he appreciated the extent to which medieval heretical groups appealed to women by offering women roles from which they were excluded by the church. But he failed to see that folk religion (folk magic, witchcraft) was another valid alternative for women. Throughout, he accepted the demonologists' definitions of witchcraft, calling it a "violent form" of "feminine discontent" involving "criminal" activity. Because he insisted on associating witchcraft primarily with heresy, rather than with folk religion, and saw it as ultimately subversive, he was forced to conclude that the alleged witch engaged in violent, even criminal, activity, leaving the issue not far from the "woman as hag" position. In a more recent work, Russell connects suspected women with hags even more strongly: ". . . in Christian Europe, the hag image was projected upon human beings. The European witch, then, must be understood not just as a sorceress, but as the incarnation of the hag. She is a totally evil and depraved person under the domination and command of Satan."

Two new comprehensive studies that cover the entire witch-hunting period, go further in searching for gender factors. In Joseph Klaits's 1985 book, misogyny is dissected as part of theology, medical attitudes, law, art, ageism, and poverty. Woman-hatred is identified in familial attitudes and in sexual exploitation. That Klaits devotes half a chapter to "sexual politics," a discussion he placed early in the book, shows that he understands the institutional nature of the problem—that the social order felt threatened by nonconformist women, felt that church and family, and even the state, were threatened. And he is one of the few (Muchembled is another) who has analyzed the sadistic impulse in the witch-hunt.

But Klaits sees not women but the Reformation (meaning both Protestant and Catholic) as the main factor in the persecutions, blaming both the religious upheaval and, chiefly, the antisexual reformism of the Reformation period for the extremes of the witch-craze, and in doing so he shifts the focus away from women. Women, after all, were not the main actors in the Reformation drama, so Klaits brings us back to looking at what men did. It matters little to witchcraft studies whether one explains witchcraft by what lawyers, judges, doctors, theologians, bishops or Reformers did—all of these explanations miss the central point, because all pull the focus away from the victims, from the women themselves. And Klaits states categorically that women are not the central issue. Even his emphasis on them as sexual objects, true though it is to the trial material, has the effect of showing us the victims from the outside.

Brian Levack's study, intended like Klaits's to be used as a textbook, affirms at one point that witchcraft was sex related, and discusses the many ways in which women were more vulnerable than men to these charges. But Levack seldom mentions gender in the rest of his book.

A model of gender analysis finally appeared in 1976, E. William Monter's study of the witch-craze in the Swiss–French borderlands. Affirming the widespread use of black and white magic in preindustrial Europe, he is sympathetic to women's use of magic as a compensation for their legal and economic disadvantages. He lays their persecution to their gender and maintains unequivocally that sex was the crucial factor, more important than poverty, age, or any other. Defining misogyny as more than the usual woman-hatred in family and in theology, Monter adds the important observation that witch prosecutions rose and fell with legal action against two other sex-linked crimes: infanticide and sodomy. Infanticide was resorted to almost entirely by single women, and both infanticide and sodomy were seen by sixteenth-century society as "unnatural." Since witchcraft was seen as "unnatural," sinful, and a single woman's crime, it is not surprising that the sixteenth century became "interested in executing women as witches." Concluding that "women were the specially designated victims," that "witchcraft, as the demonologists had repeatedly insisted, was sex-linked," Monter set the stage for the type of gender analysis which must be done on the witchcraft materials, but he did not follow through on these insights.

The late Scottish sociologist Christina Larner produced the most thorough gender investigation to date. Using her triple skills in sociology, history, and religion, Larner accepted the positive use of witchcraft by poor village females ("women embracing witchcraft"), saw the persecutions as motivated by a desire to control independent-minded (and -mouthed) women, and made male-hatred of the female body into a real, believable factor in the craze. One expects her to conclude that gender is the central issue, and she does affirm that "all women were potential witches," that "the witch hunt was part of the sex war," and that "witch-hunting *is* woman-hunting." And yet she wasn't satisfied with these formulations, and repeatedly modified them: "the reasons why witches were hunted are not directly related to their being women, but to their being thought evil"; "the crime of witchcraft, while sex-related, was not sex specific"; the hunt was "no more a persecution of women than the prosecution of killers was a persecution of men." Finally concluding, that "witch-hunting is *not* woman-hunting." Larner maintained that at any rate the questions raised by the issue of woman-hunting were too narrow. Recommending instead that we ask broader, presumably more important questions of the craze, questions about Christianity as a political ideology, about crises in law and order—that is, the more political questions—she turned away from the theory of persecution by gender, which she more than anyone had validated.

Once again women as a gender group are seen not to matter and the questions of women's history are considered too narrow. Larner's conclusions are the most disappointing of all, for she had a keen awareness of how the oppression of women works in history. She doesn't make clear why one must forego questions about woman-hunting in order to work on the political issues, nor does she see that the woman-hunting questions *are* political. Material that shows women as "threatening to patriarchal order," or religion as "relentlessly patriarchal" is neither narrow nor apolitical.

To sum up: the problems one faces in studying witchcraft as a persecution by gender are many. First one must acknowledge that folk healers and diviners were useful, sought-after members of society, pre-1500. Although they were reperceived after that as suspect, even as evil, by elite groups, and eventually by villagers as well, the historian has no grounds to caricature them as hags. Second the distinction between folk religious practices and witchcraft accusations must be observed. The latter were the grotesque distortions made by the European elite of the actual, useful functions of folk healers and counsellors, made in order to discredit them. Finally, one must distinguish between sex and gender. Despite the emphasis on female sexuality in the trial records and procedures, the historian is ill-advised to interpret the victims, no matter how sympathetically, as sex objects. Women were more than sex objects in sixteenth-century society, they served as midwives, healers, counsellors, farmers, alewives, spinners, domestic servants, assistants to their husbands in craft work, etc., and their productive, as well as reproductive, roles shaped how they were seen. Only when the historian distinguishes between gender roles and sexuality can we properly evaluate why women were perceived as a threat.

A lack of understanding of patriarchy as a historical category and of how it functions in society is another weak point in most of the works cited here. Without this understanding one doesn't see that women were accused primarily by men, tried by male juries, searched by male prickers, sentenced by male judges, tortured by male jailers, burned to death by male executioners—while being prayed over by male pastors. The patriarchal system also explains why many women accused other females: if a woman displeased or threatened the men of her community, she would also be seen as dangerous by the women who depended on or identified with those men. The internalization of "who is not acceptable" goes even deeper than that: women—and other oppressed groups—sometimes try to outdo their oppressors in scorning persons perceived as outsiders, in hope of being accepted, or tolerated, themselves. In the witchcraft trials, the poor attacked those even poorer; and poor women attacked those women even further out of power than they.

How misogyny, the hatred of women, in addition to patriarchy, the rule over women, caused females to be singled out, needs to be made clear. It was antiwoman theology that turned the attention of the inquisitional courts to women *as women*, a process that was quickly taken up by secular courts as early as c. 1400. This was not caused by something innately evil about women, nor any change in their nature; the cause was the specific connection that Dominican inquisitors and theologians (de Savigliano, Nider, Jacquier, Kramer, Sprenger) made between witchcraft and women, based on ancient Christian beliefs about the defective, evil nature of women. When historians deal with this tradition of misogyny, rather than blaming the victim for somehow "attracting" hatred, then the persecutions can be understood. Both patriarchy and misogyny are valid, and in this case essential, historical factors.

Furthermore, this is not a one-issue topic. A number of false leads have been followed, and the concept of persecution by gender has been repeatedly denied, in order to narrow down the analysis to some one key factor: the Reformation(s), community tensions, proto-capitalist agriculture, more abstract forms of justice, demographic change (more single women), plague, etc. While all of the above are factors, none of them is *the* factor. I suggest that we stop looking for a central, unifying explanation for this very complex, messy, rich phenomenon. Witchcraft, far from being odd, esoteric, or disgusting, turns out to be a capital topic for studying the transition from medieval to early modern society. By forcing the historian to focus on women's lives and how they were changed and limited by the greater power of the seventeenth-century churches and states, the witchcraft phenomenon illuminates the racism and imperialism that Europeans were beginning to export around the world. What European men and women did to the people whom they colonized, European men first did to European women. Traditional patriarchal structures and misogynistic attitudes were heightened by new legal, religious, and political arrangements. Women's lives *were* changed; some of their old roles were challenged, and as they resisted, they were made the new scapegoats for an expanding but insecure society.

This dynamic history cannot be reduced to a central cause. It must be dealt with as multifaceted, as filled with internal change and contradiction. The thread that runs through it, the only constant, is the gender of the victims. It is from the beginning, and becomes even more emphatically, a persecution of women, which sheds light on the history of persecution, criminality, poverty, religious teaching, the family, and how men and women relate to each other.

Anne Llewellyn Barstow is professor of history, retired, at the State University of New York at Old Westbury. She is the author of *Witchcraze: A New History of the European Witch Hunts* (HarperCollins, 1994).

Robert W. Thurston

The World, the Flesh and the Devil

Robert W. Thurston looks at the politics of demonology and rethinks attitudes to witches and women between 1400 and 1700.

All wickedness is but little to the wickedness of a woman . . . [She is] an evil of nature . . . [Women] are more credulous; and since the chief aim of the devil is to corrupt faith, therefore he rather attacks them . . . Women . . . are intellectually like children . . . [A woman] always deceives.

As the Dominican monk Heinrich Kramer (c.1430-c.1505) sat down to write about witches in early 1486, he must have felt desperate. He had recently been sentenced to prison for theft, blocked by other clerics as he tried to convict women of witchcraft, and scorned and threatened by a bishop. Kramer (known as Institoris in some sources) needed to recoup the respect appropriate to a papal inquisitor, his position in 'Upper Germany', a swathe of present day Germany, France and Austria.

This was the inauspicious background to the creation of the *Malleus Maleficarum* ('Hammer of Witches'). First printed in 1486, the *Malleus* is often considered to be the pivotal work for the study of both the witch hunts, which lasted roughly from the 1420s to the 1690s, and the era's commentaries on women.

The book owes much of its fame to late nineteenth- and early twentieth-century scholars who were certain that superstition and fanaticism produced the hunts, while the Enlightenment's breakthrough to reason ended them. In 1878 the President of Cornell University, Andrew Dickson White, showed an early edition of the *Malleus* to 'his shuddering class', saying that it had 'caused more suffering than any other [work] written by human pen.' The narrator of Dan Brown's *The Da Vinci Code* (2004) echoes this claim:

> The Catholic Inquisition published the book that arguably could be called the most blood-soaked publication in human history. *Malleus maleficarum*—or *The Witches' Hammer*—indoctrinated the world to 'the dangers of freethinking women' and instructed the clergy how to locate, torture, and destroy them. . . . During three hundred years of witch hunts, the Church burned at the stake an astounding five million women.

Not astounding but absurd—the old guesses of up to nine million victims have been revised downwards: recent estimates suggest 30–40,000 executions. Nor did 'the Inquisition' itself publish the *Malleus*. Germany, particularly along the Rhine, was the worst killing ground. France was a distant second, while England and even Scotland lagged far behind. Italy, Spain, and Portugal contributed relatively few victims to the pyres.

For all that estimates of the death toll have fallen recently, it still appears that females typically comprised about 75 percent of the victims. However, commentators on witchcraft between 1400 and 1700 divide sharply on three key points: whether or not women are intrinsically wicked; whether demons could perform real actions or simply create illusions; and whether witchcraft was truly practised. These divisions go far to explain why the witch-hunts were so erratic.

The reasons for the high proportion of female victims must be sought in more mundane factors than the demonologists advanced: the tasks that women performed, giving birth, suckling babies, preparing food, caring for children and washing the dead, were just the ones that contemporaries suspected could provide opportunities and substances for evil acts.

The story of the *Malleus* and its author open the way to rethinking demonology in general. In the last decade studies of European demonology have focused more on widespread anxiety about heresy than on obsessions with women. When Kramer's work is seen in the context of the wider politico-religious struggles of the era, the *Malleus* appears less an assault on women than an attempt to use them—or stock images of them—to make points about correct belief.

Kramer had been arrested in 1482 for allegedly stealing silverware and money in the course of his inquisitorial duties. The Inquisition had arisen in the late twelfth century as the Church focused on combating heresy. Managed by the papacy and the Dominican and Franciscan Orders in its early phases, the Inquisition later developed various 'Holy Offices', for example in Portugal and Rome. Kramer, operating under the Pope and his own Dominican Order, was responsible in Upper Germany for investigating, arresting and ordering the torture of suspected heretics, which by now included witches.

Before Kramer could actually be gaoled, the Archbishop of Craynensis (Albania) issued a call for a new

Church council. Kramer seized this moment to write a strong defence of papal authority in opposition to conciliarism, the movement which argued that councils possessed higher authority than the Pope. Pope Sixtus IV, recognizing that Kramer's pen could be an important force on his side, dropped all charges against the monk and returned him to his inquisitorial post.

But Sixtus died in 1484, to be replaced by Innocent VIII. At this juncture Kramer, possibly supported by his inquisitorial partner Jakob Sprenger, complained to the new pontiff that ecclesiastical officials were hampering their efforts to combat heresy. Innocent responded by issuing the Bull *Summis desiderantes affectibus* ('Desiring with supreme ardour') in 1484, in which he enjoined all secular and Church authorities in Upper Germany to aid the two inquisitors.

Armed with this Bull, Kramer arrested some fifty women on the charge of witchcraft and put several on trial in Brixen, east of Innsbruck. He denied his prisoners legal counsel and had them tortured immediately, both gross violations of inquisitorial rules. His actions provoked strong opposition from officials appointed by the Bishop of Brixen, Georg Golser. These clerics finally agreed to try the women, but the case led to Kramer's downfall. When he questioned a defendant about her sexual practices and moral standing in her community, the judges found his query irrelevant and overruled him. The trial was quickly ended and the women released, as episcopal members of the court decided that Kramer had abused his position.

Golser wrote to a priest named Nikolaus criticizing Kramer for his 'completely childish' behaviour, a result of 'his advanced age' (he was about fifty-five). Kramer 'still wants perhaps to mix in women's affairs', the bishop continued, but 'I am not letting him do that, as formerly he erred almost completely in his trial'. Instead he advised him to return to his monastery in Innsbruck. But in the autumn of 1485, Golser informed Kramer that he had now become unwelcome in Innsbruck, warning him that a popular uprising against his witchcraft cases might develop. No such revolt occurred, but after a second threatening letter from Golser in early 1486, Kramer departed for Salzburg.

He then set to work on the *Malleus*, perhaps in the hope that a new book could salvage his standing. Hastily written by Kramer alone, and with glaring lapses in presentation of the argument and grammar, the text was printed late in the year. Sprenger's name became attached to the work in a later reprinting, which may have been a ploy by Kramer to give his book more scholarly weight.

While the *Malleus* offered little new on the theory of witchcraft, it did argue vehemently that witches existed, that women were particularly drawn to witchcraft and sex with demons, and that with demons' help, witches performed evil deeds. The book also presented sensational stories. For example, Kramer reported that in a certain city beset by plague, a dead 'woman was gradually eating the shroud in which she had been buried'. The pestilence would continue until she consumed the entire cloth. When the body was exhumed, half the shroud had been eaten. Aghast, an official cut the head from the corpse and threw it out of the grave; 'at once the plague ceased'.

After the *Malleus* appeared, Kramer continued his dubious or outright criminal behaviour. He implied that the book had direct papal approval by inserting Innocent VIII's Bull as the preface to an edition printed in 1487. But Innocent had merely written a standard directive reaffirming the authority of his inquisitors. The Bull repeats the conventional wisdom of the day on the sexual depravity of heretics, but not witches—it does not mention nocturnal flight and refers to the sabbat only indirectly. It did not single out women as Satan's whores.

Nevertheless, the *Malleus* has retained a leading role in studies of the witch persecutions because of its vitriolic condemnation of women. The most important reason for the Devil's appeal to females, Kramer argued, is that a woman is 'more carnal than a man, as is clear from her many carnal abominations'. The Dominican obsessively reiterated this point, concluding that 'all witchcraft comes from carnal lust, which is in women insatiable'. He did mention 'chaste and honest women', but the remark paled beside his overall misogyny. Clearly he feared women, as shown by the many references to impotence caused by witches and even to their removal of penises.

Kramer's career after 1486 demonstrates that by no means everyone agreed with him on witchcraft. He undermined his own cause by having a forgery endorsing his book inserted among letters from the theology faculty at the University of Cologne, which had offered only limited support for his ideas. Kramer then bribed a notary to label all the letters as true documents. The letters, along with the papal Bull of 1484, were bound with the *Malleus* in some reprintings, in an attempt to give it maximum authority. When this forgery became known, Kramer's reputation plummeted, and his ex-partner Sprenger opened prosecution against him for the forgery.

Kramer then moved on to the Mosel district, where he angered his superiors by approving a local community's effort to create counter-magic against dark forces by erecting a large crucifix. The Church could not openly approve such quasi-pagan measures.

Kramer's behaviour in Brixen had so discredited the concept of diabolical witchcraft that no further witch trials took place there. In 1490, the Dominican Order condemned him for excesses in his work. Although in 1491 the Nuremberg city council requested Kramer's assistance in witch trials and he obliged by writing a treatise denouncing laxity in the pursuit of witches, the city aldermen refused to publish it, perhaps because they had finally been informed about his past. He moved yet again, this time to Bohemia, where he died in about 1505.

While the *Malleus* represents an extreme strain in late fifteenth-century male attitudes towards women, it does not support the notion that misogyny was the preeminent factor behind the witch hunts. To begin with, the extent of the book's influence is far from clear. While some later works on witches drew heavily on the *Malleus,* its publication history was erratic. It appeared in two waves (sixteen editions were published between 1486 and 1520, and about the same number between 1574 and 1621), but none in the intervening fifty years, a crucial period in the rise of the witch trials. In 1526 the Spanish Inquisition denounced the *Malleus* as worthless. Nor were there further editions during another great round of hunts between 1620 and 1665.

The book's appeal is often explained in terms of its completeness in guiding witch-hunters, down to how to lead the witch into a courtroom (backwards). Yet, especially in view of the sensationalist qualities of the *Malleus,* it cannot be assumed that readers always accepted Kramer's arguments.

Sigismund, Count of Tyrol, had been so disturbed by Kramer's conduct at the Brixen trial in 1484 that he commissioned the jurist Ulrich Molitor to clarify the issues. Molitor's *De lamiis* [or *laniis*] *et phitonicis mulieribus* ('On Female Witches and Fortune-tellers', 1489) reached the traditional conclusion that while demons exist they can only create illusions, and cannot interact physically with humans. While Molitor agreed that women were more likely than men to enlist in Satan's service and should be tried for making a pact with him, he explained female attraction to demons by referring to specific circumstances such as poverty, hatred or other unspecified temptations, rather than to general female characteristics such as lust or defective character.

A stronger counter-attack against Kramer, Johann Weyer's *De praestigiis daemonum* ('On Demonic Illusions' or 'On Witchcraft'), appeared in numerous editions beginning in 1563. Weyer too maintained that Satan could only produce illusions; violent phenomena such as sudden illnesses or hailstorms had natural, not diabolic, causes. Evidence obtained under torture was worthless, and old women's voluntary confessions of witchcraft resulted from 'melancholy'.

Reading Kramer's work within the broad context of demonology makes it clear that the genre's primary goal was to defend the reality of demons and humans' physical interaction with them. This argument underscored the need for mainstream Christianity to engage in a sharper struggle against evil. The *Malleus* begins, 'Question the First. Whether the belief that there are such beings as witches is so essential a part of the Catholic faith that obstinately to maintain the opposite opinion manifestly savours of heresy'. No wonder Kramer argued for the existence of witches.

He sought a vivid means of supporting the notion that Satan could easily recruit some humans. Sex sells, and emphasizing purported female sexual transgressions was for Kramer a way of drawing on existing negative stereotypes to make demonic activity more plausible. Since women were traditionally considered the weaker sex and the Devil was definitely male, demonic copulation had to be overwhelmingly with females. Thus *incubi,* or demons who insert a sexual member into a human body, appear about nine times as often in demonological works as *succubi,* which are sexually receptive creatures.

In this and other respects, Kramer borrowed heavily from earlier works on witchcraft, especially Johann Nider's *Formicarius* ('The Ant Heap', 1435–37). The *Malleus* cites Nider at least fifty times. Though Nider had never been a witch-hunter, he was deeply concerned with heresy, particularly with the Hussite movement. A negotiator with the Hussites at the Council of Basel in 1433, he wavered between seeking their return to the fold and urging their destruction.

Nider noted that both sexes could be witches but argued that women's sexual 'weakness' often led them into the Devil's arms. Yet in contrast to Kramer, he was unwilling to break completely with the old doctrine that insisted Satan produced illusions, not acts, on Earth: two of the five books in *Formicarius* are concerned with 'false visions' and dreams.

Nider considered that demons posed a grave problem for true Christianity, because they allied with opponents of reform within the Church. He quoted St Paul in 1 Corinthians 11:19: 'For there must be also heresies among you, that they which are approved may be made manifest among you.' Heretics of all sorts were useful to the Church by demonstrating what *not* to believe and how not to act—and this included their reported copulation with demons. As this argument unfolds in *Formicarius* amid discussion of such topics as the importance of growing rye, it becomes clear that Nider's anxiety about wanton women is a small part of his larger concerns.

Although most witch-hunts occurred in German-speaking lands, the most developed demonology arose, surprisingly, in France during the mid- to late-sixteenth century. Yet the many French treatises on demons by no means sparked large-scale witch persecutions. Indeed, trials in Francophone regions occurred mostly in eastern borderlands not then under the crown, especially Franche Comté and Lorraine. Normandy, long an integral part of the realm, did witness numerous cases, but there male witches far outnumbered females.

Lambert Daneau (1564), Jean Bodin (1580), Henri Boguet (1602), Martin Del Rio (1603 and 1611) and Pierre de Lancre (1612) were the leading French experts on witchcraft. Some of these men did think women were especially drawn to Satan. But, paralleling new work on Nider, historians such as Michael Bailey have seen these writers as preoccupied above all with political-cum-religious battles. Except for the Protestant Daneau, who fled to Geneva to write, the French authors were all zealous Catholics, writing in the wake of the Council of Trent (1545–63), which had adopted a host of new policies to strengthen the Church in the face of the Protestant challenge. They produced copious propaganda directed at the enemies of Tridentine reform: Catholic *politiques* (compromisers) as well as Protestants. How best to smear these opponents and solidify one's own ranks? Simple: by linking these enemies of the true faith to Satan.

The French demonologists directed particular fire at the Paris *parlement,* an appeals court whose jurisdiction covered a large part of the kingdom. The *parlement,* dominated for most of this period by religious moderates, was stubbornly sceptical towards the evidence for witchcraft accepted in lower tribunals. Unlike them, the Paris court used torture half-heartedly at best; of 185 appellants the court had tortured, only one confessed. The tribunal did not use physical duress in any witchcraft case after 1593. In 1624, the *parlement* required an automatic appeal to it from lower courts for all witch trials; by the 1640s the Parisian magistrates rejected witchcraft accusations altogether and even ordered that lower-court judges who tortured prisoners accused of the crime be punished themselves. The witch-hunters charged that these developments suggested the *parlement* had succumbed to diabolical influence.

Like Kramer, the French demonologists insisted that demons were real, flew about the earth and had intercourse with humans. Again like Kramer, they identified females as the likely candidates for diabolical connections. Yet they did not exhibit misogyny anything like Kramer's; most were rather even-handed about the sex of witches. In maligning all women, the *Malleus* occupied a special, perhaps unique, niche within demonology.

Since the existence of witches would confirm the earthly activities of demons, the concern to find them was, at root, related to a fear of atheism. More than a few observers argued that, if there were no witches, then the Devil might not be real either, which could mean that even God might be an unnecessary concept. Giordano da Bergamo may have been the first to say publicly that a belief in witchcraft was essential to true Christian faith. He wrote in 1470, well ahead of Kramer, and possibly he provided a stimulus for the Dominican's arguments.

The dread of atheism and its connection to discussions of witches appeared especially strongly in England. Clergyman Joseph Glanvill fulminated in 1668 against those who thought witches not real but merely 'creatures of melancholy and superstition'. To him, this was a notion fostered by 'ignorance and design'. And even though Meric Casaubon's *Of Credulity and Incredulity,* published in the same year, was sceptical regarding evidence of witchcraft, the author still believed in witches, or said he did, because to doubt was a step towards atheism. The Platonist Henry More evinced a similar concern. But as the belief that God intervened continually in the daily round of the natural world gave way in the late seventeenth century to the idea that he was the divine watchmaker, it became less important to believe that evil forces daily stalked good Christians.

The politics of belief in witches must also be seen against the background of a literary and theological debate on women known as the *querelle des femmes,* which ran from the late Middle Ages into the eighteenth century. This centred at first on the *Roman de la Rose,* a rambling poem begun by Guillaume de Lorris and completed by Jean de Meun around 1278. The poem is an allegory of courtly and carnal love but also a guide to manners, clothing, and the conquest of friends and lovers. Along the way, several characters deliver scathing attacks on women. Jealous Husband offers the worst tirade; he complains that a married woman reveals 'her evil nature'. His own wife is an 'evil bitch'. Husband defies anyone who says, 'I am overconfident in my attacks on all women'. Husband is sure that, 'All women get themselves laid', for the wish of each one 'is always to do it'.

A century later, Christine de Pizan replied to the misogyny she saw in the *Rose,* in her poem *The God of Love's Letter* (1399) and particularly in *The Book of the City of Ladies* (1404–05). She sparked a debate that dominated literary Paris in 1400–02, from which some twenty related treatises, letters and sermons survive. Prominent men arranged themselves on both sides; one of de Pizan's foremost supporters was Jean Gerson, provost of the University of Paris.

The new demonology followed closely upon the *Rose* debate and in key respects was closely intertwined with it. Thus Nider's *Formicarius* of 1435–37 and Martin Le Franc's *Le Champion des Dames* (1440–42) contributed to a new stereotype of the witch as female, sexually assertive and eager to be in league with Satan. But neither book is essentially misogynistic. Le Franc's main character is Defender (of women), who refers to the 'valiant Christine'. Le Franc describes how evil persons greet the Devil as their leader, proceed to have sex with him or each other and receive lethal powders from him. For all that, Defender maintains that women are essentially good and easily wins the debate.

Gianfresco Pico's *Strix, sive de ludificatione daemonum* ('Strix or The Deceptions of Demons', 1523), features a character who until the last page is sceptical that demons recruit humans. And in *De venificis* (1564), translated in 1575 into English as *A Dialogue of Witches,* Lambert Daneau's Theophilus also succeeds only after much talk in convincing his friend Anthony of the reality of witchcraft. These works do not insist that women are generally vile.

Alfonso de Spina, writing in 1458–60, qualified the issue of gender and demons by indicating that only old women became Satan's lovers. In 1584, Reginald Scot's influential *Discoverie of Witchcraft* all but denied the existence of demons on earth. Scot attacked the *Malleus* on logical grounds and was almost completely unconcerned with what women might or might not do. Other important voices directly defended women; Signor Magnifico in Baldesar Castiglione's *The Book of the Courtier* (1528) praises women and forgoes any mention of witchcraft.

The thorough-going misogynistic sentiments of the *Malleus* were largely discarded. While James VI of Scotland insisted in *Daemonologie* (1597), that there were twenty female witches for every male, the only reason he cited for the disproportion was women's greater frailty. After assuming the English throne in 1603, he refused to promote hunts and even stopped them on occasion.

Even as the witch-hunts intensified, powerful arguments continued to refute the idea that females were naturally evil. In the doleful story of the witch persecutions, misogyny by no means triumphed completely. Europeans could choose among competing views of the nature of women and their purported attraction to Satan. Political and religious questions often hovered just behind those debates.

For Further Reading

Richard Golden, (ed)., *Encyclopedia of Witchcraft: The Western Tradition* (ABC-CLIO, 2006); Michael Bailey, *Battling Demons: Witchcraft, Heresy, and Reform in the Late Middle Ages* (Pennsylvania State University Press, 2003); Stuart Clark, *Thinking with Demons: The Idea of Witchcraft in Early Modern Europe* (Oxford University Press, 1997); Dylan Elliot, *Fallen Bodies: Pollution, Sexuality, and Demonology in the Middle Ages* (University of Pennsylvania Press, 1999); Jonathan L. Pearl, *The Crime of Crimes: Demonology and Politics in France, 1560–1620* (Wilfrid Laurier University Press, 1999); Eric Wilson, 'Institoris at Innsbruck: Heinrich Institoris, the Summis Desiderantes and the Brixen Witch-Trial of 1485', in Bob Scribner and Trevor Johnson, eds. *Popular Religion in Germany and Central Europe, 1400–1800* (St Martin's Press, 1996).

Robert W. Thurston is Philip R. Shriver Professor of History at Miami University, Oxford, Ohio. His new book is *The Witch Hunts* (Pearson, 2012).

EXPLORING THE ISSUE

Were European Witch Hunts Misogynistic in Nature?

Critical Thinking and Reflection

1. What does it mean to be a "witch?" Often, it meant a wise woman, a herbal healer, a midwife. How did the term come to stand for evil and satanic associations? What community anxieties might have been ignited during this period that required an object? Critically examine this phenomenon.
2. What were the crimes for which women (primarily) were accused and punished? Would any of these be considered "crimes" today? Critically analyze.
3. If there is a handbook of torture used in extracting confessions, how much confidence can we have in any testimony achieved in this way? Critically discuss.
4. Does this three-century period fit the classical definition of scapegoating? If so, what fears were being allayed? If not, what accounts for the brutality and sadism of the torture? Critically discuss.
5. It has been suggested that the power of women to give birth and continue the life of the group is at the heart of a fear and hatred of women. Critically defend or challenge this assertion.
6. Supernatural power seems to be central to fears of witchcraft. In a pre-modern or early modern society, what factors might give rise to anxiety about supernatural powers possessed by some community members? Critically analyze and discuss.
7. In what ways do current examples of violence against women resonate against this background? Research and critically analyze.
8. Why is there such great disparity in estimates of the number of women killed in the European witch craze? Critically discuss.

Is There Common Ground?

Carefully read both selections, looking for factual descriptions of political, social, and religious conditions in play during this period. Are there grounds on which both authors might stand in agreement? Where they differ is primarily in the motivation they each assign to the prosecutors of witches. It may be possible that some combination of misogyny and fear of heresy combined to drive prosecutors into an obsessive hunt for witches. In the United States, the last gasp of this madness can be seen in the Salem Witch Trials. Playwright Arthur Miller, writing during the 1950s, used the Salem experience to express his outrage over the political "witch hunts" of the McCarthy era in his play "The Crucible." Which of the selections—the YES selection or the NO selection—best reflects your understanding of Joseph McCarthy's accusations that there were countless communists in the Congress, in Hollywood . . . everywhere? His "evidence" was as scanty as that against thousands of women in the past who were tortured and killed for the crime of "witchcraft."

Question: Does every "age of anxiety" seek and find an "other" to blame?

Additional Resources

An excellent primary source book which can be used to shed light on the subject is Alan C. Kors and Edward Peters, eds., *Witchcraft in Europe, 1100–1700: A Documentary Issue* (University of Pennsylvania Press, 1995), which provides among its many primary source pieces, opinions by several popes, Martin Luther, John Calvin, Cotton Mather, Michel de Montaigne, Baruch Spinoza, and countless others. See also Jonathan Barry, Marianne Hester, and Gareth Roberts, eds., *Witchcraft in Early Modern Europe: Studies in Culture and Belie* (Cambridge University Press, 1998), which contains many articles on the subject, written by leading European scholars. Finally, a recent article which brings the historiographical study of the witch hunts and gender up to date is Elspeth Whitney, "The Witch 'She'/the Historian 'He': Gender and the Historiography of the European Witch Hunts," *Women and Language* (Spring, 2000).

Internet References . . .

European Witch Hunts (15th–17th Century)

Provides brief information about the witch hunts and their ramifications; also contains a short, but relevant annotated bibliography of important sources.

http://departments.kings.edu/womens_history/witch/

Selected, Edited, and with Issue Framing Material by:
Helen Buss Mitchell, *Howard Community College*
and
Joseph R. Mitchell, *Howard Community College*

ISSUE

Was the Scientific Revolution Revolutionary?

YES: Edward Grant, from "When Did Modern Science Begin?" *The American Scholar* (Winter 1997)

NO: Steven Shapin, from *The Scientific Revolution* (University of Chicago Press, 1996)

Learning Outcomes

After reading this issue you should be able to:

- Define the phenomenon known as Scientific Revolution.
- Describe what some have called the "revolution in science."
- Describe what some have called the "evolution of science" over a period of centuries.

ISSUE SUMMARY

YES: Distinguished Professor Emeritus of history and philosophy of science Edward Grant argues that there was a revolution in science that took place in the seventeenth century; however, it might have been delayed by centuries if several key developments between 1175 and 1500 had not paved the way for it.

NO: Professor of sociology and historian of science Steven Shapin argues that we should question the idea of a Scientific Revolution, suggesting that there was no philosophical break with the past and rejecting a single time/space event we might call a Scientific Revolution.

When you open a history textbook, you will find it conveniently divided into chapters and units with titles that mark the major turning points of history. One of those titles in a text on world history or Western civilization is likely to be the Scientific Revolution. Known as periodization, this tendency of historians to provide interpretive groupings of events has recently been subjected to reappraisal. If "where you stand determines what you see," then the very act of labeling periods of history makes judgments about what is important and valuable. Traditional schemes of periodization, for instance, have taken the experiences of white men as the standard and ignored the often quite different lives of women and minorities. If only the concerns of the powerful provide the basis for interpreting historical significance, then much of history will be left out.

The assumption behind periodization is that there are moments when the path of history is rerouted, when a sharp break with the past leads to a new kind of experience or a new way of understanding the world. One of the questions historians must ask, therefore, is whether a particular event or series of events represents continuity with the past or discontinuity from it. Traditional periodization has seen the Scientific Revolution as a classic example of discontinuity—as a sharp break with the medieval past and the ushering in of the modern world. Recently, however, historians have taken a fresh look at the late sixteenth and early seventeenth centuries and wondered how scientific and how revolutionary this period actually was.

A danger historians must also remain alert to is called presentism, the tendency to judge and interpret the past by the values, as well as the standards and concerns of the present. From the perspective of the early twenty-first century, for example, we might be tempted to view the Industrial Revolution as replacing backbreaking labor with the power of machines. People living through what we have come to call the Industrial Revolution, by contrast, might have focused on the breakup of the family, as individuals left the home to do wage work, and the substitution of the factory for the productive unit in the home. One of the questions we must ask ourselves is: Did the people living in the seventeenth century think something revolutionary was going on? and How much of a break with the past did the scientific discoveries represent?

This question is a philosophical as well as a historical one. At issue are how we understand key terms such as "science" and "revolution" as well as how we interpret what philosophers call epistemology or knowledge theory. Both historians agree that key people in the past understood what they were doing as a break with the past. Where they disagree is over how to evaluate the past in the context of what we know in the present. Deconstructing or taking apart texts to reveal their hidden meanings has led many to question whether it is ever possible to have a single, universal meaning for a term like "science." What the word may have meant to people practicing it in the seventeenth century may be worlds away from what it means to people practicing it today. And those of us outside the scientific community in either period probably have even less idea about what may be at stake.

Thomas Kuhn, whose widely read 1962 book *The Structure of Scientific Revolutions* (University of Chicago, 1962, 1970) has shed some light on this controversy, combines continuity with discontinuity. Revolutions, Kuhn writes, are occasional, dramatic breaks from periods of what he calls "normal science" when everyone in the scientific community operates from within an accepted paradigm. Revolutions occur when experiments repeatedly do not yield the expected results or when data do not conform to predicted outcomes. Scientists struggle to make the new material fit the old paradigm; those who challenge the paradigm are marginalized or forced to conform. When it becomes clear that the paradigm has broken down, a new paradigm is accepted. Then everything is explained in terms of the new paradigm. Students are educated in the new paradigm; textbooks are written to reflect it; research takes it as its starting point. Has the world changed or only our way of explaining it to ourselves?

After 1700 science had incorporated Copernicus's theory of a heliocentric system, Vesalius's anatomy of the human body had spread, new worlds had been discovered in the heavens and on earth, Francis Bacon's *Novum Organum* had established the scientific method of observation and experiment, William Harvey had demonstrated the circulation of the blood, Rene Descartes had divided reality into mind and matter, and Isaac Newton had proposed the principles of classical mechanics or physics. Would these, taken together, constitute a paradigm shift?

For Edward Grant, there was undoubtedly a Scientific Revolution. He sees the fields of astronomy, cosmology, and physics undergoing "momentous changes" over the sixteenth and seventeenth centuries. However, he also documents a series of events—the translation of Greek and Arabic scientific/philosophical works into Latin, the formation of the medieval university, and the emergence of a class of theologian/natural philosophers—without which the Scientific Revolution would not have occurred when it did.

Steven Shapin begins his introduction with a boldly revisionist statement: "There was no such thing as the Scientific Revolution." Reflecting a postmodern view of the world, Shapin questions whether it is possible even to speak about an "essence" of something called "science." Instead of a single, discrete entity, he sees a wide variety of ways of understanding, explaining, and controlling the natural world. If we list the characteristics of the so-called revolution, Shapin thinks we will find that experimental method, mathematical approaches, and even mechanical conceptions of nature were both advocated and rejected by people who thought of themselves as scientists.

Both Grant and Shapin see continuity with the medieval past rather than a radical break from it. And, both would agree that the past did not become the "modern world" at a single historical moment. Summarize the difference between them in your own words. Be precise in where they part company. What constitutes the turning point for Grant? And, what permits Shapin to deny Grant's claim?

YES

Edward Grant

When Did Modern Science Begin?

Although science has a long history with roots in ancient Egypt and Mesopotamia, it is indisputable that modern science emerged in Western Europe and nowhere else. The reasons for this momentous occurrence must, therefore, be sought in some unique set of circumstances that differentiate Western society from other contemporary and earlier civilizations. The establishment of science as a basic enterprise within a society depends on more than expertise in technical scientific subjects, experiments, and disciplined observations. After all, science can be found in many early societies. In Islam, until approximately 1500, mathematics, astronomy, geometric optics, and medicine were more highly developed than in the West. But science was not institutionalized in Islamic society. Nor was it institutionalized in ancient and medieval China, despite significant achievements. Similar arguments apply to all other societies and civilizations. Science can be found in many of them but was institutionalized and perpetuated in none.

Why did science as we know it today materialize only in Western society? What made it possible for science to acquire prestige and influence and to become a powerful force in Western Europe by the seventeenth century? The answer, I believe, lies in certain fundamental events that occurred in Western Europe during the period from approximately 1175 to 1500. Those events, taken together, should be viewed as forming the foundations of modern science, a judgment that runs counter to prevailing scholarly opinion, which holds that modern science emerged in the seventeenth century by repudiating and abandoning medieval science and natural philosophy, the latter based on the works of Aristotle.

The scientific revolution appeared first in astronomy, cosmology, and physics in the course of the sixteenth and seventeenth centuries. Whether or not the achievements of medieval science exercised any influence on these developments is irrelevant. What must be emphasized, however, is that the momentous changes in the exact sciences of physics and astronomy that epitomized the scientific revolution did not develop from a vacuum. They could not have occurred without certain foundational events that were unique products of the late Middle Ages. To realize this, we must inquire whether a scientific revolution could have occurred in the seventeenth century if the level of science in Western Europe had remained much as it was in the first half of the twelfth century, before the transformation that occurred as a consequence of a great wave of translations from the Greek and Arabic languages into Latin that began around 1150 and continued on to the end of the thirteenth century. Could a scientific revolution have occurred in the seventeenth century if the immense translations of Greco-Arabic (or Greco-Islamic) science and natural philosophy into Latin had never taken place? Obviously not. Without those translations many centuries would have been required before Western Europe could have reached the level of Greco-Arabic science. Instead of the scientific revolution of the seventeenth century, our descendants might look back upon a "Scientific Revolution of the Twenty-first Century." But the translations did occur in the twelfth and thirteenth centuries, and so did a scientific revolution in the seventeenth century. It follows that something happened between, say, 1175 and 1500 that paved the way for that scientific revolution. What that "something" was is my subject here.

To describe how the late Middle Ages in Western Europe played a role in producing the scientific revolution in the physical sciences during the seventeenth century; two aspects of science need to be distinguished, the contextual and the substantive. The first—the contextual-involves changes that created an atmosphere conducive to the establishment of science, made it feasible to pursue science and natural philosophy on a permanent basis, and made those pursuits laudable activities within Western society. The second aspect—the substantive—pertains to certain features of medieval science and natural philosophy that were instrumental in bringing about the scientific revolution.

The creation of an environment in the Middle Ages that eventually made a scientific revolution possible involved at least three crucial preconditions. The first of these was the translation of Greco-Arabic science and natural philosophy into Latin during the twelfth and thirteenth centuries. Without this initial, indispensable precondition, the other two might not have occurred. With the transfer of this large body of learning to the Western world, the old science of the early Middle Ages was overwhelmed and superseded. Although modern science might eventually have developed in the West without the introduction of Greco-Arabic science, its advent would have been delayed by centuries.

The second precondition was the formation of the medieval university, with its corporate structure and control over its varied activities. The universities that emerged by the thirteenth century in Paris, Oxford, and Bologna were different from anything the world had ever seen. From these beginnings, the medieval university took root and has endured as an institution for some eight hundred years, being transformed in time into a worldwide phenomenon. Nothing in Islam or China, or India, or in the ancient civilizations of South America is comparable to the medieval university. It is in this remarkable institution, and its unusual activities, that the foundations of modern science must be sought.

The university was possible in the Middle Ages because the evolution of medieval Latin society allowed for the separate existence of church and state, each of which, in turn, recognized the independence of corporate entities, the university among them. The first universities, of Paris, Oxford, and Bologna, were in existence by approximately 1200, shortly after most of the translations had been completed. The translations furnished a ready-made curriculum to the emerging universities, a curriculum that was overwhelmingly composed of the exact sciences, logic, and natural philosophy.

The curriculum of science, logic, and natural philosophy established in the medieval universities of Western Europe was a permanent fixture for approximately 450 to 500 years. It was the curriculum of the arts faculty, which was the largest of the traditional four faculties of a typical major university, the others being medicine, theology, and law. Courses in logic, natural philosophy, geometry, and astronomy formed the core curriculum for the baccalaureate and master of arts degrees and were taught on a regular basis for centuries. These two arts degrees were virtual prerequisites for entry into the higher disciplines of law, medicine, and theology.

For the first time in the history of the world, an institution had been created for teaching science, natural philosophy, and logic. An extensive four-to-six-year course in higher education was based on those subjects, with natural philosophy as the most important component. As universities multiplied during the thirteenth to fifteenth centuries, the same science-natural philosophy-logic curriculum was disseminated throughout Europe, extending as far east as Poland.

The science curriculum could not have been implemented without the explicit approval of church and state. To a remarkable extent, both granted to the universities corporate powers to regulate themselves: universities had the legal right to determine their own curricula, to establish criteria for the degrees of their students, and to determine the teaching fitness of their faculty members.

Despite some difficulties and tensions between natural philosophy and theology—between, essentially, reason and revelation—arts masters and theologians at the universities welcomed the arrival of Aristotle's natural philosophy as evidenced by the central role they gave it in higher education. Why did they do this? Why did a Christian society at the height of the Catholic Church's power readily adopt a pagan natural philosophy as the basis of a four-to-six-year education? Why didn't Christians fear and resist such pagan fare rather than embrace it?

Because Christians had long ago come to terms with pagan thought and were agreed, for the most part, that they had little or nothing to fear from it. The rapprochement between Christianity and pagan literature, especially philosophy, may have been made feasible by the slowness with which Christianity was disseminated. The spread of Christianity beyond the Holy Land and its surrounding region began in earnest after Saint Paul proselytized the Gentile world, especially Greece, during the middle of the first century. In retrospect—and by comparison with the spread of Islam—the pace of the dissemination of Christianity appears quite slow. Not until 300 A.D. was Christianity effectively represented throughout the Roman Empire. And not until 313, in the reign of Constantine, was the Edict of Milan (or Edict of Toleration) issued, which conferred on Christianity full legal equality with all other religions in the Empire. In 392, Christianity was made the state religion of the Roman Empire. In that year, the Emperor Theodosius ordered all pagan temples closed, and also prohibited pagan worship, thereafter classified as treason. Thus it was not until 392 that Christianity became the exclusive religion supported by the state. After almost four centuries of existence, Christianity was triumphant.

By contrast, Islam, following the death of Mohammad in 632, was carried over an enormous geographical area in a remarkably short time. In less than one hundred years, it was the dominant religion from the Arabian peninsula westward to the Straits of Gibraltar, northward to Spain and eastward to Persia, and beyond. But where Islam was largely spread by conquest during its first hundred years, Christianity spread slowly and, with the exception of certain periods of persecution, relatively peacefully. It was this slow percolation of Christianity that enabled it to come to terms with the pagan world and thus prepare itself for a role that could not have been envisioned by its early members.

The time it took before Christianity became the state religion enabled Christianity to adjust to the pagan society around it. In the second half of the third century, Christian apologists concluded that Christianity could profitably utilize pagan Greek philosophy and learning. In a momentous move, Clement of Alexandria (ca. 150–ca. 215) and his disciple Origen of Alexandria (ca. 185–ca. 254) laid down the basic approach that others would follow. Greek philosophy, they argued, was not inherently good or bad, but one or the other depending on how it was used by Christians. Although the Greek poets and philosophers had not received direct revelation from God, they did receive natural reason and were therefore pointed toward truth. Philosophy—and secular learning in general—could thus be used to interpret Christian wisdom, which was the fruit of revelation. They were agreed that philosophy and science could be used as "handmaidens to theology"—that is, as aids to understanding Holy Scripture—an attitude that had already been advocated by Philo Judaeus, a resident of the Jewish community of Alexandria, early in the first century A.D.

The "handmaiden" concept of Greek learning became the standard Christian attitude toward secular learning by the middle of the fourth century. That Christians chose to accept pagan learning within limits was a momentous decision. They might have heeded the words of Tertullian (ca. 150–ca. 225), who asked pointedly: "What indeed has Athens to do with Jerusalem? What concord is there between the Academy and the Church?" With the total triumph of Christianity at the end of the fourth century, the Church might have reacted adversely toward Greek pagan learning in general, and Greek philosophy in particular, since there was much in the latter that was offensive to the Church. They might even have launched a major effort to suppress pagan thought as a danger to the Church and its doctrines. But they did not.

The handmaiden theory was obviously a compromise between the rejection of traditional pagan learning and its full acceptance. By approaching secular learning with caution, Christians could utilize Greek philosophy—especially metaphysics and logic—to better understand and explicate Holy Scripture and to cope with the difficulties generated by the assumption of the doctrine of the Trinity and other esoteric dogmas. Ordinary daily life also required use of the mundane sciences such as astronomy and mathematics. Christians came to realize that they could not turn away from Greek learning.

When Christians in Western Europe became aware of Greco-Arabic scientific literature and were finally prepared to receive it in the twelfth century, they did so eagerly. They did not view it as a body of subversive knowledge. Despite a degree of resistance that was more intense at some times than at others, Aristotle's works were made the basis of the university curriculum by 1255 in Paris, and long before that at Oxford.

The emergence of a class of theologian-natural philosophers was the third essential precondition for the scientific revolution. Their major contribution was to sanction the introduction and use of Aristotelian natural philosophy in the curriculum of the new universities. Without that approval, natural philosophy and science could not have become the curriculum of the medieval universities. The development of a class of theologian-natural philosophers must be regarded as extraordinary. Not only did most theologians approve of an essentially secular arts curriculum, but they were convinced that natural philosophy was essential for the elucidation of theology. Students entering schools of theology were expected to have achieved a high level of competence in natural philosophy. Since a master of arts degree, or the equivalent thereof, signified a thorough background in Aristotelian natural philosophy, and since a master's degree in the arts was usually a prerequisite for admittance to the higher faculty of theology, almost all theologians can be said to have acquired extensive knowledge of natural philosophy. Many undoubtedly regarded it as worthy of study in itself and not merely because of its traditional role as the handmaiden of theology. . . .

Medieval natural philosophers investigated the "common course of nature," not its uncommon, or miraculous, path. They characterized this approach, admirably, by the phrase "speaking naturally" (loquendo naturaliter)—that is, speaking by means of natural science, and not by means of faith or theology. That such an expression should have emerged, and come into common usage in medieval natural philosophy, is a tribute to the scholars who took as their primary mission the explanation of the structure and operation of the world in purely rational and secular terms.

The widespread assumption of "natural impossibilities" or counterfactuals—or, as they are sometimes called, "thought-experiments"—was a significant aspect of medieval methodology. An occurrence would have been considered naturally impossible" if it was thought inconceivable for it to occur within the accepted framework of Aristotelian physics and cosmology. The frequent use of natural impossibilities derived largely from the powerful medieval concept of God's absolute power, in which it was conceded that God could do anything whatever short of a logical contradiction. In the Middle Ages, such thinking resulted in conclusions that challenged certain aspects of Aristotle's physics. Where Aristotle had shown that other worlds were impossible, medieval scholastics showed not only that the existence of other worlds was possible, but that they would be compatible with our world.

The novel replies that emerged from the physics and cosmology of counterfactuals did not cause the overthrow of the Aristotelian world-view, but they did challenge some of its fundamental principles. They made many aware that things could be quite different from what was dreamt of in Aristotle's philosophy. But they accomplished more than that. Not only did some of the problems and solutions continue to influence scholastic authors in the sixteenth and seventeenth centuries, but this characteristically medieval approach also influenced significant non-scholastics, who reveal an awareness of the topics debated by scholastics.

One of the most fruitful ideas that passed from the Middle Ages to the seventeenth century is the concept of God annihilating matter and leaving behind a vacuum—a concept used effectively by John Locke, Pierre Gassendi, and Thomas Hobbes in their discussions of space.

A famous natural impossibility derived from a proposition condemned in 1277. As a consequence, it was mandatory after 1277 to concede that God could move our spherical world rectilinearly, despite the vacuum that might be left behind. More than an echo of this imaginary manifestation of God's absolute power reverberated through the seventeenth century, when Pierre Gassendi and Samuel Clarke (in his famous dispute with Leibniz) found it useful to appeal to God's movement of the world. In medieval intellectual culture, where observation and experiment played negligible roles, counterfactuals were a powerful tool because they emphasized metaphysics, logic, theology, and the imagination—the very areas in which medieval natural philosophers excelled.

The scientific methodologies described here produced new conceptualizations and assumptions about the world. Ideas about nature's simplicity, its common course, as well as the use of counterfactuals, emphasized new and important ways to think about nature. Galileo and his fellow scientific revolutionaries inherited these attitudes, and most would have subscribed to them.

Another legacy from the Middle Ages to early modern science was an extensive and sophisticated body of terms that formed the basis of later scientific discourse such terms as potential, actual, substance, property, accident, cause, analogy, matter, form, essence, genus, species, relation, quantity, quality, place, vacuum, infinite, and many others. These Aristotelian terms formed a significant component of scholastic natural philosophy. The language of medieval natural philosophy, however, did not consist solely of translated Aristotelian terms. New concepts, terms, and definitions were added in the fourteenth century, most notably in the domains of change and motion. Definitions of uniform motion, uniformly accelerated motion, and instantaneous motion were added to the lexicon of natural philosophy. By the seventeenth century, these terms, concepts, and definitions were embedded in the language and thought of European natural philosophers.

Medieval natural philosophy played another momentous role in the transition to early modern science. It furnished some—if, it is true, not many—of the basic problems that exercised the minds of non-scholastic natural philosophers in the sixteenth and seventeenth centuries. Medieval natural philosophers produced hundreds of specific questions about nature, the answers to which included a vast amount of scientific information. Most of the questions had multiple answers, with no genuine way of choosing between them. In the sixteenth and seventeenth centuries, new solutions were proposed by scholars who found Aristotelian answers unacceptable, or, at best, inadequate. The changes they made, however, were mostly in the answers, not in the questions. The scientific revolution was not the result of new questions put to nature in place of medieval questions. It was, at least initially, more a matter of finding new answers to old questions, answers that came, more and more, to include experiments, which were exceptional occurrences in the Middle Ages. Although the solutions differed, many fundamental problems were common to both groups. Beginning around 1200, medieval natural philosophers, largely located at European universities, exhibited an unprecedented concern for the nature and structure of the physical world. The contributors to the scientific revolution continued the same tradition, because by then these matters had become an integral part of intellectual life in Western society.

The Middle Ages did not just transmit a great deal of significantly modified, traditional, natural philosophy, much of it in the form of questions; it also conveyed a remarkable tradition of relatively free, rational inquiry. The medieval philosophical tradition was fashioned in the faculties of arts of medieval universities. Natural philosophy was their domain, and almost from the outset masters of arts struggled to establish as much academic freedom as possible. They sought to preserve and expand the study of philosophy. Arts masters regarded themselves as the guardians of natural philosophy and fought for the right to apply reason to all problems about the physical world. By virtue of their independent status as a faculty, with numerous rights and privileges, they achieved a surprisingly large degree of freedom during the Middle Ages.

Theology was always a potential obstacle, true, but in practice theologians offered little opposition, largely because they, too, were heavily imbued with natural philosophy. By the end of the thirteenth century, the arts faculty had attained virtual independence from the theological faculty. By then, philosophy and its major subdivision, natural philosophy, had emerged as an independent discipline based in the arts faculties of European universities. True, arts masters were always subject to restraints with regard to religious dogma, but the subject areas where such issues arose were limited. During the thirteenth century, arts masters had learned how to cope with the problematic aspects of Aristotle's thought. They treated those problems hypothetically, or announced that they were merely repeating Aristotle's opinions, even as they offered elaborations of his arguments. During the Middle Ages, natural philosophy remained what Aristotle had made it: an essentially secular and rational discipline. It remained so only because the arts faculty struggled to preserve it. In doing so, they transformed natural philosophy into an independent discipline that embraced as well as glorified the rational investigation of all problems relevant to the physical world. In the 1330s, William of Ockham expressed the sentiments of most arts masters and many theologians when he declared:

> Assertions . . . concerning natural philosophy, which do not pertain to theology, should not be solemnly condemned or forbidden to anyone, since in such matters everyone should be free to say freely whatever he pleases.

Everyone who did natural philosophy in the sixteenth and seventeenth centuries was the beneficiary of these remarkable developments. The spirit of free inquiry nourished by medieval natural philosophers formed part of the intellectual heritage of all who engaged in scientific investigation. Most, of course, were unaware of their legacy and would probably have denied its existence, preferring to heap ridicule and scorn on Aristotelian scholastics and scholasticism. That ridicule was not without justification. It was time to alter the course of medieval natural philosophy.

Some Aristotelian natural philosophers tried to accommodate the new heliocentric astronomy that had emerged from the brilliant efforts of Copernicus, Tycho Brahe, and Galileo. By then, accommodation was no longer sufficient. Medieval natural philosophy was destined to vanish by the end of the seventeenth century. The medieval scholastic legacy, however, remained—namely, the spirit of free inquiry, the emphasis on reason, a variety of approaches to nature, and the core of legitimate problems that would occupy the attention of the new science. Inherited from the Middle Ages, too, was the profound sense that all of these activities were legitimate and important, that discovering the way the world operated was a laudable undertaking. These enormous achievements were accomplished in the late Middle Ages, between 1175 and 1500.

To illustrate how medieval contributions to the new science ought to be viewed, let me draw upon an analogy from the Middle Ages. In the late thirteenth century in Italy, the course of the history of medicine was altered significantly when human dissection was allowed for postmortems and was shortly afterward introduced into medical schools, where it soon became institutionalized as part of the anatomical training of medical students. Except in ancient Egypt, human dissection had been forbidden in the ancient world. By the second century A.D., it was also banned in Egypt. It was never permitted in the Islamic world. Its introduction into the Latin West marked a new beginning, made without serious objection from the Church. It was a momentous event. Dissection of cadavers was used primarily in teaching, albeit irregularly until the end of the fifteenth century. Rarely, if at all, was it employed to enhance scientific knowledge of the human body. The revival of human dissection and its incorporation into medical training throughout the Middle Ages laid a foundation for what was to come.

Without it, we cannot imagine the significant anatomical progress that was made by such keen anatomists as Leonardo da Vinci (1452–1519), Bartolommeo Eustachio (1520–74), Andreas Vesalius (1514–64), and many others.

What human dissection did for medicine, the translations, the universities, the theologian-natural philosophers, and the medieval version of Aristotelian natural philosophy did collectively for the scientific revolution of the seventeenth century. These vital features of medieval science formed a foundation that made possible a continuous, uninterrupted eight hundred years of scientific development, a development that began in Western Europe and spread around the world.

Edward Grant is distinguished professor of history and philosophy of science at Indiana University, Bloomington.

Steven Shapin

NO

The Scientific Revolution

The Scientific Revolution: The History of a Term

There was no such thing as the Scientific Revolution, and this [selection is from] a book about it. Some time ago, when the academic world offered more certainty and more comforts, historians announced the real existence of a coherent, cataclysmic, and climactic event that fundamentally and irrevocably changed what people knew about the natural world and how they secured proper knowledge of that world. It was the moment at which the world was made modern, it was a Good Thing, and it happened sometime during the period from the late sixteenth to the early eighteenth century. In 1943 the French historian Alexandre Koyré celebrated the conceptual changes at the heart of the Scientific Revolution as "the most profound revolution achieved or suffered by the human mind" since Greek antiquity. It was a revolution so profound that human culture "for centuries did not grasp its bearing or meaning; which, even now, is often misvalued and misunderstood." A few years later the English historian Herbert Butterfield famously judged that the Scientific Revolution "outshines everything since the rise of Christianity and reduces the Renaissance and Reformation to the rank of mere episodes. . . . [It is] the real origin both of the modern world and of the modern mentality." It was, moreover, construed as a conceptual revolution, a fundamental reordering of our ways of *thinking* about the natural. In this respect, a story about the Scientific Revolution might be adequately told through an account of radical changes in the fundamental categories of thought. To Butterfield, the mental changes making up the Scientific Revolution were equivalent to "putting on a new pair of spectacles." And to A. Rupert Hall it was nothing less than "an *a priori* redefinition of the objects of philosophical and scientific inquiry."

This conception of the Scientific Revolution is now encrusted with tradition. Few historical episodes present themselves as more substantial or more self-evidently worthy of study. There is an established place for accounts of the Scientific Revolution in the Western liberal curriculum, and this [selection] is an attempt to fill that space economically and to invite further curiosity about the making of early modern science. Nevertheless, like many twentieth-century "traditions," that contained in the notion of the Scientific Revolution is not nearly as old as we might think. The phrase "the Scientific Revolution" was probably coined by Alexandre Koyré in 1939, and it first became a book title in A. Rupert Hall's *The Scientific Revolution* of 1954. Before that time there was no event to be studied in the liberal curriculum, nor any discrete object of historical inquiry, called the Scientific Revolution. Although many seventeenth-century practitioners expressed their intention of bringing about radical intellectual change, the people who are said to have made the revolution used no such term to refer to what they were doing.

From antiquity through the early modern period, a "revolution" invoked the idea of a periodically recurring cycle. In Copernicus's new astronomy of the mid-sixteenth century, for example, the planets completed their revolutions round the sun, while references to political revolutions gestured at the notion of ebbs and flows or cycles—fortune's wheel—in human affairs. The idea of revolution as a radical and irreversible reordering developed together with linear, unidirectional conceptions of time. In this newer conception revolution was not recurrence but its reverse, the bringing about of a new state of affairs that the world had never witnessed before and might never witness again. Not only this notion of revolution but also the beginnings of an idea of revolution in science date from the eighteenth-century writings of French Enlightenment philosophes who liked to portray themselves, and their disciplines, as radical subverters of ancient régime culture. (Some . . . seventeenth-century writers . . . saw themselves not as bringing about totally new states of affairs but as restoring or purifying old ones.) The notion of a revolution as epochal and irreversible change, it is possible, was first applied in a systematic way to events in science and only later to political events. In just this sense, the first revolutions may have been scientific, and the "American," "French," and "Russian Revolutions" are its progeny.

As our understanding of science in the seventeenth century has changed in recent years, so historians have become increasingly uneasy with the very idea of "the Scientific Revolution." Even the legitimacy of each word making up that phrase has been individually contested. Many historians are now no longer satisfied that there was any singular and discrete event, localized in time and space, that can be pointed to as "the" Scientific Revolution. Such historians now reject even the notion that there was any single coherent cultural entity called "science" in the seventeenth century to undergo revolutionary change. There was, rather, a diverse array of cultural practices aimed at understanding, explaining, and controlling the natural world, each with different characteristics and each experiencing different modes of change. We are now much more dubious of claims that there is anything like "a scientific method"—a coherent, universal, and efficacious set of procedures for making scientific knowledge—and still more skeptical of stories that locate its origin in the seventeenth century, from which time it has been unproblematically passed on to us. And many historians do not now accept that the changes wrought on scientific beliefs and practices during the seventeenth century were as "revolutionary" as has been widely portrayed. The continuity of seventeenth-century natural philosophy with its medieval past is now routinely asserted, while talk of "delayed" eighteenth- and nineteenth-century revolutions in chemistry and biology followed hard upon historians' identification of "the" original Scientific Revolution.

Why Write About the Scientific Revolution?

There are still other reasons for historians' present uneasiness with the category of the Scientific Revolution as it has been customarily construed. First, historians have in recent years become dissatisfied with the traditional manner of treating ideas as if they floated freely in conceptual space. Although previous accounts framed the Scientific Revolution in terms of autonomous ideas or disembodied mentalities, more recent versions have insisted on the importance of situating ideas in their wider cultural and social context. We now hear more than we used to about the relations between the scientific changes of the seventeenth century and changes in religious, political, and economic patterns. More fundamentally, some historians now wish to understand the concrete human *practices* by which ideas or concepts are made. What did people *do* when they made or confirmed an observation, proved a theorem, performed an experiment? An account of the Scientific Revolution as a history of free-floating concepts is a very different animal from a history of concept-making practices. Finally, historians have become much more interested in the "who" of the Scientific Revolution. What kinds of people wrought such changes? Did everyone believe as they did, or only a very few? And if only a very few took part in these changes, in what sense, if at all, can we speak of the Scientific Revolution as effecting massive changes in how "we" view the world, as the moment when modernity was made, for "us"? The cogency of such questions makes for problems in writing as unreflectively as we used to about the Scientific Revolution. Responding to them means that we need an account of changes in early modern science appropriate for our less confident, but perhaps more intellectually curious, times.

Yet despite these legitimate doubts and uncertainties there remains a sense in which it is possible to write about the Scientific Revolution unapologetically and in good faith. There are two major considerations to bear in mind here. The first is that many key figures in the late sixteenth and seventeenth centuries vigorously expressed *their* view that they were proposing some very new and very important changes in knowledge of natural reality and in the practices by which legitimate knowledge was to be secured, assessed, and communicated. They identified *themselves* as "moderns" set against "ancient" modes of thought and practice. Our sense of radical change afoot comes substantially from them (and those who were the object of their attacks), and is not simply the creation of mid-twentieth-century historians. So we can say that the seventeenth century witnessed some self-conscious and large-scale attempts to change belief, and ways of securing belief, about the natural world. And a book about the Scientific Revolution can legitimately tell a story about those attempts, whether or not they succeeded, whether or not they were contested in the local culture, whether or not they were wholly coherent.

But why do we tell *these* stories instead of others? If different sorts of seventeenth-century people believed different things about the world, how do we assemble our cast of characters and associated beliefs? Some "natural philosophers," for example, advocated rational theorizing, while others pushed a program of relatively atheoretical fact collecting and experimentation. Mathematical physics was, for example, a very different sort of practice from botany. There were importantly different versions of what it was to do astronomy and believe as an astronomer believed; the relations between the "proper sciences" of astronomy and chemistry and the "pseudosciences" of astrology and alchemy were intensely problematic; and even the category of "nature" as the object of inquiry was understood in radically different ways by different sorts of practitioners. This point cannot be stressed too strongly. The cultural practices subsumed in the category of the Scientific Revolution—however it has been construed—are not coextensive with early modern, or seventeenth-century, science. Historians differ about which practices were "central" to the Scientific Revolution, and participants themselves argued about which practices produced genuine knowledge and which had been fundamentally reformed.

More fundamentally for criteria of selection, it ought to be understood that "most people"—even most educated people—in the seventeenth century did not believe what expert scientific practitioners believed, and the sense in which "people's" thought about the world was revolutionized at that time is very limited. There should be no doubt whatever that one could write a convincing history of seventeenth-century thought about nature without even *mentioning* the Scientific Revolution as traditionally construed.

The very idea of the Scientific Revolution, therefore, is at least partly an expression of "our" interest in our ancestors, where "we" are late twentieth century scientists and those for whom what they believe counts as truth about the natural world. And this interest provides the second legitimate justification for writing about the Scientific Revolution. Historians of science have now grown used to condemning "present-oriented" history, rightly saying that it often distorts our understanding of what the past was like in its own terms. Yet there is absolutely no reason we should not want to know how we got from there to here, who the ancestors were, and what the lineage is that connects us to the past. In this sense a story about the seventeenth-century Scientific Revolution can be an account of those changes that we think led on—never directly or simply, to be sure—to certain features of the present in which, for certain purposes, we happen to be interested. To do this would be an expression of just the same sort of legitimate historical interest displayed by Darwinian evolutionists telling stories about those branches of the tree of life that led to human beings—without assuming in any way that such stories are adequate accounts of what life was like hundreds of thousands of years ago. There is nothing at all wrong about telling such stories, though one must always be careful not to claim too much scope for them. Stories about the ancestors as ancestors are not likely to be sensitive accounts of how it was in the past: the lives and thoughts of Galileo, Descartes, or Boyle were hardly typical of seventeenth-century Italians, Frenchmen, or Englishmen, and telling stories about them geared solely to their ancestral role in formulating the currently accepted law of free fall, the optics of the rainbow, or the ideal gas law is not likely to capture very much about the meaning and significance of their own careers and projects in the seventeenth century.

The past is not transformed into the "modern world" at any single moment: we should never be surprised to find that seventeenth-century scientific practitioners often had about them as much of the ancient as the modern; their notions had to be successively transformed and redefined by generations of thinkers to become "ours." And finally, the people, the thoughts, and the practices we tell stories about as "ancestors," or as the beginnings of our lineage, always reflect some present-day interest. That we tell stories about Galileo, Boyle, Descartes, and Newton reflects something about our late twentieth-century scientific beliefs and what we value about those beliefs. For different purposes we could trace aspects of the modern world back to philosophers "vanquished" by Galileo, Boyle, Descartes, and Newton, and to views of nature and knowledge very different from those elaborated by our officially sanctioned scientific ancestors. For still other purposes we could make much of the fact that most seventeenth-century people had never heard of our scientific ancestors and probably entertained beliefs about the natural world very different from those of our chosen forebears. Indeed, the overwhelming majority of seventeenth century people did not live in Europe, did not know that they lived in "the seventeenth century," and were not aware that a Scientific Revolution was happening. The half of the European population that was female was in a position to participate in scientific culture scarcely at all, as was that overwhelming majority—of men and women—who were illiterate or otherwise disqualified from entering the venues of formal learning.

Some Historiographical Issues

I mean this [selection] to be historiographically up to date—drawing on some of the most recent historical, sociological, and philosophical engagements with the Scientific Revolution. On the other hand, I do not mean to trouble readers with repeated references to methodological and conceptual debates among academics. This [selection] is not written for professional specialized scholars. . . . There is no reason to deny that this story about the Scientific Revolution represents a particular point of view, and that, although I help myself freely to the work of many distinguished scholars, its point of view is my own. Other specialists will doubtless disagree with my approach—some vehemently—and a large number of existing accounts do offer a quite different perspective on what is worth telling about the Scientific Revolution. The positions represented here on some recent historiographic issues can be briefly summarized:

1. I *take for granted* that science is a historically situated and social activity and that it is to be understood in relation to the *contexts* in which it occurs. Historians have long argued whether science relates to its historical and social contexts or whether it should be treated in isolation. I shall simply write about seventeenth-century science as if it were a collectively practiced, historically embedded phenomenon, inviting readers to see whether the account is plausible, coherent, and interesting.

2. For a long time, historians' debates over the propriety of a sociological and a historically "contextual" approach to science seemed to divide practitioners between those who drew attention to what were called "intellectual factors"—ideas, concepts, methods, evidence—and those who stressed "social factors"—forms of organization, political and economic influences on science, and social uses or consequences of science. That now seems to many historians, as it does to me, a rather silly demarcation, and I shall not waste readers' time here in reviewing why those disputes figured so largely in past approaches to the history of early modern science. If science is to be understood as historically situated and in its collective aspect (i.e., sociologically), then that understanding should encompass all aspects of science, its ideas and practices no less than its institutional forms and social uses. Anyone who wants to represent science sociologically cannot simply set aside the body of what the relevant practitioners *knew* and how they went about obtaining that knowledge. Rather,

the task for the sociologically minded historian is to display the structure of knowledge making and knowledge holding *as social processes.*

3. A traditional construal of "social factors" (or what is sociological about science) has focused on considerations taken to be "external" to science proper—for example, the use of metaphors from the economy in the development of scientific knowledge or the ideological uses of science in justifying certain sorts of political arrangements. Much fine historical work has been done based on such a construal. However, the identification of what is sociological about science with what is external to science appears to me a curious and a limited way of going on. There is as much "society" inside the scientist's laboratory, and internal to the development of scientific knowledge, as there is "outside." And in fact the very distinction between the social and the political, on the one hand, and "scientific truth," on the other, is partly a cultural product of the period [I discuss]. What is common sensically thought of as science in the late twentieth century is in some measure a product of the historical episodes we want to understand here. Far from matter-of-factly treating the distinction between the social and the scientific as a resource in telling a historical story, I mean to make it into a topic of inquiry. How and why did we come to think that such a distinction is a matter *of course?*

4. I do not consider that there is anything like an "essence" of seventeenth-century science or indeed of seventeenth-century reforms in science. Consequently there is no single coherent story that could possibly capture all the aspects of science or its changes in which we late twentieth-century moderns might happen to be interested. I can think of no feature of early modern science that has been traditionally identified as its revolutionary essence that did not have significantly variant contemporary forms or that was not subjected to contemporary criticism by practitioners who have also been accounted revolutionary "moderns." . . .

The confrontation over Newton's optical work can stand as an emblem of the fragmented knowledge-making legacies of the seventeenth century. A theoretically cautious and experience-based conception of science was here juxtaposed to one that deployed mathematical as well as experimental tools to claim theoretical certainty. Diffidence was opposed to ambition, respect for the concrete particularities of nature to the quest for universally applicable idealizations, the modesty of the fact gatherer to the pride of the abstracted philosopher. Do you want to capture the essence of nature and command assent to representations of its regularities? Do you want to subject yourself to the discipline of describing, and perhaps generalizing about, the behavior of medium-sized objects actually existing in the world?

Both conceptions of science persist in the late twentieth century, and both can trace elements of their formation back to the seventeenth century. The one is not necessarily to be regarded as a failed version of the other, however much partisans may defend the virtues of their preferred practice and condemn the vices of another. These are, so to speak, different games that natural philosophers might wish to play, and decisions about which game is best are different in kind from decisions about what is a sensible move within a given game: an accurate pass from midfield to the winger in soccer is not a bad jump shot in basketball. In the seventeenth century natural philosophers were confronted with differing repertoires of practical and conceptual skills for achieving various philosophical goals and with choices about which ends they might work to achieve. The goal was always some conception of proper philosophical knowledge about the natural world, though descriptions of what that knowledge looked like and how it was to be secured varied greatly.

Steven Shapin is professor of sociology at the University of California at San Diego. He is the author of *Leviathan and the Air Pump: Hobbes, Boyle, and the Experimental Life* (Princeton University Press, 1985).

EXPLORING THE ISSUE

Was the Scientific Revolution Revolutionary?

Critical Thinking and Reflection

1. Define periodization and explain the relevance of this term to the question raised in this issue. Critically examine whether there was a sharp turning point in the seventeenth century that merits the title, "Scientific Revolution."
2. Thomas Kuhn, in his book *The Structure of Scientific Thought* describes periods of normal science followed by periods of revolution in which experiments do not yield expected results, for example. At those points, a paradigm is overthrown and another one takes its place. Paradigms are vast, complex, coherent views of reality that are so taken-for-granted that they become invisible. With this brief explanation in mind, critically evaluate whether what textbooks typically describe as the Scientific Revolution represents a paradigm shift.
3. In the twentieth century, the discovery of quantum mechanics and relativity theory represented what many would agree was a paradigm shift. In what ways did these two theories revolutionize our understanding of "ordinary" reality? Critically research and analyze this phenomenon.
4. Were there events in the history of science that you would label "revolutionary?" What are some of them and what qualifies them to be called revolutionary? Critically discuss.
5. What key events between 1175 and 1500 does Edward Grant cite as paving the way for a revolution in science? Do you agree that these are crucial events: Critically discuss the criteria Grant uses and the criteria you would use.
6. Having read both selections, which argument do you find more compelling—the claim of continuity or the claim of discontinuity? What specific elements make one interpretation more compelling? Critically discuss.
7. It is only by taking a very long view that we are able to look back at the sweep of history and chunk it into "periods" for study and research. What clues might there be that a society is undergoing a paradigm shift in "real time?" Are we undergoing a paradigm shift now? Critically research, analyze, and make your case either for or against this claim.

Is There Common Ground?

Both historians acknowledge continuity with the medieval past rather than a radical break from it. And, both would agree that the past did not become the "modern world" at a single historical moment. Where they differ is that Grant does see a seventeenth-century turning point—although rooted in a steady forward progression—whereas, Shapin insists that every development we might label revolutionary had "significantly variant contemporary forms" or was criticized by contemporaries whom we also regard as revolutionary "moderns."

It might be worthwhile to interview several scientists or invite a speaker from within the scientific community who could evaluate whether scientists acknowledge a "scientific revolution."

Question: Is it only in hindsight that we can discern the major turning points in history?

Additional Resources

A selection from Thomas Kuhn's book is the concluding essay in *The Scientific Revolution*, Vern L. Bullough, ed. (Holt, Rinehart and Winston, 1970). The opening essay is an excerpt from Andrew Dickson White's classic *A History of the Warfare of Science with Theology*, first published in 1896. A more modern collection of essays appears in *Reappraisals of the Scientific Revolution*, edited by David C. Lindberg and Robert S. Westman (Cambridge University Press, 1990). In it, essays by philosophers of science and historians consider conceptions of science and the relationship between philosophy and science. They also examine what is included in our definition of science and question the historic marginalization of disciplines such as medicine and natural history.

Internet References . . .

The Scientific Revolution: Readings, Resources, Link

A site which explores every facet of the movement; includes essays written by professors, outlines of important material, and many useful resources, print and electronic.

www.clas.ufl.edu/users/rhatch/pages/03-Sci-Rev/SCI-REV-Home/

Selected, Edited, and with Issue Framing Material by:
Helen Buss Mitchell, *Howard Community College*
and
Joseph R. Mitchell, *Howard Community College*

ISSUE

Did the British Enlightenment Pave the Way for the Modern World?

YES: Roy Porter, from "Matrix of Modernity," *History Today* (April 2001)

NO: John Robertson, from "The Enlightenment," *History Review* (September 1997)

Learning Outcomes

After reading this issue you should be able to:

- List the key components in the term "Enlightenment."
- Describe the key characteristics of the British Enlightenment.
- Explain the conditions that were present uniquely in eighteenth-century England.

ISSUE SUMMARY

YES: Professor of Social History, Roy Porter, contends in his Royal Historical Society Gresham Lecture that British thinkers of the eighteenth century were influential in the Enlightenment turn toward a secular worldview and a focus on the future that paved the way for the Modern World.

NO: John Robertson, a University Lecturer in Modern History, finding greater geographic diversity and intellectual complexity, argues that the Enlightenment conversations that shaped modern thought did not occur in eighteenth-century England where political liberty and intellectual freedom were already in place.

In this issue, as in so many others, a lot depends on how we define The Enlightenment. Traditional descriptions stress: the power of human reason over blind faith or obedience; freedom of thought over dogma and superstition; belief in the possibility of progress and the improvement of institutions; and the assertion that human society, the self, and the universe are all rational and understandable. Since both authors in this issue challenge the traditional understanding of the Enlightenment, we are left to question whether there was a single, coherent intellectual movement whose ideas shaped the modern world.

The Enlightenment or the Age of Reason marks one of the turning points in the traditional periodization of European history (see the Introduction). Textbooks on Western civilization typically begin a chapter on the Enlightenment by citing a new reliance on human reason as a tool for modernizing beliefs and institutions. "Dare to think!" said the Prussian philosopher Immanuel Kant, who advocated bringing "light into the dark corners of the mind."

Philosophes, found in major European cities of the eighteenth century, are generally credited with simplifying and popularizing philosophical ideas and relying on the printing press to broadcast their political, literary, and journalistic texts. The term "philosophe" is French for "philosopher," and Paris is usually described as the intellectual center and heart of the European Enlightenment. Inspired by the discoveries of the Scientific Revolution (see Issue Did Martin Luther's Reforms Improve the Lives of European Christians?), historians often claim, the Enlightenment created the modern world.

In the salons of Paris, the traditional understanding of the Enlightenment explains, ideas were debated with a passion and intensity that enflamed the rest of Europe and crossed the Atlantic to America. Censorship and the power of the French monarch and Church made discussing banned books risky, but change was in the air. The public intellectuals who named themselves "philosophes," dwelled intellectually in what they called a "republic of letters," a cosmopolitan forum for ideas that crossed national boundaries.

Great Britain is not typically spoken of as the locus of the Enlightenment, though some texts might mention the "Scottish Enlightenment." However, the pathbreaking philosophical ideas of England's John Locke and Scotland's David Hume were also quite influential, especially their reliance on sense experience as the only solid basis for knowledge. Voltaire (Francois Marie Arouet) became a philosophe when he visited London, impressed with England's constitutional monarchy, the new science of Isaac Newton, and the religious toleration that permitted diversity of thought to flourish.

Unlike most of continental Europe, England had already reined in the power of both king and church. Its so-called Glorious Revolution of the previous century had overthrown the hereditary Stuart King James II. And, a century before that, Henry VIII had broken with the Roman Catholic Church, as part of the overall Protestant Reformation, and installed himself as head of a national Anglican Church. England was firmly on a path to representative government and toward increasing freedom in intellectual and religious thought.

Over the last 30 years, scholars have realized how diverse the Enlightenment actually was—geographically, intellectually, and socially. In this area of study, periodization is not a one-time thing. As our understanding grows, long-held assumptions can be challenged. And, that is what is happening in our own time with regard to the Enlightenment. Not only France, but most of Europe and the United States, it seems, were involved in a conversation about political liberty, freedom of conscience, and the nature of social structures during the eighteenth century.

To explore this issue further, it might be helpful to get a clear sense of the standard view and then explore modern challenges to it. For background on the traditional interpretation, Gertrude Himmelfarb's *The Roads to Modernity: The British, French, and American Enlightenments* (Vintage, 2005; Knopf, 2004) emphasizes the importance of the British Enlightenment, as does our YES selection. Himmelfarb's book does have a neoconservative subtext that praises George W. Bush and Tony Blair for their religious and moral paternalism, whose roots she sees in the British Enlightenment and which is irrelevant to this particular issue.

Dorinda Outram's *The Enlightenment* (Cambridge University Press, 1995) reflects recent challenges to a unified view of the Enlightenment. Outram, who thinks the Enlightenment should be seen as an intersection of debates, rather than one unified stream of thought, presents the varying ways in which the term "enlightenment" has been interpreted historically.

Both of our issue authors have full-length book treatments of this topic. Roy Porter's *Enlightenment: Britain and the Creation of the Modern World* (Penguin, 2000) further amplifies his assertion that Britain was the first enlightened, modern society. Crediting the vital contributions of John Locke, Sir Isaac Newton, and David Hume, as well as the spread of literacy and the elimination of press censorship, Porter praises his native Britain for its creation of a tolerant and secular society that remains inspirational in these respects even today. A later look at the thinking of intellectual historian John Robertson may be found in his *The Case for Enlightenment: Scotland and Naples 1680–1760* (Oxford, 2005). Here he finds commonalities in the intellectual preoccupations of thinkers in two cultures at the extreme edges of Europe. Thus, Robertson challenges the current tendency to fragment the Enlightenment into a series of country-specific events.

The British Isles had developed a confidence in knowledge based on sense experience. This reliance on contact with the world itself for knowledge gave a practical focus to British intellectual thought and probably gave Britain a head start on what historians would later call the Enlightenment. Both the YES selection and NO selection take the British Enlightenment quite seriously.

Roy Porter, author of the YES selection, makes a strong case for Britain as a key contributor to the Enlightenment and the place in which essential features of the modern world were created. The NO selection takes a much wider-ranging look at where and how Enlightenment ideas developed. After systematically dismantling the assumption that there was a single Enlightenment, John Robertson concludes by proposing a new, unifying definition of the Enlightenment that, ironically, excludes England.

YES

Roy Porter

Matrix of Modernity

This MILLENNIUM YEAR led historians to address moments in the past which represent epochs in human affairs. The Enlightenment comprised such a turning-point, since it secularised the worldview and trained eyes and attention towards the future. British thinkers played an influential part in this intellectual revolution—though that is a contribution often ignored or played down, by contrast to that of France.

In the eighteenth century, attention became focused, perhaps for the first time ever, on the future rather than the past, and the drive to create a better future generated a belief in progress. The achievements of scientists like Isaac Newton (1642–1727) and philosophers like John Locke (1632–1704) bred new faith in man's right and power to achieve knowledge of himself and the natural world, and encouraged practical action in such fields as overseas exploration, technology, manufactures, social science and legal reform. Philosophers became commited to the ending of religious strife, bigotry, ignorance, prejudice and poverty, and the creation of polite new social environments and lifestyles.

History is progressive, proclaimed the enlightened activists, 'Rousseau exerts himself to prove that all was right originally,' commented Mary Wollstonecraft (1759–97), 'a crowd of authors, that all is now right: and I, that all will be right'. Sights became trained on the future—not the Apocalypse of orthodox Christian eschatology but one continuous with the here-and-now. Indeed the Enlightenment brought the birth of science fiction—Samuel Madden's futurological *Memoirs of the Twentieth Century* (1733), for instance, or the anonymous and not too chronologically inaccurate *The Reign of George VI, 1900–1925* (1763).

The scent of progress was in the air. The Anglican Edmund Law (1703–87)professed his faith in the 'continual Improvement of the World in general', while the Glasgow Professor John Millar taught that 'one of the most remarkable differences between man and other animals consists in that wonderful capacity for the improvement of his faculties'. Improvement seemed so visible and tangible. 'Who even at the beginning of this century', asked the Unitarian minister Richard Price (1723–91), fired by rational Dissent:

> . . . would have thought, that, in a few years, mankind would acquire the power of subjecting to their wills the dreadful force of lightning, and of flying in aerostatic machines? . . . Many similar discoveries may remain to be made . . . and it may not be too extravagant to expect that . . . the progress of improvement will not cease till it has excluded from the earth most of its worst evils, and restored that Paradisiacal state which, according to the Mosaic History, preceded the present state.

Late-Enlightenment belief in progress was, to be sure, a secular theodicy but Mary Wollstonecraft's 'all will be right' was not complacent. The world, as she explained, was not perfect yet: rather it was mankind's duty to perfect it through criticism, reform, education, knowledge, science, industry and sheet energy. The dynamo of advancement, proclaimed the psychologist David Hartley, was 'the diffusion of knowledge to all ranks and orders of men, to all nations, kindred, tongues, and peoples', a progress which 'cannot now be stopped, but proceeds ever with an accelerated velocity'. And all this optimism about the future was buoyed up by the conviction, in the thinking of the likes of Hartley, Price and Joseph Priestley, that Divine Providence guaranteed such developments or that social progress was underwritten by the surge of biological evolution at large.

Traditional historical pessimism was addressed and allayed by Edward Gibbon (1737–94). Would not, as many believed, the calamities which had destroyed Imperial Rome recur in 'this enlightened age'? No: the great 'source of comfort and hope', explained the *Decline and Full,* was the permanency of improvement. From savagery, mankind had 'gradually arisen to command the animals, to fertilise the earth, to traverse the ocean, and to measure the heavens'. The 'experience of four thousand years should enlarge our hopes', soothed Gibbon, and since technical skills could never be lost, no people 'will relapse into their original barbarism'. Mankind could, therefore,

> acquiesce in the pleasing conclusion that every age of the world has increased, and still increases, the real wealth, the happiness, the knowledge, and perhaps the virtue, of the human race.

Crucial to the birth of the modern was a rethinking of economics. Greek philosophy and Christian theology had each condemned the love of money. The Churches had deemed lucre filthy, greed evil, profit without labour usurious. The Christian duty to conduct personal economic dealings in a just manner had been mirrored in Tudor commonwealth thinking at large. 'Mercantilism'—the economic outlook which dominated the Stuart century and beyond—

took good housekeeping as its model. It measured economic well-being principally in terms of a favourable balance of trade generated by export surpluses: being in pocket. Associating wealth with money or gold and silver, mercantilism's advocates approved the boarding of reserves, the promotion of exports, the limitation of imports, and the management of vital national monopolies.

Enlightened thinking attacked such policies for being unscientific and hence futile. David Hume's essay 'Of the Balance of Trade' (1741) argued that a nation never need be apprehensive of losing its money so long as it preserved its people and its industry, because an automatic self-adjusting mechanism operated which 'must for ever, in all neighbouring countries, preserve money nearly all proportionable to the art and industry of each nation'. In place of regulation, labour and consumption were to be set at the heart of the new thinking.

Mercantilism's faith in interference, critics argued, was superficial opportunistics, and often poisonous. Regulation had made bad worse. What was needed instead was an informed grasp of the macro-economics of cash transfers, the relations between wealth and bullion, money and commodities, the short and the long term.

A profound revaluation of economic activity itself was under way. The old 'moral economy' was coming under fire from a new 'political economy' which laid claim to a scientific grasp of wealth-creation and consumer satisfaction. Enlightened analysis insisted that economic activity was governed by fundamental laws of its own. Ideals such as the just price, the proper reward for labour and other aspects of the moral economy might be admirable, but they did not reflect human nature. Man was, if not nakedly rapacious, at least an accumulating creature, and to ignore such omnipresent motives was pie in the sky.

The new political economy prided itself upon being grounded on a proper grasp of motives, ends and means—natural science, in particular Newtonian physics, often being invoked to prove how economic forces 'gravitated' to an equilibrium: prices were 'continually gravitating . . . ,' wrote Adam Smith, 'towards the natural price'. Like water, economic activity would find its own level, and regulation was thus counter-productive. Since profit-seeking was only human nature, it was best to leave trade free and let the economic players get on with it. As the economist Dudley North (1641–91) opined.

> The main spur to Trade, or rather to Industry and Ingenuity, is the exorbitant Appetites of Men, which they will take pains to gratifie, and so be disposed to work, when nothing else will incline them to it: for did Men content themselves with bare Necessaries, we should have a poor World.

The pioneering figure among the liberal theorists of this school was John Locke. Not only private property but exchange and money were, in his scheme, pre-established in the state of Nature, subject to the laws of Nature and human rationality. Value itself was determined by labour. Hence economic regulation formed no part of the state's day-to-day remit. The new political economy thus repudiated moral or statesmanly to policing of wealth.

Adam Smith (1723–90) systematised the new political economy, grounding it in a science of human appetite, 'the desire of bettering our condition'. Selfishness made the world go round:

> It is not from the benevolence of the butcher, the brewer, or the baker, that we expect our dinner, but from their regard to their own interest.

His formula—let demand decide—expresses the enlightened inclination to trust in Nature. In so doing, Smith was forced to confront the old civic humanist worries about private wealth and greed. Could *enrichissez-vous* prove compatible with socio-political stability? Would not the pursuit of affluence compromise virtue, and 'luxury' subvert liberty, set class against class, and corrupt the commonwealth?

Smith's *Inquiry into the Wealth of Nations* (1776) must be assessed in terms of its wider contribution to enlightened discussions about freedom, justice, subject/state relations, and the quality of life in commercial society. Smith proposed 'opulence and freedom' as 'the two greatest blessings men can possess'. The pairing packed some punch. Two contrasting concepts of liberty had been in circulation since Antiquity. In the Stoic view, freedom was a state of tranquillity in which the cravings of the flesh were curbed by the rational will. There was also the 'civic' view, proposed by Cicero and Livy, for whom liberty lay in political activity and public service. Smith though held that the true key to freedom was commerce, and that it achieved its full expression only in a nation of shopkeepers.

Like Hume, Smith held that the proper stage for human energies was not honour and glory in the Senate, but private, self-regarding pursuits. For Graeco-Roman thinkers, time spent meeting household needs was beneath the dignity of the true male citizen; for Smith, by contrast, it was the natural business of humanity. Indeed, it was a public benefit, for economic exchange forged supportive social networks.

For Smith, dependency was corrupting—a view central to the civic humanist equation of freedom with independence. Yet he insisted that 'commerce is one great preventive' of its occurrence. Economic activity was thus not pathological but prophylactic, preservative of a sound constitution.

Science too was a mighty generator of optimism. In the wake of the great age of Newton, the culture of science spread. While the Royal Society remained the nation's senior scientific society, other bodies were added in the capital, notably the Linnean Society of London (1788) and the Royal Institution (1799). The Royal Society of Edinburgh was set up in 1783, and its counterpart, the Royal Irish Academy, in 1785, while science. Dissent and political reformism joined forces from the 1760s in literary and philosophical societies in Manchester, Newcastle and other industrial centres. Science was acclaimed as vital not just to utility but to the civilising process, the leading light in Manchester, Thomas Henry pronouncing the pursuit of natural philosophy preferable to 'the tavern, the gaming table, or the brothel'.

The most energetic of such gatherings embodying enlightened faith in science was the Lunar Society in Birmingham, formed by Matthew Boulton whose machine-tool-producing Soho factory was internationally famous. From about 1765 a group of friends—leading industrialists, scientists, educators, dissenting ministers and physicians—began to meet at Boulton's home to discuss innovations in science and technology and the new industrial order they were helping to create. They met once a month at full moon, to help light them home. William Hutton found there an ethos he had not encountered elsewhere:

> I had been among dreamers, but now I saw men awake.

Through such associations, Paul Langford tells us, 'a nation of Newtons and Lockes became a nation of Boultons and Watts'.

Scientific improvement was a label often applied to the land, serving as a code-word for capitalist farming, notably enclosure. The improving spirit in agriculture was increasingly associated with the application of science. In the 'Introduction' to his *Phytologia* (1800). Erasmus Darwin, for instance, expressed his view that agriculture had to be made businesslike, through the teachings of political economy:

> . . . for the invention of arts, and production of tools necessary to agriculture, some must think, and others labour: and as the efforts of some will be crowned with greater success than that of others, an inequality of the ranks of society must succeed.

Farming became regarded as a form of manufacturing, with Robert Bakewell's fat sheep serving, rather like Newton's prism, as icons of Enlightenment. That Leicestershire stockrearer bred sheep, cattle, and pigs as meat-producing engines, selected so as to maximise expensive cuts and minimise bones and waste: animals were thus turned into machines.

But it was another field of progress which [then] received the warmest accolades: manufacturing. Progressives had long expressed their fascination with industry in the traditional meaning of skilled work, praising *homo faber*. Manufacturing's appeal to enlightened minds was potent and many-sided. Technology was the cutting-edge of novelty. Water-wheel design became a model of experimental efficiency, and the engineer John Smeaton (1724–92) perfected the lighthouse. In 1758 the 'Improved Birmingham Coach' had blazoned on its side, a touch over-optimistically, "FRICTION ANNIHILATED', and by 1801 Richard Trevithick (1771–1833) had put a steam carriage on the road. Textiles technology was transformed and the steam engine revolutionised power. Industry was also a prime instance of disciplined rationality. Josiah Wedgwood (1730–95) 'the potter, aimed to 'make such machines of Men as cannot err', introducing clocking-on to ensure punctuality among his work-force. Surveying the progress so visible across the West Midlands, he declared.

> Industry and the machine have been the parent of this happy change. A well directed and long continued series of industrious exertion, has so changed, for the better, the face of our country, its buildings, lands, roads and the manners and department of its inhabitants, too.

Business promoted not just wealth but well-being.

Manufacturing, moreover, seemed to be producing a new breed of heroes, principally the self-made 'captain of industry'. One of the children's tales in Anna Barbauld's primly improving *Evenings at Home; Or the Juvenile Budget Opened* (1794) celebrated Sir Richard Arkwright's rise to fame and fortune. 'This is what manufacturers can do', explained Papa to his children: 'here man is a kind of creator, and like the great Creator, he may please himself with his work and say it is good'. Showing his youngsters round a factory, the fictional father insisted what fun it all was: there was 'more entertainment to a cultivated mind its seeing a pin made, than in many a fashionable diversion'.

The entrepreneur was applauded as the exemplar of modern energy. 'I shall never forget Mr. Boulton's expression to me', recalled James Boswell of a visit to the Soho works: "I sell here, Sir, what all the world desires to have—power". He had about seven hundred people at work . . . he seemed to be a father to this tribe'.

Like Boulton, his friend Josiah Wedgwood was one of a remarkable new breed of men conspicuous for applying enlightened thinking to business. Though of meagre formal education, he displayed a consummate faith in reason, and a passion for measuring, weighing, observing, recording and experimenting: all problems would 'yield to experiment'. His rational outlook extended beyond business to Unitarianism in religion and radicalism in polities—he was hostile to slavery, and a warm supporter of the American colonists and later the French Revolution. He thought big; "I shall ASTONISH THE WORLD ALL AT ONCE", he declared to his partner, Thomas Bentley, 'for I hate piddling you know'. Becoming 'vase-maker general to the universe', he died worth half a million.

It is Robert Owen (1771–1858), however, who offers the perfect illustration of the application of enlightened ideas to the empire of industry. Born in mid-Wales, Owen got his first employment as an errand-boy; then he moved into drapery, rising to a partnership in a Manchester firm, before, at the turn of the century, becoming partner and manager of the New Lanark Mills on Clydeside. For the next two decades he combined entrepreneurship with social reform. In his *A New View of Society* (1813) Owen urged rational social rebuilding on the basis of universal education. Manufacturing would provide the foundation for happiness, but only once divested of the arbitrariness of the dog-eats-dog market and reorganised according to social utility. Character could be moulded by correct environmental influence. If the labouring classes were ignorant, brutalised and criminal, they were victims and it was society that must shoulder the blame.

But Owen was no Smithian. *Laissez-faire* was useless for ensuring long-term prosperity and welfare—market forces would 'produce the most lamentable and permanent evils', unless there were 'legislative interference and direction'. Though industrialisation held out the promise of untold human benefit, under the competitive system some grew fabulously rich while others were pauperised. Co-operation was needed to effect industry's potential social advantages. Since people were products of circumstances, education would make all the difference according to Owen's plan. In his New Lanark factory village, the provision of schooling, along with such amenities as a museum, would programme workers for happiness. Here was a veritable social experiment in action, 'one which cannot fail to prove the certain means of renovating the moral and religious principles of the world, by showing whence arise the various opinions, manners, vices and virtues of mankind.' An unbeliever, Owen secularised Christian aspirations in envisaging

> . . . the foretold millennium . . . when the slave and the prisoner, the bond-man and the bond-woman, and the child and the servant, shall be set free for ever, and oppression of body and mind shall be known no more.

Owen was thus a logical terminus *ad quem* of certain strands of Enlightenment thought, envisaging comprehensive benevolent control within a scheme of industrialisation, and showing both a concern with education and discipline over his 'human machines'.

Many penned anthems to improvement, uniting science and imagination, poetry and social theory. The most notable poetic prophet of progress, however, was Erasmus Darwin. A physician first and foremost, Darwin practised for some forty years, and his magnum opus, *Zoonamia* (1794–96), was essentially a work of medical theory. Despite his busy medical practice, he poured his boundless energies into many channels. In 1771 he was dabbling with a mechanical voicebox; in the next year he had long discussions with Wedgwood and the engineer James Brindley about extending the Grand Trunk Canal; with his friend Brooke Boothby, he founded the Lichfield Botanic Society, which in time brought out translations of Linnaeus' classification system. His gardening interests also blossomed on a site west of Lichfield, where in 1778 he established a botanic garden, the inspiration of his later poem of the same name.

Uniting arts and sciences, medicine, physics and technology, Darwin was the embodiment of enlightened values. 'All those who knew him will allow that sympathy and benevolence were the most striking features', wrote Keir:

> He despised the monkish abstinences and the hypocritical pretensions which so often impose on the world. The communication of happiness and the relief of misery were by him held as the only standard of moral merit.

Darwin embraced a humanitarian benevolence hostile to Christian values and judgements. From early on, he rejected Christianity in favour of Deism. Indeed, he found the Christian Almighty quite repellent: how could a truly loving Father visit terrible diseases upon innocent children?

Politically, Darwin was a dyed-in-the-wool-liberal. His books and letters echo with condemnations of despotism, slavery and bloodshed: 'I hate war', 'I have just heard', he raged on one occasion to Josiah Wedgwood, 'that there are muzzles or gags made at Birmingham for the slaves in our island. If this be true' and such an instrument could be exhibited by a speaker in the House of Commons, it might have a great effect'. He supported the French Revolution, and after the 1791 Birmingham riots he wrote to Joseph Priestley deploring his victimisation by fanatics—while also politely advising him to quit his theological maunderings and get on with something more useful, namely scientific experiments. Darwin's politics were, however, never revolutionary. Law, order and property were essential ingredients for the social progress which would be achieved within the framework of free-market capitalism and industrialisation.

As the summation of his myriad ideas, Darwin developed the first comprehensive theory of biological evolution: 'would it be too bold to imagine, that all warm-blooded animals have arisen from one living filament, which THE GREAT FIRST CAUSE endued with animality?' The endless mutual competition of burgeoning organic forms within the terraqueous globe also resulted in death, destruction and even extinction.

Nevertheless, rather as for Adam Smith, the law of competition brought about net improvement, and the aggregate rise of population spelt not Malthusian misery but an augmentation of happiness Darwin's evolutionism provided the British Enlightenment's clinching theory of boundless improvement.

The epic of progress, implicit or explicit in most late-enlightenment opinion and given a scientific grounding by Darwin, stands in stark contrast to such earlier visions of the human condition as *Paradise Lost* (1663) and Pope's *Essay on Man* (1733–34). For Milton, what was fundamental was the relationship between God and man: Adam's offence lay in violation of God's command; man's destiny was couched in a transcendental revelation. Darwin, by contrast, painted a wholly optimistic, naturalistic and this-worldly picture, grounded on evolution, biological and social. Human capacities were the products of biological and physiological development which extended to 'the progress of the Mind'. Not only was there no Miltonic Lucifer and Fall, but to Darwin, man alone had consciousness of the natural order. Whereas Pope had scorned pride as hubristic, for Darwin pride and its triumphs had their legitimate basis in Nature.

Progress proved the ultimate Enlightenment gospel. Darwin and his peers presented a man-centred view of man making himself—a Promethean vision of infinite possibilities. God had become a distant cause of causes; what counted was man acting in Nature.

Erasmus Darwin's evolutionary theories were not accepted in his own day. Evolutionary thinking long lay under a cloud, being condemned as materialistic and atheistic and associated with that great abomination, the French Revolution. Therein lay one of the reasons why his grandson, Charles, was so hesitant about publishing his own evolutionary theory, and why, when *The Origin of Species* finally saw the light of day in 1859, it still created such a storm.

Something similar happened with many of the other key ideas of the Enlightenment. Original and challenging, they had never met with universal acceptance, and there always remained powerful groupings of High-Flying churchmen, Jacobites, Tories, traditionalists. Methodists and so forth for whom the enlightened accent on critical reason was an absurdity or an obscenity.

Undergoing socio-political growing pains and tensions, and in particular when confronted by the French Revolution, the Revolutionary and Napoleonic Wars, and their backlashes, liberal ideologies began to shiver into fragments. For some, libertarian rhetoric led to Jacobin radicalism—witness Tom Paine's very titles: *Common Sense, The Age of Reason,* and *The Rights of Man.* Bourgeois liberalism put a different face upon enlightened ideology: individualism was to obey the iron laws of political economy; social progress demanded time-and-work discipline, penology and scientific poor laws; while humanitarian impulses bled into proto-Victorian sentimentality. Meanwhile, establishment apologists began to draw conclusions of their own from enlightened premises. Malthus put a new gloss on desire, recruiting science to prove how legislative action could not, after all, relieve suffering and starvation. More dramatically, French Revolutionary turmoil led many to change sides: Wordsworth, Southey and Coleridge, for instance.

Yet, in the long run, enlightened ideologies were not discarded. They continued to inform Victorian self-help liberalism and free-market ideology. By touting rational self-help, they promised a meliorist, moralised future which immunised native radicals against Marxist creeds of class war or communitarian socialism. Phrenology, secularism and Fabianism were all, in their own ways, Enlightenment legacies.

None of these developments was without the most profound tensions. If I have argued that the Enlightenment generated the idea of progress, mine has been no simple tale of 'progress', but of the on-going war of ideas against ideas.

For Further Reading

Roy Porter, *Enlightenment: Britain and the Creation of the Modern World* (Allen Lane, 2000), David Spadafora. *The Idea of Progress in 18th Century Britain* (Yale Univ Press, 1990), Jan Golinsk, *Science as Public Culture; Chemistry and Enlightenment in Britain, 1760–1820* (Cambridge University Press, 1992); Larry Stewart, *The Rise of Public Science Rhetonic, Technology, and Natural Philosophy in Newtonian Britain, 1660–1750* (CUP). W.L. Letwin, *The Origins of Scientific Economics* (Methuen, 1963). Donald Wanch, *Riches and Poverty An Intellectual History of Political Economy in Britain 1750–1834* (CUP, 1996)

This article is the revised text of the Gresham Lecture delivered by Roy Porter in November 2000. Roy Porter is Professor of the Social History of Medicine at the Wellcome Trust Centre, University College, London.

Roy Porter (1946–2002) was a popular British author, commentator and historian whose published works covered diverse topics, ranging from the Enlightenment to the history of medicine. His dozen books include *The Creation of the Modern World: The Untold Story of the British Enlightenment* (2001).

John Robertson

The Enlightenment

Definition of the Enlightenment used to be a straightforward matter. It was a group of French philosophers, the philosophes, who along with a few curious foreign visitors gathered in Paris in the middle decades of the eighteenth century to talk and to write about ways of improving the world. While the subjects they discussed were many and varied, they shared and expounded a common set of values, prominent among which were reason, humanity, liberty and tolerance. The Enlightenment, in other words, existed in a certain time and place, was identified with a particular group of men, and was characterised by specific ideas. Over the past thirty years, however, scholars have questioned virtually all of these assumptions. The Enlightenment has been extended far beyond France, and has been associated with a wider range of intellectual interests than those which formed the staple of the Paris salons. Still more energy has been devoted to writing its social history, to identifying the parts played by its publishers and booksellers, to debating its significance for women, and to enlarging our knowledge of its institutional and cultural contexts.

Not surprisingly, the result of all this activity has been disagreement, to the point where many scholars now question whether it is helpful to continue to think in terms of a single Enlightenment; and even those who are still willing to talk of 'the' Enlightenment as a whole do so only in a loose and inclusive way. Such a gulf between new scholarly thinking and traditional assumptions is of course to be found in many fields of history. But the problem seems particularly acute in the case of the Enlightenment. As good an indication as any of its severity is the shortage of accessible and up-to-date surveys of the subject: not until 1995, when Cambridge published Dorinda Outram's *The Enlightenment* in the 'new approaches to European history' series, was there a replacement for Norman Hampson's 1968 Penguin of the same title.

A short article is not the place to resolve the problem and provide a new, instantly usable account of the Enlightenment. Even if, as I shall end by suggesting, it is still possible to present the Enlightenment as a single, coherent intellectual movement whose ideas shaped the modern world, this case cannot be made without recognising the importance of the new directions in Enlightenment scholarship, and the extent to which they have complicated and even undermined the traditional picture. The better to measure the change, I shall begin by taking a closer look at the traditional Enlightenment, as scholars understood it until the 1960s.

The Traditional Enlightenment

In fact the traditional Enlightenment had two aspects, literary and philosophical. Literary historians identified the Enlightenment almost exclusively with a small circle of philosophe and their supporters in France. These included a few indisputably great writers—Voltaire and Montesquieu, thought of as the founding fathers of the movement, Diderot and D'Alembert, editors of the *Encyclopedie,* the philosophers D'Holbach, Helvetius, Condillac and Condorcet, the political economists Turgot and Quesnay, and the profoundly original if rebellious political philosopher Jean-Jacques Rousseau. These and other men of letters who identified with them had made their way to Paris between the 1730s and the 1780s, were admitted to the salons of free-thinking ladies to discuss their ideas, and then or later made these ideas public in an array of books and pamphlets. Since the salon conversations were not recorded, it was the philosophes' publications which were taken as defining the intellectual content of the Enlightenment. Besides the *Encyclopedie* (1751–72), its characteristic works included Montesquieu's *Espirit des Lois* (1748), Voltaire's *Candide* (1759) and *Dictionnaire Philosophique* (1764), and Rousseau's *Discours sur les origines del'inegalite'* (1755), *Du contrat social* (1761) and *Emile* (1762).

Scholars who adhered to this view of the Enlightenment were aware of the need for nuance. It was well known that many of the philosophes spent more time out of Paris than in it: Voltaire was safely resident for long periods at Ferney, just over the Swiss border; Montesquieu did his work at La Brede, his chateau outside Bordeaux; Rousseau was soon alienated by the salons, and took to wandering within and beyond France. Nor was this Enlightenment ever entirely a French preserve. Visitors from as far afield as Scotland and Naples were drawn to Paris and admitted to the salons, [where] a David Hume or a Ferdinando Galiani was welcome to contribute to the discussions. There always harmonious: an apparently common set of values did not preclude sharp disagreement on specific issues. Rousseau's differences with fellow philosophes were so many and bitter, that is, [it] was increasingly hard to think of him as remaining within the Enlightenment at all, but disputes could arise between even its securest adherents, as when Galiani, supported by Diderot, unexpected[ly] attacked the Physiocrats in 1770. For all these qualifications, however, the Enlightenment of the literary scholars remained narrowly focussed on the thoughts of a small circle of writers, and on France.

A different though not inconsistent view was taken by scholars trained in the history of philosophy. For them the natural starting point was the essay which the great German philosopher, Imanuel Kant, had written in 1783 to answer the question "What is Enlightenment?". Not only did this essay provide the Enlightenment with its motto, Sapere aude, 'dare to know', it directed attention to Kant's ambition to put the whole of philosophy, and hence of knowledge, on a new, critical basis. Kant's philosophy, on which he worked continuously from the 1750s to the 1790s, could be regarded as a systematic summation of the intellectual project of the entire Enlightenment, and thus used as a framework in which to place and assess the contributions of other thinkers across a range of fields, including metaphysics, aesthetics, moral and politics. There was an obvious difficulty in combining this approach to the Enlightenment in Kantian perspective with the Franco-centric approach of the literary scholars: Kant lived and taught in Konigsberg, on the Baltic coast in East Prussia (the city now named Kaliningrad, which remains as 'enclave' of Russia within Lithuania), and he never . . . visited Paris. But the philosophical historians of the Enlightenment were prepared to concede that its works were otherwise overwhelmingly French: the point of their approach was that it enabled the thought of Montesquieu, Voltaire, Rousseau and others to be discussed systematically, and their values of reason, liberty and tolerance to be given philosophical substance.

Despite the awkwardness of Kant's geographical dislocation, the combination of literary and philosophical approaches was successful in giving the Enlightenment a clear historical identity. Knowing what the Enlightenment was and what it thought, historians could then proceed to determine its relation to other important developments in the eighteenth century. Both the influence of the Enlightenment on contemporary rulers—the problem of 'enlightened despotism'—and the connection between the Enlightenment and the French Revolution became questions to which it should be possible to deliver a firm answer. The latter question was of course complicated by the existence of a conspiracy theory, originating in the period of the Revolution itself, which attributed its outbreak to a 'philosophe plot'. But given a secure definition of the Enlightenment, it became possible for historians to concentrate on determining whether or not there was positive evidence of the influence of Enlightenment ideas on those who criticised the Ancien Regime or joined in designing the revolutionary constitutions.

The ground had begun to shift under the traditional understanding of the Enlightenment by the 1960s. Enlightenment studies then began to move in a number of new directions, which were pursued with increasing enthusiasm through the 1970s and 1980s. Though the divisions between them are not hard and fast, the new directions can be grouped under three headings: geographical, intellectual, and social. Each has enormously deepened our understanding of the Enlightenment; as I shall point out, however, they have also been taken to lengths which make it almost impossible to preserve a coherent view of the Enlightenment as a whole.

New Directions: Geographical

The first feature of the traditional Enlightenment to be questioned was its geographical concentration upon France. The decisive contribution was that of the late Italian historian Franco Venturi. Having begun by writing on *Diderot* and the *Encyclopedie*, Venturi never denied the centrality of France to the Enlightenment: what he pointed out, however, was that the Italian thinkers Beccaria and Galiani, hitherto treated as 'visiting' members of the Enlightenment by virtue of their stays in Paris, were also active proponents of Enlightenment ideas in their own country. In Milan, Beccaria had formed the II caffe group along with Pietro and Alessandro Verri; in Naples, Galiani had been the contemporary of Antonio Genovesi, holder of the first chair of political economy in Europe, and of the younger philosophers Gaetano Filangieri and Francesco Mario Pagano. Similar groups of illuministi, Venturi discovered, had emerged in Venice, in Piedmont, in Tuscany and even in the Papal States. Looking westwards to Spain, Venturi could point to Campomanes, Uztariz and Ulloa, economic reformers whose concerns were very close to those of the Italians.

Elsewhere a similar pattern emerged. In Germany the Enlightenment, or Aufklarung, was not confined to Kant. For all Frederick ll's preference for things, French, his capital, Berlin, was a centre of debate over issues of tolerance, freedom of the press and economic reform. Other smaller German courts facilitated a greater or lesser degree of discussion of these and other issues among officials and university teachers. In Hanover, whose prince was the King of Great Britain, the professors at the new University of Gottingen were in the forefront of developments in the 'state sciences' and philosophical history. Recognisably, Enlightenment ideas penetrated even the southern, Catholic principality of Bavaria. German (and Italian) participation in the Enlightenment, moreover, was not simply a passive response to the new thinking from Paris. German Aufklarer were also reading the works of the Italians, and of the Scots, both in the original and in translation. The passage of ideas in the Enlightenment, it is clear, was a multi- rather than uni-directional process.

But the most telling evidence for the geographical extension of the Enlightenment was provided by its discovery in Scotland. Before the 1960s the Scottishness of David Hume and Adam Smith was hardly remembered. Yet not only did they live and write in Scotland, but they also visited London and Paris for short periods before returning; among their Scottish contemporaries were the thinkers and historians Adam Ferguson, William Robertson,

Thomas Reid, Lord Kames and John Millar. Together these formed perhaps the strongest single concentration of Enlightenment thinkers outside Paris, enjoying a strong base in the country's universities and legal profession. Another branch of the Enlightenment in the English-speaking world which began to receive scholarly attention at about the same time was the North American. Many of the colonists who rebelled in 1776 did so believing themselves to be members of a wider Enlightenment republic of letters, and when Benjamin Franklin took up residence in Paris as the American minister he was welcomed by the philosophes as an intellectual equal.

The potential of this new direction in Enlightenment studies was spotted by two Cambridge scholars, Roy Porter and Mikulas Teich, who organised a seminar and published its proceedings as The Enlightenment in National Context (1981). The result is an extremely useful collection of survey articles on the Enlightenment in the several countries already mentioned, and also in England, the Netherlands, Sweden, Switzerland, Bohemia and Russia. But the volume (which became the model for a whole series of thematic collections 'in national context') may also be seen as a turning point. Although its title still acknowledged the existence of one Enlightenment, its implication was that each national Enlightenment could be studied as a separate phenomenon. In opening the volume with a plea for recognition of the Enlightenment in England, Porter flatly declared that the unity of the Enlightenment was a 'hallucination'. Not surprisingly, Porter's plea has been welcomed by the many historians of eighteenth-century England who do not wish their subject excluded from such an obviously good cause as the Enlightenment (or, at least, see it as a useful defence against the ancien regime of J.C.D. Clark). With less justification, scholars of the Scottish Enlightenment have shown a similar tendency to rely on the national context, neglecting to study the Scottish thinkers in a broader European setting. As a result, the geographical extension of the Enlightenment now threatens to end in something which Venturi would have abhorred, its fragmentation into a host of separate Enlightenments, each defined as best suits national historiography.

New Directions: Intellectual

The second new direction in Enlightenment studies has been towards a much more complex appreciation of its thought. The old shibboleth that the Enlightenment was 'the Age of Reason', behind which lay the awesome intellectual authority of Kant, has long since been abandoned. If anything, Kant was attempting to rehabilitate the concept of reason in response to the criticism to which it had been subjected by other Enlightenment philosophers. The idea that reason was humanity's key to knowledge and moral value was after all a commonplace of Christian scholasticism, rejecting this, almost all serious philosophers since the seventeenth century, from Descartes and Hobbes to Locke and Hume, had been sceptics. It was the passions, they argued, which dominated human nature, and of these, self-interest was much the strongest. As Albert Hirschman showed in a brilliant short book, *The Passions and the Interests* (1977), it was the assumption that these (and not reason) were fundamental which underlay the moral philosophy, political economy and historical theories of Mandeville and Hume, Montesquieu, Rousseau and Adam Smith. Even Kant started from here: if reason was conceivable a priori, and even attainable, it was 'the crooked timber of humanity' which had shaped the existing world.

As the equation of the Enlightenment with Reason was discarded, it became apparent that no single philosophical system could give intellectual unity to the movement as a whole. Disagreements were as common in philosophy as in political economy. It also became clearer that the Enlightenment was not uniformly irreligious. Although the challenge of scepticism was unavoidable, it did not necessarily lead to disbelief. Hume and D'Holbach (whose positions were by no means identical—Hume was horrified by D'Holbach's dogmatic atheism) were neither typical nor even very original in their unbelief: their arguments owed much to radical pre-Enlightenment critics of revealed religion, and even to priestly devil's advocacy, identifying arguments for atheism the better to refute them. Many more Enlightenment thinkers seem to have retained some religious beliefs, even if they were unorthodox, and many remained comfortably in Protestant or Catholic clerical orders. Historians have also pointed to a growing interest in the later stages of the Enlightenment in exploring the boundaries between the rational and the irrational, evident in the controversy over Franz Anton Mesmer's untestable hypothesis of invisible magnetic fluids.

Here too, however, a fruitful new direction in Enlightenment scholarship has been taken to lengths which seem to threaten the historical validity of the concept itself. Purely intellectual historians are liable to wonder where the Enlightenment is supposed to begin and end. Should it not be taken to start with Descartes and Hobbes? Given the continuous development of political economy after Smith, does it not carry over into the early nineteenth century? Others have asked why, if no single philosophy characterises Enlightenment thinking, some or indeed any areas of intellectual activity should be excluded from it. Not content with the seventeenth-century 'scientific revolution', historians of science have been particularly keen to see their subject raised to a central place in the Enlightenment as well. Almost any form of literature may likewise be regarded as eligible—an opening which students of English literature have not been slow to exploit. Ultimately it becomes impossible to exclude any not obviously reactionary form of thought from the Enlightenment's liberal embrace. But there is a price to pay: an Enlightenment so inclusive is in danger of losing any coherent, distinctive intellectual identity.

New Directions: Social

The third and probably the liveliest of the new directions in Enlightenment scholarship has been that pursued by the social historians of ideas. The starting point for this line of enquiry was a question to which traditional Enlightenment studies had already devoted attention: the extent to which the works of the philosophes were made available to and were read by the different classes in French society. The pioneering work on the subject, Daniel Mornet's Les origines intellectuelles de la Revolution francaise (1933) was linked directly to the issue of the Enlightenment's responsibility for the Revolution. The subsequent, much more thoroughly statistical investigations of Daniel Roche and his equipe of researchers have, however, set this issue aside, the better to explore the social impact of the Enlightenment through membership of provincial academies, and the potential readership of different types of publication. A different and undeniably more exciting approach was taken by the American historian Robert Darnton. In *The Business of Enlightenment: A Publishing History of the Encyclopédie* (1979) he exploited the rich archives of the Societe Typographique de Neuchatel to tell an extraordinary tale of entrepreneurial collaboration and rivalry between the editors, publishers, smugglers and sellers of the Encyclopédie, demonstrating that while its price was beyond the labouring poor it was within the reach of many in the middle and professional ranks.

But Darnton was also at the head of those who argued that a properly social history of the Enlightenment should not restrict itself to studying the diffusion of its works. Still thinking of the relation to the Revolution, he coined the distinction between the 'high' Enlightenment of the salons and academies and the 'low' Enlightenment of Parisian grub-street journalists, suggesting that it was the latter who turned the ideals of the 'high' Enlightenment into the slogans which were to drive the Revolution. But Darnton's sharp distinction between privileged elite and alienated hacks is increasingly contested. What he has missed, other historians argue, is the connection between the Enlightenment and the emergence of a new, broad-based culture of 'sociability'. First articulated in the widely admired and frequently copied English journals *The Spectator and the Tatler,* this was a culture which valued civilised conversation, correspondence and discussion free of political or religious partisanship. It was the culture of middle, professional and even noble classes who wished to live their lives independently, without constantly deferring to standards set for them by courts, churches and politicians. Two manifestations of this culture have received particular attention. The first is the participation of women in the salons. In one of the most thought-provoking recent contributions to Enlightenment studies, Dena Goodman has argued that the Salonnieres were not mere hostesses but the directors and arbiters of a distinctive Enlightenment culture, determining the rules of polite conversation and epistolary commerce. Unfortunately it was a culture which the men were to betray, by insisting on taking their disagreements into print, and then by devising new institutions which excluded women. Prominent among the latter were masonic lodges, the second form of sociability to attract historians' attention. Freemasonry as a self-conscious creed and set of rituals had originated in sixteenth- and seventeenth-century Scotland, and migrated to England in the early eighteenth century; thence it spread rapidly across the continent, with different lodges choosing between a variety of 'rites'. By no means every adherent of the Enlightenment was a freemason. The Scottish Enlightenment, for example, appears to have been relatively immune. But elsewhere, and particularly in the 1770s and 1780s, membership was common: almost all of the Neapolitan illuministi, for example, were masons. Quite why such [a] secretive, ritualistic creed [that] should have appealed to men (and, Margaret Jacob points out, one or two women) who were otherwise committed to the rational, public discussions of ideas may well puzzle late twentieth-century scholars. But it is important to set aside freemasonry's present connotations, and to recognise that in the still rigidly hierarchical societies of ancien regime Europe its internal egalitarianism, which its rituals helped to enforce, might have considerable appeal.

Association of the Enlightenment with a culture of sociability thus offers a plausible way of relating it to a range of institutions and practices popular with the middle, if not the lower, ranks of eighteenth-century societies. The problem with this approach is that it tends to render the Enlightenment little more than a vague social consciousness. The cultural historians who favour the approach commonly deride intellectual historians for the narrowness of their interest in a few selected 'texts': but intellectual historians may with at least equal justice reply that the cultural historians have no idea what serious thought is, and are treating the arguments of a Hume or a Diderot as if they were equivalent to those of any participant in 'polite' conversation. If sociability is to be the hallmark of the Enlightenment, there is no reason, as Darnton's most recent, brilliant study of *The Forbidden Best-Sellers of Pre-Revolutionary France* (1996) may be taken to imply, to distinguish the mechanistic philosophy of D'Holbach from the mechanistic pornography of the author of *Therese Philosophe:* and the latter, being also a best seller, can hardly be regarded as possessing less historical significance.

Reconstructing the Enlightenment

The volume and richness of new work on the Enlightenment make any return to the traditional view of it impossible. But if the implications of this work are to fragment the Enlightenment into separate national units, deprive it of intellectual identity, and reduce it to a culture of sociability, can any single account of the Enlightenment be put in its place? Many scholars would be unmoved, even puzzled, by the question: an easy going pluralism comes naturally to the liberal-minded who are drawn to study the Enlightenment, and is in tune with fashionable post-modern assumptions. In her new survey, Dorinda Outram bravely makes a virtue of the difficulty, choosing to define the Enlightenment as a series of debates, taking different forms in different national and cultural contexts, rather than as a unitary phenomenon whose ideas were generated by particular thinkers. With chapters devoted to science, the exotic and gender as well as to the social context, religion and government, the result is an excellent conspectus of the Enlightenment of today's scholarship. But is this the best we can do? Is it now impossible to reconstruct the Enlightenment as a single Europe-wide movement of thought, with an identifiable place in eighteenth-century society?

If such a reconstruction is to be attempted, it might be along the following lines. First, the geographical extension of the Enlightenment does not have to lead to its fragmentation. The strength of the case for the Enlightenment as a single intellectual movement within the European world is that its adherents not only had similar interests and objectives, but were conscious of sharing these with others, and of communicating them across frontiers and linguistic barriers. The ability to do this was not new: a European 'republic of letters' had existed at least since the Renaissance, and indeed Enlightenment writers made their communications more difficult by using the vernacular rather than Latin. Nevertheless, it is likely that the Enlightenment involved more participants, and reached further across the European world, from Russia to North America, than any previous intellectual movement not institutionally supported by the churches. Such a conscious sense of involvement in the Enlightenment was fostered in several ways. Paris played a key role as a cosmopolitan centre, attracting intellectually minded visitors and offering those who could not travel an example of intensive discussion of new ideas. But the expansion of the periodical press, the widespread ability to read French, and the increasing frequency of translation from one vernacular into another all made the books and the ideas of the Enlightenment available to a much larger readership.

There is likewise no need to abandon all hope of identifying the Enlightenment with a coherent intellectual project. Although the old belief that the works of the Enlightenment were expressions of a rationalist philosophy has had to be discarded, what remains clear is the commitment of the Enlightenment's adherents to investigating the ways of bettering the human condition on this earth. This was not a commitment which entailed open hostility to revealed religion: it simply focussed attention on this world and set aside considerations of the next. There were three main aspects to this commitment. One was concerned with the individual's relation to the law, and the rightful extent of personal liberty and security. Under this head can be gathered the Enlightenment's discussions of toleration, of property and the line to be drawn between abusive and legitimate property rights—'feudal' property being widely regarded as abusive—and of the administration of justice and punishment.

A second aspect of the Enlightenment project was the enquiry into the means and mechanisms of material betterment. Sophisticated writing on economic affairs of course predated the Enlightenment; but from the 1740s there can be seen a conscious attempt on the part of French, Italian, German and Scottish thinkers to render political economy a distinct, systematic field of investigation. No longer concerned with the aggrandisement of governments at another's expense, this was political economy whose goals were the wealth of nations (in the plural) and the improvement of the condition of all of society's members. Matching this commitment to material betterment was a third strand to the Enlightenment project, the aspiration to cultural refinement. Given humanity's capacity to 'polish' or even (as many followed Rousseau in supposing) to 'perfect' its nature, it was now possible to envisage the achievement of a new state of civilisation. The likeliest means to this end was seen as the extension of education, which should be made the subject of lay rather than clerical priorities, but Rousseau was not alone in thinking that education should be accompanied by the extension of political liberty.

To associate these concerns with a coherent intellectual project is not to say that they were accepted or even understood in the same sense by all the Enlightenment's adherents. The scope for disagreement over the definition and compatibility of these objectives, let alone over the means to fulfill them, was wide. Nor did these concerns exclude the pursuit of other intellectual interests. Many Enlightenment thinkers were also students of the natural world. It was a matter of priorities: and what characterised the Enlightenment was the primacy it accorded to human betterment, to what its thinkers called 'the progress of society'. The possibility—not the inevitability—of progress is the thread around which all the strands of Enlightenment enquiry were woven. To those who attached most importance to material betterment, the prospects for continuing progress were good; others, more concerned with culture, and more open to Rousseau's warnings, feared that refinement would lead to decadence, the progress must end in decline. Yet even those most fearful of decline accepted a central proposition: society is subject to change, and humans can better their condition. Whatever the consolations that may be waiting in the world to come, improvement is possible in this.

In addition to identifying a coherent intellectual project, a credible new account of the Enlightenment will also have to address its place in society. Instead of reducing the Englightenment to the culture of sociability, however, it may be more fruitful to focus on its role in developing the influence of public opinion. Although a number of well-known philophes were lured to the courts of contemporary rulers, the objective of Enlightenment thinkers, it may be argued, was not so much to give better counsel to princes (as the humanists had once sought to do), but to mobilise a broader body of opinion behind both specific causes and a more general expectation of change. Volataire's campaigns against miscarriages of justice in the 1760s, or Turgot's carefully co-ordinated efforts to persuade French public opinion of the merits of his liberal economic reforms in the early 1770s, are examples of what could be done in specific cases (although Turgot's abrupt fall in 1776 also exposed the limits to such persuasion on behalf of individual government policies). But for the most part Enlightenment writers sought to shape opinion less directly, by changing expectations of government and social behaviour. This was the objective of Diderot's *Encyclopédie,* of Hume in his *Essays and History of England,* and of Genovesi in his efforts to educate a new middle rank of Neapolitans by making available the works of French and English political economy.

An Enlightenment reconstructed on these terms cannot include everything which some recent scholars would want to associate with it. It does not treat every form of intellectual activity as equally characteristic of the Enlightenment, nor does it conflate Enlightenment with politeness and sociability. In identifying what was specific to the Enlightenment, such a view also accepts that it had intellectual and social limits. If its achievements become clearer, so do its limitations. An Enlightement reconstructed along the lines suggested was one whose commitment of liberty, economic development and cultural refinement made an enduring contribution to modern thought, but which by no means exhausted the political and literary culture of the eighteenth century. Its critical, reforming edge almost certainly encourage dissatisfaction with the ancien regime, in France and elsewhere; but it cannot be confused with the—perhaps more damaging—'forbidden literature' of the pornographers and libellistes, whose scurrilous gossip about the French royal family did so much to destroy its legitimacy.

Finally, an Enlightenment reconstructed on these terms is one which did not exist in eighteenth-century England. In part this was because such an Enlightenment was simply not needed in a country which already enjoyed political liberty, economic development and free public discussion, and whose philosophers, Newton, Locke and Shaftesbury, had provided so much of the original inspiration for the Enlightenment in Europe. But this was also an Enlightenment on which English public life missed out, despite the best efforts of David Hume and Adam Smith to make it available to English readers. The intensive discussion of ideas of human betterment, and their critical application to the existing social and political order, a discussion which took place almost everywhere in the European world in the mid- and late-eighteenth century, did not occur in eighteenth-century England. It was England's loss.

JOHN ROBERTSON is a Fellow of St. Hugh's College, Oxford, and a University Lecturer in Modern History. His published work includes *The Scottish Enlightenment and the Militia Issue* (Edinburgh, 1985) and the edited volume *A Union for Empire: Political Thought and the Union of 1707* (Cambridge, 1995). He is currently engaged in a comparative study of the Enlightenment in Scotland and Naples.

EXPLORING THE ISSUE

Did the British Enlightenment Pave the Way for the Modern World?

Critical Thinking and Reflection

1. What is your common sense definition/understanding of the Enlightenment? Where do you believe your ideas have originated?
2. How does your world history or European history text address the Enlightenment? Does either selection of this issue more closely follow the lead of your text? Critically research and analyze this comparative data.
3. What evidence exists that there was a single Enlightenment that began in France. Critically examine this evidence.
4. What evidence exists that there was no single, unique Enlightenment? Critically examine this evidence.
5. The basis on which England might be excluded from an emerging definition of Enlightenment is an ironic one. What is the basis for this irony? Critically discuss.
6. Why does Roy Porter write: "Crucial to the birth of the modern was a rethinking of economics?" Critically analyze and evaluate this statement.
7. John Robertson writes: "The volume and richness of new work on the Enlightenment make any return to the traditional view of it impossible." Critically evaluate and discuss this claim.

Is There Common Ground?

It has been widely claimed that "Where you stand determines what you see." Each of these writers stands within a different intellectual tradition. As we look at where both writers place their focuses, we can gain some insight into how both their views of the Enlightenment may be ably defended.

Question: How many other positions on this question might exist in the vast middle between these two poles?

Additional Resources

American historian Robert Darnton's *The Business of Enlightenment* (Harvard, 1979) looks at the publishing history of Denis Diderot's *Encyclopedie* (one of the key documents of the French Enlightenment) to demonstrate its wide dispersal and availability, not perhaps to the laboring class but to many educated readers who were not of the elite classes. Finally, Franco Venturi's *Utopia and Reform in the Enlightenment* (Cambridge, 1971) shines the light on Italy, by featuring the important contributions of Cesare Beccaria in Milan and Ferdinando Galiani in Naples.

Internet References . . .

The European Enlightenment

Many links to essays, definitions, key figures, ideas, documents. The site has depth and breadth to support research on this issue's questions.

http://doggo.tripod.com/doggenli.html